Bitemark Evidence

FORENSIC SCIENCE

Series Editor
Robert Gaensslen, Ph.D.
Professor and Director
Graduate Studies in Forensic Science
University of Illinois at Chicago
Chicago, Illinois, U.S.A.

Additional Volumes in Preparation

Bitemark Evidence

Edited by
Robert B. J. Dorion

MARCEL DEKKER   NEW YORK

Although great care has been taken to provide accurate and current information, neither the author(s) nor the publisher, nor anyone else associated with this publication, shall be liable for any loss, damage, or liability directly or indirectly caused or alleged to be caused by this book. The material contained herein is not intended to provide specific advice or recommendations for any specific situation.

Trademark notice: Product or corporate names may be trademarks or registered trademarks and are used only for identification and explanation without intent to infringe.

Library of Congress Cataloging-in-Publication Data
A catalog record for this book is available from the Library of Congress.

ISBN: 0-8247-5414-X

This book is printed on acid-free paper.

Headquarters
Marcel Dekker, 270 Madison Avenue, New York, NY 10016, U.S.A.
tel: 212-696-9000; fax: 212-685-4540

Distribution and Customer Service
Marcel Dekker, Cimarron Road, Monticello, New York 12701, U.S.A.
tel: 800-228-1160; fax: 845-796-1772

World Wide Web
http://www.dekker.com

The publisher offers discounts on this book when ordered in bulk quantities. For more information, write to Special Sales/Professional Marketing at the headquarters address above.

Forensic Science Series Introduction

In the last few decades, forensic science has begun to come into its own as an identifiable enterprise, and more particularly as a unified profession. There have always been and continue to be forensic specialty areas that do not necessarily overlap very much at a detailed level. Medicine (pathology), dentistry (odontology), anthropology, entomology, toxicology, criminalistics, chemistry, molecular biology, pattern evidence analysis and comparison, engineering, and some other endeavors can all fit under the "forensic science" umbrella. The connecting thread is that everyone in the profession would say that they ply their professional discipline in the service of the law. Because of that, and because forensic scientists are often interested in different questions than other nonforensic scientists and clinicians in the same discipline, there are some connecting threads that help define a unified professional arena.

The evolution of a profession is a relatively slow process. Sooner or later, there must be direct or indirect public support for the ambient profession. This support translates, at least in part, into resources that can be used to construct and develop professional infrastructure. An academic component is necessary for the education and training of new practitioners. Accreditation programs evolve for both the academic and practitioner endeavors, and certification programs evolve for individuals. All of these things are slowly but surely happening in forensic sciences. Many forensic scientists are not fond of the recent spate of television series and programs about forensic science because of the level of poetic license and exaggeration (some would say misrepresentation). But it must be conceded that the programs have raised public consciousness about forensic science in an unprecedented way.

Accompanying the evolution of a profession is the need for a literature: journals, reviews in various forms, and books. In specialty areas, there are journals dating back at least 200 years in Europe. With perhaps a few exceptions, those journals have primarily encompassed medicine, dentistry, anthropology, toxicology, and early serology/biology. But until the mid-20th century, there weren't many comprehensive forensic science journals in English. There have been a handful of forensic science books over the years, but until recently we have not seen a rich breadth and depth of books. Our objective in launching the Forensic Science series is to publish specialized, comprehensive, "go to" books that will serve as important references for the global forensic science community.

Forensic dentistry or odontology has been underrepresented in publishing. *Bitemark Evidence*, edited by Dr. Robert Dorion, is the first book in this series and represents the first comprehensive treatment of bitemarks. Broadly speaking, forensic odontologists do two major types of examinations: dental identifications, and bitemark analysis and comparison. Bitemark analysis and comparison shares many features in common with other pattern comparison specialties such as fingerprints, tool marks, firearms, and handwriting. Dr. Dorion has assembled a truly impressive team of individuals to cover every aspect of this important subject, from the general to the specific.

R. E. Gaensslen

Foreword

This book, *Bitemark Evidence*, is a clear and welcome reflection of the maturing of forensic odontology as a science. It is a sign that the field is evolving past its' origins in Frye-era "consensus of experts" and moving into an era of true scientific standards. It is also a signpost, pointing in directions still to be pursued. Those of us who have been in the field for some time can remember when we were hard pressed to find any reference textbooks whatsoever on the subject of forensic odontology, let alone bitemark evidence. This volume was conceived by its editor, Dr. Robert Dorion, to advance current knowledge and techniques in bitemark analysis in the cause of justice. In any branch of science, the questions to be asked must be tempered by the availability of the means to answer them.

Dr. Dorion has assembled a team of eminent forensic scientists from the disciplines of forensic odontology, DNA, pathology, and jurisprudence to present their views in the 13 parts of this much-needed and long-overdue book. The forensic community will surely appreciate the authors for the scope and depth of their knowledge of this fascinating subject. Professionals involved in the administration of justice will find this text to be an indispensable reference in any situation that confronts them with a question on the validity of bitemark evidence. The book will take the reader from the early history of bitemark investigation to the most sophisticated techniques in current use.

For years, the Frye Rule was the standard for admission of bitemark evidence. The Daubert decision in 1993 radically changed the terms of admission, and set the stage for objective and repeatable scientific standards. The decade since Daubert has been characterized by unprecedented growth in all the forensic sciences. Odontology is no exception. We have been the emergence and development of novel methods of analysis that would have seemed like pure science fiction to the founders of this field. These techniques have had very real and positive impact in courtrooms throughout the world. The evolution of bitemark investigation in the post-Daubert era is well documented in the chapters of this book. Dr. Dorion has performed an invaluable service in presenting the most up-to-date techniques of bitemark analysis in an intelligent and easily referenced manner. He has wisely chosen his contributors, whose aggregate knowledge and experience represent the very backbone of this field.

It is my privilege to have personally known Dr. Dorion since he was a young dental student. I have watched him grow into a leader in his field, and I hold him in the highest esteem. Likewise, I count the other contributors to this volume as valued colleagues and friends. Their work, as presented in these pages, will be an important and lasting contribution to the science of forensic odontology for years to come.

Arthur D. Goldman, DMD, FAGD, D-ABFO
Past-President, American Board of Forensic Odontology
Past-President, American Academy of Forensic Sciences

Preface

Forensic dentistry is described as a science that applies dental and para-dental knowledge to the solution of legal problems. This textbook, the first of its kind, covers every phase of bitemark investigation from the diagnosis to courtroom testimony with over 700 photographs.

The book will interest first responders, emergency room personnel, physicians, pediatricians, dentists, nurses, crime scene investigators, police identification and photography personnel, medical examiners, coroners, pathologists, law enforcement, forensic and social service personnel, lawyers and judges. The faculties of medicine, nursing, dentistry, and law will find this textbook an invaluable reference for their respective disciplines.

The reader will appreciate the complexity, difficulties, and problems encountered both in the field of bitemark evidence and by the expert. It is a collective work and as such reflects the knowledge, training, experience, and opinions of the contributing authors.

The protocols for photography, collection, preservation, and analysis of bitemarks are detailed. The legal implications and ramifications are discussed.

In the realm of death investigation the coroner/medical examiner/pathologist is the primary diagnostician, controller of information, and provider of access to material. The emphasis of the textbook is on diagnosis, communications, and cooperation among the different experts.

The manual unravels the mystery of bitemarks in 13 parts. The first part is a historical perspective fittingly described by Vale. His treatment begins with the earliest known bitemark references, from the Bible, the Kama Sutra, Old English Law, and the Salem Witch Trials to early cases in Canada. The era of bitemark growth and development is accentuated by significant cases from the United States, Norway, and Canada with mention of educational and organizational developments within forensic dentistry. The American Society of Forensic Odontology, the American Academy of Forensic Sciences, the Canadian Society of Forensic Science, and the American Board of Forensic Odontology all played key roles in the development of forensic dentistry in North America.

Part II, on bitemark recognition, is divided into three chapters dealing with the role of health professionals and other personnel in various fields. The teamwork approach in bitemark recognition, diagnosis, and investigation is emphasized. McDowell treats of biting associated with domestic violence, child, intimate partner, and elder abuse in the living. Davis relates the role of the medical examiner/coroner/pathologist in bitemark detection and underlines pattern variables. Delattre expresses the rationale and benefits of the teamwork approach. The importance of developing a teamwork protocol is emphasized.

In Part III, Bernstein describes the nature of bitemarks from its class and individual characteristics to anatomy, variations, and pathology. In Chapter 6, he deals with reconstructive bitemark analysis: quality of the bitemark, profiling the biter, and maintaining perspective.

Part IV, the collection of bitemark evidence, is divided into noninvasive and invasive analyses. The former is made up of six chapters dealing with photography, digital imagery, saliva swabbing – DNA, bitemark impressions, scanning electron microscopy (SEM), and, the handling of perishables and nonperishables.

In Chapter 7, Golden and Wright discuss photography in detail, beginning with the principles of reflection, absorption, fluorescence, and diffusion. The 35mm armamentaria including lenses, flash units, and film are treated at length as are conventional photographic techniques, visible light, and digital photography. Alternate light imaging (ALI), infrared, and ultraviolet photography are aptly managed. The application of photographic techniques for purposes other than the recording of bitemarks rounds off the chapter. Dorion discusses digital imagery from the perspective of the Scientific Working Group on Image Technologies (SWGIT) while explaining the areas of expertise in digital analysis, the type of work involved, standard operating procedures (SOP), chain of custody, and how digital imagery is perceived by the courts.

Sweet discusses salivary swabbing and DNA analysis in Chapter 9. The discussion of salivary flow, physiology, cellular content, stability, recovery, storage, and transportation of saliva as well as case examples more than adequately cover the theme at hand.

Bitemark impressions by Dorion include discussion of materials, techniques and storage, while David explores the rationale for use and the materials and methods employed for the SEM in Chapter 11.

The last of the noninvasive techniques is addressed by Dorion in Chapter 12 which describes the materials and methods employed in the handling, preservation, storage, and transportation of perishables and nonperishables as well as outlining the factors affecting bitemarks in perishables.

The invasive analysis is composed of two chapters: tissue specimens and, histology. In Chapter 13 Dorion discusses skin wetness and dehydration, the ring technique for tissue excision, fixation, storage, postfixation and storage, transportation, and transillumination. Practical examples are demonstrated using the microscope and transilluminated tissue. The examples serve to illustrate the significance of transillumination.

Davis eloquently introduces the histology and the ''timing'' of bitemarks in Chapter 14. He points out textbook discordance in the timing of bruises while discussing the differences between abrasion, contusion/bruise, laceration, and postmortem bruising. Histopathology, histochemical/biochemical, and critique of the literature reviews help the render to understand the complexities of this evidence. Reliance on color determination for aging bitemarks is called into question. He points out that a bitemark histopathology registry should be created.

Part V explores bitemark variables while presenting case material in four chapters. Souviron deals with animal bites in general, incorporating aquatic and carnivore animal bites, both fatal and nonfatal, as well as postmortem animal bites. He suggests an animal bite protocol.

In Chapter 16 Dorion deals exclusively with nonfatal and fatal dog bites. He presents a case, ''forensic nightmare – misdiagnosis,'' in which he exposes how a simple dog bite case ended up with criminal charges against a parent and four years later with civil litigation against the pathologist and odontologist. There is discussion of the significance of pattern distribution, wound patterning, clothing, ''blood wiping,'' tissue avulsion, and transillumination in case evaluation. Autopsy failures and forensic lessons learned conclude the chapter.

Factors affecting bitemark dynamics introduce Chapter 17 on human bitemarks. Of the 90-odd factors involved in bitemark dynamics, Dorion specifically deals with case presentations, cross-referencing several in other chapters. Hair, orifices, amputation/avulsion, pigmentation, healing, clothing, self-inflicted bitemarks, and erectile tissue are among the subjects discussed.

Dorion and Souviron team up in Chapter 18 to resolve issues of patterns, lesions, and trauma mimicking bitemarks. They discuss healing and healed lesions as well as patterned injuries on the deceased. The reader is warned of the potential for misinterpreting emergency medical treatment or autopsy trauma as bitemarks. It also addresses the question of unspecified marks and lesions.

Part VI comprises the collection of evidence from the suspect. Johnson explains questions of court order vs. informed consent as well as means and methods of obtaining the suspect's dental history, intra- and extraoral photographs, impressions, and DNA.

Part VII, on methods in bitemark comparison by Dailey, introduces the concept of test and static bites. Bite exemplars in wax, Styrofoam, and animal skin and dynamic test bites on volunteers as well as standard dental impression materials are evaluated. Methods of direct comparison and the avoidance of technical problems regarding dental nomenclature and dental cast inversions in comparison techniques are addressed. The issues of simple vs. computer-generated overlays and the respective problems of metric and digital analysis are effectively conveyed. Other comparison techniques, three-dimensional pattern analysis, ink immersion, and other methods of computer aided visualization concludes Chapter 20.

In Part VIII, Bernstein discusses report writing: its goals, objectives, basic qualities, preparation, content, perspective, and security. He suggests measures for maintaining objectivity and addresses the issue of the components for a standard bitemark report.

Stimson points to issues of prevention and contamination in Part IX. Various subjects are addressed, from personnel to autopsy protocol, instruments, and equipment, to bitemark and dental impressions and casts.

Part X deals with legal considerations and the courtroom. The four chapters cover science and the law, case law, courtroom aids in bitemark evidence, and the legal liability of the expert witness. Chapter 23 introduces the reader to the legal system by explaining science and the law, justice vs. truth, the adversarial system, and evidentiary restrictions. Mincer and Mincer further discuss the principles of differentiating good from junk science, the importance of objectivity, the interplay/tension between science and advocacy, and how to approach serving as an expert witness in a bitemark case. Barsley discusses the foundation of case law in Chapter 24, the qualification of the expert, and the concept of ''degree of certainty.'' He delves into the battling experts, qualifying to testify, the expert's testimony in opinion, and ''linkage.'' Kenny introduces the topic of courtroom aids in bitemark evidence by emphasizing the need for simplicity, clarity, and conciseness on the part of the testifying expert witness. In the early 1970s the analysis of bitemark evidence consisted of analyzing black-and-white photographs of dubious quality and producing hand-drawn overlays of the suspect dentition for comparison. He itemizes different methods and materials that, historically, have been used in courtroom presentations by forensic dental experts in bitemark cases. The eye-opening Chapter 26 describes the legal liability of the expert witness with specific reference to dentists. Pitluck emphasizes the reasoning behind absolute immunity and the changing concepts regarding that immunity and what to expect in the future.

Part XI, on contentious issues, is divided into two chapters: the reliability of bitemark evidence and, unresolved issues in bitemark analysis. Chapter 27 introduces concepts of reliability, validity, accuracy, sensitivity and specificity, receiver operator characteristics, and positive and negative predictive values. The effects of *Daubert* and other judicial rulings, and the various research projects in bitemark evidence and their effect on statistics, are alluded to. Chapter 28, by the same author, Pretty, discusses the human skin as a bitemark registration material and methods of analysis—both physical comparison and molecular biological techniques. Further discussion on the levels of conclusion and uniqueness of human dentition conclude the chapter.

Part XII is divided into two chapters. The first, by Dorion, is on research projects and recent developments and discusses the historic development of research in bitemark evidence as well as recent endeavors that have led to developments in other fields. Tompkins' Chapter 30, on genotypic comparison of oral bacteria isolated from bitemarks and teeth, discuss oral microbiology and the recovery and genotypic identification of oral streptococci and its application to bitemarks.

Lastly, Part XIII is composed of five appendices that will undoubtedly benefit the reader with their brevity, conciseness, and checklist approach.

Robert B. J. Dorion

Acknowledgments

I would like to thank all those who have contributed directly and indirectly to this project and in particular to my 20 contributors, without whom this book could not have been realized.

To Dr. Jean Paul Valcourt, former director of pathology at the Laboratoire de médecine légale et de police scientifique, who fostered the development of forensic dentistry in Quebec, thank you.

Thank you to Dr. André Lauzon, the section chair of pathology at the Laboratoire de sciences judiciaires et de médecine légale, Ministry of Public Security for the Province of Quebec in Montreal for his professionalism, dedication, cooperation, and encouragement over the past 31 years.

To my forensic pathologist colleagues at the lab, all of whom have become bitemark inquisitors and diagnosticians, thank you. A motto written on the wall at the entrance to our forensic laboratory is attributed to our first director. Dr Wilfrid Derome (1877–1931): ''N'avance rien que tu ne sois capable de prouver.'' I have always attempted to uphold this position in my forensic career.

I undertook the current project knowing that I had the cooperation of another indispensable collaborator. Dr. Serge Turmel, former chief coroner for the province of Quebec. Pictures are worth 1000 words and when coupled with case histories, a learning experience results. Hopefully the readership will agree.

Experienced forensic photographers in the identification section of the Quebec Provincial Police take most of the autopsy photographs at our forensic lab. Thanks to these dedicated persons for their professional attitude and product. Other photographs were taken by various police agencies, including the identification section of the Service de Police de la Ville de Montréal (SPVM), the Royal Canadian Mounted Police, the Ottawa-Carleton Police, the Winnipeg Police, and the Bermuda Police.

Thank you to the Office of the Chief Medical Examiner of the Commonwealth of Kentucky and to the Office of the Commonwealth Attorney of the Commonwealth of Kentucky, for their cooperation.

Special recognition goes to Louise Reynolds, Felicity Hawthorn, and Terry Maxwell for their cooperation and assistance.

Lastly, I thank the various local, national, and international friends and colleagues for the encouragement expressed and/or the cooperation received in the writing of this book.

Contents

Part IV. Collection of Bitemark Evidence

NONINVASIVE ANALYSES

INVASIVE ANALYSES

Part V. Bitemark Variables and Cases

Part VI. Collection of Evidence from the Suspect

Contents

Contributors

Robert B. J. Dorion, B.Sc., D.D.S., D-ABFO   Editor; Director of Forensic Dentistry, Laboratoire de sciences judiciaires et de médecine légale, Ministry of Public Security for the Province of Quebec, Montreal, Quebec, Canada; Assistant Professor, Faculty of Dentistry, Mc Gill University; Past president American Board of Forensic Odontology; Past president Canadian Society of Forensic Science; Distinguished Fellow, American Academy of Forensic Sciences; Fellow, Canadian Society of Forensic Science

Robert E. Barsley, D.D.S., J.D., D-ABFO   Forensic dental consultant to the Orleans Parish Coroners Office and the Jefferson Parish Coroners Office, New Orleans (mero area), Louisiana; Professor of Oral Diagnosis, Medicine and Radiology, and Director, Dental Health Resources, ISUHSC School of Dentistry, New Orleans, LA; Past President, American Society of Forensic Odontology; Member, Board of Directors, American Academy of Forensic Sciences; Fellow, American Academy of Forensic Sciences

Mark L. Bernstein, D.D.S., D- ABOMP, D-ABFO   Professor of Oral and Maxillofacial Pathology, University of Louisville School of Dentistry. Louisville, KY; Forensic Dental Consultant to Chief Medical Examiners Office, Commonwealth of Kentucky; Fellow, American Academy of Forensic Sciences

Jon Curtis Dailey, D.D.S., D-ABFO   Colonel, Dental Corps, U. S. Army; Assistant Director, Prosthodontic Program, Fort Gordon, Georgia; Forensic Odontology Consultant, State of Georgia Medical Examiner; Adjunct Faculty, Armed Forces Institute of Pathology; Fellow, American Academy of Forensic Sciences

Thomas J. David, B.S., D.D.S., D-ABFO   Medical Examiner Consultant, State of Georgia; Forensic Odontology Consultant, Georgia Bureau of Investigation, Division of Forensic Sciences; Fellow, American Academy of Forensic Sciences

Joseph H. Davis, M.D.   Retired Chief medical examiner, Miami-Dade County, Florida; Professor of Pathology Emeritus, University of Miami; Certified by the American Board of Pathology in Pathologic Anatomy and Forensic Pathology; Past President, American Academy of Forensic

Sciences; Past President, National Association of Medical Examiners; Distinguished Fellow, American Academy of Forensic Sciences

Veronique F. Delattre, B.Sc., D.D.S., F.A.G.D.   Chief Forensic Dental Consultant, Office of the Medical Examiner of Harris County, Joseph A. Jachimczyk, Forensic Center, Houston, Texas; Associate Professor, University of Texas, Houston Health Science Center Dental Branch, Houston, Texas

Gregory S. Golden, D.D.S., D-ABFO   Chief Odontologist/Deputy Coroner, County of San Bernardino, California; Assistant Professor, School of Dentistry Loma Linda University, Loma Linda, California; Fellow, American Academy of Forensic Sciences

L. Thomas Johnson, D.D.S., D-ABFO, SCSA   Associate Medical Examiner, Milwaukee County Medical Examiner's Office, Milwaukee, Wisconsin; Professor, Dental Science, Forensic Dentistry & Public Health, Marquette University School of Dentistry, Milwaukee, Wisconsin; Past president, American Board of Forensic Odontology; Consultant, Wisconsin Department of Justice, Crime Laboratory Bureau; Fellow, American Academy of Forensic Sciences; Certified Senior Crime Scene Analyst, International Association for Identification, Crime Scene Certification Board

John P. Kenney, D.D.S., M.S., D-ABFO, SCSA;   Deputy Coroner and Director of Identification Services, Du Page County, IL. Coroner's Office; Associate Clinical Professor of Surgery, Northwestern University Medical School; Consultant, US Army Central Identification Laboratory, Hawaii; Odontology Member, Forensic Oversight Group, USPHS D-MORT Teams; Consultant, Joint POW-MIA Accounting Command Central Identification Laboratory, Hawaii; Past President American Board of Forensic Odontology; Fellow, American Academy of Forensic Sciences; Fellow, American Academy of Pediatric Dentistry

John D. McDowell, D.D.S., M.S., D-ABFO   Director, Oral Medicine and Forensic Sciences, University of Colorado School of Dentistry; Chairman, Oral Diagnosis, Oral Medicine and Oral Radiology, University of Colorado School of Dentistry; Past President, American Academy of Forensic Sciences; Past President, American Society of Forensic Odontology; Fellow, American Academy of Forensic Sciences

Harry H. Mincer, D.D.S, Ph.D., D-ABFO   Dental Consultant to the Medical Examiner, Shelby County, Tennessee; Professor and Division Director Oral and Maxillofacial Pathology, University of Tennessee College of Dentistry; Past president American Board of Forensic Odontology; Fellow, American Academy of Forensic Sciences

Richard A. Mincer, J.D.   Hirst & Applegate, P.C., Cheyenne, Wyoming; Managing Editor, University of Memphis Law Review; Past President, Defense Lawyers Association of Wyoming

Haskell M. Pitluck, J.D.   Retired Circuit Court Judge (Illinois); Past President American Academy of Forensic Sciences; Fellow, American Academy of Forensic Sciences

Iain A. Pretty, B.D.S. (Hons), M.Sc., Ph.D.,   Forensic Dentist to the North West Coroner's Services; Forensic Consultant to Merseyside and Cheshire Police Forces; Lecturer in Restorative Dentistry, Unit of Prosthodontics University of Manchester, England

Richard R. Souviron, D.D.S., D-ABFO   Chief Forensic Odontologist, Miami-Dade County Medical Examiners' Office, Florida; Associate Medical Examiner, Miami-Dade County, Florida; Adjunct Professor Pathology, University of Miami School of Medicine; Past president American Board of Forensic Odontology; Fellow, American Academy of Forensic Sciences

Paul G. Stimson, D.D.S., M.S. D-ABFO   Senior Forensic Consultant, Harris County Medical Examiner, Harris County, Houston, Texas; Professor emeritus, University of Texas Dental Branch at Houston, University of Texas Health Science Center at Houston; Past President American Board of Forensic Odontology; Odontology Member, Forensic Oversight Group, USPHS for DMORT Teams and DMORT Team Member; Fellow, American Academy of Forensic Sciences

David Sweet, D.M.D., Ph.D., D-ABFO.   Director, Bureau of Legal Dentistry Laboratory. University of British Columbia, Vancouver, Canada; Associate Professor, Faculties of Dentistry and Medicine, University of British Columbia, Vancouver, Canada; Consultant Forensic Odontologist, Office of the Chief Coroner, British Columbia Coroners' Service, Burnaby, Canada; Consultant Forensic Odontologist, Royal Canadian Mounted Police Forensic Laboratory Services Directorate, Ottawa, Canada; Fellow, American Academy of Forensic Sciences

Geoffrey R. Tompkins, Ph.D.   Senior Lecturer, Department of Oral Sciences and Orthodontics, University of Otago, Dunedin, New Zealand

Gerald L. Vale, D.D.S., M.D.S., M.P.H., J.D., D-ABFO   Senior Forensic Dental Consultant, County of Los Angeles. Department of Coroner; Clinical Professor (Ret.), University of Southern California, School of Dentistry; Past president American Board of Forensic Odontology; Distinguished Fellow, American Academy of Forensic Sciences

Franklin D. Wright, D.M.D., D-ABFO   Forensic Dental Consultant, Hamilton County Coroner's Office, Cincinnati, Ohio; Fellow, American Academy of Forensic Sciences

I
A Historical Perspective

1

History of Bitemark Evidence

Gerald L. Vale
Department of Coroner, County of Los Angeles, Los Angeles
California, U.S.A.

1. INTRODUCTION

The teeth are remarkably versatile tools. They are used to chew food, to help produce speech sounds, to enhance the smile, and to maintain the vertical dimension of the face. They may also be used to cut a piece of thread or to hold a pipe, pencil, or carpentry nails. And on special occasions, they may be used in making love or as weapons of attack or defense. There is reason to believe that this has been the state of affairs since the origin of the human species.

2. EARLY HISTORY OF BITEMARKS

2.1. The Bible, Kama Sutra, and Old English Law

It is always tempting to suggest that the history of bitemark evidence began with the eating of forbidden fruit in the Garden of Eden. Indeed, the Book of Genesis provides a basis for arguing that bitemark evidence was created when the serpent induced Eve to eat the forbidden fruit [1,2]. She, in turn, gave it to Adam. However, the record shows that the bitemark evidence was not used—nor was it needed. When accused, Adam confessed and blamed Eve. Eve confessed and blamed the serpent. As a result, the serpent was commanded to crawl on his belly and eat dust for all the days of his life. The woman was told that she would suffer pain in childbirth and would be ruled by her husband. The man was condemned to a lifetime of toil to earn his sustenance. In light of the penalties assessed, one might hope that the fruit was tasty.

Harvey references the early history of biting with this colorful quotation from the Kama Sutra, said to have been written between AD 100 and AD 600: "All the places that can be kissed, are also the places that can be bitten, except the upper lip, the interior of the mouth and the eyes." Harvey comments that assailants in actual cases are obviously unaware of these limiting words [3].

Early recognition of the teeth as weapons is seen in old English law. For example, in the 18th century, English law defined the crime of mayhem as "an assault whereby the injured person is deprived of a member proper for his defense in fight" [4]. This definition was taken to include arms, legs, and anterior teeth as "members proper for defense." Because the 18th-century punishment for mayhem was death, a barroom fighter with a habit of punching out his opponent's front teeth would be an extremely poor insurance risk. The penalty in modern law has, of course, lessened, and the definition of the crime has changed. In California, for example, the present definition of mayhem describes depriving a human being of ''a member of his body ...'' without requiring that the body part qualify as a defensive weapon [5].

2.2. Salem Witch Trials, 1692

Pierce discusses the first known bitemark case in North American courts [6]. This landmark case was a part of the infamous Salem Witch Trials that resulted in, among other things, the conviction and hanging of the Rev. George Burroughs on August 19, 1692.

Two teenage girls in Salem had entered into a state of ''hysterical illness''—moaning, shrieking, and writhing on the ground. These bizarre symptoms spread among the children of Salem. The adults concluded that the children had been bewitched. Burroughs was one of those suspected of soliciting young women into witchcraft. His methods allegedly included pinching, choking, biting, and otherwise tormenting his victims.

Cotton Mather's fascinating description of Burroughs' trial, published in 1693, stated, ''Whereas Biting was one of the ways which the Witches used for the vexing of the Sufferers, when they cry'd out of G.B. biting them, the print of the Teeth would be seen on the Flesh of the Complainers, and just such a sett of Teeth as G.B.'s would then appear upon them, which could be distinguished from those of some other mens'' [7].

Several injured victims came to Burroughs' trial with toothmarks on their arms. Burroughs' mouth was reportedly pried open in the presence of the judges and spectators and ''his teeth were compared not only with the bites but with the teeth of others in the room.'' Pierce notes that the judges readily accepted the bitemark evidence to substantiate the allegations, although previously reluctant to accept the unsupported word of the accusers [8,9].

Although convicted, it is important to note that Burroughs was reportedly in prison at the time that he allegedly bit his victims. The cause of the hysteria in Salem has never been satisfactorily explained, nor has there been a plausible explanation for the marks seen on the arms of Burroughs' alleged victims. Aldous Huxley has referred to the events in Salem as ''an explosion, within a tiny colonial society, of pent-up malice and ancient superstition; a series of absurd travesties of justice culminating in a score of public hangings ...'' [10]. Fifty years after the incident, the colony awarded cash settlements to the survivors of those executed in 1692. Thus, the Salem Witch Trials provide a thought-provoking backdrop for the introduction of bitemark evidence into the American judicial system.

2.3. Ohio v. A.I. Robinson, 1870

As also reported by Pierce, A.I. Robinson was a well-regarded member of his community who was suspected of murdering his mistress [11]. Five distinct bitemarks were found on her arm, each clearly showing individual tooth marks. One of the examining dentists reportedly bit the woman's arm in order to compare his tooth marks to those on the arm. He later had Robinson bite the dentist's own arm to compare Robinson's teeth to those on the body.

The bitemarks on the body showed only five anterior teeth in the maxilla. One suspect had a full complement of teeth and was therefore excluded. However, Robinson had only five anterior maxillary teeth. Dr. Jonathan Taft, the future first Dean of the University of Michigan School of Dentistry, testified that he placed the cast of Robinson's teeth on the marks and ''it was a surprising good fit.'' He opined that Robinson's teeth matched the injury in every significant way. It is interesting that defense arguments in this case were similar to arguments heard 100 years later. For example, there was testimony that it was unlikely that tooth marks in skin would be sufficiently clear to establish individual identity; also, that the dentition was not very unusual. In addition, there was testimony that "you can fit the five front teeth of any mouth into the marks of five front teeth of any other mouth." The jury found Ansil Robinson not guilty.

2.4. Other Early Cases

Despite the outcome in the Robinson case, there is evidence that the value of bitemark evidence was well recognized in scientific circles by 1890. For example, Keiser-Neilsen discussed an 1890 case in which an elderly woman was murdered near Paris [12]. Knowing that strangulation victims sometimes manage to bite their attacker, the autopsy surgeon had impressions and casts made of the victim's defective and malaligned teeth. Almost a week later a young Frenchman was arrested in Belgium for a minor offense, and possible toothmarks were seen on one of his hands. He was sent to Paris, where it was demonstrated that the marks on his hand "perfectly matched" the teeth in the victim's dental cast.

In another 1890 case, an expensive cigar holder was found near the body of a wealthy banker who had been murdered in St. Petersburg. Near the tip of the cigar holder were apparent tooth marks, one deeper than the other. Keiser-Nielsen reported that during the inquest the judge noticed that the victim's cousin, who was testifying, had a lower incisor that was clearly shorter than the adjacent tooth. The witness angrily refused the judge's request to "try on" the cigar holder. However, he was arrested on the spot, and it was quickly determined that his lower incisors "fit exactly" into the mouthpiece.

Harvey has reported a number of historical cases from England, Scotland, and elsewhere [13]. The early reported cases frequently involved bites in foodstuffs, rather than on human skin. One such was a 1906 case in which a burglar was convicted on the basis of his toothprints left in cheese at the crime scene. Of even greater interest was the 1921 conviction of a man convicted by his bite in roast pork. Harvey also reported a 1929 case in which hypoplastic pits on a lower incisor left accurate marks in an apple made of soap, which the burglar apparently believed to be a real apple. In addition, there was a 1938 case in which a bite into cheese recorded a missing incisor tooth. Harvey pointed out that some foods, such as butter and icing on a cake, record teeth well. He cited a 1949 case in which thieves broke into a doctor's home and left bitemarks of very irregular teeth in some chocolate. He pointed out that in this case, as in others, the sight of the bitemark evidence obtained by the police caused the perpetrator to make a confession. Harvey also mentioned the practice of using bitemarks in wax as a dental signature. One might write, for example, in the language of an earlier era, "In proof that this is sooth I bite the wax with my wang tooth."

It should be noted that the cases reported in the early years of the 20th century included bites in human skin, as well as bites in foodstuff or wax. Gustafson, for example, discussed a 1925 report by Keyes involving bitemarks on the arm of a murdered man [14]. The marks matched well with casts of the suspect's teeth. And in a 1929 report, deep bites in the breast of a murder victim demonstrated that a maxillary central incisor was rotated about 80°. A similar rotation was found in the teeth of the suspected biter.

2.5. Early Cases in Canada

Canada's first known bitemark case occurred in the Atlantic Coast community of Sheet Harbor, Nova Scotia [15]. In this small, picturesque fishing village on the eastern shore of Nova Scotia, a break-in and robbery took place on November 14, 1924. A large quantity of merchandise was stolen from a clothing store, and a man named William Steele was eventually charged with the deed. Drs. J. Stanley Bagnall and A.W. Faulkner, local dentists, were asked to identify the impressions of toothmarks in an apple left in the burglarized store and compare them with the

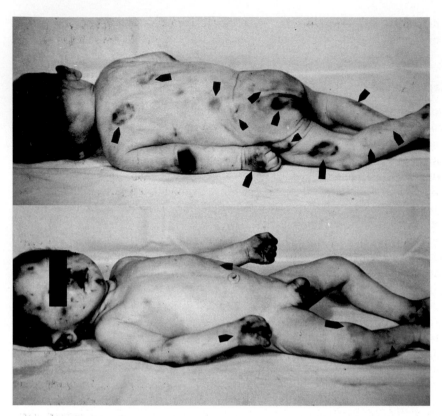

Figure 1   Multiple bitemarks in infanticide case. (Photographs courtesy of Dr. Robert Dorion).

dentition of Mr. Steele. They were able to correlate the tooth marks to the teeth of the accused, who was subsequently convicted of the crime. The provincial treasury of Nova Scotia remunerated each dentist with a payment of $25.

A case of even greater historical significance occurred in 1930 in Quebec. It involved the murder of an infant (R. Dorion, personal communication, 2003). Figure 1 shows multiple human bitemarks on the child's body. This is the first known case of a bitemark on human skin documented in Canadian forensic archives, and these may be the earliest documented photographs of bitemarks on human skin in North America. It should be noted that Canada has a long history in forensic sciences. In 1914, Quebec founded what is believed to be the first forensic laboratory under legislative authority in North America. Known today as the "Laboratoire de sciences judiciaires et de médecine légale," it is located in Montreal.

3.   THE ERA OF "BITEMARK GROWTH AND DEVELOPMENT"

3.1.   Overview of the Upward Trend

Although the history of biting may be as old as the history of mankind, the number of cases reported prior to 1950 is very small in comparison to the more recent experience. Significantly, a very large portion of the activity reported in the early years originated in Europe and in Japan. However, starting in about the middle of the twentieth century the number of reported cases began to accelerate, and many of these cases originated in the United States. Indeed, Harvey was fascinated by the number of bite cases originating from this source [16]. He noted "New York's record of 57 murders in a week, Glasgow's 16 murders in a year, no murder in Gibraltar for 15 years, and in living memory the only man in Pitcairn Island's jail is the man who cleans it out."

It is noteworthy that the formation of the American Academy of Forensic Sciences (AAFS) in 1948 played a significant role in the emergence of the United States as a major participant in the development of modern forensic sciences. This was due to the organization's outstanding annual meeting, its highly regarded forensic journal, its development of organizational sections for each of the forensic specialties, the development of specialty certification boards, and numerous other activities. All served to stimulate further development of the forensic sciences, and establishment of forensic standards. Significantly, these activities also encouraged international communication and cooperation. Forensic scientists from many nations attend and give presentations at AAFS meetings. For example, at the 2003 meeting in Chicago, 16 (34%) of the 50 papers presented at the Odontology Section's scientific sessions originated in Canada, England, Hungary, Italy, Belgium, Finland, Mexico, Sweden, and Switzerland. Thirty-four were from participants in the United States [17]. The visiting scientists not only share valuable forensic information, they often also announce meetings in other parts of the world, thereby helping to stimulate interest in international travel and exchange of information.

Forensic odontology has become a major section in the AAFS, with more than 400 members listed in the Academy's 2002 directory. Drs. Lowell Levine, Arthur Goldman, Homer Campbell, and John McDowell have served as president of the Academy. The Academy has honored Drs. Homer Campbell, Robert Dorion, Norman Sperber, and Gerald Vale as "Distinguished Fellows."

3.2. First "Reported Case" in the United States: Doyle v. State, 1954

The first "reported" bitemark case in the United States is the 1954 Texas case of Doyle v. State [18]. In legal terms, a "reported case" is one that has been certified by the court for publication in the official reports that record and archive significant cases. These are generally appellate level or Supreme Court cases.

According to the Doyle court's very brief discussion of the dental evidence, police investigating the burglary of a grocery store found a piece of cheese on the meat counter containing "pronounced tooth marks." Police officers then asked the suspect to bite into a piece of cheese and he voluntarily did so. A firearms examiner made photographs and plaster casts of the crime scene cheese and the cheese bitten by the suspect. In the words of the court decision, both the firearms examiner and "Dr. Kemp, a dentist of Haskell" testified that both pieces of cheese had been bitten by the same set of teeth. "Dr. Kemp" has been further identified as Dr. William J. Kemp, a long-time member of the Texas Board of Dental Examiners (P. Stimson, personal communication, 2003). In appealing the subsequent conviction, Doyle's lawyer raised the sole objection that the defendant's voluntary bite into the cheese constituted a confession made without the required statutory warning. The court rejected this argument and upheld Doyle's conviction.

Although the 1954 Doyle case "broke the ice" in terms of significant court recognition of bitemark evidence in the United States, nearly 20 years would elapse before another bitemark case was reported in the United States legal literature. This was the 1972 case of People v. Johnson [19]. Milton Johnson was convicted of rape and aggravated battery. The victim's identification of Johnson was supported by physical evidence, which included bitemarks on her breasts. Dr. Paul Green, a Joliet (IL) dentist, testified as to similarities between the bitemarks and the defendant's teeth. However, he did not identify the defendant as the person whose teeth were reproduced in the dental casts. The court ruled that it was not prejudicial error to recall Dr. Green the next day for the sole purpose of establishing the defendant's identity.

3.3. Norway's Long-Running Torgersen Case

The Torgersen case has been referred to as the most famous bitemark case in Scandinavia by at least one observer (H. Soomer, personal communication, 2003). It began with the murder of a 16-year-old girl in Oslo in 1957. It was reportedly active as recently as 2001—a span of some 44 years.

The victim's body was found by firemen under a pile of smoldering debris in the cellar of her home on December 7, 1957 [20]. Autopsy revealed that she had been sexually assaulted and had probably died of manual strangulation. A dental expert confirmed that there was a bitemark around the nipple of her left breast. He took photographs and impressions, and charted the injury. Ludvig Fasting Torgersen, who was arrested near the scene of the crime, was accused of committing the murder, piling debris on top of the body and igniting it in an attempt to conceal the crime.

After first refusing to have impressions taken of his teeth, Torgersen finally consented on the condition that if the dental study did not exclude him as the biter, a second expert would be utilized. However, both the initial examiner and the second examiner concluded that the characteristics of the bitemark were all present in Torgersen's teeth. At trial they testified that Torgersen was the originator of the bitemark. He was convicted of murder in the first degree and sentenced to life in prison. The decision was appealed, but was upheld by the Supreme Court on November 1, 1958. In 1970, after 12 years in prison, Torgersen reportedly barricaded himself in a prison office with a hostage, whom he had badly beaten. Torgersen was subsequently overpowered and placed in solitary confinement for 2 years. Surprisingly, the incident generated wide debate and a large following of advocates for Torgersen's cause [21]. In 1974, after 16 years in prison, Torgersen was released. He then filed a petition for retrial. Before deciding on the matter, the court determined that the toothmarks should be reexamined, and appointed Professor Gisele Bang for that purpose.

Materials from the 1957 examinations were available, and were utilized in this 1975 study. This included the injured breast, fixed in Kaiserlings solution, and impressions of the toothmarks and models of the appellant's teeth, both in plaster of Paris. In addition, there were scene photographs, photos of the breast with the toothmarks and of the casts of the toothmarks and the purported biter's teeth [22]. Using elastomeric impression materials, new models were made of the tooth marks and of the appellant's teeth. Models were then produced in Xantopren Blue and hard dental stone (Vel-Mix). Subsequent analysis included visual inspection, stereophotography, and scanning electron microscopy. In addition, stereometric graphic plotting, which had not previously been employed in the analysis of tooth marks in humans, was used. In this method, the outline of a toothmark or biting edge of a tooth can be recorded in three-dimensional detail in the form of a contour map. Professor Bang concluded that it is highly probable that the teeth of the accused made the tooth marks in the breast.

This, however, was not the end of the case. The matter has been reexamined in the recent past, and additional investigation of the dental evidence has been reported as recently as 2001 (personal communication, C. Bowers, 2001, and H. Soomer, 2003).

3.4. Canada's First Bitemark Serial Killer: Wayne Clifford Boden

The Wayne Clifford Boden murders are noteworthy for several reasons. The 1924 Nova Scotia case referenced 2.5 was the first bitemark case in the Canadian judicial system; it involved toothmarks in an apple. The Wayne Clifford Boden murder of Elizabeth Porteous, which took place some 47 years later, is the first known case in the Canadian courts in which toothmarks in human skin were used to identify the perpetrator of a bite [23]. Also, it was the first Canadian case in which bitemarks occurring in far distant geographic locations were used to help link crimes to a single individual. In addition, the point count system used in presenting the evidence in these cases helped to spark subsequent efforts by the American Board of Forensic Odontology (ABFO) to quantify the value or weight of bitemark evidence in a given case [24].

Elizabeth Ann Porteous, a popular and attractive schoolteacher, was found lifeless on the floor of her Calgary apartment on May 20, 1971. Bitemarks were discovered on her breasts and neck. Wayne Clifford Boden, an itinerant salesman, became the primary suspect. On May 21, the police contacted Dr. Gordon C. Swann, a Calgary orthodontist, and requested his assistance in their homicide investigation. Dr. Swann compared the casts of Boden's teeth to the bitemarks on the right breast and left neck, using a system of direct geometric progression modified from the method described by Furness [25]. Dr. Swann reported, ''The analysis indicated clearly a total of 29 points of similarity which led to the positive conclusion that the bitemarks on the body of the Elizabeth Ann Porteous were indeed inflicted by the teeth of the accused Wayne Clifford Boden.'' The Chief Justice stated that Dr. Swann ''found such a large number of similarities in the way of characteristics that in reason one cannot fail but accept as probative and conclusive his evidence. ... I therefore sentence the accused to imprisonment for life.''

Dr. Swann was then asked to review the evidence related to three young women who were sexually assaulted and strangled in Montreal in late 1969 and early 1970. He determined that there were no bitemarks on one of the three victims. There were bitemarks on both breasts of a second victim, but the photographs, which were taken postautopsy, were extensively distorted. However, bitemarks on the right breast of Shirley Audette were similar to those on Elizabeth Porteous. Detailed study of Boden's teeth in relation to the mark studied on the victim's breast demonstrated 17 points of similarity. Swann stated his opinion that ''this evidence clearly points to a positive identification of Wayne Boden as the perpetrator of this assault.'' Brought back to Montreal for trial of the three murders, Boden was visited by a fourth-year dental student, Robert Dorion. His mentor, Dr. Araceli Ortiz, took Boden's dental impressions at the infamous maximum-security Saint Vincent-de-Paul penitentiary (R. Dorion, personal communication, 2003). Boden pleaded guilty to the three Montreal murders.

After receiving four life sentences, Boden escaped custody in 1984 through the restroom window of the famous Montreal Sheraton's hotel restaurant, the Kon Tiki, while on an escorted day pass from the maximum-security prison. In a sequence of events worthy of a Hollywood scenario, he was recaptured the next day on the same street, in a bar where he had picked up his victims 15 years earlier (R. Dorion, personal communication, 2003).

3.5. The Increasing Volume of Bitemark Cases

Starting in the 1970s, there has been a dramatic increase in the use of bitemark evidence in U.S. courts. Pitluck has, for many years, painstakingly compiled and updated a listing of reported bitemark cases (H. Pitluck, personal communication, 2003). Figure 2, which the present author derived from Pitluck's data, graphically displays the increase in reported cases that has occurred during the past five decades. In brief summary, bitemark evidence made its formal appearance in U.S. courts in the 1950s, gained significant momentum in the 1970s, and then experienced a relative explosion into the legal arena in the 1980s and 1990s. This time-related assessment is not precise because, among other things, the time lag between the date of the crime and the date of the report is highly variable and tends to be lengthy. For example, in the case of People v. Marx, the crime occurred in 1974 and the appellate decision was reported in 1975. However,

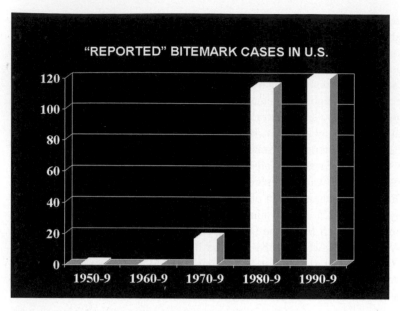

Figure 2   Illustration of the dramatic increase in the use of bitemark evidence in U.S. courts from the 1970s forward.

in the Milone case, the crime occurred in 1972, and reports of the higher courts appeared in 1976, 1992, and 1994.

3.6.   Educational and Further Organizational Developments

A major development in the history of bitemark investigation occurred in 1962 with the establishment of courses in forensic odontology at the Armed Forces Institute of Pathology (AFIP) in Washington, DC (Personal communication, AFIP staff office, 2003). Drs. Albert Dahlberg, Louis Hansen, John Salley, Viken Sassouni, and David Scott gave presentations in the initial 4-day course. Within the first few years, the course became an annual event. Drs. Curtis Mertz, Edward Comulada, Lowell Levine, Lester Luntz, and Paul Stimson were among those who were active in the early implementation of the AFIP program (A. Norrlander, personal communication, 1997). Over the years, attendance at one of these well-organized AFIP courses became almost a mandatory requirement for those seriously interested in forensic odontology.

Another event affecting the development of forensic dentistry occurred in 1966, with the publication of Gustafson's English text, ''Forensic Odontology,'' which had a substantial chapter on bitemarks [26]. Surprisingly, this was the first major text on the subject since Amoedo's 1898 landmark work, ''L'Art dentaire en médecine légale'' [27].

The year 1970 was truly momentous for forensic odontology. In 1970, forensic odontology gained important recognition as a specialty of the forensic sciences with formation of the Odontology Section of the AAFS. This created a valuable forum for the emerging specialty, and gave forensic odontology representation in the operation and leadership of AAFS. The Odontology Section was created primarily by recruiting dentists from the General and Pathology Sections. Drs. Lowell Levine and Edward Woolridge were the first section chairman and secretary, respectively [28].

The American Society of Forensic Odontology (ASFO) was also formed in 1970 under the leadership of Col. Robert Boyers [29]. From the early 20 or so members, who were largely faculty of the AFIP forensic odontology course, the Society has grown to become one of the largest forensic organizations in the world, with 1200 members in 2002 (P. Stimson, R. Dorion, personal communication, 2003). Membership is available to all who have an interest in this field. The organization provides significant educational information through its annual educational programs and widely distributed informational materials, including several editions of the ''Manual of Forensic Odontology.''

Also in 1970, the Canadian Association of Forensic Odontology merged with the Canadian Society of Forensic Odontology. By 1972 this new organization had merged with the Canadian Society of Forensic Science to form an Odontology Section. By 1976 the section was 85 members strong (R. Dorion, personal communication, 2003). It is noteworthy that odontologists from Canada have worked closely with their counterparts in the United States throughout the development of odontology. For example, Drs. Robert Dorion, David Sweet, John W. Blair, George Burgman, and Laurence Cheevers, among others, have contributed significantly to development of the specialty and its associated organizations.

Schools of dentistry began showing an increased interest in forensic dentistry at about this time. In 1971, under the auspices of the office of the Chief Medical Examiner of New York, a symposium on forensic odontology was held in conjunction with New York University. Speakers included Drs. Michael Baden, Robert Boyers, John Devlin, Elliott Gross, Milton Helpern, James Helbock, Soren Kieser-Nielsen, Lowell Levine, Lester Luntz, David Scott, Inder Singh, and Knud Petersen (R. Dorion, personal communication, 2003).

Another educational landmark occurred 2 years later, with the publication of the ''Handbook for Dental Identification,'' authored by Lester and Phyllys Luntz. It is believed to be the first text on forensic dentistry by an American author, and included a chapter on bitemarks [30].

3.7. People v. Marx, 1975

People v. Marx [31] has been described by Giannelli and Imwinkelreid as ''the leading bitemark case'' [32] and by Bowers as the ''the seminal case for bitemark analysis'' [33]. It was the first reported bitemark case in California and the fifth in the nation [34].

An elderly lady was found dead in her Torrance, CA, home on February 2, 1974. She had been strangled and sexually mutilated. There were deep lacerations on the dorsum of the nose and lesser injuries on the base of the nose [35] (Figs. 3, 4). Following autopsy, the body was released to the family, embalmed, and buried. Walter Marx, who rented space in the victim's home, admitted being with her on the evening of her death, but denied involvement with the crime. Marx refused to comply with the court order to have dental casts made. Consequently, he was held in jail for contempt of court for about 6 weeks. On March 20, he agreed to comply with the court order; impressions were made of his teeth, and he was released from custody.

The victim's body, which had been buried in Texas on February 7, 1974, was exhumed on March 23. Dr. Irving Stone at the Forensic Science Institute in Dallas County took impressions and photographs of the injured nose. After carefully cleaning the injury with saline, it was found that the markings were remarkably clear and deep, and could be compared with the casts of the suspect's teeth. Torrance detectives returned the evidence to Los Angeles.

On March 27, Los Angeles County Deputy District Attorney James Ideman contacted Dr. Gerald Vale, who agreed to study the bitemark evidence. Dr. Vale suggested that it be brought to a meeting he had previously scheduled for that afternoon with Drs. Reidar Sognnaes and Gerald Felando. This would provide the benefit of a team approach.

The remarkable depth of the tooth markings can be seen in Figure 5. The cast of the nose (Vel-Mix) was made from a polysulfide rubber impression taken 7 weeks after death. It was concluded that the wound was consistent with a human bitemark on the basis of the overall

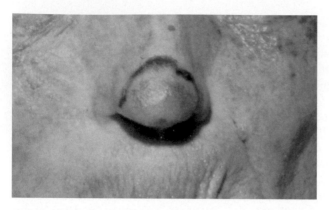

Figure 3   Deeply lacerated bitemark on the dorsum of the nose at autopsy. (Courtesy of ASTM.)

pattern, the orientation of the maxillary and mandibular arch imprints, the size, shape, characteristics, and spatial relationship of the indentations. Several methods were used to compare the suspect's teeth to the injury. As noted above, three-dimensional preliminary comparison was made following exhumation by comparing dental casts directly to the body. Subsequently, the casts were duplicated and mounted on an adjustable articulator to facilitate study of the defendant's Class III occlusion and jaw movements. The suspect's dental casts were compared to photographs of the victim's bitemark two-dimensionally, and were compared three-dimensionally to casts of the victim's nose. Casts of the nose were made in dental stone, silicones, wax, clay, and epoxy resin. Flexible rubber noses were also made using material known as Dermathane 100. In addition, acetate overlays were used to compare marks made by the suspect's dental casts to the marks on the victim's nose. Figures 6 and 7 show ivory-colored epoxy casts

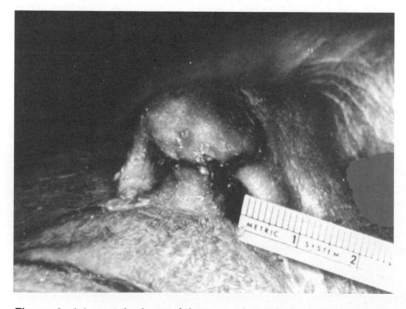

Figure 4   Injury at the base of the nose photographed post-exhumation. (Courtesy of ASTM.)

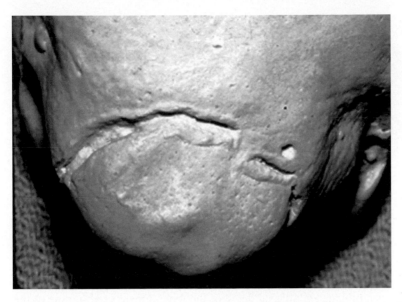

Figure 5 Depth of the lacerated toothmarks is evident on stone cast of victim's nose.

of the suspect's teeth adjacent to corresponding markings on epoxy casts of the victim's nose. The markings had been darkened with black powder prior to photography.

Using the suspect's cast, a series of test bites were made into replicas of the victim's and volunteers' noses. Other test marks were made in a kosher frankfurter, and then on the forearm, and finally on the nose of a brave volunteer—one of the homicide detectives. Scanning electron

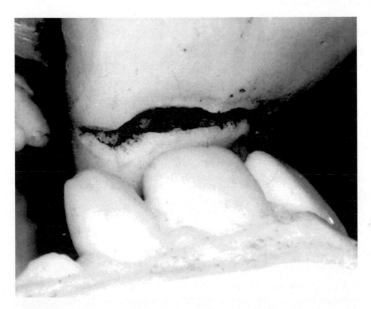

Figure 6 Casts of Marx's left maxillary central and lateral incisor in proximity to corresponding toothmarks on epoxy model of victim's nose. (Courtesy of ASTM.)

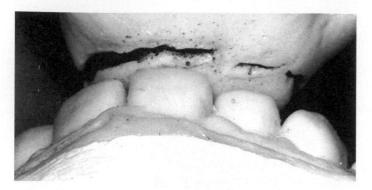

Figure 7   Casts of Mark's maxillary right central and lateral incisor in proximity to corresponding toothmarks on epoxy model of victim's nose. (Courtesy of ASTM.)

microscope studies provided further information on the adequacy of the postmortem epithelial tissue preservation. They also provided additional detail of the three-dimensional outline of the incisor teeth in relation to the marks on the nose. In addition, silicone matrices were produced showing the labial-incisal characteristics of the suspect's teeth. They could be placed directly on the cast of the nose, adjacent to the corresponding tooth marks. This facilitated comparison between details of the suspect's teeth and the corresponding tooth marks on the nose.

In all studies, a high degree of similarity was noted between the features of the bitemark on the victim's nose and Walter Marx's teeth. The prosecution experts' report detailed 18 points of similarity involving eight of the suspect's teeth, with no discrepancies. At trial, Drs. Reidar Sognnaes, Gerald Vale, and Gerald Felando, each in his own words, stated their opinion that the bitemark on the victim's nose was inflicted by Walter Marx's dentition. Marx was found guilty and convicted of voluntary manslaughter.

In upholding the conviction and the admissibility of bitemark evidence, the appellate court indicated that it was not necessary in this case to follow the usual requirement that the scientific principle involved had gained general admissibility in the field to which it belonged (the Frye standard, which is still followed in California in modified form). The opinion further indicates that the trial court was shown sufficient comparative material so that it could see the extent to which the wounds changed (or, according to the evidence, did not change) between autopsy and exhumation. The court could also see the "the extent to which the purported bitemarks appear to conform generally to obvious irregularities in defendant's teeth." Thus, the basic data were verifiable by the court, and "the court did not have to sacrifice its independence and common sense in evaluating it." Giannelli and Imwinkelried comment that, "In light of the 'battle of experts' that often surface in later cases, the court's reliance on the jury's ability to verify the expert's findings seems misplaced" [36].

3.8.   Formation of ABFO, 1976

The need to identify forensic scientists unequivocally qualified to provide essential professional services for the nation's Judicial and Executive branches of government has long been recognized. In response to this need, the American Board of Forensic Odontology (ABFO) was organized in 1976 to provide, in the interest of the public and the advancement of the science, a program of certification in forensic odontology. In its purpose, function, and organization, ABFO is analogous to the certifying boards in various medical specialties and scientific fields.

The Board's objective is to establish, enhance, and revise (as necessary) standards of qualification for those who practice forensic odontology, and to certify as qualified specialists the voluntary applicants who comply with the requirements of the Board. In this way, the Board aims to make available a practical and equitable system for readily identifying those persons professing to be specialists in forensic odontology who possess the requisite qualifications and competence. Certification is based on the candidate's personal and professional record of education, training, experience, and achievement, as well as the results of a formal examination [37]. The charter members of the Board were Drs. Edward Woolridge, Richard Souviron, Curtis Mertz, Arthur Goldman, Gerald Vale, Stanley Schwartz, Lowell Levine, Robert Dorion, Paul Stimson, David Scott, Manuel Maslansky, and George Ward [38].

Dr. Curtis Mertz served as the first president. He was succeeded by Drs. Arthur Goldman, Lowell Levine, William Giles, Gerald Vale, David Scott, Robert Dorion, Raymond Rawson, Richard Souviron, Thomas Krauss, Stanley Schwartz, David Sipes, Paul Stimson, William Alexander, Wilbur Richie, Gary Bell, Jack Kenney, Ann Norrlander, George Isaac, David Averill, Harry Mincer, L. Thomas Johnson, Michael Tabor, Joseph Gentile, Bryan Chrz, and John Lewis (2003).

3.9. People v. Milone, 1976

It seems appropriate that the often quoted Milone bitemark case was first reported in the same year that the ABFO was formed. It is one of the most controversial bitemark cases, both in terms of conflict over the dental findings and the long tortuous path it has followed through the legal system from 1972, when the crime occurred, to at least 1995 [39].

On September 12, 1972, 14-year-old Sally Kandel went for a bicycle ride and never returned. Her body was found the next morning. She had severe head injuries and a human bitemark on the inner right thigh inflicted "some time after the heart stopped beating." Nearby was a shopping cart handle that was later determined to be the murder weapon. It was traced to a D-C Warehouse in Addison, IL, and eventually to Richard Milone, an employee [40]. The case became one of many that featured teams of experts on each side. Here, three experts testified for the prosecution and four testified for the defense.

According to the 1976 appellate court report, the State expert witnesses asserted that, in their opinion, "Richard Milone was without a doubt the perpetrator of the bite on the victim's thigh." Dr. Lester Luntz reportedly enumerated 29 points of comparison leading to the positive identification. Dr. Harold Perry, Chair of Orthodontics at Northwestern University School of Dentistry, noted the correlation between a fractured left central incisor in both the defendant's teeth and the bitemark. He pointed out that less than 1% of the population would have a fracture of that tooth. Dr. Irwin Sopher testified that the bitemark in question was good in terms of "definity [sic] of points, clarity, lack of distortion, and lack of decompositional change." He also found numerous unique and specific points of identification supporting the positive identification of Richard Milone as the biter.

The experts for the defense concluded that "no positive correlation could be made between the defendant's dentition and the bitemark in question." Defense experts (of whom only Dr. Lowell Levine is mentioned by name in the court report) noted that it is far easier to exclude than to identify through bitemark comparison. All four defense experts pointed out inconsistencies between the bitemark and the defendant's casts, and therefore either denied that a positive identification could be made or ruled out the defendant as the biter. On rebuttal, the State witnesses offered explanations for the inconsistencies [41]. Milone was convicted and given a sentence of 90–175 years in prison [42]. The appellate court upheld Milone's conviction in 1976, citing the recent Marx case and others as a basis for admitting the bitemark evidence.

The court also cited the excellent quality of the bitemark evidence in the Milone case [43]. The Illinois Supreme Court denied leave to appeal, and no petition for a writ of certiorari to the U.S. Supreme Court was filed at that time.

In 1986, 10 years after his state court appeal, Milone petitioned the federal district court to issue a writ of habeas corpus. The parties agreed to stay the federal proceedings while Milone pursued executive clemency [44]. In his request to the Governor for unconditional pardon, Milone claimed, among other things, that it was Richard Macek and not Milone who murdered Sally Kandel in 1972. In support, he offered two written confessions and a number of oral ''confessions'' made by Macek [45]. However, in his statement on the matter, the Governor found that because of internal inconsistencies and Macek's disturbed state of mind and subsequent recantations of the ''confessions,'' they could not be considered credible. In light of the conflicting dental opinions, the Governor directed the state police to submit the forensic evidence to credible unbiased experts in forensic odontology. According to the Governor's report, three additional experts in forensic odontology who were not connected with any of the previous trials expressed the shared opinion, based on the evidence made available to them, that ''Richard Milone inflicted the bitemark on the leg of Sally Kandel,'' and that ''there were distinguishing irregularities between the bitemarks found on Macek's victims and Sally Kandel.'' Governor Thompson denied the petition for unconditional pardon in April 1989.

Following additional legal proceedings, the petition for habeas corpus was also denied by the U.S. District Court in Illinois in 1992 [46,47]. Milone then appealed to the U.S. Court of Appeals, Seventh Circuit [47]. He claimed that at the time of his 1973 trial bitemark evidence was unreliable, and failed both the Frye and Daubert tests for admissibility [48]. Secondly, he asserted that expert testimony was then available (and reliable because of advances in forensic odontology in the past 20 years) tending to show that the bitemark on Sally Kandel's thigh could not have been made by Milone. Moreover, the bitemark could now be shown to match the dentition of a known serial murderer, Richard Macek. Richard Macek reportedly confessed to the murder of Sally Kandel several times before committing suicide in his jail cell in 1987. However, the parties disputed whether Macek also recanted these confessions.

The Court of Appeals noted that Milone had recently been paroled after serving almost 20 years of a 90-to-175-year sentence [49]. The court determined that it could take Milone's newly discovered evidence into account only insofar as it bore upon his constitutional claims: ''the existence merely of newly discovered evidence relevant to the guilt of a state prisoner is not a ground for relief on federal habeas corpus'' [50]. On April 21,1994, the Court of Appeals held that ''(1) habeas corpus relief was not warranted by (Milone's) credible claim that newly discovered evidence would not only cast doubt upon his guilt of murder for which he was convicted but in fact would exonerate him and (2) [Milone] failed to show that any consitutitonal error occurred during state court proceedings. Consequently, in 1994 the Court of Appeals affirmed the U.S. District Court's denial of Milone's petition for a writ of habeas corpus. In 1995, a writ of certiorari was also denied [51].

3.10 1979—A Banner Year

In July 1979, Theodore Bundy (Fig. 8) was convicted of murder in what may have been the most widely publicized of all cases involving bitemark evidence [52]. Bundy was one of the most notorious serial killers in U.S. history. He reportedly could have been responsible for the deaths of as many as 36 young women from Florida to the state of Washington [53].

Theodore Bundy was convicted of entering a Chi Omega sorority house in Florida in January 1978, where he murdered two coeds and attempted to murder two others. He then entered a nearby house and bludgeoned a third female victim. Several days after the crime

Figure 8   Theodore Bundy, one of America's most notorious serial killers. (Courtesy Dr. Richard Souviron.)

occurred, Dr. Richard Souviron was asked to come to Tallahassee to examine bitemark evidence that had been discovered on the body of one of the victims (R. Souviron, personal communication, 2003). He found that it consisted of tissue from a breast and buttocks that had been excised and placed in fluid without retaining rings. While these materials were of limited value, Dr. Souviron was able to determine that the biter would have had poorly aligned teeth. This information helped to establish the element of probable cause, necessary for obtaining a search warrant. When this was accomplished. Dr. Souviron was able to take dental impressions, bite records, and photographs of Bundy's dentation (Fig. 9). Dr. Souviron was then provided a photograph of the bite injury.

     Following Dr. Souviron's study of the available evidence, it was also examined independently by Drs. Lowell Levine and Norman Sperber. All three examiners found that the evidence implicated Bundy as the perpetrator of the bitemarks. Drs. Souviron, Levine, and Sperber then spent approximately a week in Tallahassee at a Frye hearing on the admissibility of the bitemark evidence. Dr. Souviron reported that both the Marx case and Milone case were cited at the hearing, with Marx considered the "gold standard" (R. Souviron, personal communication, 2003).

     After admissibility of the evidence was determined, Dr. Souviron presented a series of slides to the grand jury. Subsequently the grand jury issued an indictment. Theodore Bundy acted as his own attorney during much of the legal process. As a result, Dr. Souviron was treated to the unique experience of spending a day in a Tallahassee prison cell with a serial killer, with the prisoner taking Dr. Souviron's deposition.

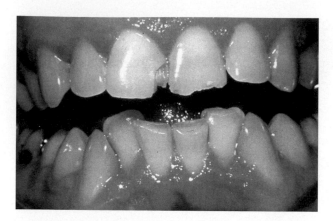

Figure 9 Bundy's teeth have distinctive features that were recorded in the bitemark. (Courtesy Dr. Richard Souviron.)

Due to voluminous pre-trial publicity there was a change of venue from Tallahassee to Miami. Drs. Souviron, Levine, and Homer Campbell testified at the trial, with Dr. Campbell providing computer enhanced images of the bite patterns. Bundy was convicted on all seven counts. He was subsequently executed for the murder of a 12-year-old girl in another case.

It is noteworthy that, while the Bundy and Marx cases differ in many respects, they have at least four important features in common. Each was a landmark case. Marx established bitemark analysis as an admissible form of evidence in the nation's most populous state, providing important legal precedent. The Bundy case helped bring a notorious serial murderer to justice, and played a major role in educating both the legal system and the general public about the importance of bitemark evidence. Secondly, each case illustrated that bitemark evidence can be the crucial evidence that determines whether a case will be adjudicated. In Marx, the prosecutor made it clear that he would not have taken the case to court if it were not for the bitemark evidence. And in Bundy, a member of the grand jury stated that they would not have been able to bring an indictment without the bitemark evidence. Thirdly, both cases illustrate a continuing issue that forensic odontologists must learn to face. In each case, the odontologist was brought into the matter after the bitemark evidence had already been collected. Both cases illustrate the challenges that can arise when this occurs. Finally, both cases illustrate a fundamental principal of bitemark investigation: If (1) a bitemark contains detailed information about the dentition of the biter, and (2) the biter's dentition shows distinctive or unusual features, then the examiner is presented with an opportunity to compare a suspect's dentition and reach a conclusion that should be valid and reliable, and that can be confirmed independently by other examiners. In addition, it should be eminently supportable at the time of trial.

The year 1979 also witnessed a landmark case in the military courts in U.S. v. Martin. Here, the military courts joined at least eight jurisdictions in the United States that had considered and accepted the admissibility of bitemark evidence [54]. Dr. Norman Sperber testified for the prosecution. Drs. Gerald Vale and John Beckstead testified for the defense. Dr. Vale also testified for the prosecution as to the admissibility of bitemark evidence [55].

The year 1979 was also the year that the University of Texas Health Science Center at San Antonio Dental School instituted the Southwest Symposium on Forensic Dentistry. As with the AFIP course, the excellent program in Texas soon earned the reputation of being one of the "must take" courses for those seriously interested in forensic dentistry. Other programs that offer valuable training in forensic dentistry (including bitemark analysis) have also become available. One such is the 3-day course given at the Wayne County, Michigan, Medical Examiner's Office, which includes both didactic material and a hands on bitemark exercise (A. Warnick, personal communication, 2003).

Yet another significant development occurred in 1979 when the ABFO conducted its first examination for applicants applying for ABFO certification. The examination was conducted at the Dade County Medical Examiner's Office in Florida (R. Souviron, personal communication, 1997).

Following hard on the heels of the 1979 events, an important educational resource became available in 1980 with the publication of the first edition of the ASFO's ''Manual of Forensic Odontology.'' It was edited by Drs. Robert Seigel and Norman Sperber. The second edition (1991) was edited by Dr. David Averill, and the third edition (1995) was edited by Drs. C. Michael Bowers and Gary Bell. The manual has evolved into a periodically updated compendium of current information on forensic dentistry, including bitemark analysis. The compendium is available internationally.

3.11. Development of Guidelines for Bitemark Analysis

The year 1984 was pivotal in the history of bitemark evidence, as it brought to fruition several years of effort to develop bitemark guidelines. A 1975 study by Whittaker indicated that bites made into a good recording medium, such as wax, could produce accurate identification of the biter in a high percentage of cases, but that identification from bites made into pigskin was considerably less reliable [56]. This study and others supported the concept that additional research and the development of standards for bitemark investigation were in order. A step in that direction had been taken in 1977, when the Odontology Section of the AAFS received a report from its committee on recommended methods, chaired by Dr. Robert Dorion. However, that report did not appear in the scientific literature until the present publication (this volume, Chapter 29). Increased impetus to develop guidelines occurred in 1978, when a legal journal published an article recommending that the use of bitemark evidence should be curtailed pending the establishment of a committee to develop standards for the use of this type of evidence [57].

Recognizing a need, in 1980 the Odontology Section of AAFS appointed a Bitemark Standards Committee [58]. It consisted of Drs. Norman Sperber (Chair), Gerald Vale, Raymond Rawson, and Roddy Feldman (N. Sperber, personal communication, 1980). The committee started its work in June of that year by drafting standards for the collection of evidence. In addition, on January 7, 1981, the committee initiated a study at the University of Southern California in which dental casts of eight individuals were used to create bitemarks on an anesthetized dog. In 1981, ABFO determined that it, too, would launch a program to improve methodology in bitemark analysis [58]. This resulted in the formation of a conjoint committee that was given the assignment of developing bitemark guidelines. The Committee on Bitemark Guidelines was chaired by Dr. Gerald Vale and included Drs. Raymond Rawson, Norman Sperber, and, later, Edward Herschaft.

The committee first used a consensus approach to develop tentative guidelines for collecting evidence from the victim and from the suspect. The committee then addressed the thorny question of how strong the evidence must be in order to reliably determine whether a bitemark was inflicted by the suspect dentition. To answer this question, the committee attempted to develop a quantitative approach to measuring bitemark evidence. The committee planned to first define what constitutes a matching point, and then assess the number of matching points needed to reliably identify a biter.

Despite obvious difficulties, it was considered essential to attempt to measure the weight or value of bitemark evidence because of the extreme differences of opinion that qualified experts were expressing on bitemark cases in court. Therefore, the committee drafted tentative definitions of ''matching points,'' then drafted tentative scoring guidelines to assist in determining the degree of match. The committee members then tested the guidelines on sample cases as a group. Other studies were conducted to evaluate the reliability of the scoring system, and were published in the scientific literature [59].

At the recommendation of Dr. Thomas Krauss, the ABFO decided to conduct a bitemark workshop on February 18–20, 1984, in Anaheim, CA, for the purpose of formally establishing guidelines for use in bitemark analysis. Dr. Krauss, a dedicated and tireless worker, was a driving force in the field of forensic dentistry (Fig. 10). His role in initiating the development of guidelines, codeveloping the internationally used ABFO No. 2 Reference Scale, and accom-

Figure 10 Dr. Thomas Krauss, Program Chair of the first workshop to develop guidelines for the use of bitemark evidence. (Courtesy Mrs. Anne Brockhoff.)

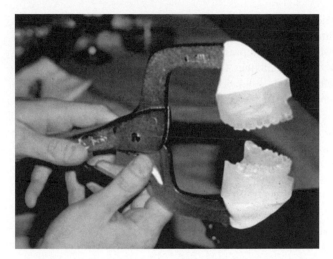

Figure 11   Models mounted on clamping device for biting exercise at First Bitemark Workshop in Anaheim, CA, 1984. (Courtesy Dr. Frank Morgan.)

plishing numerous other innovative projects left a rich legacy [60]. He died in a tragic accident at his ranch on April 25, 1994, at age 61. The well-attended annual Bitemark Breakfast at the AAFS meeting has been named in his honor.

Although there had been a small bitemark workshop in 1977, the 1984 workshop is believed to be the first organized effort to develop guidelines for the use of bitemark evidence and it is referenced in ABFO literature as the first bitemark workshop. More than 30 forensic dentists participated in the 1984 workshop. All were diplomates of ABFO or board-eligible applicants. Dr. Krauss was program chairman, and Dr. Paul Stimson assisted in program preparation. Dr. Krauss assigned to Dr. Gerald Vale, chair of the committee that drafted the guidelines, the task of organizing and facilitating the workshop discussions, and editing the drafts. Dr. Raymond Rawson performed the extensive task of organizing, preparing, and conducting the clinical portion of the meeting, and evaluating the resulting data. The activities included a study in which dental casts were used to produce experimental bitemarks on the workshop participants (Figs. 11, 12).

Figure 12   Workshop bitemark of exceptional evidentiary value produced on the arm of Dr. John W. Blair. (Courtesy Dr. Frank Morgan.)

During the workshop, the participants met in plenary session and in small groups to discuss and revise the bitemark committee's first draft of the guidelines. Based on this input, the committee wrote a second draft, which was then presented to the plenary session for further discussion. After additional revisions, the "Guidelines for Bite Mark Analysis" were adopted by the workshop participants on February 20, 1984. They were adopted by the ABFO the following day. The guidelines have been widely published [58,61,62], and an outline of the current bitemark guidelines is reproduced in the Appendix.

The 1984 guidelines include the ABFO attempt to quantify bitemark evidence by means of a scoring system [58]. However, in January 1988, the members of the original Committee on Bitemark Guidelines published a letter in the Journal of Forensic Sciences which included the following statement:

> While the Board's published guidelines suggest use of the scoring system, the authors' present recommendation is that all odontologists await the results of further research before relying on precise point counts in evidentiary proceedings. This does not mean that the investigator should not use the scoring system or other method of analysis that he or she may find helpful. It does mean that the authors believe that further research is needed regarding the quantification of bitemark evidence before precise point counts can be relied upon in court proceedings [62].

3.12. The "Golden Rule" and Additional Bitemark Workshops

In March 1988, William Hyzer and Dr. Thomas Krauss formally introduced a scientific tool that would become an international standard for excellence in forensic investigation [63]. In their article entitled "The Bite Mark Standard Reference Scale—ABFO No. 2," they described the development of an L-shaped scale that enables accurate measurement in both vertical and horizontal directions. It also contains circular references to facilitate the determination and correction of photographic distortion and a gray scale for photographic color corrections. The device is remarkably simple to use, simple in design, durable in construction, and inexpensive. Designed primarily for bitemark photography, the scale has been adopted almost universally for this purpose. In addition, because of its accuracy and practicality, it is also being used increasingly by other scientific disciplines.

Ten years after the 1984 workshop, ABFO conducted Bitemark Workshop No. 2 on February 12–14, 1994, in San Antonio, TX. Dr. Gary Bell was chair. The purpose was to establish guidelines and standards regarding bitemark terminology and bitemark methodology and, in addition, to review application of the scientific method [64].

The workshop began with a presentation and discussion led by Dr. Mark Bernstein on bitemark terminology. It focused on an in-depth survey in which 45 respondents expressed their views on the use of language utilized in bitemark analysis. Dr. Bernstein accepted responsibility for collating this material and proposing guidelines for bitemark terminology. The workshop also included a presentation by Dr. John McDowell on scientific methodology related to bitemark investigation. In the afternoon, Dr. Robert Dorion led a discussion of the survey that had been conducted on collection of bitemark evidence and methods of analysis, which had a 41% response rate. Drs. Gary Bell, Gregory Golden, and Raymond Rawson presented on methods of comparison, after which Dr. Rawson presented sample cases. This was followed by individual case reviews.

The second day consisted of group evaluation, discussion, and presentation of bitemark cases provided by Drs. Gregory Golden, Thomas Krauss, Donnell Marlin, Richard Souviron, and Allan Warnick. The third day involved presentation of the "ideal" bitemark case, using information developed at the workshop. The meeting ended with a summary of the workshop, discussion, and conclusions.

The material developed at this second bitemark workshop was studied by the workshop committee and used to establish the bitemark guidelines and standards regarding terminology and methodology. Following review and discussion by the ABFO Diplomates at their annual meeting in Seattle in 1995, the guidelines and standards on terminology and methodology were adopted. They are found in the ABFO Diplomates Reference Manual and are also available on the ABFO website (www.abfo.org).

At this point, the board had established a common language, and had agreed upon acceptable methods of comparison. However, it was determined that continued study was needed to develop consistent findings in the study of bitemarks. To that end, a third bitemark workshop was organized. (G. Bell, personal communication, 2003). ABFO Bitemark Workshop No. 3 was held in New York on February 16 and 17, 1997 [65]. It was chaired by Drs. Gary Bell and Robert Dorion. The purpose was to review past and current literature on bitemark analysis, to attempt to establish guidelines for injury analysis related to the amount and quality of evidence collected, and to establish bitemark report writing guidelines.

The workshop began with discussion of 23 bitemark-related articles and texts published from 1966 to 1995. In the opinion of the reviewers, most of these works were out of date and/ or contained inaccurate information. In their view, only the latest articles and texts were found to be of value in the analysis of bitemark information.

The participants then focused on injury analysis. The goal here was to develop a list of criteria that would assist in determining whether an injury is a bitemark. Next was the effort to determine the evidentiary value of the injury. Breakout groups analyzed 33 cases. Results were reviewed, and suggestions were made to modify the questions that would be used to help determine whether an injury is a bitemark and, if so, its degree of value as evidence.

On the second day, the participants addressed the issue of report writing. A tentative draft was presented for review and discussion. Revisions were made on the basis of this review (G. Bell, personal communication, 2003). The ABFO Bitemark Report Writing Guidelines were adopted following presentation and discussion at the ABFO's annual meeting in Orlando in 1999. They are published in the ABFO Diplomates Reference Manual [66] and on the ABFO website (www.abfo.org).

The fourth ABFO Bitemark Workshop was held in Orlando, Florida on February 14–15, 1999 [67]. Dr. Gary Bell chaired it. The purposes were to review and update bitemark evidence collection as it relates to the dentition responsible for the bite injury; practical use of previously established guidelines and standards of case analysis and methods of comparison; and the use of the Bitemark Report Writing Guidelines.

After reviewing the statistical analysis of the previous workshop, participants focused on the topic of collecting evidence of the dentition. No changes from the 1984 Bitemark Workshop evidence collection guidelines were recommended. Subsequently, there were breakout sessions on the subject of case analysis and the methods used in this process.

The second morning was devoted to review of the four cases that had been sent to the participants in advance for their analysis, completion of questionnaires, and preparation of materials to defend their opinions and method of analysis. Participants were required to consider seven sets of casts as representing suspected biters in each of the four cases. They were also required to mark the position of individual teeth on copies of the bitemark photographs. The first objective was to have participants use the guidelines that had been developed for terminology, methodology, and report writing. The second objective was to determine if there was a correlation between the forensic value of the bitemark evidence and the extent of agreement in the participant's opinions. It was logically expected that good evidence would yield common opinions. Gross analysis of the results indicated that this hypothesis was true. The case with the best evidence yielded a high level of agreement when casts were compared to bitemarks. Similarly, the case with the least amount of evidence (lower evidentiary value) yielded more disagreement as to identification of the biter. However, even in the best case a few of the participants disagreed with the majority. It was felt that this justifies further study of the analysis of bitemark evidence. It was suggested that the disagreement may have resulted from failure on the part of some of the participants to spend adequate time analyzing the available information, but this hypothesis was unproven (G. Bell, personal communication, 2003) (see this volume, Chapters 27–29 for additional comments).

In the afternoon, participants continued the project of report writing. They used an outline developed from the previous workshop that listed the recommended components of a bitemark analysis report. The outline included introductory material, such as the agency requesting service, date of the request, an inventory of the evidence received, and a description of the evidence collection procedures if performed by the report writer. This was followed by analysis of the injury evidence, analysis of the subject dentition, the comparison procedures, and the resulting opinions.

3.13. Wilhoit v. Oklahoma, 1991

Oklahoma's Wilhoit case is unique in several respects, one of which is that the peer-reviewed opinion of 11 ABFO diplomates played a significant role in reversing the death penalty conviction of a man who had been found guilty of murdering his estranged wife [68]. Gregory Wilhoit was charged with first-degree murder in 1987. Because the prosecution contended that bitemark evidence on the victim matched Wilhoit's teeth, his family contacted Dr. Thomas Krauss to serve as a defense expert [69]. However, the trial attorney failed to provide Dr. Krauss with access to the evidence or to use his testimony in court. Wilhoit was convicted and given the death penalty. Dr. Krauss was subsequently asked by the family to work with the public defender. This began a 3-year odyssey that ultimately resulted in reversal of the murder conviction and remanding the case for a new trial.

After studying the evidence he was able to obtain, Dr. Krauss asked Drs. Wilbur Richie and Gerald Vale to each review it independently [69]. Finding that all three experts disagreed with the prosecution position, he obtained additional opinions. Ultimately, 11 ABFO odontologists stated their disagreement with the prosecution expert's findings and submitted affidavits to that effect [70]. On July 3, 1990, the Court of Criminal Appeals ordered an evidentiary hearing by the District Court, which was held in August, October, and December of that year. Since there was an issue regarding the significance of finding *Candida albicans* and *Bacteroides* on the victim, a microbiology professor testified that these organisms are extremely common in the human mouth. Dr. Richard Souviron testified regarding bacterial and bitemark comparisons, and Dr. Krauss testified regarding his activities in the case and the evidence itself.

According to the district judge who conducted the hearings, "The most important item of circumstantial evidence tending to prove that the defendant was the perpetrator of said crime … was the testimony of two prosecution experts regarding the bitemark evidence and the identity of the perpetrator of the bite" [70]. He determined that the trial attorney for the defense had failed to use an expert even though the family had made one available, and that there was no strategic reason for this action.

The district judge found that the defense attorney was deficient because of his failure to investigate the bitemark evidence, and that there was a reasonable probability that the trial result would have been different had he used an expert. Therefore, Wilhoit had been denied a fair trial, and the sentence was reversed and remanded for new trial. Although additional factors were involved, the case demonstrates that failure to obtain expert assistance when needed can be grounds for arguing ineffective assistance of counsel and lack of a fair trial. The Osage

County Court clerk reports that the case against Gregory Wilhoit was dismissed on March 31, 1993 (J. Burd, personal communication, 2003).

3.14. The Bureau of Legal Dentistry, 1997

A noteworthy event occurred on April 28, 1997, when the Bureau of Legal Dentistry (BOLD) officially opened its doors in Vancouver, BC, Canada [71]. BOLD is said to be the only laboratory in the world dedicated to full-time forensic odontology research and casework [72]. It was made possible by a $500,000 contribution from the provincial government in conjunction with the provision of salaries, space, and administrative support by the Faculty of Dentistry of the University of British Columbia. Dr. David Sweet, a leading participant in scientific and organizational activities in forensic dentistry, is the director of BOLD [73].

To date, scientists affiliated with BOLD have been major contributors to the forensic literature and to programs at professional meetings. BOLD has increased the credibility of bitemark analysis by emphasizing in its publications the need for a scientific approach to bitemark investigation, using DNA and digital technology whenever possible. BOLD has also advocated eliminating examiner bias through the use of methods such as the "dental lineup." Along with other research centers, the Bureau is developing a database that is expected to make it possible to determine the degree of uniqueness of an individual's dentition. BOLD has also broadened educational opportunities by offering advanced training and advanced degrees in forensic science. Thus, the development of this organization represents a large step forward for forensic dentistry in terms of increased emphasis on science, improved service to the community, and greater credibility for forensic dentistry in general, and bitemark analysis in particular.

4. CONTROVERSIES IN BITEMARK ANALYSIS

4.1. The Dichotomy

The history of bitemark analysis contains an interesting dichotomy. On the one hand, there is remarkable consistency in the acceptance of bitemark evidence in the legal system in U.S. courts. Indeed, bitemark evidence is now accepted in at least 37 U.S. jurisdictions and has not been rejected in any state [74]. Despite this widespread acceptance into the judicial system, bitemark evidence has not been without controversy. Two areas of interest will be touched on briefly here from a historical perspective.

4.2. "Battles of the Experts"

Legal commentators have discussed the "battles of experts" that have occurred in a number of bitemark trials [75,76]. Faigman, for example, cites eight cases to support the statement that, "In numerous cases, forensic odontologists have disagreed about whether a particular mark on a victim was a bite mark or not. He then cites 12 cases to support the statement that "The other issue, whether a defendant was the source of a bitemark, has generated at least as much disagreement between experts." While these observations are accurate, they do not lead to the conclusion that bitemark evidence is unique in having qualified experts take opposing positions. One need only look to some of the most widely publicized trials of the past century to find case after case in which experts in various forensic disciplines held markedly differing views. For example, disagreement among forensic entomologists was a prominent feature in the California murder trial of David Westerfield. And millions of viewers of the criminal trial of O.J. Simpson heard eminent scientists on both sides disagree about the significance of the DNA evidence.

Similarly, differences of opinion among experts in forensic psychiatry, forensic pathology, and the examiners of questioned documents, to name a few, occur frequently.

More significant is Faigman's statement that "there have been numerous reports of forensic odontologists reaching opinions that disagreed with the results of DNA and other forensic analysis." He cites four cases, and others have occurred subsequently.

4.3. Challenges to the Validity of Bitemark Evidence

A second, related area of controversy is found in the literature that has questioned the validity and reliability of bitemark evidence. Validity is the ability of a test to measure what it is supposed to measure. For example, if the underlying hypothesis that it is possible to accurately identify a biter from marks left on skin is correct, then this type of analysis is valid. If the underlying hypothesis is incorrect, the test is invalid. Reliability deals with the consistency of obtaining the same results each time the test is performed [77,78]. Unfortunately, these terms are often used interchangeably in the legal literature.

One of the earliest law review articles questioning the use of bitemark evidence appeared in the Southern California Law Review in 1978, just 3 years after publication of the Marx case [79]. Authored by Adrienne Hale, this 25-page "Note" argued that admission of bitemark evidence may result in the use of irrelevant, prejudicial evidence. It also argued that the subjective nature of bitemark evidence hampers the jury in assessing the weight to be accorded that evidence. The author proposed that admissibility of bitemark evidence be barred, pending the establishment of standards of admissibility by a committee of forensic odontologists. The committee's primary function would be to establish a minimum standard for admissibility by determining how many concordant points of similarity are necessary and by setting uniqueness or quality values for specific points. Secondarily, it would certify accurate and uniform methods of comparison. Interestingly, the ABFO embarked upon this journey with its 1984 workshop. The author concluded by noting the intent was not to disparage the courtroom use of bitemark analysis, but to enlist a scientific committee to conclusively establish its value.

A 1987 article in American Criminal Law Review by Robert A. DeLaCruz had the provocative title, "Forensic Dentistry and the Law: Is Bite Mark Evidence Here to Stay?" [80]. DeLaCruz cited "at least" 23 appellate jurisdictions that have allowed bitemark evidence in criminal proceedings. However, he stated that "Many commentators and defense attorneys have criticized bite mark identification, arguing that the scientific process involved is unproven" [79,81]. After examining legal issues, the author determined that "despite its uncertain accuracy, bite mark evidence is not likely to be excluded from the court room." Interestingly, this article recommends that courts should adopt the procedures used in State v. Stokes [82]. In that case, "a Louisiana trial court directed that dental impressions from four male Caucasians within 10 years of age of the defendant, two picked by the prosecution and two by the defense, be sent to the state's expert along with the defendant's impression." The objective was to eliminate "impermissible suggestiveness."

The 1993 case of Daubert v. Merrell Dow Pharmeceuticals raised questions about the admissibility of scientific evidence that had implications for all the forensic sciences, including bitemark evidence [83]. Previously, courts in 45 states followed the Frye rule, which required that in introducing a new technique, there must be general acceptance of the underlying scientific principle or discovery in the field in which it belongs [84]. However, under Daubert the expert's task is to prove that the method used is scientifically valid and is relevant. In jurisdictions that have adopted Daubert, the court must examine whether the methodology can be tested and has actually been tested. Peer review and publication are persuasive, but not essential. Consideration is also given to whether there is a known error rate and standards for applying the method.

Under Daubert, "general acceptance by the scientific community" is one of the considerations, but is not determinative by itself.

How does bitemark evidence fare if attacked under the Daubert rule? In discussing the Minnesota case of State v. Hodgson, Faigman notes that the court swept aside the opportunity to determine whether it should continue to follow its modified version of the Frye test or should adopt its own version of Daubert [85,86]. In considering the challenge to bitemark evidence on the ground that it was not generally accepted, the court simply said that the challenge need not be addressed because bitemark analysis is not a novel or emerging type of scientific evidence.

Faigman points out that some courts have critically evaluated, rather than blindly accepted the assertions of forensic odontologists about the scientific validity and evidentiary reliability of bitemark evidence [87]. He cites Howard v. State [88], in which the Mississippi Supreme Court noted that while courts have generally admitted bitemark evidence, "numerous scholarly authorities have criticized the reliability of this method ... ." The court noted, "There is little consensus in the scientific community on the number of points which must match before any positive identification can be announced." The court stated that "it is certainly open to defense counsel to attack the qualifications of the expert, the methods and data used to compare the bite marks ... and the factual and logical bases of the expert's opinions. Also, where such expert testimony is allowed by the trial court, it should be open to the defendant to present evidence challenging the reliability of the field of bite-mark comparisons."

In light of the subjectivity involved, Bowers [89] has suggested that "the strongest opinion linking bite marks to suspects be limited to 'possible' until such time that bitemark analysis is more satisfactorily tested in relation to reliability, error rate, scientific validation of historical bitemark analyses, and perhaps comes to be conducted pursuant to court appointed, rather than adversarial, expert testimony." Bowers also quotes Sweet as recommending that the odontologist perform the pattern analysis bitemark comparison before the DNA analysis is performed. This would prevent having the subjective pattern analysis biased by the DNA results and would provide the court with the benefit of two independent assessments of identity.

5. QUO VADIS BITEMARK EVIDENCE

What will be the role of bitemark evidence in the future? Will the much-lauded virtues of DNA drive pattern analysis into obscurity? Will the continued challenges to the validity and reliability of bitemark analysis exclude this form of evidence from the courtroom—or severely limit its use? A strong argument can be made that the answers to the above questions, in sequence, should be "Vigorous," "No," and "No."

It is indisputable that bitemark evidence has become established as an important and useful tool in the administration of justice. In this process, the courts have already considered most of the concerns discussed above, particularly in a jurisdiction's first bitemark case. And, as previously noted, bitemark evidence has been accepted in every state in which it has been considered. This now includes more than 37 jurisdictions in the United States, as well as the military court system [90]. In addition, high-profile cases such as Bundy help to make both the public and the legal profession aware of the value of this form of evidence. And television is currently flooded with forensic programming, much of which portrays bitemark evidence as a powerful tool.

Practical considerations further strengthen the expectation for continued use of bitemark pattern analysis. Among other reasons, this form of analysis is relatively fast and available, particularly when compared to DNA analysis. In addition, salivary DNA evidence may not be recovered in a given case, or it may be compromised. Also, the investigating agency's DNA laboratory may be have a severe backlog of cases, or funding problems may limit the use of DNA analysis. Further, even DNA evidence, despite its well-established scientific basis, is subject to attack on various grounds, such as mishandling evidence or using inappropriate methods of analysis [91]. As a result, even in the presence of DNA evidence, bitemark pattern analysis has continued to be used as a valuable form of adjunctive evidence in investigation and trial [92–94].

Despite the strength and value of pattern analysis, vigilance is in order. Forensic odontology cannot be indifferent when the public and legal profession read about cases in which bitemark pattern analysis has pointed to the guilt of individuals who are released from prison years after conviction, when DNA evidence points to their innocence. Nor can the specialty ignore criticism that it has not yet established a sufficient scientific basis to assure validity and reliability.

Significantly, a number of the articles that have criticized the scientific basis for bitemark evidence have also applauded the steps that the specialty has taken to address these concerns. Forensic odontology has done much to improve the scientific status of bitemark analysis in recent years. The development of guidelines and standards, the implementation of periodic workshops to improve the application of current knowledge, the development of a mandatory recertification program and voluntary competency testing for board diplomates, the funding of research projects, and efforts to discipline diplomates are all laudable and generally productive steps that have been taken.

In planning for the future, a recent article related to firearm and toolmark identification is relevant. Nichols emphasizes that one must first recognize and appreciate what has been already been accomplished. This helps to clarify what can be said and what remains to be accomplished. The next step is to define the future course of action in a manner that is consistent with sound scientific practice and that can be effectively communicated to the end user of the discipline [95].

Clearly, the research that has begun to flower in recent years must be supported and expanded. The studies to establish a database for tooth alignment must continue and the results must become widely available. The dentist testifying in court must be able to state, based on documented evidence, that the likelihood of another individual having a dentition similar to the defendant's is only some known figure. This knowledge will go a long way to making bitemark conclusions more meaningful, more applicable, and more evidence based. Future workshops should focus on applying the knowledge gained from current research to casework methodology. Further efforts should be made to develop more meaningful standards for periodic recertification of board diplomates.

It also seems clear that bitemark pattern evidence must become symbiotic with DNA evidence. These forms of evidence should not be considered independent entities, but members of a team [96]. They should be married, not divorced. After all, the first step in the bitemark protocol (after photography) is the collection of saliva evidence for DNA analysis [97].

If bitemark pattern analysis is completed before an anticipated report on DNA evidence is returned, the forensic dentist should recognize that the DNA evidence could be at odds with the conclusions based on pattern analysis. And, because of its known error rate and far greater research base, the DNA evidence will be considered the more reliable form of evidence. The forensic dentist should share this information with the investigative team in advance. He/she should also consider submitting the pattern analysis conclusion as a preliminary report, to be confirmed or refuted by the DNA findings. This is a realistic and honest approach that protects the interests of both the accused and the investigating agency.

Finally, the ABFO can further improve its credibility by strengthening its efforts to assure that its members adhere to the laudable standards articulated in the board's bylaws, code of ethics, and other published materials. The board has recently taken a step in this direction by deciding to initiate a review of current procedures with the goal of improving methods of assuring adherence to board policies.

In brief summary, bitemark pattern analysis has become an established and significant part of the justice system. Even with the emergence of DNA technology, it has been shown that pattern analysis continues to have a vital role to play. It is important to continue to move the development of this evidence in a scientific direction, and to assure that it is applied in this manner in the administration of justice.

ACKNOWLEDGMENTS

The author expresses appreciation to Drs. Robert Dorion, Gary Bell, Paul Stimson, Richard Souviron, Helena Soomer, Michel Perrier, and Frank Morgan for their valued assistance in preparing this chapter.

REFERENCES

1. The Holy Scriptures, Masoretic Text. Philadelphia: Jewish Publication Society of America, 1917: 5,6.
2. The Holy Bible, King James Version. Salt Lake City: Church of Jesus Christ of Latter Day Saints, 1989:5,6.
3. Harvey W. Dental Identification and Forensic Odontology. London: Henry Kimpton, 1976:90.
4. Encyclopedia Britannica. 11th ed.. University of Michigan website, www.umich.edu~ece/student_projects/bonifield/mayhem2.html. Vol. 17. New York: Encyclopaedia Britannica Co., Dec. 19, 2002.
5. California Penal Code, Section 203.
6. Pierce L. Early history of bitemarks. In Averill D, Ed. Manual of Forensic Odontology ed 2. Colorado Springs: American Society of Forensic Odontology, 1991:127–128.
7. Mather C. The wonders of the invisible world. In Burr G, Ed. Narratives of the Witchcraft Cases 1648–1706. New York: Charles Scribner's Sons, 1914:216–223.
8. Morley J. Crimes and Punishment. Vol. 2. London: Phoebus Publishing, 1974:51.
9. Pierce L. Early history of bitemarks. In Averill D, Ed. Manual of Forensic Odontology ed 2. Colorado Springs: American Society of Forensic Odontology, 1991:128–129.
10. Huxley A. Introduction. In Starkey M, Ed. The Devil in Massachusetts. New York: Time Inc. Book Division, 1963:p. xv.
11. Pierce L. Early history of bite marks. In Averill D, Ed. Manual of Forensic Odontology ed 2. Colorado Springs: American Society of Forensic Odontology, 1991:129–130.
12. Keiser-Nielsen S. Teeth That Told. Odense. Denmark: Odense University Press, 1992:17.
13. Harvey W. Dental Identification and Forensic Odontology. London: Henry Kimpton, 1976:88–89.
14. Gustafson G. Forensic Odontology. New York: American Elsevier, 1966:159.
15. Sykora O. How a munched apple gave a robber away. Am Acad Hist Dent 1987; 35(1):64–65.
16. Harvey W. Dental Identification and Forensic Odontology. London: Henry Kimpton, 1976:94.
17. Proceedings of the American Academy of Forensic Sciences, Annual Meeing, Chicago, Colorado Springs: AAFS, 2003:159–186.
18. Doyle v. State, 159 Tex. C.R. 310, 263 S.W.2d 779.
19. People v. Johnson, 8Ill.App.3d 457, 289 N.E.2d 722 (Nov. 16, 1972).
20. Keiser-Nielsen S. Teeth That Told. Odense. Denmark: Odense University Press, 1992:52.
21. Keiser-Nielsen S. Teeth That Told. Odense. Denmark: Odense University Press, 1992:52–56.
22. Bang G. Analysis of tooth marks in a homicide case. Acta Odontol Scand 1976; 34(1):1.
23. Swann G. The Wayne Boden murders. Int J Forens Dent 1974; 2(4):32–42.
24. ABFO. Guidelines for bitemark analysis. J Am Dent Assoc 1986; 112:385–386.
25. Furness J. A new method for the identification of teeth marks in cases of assault and homicide. J Br Dent Assoc 1968:261–267.
26. Gustafson G. Forensic Odontology. New York: American Elsevier, 1966:140–165.
27. Amoëdo O. L'Art dentaire en médécine légale. Paris: Masson & Cie, 1898.

28. Fields K. History of the American Academy of Forensic Sciences. West Conshohocken. PA: ASTM, 1998:61.
29. ABFO Diplomate Reference Manual, Colorado Springs: ABFO, Sec. V, 2004:25.
30. Luntz L, Luntz P. Handbook for Dental Identification. Philadelphia: Lippincott, 1973:148–162.
31. People v. Marx, 54 Cal. App. 3d 100, 126 Cal. Rptr. 350.
32. Giannelli P, Imwinkelried E. Scientific Evidence. 2nd ed.. Vol. I. Charlottesville. VA: Michie Co, 1993:357–371.
33. Bowers CM. The scientific basis for bitemark probability determination. ASFO News, p 14, Summer, 1998.
34. Pitluck H. Bitemark Citations. Las Vegas: Pitluck, 2000:1.
35. Vale G, Sognnaes R, Felando G, Noguchi T. Unusual three-dimensional bite mark evidence in a homicide case. J Forens Sci 1976; 21:642.
36. Giannelli P, Imwinkelried E. Scientific Evidence. 2nd ed.. Vol. I. Charlottesville. VA: Michie Co, 1993:366–367.
37. ABFO Diplomate Reference Manual, Colorado Springs: ABFO Sec. II:3.
38. ABFO Diplomate Reference Manual, Colorado Springs: ABFO Sec. V:26.
39. People v. Milone, 43 Ill. App. 3d 385, 356 N.E.2d 1350:394.
40. People v. Milone, 43 Ill. App. 3d 385, 356 N.E.2d 1350:386–387.
41. People v. Milone, 43 Ill. App. 3d 385, 356 N.E.2d 1350:392–394.
42. People v. Milone, 43 Ill. App. 3d 385, 356 N.E.2d 1350:386.
43. People v. Milone, 43 Ill. App. 3d 385, 356 N.E.2d 1350:386–399.
44. Milone v. Camp, 22 F.3d 693 (7th Cir. 1994), 698.
45. Statement of Gov. James R. Thompson in the Matter of the Executive Clemency Petition of Richard Milone. April 20, 1989:8–16.
46. Shepard's 43 Ill. App.3rd 385.
47. Milone v. Camp, 22 F.3d 693 (7th Cir. 1994):693–706.
48. Milone v. Camp, 22 F.3d 693 (7th Cir. 1994)702.
49. Milone v. Camp, 22 F.3d 693 (7th Cir. 1994):697.
50. Milone v. Camp, 22 F.3d 693 (7th Cir. 1994):701.
51. Shepard's 43 Ill. App.3rd 385.
52. Bundy v. State 455 So 2d 330 (Fla. 1984):349.
53. Bundy: guilty. Time Magazine, August 6, 1979:22.
54. Pitluck H. Bitemark citations. Bite Mark Management and Legal Update: Las Vegas, 2000:2.
55. U.S. v. Martin, 9 M. J. 731 (NCMR 1979) (Aug. 7, 1979).
56. Whittaker D, Watkins K, Wiltshire J. An experimental assessment of the reliability of bite mark analysis. Int J Forens Dent 1975; 3(7):3–7.
57. Hale A. Admissibility of bite mark evidence. So Cal Law Rev 1978; 51:309–334.
58. ABFO. Guidelines for bitemark analysis. J Am Dent Assoc 198; 112:383–386.
59. Rawson R, Vale G, Sperber N, Herschaft E, Yfantis A. Reliability of the scoring system of the American Board of Forensic Odontology for human bite marks. J Forens Sci 1986; 31(4):1235–1260.
60. Mishap on ranch results in death of Dr. Thomas C. Krauss. Am Soc Forens Odont News, 1994:1.
61. ABFO Diplomates Reference Manual. Colorado Springs: ABFO, 1997, Sec. IIC Bowers, G Bell.
62. Manual of Forensic Odontology, Colorado Springs: ASFO, 1995:334–35.
63. Hyzer W, Krauss T. The bite mark standard reference scale – ABFO No. 2. J Forens Sci 1988; 33(2): 498–596.
64. Am. Bd. of Forensic Odontology, Workbook, ABFO Bitemark Workshop #2. San Antonio: Texas, Feb. 12–14, 1994.
65. Am. Bd. of Forensic Odontology, Workbook, ABFO Bitemark Workshop #3. New York. NY, Feb. 16 & 17, 1997.
66. ABFO Diplomates Reference Manual, Colorado Springs: ABFO, 1997, Sec. II.
67. Am. Bd. of Forensic Odontology, Workbook, ABFO Bitemark Workshop #4, Orlando, FL, Feb.14–15, 1999.
68. Wilhoit v. State of Oklahoma, 809 P.2d 1322 (Okl.Cr. 1991).

69. Krauss T. Script of presentation at Bitemark Breakfast. Am Acad Forens Sci Feb. 1972:1–13.
70. Pearman J. Oklahoma vs. Wilhoit. Findings of fact and conclusions of law re: evidentiary hearing of Aug, Oct, Dec 1990:1–10.
71. University of British Columbia Media Release, April 28, 1997:1.
72. BOLD informational brochure. Vancouver. BC: BOLD, 2003:1.
73. Good Impressions. Univ Brit Colum Fac of Dent p1, Spring, 1996.
74. Pitluck H. Bitemark citations. Bite Mark Management and Legal Update: Las Vegas, 2000:1–13.
75. Giannelli P, Imwinkelried E. Scientific Evidence. 2nd ed.. Vol. I. Charlottesville. VA: Michie Co, 1993:363.
76. Faigman D, Kaye D, Saks M. Modern Scientific Evidence. Vol. 2. St Paul: West Group, 1999 Pocket Part:17–19.
77. ABFO Diplomates Reference Manual, Colorado Springs: ABFO, 1997, Sec. II:23–24.
78. Giannelli P, Imwinkelried E. Scientific Evidence. 2nd ed.. Vol. I. Charlottesville. VA: Michie Co, 1993:1.
79. Hale A. Admissibility of bite mark evidence. So Cal Law Rev 1978; 51:309–334.
80. DeLaCruz R. Forensic dentistry and the law: is bite mark evidence here to stay. Am Crim Law Rev 1987; 24:983–1005.
81. Wilkinson A, Gerughty R. Bite mark evidence: its admissiblity is hard to swallow. West State Univ Law Rev 1985; 12(2):519, 560.
82. State v. Stokes, 453 So. 2d 96 (La. 1983).
83. Daubert v. Merrell Dow Parmaceuticals, 509 U.S. 579, 113 S.Ct. 2786, 125, L.Ed2d 469 (1993).
84. Giannelli P, Imwinkelried E. Scientific Evidence. 2nd ed.. Vol. I. Charlottesville. VA: Michie Co, 1993:366.
85. Faigmany D, Kay D, Saks M. Modern Scientific Evidence, Vol. 2. St. Paul: West Group, 1999 Pocket Part 15–17.
86. State v. Hodgson, 512 N.W.2d 95 (Minn.1994).
87. Faigmany D, Kay D, Saks M. Modern Scientific Evidence, Vol. 2. St. Paul: West Group, 1999 Pocket Part 17.
88. Howard v. State, 701 So.2d 274, 288 (Miss.1997).
89. Bowers C. in Modern Scientific Evidence, 1999 Pocket Part:20–30.
90. Pitluck H. Bitemark citations. Bite Mark Management and Legal Update: Las Vegas, 2000:1–13.
91. Thompson Wet al. How the probability of a false positive affects the value of DNA evidence. J Forens Sci Jan 2003; 48(1):48.
92. People v. Castro, Los Angeles Coroner Case 96–03494.
93. People v. Baires, Los Angeles Coroner Case 99–02819.
94. People v. Lopez, Los Angeles County Case KA-0563220.
95. Nichols R. Firearm and toolmark identification criteria: a review of the literature, part II. J Forens Sci 2003; 48(2):318–327.
96. Smith B, Holland M, Sweet D, Dizinno J. DNA and the forensic odontologist. In: Manual of Forensic Odontology. Colorado Springs: ASFO, 1995:283–294.
97. ABFO Diplomates Reference Manual, Colorado Springs: ABFO, 1997, Sec. II:7.

II
Bitemark Recognition

2

Role of Health Professionals in Diagnosing Patterned Injuries from Birth to Death

John D. McDowell
University of Colorado School of Dentistry
Boulder, Colorado, U.S.A.

1. OVERVIEW OF BITING ASSOCIATED WITH DOMESTIC VIOLENCE

North Americans and Europeans continue to report that violence in society is one of their main concerns, yet domestic violence is continuing to increase in both locations. Whereas the home should be a safe haven from violence, the family is anything but safe for many individuals. Children, women, the disabled, and the elderly are more likely to be victims of intentional trauma within their own homes than they are at any other single location. Most domestic violence goes unreported and therefore undocumented.

Citing the work of Tjaden and Thoennes [1], the National Center for Injury Prevention and Control, a division of the Centers for Disease Control and Prevention, has reported that in the United States: (1) approximately 1.5 million women and 0.8 million men are raped and/or physically assaulted by an intimate partner each year; (2) more than 500,000 women injured during IPV (intimate partner violence) require medical treatment; and (3) One in four women has been physically assaulted or raped by an intimate partner, and one in 14 men reported assault or rape by an intimate partner.

Because intentionally inflicted trauma can be perpetrated upon any member of the family, it is difficult to separate one form of domestic violence from another. Battered women are arguably the most common subset of domestic violence victims within dysfunctional families. Not surprisingly, a battered woman is at greater risk of generating a battered child. A child reared within a loving, supportive, nonviolent home is less likely to become an abuser. Concurrence rates of intimate partner abuse/child abuse (an abused mother with an abused child/children) have been reported approximating 50% [2,3]. Witnessing violence is a risk factor for long-term mental and physical health including being a victim of abuse or perpetrating abuse [4,5]. Without intervention, inflicted trauma tends to persist throughout the time that families live together. Some abused children learn that violent behavior is a way of accomplishing short- or long-term goals. Abused children might grow into abused or abusive adults. This violent learned behavior can lead to dysfunctional and abusive relationships that may continue for years, even beyond the seventh and eight decades of life.

Regardless of age or ability, the individual within a violent relationship can be the recipient of any number of different injuries. These include shooting, stabbing, hitting, slapping, kicking, pushing, and biting. Biting as a means of inflicting injury has been reported in nearly every developed country. Excellent articles on recording and analyzing bitemark evidence originate from the United States, Canada, all of the countries within the United Kingdom, India, Russia, and Germany to name a few [6–14]. Bitemarks injuries appear to be a universal problem.

2. CHILD ABUSE

Child abuse is a major public health threat in North America. Most reporting agencies indicate that approximately 1 million American children suffer nonfatal intentionally inflicted physical injuries during any given year. For the past several years, the National Center for Injury Prevention and Control has consistently reported that homicide is the fourth leading cause of death in children between the ages of 1 and 10 years and the third leading cause of death for children aged 10–14. Approximately 1200 children die in the United States every year from abuse and neglect, many dying because of physical injuries inflicted by one or both parents. Among many other forms of trauma, evidence of biting is frequently seen in fatal and nonfatal child abuse cases.

Bitemarks can take many forms and can be seen in various stages of healing in the living abused child. Figure 1 reveals a recent cheek bitemark on a 3-year-old African-American. According to the mother, the child was left in the care of the boyfriend for a brief period. Upon her return, the child had been badly burned by water immersion. The mother immediately noticed the cheek injury and made sure that medical personnel attending to the child's burns photographed the bitemark. The bite is reportedly less than 2 hours old.

Figures 2 and 3 demonstrate two separate bitemarks in a child abuse victim with significant head injuries. Figure 2 shows a bitemark on child's left upper arm and attests to the importance

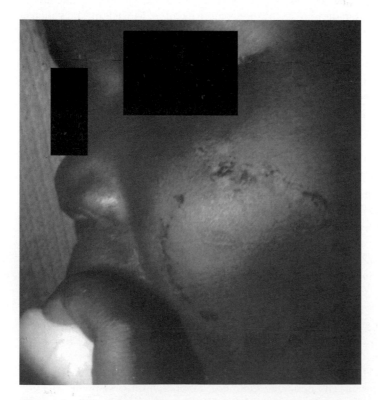

Figure 1   Cheek bitemark.

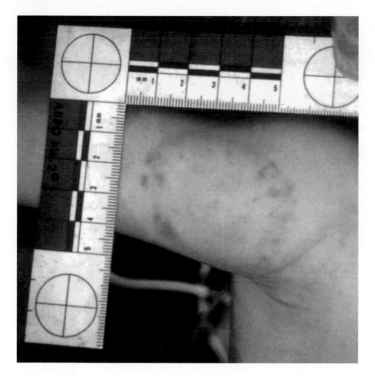

Figure 2 Bitemark on an arm. Also see color photograph insert section.

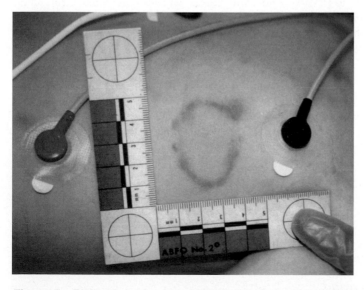

Figure 3 Bitemark on the upper chest. Also see color photograph insert section.

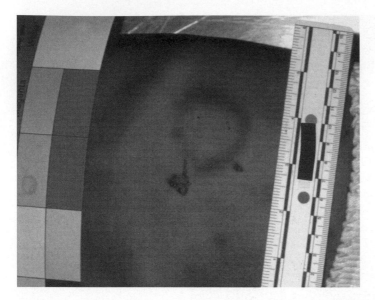

Figure 4   Diffuse bitemark on the abdomen. Also see color photograph insert section.

of making several photographs of the bitemark on a curved surface. The photograph should include as much of the dental arches as possible in one frame while remaining perpendicular to majority of the bitemark. In this example, the canine-premolar region is recorded but the incisor regions are unclear. Figure 3 illustrates the proper photographic technique for localizing and orienting the bitemark with the ABFO No. 2 scale. It is also recommended that additional photographs be taken from a more distant vantage point without scale and with the removal of any materials/equipment.

Although some bitemarks associated with child abuse may be reasonably clear, more commonly the diagnosed bitemark is a diffuse ecchymosis that may initially appear to be of little evidentiary value. Notwithstanding the limitations rightfully associated with these diffuse injuries, valuable evidence may also be associated with these marks. Figure 4 shows a diffuse abdominal bitemark on a 4-year-old homicide victim. There are few individual dental characteristics detected within the class characteristics. However, the bitemark may contain significant evidence in the form of saliva from which the perpetrator's DNA can be recovered.

Color and black-and-white photographs are not the only bitemark recording media. Bitemarks and other healing pattern injuries might be recorded by imaging techniques not commonly available to medical emergency personnel. Infrared, ultraviolet, and alternate light recording systems might be available through law enforcement, forensic lab, or medical examiner offices. These imaging systems record beyond the visual light spectrum.

It is also important to note that the ABFO No. 2 scale (available through Lightening Powder Company) in Figures 2 and 3 references the bitemark metrically. Whether recorded on film or digitally [15], an additional gray-scale reference is present for density reproduction of the captured image. The less acceptable, one-dimensional ruler in Figure 4 also shows a Kodak Color Control Patch used by some photographers to verify color accuracy.

3   INTIMATE PARTNER ABUSE

Intimate partner abuse (also called spouse or spousal abuse) is the commonest form of domestic violence. There has been much debate over which gender is the more likely to commit abuse or which member in the partnership is most likely to be abused. Historically, most authors have reported that women are most frequently recipients of abuse and receive the most severe injuries. However, several recent studies including meta-analyses conclude that men are just as likely to be abused as women [16–21]. A review of the behavioral science literature indicates that some studies report that women were more likely than men to commit acts of aggression and more frequently use aggressive acts [22–26]. It does not matter whether the man or the woman is more likely to be physically aggressive; that both may commit acts of violence against an intimate partner is important. This includes biting [27–29].

As in child abuse, bitemarks associated with spouse abuse may be found on any part of the body. Figure 5 reveals an ill-defined bitemark on the mons pubis. After collecting other physical evidence and extensively photographing the area under various lighting conditions, the pubic hair was shaved to more clearly demonstrate the diffuse bruising. The maxillary canines produced the prominent contusions.

When detected by health care providers, law enforcement personnel or others, bitemarks should be treated and documented in accordance with standard institutional practices. Additionally, any forensic evidence should be recovered including, when indicated, collecting salivary evidence from the wounds. Photography remains a significant means of evidence collection and preservation. When curved surfaces like breast tissue or extremities are photographed, it is often necessary to take photographs in two or more planes. Figure 6 demonstrates one technique for aligning the film plane with the bitemarks. Figure 7 shows a bitemark on the woman's upper back. Note how the bitemark can be recorded in one photographic frame.

Depending on the biter's force and movement, avulsive injuries can occur. Bitemark analyses are often more complex when tissue has been distorted or removed. The problem may be compounded by medical intervention including suturing and bandaging, inflammation, and the healing process itself. Figure 8 displays a bitemark on an abused woman's upper right chest. Although the victim was very specific on the perpetrator's identity and timing of the event, the bitemark analysis could not provide identity confirmation.

Figure 9 depicts a nose bitemark produced during a violent struggle. The bite was so deep that the tip of the nose was nearly lost in transport.

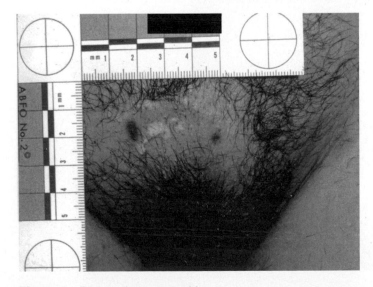

Figure 5   Bite on the mons pubis.

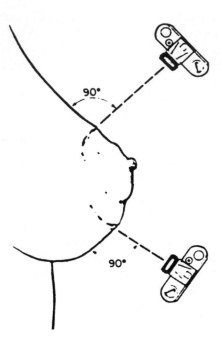

Figure 6 Photographic angulation.

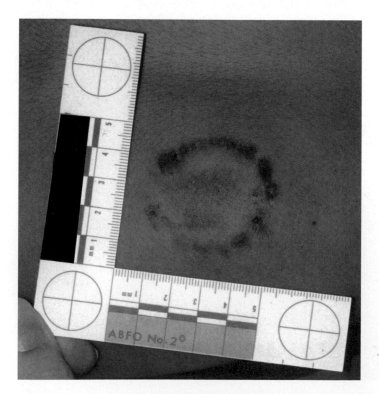

Figure 7 Bitemark on the back. Also see color photograph insert section.

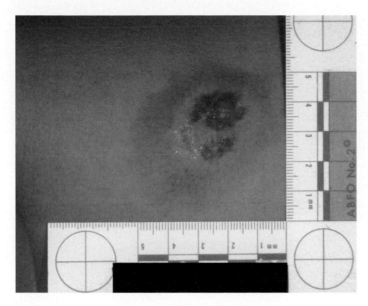

Figure 8   Bitemark on the upper right chest. Also see color photograph insert section.

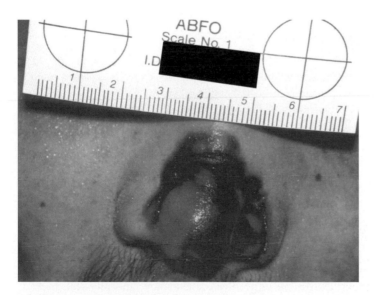

Figure 9   Nose bitemark.

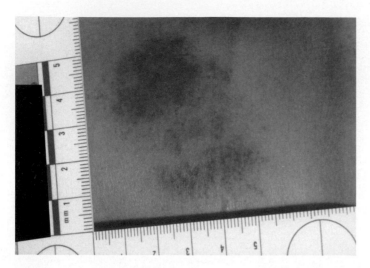

Figure 10   Diffuse neck bitemark.

Figure 10 demonstrates a neck bitemark inflicted during domestic violence. Several hours after the assault, the woman presented to the emergency department for treatment of other injuries. When asked about the neck bruise, the woman admitted she had been bitten. Individual teeth marks cannot be identified within the inflammation; however, serial photographs should be taken with various films and light source.

4. BITEMARKS IN ELDER ABUSE

The 2000 census reveals that more than 20% of the U.S. population is 65 years of age or older. Most of these individuals reside in homes where the quality of life exceeds that of previous generations. As they age, some will remain in good health; others will develop chronic and disabling diseases that limit their daily activity. A few will eventually become totally dependent on others. Unfortunately, some will be subjected to abuse and neglect. A recent estimate indicates that nearly 500,000 elderly persons annually experienced abuse, neglect, or both in the domestic setting [30].

In the United States, self-neglect, the condition where an elderly self-sufficient person loses autonomy, is prevalent. Another common form of neglect is unintentional neglect, the condition whereby a person is incapable of caring for another. Intentional neglect arises with the deliberate withholding of essential services, medications, or support necessary to maintain a good quality of life. As in child neglect, elderly neglect can result in injury, disease, or death whether intentional or not.

Abuse and neglect often result from familial conflict. Factors contributing to intrafamily elder abuse include postretirement depression, infirmities, dependency, and physical, mental, and emotional illness [28]. Fortunately, a stressful situation does not often result in physical trauma to the aged. Although spouse abuse may begin late in life out of frustration or anger, it more likely involves a long history.

The diagnosis of intentional trauma can be more difficult in the aged population. Systemic diseases and medications can lead to increased bruising. Medications, hypotension, visual deficiencies, arrythmias, and vertigo can lead to falls. Caretakers or persons in authority might misinterpret the accidental self-induced trauma. All cases of suspected elder abuse should be evaluated by a team of knowledgeable and experienced medical, dental, nursing, social, and

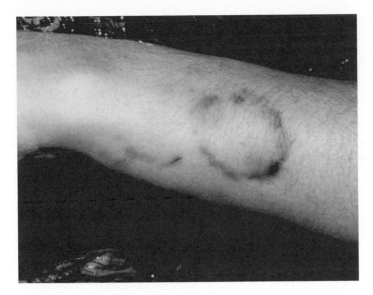

Figure 11 Bitemarks on the arm.

law enforcement personnel in a supportive, nonaccusatorial manner. The elderly abused often exhibit denial and shame, and might even minimize the sequelae of an assault.

Whenever bitemarks are detected, they should be handled in a like manner as those of child and spousal abuse. Figure 11 shows two arm bitemarks on an elderly homicide victim. Note that the proximal mark is quite clear as there was little inflammatory response.

Figure 12 exhibits a mark on the back of the same victim. Notice how the dependent lividity, resulting in blood pooling within the individual tooth imprints, has caused the marks

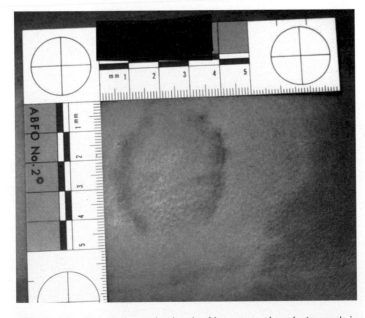

Figure 12 Bitemark on the back. Also see color photograph insert section.

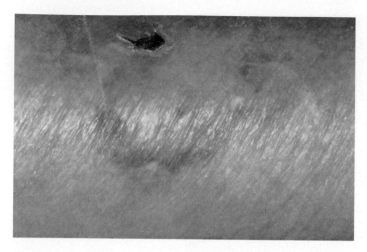

Figure 13 Bitemark on the forearm.

to become quite clear. Figure 13 illustrates a bitemark on the forearm of an 83-year-old Caucasian man. This 4-day-old mark should be compared to the victim's dentition to eliminate a self-inflicted injury.

A bitemark on the upper right chest of a 77-year-old Hispanic man is shown in Figure 14. The nursing-home resident, assaulted by his roommate, received at least two bites in addition to other injuries. The bite was inflicted about 3 days prior to this photograph. Figure 15 shows the forearm of the same patient who claimed that the bitemarks were inflicted at the same time. Note the difference in healing.

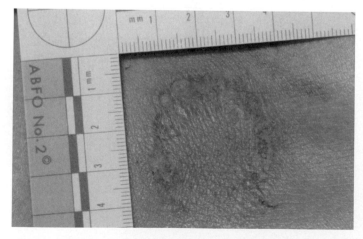

Figure 14 Bitemark on the upper chest. Also see color photograph insert section.

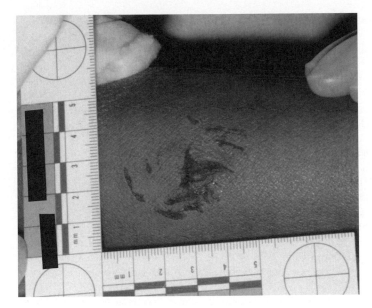

Figure 15 Bitemark on the arm. Also see color photograph insert section.

5. CONCLUSION

Whenever there is direct, violent contact between individuals, many forms of trauma can occur, including evidence of biting. Several studies have shown that bitemarks are seen in every form of domestic violence. The first step in bitemark analysis is recognition. The unrecognized bitemark will usually go undocumented and potentially lost as a valuable piece of forensic evidence. When bitemarks yield individual dental characteristics, identification of the perpetrator is possible.

REFERENCES

1. Tjaden P, Thoennes N. Extent, nature and consequences of intimate partner violence: findings from the National Violence Against Women Survey. Report for grant 93-IJ-CX-0012, funded by the National Instate of Justice and the Centers for Disease Control. Washington. DC: NIJ, 2000.
2. McKibben L, DeVos E, Newberger E. Victimization of mothers of abused children; a controlled study. Pediatrics 1989; 84:531–535.
3. Wright RJ, Wright RO, Isaac NE. Response to battered mothers in the pediatric emergency department; a call for an interdisciplinary approach to family violence. Pediatrics 1997; 99:186–192.
4. Felitti V, Anda R, Nordenberg D, Williamson D, Spitz AM, Edwards, et al. V. Relationship of childhood abuse and household dysfunction to many of the leading causes of death in adults. Am J Prevent Med 1998; 14(4):245–258.
5. Holtzworth-Monroe A, Bates L, Smutzler N, Sandin E. A brief review of the research on husband violence. Part I: maritally violent versus nonviolent men. Aggress Violent Behav 1997; 2(1):65–99.
6. Fenton SJ, Bouquot JE, Unkel JH. Orofacial consideration for pediatric, adult and elderly victims of abuse. Emerg Med Clin North Am 2000; 18(3):601–617.
7. Lee LY, Ilan J, Mulvey T. Human biting of children and oral manifestations of abuse: a case report and literature review. J Dent Child 2002; 69(1):92–95.
8. Sweet D, Pretty IA. A look at forensic dentistry. Part 2: teeth as weapons of violence—identification of bitemark perpetrators. Br Dent J 2000; 190(8):415–428.

9. Pretty IA, Sweet D. The scientific basis for human bitemark analyses—a critical review. Sci Justice 2001; 41(2):85–92.
10. Dhar V, Tandon S. Bite mark analysis in child abuse. J Indian Soc Pedodon Preve Dent 1998; 16(3): 96–102.
11. Mailis NP. Bitemarks in forensic dental practice: the Russian experience. J Forens Odonto-Stomatol 1993; 11(1):31–33.
12. Trube-Becker E. Bite-marks on battered children. J Legal Med (Germany) 1977; 79(1):73–78.
13. Simon PA. Recognizing and reporting the orofacial trauma of child abuse/neglect. Texas Dent J 2000; 117(10):21–31.
14. Senn DR, McDowell JD, Alder ME. Dentistry's role in recognition and reporting of domestic violence, abuse and neglect. Dent Clin North Am Forens Odontol 2001; 45(2):343–363.
15. Bowers CM, Johansen RJ. Digital analysis of bite marks and human identification. Dent Clin North Am Forens Odontol 2001; 45(2):327–339.
16. Archer J. Sex differences in aggression between heterosexual partners: a meta-analytic review. Psychol Bull 2000; 126:651–680.
17. Carrado M, George MJ, Loxam E, Jones, et al. L. Aggression in British heterosexual relationships: a descriptive analysis. Aggress Behav 1996; 22:401–405.
18. Coney NS, Mackey WC. The feminization of domestic violence in American: the woozle effect goes beyond rhetoric. J Mens Stud 1999; 8(1):45–58.
19. Fiebert MS, Gonzalez DM. Women who initiate assaults: the reasons offered for such behavior. Psychol Rep 1997; 80:583–590.
20. George MJ. A victimization survey of female perpetrated assaults in the United Kingdom. Aggress Behav 1999; 25:67–79.
21. Goodyear-Smith FA, Laidlaw TM. Aggressive acts and assaults in intimate relationships: towards an understanding of the literature. Behav Sci Law 1999; 17:285–304.
22. Lalmuss D. The intergenerational transmission of marital aggression. J Marriage Fam 1984; 46: 11–19.
23. Margolin G. The multiple forms of aggressiveness between marital partners: how do we identify them. J Marital Fam Ther 1987; 13:77–84.
24. Milardo RM. Gender asymmetry in common couple violence. Pers Relationships 1998; 5:423–438.
25. O'Leary KD, Barling J, Arias I, Rosenbaum A, Malone J, Tyree A. Prevalence and stability of physical aggression between spouses: a longitudinal analysis. J Consult Clin Psychol 1989; 57: 263–268.
26. Russell FH, Hulson B. Physical and psychological abuse of heterosexual partners. Pers Indiv Diff 1992; 13:457–473.
27. Murphy JE. Date abuse and forced intercourse among college students. In Hotaling, Finkelhor, Kirkpatrick, Straus (Eds). Family Abuse and Its Consequences: New Direction in Research. Thousand Oaks. CA: Sage Publications, 1988:285–296.
28. McDowell JD. Domestic violence: recognizing signs of abuse in patients. Dent Teamwork 1994: 23–25.
29. McDowell JD, Miller EH. The dental team's role in recognizing and reporting domestic violence. J Colo Dent Assoc 1996; 1:21–37.
30. National Elder Abuse Incidence Study. Final Report Prepared for the Administration on Aging. Washington. DC: U.S. Department of Health and Human Services, 1998.

3

Role of the Medical Examiner/Coroner/Pathologist

Joseph H. Davis
Retired Chief Medical Examiner, Miami-Dade County
Florida, U.S.A.

1. DEATH INVESTIGATIVE SYSTEMS

Most death investigators, including consultant forensic odontologists, are familiar with their own jurisdiction but may not be aware of the variables that exist throughout the world including the United States. In general, systems tend to fall into three broad categories. Most common throughout much of the non-English-speaking world is a system where a magistrate or prosecutor supervises the death investigation. When an autopsy is needed, it may be provided by governmental or university sources. The English-speaking nations tend to follow the coroner system, the coroner being appointed as a quasi-judicial agent who supervises death investigation and may conduct inquests of the dead. When the colonies broke away from Britain, the coroner system was brought to the United States, usually as a county elective office. In some states, a justice of the peace office was combined with coroner functions. Medical qualifications were not required.

Some elected coroner systems of the United States have been replaced by an appointed medical examiner system. The first system with a pathologist supervisor and a central laboratory in the United States was in New York City, circa 1915. Maryland replaced its elected lay coroner system with an appointed pathologist medical examiner system in 1939. Other jurisdictions followed in the period following World War II. Today the United States has a varied mix of systems including sheriff-coroners in some parts of California, and medical examiners in other parts. Some states have only medical examiners, and others a mix of coroners and medical examiners [1]. In some jurisdictions the coroner may be called a medical examiner even though a nonpathologist. Historical, political, and economic factors seem to determine what system exists. Canada has generally followed the coroner model, although some jurisdictions follow the medical examiner model [1].

2. A COMPLETE MEDICAL EXAMINER SYSTEM

It might be well to define a complete medical examiner system as one where the agency director is an appointed pathologist with authority to carry out scene investigations and to authorize and perform autopsies of public concern. The usual statute defines such deaths as apparent homicide, suicide, accident, suspicious, sudden when in apparent good health, unattended by a licensed physician, of occupational origin, of public health threat, and so forth. In some states coroners must be physicians, others not. A recent trend is the election of forensically trained nurses as coroners. A universal awareness of the need for training exists. A national guideline for death scene investigation was produced only recently [2].

3. THE FLORIDA MODEL

A model for a large state is Florida, where a system of districts, each headed by an appointed pathologist district medical examiner, serves the entire state [3]. A commission provides oversight with rule-making authority. About 12% of the total deaths in Florida fall into one or more of the above categories. About 53% of all medical examiner–certified cases are violent—either accident, suicide, or homicide. The remainder are natural. Some statutes require the medical examiner to approve all cremations, an increasingly popular means of final disposal. If cremation approvals are included as a medical examiner function, over half of all deaths within Florida come to the attention of the medical examiners [4]. Homicides constitute about 0.6% of total deaths in Florida. Within that small pool are found those few homicides associated with bitemarks.

4. CASE INVESTIGATIVE PRINCIPLES

Proper case investigative principles do not deviate regardless of the system. However, system variations may adversely prevent the implementation of proper principles. The objective of a death investigation is to derive sufficient data to determine cause and manner of death, to assure civil and criminal justice, and to assure proper certification and disposal of the dead. A system that favors total expeditious investigations by educated, trained, and ethically impartial professionals is preferred. Oversight and review mechanisms ought to exist. In Florida the Medical Examiners Commission designates district boundaries, participates in the nomination process for district medical examiners, and has disciplinary and rule-making authority. It has set standards for mandated performance of autopsies in certain types of cases and for record preparation and preservation, and even specifies personal participation of the pathologist during the autopsy procedure [5]. Not all systems in the United States operate with these controls, leaving room for variations based on personal whim. Such systems may fail to adhere to proper principles of investigation. A positive influence upon investigative quality is participation in the American Academy of Forensic Sciences and the National Association of Medical Examiners.

A death investigation involves different agencies with varied personnel. All must act together in harmony to produce a correlated investigation. The death investigation requires a synthesis of information derived from scene and witnesses, past medical and social history, and examination of the environment in which the death or injury occurred. Participants in this process are police, crime scene technicians, crime laboratory scientists, medical examiner or coroner investigators, pathologists, toxicologists, and various consultants—forensic odontologists, anthropologists, entomologists, engineers, and so forth. In general, most investigative and decision processes are shared between two agencies, police and coroner/medical examiner. All investigations must be sufficient to develop a database that assures answers for future questions, those of criminal, civil, scientific, family service, and public concern. The key to success is the correlative and cognitive capabilities of the supervisors on both sides.

5. FORENSIC ODONTOLOGY SERVICE NOT AVAILABLE

The genesis of forensic odontology service within a busy medical examiner practice may be exemplified by the following personal experience. It began nearly a half-century ago in cramped quarters with a limited budget and no prior local experience to forecast needs. The earliest forensic dental identification problem concerned a 35-year-old intoxicated male, blood alcohol 0.22 g percent, who perished from smoke inhalation while smoking in a parked automobile. The body was charred beyond recognition (Fig. 1). Papers in a wallet and witnesses furnished presumptive identity. Police telephoned the chief dental officer of the Bureau of Medicine and Surgery, Department of the Navy in Washington, DC. He in turn telephoned the Naval Records Management Center in St. Louis for a record dated July 24, 1946. The information was relayed to the dental officer at the Marine Corps Air Station in Miami, who prepared a chart and compared it with the victim's teeth. The transmission of record information from the initial inquiry to receipt in Miami was accomplished in only 20 min.

The initial "bite" case for the office concerned a brawl in which a man struck a mouth with his fist. Lacerations on his hand became infected. He delayed seeking medical care, gas gangrene set in, and he died.

Local knowledge of bitemark analysis was nil in those days. In 1959, a 53 year-old murdered spinster was found strangled in her bedroom. A breast had been amputated and the vaginal area was mutilated after death. Found later at the morgue, beneath dense pubic hair on the skin of the mons pubis, was a curvilinear arc of faint indistinct focal markings that raised a question of a bitemark (Fig. 2). The overlying pubic hair could have acted as an intermediary to obscure fine detail.

At that time the possibility of a bitemark was discussed but not pursued. Twelve and a half years later, the assailant confessed to the murder. A partial palm and a fingerprint documented his presence at the crime scene. The medical examiner file does not indicate whether his confession mentioned any biting.

Figure 1 Body of the first dental identification case in Miami.

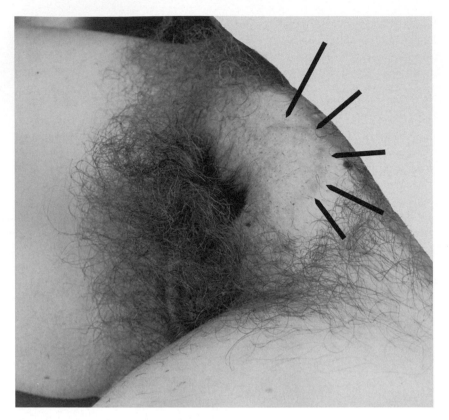

Figure 2   Miami's first questionable bitemark case on the murdered victim's mons pubis.

When skeletal remains were found, the treating dentist confirmed the identity. In one case, a canvas bag containing a skeleton, including skull, was found in a small lake. The initial examination by a dentist noted new gold crowns. The lack of wear facets (Fig. 3) indicated that they were inserted less than 2 months from death. Eventually, the treating dentist identified the body.

The murdered victim had been buried in a shallow grave, exhumed by the killers, and dumped in the lake. In many skeletal investigations there are sufficient identity markers apart from the teeth. Dental consultations in those days were limited. The medical examiner would examine the teeth for consistency with known characteristics of the presumed victim. There was no dental profiling nor was there National Crime Information Center (NCIC) dental queries for possible matches of the missing to the unknowns. In one presumed identity case, the victim presented with amalgam fillings placed at 11 years of age. The dentist had drawn their outlines on an odontogram (three-dimensional drawing of the dentition) (Fig. 4). About 15 years later, the match between ante- and postmortem records was confirmed and the victim identified.

Gustafson's 1966 textbook [6] was at the time most useful in the assessment. Today, one might consider the Manual of Forensic Odontology, a publication of the American Society of Forensic Odontology [7]. An internet search might provide information on bitemarks, but knowledge of the source, applicability, and veracity of the information must be verified.

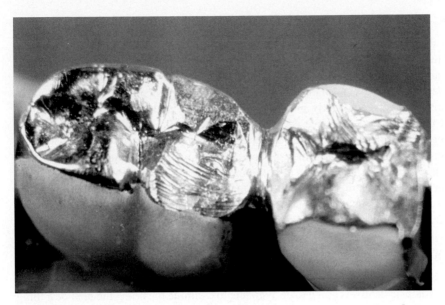

Figure 3 Lack of wear on gold crowns indicates that death probably occurred within 2 months of dental treatment.

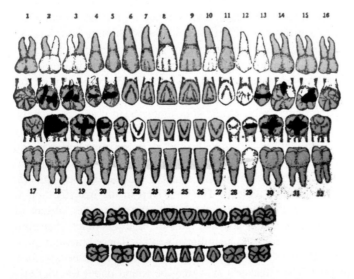

Figure 4 Meticulous charting of amalgams at age 11 permitted matching to the teeth of a decomposed adult murdered 15 years later.

6. FORENSIC ODONTOLOGY SERVICE BECOMES AVAILABLE

Subsequently, a dentist involved in a skeletal identity of a former patient expressed interest in forensic cases. He volunteered his services, became proficient, and is now an open-ended contractual consultant, an arrangement that encourages visits. Frequency of participation by an unpaid volunteer or a fee-for-service consultant is restricted by the reimbursement system. Medical examiner case investigations frequently involve the mouth. The present consultant is notified for all things of dental interest even if it is an obvious pseudo-bite pattern. Whether or not a dental consultant is used depends upon the interest of the consultant and the lack of fiscal restraints on consultations. The more times a dental consultant is encouraged to spend in a medical examiner's office, the more frequent is the use of dental expertise in problem solving and teaching. The optimum is a relationship that facilitates the use of dental consultations rather than restricts. As a result of this policy, our dental consultant, Richard R. Souviron, DDS, has examined over 2000 cases in the Miami-Dade County Medical Examiner Department.

7. BITEMARKS

Suspect bitemarks merit special consideration. If the medical examiner/coroner lacks dental resources, and no forensic dentist is going to be available to examine the body, the next best thing is to document so that future study may be feasible. The marks should be carefully scrutinized for evidence of abrasions, contusions, petechia in skin, and impressions left by teeth. The bite should be swabbed for DNA, making certain that the swabs and containers are not cross-contaminated. Orientation and closeup photographs must be arranged. A quality camera and film sufficient for future enlargements is needed. Digital photography may suffice if camera resolution permits enlargements without distortion. Color slide film has greater resolution than print film. A series of photographs without a scale and a series of photographs with scale in the same plane as the mark are essential. The ABFO No. 2 scale is preferred. Composition, lighting, color balance (use a color scale in pictures), and focus are critical. A macro lens is useful for the closer views. When satisfactory photographs are completed, a cast or other form of documentation may be made of the bitemark in the event that indentations are present [8]. Local police crime scene personnel or a local dentist may be able to assist. After all documentation to scale is completed, careful total excision of the bitemark is made, avoiding tissue distortion through shrinkage or other means (Editor's note: see Chapter 13), for two ulterior purposes: to preserve photographically the color and depth of the underlying contusion, and for microscopic slide preparations. Eventual histopathological examination is desirable and is outlined in Chapters 13 and 14. Microscopic slides must be identified as to source. It is well to have the report contain a chart of the bite and the identified sites from which microscopic slides have been prepared. Ideally, a forensic odontologist should participate.

The attacker may transfer personal identity substrates to the victim or vice versa, which may include blood, sperm, sweat, or hair. While human bitemarks may be visible, DNA containing saliva is usually not. The crime scene and circumstances might indicate a potential oral transfer regardless of the state of the persons involved. The first step in the investigation is recognition that a set of circumstances might indicate potential for mouth contact absent of teethmarks. If conscious, the patient might indicate possible sites of mouth contact. If unconscious or dead, exposed portions of skin may indicate a similar potential. These potential areas should be protected and swabbed for DNA as soon as possible. Clothing should be carefully preserved and not further contaminated. The attacker's skin may be found under the victim's fingernails.

One may not assume that first responders thought of this potential. Only in recent years has the value of DNA evidence from saliva been appreciated. Police may focus on bloodstains or obvious injury patterns but may overlook the potential for saliva transfer at other points. Those who follow in the investigative steps must be concerned despite the fact that they were not involved in the initial investigative phase.

In fatal events, sooner or later coroner/medical examiner personnel enter into the investigation. Systems, response of personnel, and training and experience of personnel are not uniform from one jurisdiction to another. Yet the principles of proper investigation remain the same throughout all jurisdictions. Accordingly we should familiarize ourselves with the investigative systems in our jurisdictions and be prepared to respond properly.

The coroner/medical examiner investigator may be part of the initial response, although not always. The first rule is that the scene remains undisturbed until crime scene evidence technicians have documented by proper photography the relationship of the body to its surroundings. Any items of potential evidence must be documented. At some point the body is examined. This critical examination may disclose the potential for saliva transfer to any part of the body, the potential for patterns of teeth injury, the potential for fingernail scraping evidence, and even latent fingerprints upon skin. Latent fingerprints upon skin, long thought to be impossible, are possible under certain circumstances [9]. An example is a deceased young woman who was found at her place of employment. Her nude body was dusted for fingerprints and a set appeared on a leg above the ankle. Police photographed the prints with a Rolliflex camera equipped with auxiliary clip on magnifying lenses and used print film. The medical examiner used a Nikon with an expensive macro lens and color slide film. Only the medical examiner's photographs revealed resolution detail sufficient for classification of the prints. Two lessons were learned: it is wise to build redundancy into the documentation process, and resolution is essential. Camera and film quality must meet specific needs. Police subsequently switched to Nikon cameras with quality lenses. Another lesson learned was that ambient temperature plays a role in the detection of fingerprints on human skin [9]. Similar high-resolution quality photographs must also apply to bitemark evaluation.

Clothing may or may not be removed from the body prior to transport. If removed, pathologist and especially the bitemark specialist must know the nature of the clothing and the areas covered by the clothing. A recent example concerned a forensic odontologist who rendered an erroneous bitemark opinion because he failed to require police crime scene photographs. Magnification of the skin may reveal a cloth weave pattern. Also, when clothing is interposed between teeth and skin, saliva DNA should be expected upon the clothing, not the underlying skin. Pathologists and their consultants must therefore be certain that all pertinent circumstantial information be furnished before rendering an opinion. If clothing interposition is suspected, the suspicion must be immediately related to the police and the forensic laboratory to search the clothing for DNA.

It is incumbent upon all first responders, treatment personnel, police, crime scene investigators, medical examiner/coroner, pathologist to realize the potential interpersonal victim-assailant linkage with the crime scene and circumstances.

8. CONSULTATIONS

A pattern injury may clearly be a bitemark, a suspicious bitemark, or clearly not a bitemark. In any case, a forensic odontologist should be given the opportunity to examine the lesions and judge their relevance. The problem is that not all pathologists or dentists are equally trained, knowledgeable, or experienced. For these reasons, it is prudent to have a qualified set of eyes review the evidence.

Two murder victims were found in an adjacent jurisdiction. To the pathologist and the consultant odontologist, some patterns on a body appeared to be human bitemarks. Prudence prevailed and they sought the assistance of a more experienced forensic odontologist who brought the present author along. Although some patterns might suggest human teethmarks, an incision into the suspect area clearly demonstrated the superficial nature of surface erosions caused by ants. Prudence on the part of the investigators resulted in a proper final opinion as to the cause of the patterns. Unfortunately, wrongful criminal charges can result when evidence is weak and opinions are strong. Ant bites erosions and irritative dermatitis patterns have been equated with human bite patterns by some odontologists and pathologists with dire consequences. A wise pathologist is familiar with patterns and should judge the validity of consultant opinions. The police and prosecuting attorney are not expected to possess this talent. The forensic pathologist retains accountability and liability for pathology opinions and in some jurisdictions might be liable for consultant opinions (Editor's note: see Chapters 24, 26).

9. PATTERN VARIABLES

Scene investigators, pathologists, and odontologists recognize that bitemarks can present variable patterns. The inflicted violence is variable. At one end of the spectrum there is licking, mouthing, or sucking without any abrasive or crushing action by teeth. Circumstances must be carefully evaluated before rendering an opinion that potential DNA sites are absent. At the other end of the spectrum is the avulsive bite. An example is the notorious highly publicized example of boxer Mike Tyson who bit off part of his opponent's ear.

Sites may be located anywhere on the body. One study suggests that 40% of cases had two or more bites. Males were bitten more commonly on arm or shoulders while females on breast, arms, and legs. This differs from live clinical studies where hands and fingers were more common reflecting the nature of the problem, altercation [10].

Skin thickness varies widely from thin eyelids, nipple, scrotum and penis to thick skin of the back, the nose overlying cartilage, calloused palms and feet. Skin varies with age from the thin skin of the infant to the atrophic fragile skin of the elderly.

The pattern injury produced by teeth will vary depending on surface contour and interpersonal positions. The observed pattern on a body lying flat on the autopsy table may or may not reflect the pattern of infliction in positional relationship at the precise moment of attack. A bite in the region of the axillary fold will vary with positional change (Fig. 5).

The same victim, the same attacker, more than one bite, the patterns may appear to be from different sources to the untrained eye. Alternatively, a dental impression on the back of the hand or forearm may be caused by the victim's own mouth resting on that portion of the anatomy after collapse.

The pathologist and consultant should anticipate future questions that may arise as the investigation unfolds and wends its way through court. Was the bite inflicted before, during, or after death?

MacDonald, commenting on circumstances of a bite, points out a spectrum from amorous to aggressive [11]. One may anticipate a defense claim that a bite was consensual and not associated with the crime. Would a bite leave permanent marks or scarring? In a living victim, permanence of damage may constitute the difference between a third-degree battery and a second-degree battery and thus affect the criminal charges.

10. EXPERT DISCORDANCE

What happens when experts disagree on bitemark interpretation? Theoretically, equally well trained experts ought to come to the same conclusions. The first consideration is to determine whether they examined the exact same evidence. For example, original slides and duplicates

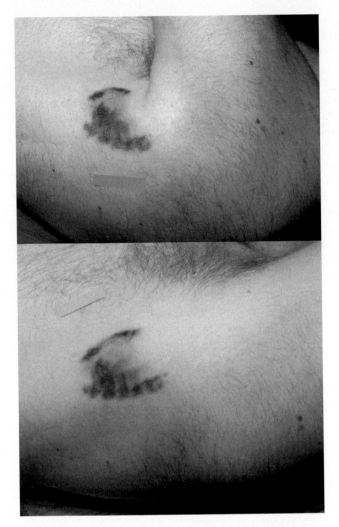

Figure 5   Posterior axillary fold bitemark without arm extension (top) and arm raised (bottom).

are not necessarily the same. Original photos that have been digitized are not originals. That being so, the next step is to determine if one of the experts is a pseudo-expert whose motives may be suspect. Starrs, in an informative and entertaining fashion including the title ''Mounte-banks Among Forensic Scientists'' presents 12 case examples with ample references from trial testimony [12]. In reviewing the cases, it is noteworthy that untrustworthy testimony often includes exaggeration of credentials. Aberrant opinion may be difficult to challenge, but falsifica-tion of credentials is easy to detect.

The greatest problem is when the differing experts are equally well trained, knowledgeable, experienced, and well respected. In theory, discordance of interpretation should be lacking. Nordby, whose background includes medical examiner death scene investigation, has a unique qualification—a doctorate in philosophy with a dissertation on logic. One needs to study his analysis of the factors leading to disagreement between forensic experts, including odontologists [13]. The eyes see but the viewer observes. Observation is affected by investigative expectation. From observation is derived opinion which may have been affected by an artifact induced by expectation. The Nordby paper deserves repetitive study. (Editor's note: Chapters 23, 27, and 28 address some of the issues raised by the author.)

11. SUMMARY

The medical examiner/coroner is usually the person to notify a consultant forensic odontologist that a suspect bitemark is present. Police or coroner/medical examiner investigators are most likely the first to notice suspect patterns. If they fail, the forensic pathologist is the next step in the detection. At this point the full resources of forensic odontology must prevail. The role of the forensic odontologist as part of the death investigative team is today an accepted fact.

A complex bitemark case may occur in any police or coroner/medical examiner jurisdiction, large or small, rural or urban. Lack of local resources is no excuse for an inadequate investigation. Local egos must never override a need to seek consultation. Police, forensic pathology, and forensic odontology networks exist. Initial "what to do" consultation is only a telephone call away. If an arrest is made and a criminal trial ensues, courts will not tolerate a lack-of-resources excuse for an inadequate investigation. Coroner/medical examiners and their forensic pathologists must plan for this eventuality if their community and justice will be served. Ideal planning should encompass the total death investigation system including infrastructure and training, professional standards and quality, the criminal and civil justice systems, public health needs, disasters, and homeland security [14].

REFERENCES

1. Combs DL, Parrish RG, Ing R. Death Investigation in the United States and Canada. Atlanta; U.S. Department of Health and Human Services, Public Health Service, Centers for Disease Control and Prevention, August, 1995.
2. National Medicolegal Review Panel. Death Investigation: A Guide for the Scene Investigator. National Institute of Justice, Nov 1999. http://www.ncjrs.org/txtfiles/167568.txt.
3. Chapter 406, Medical Examiners, Florida Statutes.
4. Medical Examiners Commission Annual Report 2000, Tallahassee, FL: Florida Department of Law Enforcement.
5. Florida Administrative Code 11G 1–5.
6. Gustafson G. Forensic Odontology. London: Stapler Press, 1966.
7. Bowers DM, Bell G, Eds. Manual of Forensic Odontology. 3rd ed. Montpelier. VT: Printing Specialists, 1995.
8. Rao VJ, Souviron RS. Dusting and lifting the bite print: a new technique. J Forens Sci 1984; 19(1): 326–330.
9. Sampson WC. Latent finger print evidence on human skin (Part 1). J Forens Ident 1996; 46(2): 188–195.
10. Vale GL, Noguchi TT. Anatomical distribution of human bitemarks in a series of 67 cases. J Forens Sci 1983; 28(1):61–69.
11. MacDonald DG. Bitemark recognition and interpretation. J Forens Sci 1974; 14:229–233.
12. Starrs JE. Mountebanks among forensic scientists in Safferstein R, Ed. Forensic Science Handbook. Vol. II. Englewood Cliffs. NJ: Prentice Hall, 1988.
13. Nordby JJ. Can we believe what we see, if we see what we believe? Expert disagreement. J Forens Sci 1992; 37(4):1115–1124.
14. Committee for the Workshop on the Medicolegal Death Investigation System. Medicolegal Death Investigation System Workshop Summary. Washington: National Academies Press, 20001, 2003.

4

Teamwork in Bitemark Investigation

Veronique F. Delattre
Office of the Medical Examiner of Harris County
Houston, Texas, U.S.A.

1. RATIONALE

Integrating the philosophy of teamwork during bitemark investigation of the deceased can serve as the basis for success in the recognition, collection, chain of possession, storing, analysis, and court presentation of the evidence. Despite recent advances in bitemark analysis, the most important asset is a thorough and well-planned investigation. Even in the presence of unlimited resources, high-tech equipment, and modern laboratory facilities, an investigation can only benefit from the interaction of competent personnel.

2. BENEFITS OF TEAMWORK DURING BITEMARK INVESTIGATION

Teamwork can reduce if not eliminate feelings of disjointedness among the first responders, treatment personnel, police, crime scene investigators, medical examiner/coroner, pathologist, odontologist, and other forensic scientists working the same case. Teamwork also assures that one forensic specialty's methods of evidence collection will not undermine the efforts of others, or damage the particular evidence needed in each specialty. Even the most modern, high-tech methods may be of no evidentiary value if the evidence is undiagnosed, overlooked, altered, damaged, or destroyed before each expert is able to complete his/her portion of the investigation. The teamwork approach allows each member of the team to hold specific duties, limits and responsibilities. These should be clearly spelled out, preferably in a written protocol, so as to minimize confusion, duplication, and errors. This approach will potentially enhance the perceived validity of the various forms of evidence presented to the jury [1].

3. DEVELOPING A TEAMWORK PROTOCOL

Initially, when developing a teamwork protocol in bitemark investigation of the deceased, it may be wise to have as many potential members of the team as possible attend the complete simulated postmortem training process to assure that each member clearly understands his/her duties, limits, and responsibilities. It should quickly become apparent that a team leader (first responders, police, medical examiner/coroner, crime scene investigator, pathologist, odontologist) orchestrates part of the investigation and that a certain flow of duties results. The team may need to identify specific roles, the order in which each will function, and the evidence to be collected. For example, who will collect DNA samples? How? At the scene or at autopsy? If at autopsy, how is the body protected from further contamination during transportation? Who records the chain of possession? How is it registered? Who is responsible for the transfer of evidence?

Once the protocol is established, it generally means that a specific member will enter the investigation at a specific time. However, it is essential that all agree and understand the protocol to be followed. Protocol adjustments may be needed from time to time for some particular problem.

Each member provides a report of findings to the person in charge of the investigation, usually the medical examiner/coroner, with additional reports to law enforcement personnel, other appropriate authorities, prosecutors, and defense counsel.

4. POTENTIAL TEAM MEMBERS

1. In the living individual, first responders such as paramedics, emergency medical technicians, forensic nurses, and emergency room physicians may be the first to recognize a suspected bitemark and in the initial collection of evidence. As primary diagnosticians, they can alert law enforcement officials, social services, and other forensic experts including the forensic dentist.

2. Crime scene investigators, homicide detectives, and law enforcement personnel are responsible for securing, evaluating, and photographing the scene; packaging physical evidence for scientific evaluation and comparison; and preparing detailed reports on crime scene observations and interviews.

3. A medical examiner is a physician pathologist who investigates persons who died a sudden, unexpected, or violent death. A coroner is a public official whose duty is to inquire into deaths of certain categories of deaths. (Editor's note: See previous chapter for a more complete description.)

4. A pathologist evaluates tissue specimens collected during an autopsy. In the course of bitemark investigation, the pathologist may evaluate the tissue injury to determine timing and extent of the injury.

5. The forensic dental consultant is integral to any bitemark investigation. His/her duties include the recognition, recording, collection, preservation, analysis, and comparison of pattern injuries and, more specifically, bitemarks.

6. A forensic photographer visually records crime scene and body for ulterior study and court presentation.

7. A forensic chemist analyzes crime scene/autopsy-related material.

8. The forensic DNA analyst extracts, amplifies, and compares DNA samples to determine if there is a correlation between them.

9. District attorneys, defense attorneys, and judges are individuals who are involved with the end product of an investigation, the trial.

5. FACTORS AFFECTING THE TEAM CONCEPT

Major factors affect the development and use of the team concept including jurisdictional rivalries and human and financial resources. There are as many organizational models as there are cities, counties, states, and countries.

6. FIRST RECOGNITION OF THE SUSPECTED BITEMARK

The sooner a bitemark pattern injury is recognized/suspected and reported, the better the evidence collection and chain of evidence will be. Any of the following individuals may be the first to recognize a suspected bitemark:

6.1. Live Victim Hospital Attended Case

1. First responders, such as paramedic or emergency medical technician
2. Law enforcement officer investigating the scene
3. Emergency room physician or nurse
4. Forensic nurse
5. Forensic dentist

This overview scenario does not by any means cover all possibilities. The dentist, for example, may be the first to diagnose a potential child abuse case in his private office. A caretaker or family member may suspect and report elder abuse of a confined parent. A parent may report the child suspected abuse occurring in a day care center.

6.2. Deceased Victim

1. Law enforcement officer
2. Medical examiner/coroner
3. Crime scene investigator
4. Forensic pathologist
5. Forensic dentist

If all of the above individuals have been involved in preplanning and training, each will be aware of proper collection and preservation of evidence that could otherwise be overlooked or lost. Particularly important are the DNA swabs of the suspected bitemarks. The potential evidence can easily become contaminated through emergency medical procedures, bodily movement and transportation, and environmental factors such as bacteria, rain, etc.

7. SAMPLE TEAM PROTOCOL FOR COLLECTING PATTERNED INJURY EVIDENCE

7.1. At the Scene

1. Document the suspected bitemark injuries.
2. Photograph the suspected bitemark injuries.
3. Depending on established jurisdictional protocol, collect DNA samples at the scene.
4. Cover any body part suspected of trace evidence material: bag hands and feet, cover breasts, etc.
5. Place deceased in a new (preferable) or totally decontaminated sealed body bag.
6. Transport body to the morgue.

7.2. At the Morgue

1. Routine check-in procedures.
2. Body is issued a case number.
3. In some jurisdictions, full-body radiographs are taken through body bag before unsealing.

4. Body bag's seal is removed and the body bag is opened in the presence of the medical examiner/forensic pathologist.
5. Photographs are taken throughout the checkin procedures, weighing, unclothing, etc.
6. Full-body radiographs.
7. Examination, etc.

7.2.1. Trace Evidence Detection and Collection

1. Trace evidence collection begins with the bagged body parts.
2. Evidence detection proceeds using white light, ultraviolet, and alternate light source.
3. Fluorescent areas and obvious injuries are marked on diagram sheets.
4. Fluorescing items, such as dried bodily fluids, are photographed in vivo, catalogued, and collected using sterile saline, and are appropriately stored for DNA analysis.
5. Collected items and trace evidence swabs are labeled with case number, date, and collector initials, and are placed in appropriate sealed and labeled containers.

7.2.2. Forensic Dental Evaluation and Evidence Collection

1. Determine if injury is a potential bitemark [2].
2. Swab the injuries if not certain that they have previously been processed [3]; this is where a clear protocol would avoid duplication and confusion.
3. Photographic documentation of the potential bitemark [4,5].
4. Take impressions of the potential bitemark [6].
5. Total excision, preservation, fixation of bitemark specimen [7].

7.2.3. Pathology or Histology Evidence Collection and Evaluation

1. Histological sections of the injury [8].

8. TEAMWORK IN SMALLER JURISDICTIONS

In smaller jurisdictions, only a few people may constitute the entire "team" by becoming familiar and trained in the rudimentary skills involved in recognition, proper collection, and storage of all types of evidence for ulterior evaluation by outside consultants. The reader is encouraged to refer to the appropriate chapters in this book for detailed instructions on the collection, preservation, and interpretation of bitemark evidence in the living/deceased.

9. CONLUSION

Teamwork requires that each investigator/scientist perform a specific task efficiently in order to produce the requisite unbiased scientific result. Each member is interdependent yet result independent. Teamwork can only increase the potential for success in bitemark investigation.

REFERENCES

1. Delattre V, Reynolds R, Santos A, Stimson P. Teamwork in action—integration of the forensic sciences during bitemark investigations, Proceedings of the American Academy of Forensic Sciences Annual Meeting, Atlanta, 2002.
2. Delattre V, Stimson P. Bite marks vs. other injuries—forensic odontological evaluation of a homicide, Proceedings of the American Academy of Forensic Sciences Annual Meeting, San Francisco, 1998.

3. Chapter 9, Salivary Swabbing—DNA.
4. Chapter 7, Photography.
5. Chapter 8, Other Photographic Considerations.
6. Chapter 10, Bitemark Impressions.
7. Chapter 13, Tissue Specimens.
8. Chapter 14, Histology and Timing of Injury.

III
Description of the Bitemark

5
Nature of Bitemarks

Mark L. Bernstein
University of Louisville School of Dentistry
Louisville, Kentucky, U.S.A.

1. DEFINITION

A bitemark can be generally defined as a pattern made by teeth in a substrate. Since the teeth can be of human or animal origin, and the substrate can be skin, food, or a firm but compressible substance, more specific definitions are needed. Most bitemarks of forensic interest involve the contact between human teeth and skin. The American Board of Forensic Odontology defines the human cutaneous bitemark as follows: ''An injury in skin caused by contacting teeth (with or without the lips or tongue) which shows the representational pattern of the oral structures'' [1].

The definition excludes other nonpatterned injuries made by teeth contacting skin such as might be encountered by a fist to the mouth. It also excludes the closing action of jaws during intended biting if a recognizable pattern is not produced. These other tooth-to-skin interactions are still important even if not distinguished by the term ''bitemark'' because they can be responsible for infection, tissue destruction, or transmissible diseases, and can transfer DNA in saliva. However, by convention, the term ''bitemark'' signifies to the forensic odontologist an injury that, by its pattern, helps establish its origin from teeth.

2. SPELLING

Three terms, bitemark (one word) [2], bite mark (2 words) [3–8], and bite-mark (hyphenated) [9–12] appear in the literature. ''Bite mark'' is most widely used. This form implies a type of mark whereas ''bitemark'' connotes an entity unto itself and recognizable as such. It is considered to be a more progressive term, signifying that odontologists have accumulated a sufficient body of knowledge to dignify the form. ''Bite-mark'' should be reserved for use as a compound adjective as in ''bite-mark analysis'' [1]. The point may be moot since all forms are acceptable, yet it is important to consider all terms when performing a computer literature search. (EDITOR'S NOTE: For the purposes of this book the term ''bitemark'' has been adopted excepting cited quotations and references when spelled differently.)

3. EVIDENTIARY VALUE

The presence and recognition of a bitemark in a living or deceased individual or in a substrate at a crime scene is relevant in both civil and criminal cases. The mere presence of an identifiable bitemark in a purported crime is significant even if the pattern fails to implicate a specific biter. In a case of disputed child abuse, where the injuries are arguably accidental, the presence of a bitemark supports an accusation of abuse. In alleged sexual assault, when DNA evidence is apt to confirm the identity of the accused, the defense of consensual sex is less believable if bitemarks are found. Even a poor-quality bitemark, if recognized, can prompt trace evidence collection for salivary DNA and amylase.

Many bitemarks do record the distinctive morphologic features of the biter's dentition, offering an opportunity to identify the biter based on metric and pattern analysis. The discovery of bitemarks, like fingerprints, offers hope of perpetrator identification but there are important differences between the two. When latent fingerprints are discovered at a crime scene, it means only that a certain person touched something at an unspecified time. There is not necessarily a link to the crime. In contrast, the presence of a bitemark in skin indicates a violent interaction between individuals as well as a rough temporal connection to the event.

4. DEMOGRAPHICS

Bitemarks are seen in crimes of passion—homicide, rape/sexual assault, domestic violence (child, partner, elder abuse), and battery. The perpetrator may bite the victim or the victim may bite the assailant in self-defense. Rarely, self-biting has been reported in association with mental retardation, psychological disturbance, organic brain disease [13], severe pain [14], epileptic seizures, an attempt to frame another individual, or forcible insertion of an arm into the victim's mouth during a fight to subdue the victim or prevent crying out [10,15]. An unusual one-arched bitemark was reported in a woman who fell on her denture [16]. Other sources of human bitemarks include partly eaten food or chewing gum discarded during robberies, or teeth contacting inanimate objects during fights. Animal bites, particularly from dogs but also from other mammals, reptiles, and fish, are of forensic interest including postmortem predation from field animals and insects.

Bitemarks may appear on any skin surface [7,9,17] although with greatest frequency on the breasts, arms, legs, and head. Females are bitten four times as often as males. In heterosexual assaults on women, breasts, arms and legs, face and neck, pubic area, and buttocks are frequent sites while in male homosexual attacks, the upper back, shoulders, axillae, penis, and scrotum are favored. Abused children are randomly bitten with frequent bites on the face and back [6,7]. Rawson reported that 43% of bites on children occurred in the head and neck [18]. In Pretty and Sweet's study, all male children had genital bites [19]. Meta-analysis of these multiple studies is not entirely accurate because they derived cases from different sources—hospital-based population [18,20], coroner's cases [9], and court cases [19]. Forty percent to 48% of bitemark cases show multiple bites [19,20]. Pretty and Sweet caution that, when one bite is detected, others should be sought [19].

In dog maulings where multiple bites are sustained, the extremities are bitten and deep perforating bites of the neck and avulsive bites of the scalp are common (Fig. 1).

5. PATHOLOGY OF THE CUTANEOUS BITEMARK

Fingerprints, impressions, and patterned injuries all represent a transfer of a pattern from one medium to another. This is where the similarity ends. The visibility of a fingerprint derives from deposits of sweat and dirt on the crests of the friction ridges that are passively transferred to a smooth surface. The deposit faithfully reproduces the anatomy of the ridge detail in much the manner of a rubber stamp imprint. An impression is a three-dimensional indentation occurring when a hard material displaces a softer material that retains the depression after the two materials

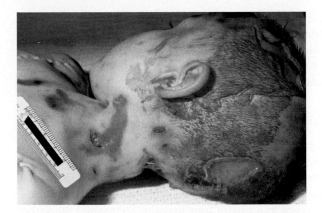

Figure 1 Fatal neck perforation and avulsion of scalp in a dog mauling.

are separated. A patterned injury such as a bitemark is made visible not by a transfer of material and not often by indentations but rather by a vital response of the bitten tissue. It is the superficial scraping of the epithelium by the contacting teeth (abrasion), the bleeding within skin by the pressure of the teeth (contusion), or the tearing of skin by teeth (laceration) that renders the bitemark visible. Bleeding or scraping of skin under assault are not obliged to conform precisely to the anatomy of the object that produced it. The bleeding can extend beyond the toothmarks. Conversely, bitten skin may not have been sufficiently damaged to react at all. The bitemark is not an imprint or impression but a reactive response generated by injured skin that is invariably less precise than a direct recording. A myriad of other unpredictable and nonreproducible variables further confound the patterns displayed in a bitemark. These include skin thickness, elasticity, curvature, texture, vascularity, pigmentation, underlying support, and position during biting. Also important are the age and gender of the victim, and the presence of systemic diseases and medications. The dynamics of biting—force and direction—affect the resulting pattern as do surface characteristics of contacting teeth. In spite of all these variables, it remains a maxim of forensic pathology that abrasions and contusions often reproduce the pattern of the offending agent. It is this observation that affords odontologists the opportunity to determine whether or not a specific dentition might have produced a given bitemark.

6. ANATOMY OF THE TYPICAL CUTANEOUS HUMAN BITEMARK

The human dental formula is I2/2, C1/1, P2/2, M3/3 indicating two incisors, one cuspid, two premolars and three molars in each upper and lower quadrant. The 16 maxillary and 16 mandibular teeth are arranged along parabolic arches. Typically, it is only the six anterior teeth in each arch (incisors and cuspids) that participate in a bitemark. Occasionally first premolars and, rarely, molars mark. During biting, the jaws approximate one another, the biting (incisal) surfaces of the teeth contact skin with various degrees of force, and the skin reacts, registering a pattern that resembles a mirror image of the incisal signature.

   Our genetics determine the general characteristics that define the size, shape, and arrangement of our dentition. All humans are expected to share these basic dental characteristics, which are similarly reproduced in well-inflicted bitemarks. This enables the forensic investigator to examine a patterned injury and, by virtue of these characteristics, identify it as a human bitemark. "Class characteristics" is a term borrowed from tool mark analysis [6]. It refers to those morphologic features in a transfer pattern that are expected to be reproduced by any and all members of a certain class or set and serve to identify the set from which it was derived. Thus, a certain pattern in a footprint or tread mark would enable the identification of the brand of sole or tire. For our purposes, class characteristics of the human dentition are those features that, when seen in a patterned injury, allow its identification as a generic human bitemark.

7. CLASS CHARACTERISTICS OF THE HUMAN CUTANEOUS BITEMARK

The classic human bitemark in skin appears as a circular or oval ring-shaped or doughnut-shaped injury composed of two opposing U-shaped arches facing one another and separated from each other at their bases. Each arch features an alignment of individual contusions, abrasions, and/or lacerations that approximate the size, shape, and arrangement of human teeth. The incisors, located toward the center of each arch, record as a row of four linear or rectangular marks per arch. The cuspids (or canines) produce circular, triangular, or diamond-shaped marks toward the edges of the arches, with their size determined by their incisal surface area and depth of penetration of their conical cusps. If a premolar marks, it produces a cuspidlike marking aligned with the arch and possibly a second mark a few millimeters within the arch, representing the lingual cusp.

Since the upper and lower arches have distinguishing features, class characteristics can be defined for the maxillary and mandibular dentitions. Upper central incisors are broad and can be expected to leave linear markings measuring 8–9 mm. The narrower lateral incisors leave similar marks of 6–7 mm. Since lateral incisors do not typically reach the occlusal plane, these shorter teeth do not place as much pressure on skin and may leave less intense marks or no marks at all. The longer, pointed cuspids often leave well-defined marks. Their position at the corners of the arch marks the area where the arch curves most sharply. In the lower arch, the incisal widths of the central and lateral incisors are less disparate, measuring $\sim$ 5.5 and 6.0 mm, respectively. If lower premolars mark, only the buccal cusps are likely to record since the lingual cusps are diminutive. The measurements are based on the study of Moorrees et al. [21], which should be consulted for more precise values, standard deviations, and ranges.

The upper arch is larger than the lower, and its intercuspid distance averages 32.3 mm [22] to 33.6 mm [23] ± 2.5 mm for 1 SD. The range, based on nearly 400 cases was 21.3–41.0 mm [22]. The mandibular intercuspid distance averages 25 mm [22,23] ± 1.85 mm for 1 SD and ranged from 11.6 to 33.0 mm [22]. Barsley obtained slightly higher mean intercuspid distances of 35.9 ± 3.3 mm (maxillary) and 28.1 ± 2.9 mm (mandibular) because he measured from the disto-occlusal aspects of worn canines rather than the cuspal midpoints [24]. He also found that 98.7% of all mandibular arches measured < 35 mm and 78% measure < 30 mm. For maxillary arches, 3.4% are less than 30 mm and 38.8% are less than 35 mm from cuspid to cuspid. The differences between male and female intercuspid distance averaged 1.6 mm for the maxilla and 1.0 mm for the mandible, but there was considerable overlap. Racial and age differences over the age of 12 were also insignificant [24]. Thus race, gender and age cannot be predicted from an adult bitemark. The entire adult bitemark injury usually measures in width from 3.5 to 4.0 cm when a full complement of anterior teeth is involved. Its length, measured from upper to lower incisors, varies with degree of jaw opening and amount of skin gathered during the bite. The average maximal opening diameter is $\sim$ 42–45 mm but can exceed 70 mm. The amount of skin gathered will be less on flat, taut surfaces than on curved or pliable surfaces such as extremities, breasts, and buttocks.

The dynamics of biting usually cause the mandibular bitemark to appear more intense and more sharply defined than the maxillary. This has been attributed to the fact that the lower is the movable jaw or, as Sperber opined, that the skin contacting the upper teeth during biting is

├──── 3.5-4.0 cm ────┤

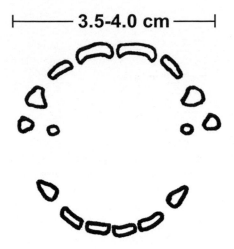

Figure 2 Diagram of a prototypical human bitemark showing class characteristics.

not squarely pressed against the incisal edges as in the lower, but along the broad slope of the lingual surfaces of the overlapping upper teeth [25]. The idealized bitemark is diagramed in Figure 2.

The value of defining class characteristics for the human bite is twofold: first, it defines objective criteria upon which to distinguish the human bite from other patterned injuries; second, the data suggest that many bitemarks will be similar based on shared characteristics and that a "match" between a bitemark and suspect based on these nonspecific class characteristics does not necessarily "identify" the biter. A bitemark with a maxillary and mandibular intercuspid distance of 34 mm and 25 mm, respectively, 9.0 mm maxillary central incisors, 5.6 mm mandibular incisors, and aligned arches will accommodate a large percentage of human dentitions.

Bites inflicted by children also bear class characteristics that define this subset. Compared to adult teeth, the deciduous dentition of children below the age of 6 years typically features smaller, rounded, bowlike arches, smaller teeth, and spacing between teeth. Upper central incisors, at an average mesiodistal width of 6.5 mm, are only slightly larger than lateral incisors at 5.3 mm. Lower incisors measure about 4–4.5 mm [21,26]. The mean maxillary intercuspid distance measures 28–29 mm from ages 3–6 years, and the mean mandibular intercuspid distance is ~ 22.6 mm. This is about 4.4 mm and 2.5 mm smaller than the respective intercuspid distances of adults [23]. Reflecting these attributes, bitemarks from children are typically smaller than adult bitemarks (3–3.5 cm), with spaces between the teeth (Fig. 3). Marks from the upper centrals are only slightly larger than other incisors. Children between the ages of 7 and 11 have a mixed dentition, which effaces the anterior spacing once the larger permanent incisors erupt. This causes the anterior segment to widen while the narrower posterior segments are relatively constricted lingually [26].

8. VARIATIONS OF BITEMARK PATTERNS

Unfortunately, a well-inflicted, nondistorted bitemark showing 12 or more teeth is uncommonly seen. There are variations in bitemark morphology due to additional injury patterns sustained

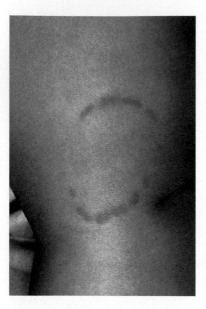

Figure 3 Typical bitemark from a child showing small, spaced teeth. Also see color photograph insert section.

during the dynamics of biting as well as degradations and deficiencies due to distortion or partial recording.

8.1. Central Contusion

A central area of contusion or ecchymosis is frequently noted within the confines of the bite ring (Fig. 4). This has long been attributed to suction with or without the pressure of tongue thrusting, and its etiology has been ascribed to prolonged, sadistic, sexual biting activity. Another proven and probably more frequent pathogenesis for central contusion is the mere compression

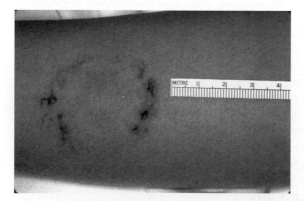

Figure 4 Bitemark showing central contusion with pale area from tongue thrusting. Note continuous ring due to approximation of maxillary and mandibular arches. Also see color photograph insert section.

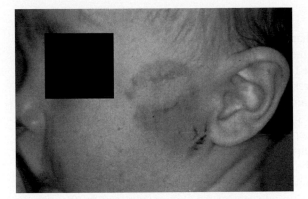

Figure 5   Drag marks left by mandibular teeth scraping across face. Also see color photograph insert section.

of tissue squeezed in between the upper and lower teeth, which causes rupture of capillaries. The mechanism has been witnessed at the 1984 ABFO Bitemark Workshop when a set of models on an articulator compressed abdominal tissue of a volunteer, causing an instant and intense central bruise. There was no possible suction. The literature persists in calling these bruises ''suck marks'' [8] with the implication of a sexual motivation. Such a deduction is not necessarily appropriate. Both mechanisms, positive and negative pressure, contribute to central contusions. The appearance of central contusion is not helpful in identifying a biter since it is non-patterned and not made by teeth. However, it does help support that the lesion represents a bitemark.

8.2.   Linear Abrasions/Contusions

A series of linear abrasions or contusions is often found radiating at right angles to the arches external to the periphery of the bitemark. These represent the action of teeth scraping as they slip across skin during closing or as the victim attempts to pull free. These ''drag marks'' distort the anatomy of the teeth and are not welcome in terms of biter identification but they do help corroborate the nature of the injury as a bite (Figs. 5 and 6).

Figure 6   Three drag marks in a bitemark made by mandibular left teeth. Also see color photograph insert section.

8.3. Lingual Markings

Occasionally, short linear or gumdrop-shaped patterns appear centripetally, radiating inward from the arches. These represent the outlines of the lingual surface of teeth. Entire outlines of embrasures, gingival margins, and papillae can be reproduced. Harvey attributed these markings to tongue thrusting in which the tongue pressed the captured skin against the teeth [9]. Sperber, noting that lingual markings were more common on upper teeth, related their presence to pressing of skin by lower teeth against the lingual surfaces of overlapping upper teeth when bites were inflicted in centric relationship [25]. Other potential factors contributing to lingual markings include soft skin, thin skin supported by adipose and labially inclined anterior teeth. The pressure of the lingual surfaces does not have to be great to register markings; some lingual markings may not represent a wound at all but rather an area of sparing when central contusion follows a path of least resistance and flows into skin adjacent to the skin compressed by the cingula and marginal ridges of the incisors. The incisor imprints appear pale, outlined by thin red tracts of contusion where relief was afforded by embrasures and gingival soft tissue (Figs. 7 and 8).

8.4 Tongue Thrusting

The tongue can leave a pale area within central contusion where its pressure against the skin either forced out or failed to admit the blood extravasated during central contusion formation (Fig. 4).

8.5. Acute Inflammatory Reaction

A bitemark may show the hallmarks of acute inflammation within minutes of infliction. This includes the wheal and flare reaction where redness and swelling predominate. The bitemark appears diffusely erythematous and slightly raised. The ring appearance may be replaced by a solid red oval that obliterates the arches and tooth marks. The acute reaction subsides within

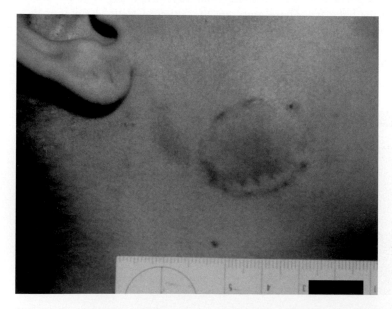

Figure 7 Lingual markings formed when pressure from mandibular cingula prevented spread of central contusion. (From ABFO Bitemark Workshop.) Also see color photograph insert section.

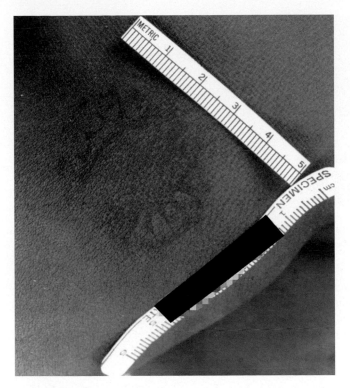

Figure 8 Five maxillary and five mandibular teeth recorded as lingual markings. Also see color photograph insert section.

hours to a day, restoring the identifying class characteristics [15]. Such events are most common on the faces of children (Figs. 9 and 10).

8.6. Uninterrupted Arches

Most bitemarks show a separation between the maxillary and mandibular arches, representing the unbitten skin that curves between two arches. If the skin is sufficiently thin and the bite

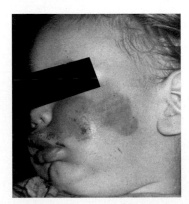

Figure 9 Acute inflammation and swelling account for solid appearance of bitemarks photographed within hours of infliction. Also see color photograph insert section.

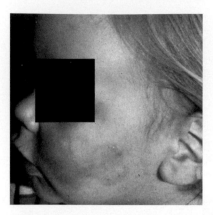

Figure 10   Same bitemarks as Figure 9 photographed a day later, when subsiding inflammation revealed the ring pattern of arches. Also see color photograph insert section.

force is intense, the upper and lower teeth at the posterior margin of the bite can nearly approximate, causing a continuous, uninterrupted ring of tooth marks, representing both arches (Fig. 4). Since similar patterns can be made by oval and round objects like rings, care must be exercised in designating an origin from such patterns.

8.7.   Tooth Indentations

Actual depressions representing impressions of teeth in skin do occur at the moment of biting and do not require much force. Because of the elastic memory of skin and the swelling that might occur in the acute phase, these indentations usually smooth out within 20 min and are seldom available for evaluation (Fig. 11).

8.8.   Double Bite

Literally a bitemark within a bitemark, this variant occurs when a mass of skin captured between teeth is grasped and the victim partly pulls free, followed by a reapplication of biting force. The result is two concentric sets of arches with duplication of the bite pattern. Accompanying drag marks might be seen (Fig. 12).

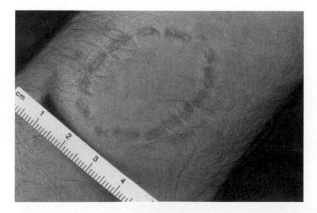

Figure 11   Temporary indentations of teeth in a bitemark photographed minutes after infliction.

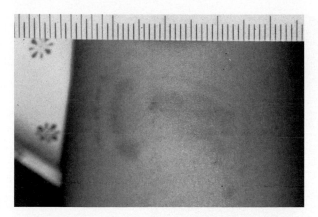

Figure 12 "Double bite" occurring as teeth slipped, followed by reapplication of force, creating concentric duplication of pattern. Also see color photograph insert section.

8.9. Multiple and Superimposed Bites

Forty percent to 48% of bitemark cases show two or more bites [19,20]. Multiple bites made by the same biter allow the odontologist to search for reproducible patterns among the bites that can then be considered nonartifactual stable characteristics (Figs. 13–15). Superimposed bites, on the other hand, can confound bitemark analysis because they overlap and degrade detail (Figs. 13 and 16).

8.10. Weave Patterns

Bitemarks through clothing can leave the weave pattern of the fabric embossed in contusion. Clothing can also dull or eliminate the detail of tooth marks and prevent saliva/DNA deposition that must then be obtained from the garment (Fig. 17).

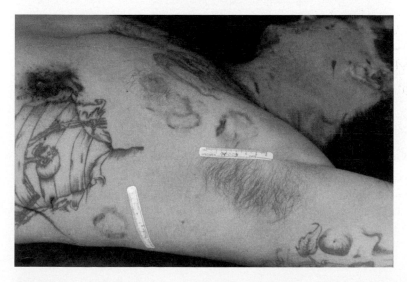

Figure 13 Multiple bites in a gunshot homicide victim. Superimposed bites and two single bites are seen.

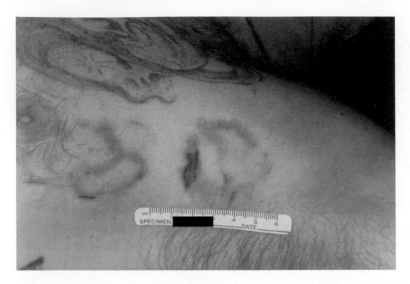

Figure 14 Closeup of bitemark medial to axilla in Figure 13, showing distinctive pattern of individual characteristics.

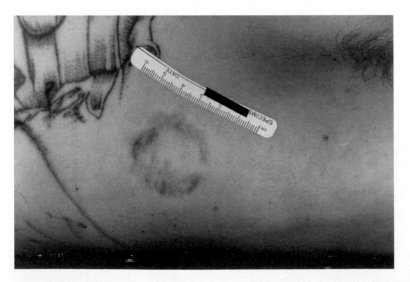

Figure 15 Closeup of bitemark inferior to axilla in Figure 13, showing repetition and improvement of pattern seen in Figure 14. Note severe labial crowding and rotation of No. 27, overlapping of 26, 25, and 24 (Universal System), and drag marks of entire anterior maxillary arch. Also see color photograph insert section.

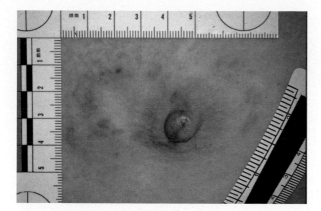

Figure 16 Two superimposed bites converging at the nipple. Also see color photograph insert section.

8.11. Excessive Ecchymosis and Abrasion

Excessive bleeding outside the confines of the bitemark can obscure pattern details and cause the bitemark to appear larger than normal. Secondary injury unrelated to biting, such as holding of the part being bitten, may account for some examples. Ostensibly, biting of previously injured skin can cause peculiar patterns. Levine reported a case in which the biter inflicted abrasions in an attempt to obliterate the bite pattern [7]. Excessive bleeding is also encountered in those who bruise readily (females, elderly, children, thin skin, skin supported by adipose, patients on steroids, anticoagulants, or those with coagulopathies or liver disease). Care is necessary to find the characteristic arch form and tooth marks so the injury can be properly identified (Fig. 18).

8.12. Partial Bitemarks

If skin is not squarely bitten, only portions of the dentition mark. Resulting variants include unilateral (one-sided) bitemarks (Fig. 19) in which only the left or right side of both arches

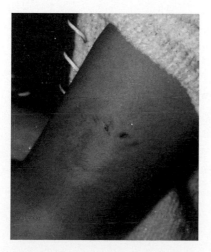

Figure 17 Linear arrangement of tiny contusions reflecting the weave pattern in the sweater in this bitemark through clothing.

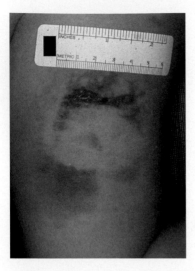

Figure 18 Excessive hemorrhage surrounding bitemark. (Courtesy Dr. William Smock.) Also see color photograph insert section.

mark, one-arched bitemarks (Fig. 20) showing only an upper or lower arch, or bitemarks showing only a few teeth (Fig. 21). Unilateral bitemarks occur when the bite is skewed or the anatomy of the bitten tissue curves away from the teeth on one side. Bitemarks showing few teeth can be due to a poorly inflicted bite, superimposed clothing, highly curved skin contours, variations in underlying skin support within the bitten tissue, or missing teeth in the biter. Single-arched bitemarks are most likely to be disputed. Logic predicts that both arches are needed to produce the required pressure, however bitemarks with one arch are documented, despite the fact that the biter had a full dentition [7]. Interposed clothing, dull surfaces of teeth, variations in skin and skin support, more rapid fading of one arch (usually the upper), can all account for single-arched marks. Falling upon a removable denture has produced a one-arched bite pattern [16].

8.13. Indistinct/Faded Bitemarks

''Toothless'' bitemarks frequently appear. The class characteristic of facing arches is present, but individual teeth are not seen. There may be a suggestion of scalloping, indicating a fusion

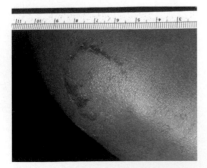

Figure 19 Partial bitemark created by left maxillary and mandibular arch. (Courtesy Dr. William Smock.) Also see color photograph insert section.

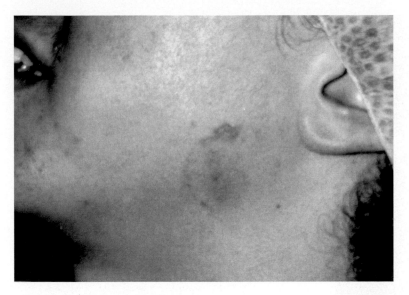

Figure 20 One arched bitemark. (From ABFO Bitemark Workshop.)

of indistinct toothmarks or merely a uniform contusion with little or no abrasion. Such bitemarks occur when the collective pressure of teeth within an arch leaves a continuous curved contusion. This is most often seen in soft yielding skin (children, women) and skin cushioned by abundant adipose, which is very vascular and easily bruised. It also occurs as bitemarks heal. An otherwise well-defined bitemark can show fading of the tooth marks before the background contusions (Fig. 22).

8.14. Avulsive Bite

Severe, vicious bitemarks can lacerate and avulse tissue to the point of loss of soft tissue. This results in gaping wounds that are not readily identifiable as bitemarks and rarely permit identification of a perpetrator. Avulsive bites, common in dog maulings, are infrequent in human

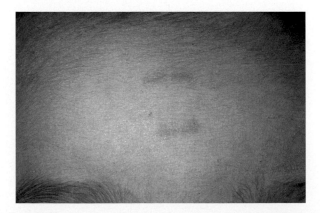

Figure 21 Bitemark showing only two maxillary and two mandibular incisors.

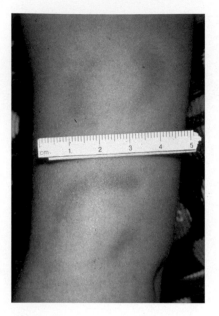

Figure 22   Toothless bitemarks showing only arch form and size as class characteristics. Also see color photograph insert section.

bites. They are most apt to occur on projecting anatomic areas such as nipples, noses, ears, fingers, genitals [9,15,27] or tongues (Fig. 23).

8.15.   Healed Bitemarks

Any injury can heal with more, less, or the same amount of melanin as the surrounding skin. Increased melanin is known as postinflammatory pigmentation. Decreased melanin is seen in some scars. Both phenomena are more readily appreciated in dark-pigmented individuals. These pigmentary changes may maintain the pattern of a bitemark for many months (Fig. 24). Some-

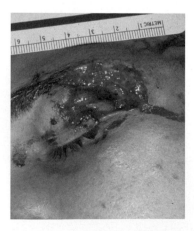

Figure 23   Avulsed human bitemark in soft tissue above the eyelid. (Courtesy Dr. William Smock.)

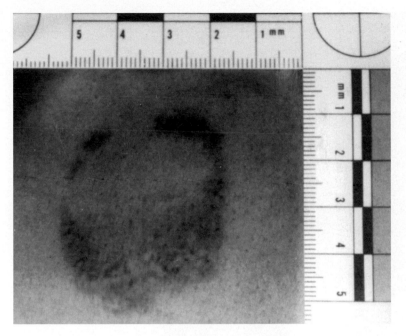

Figure 24 Old healed bitemark showing postlesional pigmentation. (Courtesy Dr. Richard Souviron.) Also see color photograph insert section.

times the pigmentary patterns are too subtle to be seen visibly and are present as latent injuries that can be imaged only by ultraviolet photography.

8.16. Postmortem Bitemarks

Bitemarks created after death do not show the vital responses that facilitate visualization of the injury. Postmortem abrasions lack the scab composed of serum, fibrin, and red blood cells formed in a living subject. They appear yellow, translucent, and parchmentlike [28]. It should be noted that a severe blow inflicted within a few hours of death might produce contusions [29]. It is not known whether or not postmortem bitemarks can produce contusions.

9. INDIVIDUAL CHARACTERISTICS OF THE HUMAN BITEMARK

An individual characteristic is a feature or pattern that represents a departure from an expected finding within a defined group. It represents an individual variation that serves to identify a particular member of the group. A tear or wear pattern in a tire or shoe sole that imprints in a tread mark or footprint is an example. For bitemarks, a tooth malposition or diastema can produce individual characteristics. Such characteristics are due to a combination of genetics and environment. When seen in bitemarks, individual characteristics allow the forensic dentist to eliminate, narrow down, or identify suspects depending on their degree of distinctiveness.

10. DOG BITES

Large dogs, most notably rottweilers, pit bulls, chows, shepherds, and Dobermans, account for most serious or fatal bites in the United States. Canine dentitions show considerable variations

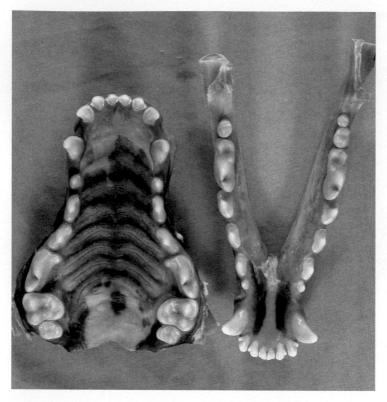

Figure 25   Occlusal views of the canine dentition. Note constriction of arch posterior to the cuspid followed by flaring beginning in the premolar region.

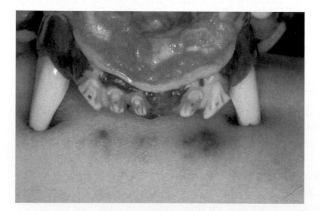

Figure 26   Flared mandibular cuspids fit into perforations in this dog bite. Note concordance of incisor injuries to the arrangement and anatomy of incisor teeth.

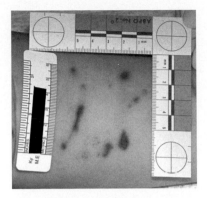

Figure 27 Dog bite showing constriction and flaring of mandibular arch including molar teeth.

among breeds with regard to tooth and arch size and arch shape. Such dogs as collies and Dobermans have long muzzles while rottweilers, chows, and pit bulls have wider arches. Yet in spite of variations, there are defining class characteristics that allow identification as a dog bite. The canine dental formula is I3/3, C1/1, P4/4, M2/3 (Fig. 22). Each arch has six small incisors aligned in a gentle curved arch. Following a space (largest in the maxilla), two long, pointed cuspids are positioned at the corners of the arch at which point the arch turns sharply posteriorly. Beyond the cuspids, there is a space followed by a small first premolar. The second, third, and fourth premolars are spaced and become increasingly larger. The first molar is the largest molar followed by progressively smaller molars (Fig. 25). Dogs and other carnivores possess tritubercular posterior teeth in which premolars and molars have three aligned cusps or tubercles forming a triangle [26]. Upper and lower cusps slide past and interlock with each other during biting, allowing these teeth to grasp and lacerate.

The well-inflicted dog bite shows a long, narrow arch compared to a human bite. The small incisors may not produce markings, but if all six incisors of an arch mark, they serve to exclude a human bite. The long, fanglike cuspids produce prominent markings, often deep punctures or lacerations that may not conform to the intercuspid distance of the bites since dog canines flare occlusally (Fig. 26). The bitemark turns sharply posteriorly to the cuspids and

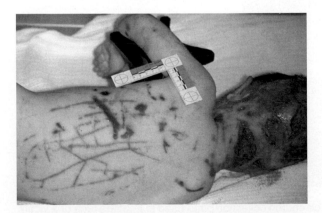

Figure 28 Dog claw marks across back of victim of dog mauling.

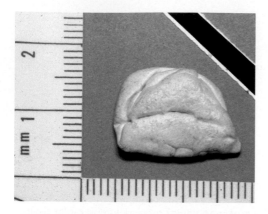

Figure 29 Bite pattern of mandibular anterior teeth deliberately recorded in chewing gum by a clever rape victim during her incarceration in the trunk of a car. The gum was left in the car to confirm her ordeal.

converges lingually then flares buccally. Premolars and molar markings are common since the dog's jaws can open widely (Fig. 27).

In a defensive or anger bite, a dog may snap and let go. In these bites, anterior tooth marks predominate and can show superficial similarity to a human bite. In a mauling or predatory bite, the dog will grasp a large segment of tissue using posterior teeth and, by pulling and shaking, cause drag marks and lacerations. If the grip loosens, the dog attempts to thrust its head forward to seize more tissue, thus creating double or superimposed bites. Laceration and avulsions caused by large carnivores can be so sharply defined as to be mistaken for incisions (see Chapter 15, Fig. 10). Accompanying long abrasions from claws may be seen in some cases (Fig. 28).

11. BITEMARKS IN OTHER SUBSTRATES

Food and other compressible objects record a bitemark in the same manner as impression material, its accuracy determined by the substrate and its tendency to deform, dehydrate, or decompose

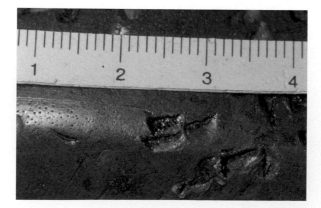

Figure 30 Toothmarks left in a hardwood church collection plate used to beat the face of a victim of traumatic death.

following the bite. Foods like cheese, chewing gum, cake icing, chocolate and other candy can produce useable three-dimensional impressions under favorable conditions (Fig. 29). Fruits, vegetables, butter and preserved meats can also record identifiable bitemarks but with more opportunity for distortion. Tooth indentations have also been recorded in wood and plastic (Fig. 30).

REFERENCES

1. ABFO Bitemark Terminology Guidelines, American Board of Forensic Odontology, Seattle, WA, 1995.
2. Sweet DJ, Dorion R, Dailey JC, Shernoff AF, Gelles JHW, Spencer D, David TJ. Bitemark evidence. In Bowers CM, Bell GL, Eds. Manual of Forensic Odontology. 3rd ed. Colorado Springs: American Society of Forensic Odontology, 1995:148–190.
3. Sopher IM. Forensic Dentistry. Springfield. IL: Charles C. Thomas, 1976:125–152.
4. Gladfelter IA. Dental Evidence: A Handbook for Police. Springfield. IL: Charles C. Thomas, 1975: 31–47.
5. Stimson PG, Mertz CA. Bite mark techniques and terminology. In Stinson PG, Mertz CA, Eds. Forensic Dentisry. Boca Raton. FL: CRC Press, 1997:137–159.
6. Levine LJ. Bite mark evidence. In Cottone JA, Standish SM, Eds. Outline of Forensic Dentistry. Chicago: Year Book Medical Publishers, 1982:112–127.
7. Levine LJ. Bite mark evidence. In Standish SM, Stimson PG, Eds. The Dental Clinics of North America—Symposium on Forensic Dentistry: Legal Obligations and Methods of Identification for the Practitioner. Philadelphia: W.B. Saunders Company, 1977:145–158.
8. Clark DH. Practical Forensic Odontology. Oxford: Wright, 1992:128–205.
9. Harvey W. Dental Identification and Forensic Odontology. London: Henry Kimpton Publishers, 1976: 88–140.
10. Luntz LL, Luntz P. Handbook for Dental Identification: Techniques in Forensic Dentistry. Philadelphia: J.B. Lippincott Company, 1973:148–162.
11. Gustafson G. Forensic Odontology. London: Staple Press, 1966.
12. Cameron JM, Sims BG. Forensic Dentistry. Edinburgh: Churchill Livingstone, 1974:129–145.
13. Sobel MN, Perper JA. Self-inflicted bite mark on the breast of a suicide victim. Am J Forens Med Pathol 1985; 6(4):336–339.
14. Warnick AJ, Biedrzycki L, Russanow G. Not all bite marks are associated with abuse, sexual activities or homicides: a case study of a self-inflicted bitemark. J Forens Sci 1987; 32(3):788–792.
15. Whittaker DK, MacDonald DG. A Color Atlas of Forensic Dentistry. Ipswich: Wolfe Medical Publications Ltd, 1989:108.
16. Levine LJ. Forensic odontology. Int Microform J Leg Med. 1971; 6(3, Card 5B4–13).
17. Vale GL. Bite mark evidence in the investigation of crime. CDA J 1986; 14(3):36–42.
18. Rawson RD, Koot A, Martin C, Jackson J, Novosel S, Richardson A, Bender T. Incidence of bite marks in a selected juvenile population: a preliminary report. J Forens Sci 1984; 29(1):254–259.
19. Pretty IA, Sweet D. Anatomical location of bitemarks and associated findings in 101 cases from the United States. J Forens Sci 2000; 45(4):812–814.
20. Vale GL, Noguchi TT. Anatomical distribution of human bite marks in a series of 67 cases. J Forens Sci 1983; 28(1):61–69.
21. Moorrees CFA, Thomsen D, Jensen E, Yen PK. Mesiodistal crown diameters of the deciduous and permanent teeth in individuals. J Dent Res 1957; 36(1):39–47.
22. Rawson RD, Ommen RK, Kinard G, Johnson J, Yfantis A. Statistical evidence for the individuality of the human dentition. J Forens Sci 1984; 29(1):245–253.
23. Moorrees SFA. The Dentition of the Growing Child: a Longitudinal Study of Dental Development Between 3 and 18. Cambridge: Harvard University Press, 1959:92–106, 203.
24. Barsely RE, Lancaster DM. Measurement of arch widths in a human population: relation of anticipated bite marks. J Forens Sci 1987; 32(4):975–982.

25. Sperber ND. Lingual markings of anterior teeth as seen in bite marks. J Forens Sci 1990; 35(4): 838–844.
26. Ash MM, Nelson SJ. Wheeler's Dental Anatomy, Physiology and Occlusion. 8th ed.. Philadelphia: W.B. Saunders Company, 2003:75, 101–102, 160, 168, 181,188.
27. Rawson RD. Child abuse identification. CDA J 1986; 14(3):21–25.
28. DiMaio DJ, DiMaio VJM. Forensic Pathology. 2nd ed.. Boca Raton. FL: CRC Press, 2001:92–104.
29. Robertson I, Mansfield RA. Antemortem and postmortem bruises of the skin: their differentiation. J Forens Med 1957; 4:2–10.

6
Reconstructive Bitemark Analysis

Mark L. Bernstein
University of Louisville, School of Dentistry
Louisville Kentucky, U.S.A

1. ORGANIZATIONAL CONSTRUCTION FOR INITIAL ANALYSIS

Routinely, when called to examine a patterned injury, the odontologist follows a standard protocol asking a series of increasingly specific questions:

1. Is it a bitemark?
2. Is it human or an animal?
3. Can it be ascribed to an adult or child?
4. Can upper and lower arch be discriminated?
5. Are there individual characteristics that help to profile the biter's dentition?

The answer to each question is neither intuitive nor based on an educated guess but derives from the fulfillment of criteria that can be explained, demonstrated, and justified. In a well-inflicted, characteristic bitemark, these determinations can be made.

2. QUALITY OF THE BITEMARK

Many odontologists assign a quality rating to bitemarks. Since the standards for quality have not been formalized among odontologists, each investigator is free to make subjective or objective assessments based on personal criteria. This has the potential for inconsistent determinations and miscommunications. If we define bitemark quality as an assessment of value referenced to a criteria-based goal or standard, the exercise may be more meaningful. First we must define what a quality assessment is intended to measure. If the objective is simply to identify a pattern as a bitemark, then quality can be expressed as the ability of the pattern to reproduce the class characteristics of the human bite. If instead, ''quality'' is intended to communicate anticipated evidentiary value in perpetrator identification, then both class and individual characteristics must be evaluated. Since the most useful outcome of a bitemark interpretation is its ability to discriminate the biter and exclude others, this goal will frame our discussion of quality.

Determining the quality of a bitemark is an exercise that is performed in the reconstructive phase, prior to a comparison of suspect casts. It is intended to predict a bitemark's anticipated value in perpetrator identification. The individual criteria used to determine quality are objective, yet an overall appraisal of quality is an algorithmic judgment based on these criteria.

A bitemark deemed to be of exceptional quality would show the idealized class characteristics recorded in a distortion-free pattern. The incisal edges of individual teeth would be outlined and distinct, unencumbered by drag marks, superimposed distractions, or inaccuracies caused by skin elasticity. Each tier of specificity (identification as a bitemark, discrimination of animal vs. human, adult vs. child, and upper vs. lower arch) would be determinable. If the only objective in a case were recognition as a bitemark, these criteria would confer a bitemark of exceptional quality. But since we have defined quality as potential ability to identify the biter, more is needed. Individual characteristics would have to show sufficient quantity or deviation from the norm so as to constitute a distinctive or unique pattern (see Fig. 15 in Chapter 5). All things being equal, the greater the quantity of features in a bitemark, the more opportunity there is for higher quality. However, for discriminating out a biter, the quantity of participating teeth is not as important as their degree of abnormality. Six well-aligned teeth in an arch will render a bitemark of less quality than one with fewer teeth if some are malapposed. Similarly, since arch size and shape are relatively consistent among people, only clearly deviant arches would add quality to the bitemark.

A bitemark is considered to be poor or marginal in quality when the toothmarks are absent, uncertain, smudged, indistinct, faded, or distorted to the extent that incisal edge morphology is effaced. Partly inflicted toothmarks or sparse marks that fail to show a relationship between adjacent teeth also degrade the value of the bitemark.

Bitemarks showing features intermediate in value between these two extremes may be considered of good or fair quality. Thus, the discriminating value of any individual characteristics has to be weighed against the minimizing effect of any distortions or deficiencies. Well-inflicted bitemarks that are clear and distinct yet lack individual characterization may also be considered in this category since their value in assailant identification is conditional. Where odontologists rarely disagree on interpretations of exceptional or poor-quality bitemarks, judging the value of good or fair quality bitemarks is more inconsistent. There are no guidelines to assist odontologists in reliably constructing a precise hierarchy of bitemark quality.

The initial assessment of bitemark quality should serve only as a guide to approaching the case and not a formal and final determination. Other investigations may impact on this initial judgment. Transillumination of the bitemark, nontraditional photographic studies for discovery, scanning electron microscopy, and computer enhancement are but a few of the tertiary techniques that may add information to elevate the quality of the bitemark. The finding of other bitemarks on the body enhances the value of each component bitemark because individual features can be cross-referenced among the bitemarks to determine their stability and reliability (Figs. 14, 15 in Chapter 5).

3. PROFILING THE BITER

It is tempting to ''read'' a bitemark and make predictions about the teeth that produced it, but this can be a two-edged sword. Levine has urged against such profiling, cautioning that bitemark patterns can defy logic (1,2). A space in a bitemark might merit a spurious comment such as ''look for a person with a missing tooth,'' only to be discredited when the tooth is present in the biter. The reason for its not appearing could be that it was chipped, did not reach the occlusal plane, was blunted, was loose, or was buffered by superimposed clothing. Skin factors such as folding during the bite and lack of bony support can account for a tooth not leaving a mark (Figs. 1 and 2). Likewise, if individual teeth in a bitemark are not clearly identifiable or if maxillary and mandibular arches cannot be discriminated with certainty, these determinations should not be formalized or communicated. Such speculation can be the odontologist's albatross. On the other hand, a prediction that correctly identifies an unusual characteristic in a suspect inspires confidence in the odontologist because it is objective and criteria based. Recalling that

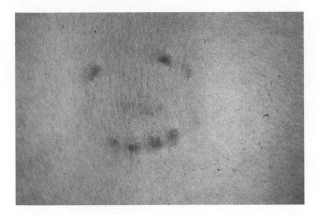

Figure 1 Witnessed bitemark of a child showing apparent missing maxillary central incisors.

a bitemark represents a mirror image of the dentition, the odontologist must be careful to correctly identify the participating teeth.

4 MAINTAINING PERSPECTIVE

When an odontologist is asked to inspect a pattern in an injury or object, he or she will formulate an initial assessment by applying the criteria reviewed in this chapter. Some patterns will fulfill enough criteria to merit distinction as a bitemark or probable bitemark. Others will simply fail to reach a threshold of characteristics that would allow a designation of bitemark, let alone perpetrator identification. The odontologist is advised not to automatically dismiss such injuries. Even bitemarks deemed to be of poor or marginal quality have proven to be relevant. A poorly or partially registered tooth-to-substrate mark might have saliva trace evidence sufficient for perpetrator identification. Similarly, identifiable bitemarks that lack individual characteristics should be given full attention and photographic documentation. The manner in which the case unfolds might make such a bitemark critical evidence. As mentioned earlier, a nondescript bitemark helps support the nature of some crimes even if it cannot implicate a particular perpetrator. A final determination of usefulness of a bitemark must consider the comparison of suspects'

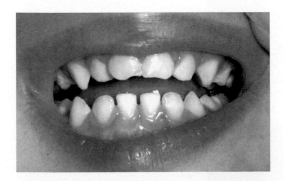

Figure 2 The biter of Figure 1 has nonmobile central incisors that did not imprint because the skin was folded and clothed in the act of biting.

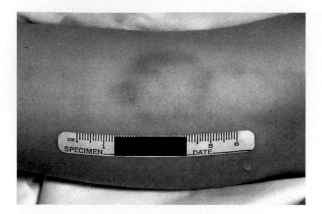

Figure 3 This toothless bitemark is nondescript except for its relatively small, rounded arches.

teeth. In some crimes, particularly child abuse cases, it might be shown that only a limited number of people had opportunity to bite (2). A nondescript bitemark in such a case could be used to rule out individuals if there are gross and unexplainable discrepancies, or be used to implicate a suspect by exclusion of all others (Figs. 3–5). Even an injury that mimics a bitemark should be fully documented and analyzed by a forensic odontologist. If such a lesion is disregarded because it is attributed to some other cause, opposing attorneys could capitalize on such

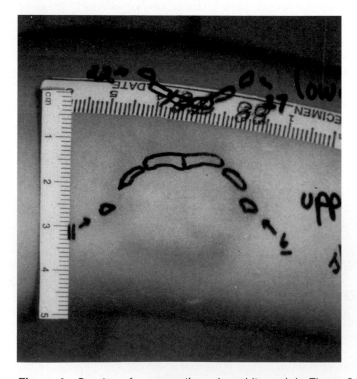

Figure 4 Overlay of a suspect's arch on bitemark in Figure 3 shows nonspecific similarity.

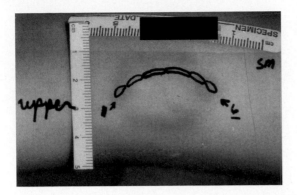

Figure 5 Overlay of a second suspect's arch on bitemark in Figure 3 shows incompatible arch size and form. Three other suspects were similarly eliminated. The dentition in Figure 4 was identified as the biter by exclusion of all other suspects.

a mark by identifying it as a bitemark that mismatches the dentition of the accused (see Figs. 31–32 in Chapter 18). In some cases, a biter's dentition might be so aberrant that his bitemark is unrecognizable as such and is overlooked. Failure to document such an injury could be a missed opportunity to record a unique pattern that would have generated convincing assailant identification. As is evident from these examples, the initial assessment of evidentiary value of a bitemark might have to be modified once the comparison is performed.

5. SUMMARY

Bitemarks are patterned injuries or impressions that can be relevant in the determination of the nature of crimes and the identification of perpetrators. The collective wisdom of odontologists gained over 30 years of judicious and organized study of bitemarks has provided objective criteria upon which to evaluate these patterns. The subject is complex and fastidious techniques must be applied both technically and analytically. Because the odontologist can never anticipate the outcome of a given case, all patterned injuries or impressions of questioned dental origin should be treated as bitemarks and processed accordingly whether or not the odontologists initially suspects etiology from teeth. This also applies to nondescript injuries in which victims claim to have been bitten.

REFERENCES

1. Levine LJ. Bitemark evidence. In Cottorne JA, Standish SM, Eds. Outline of Forensic Dentistry. Chicago: Year Book Medical Publishers, 1982:112–127.
2. Levine LJ. Bitemark evidence. In Standish SM, Stimson PG, Eds. The Dental Clinics of North America—Symposium on Forensic Dentistry: Legal Obligations and Methods of Identification for the Practitioner. Philadelphia: W. B. Saunders Company, 1977:145–158.

Figure 4 ...

IV
Collection of Bitemark Evidence

7
Photography
NONINVASIVE ANALYSES

Gregory S. Golden
Coroner's Office, County of San Bernardino
San Bernardino, California, U.S.A.

Franklin D. Wright
Hamilton County Coroner's Office
Cincinnati Ohio, U.S.A.

1. INTRODUCTION

The elementary principles of forensic photography have remained stable and unaltered for decades. What continuously change are the technological aspects of forensic photography. Any treatise or chapter that addresses current levels of phototechnology and imaging risks obsolescence by the time publication places it into the public domain. The technology of photographic imaging is expanding that rapidly.

What the authors hope to accomplish in this chapter on advanced photographic methods is to provide the reader with the fundamental building blocks necessary to understand each method's protocol, the variations among techniques, and their applications in bitemark evidence documentation. The primary intent is to convey the information necessary to allow anyone with a basic comprehension of photography to document what happens biologically in injured tissue.

A discussion of equipment requirements for each technique will be included as well as an explanation of why certain parts of the visible and nonvisible spectrum produce images of the same bitemark that appear entirely different from each other. The authors' mutual goal is to assist the reader in ultimately becoming a better photographer, thereby improving one's expertise for capturing and reproducing accurate photographic bitemark evidence.

It is beyond the scope of this chapter to teach the basic fundamentals of photography. Many high-quality introductory photography textbooks have been written and are readily available at book and photography stores. This writing takes information from the basics of photography and integrates it with the special technical requirements associated with forensic photography. Unless otherwise specified, the scientific data and techniques described within will apply to forensic photography as related to the photographic documentation of bitemark injuries in skin.

2. ELECTROMAGNETIC SPECTRUM: WHAT IT MEANS TO FORENSIC PHOTOGRAPHY

The electromagnetic spectrum runs from very short wavelength ultraviolet light in the 200-nm range through the visible light range of 400–700 nm into the infrared range of 700–900 nm.

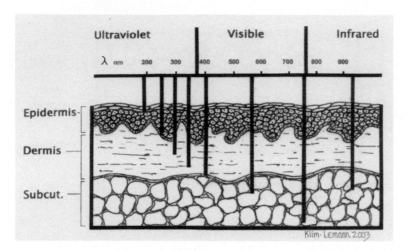

Figure 1 Penetration of light into skin with different wavelengths of the electromagnetic spectrum.

A nanometer (nm) is 10^{-9}m. Since the human eye cannot capture light outside the visible range, special photographic techniques using ultraviolet and infrared light have been developed for this purpose [1]. With varying light wavelengths illuminating the photographed object, very different appearances of the object can be portrayed. This is especially relevant in documenting patterned injuries such as bitemarks, stab and gunshot wounds, fingernail scrapes, etc. The techniques can highlight damaged from normal tissue. Ultimately, a more complete and comprehensive collection of photographic evidence is obtained (Fig. 1–6).

When full-spectrum light strikes skin, four resultant events occur: reflection, absorption, diffusion, and fluorescence [2]. By changing the wavelength of the incident light, each of these

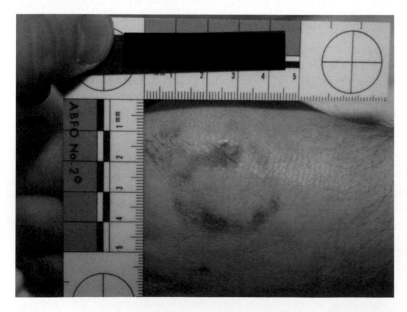

Figure 2 Typical photograph of bitemark on hand. Also see color photograph insert section.

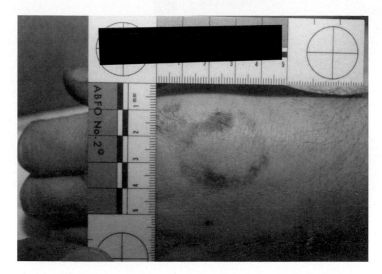

Figure 3   Same bitemark on hand as in Figure 2, in black-and-white photograph.

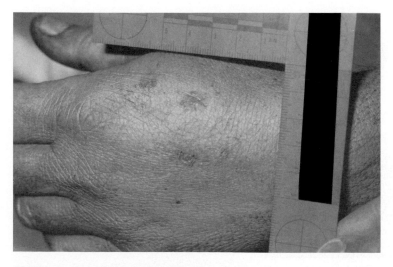

Figure 4   Same bitemark on hand as in Figure 2, in ultraviolet (UV) photograph.

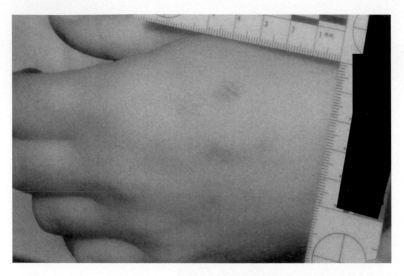

Figure 5   Same bitemark on hand as in Figure 2, in infrared (IR) photograph.

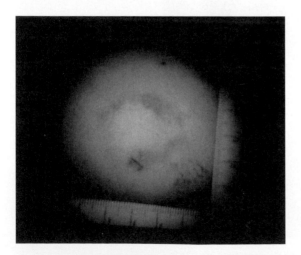

Figure 6   Same bitemark on hand as in Figure 2, in alternate light imaging (ALI) photograph. Also see color photograph insert section.

four possible effects can be emphasized to reveal differing amounts of detail in the resultant images.

2.1. Reflection

Reflection of incident light occurs when a portion of the incident light hits a surface and bounces back, thereby not penetrating the surface. The complex properties of skin as well as the wavelength of incident light determine the amount of reflection. Light that is not reflected penetrates into the skin and becomes absorbed as it diffuses. Measurements of penetration of light into skin have been made and compiled in Beers' Law (Fig. 7).

Skin surface detail is best captured using ultraviolet (UV) light [3]. When UV light hits skin, neither reflection nor fluorescence can be seen with the unaided human eye. The fluorescent properties of light on skin are better captured using another technique, alternate light imaging (ALI), which is described further in this chapter. In surface skin disruption, such as in biting, the reflective UV photograph highlights the differences between normal and damaged tissue (Fig. 8–9).

2.2. Absorption

Some light energy penetrates below the epidermis, particularly the longer wavelengths of light. Once in the dermis, light absorption occurs. The physical elements in the dermis (vascular bundle, nerves, hair and sweat cells) and products associated with the bitemark injury are responsible for absorption. The longer the wavelength of light, the further into the dermal layer it travels. If a bite has sufficient force to cause bleeding in the deeper skin layers, the properties of the long-wavelength infrared (IR) light can be used. IR light penetrates up to 3 mm below the surface of the skin [4] and is highly absorbed by blood products associated with bruising. IR light, while not visible to the unaided human eye, can assist in visualizing where bleeding occurred well below the surface of the skin (Fig. 10–11).

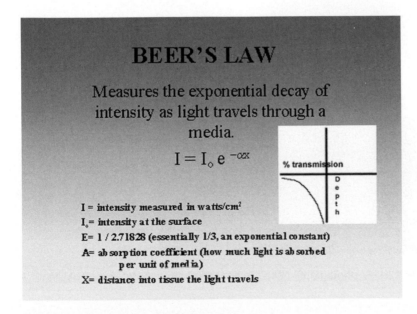

Figure 7 Explanation of Beer's Law.

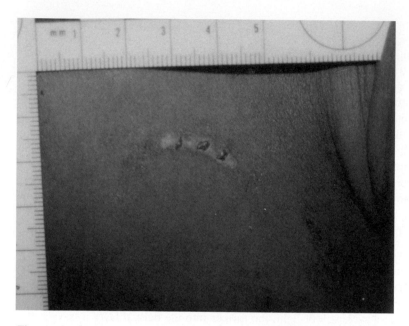

Figure 8 Single-arch bitemark on shoulder in photograph. Also see color photograph insert section.

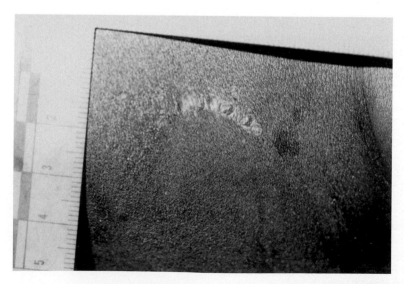

Figure 9 Same bitemark in UV photograph. Note the enhanced surface detail with UV light.

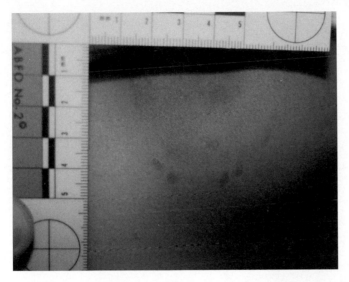

Figure 10 Photograph of bitemark on shoulder taken the day of the incident. Also see color photograph insert section.

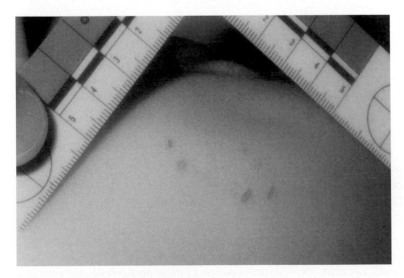

Figure 11 IR photograph of Figure 10.

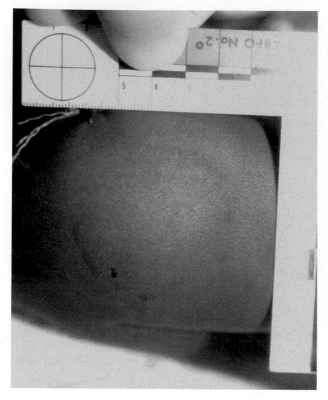

Figure 12 Black-and-white photograph taken 1 day after the homicide.

2.3. Fluorescence

Light energy striking skin also creates an excitation at the molecular level. As the molecules return to a normal energy state, they leave behind a faint visible glow known as fluorescence. This phenomenon lasts for ~ 100 ns (10^{-9} s) [5]. ALI is required for the eye to see fluorescence. This technique also accentuates differences between the injured and uninjured tissue (Figs. 12–14).

2.4. Diffusion

The final event that occurs as light contacts skin is called diffusion, also sometimes referred to as transmission. This event involves the scattering of light within tissue when skin is illuminated. Because light diffuses through skin, it is not recovered or seen in the photograph.

2.5. Summary

In traditional color photography, visible light that strikes skin exhibits four phenomena: reflection, absorption, fluorescence, and diffusion. The combination of these phenomena characterizes what appears in the bitemark photograph. The dark areas associated to the bitemark represent absorption; the light areas, reflection. Although fluorescence occurs, it is not observed in the photograph without using special techniques with filters and monochromatic light. The diffusion of light within skin is not recoverable and therefore not a component of bitemark photographs. The following set of photographs (Figs. 15–18) familiarizing the reader with the different appear-

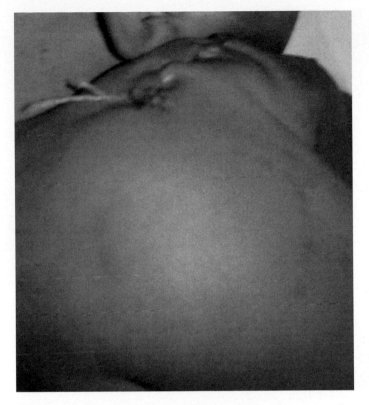

Figure 13 ALI photograph of Figure 12. Also see color photograph insert section.

ance of bitemarks using different photographic techniques. These images were all taken during the same photographic session.

In some instances, even the best photographic efforts cannot improve the quality of a poor bitemark regardless of the wavelength of light used, as witnessed by the four photographs of the same bitemark on the arm of a homicide victim (Figs. 19–22). All photos were taken during the same session.

3. CONVENTIONAL PHOTOGRAPHS

By far the most common method of documenting bitemarks involves the use of conventional camera equipment manufactured for the visible light spectrum. While photographic film is the current standard means of capturing bitemarks, digital photography is gaining popularity and respectability and is accepted by the courts under specific conditions. The reader is referred to the following chapter for more information. Both camera systems are optically designed to work within the visible light spectrum of electromagnetic radiation. Under normal conditions, creating a photograph is relatively simple, predictable, and affordable.

The variety of available cameras, lenses, flash units, and image capture devices is ever increasing. It is possible to take very high quality photographs using different combinations of camera equipment. Bitemark documentation requires that the resultant photographs accurately depict the bitemark pattern on skin. This requirement precludes the use of lower-quality cameras

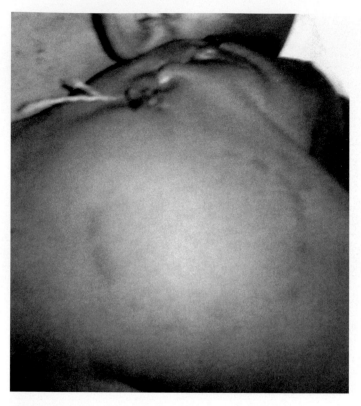

Figure 14 ALI photograph from Figure 13 digitally changed to black-and-white and enhanced. Note the detail of the individual teeth in the bitemark.

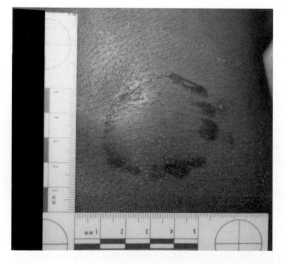

Figure 15 Photograph of a bitemark on the neck on the day of the homicide. Also see color photograph insert section.

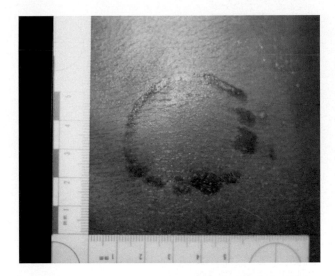

Figure 16   Black-and-white photograph of the same bitemark as Figure 15.

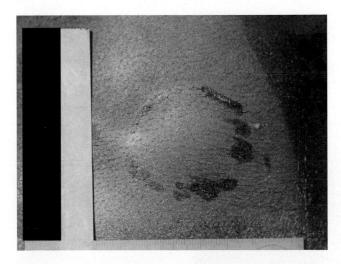

Figure 17   UV photograph of the same bitemark as Figure 15.

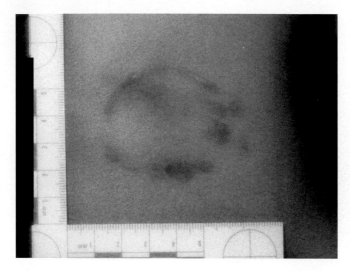

Figure 18   IR photograph of the same bitemark as Figure 15.

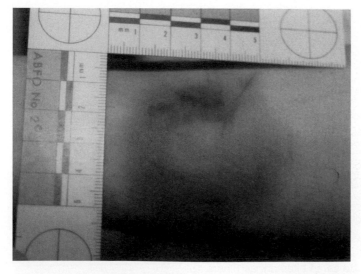

Figure 19   Photograph of poor-quality bitemark on an arm. Also see color photograph insert section.

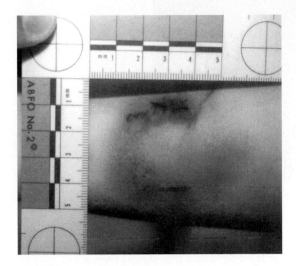

Figure 20   Black-and-white photograph of Figure 19.

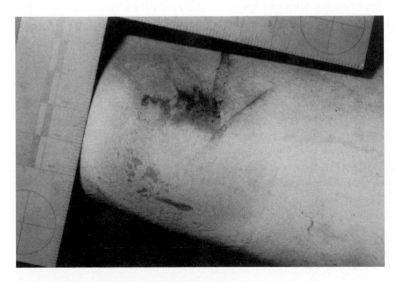

Figure 21   UV photograph of Figure 19.

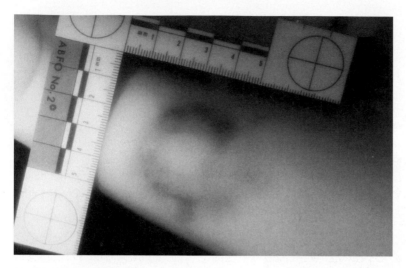

Figure 22 IR photograph of Figure 19.

and inferior-quality optical systems. However, it must be stated that should only a low-quality camera be available, such as a disposable camera, the requirement of photographing the bitemark cannot be disregarded. This may be the only opportunity to record the injury.

Conventional film-based photography is still the single best method of documenting bitemarks today. As the digital era of photography unfolds, many potential problems need addressing. Certain advantages and disadvantages of digital imagery will be discussed later in this chapter. By comparison, traditional photographic film and resultant prints are time tested and archivable with little loss of detail. Though film-based cameras are universally available, and, for the most part, simple to use, the film itself should be properly processed and stored or it will degrade with time. Film-based photography can also present other problems. Improper film handling can ruin the roll. Unlike digital photography, where images can be viewed immediately, there is a time delay in image capture/processing/printing and viewing. Choosing the wrong film for bitemark documentation can provide less than adequate photographs. Instant self-developing photographs, such as Polaroid systems, present additional concerns in bitemark documentation. Polaroid photographs cannot be duplicated or reprinted and do not archive well.

The authors' suggest the use of a 35-mm film-based camera using color and black-and-white photographs at the slowest film speed possible for the lighting available. For digital photography, use the highest resolution the camera offers. Following these recommendations will allow the photographer the opportunity to capture many images in a short period of time and potentially increase the amount of evidence recovered.

4. ARMAMENTARIA FOR CONVENTIONAL 35-MM PHOTOGRAPHY

4.1. Cameras

The 35-mm film-based single-lens reflex (SLR) with through-the-lens (TTL) capability is the ideal camera. What you see framed in the viewfinder is what you get in the photo. There are many reasonably priced high-quality camera bodies that work with fixed or interchangeable lenses. Most of the less expensive 35-mm cameras (so-called ''point and shoot'') are capable of taking good-quality photographs but have a non-TTL viewfinder. The lack of TTL introduces a parallax problem when framing the image to photograph. This problem may not manifest itself until prints are in hand. Parallax problems and poor optical properties of plastic lenses are inherent to disposable cameras. As previously paraphrased, a poor-quality picture is better than none at all.

4.2. Lenses

The lens transmits and focuses light onto the film emulsion to create the image. The higher quality the lens, the more precise and sharp the image that is created. Glass lenses work better than plastic ones. Compound multiple element lenses are best for highly detailed and sharply focused photographs. Lenses range in quality and cost; typically, the higher the cost, the better the quality. If the camera uses interchangeable lenses, consider a lens that has both zoom capability and a calibrated macro setting for closeup photographs. Utilizing a combination lens permits the acquisition of subject orientation and closeup photographs with the same lens. Additionally, they have often special fluorite coatings that block all wavelengths except visible light. The photographer will need to experiment with the lens to know its capabilities prior to case use.

4.3. Flash Units

The required light to properly expose an image can be supplemented with the use of a flash. When properly connected to the camera body and synchronized, the flash unit will strobe simultaneously during exposure to add sufficient light to create the optimal image. For macrophotography, adjustable flash units, or nonadjustable flashes with a guide number of 35–40, provide adequate light. Too much light leads to overexposure; too little light leads to underexposure. Since all cameras and flash units are not the same, the photographer should experiment with exposure settings and flash for the best results.

Many commercially available cameras have built-in self-control flash units; others lack user controls, while still others are fully programmable. Automatic fill flash provides light when conditions require it. User override of the fill flash feature is required in macrophotography. Other disadvantages of built-in flash units are their limited capacity for under or overexposure and nondetachability. The ability to change both exposure setting and flash angle are desirable properties in photographing three-dimensional bitemarks. This specialized flash driven technique is not available with a fixed (permanently attached) camera controlled flash (Fig. 23).

Using a detachable flash, the photographer has the ability to not only manually adjust the flash time, but also move the flash position to angles other than perpendicular (Fig. 24). Too much light from a pure perpendicular angle may cause a ''flash burnout'' where the reflection of indirect light from the flash floods the injury and no detail is recorded in the image. This becomes more of a problem when the flash is fixed on the camera by the manufacturer and metered by the camera. The type and intensity of the light emitted by the flash as well as the direction from which the light strikes the bitemark will have a definite impact on the appearance of the injury. It is recommended that a detachable flash unit be used in bitemark photography to provide the photographer maximum versatility. Too little or too much light can make the bitemark appear vague or ill defined (Fig. 25–26).

4.4 Film

There are many high-quality 35-mm films available such as those made by Kodak and Fuji (Fig. 27). Films come with an ASA/ISO number rating. In its simplest form, the ASA/ISO rating is a determination of the handling characteristics of the emulsion layers on the film relative to the amount of expected light available when the image is created. In general, the lower the ASA/

Figure 23   Camera-based flash system.

Figure 24   Detachable flash system.

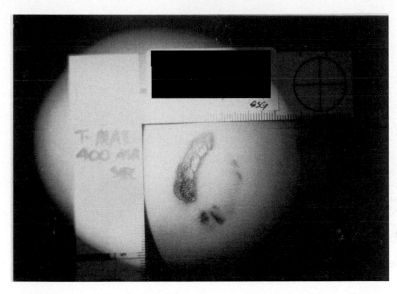

Figure 25   Taken with a light source at perpendicular angle to the bitemark.

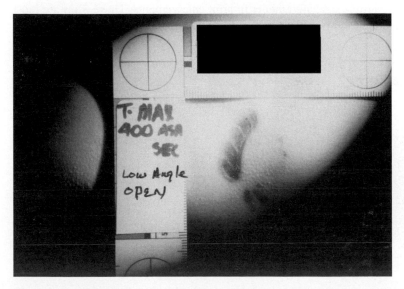

Figure 26   Same bitemark as in Figure 25 with a low-angle light source. Note pinched tissue at tooth embrasures.

Figure 27 Typical 35-mm films used in bitemark photography.

ISO number, the more densely packed the emulsion layer is with the photosensitive grains. The lower-speed films require more light to expose the film but produce a sharper image, thus greater enlargement capabilities without graininess and sharper contrast. Conversely, higher-speed (faster) films, such as ASA/ISO 800–1600, require less light but sacrifice detail and contrast and, because of the larger particle size, are grainier in print enlargements. These films are most useful when adequate lighting is unavailable. For bitemark photographs, the authors recommend

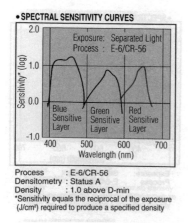

Figure 28 Typical electromagnetic sensitivity of color reversal (slide) film. Note this film would *not* work in UV or IR photography since it has no sensitivity to either UV or IR light.

using 25–100 ISO film speed. In less than ideal conditions, higher-speed films are acceptable, particularly when adequate lighting conditions are not under control of the photographer (Fig. 28–30).

5. CONVENTIONAL PHOTOGRAPHIC TECHNIQUES

Understanding the spectrum of electromagnetic radiation and the types of photographic equipment available, the photographer now needs to develop a specific technique for bitemark documentation [2]. A typical standard technique would be structured as follows: film-based color orientation photographs, color and black-and-white closeup photographs with and without a photographic scale, digital photographs, infrared and ultraviolet photographs, alternate light imaging photographs (Fig. 31–33).

Photography is the first of the noninvasive techniques and may be the only opportunity for the investigator to document the injury. The use of a photographic scale is mandatory because it provides a visible reference showing the dimensional size of the bitemark; without it, life-size enlargements cannot be accurately reproduced. Care should be taken to avoid placing the scale so that it obstructs any part of the injury.

Krauss said, "In photographic bitemark evidence collection, the camera's film plane and the ruler used for scale should be … parallel for maximum accuracy" [6]. Accomplishing both of these requirements ensures capture of size and orientation of the bitemark. Lack of parallelism will create photographic distortion and diminish the evidentiary value of the bitemark. There are digital techniques for the correction of distortion, but proper orientation of the scale alleviates this necessity. If used improperly, computerized techniques for correcting perceived photographic distortion may in fact further distort the bitemark [7].

There are numerous types of photographic scales used for forensic photography. The ABFO No. 2 scale (Fig. 34) designed by Hyzer and Krauss is strongly recommended for bitemark photography [6].

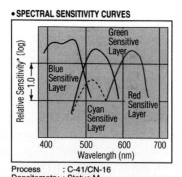

FUJICOLOR SUPERIA REALA [CS]

• SPECTRAL SENSITIVITY CURVES

Process : C-41/CN-16
Densitometry : Status M
Density : 1.0 above minimum density
*Sensitivity equals the reciprocal of the exposure (J/cm²) required to produce a specified density

Figure 29 Typical electromagnetic sensitivity of color negative film. This film is *not* useful in UV or IR photography.

FILM	TECHNIQUE	ASA/ISO SPEED	SENSITIVITY	PROCESSING
Black and White Films				
Kodak TMAX	B&W prints, UV	100 or 400	250-700 nm	TMAX, D-76, HC110
Kodak TMAX CN	B&W prints, UV	400	250-700 nm	C-41
Kodak Plus X	UV	125	250-700 nm	D-76, HC110
Kodak High Speed Infrared	IR *handle in complete darkness	Manual set to 25 or 64	250-900 nm	D-76, HC110
Color Negative Films				
Kodak Gold	Color prints	100, 200, 400, 800, 1600	250-700 nm	C-41
Fuji Superia or Reala	Color prints	100,200,400,800,1600	250-700 nm	C-41
Color Reversal Films				
Kodak Kodachrome	Color slides	64	250-700 nm	K-14 (send to Kodak)
FujiChrome Sensia	Color slides	100, 200, 400	250-700 nm	E-6
Kodak Elite	Color slides	100, 200, 400	250-700	E-6

* Underlined - ASA speed recommended if proper photographic conditions exist.

Figure 30   Recommended Commercial 35mm Films for Bitemark Photography.

This multifunctional scale assures both dimensional and color references. The right-angled shape provides a reference for measuring (correcting) photographic distortion in two planes. If an ABFO No. 2 scale is unavailable, reference objects such as rulers, coins, or paper clips can also be used. Any object used in the photographs as a reference other than an ABFO No. 2 scale should be kept as evidence and maintained in the "chain of evidence."

6. VISIBLE LIGHT PHOTOGRAPHY

The most commonly employed photographs taken in bitemark cases are film-based visible light photographs. The photographs capture the details of the bitemark as seen by the human eye.

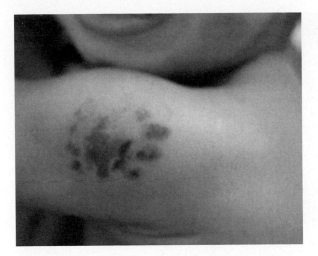

Figure 31 Orientation photograph of bitemark on the deltoid.

The resultant image appears exactly the same as it did in real life when photographed. Evidentiary preservation using photographs is readily accepted as an accurate and reliable depiction of the details of the bitemark in the legal system.

6.1. Visible Light Photography Technique

In the vast majority of bitemark cases, traditional visible light photography will be the only photography used. Realistically, most forensic photographers may not have access to or expertise in specialized techniques using ALI or nonvisible light. This places an additional burden on the photographer for the technique to be done right the first time.

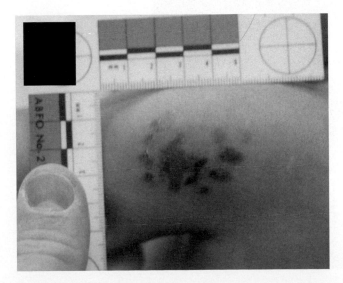

Figure 32 Closeup with scale in place. Also see color photograph insert section.

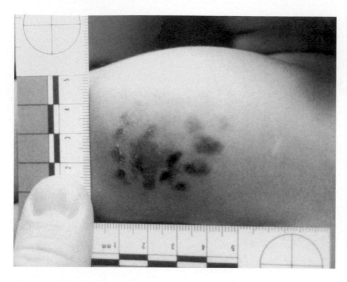

Figure 33   Black-and-white closeup.

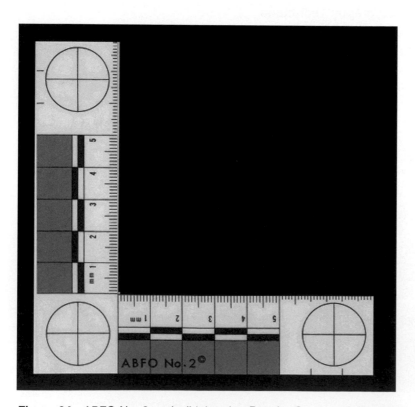

Figure 34   ABFO No. 2 scale (Lightening Powder Co., Inc., Salem, OR).

Evidence collection in the living and deceased using traditional color film begins with orientation photographs that demonstrate the location of the injury. Sequential views of the bitemark with and without scale are followed by macrophotography. If the bitemark has three-dimensional characteristics, additional photographs are produced with the flash positioned at a low angle to highlight details (Fig. 26). The film should be developed and processed as soon as possible. In the living, it might be important to perform serial photography at different times to observe the healing process (Figs. 35–36).

Once orientation photographs are completed, macrophotographs are taken in the visible light range of the spectrum using a 35-mm TTL SLR camera. Closeup (macrophotography) armamentaria include a macro lens, synchronized detachable flash, and the slowest-speed film the conditions will allow. Digital photography can also be employed. The authors recommend that digital and film photography be utilized in the event that the latter technique fails.

Upon completion of the color photography, a second session should be done using black-and-white film. While it may appear to be redundant to take similar photographs in black-and-white that were taken in color, it is not. Because the retina of the eye has more rods (differentiates black and white) than cones (differentiates color), removing the color can at times enhance minute details within the bitemark. In the same fashion, color and black-and-white film do not have the same photosensitivity, so subtle differences between color and black-and-white prints exist. Black-and-white film emulsion is, moreover, typically smaller in particle size, finer in layer detail, and denser than color film emulsion.

The technique for taking black-and-white photographs is the same as for the color film-based protocol. There is no need to retake the orientation photographs in black-and-white if

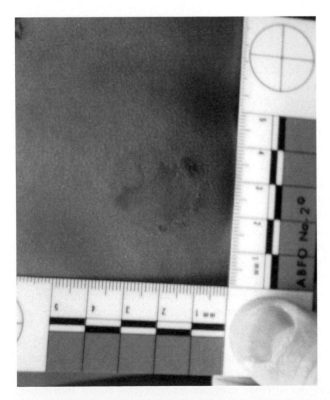

Figure 35 Photograph of bitemark on the back. Also see color photograph insert section.

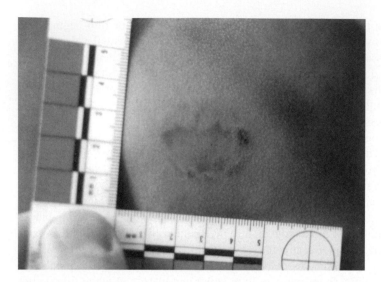

Figure 36   Black-and-white photograph of same bitemark in Figure 35. Note the more detailed appearance of the lingual markings of the upper teeth and the individual markings of the lower teeth.

they were taken in color. The photographic scale and the film plane should be parallel to the bitemark to minimize photographic angular distortion.

7. DIGITAL PHOTOGRAPHY

Digital technology has had a tremendous impact on the field of photography. Digital cameras are now employed for every professional and nonprofessional purpose. The influence of digital photography in law enforcement, commercial photography, and in the public domain has lead to a paradigm shift in archetypical standards and criteria for accumulating images. As a result, more forensic photographers are making the transition from film to digital imaging for a variety of reasons. In odontology, "the use of digital imagery is becoming more common with almost 45% of all respondents reporting some use of digital cameras" [8].

In forensic photography too, the transition from film-based to digital recording of evidence is on the rise. Applications in surveillance photography, questioned documents, crime scenes, forensic pathology, and odontology are all involved to some extent, some more than others. Documentation of bitemark injuries naturally favors this venue since image transfer, enhancement, distortion rectification, overlay production, and comparisons can be performed in a totally digital environment by using digital cameras, scanners, and computers.

Conversion of analog image information to digital information can be accomplished in numerous ways: digitized (scanned) pictures, slides, and prints; digital still photographs; digitized videotape (video capture); and digital video are the primary methods. Digital imaging represents a process that involves much more than just a digital camera.

Even though some 35-mm digital cameras appear to be similar to film-based cameras (Fig. 37), three fundamental components of a digital camera make it unique. The first component is the capture element that gathers light reflected from the subject through the lens. The second is an analog-to-digital (ADC) processor and software program that converts analog into digital information. The third is storage. Images in conventional film-based photography are stored on

Figure 37   Typical 35-mm digital camera (Courtesy of Fuji).

film emulsion, while in the digital environment the images are stored on magnetic media, in RAM, or on a memory card in the same fashion as a computer's hard drive.

There are many advantages of digital imaging including instant viewing, printing, extremely low cost per image, no film use, lack of processing or reloading, control of chain of custody, and portability of images; potentially an infinite number of photographs can be produced, shared, transferred, duplicated, etc.

The language in digital photography is specific, and there needs to be an understanding of several terms. The following terms describe the fundamental building blocks of digital imaging.

8.   CCD VERSUS CMOS SENSORS

When discussing digital cameras, the image capture elements are usually either CCD or CMOS type electronic chips. Not all sensors are created equal. The acronym CCD stands for "charge-coupled device." A CCD is: "A semiconductor device that is used especially as an optical sensor and that stores charge and transfers it sequentially to an amplifier and detector [9]." CCD sensors are made of silicon and are quite expensive to produce. Their size and quality have a direct effect on the price of the camera. Additional advantages of the CCD are the capacity for high ISO (similar to film speed), good color quality, and low electronic noise at long or low-light exposures (Figs. 38).

Figure 38   Capture elements (Courtesy of Kodak).

The biggest disadvantage of the CCD is its slow transfer of data to the recording media. However, "with CCDs, production of a quality image remains their selling point, whether the sensors are used with a microscope, the Advanced Camera for Surveys [ACS] on the Hubble Space Telescope, or your cell phone. In all cases, time is of the essence" [10].

The other digital image capture device, known by the acronym CMOS (complementary metal oxide semiconductor), converts light energy into electrical signals [11]. The CMOS sensor is less expensive to produce, but does not give as high an ISO rating as a CCD. The color quality is not quite as accurate as a CCD. Generally, there is a higher noise capability, although most CMOS cameras have noise-limiting algorithms built into the software. The big advantage of CMOS over CCD is the rapid transfer of data. The term "burst rate" describes how quickly the sensor writes data to storage. The burst rate usually indicates how many frames per second a still camera can acquire images during continuous shooting mode.

9. PIXELS AND COLOR

Capture elements (sensors) are produced in varying sizes. The size of the sensor dictates the cost of the camera, color accuracy, speed (ISO), light-gathering capability, and the magnification of the lens. Sensors have microfilters that interpolate a monochrome image (256 levels of gray) into an accurate color image. These microfilters make up the basic components in a sensor and are referred to as "pixels." In its simplest form, think of a pixel as a grain of emulsion on a strip of film. Pixels can interpolate the color several ways, depending on the manufacturing process. The two most common are red-green-blue (RGB) and cyan-yellow-magenta (CYM). Still, others capture YC (chrominance and luminance) values indirectly from the sensor. In a typical RGB sensor (Fig. 39) there are several thousand clusters of four-element pixels per each "color cell." Two of the elements are green, one is blue, and one is red.

Figure 39   Typical array of RGB Pixels. (Courtesy Linear Systems Inc.)

These subgroups are distributed over the entire sensor and each of the color cells form a "committee" to decide which color all four of the cells will be. The pattern is designed to match the color sensitivity of the human eye and is often referred to as the "Bayer" pattern [12]. For example, in the case of a blue area of color, only the blue part of the cluster will record the light; the group reports no green or red. The end result is that the entire area (all four pixels) records blue. To get a reverse situation (a yellow area), the red- and green-filtered pixels would respond but not the blue pixel.

There is an inherent problem with this type of filtering system, particularly when the frequency of information is greater than the frequency of the filter groups, leading to an effect called "aliasing." Aliasing can appear as a white area in a particularly detailed area of the image, surrounded by red-, green-, and blue-colored pixels. Two methods for correcting aliasing include optical correction, usually by using quartz filters on the CCD, and software correction. The use of the quartz filter can directly and significantly affect the cost of the imaging system.

10. ASPECT RATIO

Most 35-mm digital still cameras have an aspect ratio of 3:2, which corresponds to the size of the sensor (width vs. height). Printing enlarged images will become sized in multiples of the same aspect ratio as the sensor: 4 × 6, 8 × 12, 16 × 24, etc. This feature can become problematic if a printed presentation is going to be formatted in traditional film dimensions. For example, a typical film enlargement can be printed as 8 × 10 inches without peripheral loss. A digital camera will create a file whose aspect ratio prefers enlargement to 8 × 12 size, but may get printed as 8 × 10 inches during commercial enlargement. Hopefully, any crucial information contained in the image is not located at the edge that will be cropped during the enlargement and printing process.

11. RESOLUTION AND COMPRESSION

Digital still cameras are able to save files (images) in several formats. Some images are saved with compression, a method that squeezes the data into a smaller file. Resolution represents the quality of an image printed at a specific size. Both resolution and compression are important components of the image and will determine to what size it can be enlarged. It is possible to determine from the size of the print what file size and resolution are needed for the saved image by using the mathematical equation: height (in) $\times$ width (in) $\times$ pixels/in/1000 $=$ file size (megabytes). For example at 300 pixels per inch: an $8 \times 10 = 80 \times 300$ pixels/in $=$ 24,000/1000 $=$ 24 megabytes (MB).

One may also derive the file size by the actual pixels. This is usually a ratio of 1:3. For example, an RGB.tif file with no compression and a raw image of 1.2 million pixels will result in a 3.6-MB file. These terms must be understood before an intelligent choice can be made on fulfilling the photographer's needs.

12. ISO EQUIVALENCE

The ISO setting on a digital camera is nothing more than an emulation of film properties. Digital cameras have an advantage in that some can shoot images at incredibly high ISO equivalence settings. For example, a digital camera that has the capacity to capture an image at 6400 ISO can be set to shoot one stop faster than film rated at the same ISO, thereby increasing the digital ISO to 12,800. Moreover, some digital cameras have the capability to pull or push the images up to two additional full stops, resulting in a virtual ISO of 50,000. These images can be either monochrome or color. The greater the ISO, the more ''dark current noise'' is introduced into the image (Fig. 40). This is equivalent to an increased graininess associated with high ISO rated traditional film.

Some cameras can eliminate dark current noise by the application of a filter inside the camera. Other cameras eliminate the noise by applying a filter inside the software. Even more sophisticated, some cameras eliminate the noise by acquiring two separate images during the exposure, one with the shutter closed [13]. Employing the application of a noise subtraction algorithm, the software eliminates the dark current noise.

13. LENS MAGNIFICATION

If the sensor size is physically smaller than the actual film size the camera body was designed for, i.e., traditional 35-mm film-based cameras, this decreased size will magnify the image from

Figure 40 Increasing ISO increases "current noise." (Courtesy Kodak.)

Figure 41 Actual sensor size.

the lens (Figs. 41–42). Magnification in sensors is typically a factor of 1.2:1 or 1.7:1. To understand the effect of magnification on image, a 50-mm lens gives a magnification 1.5:1. The image equivalent will be of a 75-mm lens. Similarly, a 100-mm lens will give an equivalent digital image of a 150-mm lens. This presents an advantage during long-range surveillance and closeup photography since there is no loss of light in magnification.

14. STORAGE DEVICES

Electronic images are stored via smart memory in the camera, removable compact flash cards, type II and type III PCMCIA cards, and microdrives that have large gigabyte capacities (Fig. 43). Once the image (data) is on the card, it can be transferred to a computer's imaging software where it can be modified or saved in the file format in which it was acquired. Care

Figure 42 Effect of magnification by sensors. (Courtesy Linear Systems Inc.)

Figure 43 Storage devices. (Courtesy of Linear Systems Inc.)

should be taken when handling compact flash cards, since magnetism or other electrical fields can damage the data. Many consumer cameras are sold with an accompanying software imaging program that allows the user to download images from the camera by the plug and play method, utilizing a serial, USB or firewire port on the computer. Other cameras and software programs use the ''firewire'' method, which is the next most rapid method of transferring large digital files to an existing hard drive. The fastest technique is by way of direct access. This process requires the installation of a PCMCIA card reader drive with the accompanying software on board the computer itself. For digital cameras that save images as JPEG files, the transfer of images can easily be accomplished with the Windows operating system or the iPHOTO MacIntosh program. Files are moved into the computer by simply copying or downloading the files from the flashcard to the hard drive folder that the user creates for storage.

15. FILE TYPES

A ''RAW'' file is an image saved directly from the camera's imaging sensor and contains the most information of all file types. Usually it is a secure file format that prohibits modification in imaging software applications. The RAW file also offers the ability of post exposure compensation and color correction. A ''JPEG'' file is one that has been compressed from the RAW data into a smaller size for storage maximization and saved with a JPG file extension. JPG files are not secure and the user cannot change the values for exposure or color from the raw data. Most professional digital still cameras produce either a RAW or JPG file and some produce both files simultaneously.

The secure file format is a source for debate among forensic scientists, the legal community, and investigative agencies alike. Although it is a ''loss-less compression'' type of file, a secure file is one directional and can be viewed, edited, and modified in a software program. When edited it cannot be written back to a secure file format. If the software does save the file under the same name and extension, the image was not an original to begin with.

Secure file formats contain more information than any other file type. The information can include time of day, date, serial number of the camera, exposure number, and camera settings for each exposure. Working in a secure file format minimizes chain of custody issues because the authenticity of the image is provable. The most advantageous feature of a secure file format is that it becomes insurance against challenges of authenticity, an issue that could be raised in judicial proceedings.

The question of when to use a secure file format is based on a number of considerations. Who will be getting access to the files? Where are they? How are they handled, where, and when? To whom will they be distributed? Who has access to the originals? These questions are important when the exchange of files (evidence) will occur inside law enforcement agencies, forensic labs, among experts, lawyers, and/or the courts. The same problems are encountered should the defense produce digital information in judicial proceedings.

16.   SCANNERS

One way of converting analog images to digital data is by scanner. There are optical scanners that are designed specifically for reading film, slides, printed material, or all. In the typical flatbed scanner, the scanned material is placed on a glass platen. An optical sensor under the glass moves past the object and records it as a digital image. The sensor reads the object very much like a photocopier; however, in this case, instead of producing a print on paper, the software creates an image file that can be stored and managed.

There are several important scanner applications relevant to bitemark investigation. Dental study models (casts) of suspects' teeth can be imported as image files using a flatbed scanner (see Fig. 44). Many odontologists use the image of scanned study models to create hollow volume and/or compound overlays for comparison to life-size bitemark digital images or standard photographs. Images of a pattern injury can also be imported into an imaging software program such as Adobe Photoshop via scanned film, color print enlargement, or actual digital files. Once digitized, the image can be corrected for rotation, size, and photographic distortion [7]. The entire bitemark comparison and analysis can then be demonstrated on computer, printed, or projected via a laptop computer connected to an LCD projector.

17.   CONSIDERATIONS FOR DIGITAL PHOTOGRAPHY IN ORDER OF IMPORTANCE

The first consideration is output. If the main intent is to print the images, how big the actual prints are going to be will determine file size, camera capabilities, and printer features. Larger prints of digital images require larger files with more resolution, which means more sophistication and advanced features in the camera. Are the images going to be subject to electronic distribution? If so, will it be through a network, server, or internet email? The larger the file size, the more time is required for image transfer. Many internet service providers limit the maximum file size they will accept. Some raw image files may be too large to send via electronic distribution.

The second consideration is storage. Will the images be stored temporarily on a flash card, on line, with a hard drive or RAID array or near line via a network server or DVD jukebox (Fig. 45)?

The file size and number of files to be stored will dictate the requirements for storage hardware. For personal usage, a CD burner may be more than adequate. A major metropolitan law enforcement agency may accumulate thousands of images daily. For this situation, a multiuser access drive with multiterabyte capacity may be necessary for storage (Fig. 46).

The third consideration is retrieval. Who is going to maintain the software to download the images? Will it be one person or several people? Will that software be the same as the one that is used to find the image and work with it? How will the files be indexed, sorted, named, and saved? These questions are critical for multiuser input settings and must be answered before beginning to integrate digital imagery in forensic applications.

The fourth consideration is hardware requirements. The type of computer one uses for viewing and creating images and graphics must be adequate to fulfill the requirements of the job. The components should include a large amount of RAM, a big hard drive, a fast processor,

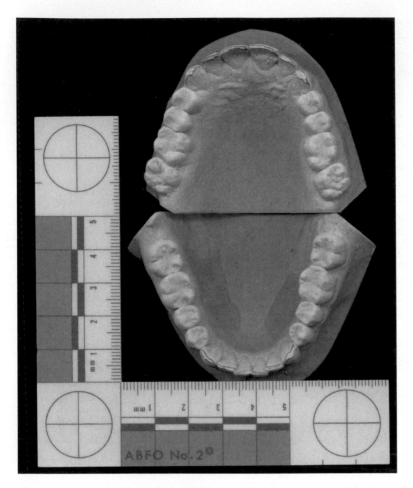

Figure 44   Scanned dental casts.

DVD or CD reader/writer, and a PCMCIA drive or firewire for faster downloading of images. Some additional considerations might include a wireless transmitter or cell connectivity, battery operation in case of power failure, and, last but not least, a contingency plan in case there is a general failure of digital imagery. The remote but possible failure of an application of digital imagery in a specific case reinforces the suggested redundancy by the authors of incorporating both film-based and digital photography.

The final consideration involves decisions to be made regarding the type and capabilities of the camera. Will a secure file format be necessary? How big a file will be needed and what size enlargement for working cases? What applications are available from the manufacturer for downloading and working with the images? How are images to be stored? There is currently at least one 35-mm digital camera that has a 13.89 millionpixel CMOS image sensor capable of creating a 41-MB full-resolution TIFF file (Fig. 47) [14]. Downloading and storing images on a home PC under these circumstances might create more problems than anticipated.

Software selection is critical. What are the needs of the investigator? Eventually one can count on outgrowing the next release of any imaging software package. Will it be upgradeable and appropriate to other applications? The worst-case scenario would be changing either record

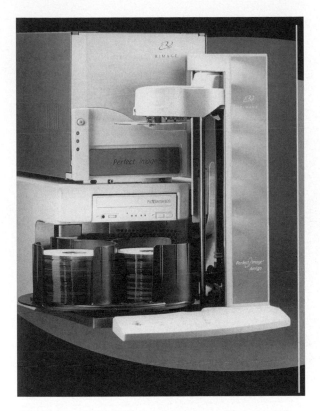

Figure 45 DVD/CD storage system. (Courtesy Rimage.)

management systems and/or operating systems. The user will need to know if the software is compatible with subsequent releases of operating systems such as Windows or Mac OS.

Another important aspect of software consideration is the ability to manipulate or enhance the images rendered. As previously mentioned, Adobe Photoshop is one of many very powerful image management systems. This multipurpose imaging software suite has algorithmic options that offer total control over how the image is presented. Digital enhancement can frequently improve the appearance of bitemark images. Figure 48 was scanned from a color slide and represents the maxillary arch on the sole of a child's foot. Using Adobe Photoshop the image was converted to grayscale and the bite isolated using the marquee tool. Enhancement of the bite pattern by altering levels of contrast and brightness resulted in Figure 49.

Another impressive enhancement software manager is LucisPro [15]. This program was developed for a variety of applications and offers a simple user-friendly system for bringing out details of bruises in bitemarks by means of two separate cursor algorithms. Figure 50 is a scanned color slide of the right calf of a female child abuse victim. Figure 51 is the same photo enhanced with LucisPro software with the large cursor set at 57 and the small cursor at 11. Note the improved visibility of the dental arches even though this bite was inflicted through the child's clothing as is evident by the elastic band imprint.

In summary, before purchasing digital equipment, the authors suggest consulting with an experienced vendor that can integrate all components of a digital system, and provide technical support when needed. Sooner or later that support will be needed, guaranteed!

Figure 46   Multiterrabyte storage array. (Courtesy Plasmon.)

The **KODAK PROFESSIONAL**
DCS PRO 14N DIGITAL CAMERA

- 13.89 million total pixels with true 3000 x 4500 pixel resolution
- 3-, 6-, and 14-megapixel variable resolution
- Full-frame, 35 mm-size CMOS sensor; no lens magnification factor
- Compatible with NIKON lenses and accessories
- KODAK PROFESSIONAL Extended Range Imaging Technology (ERI) to safeguard images
- Ability to save images as DCR RAW files or ERI-JPEG files
- Competitively priced

Figure 47   Kodak 14N Digital Camera. (Courtesy Kodak.)

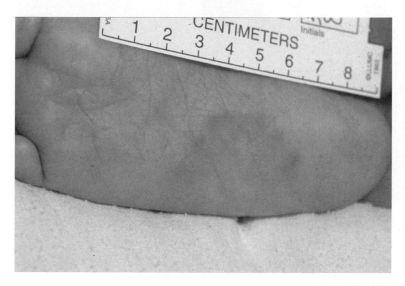

Figure 48 Unretouched image scanned from a slide. Also see color photograph insert section.

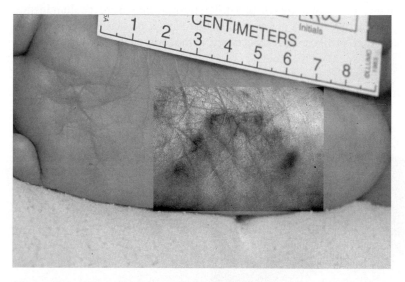

Figure 49 Enhanced image of Figure 48.

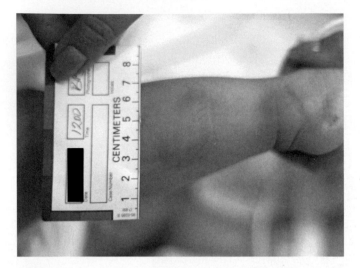

Figure 50 Scanned from original color slide with no modifications. Also see color photograph insert section.

18. ALTERNATE LIGHT IMAGING

Alternate light imaging (ALI), fluorescent photography, forensic light source photography, narrow-band illumination—these are all synonymous for the process of recording a photographic image with the aid of a monochromatic light and a blocking filter. The technique of ALI is founded upon a phenomenon entitled the "Stokes shift" after professor G.G. Stokes [16], who discovered that the remitted wavelength of light is of a different frequency from the illuminating source (Fig. 52). Part of the energy of light at a particular frequency (measured in nanometers) is absorbed by the subject matter it strikes. Once that energy, in the form of electrons, is absorbed,

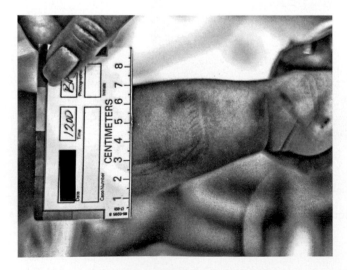

Figure 51 Same photo after enhancement with LucisPro. Also see color photograph insert section.

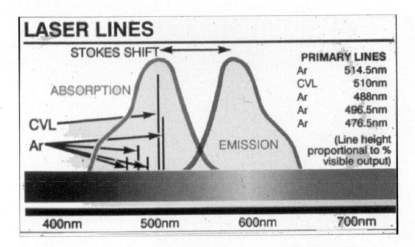

Figure 52   (Courtesy of Omnichrome Inc.)

it creates a molecular excitation that seeks to return to its unexcited state. The return of the electrons to their resting state releases that energy as fluorescence. The remitted light (fluorescence) is of a higher frequency and lower intensity, and cannot be seen in ambient conditions. It can, however, be observed by using filters that pass the remitted light and block the incident light.

The equipment requirements for ALI are similar to other forms of macrophotography with the exception that one must employ a forensic light source for the incident light and a blocking filter over the lens to capture the fluorescent image. A tripod-mounted 35-mm camera and macrolens are part of the standard armamentaria.

Figure 53 shows the ALI technique and how fluorescent images are captured photographically. Several companies manufacture forensic light sources. The authors' experiences have been primarily involved with the Omniprint 1000 manufactured by Melles Griot Laser Group, Carlsbad, CA [17]. (Fig. 54). This is a tunable light source with varying frequencies of light illumination. The Plexiglas goggles are for the observer to detect latent evidence and view enhanced fluorescent objects. The color of source light and shade of goggles used depends on the subject matter being illuminated and photographed.

Alternate light imaging is firmly anchored in numerous applications of forensic investigation. Crime scene analysts and forensic photographers learn to utilize the appropriate light wavelengths to illuminate blood spatter, illicit drugs, fibers, fingerprints, and body fluids including semen, vaginal secretions, and saliva [2].

Figure 55 is a preautopsy color photograph of the lower leg of a homicide victim taken with a strobe flash. Figure 56 is a close-up of the same leg taken with 450 nm blue light and filtered with a Tiffen No. 15 yellow filter. A previously undetected semen stain is fluorescing in the central area of the photo.

Virtually any organic compound found in nature can be made to fluoresce. What peak level of excitation a compound exhibits when illuminated depends on the wavelength of the illuminating light and the chemical components of the substance [18]. Early research on the bioluminescence of human skin detected a peak excitation at 430–450 nm [19,20]. This range of visible light is coincidentally very near the long UVA range, but is actually in the deep blue color of the visible spectrum. Illuminating tissue with the ALI technique provides a distinctive advantage when photographing bruises, pattern injuries, and bitemarks on skin. When utilizing

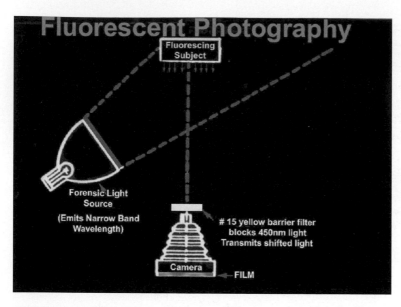

Figure 53 Fluorescent protocol.

the ALI technique, the net overall effect of obtaining the fluorescent image of a bitemark is to enhance the visibility of the injury [21].

The biochemical explanation of how this image enhancement occurs is revealed in the differences between normal and abnormal (injured) tissue substances. Certain organic components such as collagen, keratin, and subcutaneous fat in the layers of the skin (dermis and epidermis) are bioluminescent and readily transmit light [22]. Other components such as bilirubin, hemoglobin, and melanin absorb light. Uninjured epidermis, rich in keratin, is a highly bioluminescent. Contrasting blood components of hemoglobin and melanin that have collected in the injured areas of the bitemark are seen as dark areas of contusion. This difference in light absorption due to blood products and high light remittance of uninjured tissue is what creates

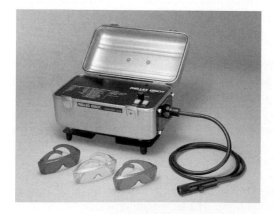

Figure 54 Omniprint 1000BR. (Courtesy Melles Griot).

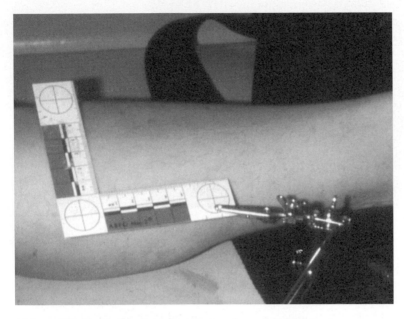

Figure 55 Lower leg photographed under normal light.

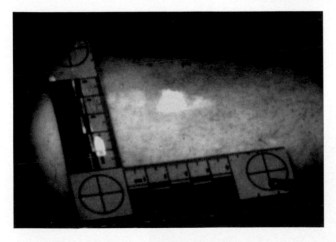

Figure 56 Leg closeup with ALI showing presence of fluorescing semen. Also see color photograph insert section.

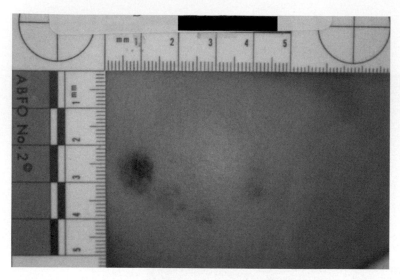

Figure 57 Bitemark taken with normal flash, visible light.

the enhanced appearance of the bitemark. Figure 57 is a digital image of a bitemark on the left shoulder of a young Caucasian female homicide victim, taken with normal flash.

The same bitemark depicted in Figure 57 and with ALI in Figure 58 reveals the more distinctive gross features of both dental arches. ALI is most useful in situations where there is minimal visible bruise pattern information present on the surface of the tissue, but below the epidermis there is significant bruising.

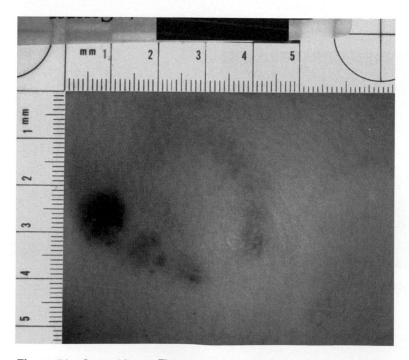

Figure 58 Same bite as Figure 57 taken with ALI. Also see color photograph insert section.

Film selection and exposure factors vary depending upon the individual situation. Unlike UVA and IR photography, ALI must be achieved in total darkness excepting the light source. Any ambient light will interfere with the image capture, particularly when using the higher speed films.

19. ALI TECHNIQUE FOR BITEMARK PHOTOGRAPHY

Routinely the photographer should be able to capture an adequate image with a minimum of 100 ISO film or the equivalent digital setting. Exposure times can vary depending on several factors that will be discussed herein. With 100 ISO film, typical exposures range between 1/4 sec to 2 sec at f-stop settings of f/4 to f/5.6 aperture. The light source and camera ideally should be placed at distances of 12–18 in from the subject. Before exposure, the camera should be tripod mounted with the film plane parallel to the injury and the ABFO No. 2 scale. It is advisable to prepare the shot and focus prior to turning out the overhead lights. The light meter readings are then taken through the No. 15 yellow filter mounted to the lens while illuminating the subject with the light source only and no other ambient lighting. The forensic light source should be set to 450 nm monochromatic light. The light guide or fiberoptic cable coming from the light source may be either tripod mounted or hand held. Exposures should be bracketed by increasing and decreasing shutter speed.

With a little practice, one may discover that with ALI, slightly underexposed images may contain more information than normal or overexposed images. Some light meters are unaccustomed to reading monochromatic light. The result is that the meter misreads the intensity of 450 nm illumination and adjusts by allowing more light than is necessary for an accurate exposure. This problem can be corrected by changing the aperture setting and/or the exposure time.

Many variables affect exposure factor. A person with a dark complexion (more melanin) will require increased exposure times due to more absorption and less reflection of light. Light source manufacturers create forensic light units with different strengths and bulb wattage; some have brighter output. The conveyance of light, whether it is through a fiberoptic cable, liquid light guide, or direct optics, determines how much luminance is transferred from the source.

Photographing living bite victims presents some interesting problems since motion must be avoided and long exposure times are required. Consequently higher speed films are chosen. Typically, 400–1600 ISO is needed for capturing bitemarks with ALI in the conscious, living person, and absolute darkness is required. Any ambient light will create fogging of the pictures.

As a rule, photographers attempting fluorescent photography should become familiar with their camera equipment, its capabilities, and the appropriate exposure settings prior to actual casework. Pretesting equipment under controlled conditions is highly recommended.

19.1. Case Presentation 1

This demonstration of normal vs. ALI photography was obtained during an officer-involved shooting. Responding to an emergency call for a domestic dispute, the sheriff's deputy was confronted at the door of the residence by a 19-year-old Hispanic female wielding a knife. After several warnings to put the knife down, the female lunged at the officer, who responded by shooting her with his service revolver. The author (G.G.) was requested to document multiple bitemarks for the purpose of validating the initial altercation between the victim and her boyfriend (Figs. 59–68).

19.2. Case Presentation 2

An attempted rape and homicide was committed on a young enlisted Navy aircraft maintenance specialist while she was on R&R (rest and relaxation) from a tour of duty in Afghanistan. The

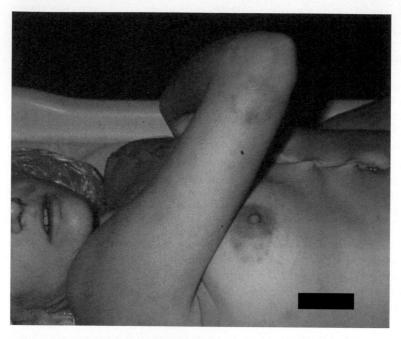

Figure 59 Orientation photo. Note bitemarks near right elbow and on breast and left cheek. Also see color photograph insert section.

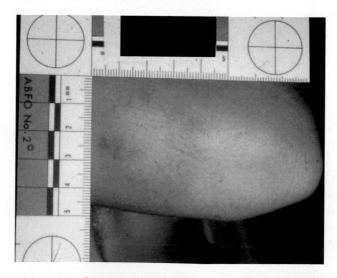

Figure 60 Closeup of right elbow, normal light. Also see color photograph insert section.

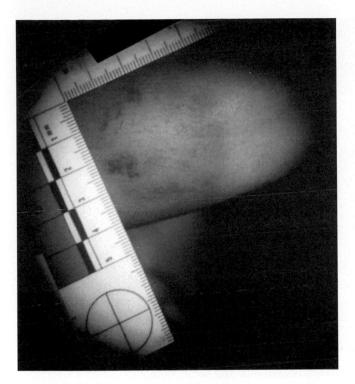

Figure 61   ALI photo of right elbow. Also see color photograph insert section.

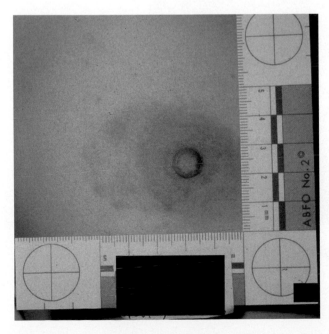

Figure 62   Flash photo of bitemark on right breast. Also see color photograph insert section.

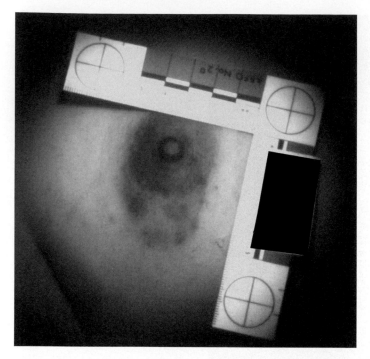

Figure 63 ALI photo of bitemark on right breast. Also see color photograph insert section.

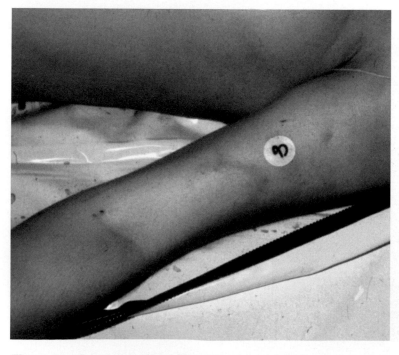

Figure 64 Orientation photo. Note bitemark on left bicep.

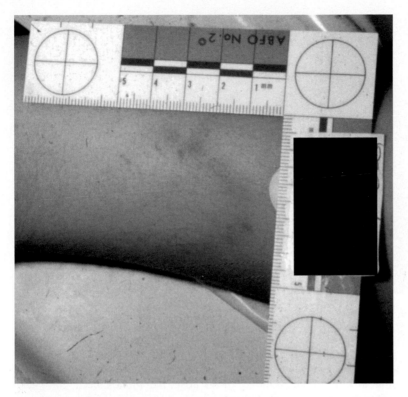

Figure 65   Closeup of bitemark on left bicep. Also see color photograph insert section.

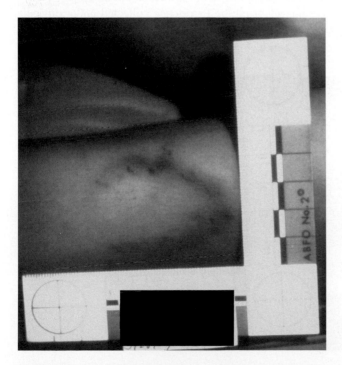

Figure 66   ALI photo of bitemark on left bicep. Also see color photograph insert section.

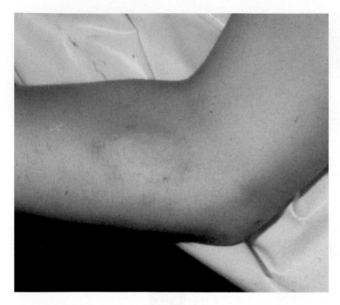

Figure 67   Bitemark on right forearm.

perpetrator, a U.S. Marine, admitted to the attack after indictment. At least 13 sustained bitemarks were documented, including an avulsed bite to the tip of the nose, facial bites, neck, ear, back, and both breasts. Photographic documentation of all these injuries consumed an entire afternoon, including several breaks for the victim and resetting equipment for different photographic protocols. Figures 69–75 constitute but a few images of the best evidence collected under difficult circumstances. Acknowledgement goes to Dr. N.D. ''Skip'' Sperber for assisting with this case.

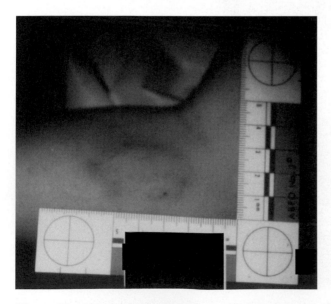

Figure 68   ALI photo of bitemark on right forearm. Also see color photograph insert section.

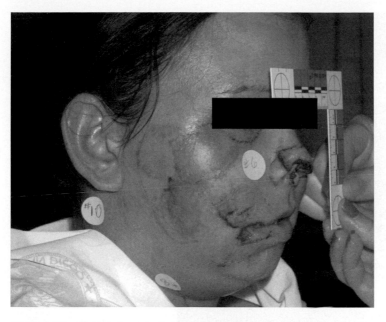

Figure 69 Orientation photo. Note numerous overlying bites on face, avulsed bite to nose. Also see color photograph insert section.

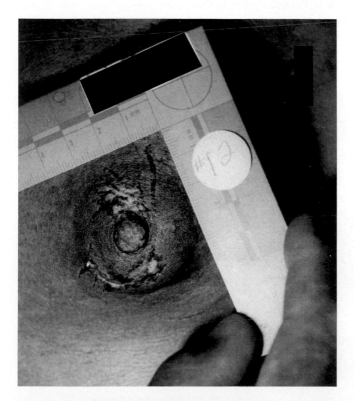

Figure 70 UV photo of bite on the left breast.

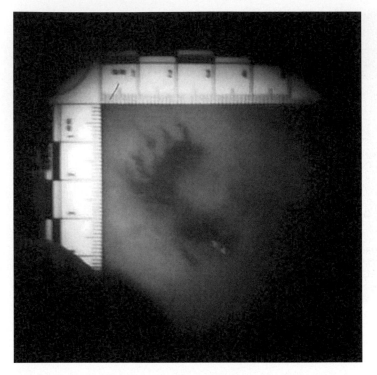

Figure 71   ALI black-and-white photo of the bite on the back.

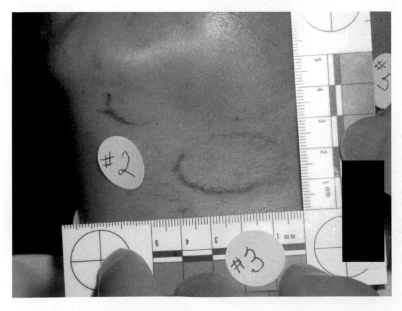

Figure 72   Photo of the bite on the neck. Also see color photograph insert section.

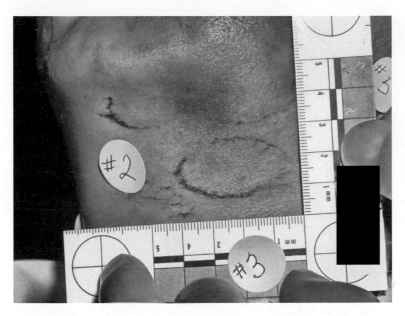

Figure 73 LucisPro enhanced image. Also see color photograph insert section.

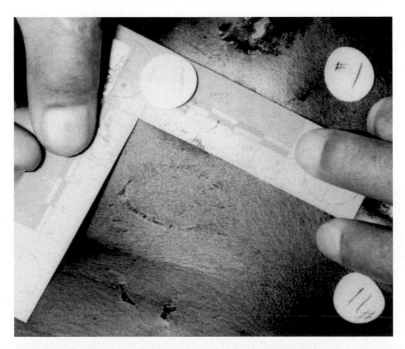

Figure 74 UV photo of same bite on the neck. Note the surface detail of the injury, and not the bruise pattern.

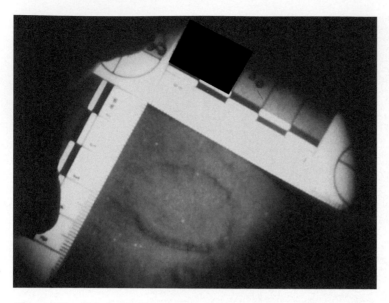

Figure 75 ALI photo of same bite on the neck as Figure 74. Also see color photograph insert section.

20. NONVISIBLE LIGHT PHOTOGRAPHY: INFRARED TECHNIQUE

Infrared (IR) light possesses special properties when directed on injured skin. It is possible to capture extravasation of blood beneath the skin surface (when present) using IR photography. While patterns may not appear as sharply focused in IR as in visible or UV photographs, they can provide yet another source of photographic bitemark documentation.

Subdermal hemorrhage can occur when teeth or other objects crush tissue. The IR technique takes advantage of light absorption in areas of bruising that consequently appear black in the resultant photograph. Frequently the individual groupings of blood patterns recorded in the IR photographs record the biter's dental signature.

The appearance of IR photographs is different from those of the same injury with visible, UV, and ALI light photographs. Because the focus point of IR photographs is up to 3 mm below the surface of the skin, the IR photographs often appear "grainy" and blurry as compared to those taken in other light media [4,26]. Failure of a bitemark to appear in an IR photograph may not be the result of poor technique. The more likely cause is the lack of bleeding below the skin surface [2]. Because the unaided human eye cannot see details of the bitemark captured in IR photography, it is the recommendation of the authors that IR photography be utilized whenever possible in the collection of bitemark evidence as part of the process to "see all that is there" [6].

20.1. Armamentarium for Infrared Photography

IR photography requires the use of special equipment. This includes a tripod, a standard 35-mm TTL SLR camera body, a lens that passes IR light, an IR light source, film sensitive to IR light, and a No. 87 Wratten gel filter (Fig. 76).

Any 35-mm camera body with a manual mode setting will work well for IR photography. While there are many commercial lenses that pass IR light, the Nikon Nikkor UV105 lens has

Figure 76 Kodak Wratten No. 87 gel filter.

been specially designed for passing both visible and nonvisible light, including IR light (Figs. 77, 78) Nikon also manufacturers the SB140 flash unit that is a full spectrum light source that emits good quantities of UV, visible and IR light. The SB140 has separate settings for each of these light specta and must be manually selected.

The most readily available IR film is Kodak High-Speed Infrared Film. This film does not come with a preset ASA/ISO setting and requires the photographer to set the camera's ISO to 25. When the film is developed, it can be "pushed" one or two stops to increase the contrast of the image. The term "pushing" refers to leaving the film in the developer longer than usual. Because Kodak high-speed infrared film is a full-spectrum film, it is very susceptible to visible and UV light, both of which fog the film, degrade it, and possibly even render it useless. Therefore, when using IR film it is critical that all handling be done in total darkness, including camera loading, unloading, and processing. This film must also be stored in either a refrigerator or freezer until it is to be used. After removal from cold storage, it should be allowed to warm up for a minimum of an hour before use [4].

Typically, the Kodak High-Speed Infrared Film is developed and printed as a contact sheet showing all exposures on the roll. This offers the photographer a choice of prints be it 3×5 or 4×6 format while viewing all images on a single sheet. Henderson describes a novel technique using a T-MAX 100 Direct Positive Film Developing outfit that can be used to develop the Kodak High-Speed Infrared Film directly to positive transparencies (slides), thus eliminating a step in the process [24]. There are many sources of IR light for IR photography. Many commercial flash units emit sufficient amounts of IR light, as do typical tungsten lamps and quartz-halogen lamps. Experimentation with different light sources and flash settings is imperative if one does not have access to a Nikon SB 140 flash.

Figure 77 Nikon 35-mm camera body with SB 140 full-spectrum flash and Nikon Nikkor UV105 lens.

Figure 78 Nikon camera setup with UV, IR, and visible light flash filters.

20.2. Infrared Photography Technique

IR photography requires the use of a tripod with the camera. Because IR light penetrates below the surface of the skin, the camera is set up so there is increased depth of field with the aperture set to f-16 or f-22 and the exposure time starting from 1/250th of a second to 1 sec, via bracketing, for each f-stop used. This will work to ensure that by slightly underexposing the images (1/250th sec) to slightly overexposing (1 sec), the details present in the bitemark using IR light will be captured. The camera is positioned so that the front of the lens, film, scale, and bitemark are all in the same parallel plane. Using the TTL viewing properties of the camera, the visible focus is established, the IR focus shift applied, and the Kodak Wratten No. 87 gel filter placed in front of the lens. To specify the exact wavelengths of light that are passed through the lens to the film, a band pass filter is used in IR photography. The Kodak Wratten No. 87 gel filter is specific for passing only infrared light. The filter is placed tight against the lens after focusing. Using an IR emitting light source, the image is created on the Kodak high-speed infrared film. A reminder that Kodak High-Speed Infrared Film must be loaded/unloaded in complete darkness, and the camera must be manually set to ASA/ISO 25.

20.3 Focus Shift

Most commercially available lenses are manufactured to optimally perform within the visible spectrum of light, the range for which the focusing properties of the lens are calibrated. Additionally, the manufacturers place fluorite coverings on the lenses which allow only the transmission of visible light. When photographing outside of the visible light spectrum, it may be necessary to make small adjustments to the focus point of the lenses to account for the non-visible light focus [25]. The process of refocusing after establishing the visible focus is referred to as the ''focus shift (Figs. 79).''

As previously mentioned, the focus for IR photography is up to 3 mm below the surface of the skin. Therefore, IR photography must account for the change in the visible focus by moving the lens slightly away from the object [4,26]. Many lenses have a small dot on the focus ring located to the right of the visible focus point that marks the infrared focus shift point. A focus shift is required for all IR photographs.

In contrast to IR photography, UV photography highlights the surface details of the bitemark. Thus, the focus point in UV is closer to the front of the lens than the visible focus, and, if a focus shift is required, the lens is moved slightly toward the object being photographed. While others have championed the need for a focus shift of the same amount as infrared but in the opposite direction when taking UV photographs, it has been this author's experience (F.W.) that a focus shift was generally unnecessary.

Practically speaking, once the photographer has the necessary equipment to begin UV and IR photography, it will take several photographic sessions of experimentation to determine the specific needs and techniques that will be required for optimal nonvisible light photography.

21. ULTRAVIOLET PHOTOGRAPHY

The primary advantage of reflective ultraviolet (UV) photography is the ability to accentuate surface details of disrupted skin. Frequently during the act of biting, there is damage to the surface of the skin as well as the subepithelial structures. The injury causes blood products such as hemoglobin and melanin to be released throughout the wounded area. These products eventually migrate toward the periphery of the injury as it heals. The increased melanin deposition is responsible for the increased absorption and less reflection of UV light. The net effect is an

Figure 79 IR focus mark on Nikon UV 105 lens. The large black dot in the top picture represents the visible focus. The small dot to the right of the visible focus highlighted in the bottom photograph represents the IR focus. (Photograph courtesy of Nikon, Inc.)

enhancement in the appearance of the injury pattern as observed in UV photographs [27]. Disruption of the normal skin surface where the teeth touch during biting creates a physiological difference between the damaged areas and the undamaged adjacent skin. UV light captures these subtle differences on film emulsion that cannot be seen with the unaided human eye. UV light does not effectively penetrate the surface of the skin and is, for the most part, reflected. As an added bonus, reflected UV light creates a sharper image on the film [28]. This fact makes UV photography advantageous for visualizing the enhanced irregularities of the damaged tissue surface.

There is some controversy in the literature regarding the optimum timing for the use of UV photography. This author (F.W.) has documented several bitemark cases in living victims who were serially photographed for 1 month and found that the greatest enhancement offered by UV photography occurs between 7 and 9 days after the injury [29]. There are documented and reported cases of bitemark injuries being captured using UV photography months and even years after the injury occurred. David et al. [30] reported a bitemark injury photographed with reflective UV photography that was visible more than 6 months after the injury occurred. This author (F.W.) photographed a bitemark injury almost 20 months postoccurrence [31]. In both of these cases, as they were reported, there was no visible evidence of the bitemark at the time the UV photographs were taken (Figs. 80–82).

There is no need to retake orientation photographs in UV photography since they have been taken in the color film or digital series. Only closeup exposures with the scale in place should be taken during the UV series, since the overall size and pattern of the injury are the most important characteristics desired in UV photographs.

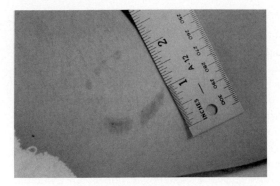

Figure 80 Bitemark on thigh taken the same day as the assault.

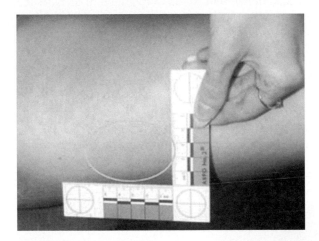

Figure 81 Photograph of same area 20 months after the assault. Also see color photograph insert section.

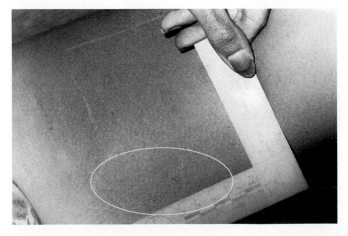

Figure 82 UV photo of same area 20 months after the assault. The UV photograph depicted does show the bitemark.

21.1. Ultraviolet Photography Armamentarium

UV photography requires the use of specialized photographic equipment and techniques. The equipment for film based UV photography includes a basic 35mm SLR camera body with a lens that transmits UV light, a UV light source, a UV specific band pass filter (Kodak wratten 18A glass UV filter) and film sensitive to UV light (Fig. 83).

Once the photographer acquires the essential equipment, predictable, reliable, and accurate UV photographs will be obtained through experimentation. It is imperative that the photographer should be familiar with the UV technique before a real bitemark case is attempted. Failure to collect all the available evidence in the bitemark case could otherwise result. The recommendation that UV photography be used does not imply that it should be employed in every bitemark case. However, it is the responsibility of the investigator to attempt to collect all available evidence when possible, and UV photography does represent one additional avenue of evidence collection.

An ideal UV photography setup has been offered from Nikon Corporation. It includes the Nikon SB 140 full-spectrum flash unit and the Nikon Nikkor UV105 lens. The UV 105 lens allows 75% transmission of UV and IR light. Its construction utilizes compound quartz glass unfiltered components that exploits visible light focus to coincide with the UV focus [2,32]. This feature eliminates the need for shifting the focal length from its point for full-spectrum light to UV; however, a focal shift is still required for IR photographic correction.

21.2. Camera

For UV photography, the use of a camera mounted on a stable tripod is required. The camera must be set to manual mode, allowing the photographer to control both the aperture and exposure

Figure 83   Kodak Wratten 18A glass filter in Nikon UR-2 filter holder.

time. The camera's built-in metering feature will not detect any light once the Kodak Wratten 18A UV filter is placed in front of the lens because the filter blocks all visible light. Because the surface details are being captured in UV photographs, the aperture is to a minimal depth of field. Usually, the aperture is set from f-5.6 to f-8 with exposure times ranging from 1/250th sec up to 1 sec. This is referred to as "bracketing." By varying the exposure times, properly exposed as well as under- and/or overexposed images will be taken. Bracketing can be accomplished using one f-stop on either side of f-5.6 with several exposure times in each f-stop for each bitemark. This technique helps ensure that the photographer has captured a range of photographic evidence that includes the best UV image available.

21.3 Flash

Although there is abundant UV light in bright sunlight, it lacks the concentrated focal intensity required for bitemark photography. Therefore, a UV emitting flash unit or other strong UV light source must be utilized. The Nikon SB 140 flash was specifically designed for UV photography. Other flashes may also emit sufficient UV light to be used in UV photography but will require experimentation by the photographer. Ideally, the flash unit should have both camera-mounted capability and remote detachability to highlight any three-dimensional properties the bitemark may exhibit whenever they exist.

21.4 Lenses

To facilitate UV photography, the lens must be capable of transmitting UV light. The website http://www.naturfotograf.com/lens_surv.html has an extensive list of commercially available lenses that can be used in nonvisible light photography. While many of the lenses listed are purported to have fluorite coatings that prevent UV and IR light transmission, many do, in fact, pass nonvisible light. It is readily accepted that the Nikon Nikkor UV105 lens is one of the best pure commercial lenses for UV, visible, ALI, and IR photography in an all-in-one package. It is expensive when it can be found. However, there are other lenses that can do the job as well.

It is important to remember that UV photographs require a macro setting on the lens. The main focus of interest in the UV photographs lies in the surface details associated with the bitemark, and these details are best captured with the lens in the macro setting.

21.5 Film

The film must be a panchromatic film with emulsions that are sensitive to UV light. Most commercially available black-and-white films have sensitivity to light well into the UV range. By far, the most popular black-and-white films used in UV photography are Kodak TMAX and Kodak Plus X. Both films record excellent UV images when the proper techniques and equipment are used (Figs. 84).

22. APPLICATION OF PHOTOGRAPHIC TECHNIQUES OTHER THAN FOR BITEMARKS

There are other areas of forensic investigation where the techniques described in this chapter can be applied. Documentation of tattoos, scratches, or toolmarks on decomposed tissue is an

	Color Prints	Color Slides	B&W	IR	UV	ALI
Film Recommendation	Kodak Gold or Select; Fuji Superia	FujiChrome; Kodak Kodachrome Lite	Kodak TMAX or Kodak TMAX CN	Kodak High Speed Infrared	Kodak TMAX or Plus X 125	Kodak Gold or Select; Fuji Superia
Film Processing	C-41	E6	TMAX: D-76 or TMAX; TMAX CN C-41	D-76	TMAX or D-76	C-41
Filters	-none-	-none-	-none-	Kodak gel 87	Kodak Wratten 18A	Kodak class of gel 15
Light Wavelength	400-700 nm	400-700 nm	400-700 nm	700-960nm	200-390nm	450nm
f-stop setting	Auto per camera manufacturer	Auto per camera manufacturer	Auto per camera manufacturer	$f\,11$-$f\,22$	f-4.5 – $f\,8$	f-4.5 – $f\,8$
Shutter speed	Auto	Auto	Auto	Bracket1/125th to 2 seconds	Bracket 1/125th to 2 seconds	Bracket 1/2 to 2 seconds
Film ASA/ISO	100-400	100-400	100-400	24-64	100-400	100-1600

Figure 84 Summary of components and protocol for bitemark photography.

applicable venue for IR. Similarly, UV and IR techniques can be applied to tattoos (Figs. 85, 86) scratches, gunshot injuries (Figs. 87–89), stab wounds (Figs. 90–92), ligature restraints (Figs. 93–96), hanging/suspension injuries, and many other types of patterned injuries. The ALI technique is applicable for examination of bruises associated with ongoing abuse or assaults, or in instances where a history of multiple ageing injuries needs to be documented.

23. CASE PRESENTATION 1

The victim was severely beaten and raped over 11 hours, and more than 30 bitemarks were sustained. The injuries were photographed over 28 days beginning with color, black-and-white, IR, and UV photographs on the first day. By the eighth day only color, BW, and UV were

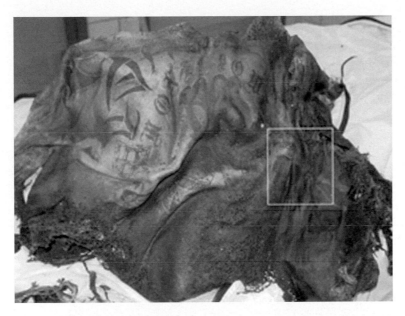

Figure 85 Skin recovered from the back of a partially skeletonized homicide victim.

Figure 86 IR photograph showing details present on recovered skin not viewable under visible light.

Figure 87 Homicide victim with a bullet hole in the neck (encircled).

Figure 88 UV photograph of the same bullet hole in the neck (encircled).

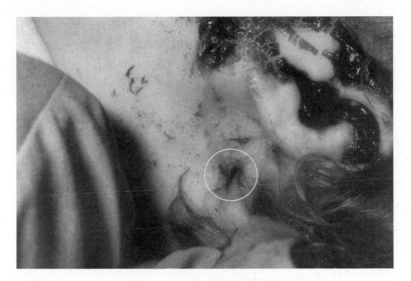

Figure 89 IR photograph focusing below the skin surface. The IR technique makes the blood on the surface of the skin seem to "disappear."

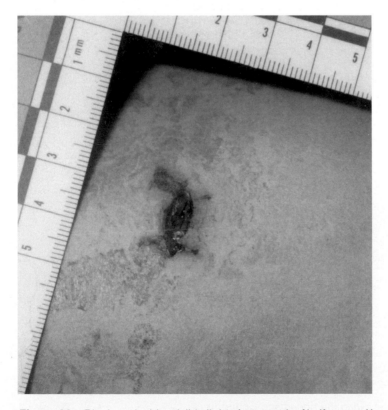

Figure 90 Black-and-white visible light photograph of knife wound in abdomen of homicide victim.

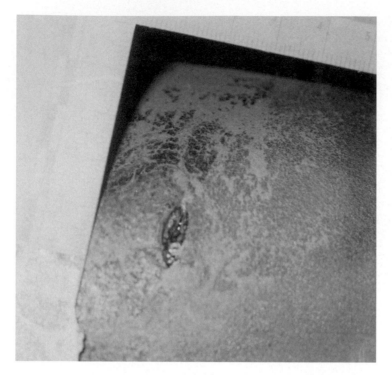

Figure 91   UV photograph of the same wound as in Figure 90.

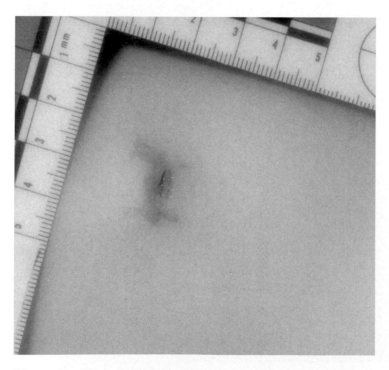

Figure 92   IR photograph showing the underlying wound track.

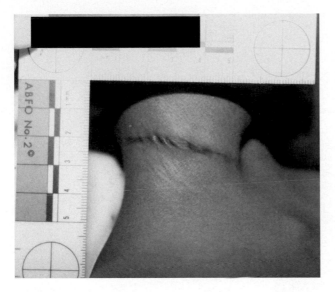

Figure 93   Ligature wound on neck.

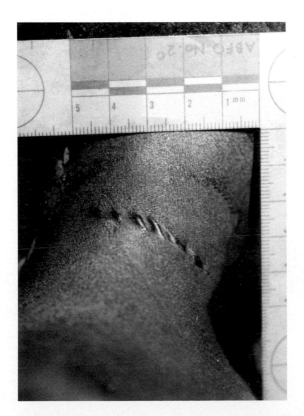

Figure 94   UV photograph showing a twining pattern (rope).

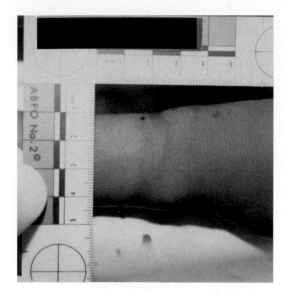

Figure 95   Photograph of ligature pattern on the victim's wrist.

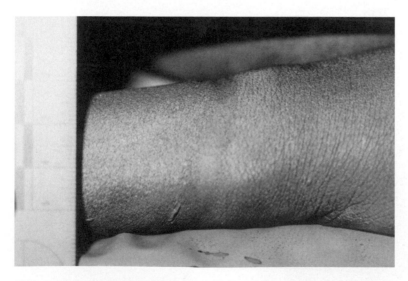

Figure 96   UV photograph of Figure 95.

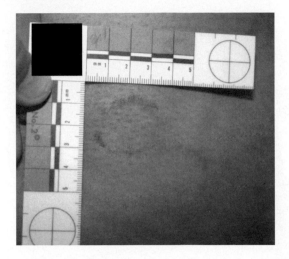

Figure 97 Photograph on the abdomen on the day of the incident. Also see color photograph insert section.

made. At day 28, no injuries were visible, but several UV photos were made. A few of the bites are depicted over time under different conditions. All bites were inflicted during the same incident by the same biter (Figs. 97–115).

The following case depicts a child abuse victim who died from dehydration while bound and restrained in a closed automobile for > 7 hours on 3 consecutive days. The patterned injuries on the child contradicted the suspect's statement of occurrence. Advanced photographic techniques documented the injuries to the neck and wrists.

24. CASE PRESENTATION 2

The victim was assaulted and bitten twice during a break-and-enter in her home. She escaped and contacted authorities allowing the injuries to be photographed three times over 29 days.

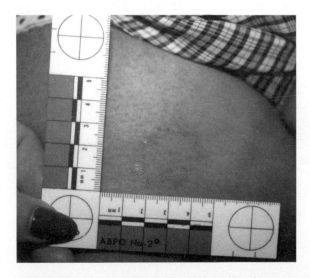

Figure 98 Photograph on the eighth day. Also see color photograph insert section.

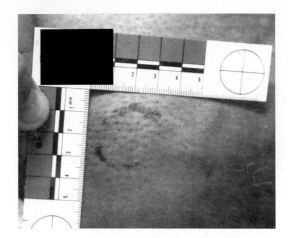

Figure 99 Black-and-white photo on the day of the incident.

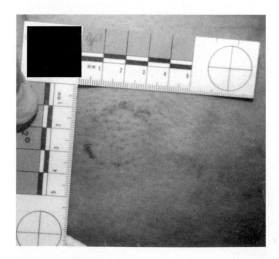

Figure 100 Black-and-white photo on the eighth day.

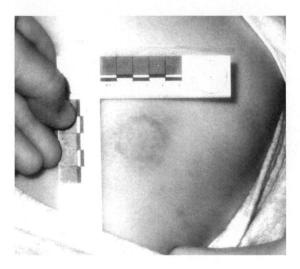

Figure 101   IR photograph on the day of the incident.

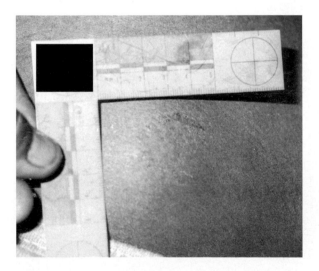

Figure 102   UV photograph on the day of the incident.

Figure 103   UV photograph day on the eighth day.

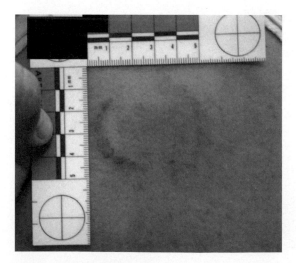

Figure 104   Photograph of the bitemark on the back on the day of incident. Also see color photograph insert section.

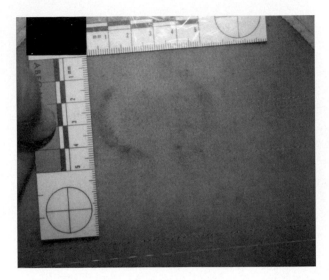

Figure 105 Photograph on the eighth day. Also see color photograph insert section.

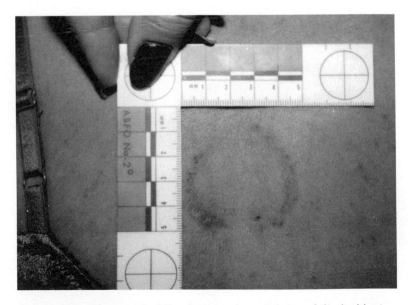

Figure 106 Black-and-white photograph on the day of the incident.

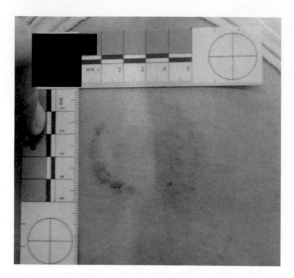

Figure 107 Black-and-white photograph the eighth day.

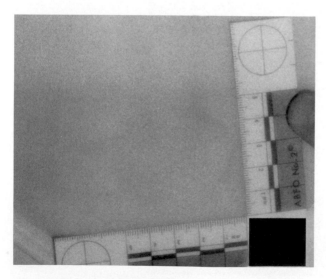

Figure 108 IR photograph the day of the incident.

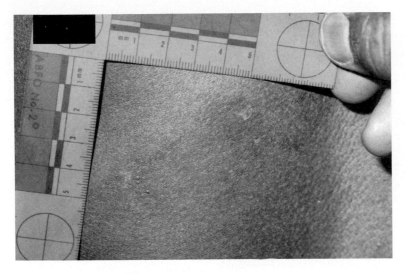

Figure 109 UV photograph day of the incident.

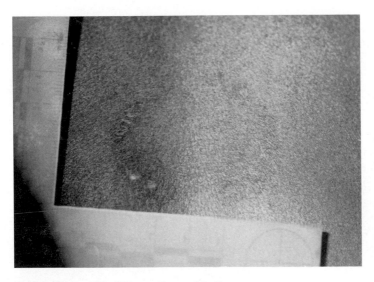

Figure 110 UV photograph on day 8.

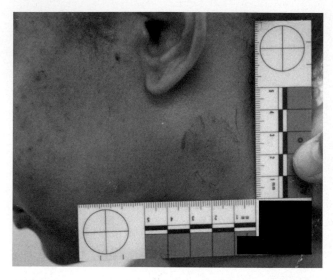

Figure 111   Photograph on the neck on the day of the incident. Also see color photograph insert section.

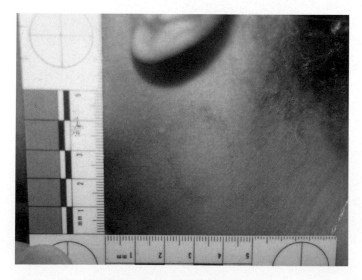

Figure 112   Photograph on the eighth day. Also see color photograph insert section.

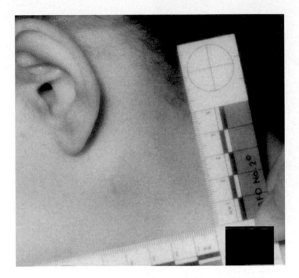

Figure 113   IR photograph the day of the incident.

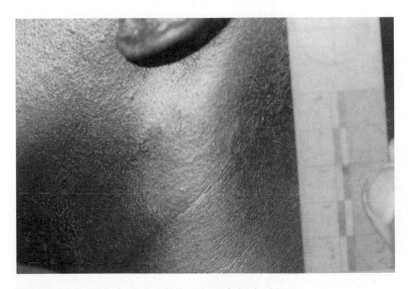

Figure 114   UV photograph the day of the incident.

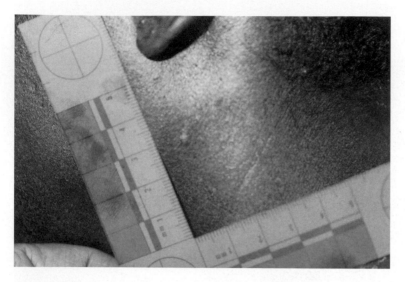

Figure 115   UV photograph on the eighth day.

The day of the incident, color, BW, UV, and IR images were taken. On the eighth day, color, BW, and UV images were captured. The same perpetrator made all bitemarks (Figs. 116–128). Figure 10 depicts a color photograph of the bitemark on the shoulder taken the day of the incident; Figure 11, an IR photograph on the same day.

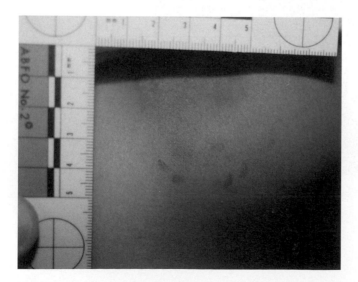

Figure 116   Photograph of bitemark on the shoulder taken the day of the incident.

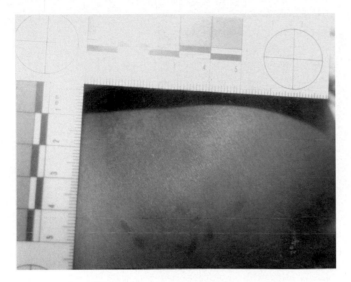

Figure 117 BW photograph taken the day of the incident. Note a second bite above and to the right of the darker bite.

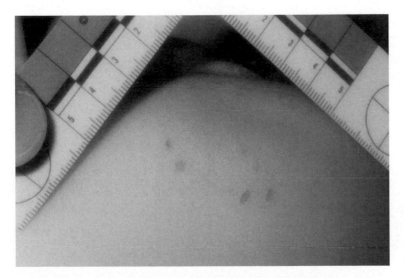

Figure 118 IR photograph taken on the day of the incident.

Figure 119 IR photograph on the eighth day. Image has no real pattern or any evidentiary value.

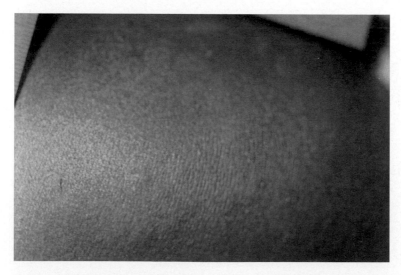

Figure 120 UV photograph taken the day of the incident.

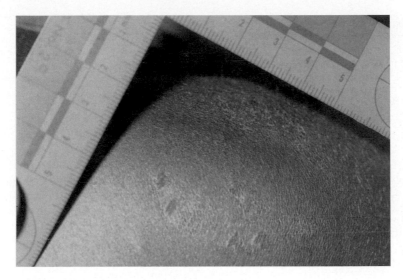

Figure 121 UV photograph taken on day 8.

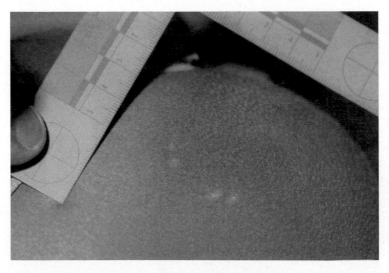

Figure 122 UV photograph taken on day 29 No injury is visible with the naked eye under normal lighting conditions

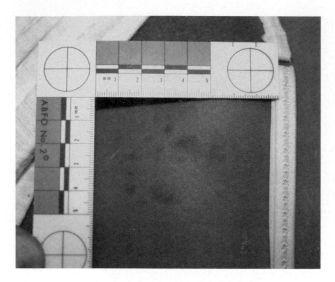

Figure 123 Photograph of a bitemark on the back taken on the day of the incident. Also see color photograph insert section.

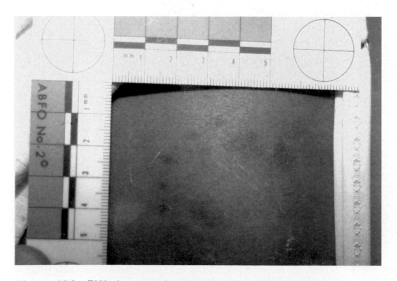

Figure 124 BW photograph taken the day of the incident.

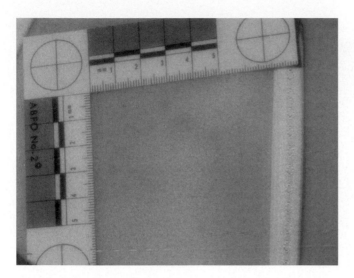

Figure 125   IR photograph taken the day of the incident.

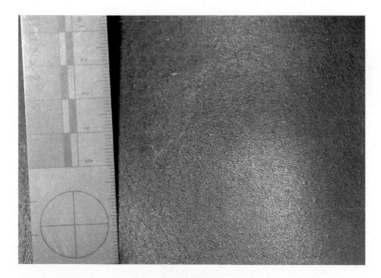

Figure 126   UV photograph taken the day of the incident.

Figure 127 UV photograph on the eighth day.

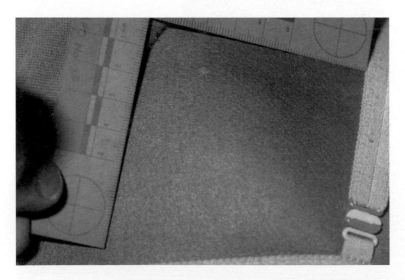

Figure 128 UV photograph on day 29. No injury was visible to the naked eye.

ACKNOWLEDGMENTS

The authors wish to thank Dr. David Senn, University of Texas, San Antonio; Chris Parsons, CEO of Linear Systems Inc.; and Dr. Anne McNamee, Bureau of Legal Dentistry, Vancouver, British Columbia, Canada, for their assistance in the research and contributions associated with this manuscript.

REFERENCES

1. Wright FD. Photography in bite mark and patterned injury documentation. Part I. J Forens Sci 1998; 43(4):877–879.
2. Wright FD, Golden G. Forensic Dentistry. InStimson P, Mertz C, Eds. Boca Raton. FL: CRC Press, 1997:102–106, 123, 132.
3. Bachem A&, Reed CI. The Penetration of Light Through Human Skin. Publication of The University of Illinois, College of Medicine, Chicago:7/7/1930.
4. Kodak Infrared Films, Kodak Publication No. N-17, p. 4.
5. Ultraviolet & Fluorescence Photography. Kodak Publication No. M-27.
6. Krauss T. Photographic techniques of concern in metric bite mark analysis. J Forens Sci 636(2): 1984.
7. Johansen R&, Bowers CM. Digital Analysis of Bite Mark Evidence Using Adobe Photoshop, Forensic Imaging Services. 2000:17–44.
8. McNamee A&, Sweet D. Adherence of forensic odontologists to the ABFO guidelines for victim evidence collection. J Forens Sci 2003; 48(2):382.
9. Merriam Webster's online dictionary: www.merriamwebster.com.
10. Powell PM. CCD Imaging: When Every Photon Counts, Photonics Spectra.. Pittsfield, MA:: Laurin Publishing Co. Inc., 2003:p.54.
11. Canon U.S.A. Inc., EOS 10D Digital Camera Brochure, 2003, p. 12.
12. Noble SA. The Technology Inside the New Kodak DCS 620x Digital Camera, Kodak Publication, 2000, http://www.dpreview.com/news/0005/kodak_dcs620x_tech_paper.pdf.
13. Canon U.S.A. Inc., D60 Digital Camera Brochure, 2003.
14. Kodak DCS PRO 14N 35 mm Digital Camera Brochure, PPI-940 CAT 838-9744.
15. LucisPro Software, Image Content Technology LLC , PMB #203, 430 Franklin Village Drive, Franklin, MA 02038-4007, www.lucispro.com, www.lucisart.com.
16. Stokes GG. On the Change of Refrangibility of Light. Phil Trans R Soc Lond 1853:385–396.
17. Melles Griot, Laser and Electro-Optics Group, 2051 Palomar Airport Rd., 200, Carlsbad, CA 92009, E-mail: sales@carlsbad.mellesgriot.com.
18. Guilbault G. Practical Fluorescence. New York: Marcel Dekker, 1973.
19. Devore D. Ultraviolet Absorption and Fluorescence Phenomena Associated with Wound Healing, PhD Thesis, University of London, Department of Oral Pathology, Oct. 1974.
20. Dawson JB. A theoretical and experimental study of light absorption and scattering by in vivo skin. Physiol Med Biol 1980; 25(4).
21. Golden G. Use of alternate light source illumination in bite mark photography. J Forens Sci 1994; 39(3).
22. Regan JD, Parrish JA. The science of photomedicine. In:. Optical Properties of Human Skin. New York: Plenum Press, 1982.
23. Wright FD. The trials and tribulations of bite mark analysis: seeing what is really there. AAFS Annual Meeting Seattle, 2001, Presentation F23..
24. Henderson JW. Infrared photography revisited. J Audiovisual Media Med 1993; 16:161.
25. Nieuwenhuis G. Lens focus shift required for reflected ultraviolet and infrared photography. J Bio Photo 1991; 59(1):17–20.
26. Medical Infrared Photography, Kodak Publication no. N-1, pg 26.
27. Krauss TC, Warlen SC. The forensic science use of reflective ultraviolet photography. J Forens Sci 1985; 30(1):264–265.

28. Cutignola L, Bullough P. Photographic reproduction of anatomic specimens using ultraviolet light. Am J Surg Pathol 1991; 15(11):1096.
29. Wright FD. Photography in bitemark and patterned injury documentation. Part 2: A case study. J Forens Sci 1998; 43(4):881–887.
30. David TG, Sobel MN. Recapturing a five month old bitemark by means of reflective ultraviolet photography. J Forens Sci 1994; 36(6):1560–1567.
31. Unpublished case. State of Ohio v Ramadugu, case 99CR053480, Lorain County, Ohio.
32. Krauss T. Forensic evidence documentation using reflective ultraviolet photography. Photo Electronic Imaging Feb 1993:p 22.

8
Digital Imagery
NONINVASIVE ANALYSES

Robert B. J. Dorion
Laboratoire de sciences judiciaires et de médecine légale,
Ministry of Public Security for the Province of Quebec,
Montreal, Quebec, Canada

1. INTRODUCTION

A variety of image capture devices have been used in recording autopsy proceedings. Bitemark photography is usually a time-constrained activity with only one opportunity to correctly complete the task. Photographs must accurately represent the details and colors of the bitemark in standard and closeup images with accurate spatial relationships. The ABFO No. 2 reference scale serves, in part, in accomplishing this task. Photographs might also record information that might initially have been overlooked or thought to be unimportant at the time of capture.

The primary image capture device is still the silver-based 35-mm (SLR) camera capable of manual override, interchangeable lenses, off-camera flash, and tripod mount. Technical developments in the field of video recording have gone from analog VHS to 8-mm formats, to Super VHS and High video 8. Beta SP and MII formats are professional-broadcast quality, the best analog formats available, and the least used at autopsy. Digital video quality varies; the high end is better than analog systems. Video cameras should have the ability to disable on-camera audio when used during autopsies. One of the advantages of certain digital video cameras is the ability to take infrared images/photographs without having to add special lenses.

Digital cameras have recently flooded the marketplace and are currently used in a supplementary capacity, as are video cameras, to the standard 35-mm camera. Digital still imaging can be used as the primary image capture device when the performance of the equipment can be shown to meet anticipated needs. Technology is so rapidly changing as to render current writings obsolete by the time they are published. There is, however, little question that high-quality digital images is comparable to what is produced in standard photography. The quality of digital photography might even surpass standard photography in the not-too-distant future.

Rather than discussing product availability, it would be more practical to discuss the technology as a whole, its application to bitemark evidence, and its admissibility in court.

2. SCIENTIFIC WORKING GROUP ON IMAGE TECHNOLOGIES

The Scientific Working Group on Image Technologies (SWGIT) was created in 1997 by the Federal Bureau of Investigation (FBI) in response to questions on digital imagery. The group is made up of more than 40 imaging professionals drawn from federal, state, and municipal law enforcement organizations, as well as academic institutions. The work products are not intended to represent the formal policy of any one agency, but rather it a consensus opinion developed by individual experts from a broad sampling of agencies and experiences. SWGIT's mission is "to facilitate the integration of imaging technologies and systems within the Criminal Justice System (CJS) by providing definitions and recommendations for the capture, storage, processing, analysis, transmission, and output of images. These imaging technologies include, but are not restricted to those which utilize film, video, and digital cameras and output devices" [1].

2.1. Areas of Expertise

SWGIT has identified three areas of digital expertise within the field of Digital Evidence:

1. Computer forensic examinations requiring competency in such areas as computer systems architecture, operating systems, programming, and storage devices. These experts recover digital information from hard disks, for example.

2. Image and video examinations requiring competency in such areas as photography, optics, image capture, and image processing. Forensic dentists using digital imagery fall into this category of expertise. Within the subdisciplines of image and video examinations are included Fixed Closed Circuit Television (CCTV) security systems, both analog and digital. These devices are found primarily in commercial institutions such as banks and convenience stores, and in private home security systems. Issues, recommendations, and guidelines to optimize image quality, lighting, etc., and to facilitate the identification of unknown individuals or objects, are specifically addressed.

3. This category involves experts in the field of audio analysis that are involved in authenticating audiotapes of Osama bin Laden and Saddam Hussein, for example.

Qualified individuals in one of the subdisciplines may not be qualified to conduct examinations in another. Moreover, a forensic photographer, for example, need not be accredited within the discipline of digital evidence unless he/she performs forensic image or video analysis. It is SWGIT's belief that accreditation issues related to imaging functions performed by a board certified person within a specific discipline, such as a Diplomate of the American Board of Forensic Odontology, should be addressed within that discipline. For example, an image enhancement used to improve the visibility of a bitemark is an intrinsic component of bitemark analysis, regardless of whether the enhancement is performed on a computer or in the darkroom. The same would apply when using digital imagery for comparison of facial or dental superimposition/ approximation. Thus, the dental expert who uses enhancement technology should be in a position to explain what he/she has done and must be able to produce the same results by repeating the same steps initially undertaken.

2.2. Type of Work

Digital evidence is information of probative value stored or transmitted in binary form (digital format). When digital imaging is practiced in disciplines such as odontology, pathology, DNA, question documents, latent fingerprints, firearms, etc., it does not fall under the discipline of digital evidence. Digital evidence applies imaging science and technology of systems and procedures to duplicate, recover, handle/preserve, and examine digital evidence. Persons utilizing imaging science should have a working knowledge of hardware and software used in digital evidence examination/comparison. There are three basic types of work performed in digital imagery: analysis, examination, and technical preparation.

2.3. Standard Operating Procedures

The successful introduction of forensic imagery as evidence in a court of law is dependent upon the following four legal tests: Reliability, Reproducibility, Security, Discovery [2]. Organizations which produce images for use in the criminal justice system should therefore have documented procedures that include not only a description of how they produce their images, but also how they document that process.

They should establish specific step-by-step procedures for image processing according to agency requirements using SWGIT guidelines. These procedures should address the following topics:

1. Capture
2. Processing
3. Storage/archiving
4. Image management
5. Security, and
6. Output

The elements of standard operating procedures (SOP) also include: the purpose, the equipment/materials/standards/controls, procedures, calibration, calculation, limitations, safety, and references for the procedures. Approved SWGIT documents are published in electronic format at the FBI's online journal, Forensic Science Communications (FSC). It can also be accessed at www.fbi.gov using the search criteria SWGIT.

2.4. Chain of Custody

For digital images, the chain of custody should document the identity of the individuals who had custody and control of each primary digital image file from the point of capture to the creation of the archived image. Once the file has been archived, the chain of custody should document the identity of the individuals who had custody and control of the archive images.

2.5. Recommendations and Guidelines

The objective of SWGIT's guidelines and recommendations is to ensure the successful introduction of forensic imagery in a court of law. This can be accomplished provided:

1. The original image is downloaded, preserved untouched in an "original image file," and archived.
2. The original image is then duplicated, not copied, into a "working file."
3. The processing steps that the duplicate image undergoes are logged when they include techniques other than those used in a traditional photographic darkroom developing procedures.
4. The end result is presented as an enhanced image, which can be reproduced by applying the logged steps to the original image.
5. Other committee recommendations are followed such as archiving the enhanced image.

Thus, opposing counsel/expert would receive the original image, the processed/enhanced image, and the logged entries to arrive at the final product. The recommendations and guidelines for the use of digital image processing [2] is an invaluable document although not dealing specifically with bitemark evidence. It includes:

1. Standards and guidelines
2. Recommendations and guidelines for the use of digital image
3. Processing in the criminal justice system

The purpose, background, introduction, definitions, image enhancement, image restoration, image compression, and quantitative image analysis are included in the subject matter. While it is not within the scope of this chapter to introduce the ever-changing standards and guidelines of digital imagery, it is recommended that the reader be aware of the current committee recommendations.

2.6. End Use of Images

The degree to which procedures are documented depends on the intended end use of the image. The end use can be classified as:

1. Images utilized to demonstrate merrily what the photographers saw or witnessed. These can include, but are not limited to, the following: crime scene and surveillance images, autopsy photographs, documentation of items for evidence in a laboratory, arrest photographs, search warrant, and warrant execution images.

2. Images utilized for scientific analysis by subject matter experts. These can include, but are not limited to, images that depict the following: latent prints, questioned documents, impression evidence, pattern evidence, and surveillance images.

2.7. Image Enhancement Category 1

There are related legal considerations that can be categorized into the following: image enhancement, image restoration, image compression, and image analysis. Image enhancement is any process intended to improve the visual appearance of an image. The enhancement techniques that have direct counterpart in traditional darkroom processing. These enhancement techniques are referred to as Type 1 or Category 1 enhancements that include the following procedures:

Brightness adjustments
Color balancing
Contrast adjustments
Cropping
Dodging and burning
Spotting
Color processing
Linear filtering techniques include: sharpening, deblurring, edge enhancement, and deconvolution
Nonlinear contrast adjustments include: gamma correction, grayscale transformation, curves, and lookup tables
Pattern noise reduction filters
Random noise reduction techniques including: low pass filters, blurring filters, median filters, and despeckling

The techniques might be applied to the entire image or to a localized area within an image. The technique of ''dodge and burn,'' for example, has been traditionally utilized in photographic darkrooms on the selective overexposure (burning) or underexposure (dodging) that would otherwise be too bright (see Fig. 17 in Chapter 16) or too dark on the final print. Other techniques might also include video image deinterlacing, video format conversion, video standard conversion, and video demultiplexing.

Does the result of processing increase ones ability to perceive features that would otherwise not be seeable? Is the process repeatable? If the conclusion/analysis depends on specific basic image adjustments, then those specific adjustments should be documented. However, if the conclusions/analysis are unaffected by basic image adjustments, their application can be documented by way of a general procedure.

2.8. Image Enhancement Category 2

Category 2 image enhancements utilize advanced techniques such as frame averaging, FFT, Deblur, image stabilization, noise reduction, image restoration, color channel selection and subtraction, prospective control/geometric correction, and unsharp mask.

The use of advanced techniques should be documented in every case. In some cases, the application of basic image adjustments prior to the use of advanced techniques can impact the result of the application of the advanced technique. In such cases, the use of basic adjustments should also be documented along with the advanced techniques.

2.9. Reproducibility and Repeatability

What does the term "reproducibility" mean in digital enhancement? Quality Dictionary by Tracy Omdahl (1997) defines reproducibility as a quantitative measure of closeness of agreement between individual measurements of the same physical quantity, property, or condition, when the individual measurements are made under defined conditions and identical test material, but with different operators. It is a form of accuracy. Does this mean a pixel-for-pixel or mouse-click-by-mouse-click reproduction? No, it means that the images are visually indistinguishable. In other words, by following the logged step-by-step procedure from original digital image to final enhanced image, anyone else following the same steps can arrive at the same end product. There might be minuscule pixel differences, but the end product is visually indistinguishable in both cases.

"Repeatability," on the other hand, is defined as the ability to produce the same result when trying again. It is closeness of agreement between successive results from the same method using identical test material and under the same conditions. It is a form of precision. Lastly, "quality" incorporates the PARCC elements (precision, accuracy, reproducible, comparable, complete).

What does "logged" mean? When working in traditional darkroom photography, it is common to use a trial-and-error method to get the "right" print. Bad prints are typically discarded. Thus, in conducting image enhancements digitally, to discard intermediate steps that do not produce the desired improvement/effect would not be recorded.

2.10. The Courts

Processed/enhanced images are not produced to mislead the trier of fact but rather to provide information to the expert that can then be conveyed and explained to the judge/jury. Category 1 enhancement of digital images is comparable to standard darkroom photographic developing/printing techniques. For example, if a photographic negative is overexposed, the print will be "burnt" to obtain a "normal" photograph (less brightness, more contrast). The process is never "logged" or "archived" and is rarely if ever mentioned in court. Should similar modifications in digital image be treated differently?

Dr. William Oliver, a member of SWGIT, opines that the requirements for presentation of digital images in a court are quite different from those required for a scientific publication. "The biggest determinant is whether or not the expert opinion is based on the processed image or whether the processed image is used merrily to illustrate an opinion" (W. Oliver, personal communication, 2003). In the former case, there are rigorous rules for new scientific techniques that are subject to admissibility hearings under Frye v. United States, 293 F. 1013 (1923, D.C. Circuit Court) or the more restrictive federal test (utilized in a number of state jurisdictions) in *Daubert v. Merrell Dow Pharmaceuticals Inc.*, 113 S. Ct. 2786 (1993, United States Supreme Court).

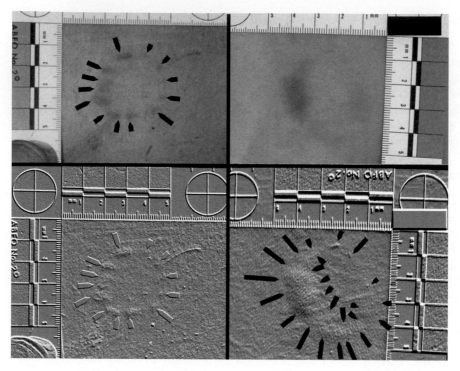

Figure 1 Bitemark on stomach (UL) and back (UR) and corresponding embossed photos (LR, LL).

3. DIGITAL SOFTWARE PROGRAMS

Whatever the software used, comparably trained personnel should achieve similar results in the processing and the analysis of digital images. (Legal note: manufactures of software used for image processing may be required to make software source code available to litigants, subject to an appropriate protective order from a judge designed to protect the manufacturer's proprietary interests.)

It is important to know the category of image enhancement for "logging" purposes. Nonlinear contrast adjustments include grayscale transformation (Figs. 1 and 2), and Lookup Tables (Fig. 2) fall into Category 1 enhancements. Embossing (Fig. 1), on the other hand, is a Category 2 enhancement. Certain parts of the picture may appear raised or lowered.

4. POWERPOINT PRESENTATION VERSUS PRINT

The reader is reminded that doing a PowerPoint presentation with digital images is not the same as analysis of digital images in an expertise. The ideal display for a PowerPoint presentation is 800×600 pixels at 72 dpi, 640×480 pixels would also be acceptable (T. Marcoux, personal communication, 2003). If the quality of the image is >72 dpi, it would simply take longer to load the PowerPoint presentation. The onscreen visual presentation would not be markedly different at 72 dpi "JPG" (compressed) format than at 600 dpi "TIF" (uncompressed) printed image. In addition, if the initial image was 893-kB "JPG" for example, Photoshop could further reduce the weight of the image by a manual compression and elimination of unnecessary information

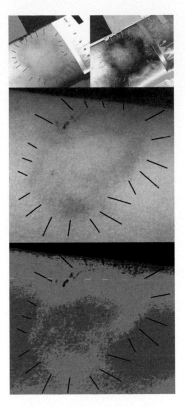

Figure 2 Healing bitemark: "grayscaled" and "Lookup Tables" application in SigmaScan.

tagged with the file itself without compromising on projection quality under the file menu "Save for Web." Once the working image is reduced to an 800 × 600 pixel at 72 dpi format, and a "sharpen" or "unsharp mask" filter is applied to further clear the image, the file size of this image can be reduced to a maximum while retaining 100% of its viewing quality with the use of the "Save for Web" function.

The above situation is entirely different from producing a high-quality print. For example, the maximum allowable size of image produced for this publication was 11.5 × 16 cm. The largest images produced were normally 10 × 14 cm at 600 dpi "TIF" format. A grayscale image (black and white) of that size, quality, and format contains 7.46 MB, while an RBG image (color) 22.4 MB. The latter, at 1200 dpi, contains 89.4 MB, an enormous file. The end use of the image is therefore important.

5. ABFO NO. 2 SCALE AND OTHER AIDS

The ABFO No. 2 scale is the standard ruler used in bitemark photography [3]. Many other disciplines have adopted this reference scale. The scale should be placed adjacent and parallel to the bitemark (Fig. 3).

When the bitemark is on a curved surface it is literally impossible to place the scale parallel to the entire bitemark. For this reason, multiple photographs are needed from different viewpoints. Photographic distortion can then be corrected by adjusting the photograph for the presence of three circles on the ABFO No. 2 scale rather than ellipses [4–6]. It is important to

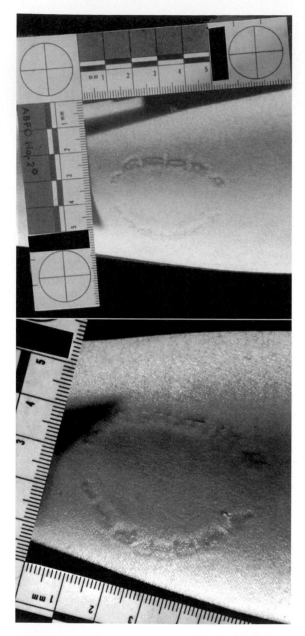

Figure 3 "Ideal three-dimensional" bitemark on arm photographed from different angles.

realize that the process leads to photographic correction of the scale, not the bitemark. If the scale is not placed perfectly parallel to the bitemark, correcting for photographic distortion of the reference scale will not provide the desired effect.

Krauss measured the accuracy of so-called "standard" rulers found in forensic laboratories and Medical Examiner facilities, and distributed as publicity handouts at forensic conferences. They were notoriously inaccurate. The ABFO No. 2 scale is standardized and accurate and can be placed in sodium hydrochloride solution (Dakins), pure Javex or activated beta-gluteraldehyde for disinfection/sterilization. If any other scale/ruler is used, it should be labeled for identification purposes, preserved as an exhibit, verified for accuracy, and made available for future reference which includes verification by the opposing attorney, expert, and the court.

Figure 4 depicts several nonstandard scales. The upper left photograph shows a pliable transparent acrylic scale with concentric circles used by dermatologists to measure the diameter of lesions. The bottom left photograph demonstrates a clear pliable acetate transparency incorporating 1-mm squares [7]. A red cross centers the transparency, dividing it in quadrants. The use of this scale can help in the orientation of the bitemark, distinguishing upper from lower quadrants, and the centrals within the arches. The two photographs on the right illustrate rulers that adhere to skin.

Figure 5 illustrates the use of two ABFO No. 2 scales on a highly curved surface, and a caliper measuring the linear distance between points on a curved surface (bottom photo). The latter measurement usually equates to the perpetrator's incisal opening diameter, that is the distance between the upper and the lower central incisors in maximum opening. There are exceptions to the tenet that the linear distance represents the opening diameter, however. Of note, if the bitten tissue can be easily compressed, say a large breast or a child's leg, a normal human adult Caucasoid male has an opening diameter in the 35–45 mm. range. The example in Figure 5 bottom photograph exceeds that figure because the tissue has been compressed. There were multiple human adult bitemarks on the leg (Fig. 12 in Chapter 13).

Figure 6 depicts two photographs and the use of a caliper for measuring distances between points of the avulsed tissue. The leg tissue avulsion is the result of a directed pit bull attack by the dog's owner. Exsanguination was a contributory cause in the mode of death.

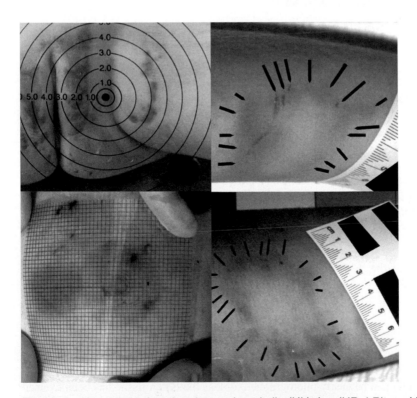

Figure 4 Nonstandard scales: leg and genitalia (UL), leg (UR, LR), and breast (LL)

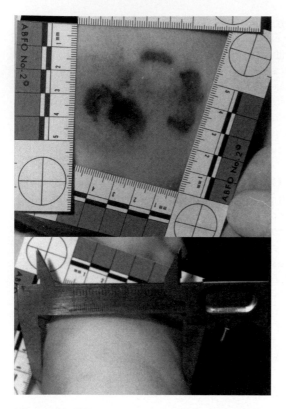

Figure 5 Measuring aids: two No. 2 ABFO scales on the breast, and caliper on the leg.

Figure 7 displays a scale that adheres to skin. It facilitates the measure of the circumferential distance between the upper and the lower dental arches represented in the bitemark. The measurement is basically meaningless since the important measurement is the linear distance.

Fig. 8 illustrates a clear acetate scale with 1 mm squares and identified by alpha columns and numeric rows.

The ABFO No. 2 scale is the gold standard for use in bitemark photography, but it does have some disadvantages according to Kaminski. While it does allow for life-size reproduction and limited correction of distortion (due to improper alignment of camera to evidence), it is unable to represent a three-dimensional object in the two dimensions of a photograph.

The Kaminski Cross (J. Kaminski, personal communication, 2003) (Fig. 9) advantages include:

1. No alteration of the ABFO No.2 scale.
2. Its dimensions are to manufacturer's specifications, and the modulus of elasticity/deformation of the material is known.
3. Free-standing.
4. Easily retained as evidence.
5. "Z-axis" allows multiple spatial relationships to be evaluated.

The disadvantages include its acceptability in bitemark photography since the bitemark is rarely in an area of the body that can be easily photographed, unless the bitten tissue has been excised or is amputated. Lastly, the cost and bulkiness are additional deterrents.

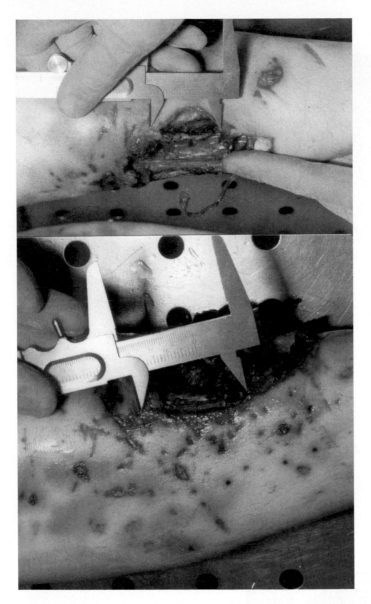

Figure 6 Caliper for measuring linear component of avulsed tissue on a leg.

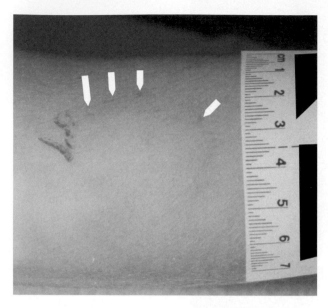

Figure 7 Adhesive scale circumscribing a child's leg.

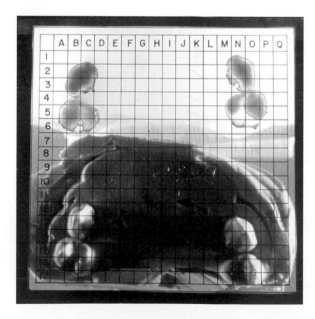

Figure 8 One-millimeter square scale.

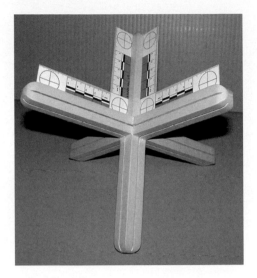

Figure 9 Kaminski cross with ABFO No. 2 scales.

REFERENCES

1. Bylaws for the Scientific Working group on Imaging Technologies (SWGIT), Article I, Section 2.
2. Recommendations and Guidelines for the Use of Digital Image Processing in the Criminal Justice System. Forens Sci Communication Jan. 2003; 5(1).
3. Hyzer WG, Krauss TC. The bite mark standard reference scale—ABFO No. 2. J Forens Sci 1988; 33(2):498–506.
4. Bowers CM, Johansen RJ. Photographic evidence protocol: the use of digital imaging methods to rectify angular distortion and create life size reproductions of bite mark evidence. J Forens Sci 2002; 47(1):179–186.
5. Krauss TC. Photographic techniques of concern in metric bite mark analysis. J Forens Sci 1984; 29(2): 633–638.
6. Bernstein ML. Two bite mark cases with inadequate scale references. J Forens Sci 1985; 30:958–964.
7. Dorion RBJ. Experimental three-dimensional ruler for use in bite mark evidence, AAFS meeting, odontology section, San Diego, Feb 16–21, 1987.

9
Bitemarks as Biological Evidence
NONINVASIVE ANALYSES

David Sweet
University of British Columbia
Vancouver, Canada

1. INTRODUCTION

In an attempt to develop objective methods to analyze bitemarks, attention has been focused on the potential use of salivary evidence deposited during biting to identify the perpetrator. Historically, most forensic uses of saliva have relied primarily on the identification of blood group antigens from secretor individuals and, in some cases, on the analysis of isoenzymes and polymorphic proteins present in the saliva or saliva-stained objects found at the scene of a crime [1]. Other substances in saliva have also been used as the basis of identification tests, including thiocyanate ion, nitrite ion, and the alkaline phosphatase and amylase enzymes. Tests of the presence in saliva of amylase are by far the commonest conventional tests [2]. Amylase tests can be used not only to reveal the presence of saliva in forensic stains but also as presumptive tests to search for saliva-containing stains, especially on clothing [3,4].

Serologists estimate that $\sim 80\%$ of the human population secretes water-soluble antigens called agglutinins in their body fluids (saliva, semen, tears, and perspiration) that can be used to determine the ABH blood group classification of a person [4–7]. Also, finding salivary amylase on an injury site might confirm the injury is a bitemark when this is not readily apparent from the physical appearance of the wound [8–11].

It was previously assumed that a saliva stain from a nonsecretor (20–25% of the human population) could not be typed for blood group agglutinins. But studies have shown that it may be possible to identify the origin of a saliva stain using certain snail antibodies and monoclonal anti-A antibodies, even in a nonsecretor [12].

Methods to discriminate the origin of a saliva sample using conventional saliva markers are not highly sensitive, and the limited detectability of these markers due to the low concentrations of the antigens, isoenzymes, and proteins of interest is an inherent problem. Additionally, because of the wide acceptance of forensic DNA analysis, interest in saliva has shifted away from these conventional markers toward the value of saliva as a potential source of DNA evidence.

Using DNA analysis it is possible to establish the origin of a sample that is isolated from biological materials [13,14]. It has been demonstrated that saliva, blood, semen, hair roots, tissue, teeth, and bones are good sources of DNA for identity testing [15–20].

The importance of saliva, blood, and semen as sources of valuable evidence is increasing with respect to forensic odontology examinations. Today, it is possible to recognize the location of a bitemark and recover saliva deposited at the site. Significantly, because of the refinement of techniques using alternative light sources to locate body fluids, it is also possible to find stains of saliva deposited by sucking or kissing, even in the absence of marks from teeth.

2. SALIVA

The fluid normally present in the mouth is termed "whole saliva". It is a complex mixture derived from four different types of salivary glands. In addition to the paired parotid, submandibular, and sublingual glands, there are numerous minor mucous glands located in most areas of the oral mucosa except the anterior part of the palate and the gingivae [21].

Whole saliva also contains a variety of nonsalivary components such as gingival crevice fluid, epithelial cells and leukocytes in various stages of disintegration, bacteria, and, occasionally, dental plaque and food debris [21]. Whole saliva tends to be very viscous, heterogeneous, contaminated with bacteria and other extraneous materials, and to consist of variable contributions from different glands.

The secretions of the major salivary glands differ in composition. The relative contribution of each gland to the mixed saliva present in the mouth varies with conditions and total flow rate [22,23]. Salivary flow is stimulated mainly by unconditioned reflexes (not requiring higher nerve centers) via proprioceptors in the periodontal ligament and the muscles of mastication. Conditioned reflexes, which rely on previous experiences, account for a smaller component of stimulation [24]. Olfactory stimuli, oral pain and irritation, and pharyngeal and psychic factors have also been shown to affect salivary flow rate [25].

Saliva is a viscous fluid that can be drawn out into long elastic threads; this viscosity varies with the degree of stimulation of the salivary glands. For example, stimulation under test conditions by chewing wax that results in secretions mainly by the parotid gland produces a fluid with a lower viscosity than that of resting saliva [23].

2.1. Unstimulated Salivary Flow

Several large studies of the unstimulated salivary flow rate in human subjects have been undertaken in the past 40 years. Results from studies by Enfors in 1962, Shannon in 1967, Shannon and Frome in 1973, and Heintze et al. in 1983 concluded that the average unstimulated salivary flow rate is 0.3 mL/min, but the range is very large [26–29].

There are many factors that affect the unstimulated salivary flow rate. The most important factor is the relative hydration of the body. When the water content of the body is reduced by 8%, the salivary flow rate decreases to virtually zero. For a man of 70 kg, comprising about 50 kg of water, 8% dehydration means a loss of 4 L of water. In contrast, hyperhydration will increase the salivary flow rate [26].

Other factors affecting flow rate include body posture (standing or lying will increase or decrease flow rate respectively), ambient light conditions (darkness decreases flow rate), cigarette smoking, and olfactory stimulation (both increase flow rate).

The amount and composition of saliva change during a 24-hour period following a circadian rhythm [26]. Flow rate peaks during the afternoon and drops to its lowest rate during sleep. These changes do not appear to have important implications for the forensic uses of saliva since the minimum flow rate during waking hours does not fall below 0.3 mL/min. The lowest flow rate, $\sim$ 0.1 mL/min, occurs during the night (Fig. 1).

Studies by Dawes and Jenkins concluded the flow rate of parotid saliva also varies according to a seasonal circadian rhythm, with a peak value in winter [21,22,30]. Flow rate can also decrease as a potential side effect of many drugs (Fig. 2).

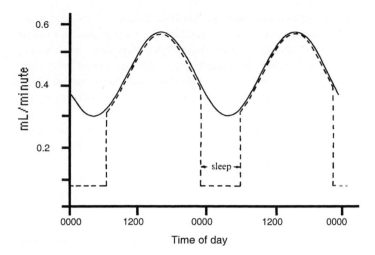

Figure 1 Daily circadian rhythm of unstimulated salivary flow. Solid line represents the mean curve, and dashed line represents the idealized effect of sleep from 2300 to 0700 hours.

2.2. Stimulated Salivary Flow

Several studies of stimulated salivary flow rate have been completed in healthy subjects [27–29,31,32]. Results show a wide variation among individuals, but it is not possible to compare directly the results from these studies because a variety of nonstandardized stimuli were used.

Many factors influence stimulated salivary flow rate. Although results from studies vary, the maximum stimulated flow rate is reported to be 7 mL/min for whole saliva [30]. The factors influencing rate include mechanical stimulation (chewing in the absence of any taste), acidic tastes (the most potent stimulator of the four taste stimuli), salivary gland size (directly proportional), and foods.

For many years it was believed that both the unstimulated and stimulated salivary flow rates decreased with age. This was mostly because studies were completed on institutionalized,

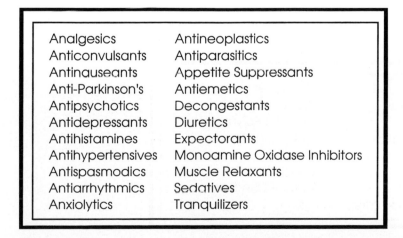

Figure 2 Drugs that cause reduced unstimulated salivary flow rate. (From Ref. 26)

medicated patients. But it also has been shown now that age has little effect on flow rate in the normal healthy population [26]. For example, a study of 700 people who were picked at random on a street in Rochester, NY, assessed the stimulated and unstimulated flow rates in people of all ages up to 80 years. The study found stable flow rates across this age range in healthy individuals. Apparently only people on medication exhibited diminished salivary flow rates [30].

This leads to a basic question: What is the total daily volume of saliva secreted by the average individual?

1. The minimum unstimulated flow rate over a waking period of 16 hours is about 0.3 mL/min, or a total of $\sim$ 300 mL of saliva. During sleep, the flow rate falls to 0.1 mL/min, producing $\sim$ 50 mL of saliva [26].

2. Studies of the effects of stimulation with various foods on flow rate suggest an average flow rate during chewing of 4 mL/min. The average time spent chewing each day is estimated to be 54 min [30]. Therefore, saliva production stimulated by chewing results in just over 200 mL/d.

Therefore, the total daily flow of saliva amounts to $\sim$ 550 mL/24 h. This estimate, from Dawes, is much less than the 1000–1500 mL/24 h that was concluded from the work of others and extensively quoted in many textbooks [24,25,32–35].

2.3. Saliva Physiology

Many factors can affect the composition of saliva (Fig. 3), including which specific gland is producing the saliva. Virtually all amylase in saliva is produced by the parotid glands whereas blood group substances derive mainly from the submandibular and sublingual glands and minor mucous glands [24,25]. However, the main factor affecting salivary composition is the ''flow rate.'' As flow rate increases, the concentration of some constituents also increases (e.g., protein, sodium, chloride, and bicarbonate) while the concentration of others decreases (e.g., phosphate and magnesium) [26]. The parotid gland normally produces 20% of the total volume of unstimulated saliva secretion while the submandibular gland contributes 65%, the sublingual 7–8%, and the minor mucous glands 7–8%, At high flow rates, the parotid becomes the dominant gland contributing $\sim$ 50% of salivary secretion [30].

The nature of a stimulus that causes an increase in flow rate also has an effect on composition. For example, the taste of salt stimulates the highest protein content. The type of stimulus has virtually no effect on the electrolyte composition.

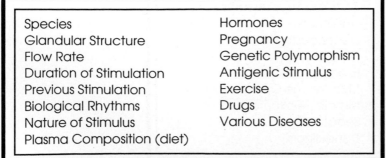

Species	Hormones
Glandular Structure	Pregnancy
Flow Rate	Genetic Polymorphism
Duration of Stimulation	Antigenic Stimulus
Previous Stimulation	Exercise
Biological Rhythms	Drugs
Nature of Stimulus	Various Diseases
Plasma Composition (diet)	

Figure 3 Factors affecting salivary composition. (From Ref. 26.)

3. CELLULAR CONTENT OF SALIVA

It appears that the cells that are present in saliva originate from three distinct sources [36]:

1. Buccal and lingual epithelial cells that are sloughed from the mucosal surface as a normal consequence of mastication
2. Leukocytes that migrate into the saliva from the gingival fluids and tissues as a consequence of chronic gingival inflammatory disease present in the host
3. Bacteria that form both the normal and pathogenic fauna of the oral cavity

Of the cells present in saliva, epithelial cells occupy the largest volume [37] (Fig. 4). Watanabe et al. concluded that there are $\sim 4 \times 10^5$ epithelial cells per milliliter in dentate patients [38]. The majority of these cells are sloughed from the surface of the buccal and lingual mucosa while a minor component is made up of crevicular or periodontal pocket epithelial cells [39]. Exfoliated epithelial cells can be separated from leukocytes by ultrafiltration under pressure and washing the cells with physiological saline [40].

The number of leukocytes in saliva has been widely investigated. Several studies estimate the number at between 1×10^5 and 4×10^5/mL [41–43]. Leukocytes continuously migrate into the dentate mouth at a rate of about one million per minute [40]. The gingival crevice is their major site of entry [44]. The largest component of the leukocyte count is composed of polymorphonuclear leukocytes (PMN). These cells are derived principally from the gingival crevice with a small contribution from the oral mucosa and the tonsils [39]. In the gingival tissues and gingival fluid, most leukocytes have the appearance of intact cells that resemble

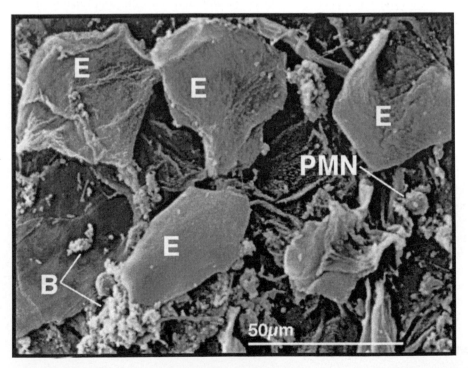

Figure 4 Scanning electron photomicrograph of cells in human saliva. E, oral epithelial cells; PMN, polymorphonuclear leukocyte; B, bacteria.

those present in the blood [45]. Of oral leukocytes, 98–99% are PMN neutrophils, and ~ 1% are lymphocytes [44].

Although there have been many studies on the bacterial composition of dental plaque, there have been few studies in relation to plaque bacteria in saliva [39]. It is known that dental plaque is a complex habitat. When one considers saliva in a forensic context, it is not necessarily informative to study the dental plaque organisms since only human-specific forensic DNA primers are utilized.

3.1. DNA Evidence from Saliva

Conventional serological methods of analyzing saliva stains are limited to certain traditional marker systems. But several studies were able to isolate saliva from objects and identify the origin of the stains using genetic typing systems [18,46–52]. In 1993, Ohashi et al. detected 17–500 desquamated buccal cells per microliter (μL) of saliva in experimental samples. Using the polymerase chain reaction (PCR) technique, the origin of the test samples at the D1S80 locus was discriminated [53].

Hochmeister *et al.* in 1991 successfully isolated and analyzed genomic DNA from cigarette butts [54], and the FBI Laboratory analyzed salivary DNA evidence in forensic casework involving envelopes and postage stamps [55].

Also in 1991, Comey and Budowle studied the efficacy of the HLA-DQA1 locus using the polymerase chain reaction on several types of body fluid stains including a mixed stain of blood and saliva on clothing. Results revealed that in a mixed stain composed of 10 μL of blood and 10 μL of saliva, the saliva component typed significantly stronger than the blood component. In fact, the typing strengths were only the same when the saliva concentration in the stain ratio was reduced by 10 times with respect to the blood concentration. This illustrates that the DNA typing strength of 1 μL of saliva is equal to 10 μL of blood [47]. The observations of Comey and Budowle point out the forensic significance of DNA from saliva. Subsequently, Sweet *et al.* in 1995 isolated sufficient salivary DNA evidence to use multiplex PCR-based tests to identify the origin of saliva stains on human skin [14,56,57].

3.2. Locating Saliva Evidence

The presence of saliva is normally implied from the discovery of considerable numbers of nucleated epithelial cells [58] and a substantial amylase activity [3,11].

Amylase activity is traditionally identified by reference to the hydrolysis of starch [4]. Amylase will also hydrolyze soluble starch-dye complexes. Sax *et al.* developed a soluble amylopectin–Procion Red complex. This complex was later precipitated on to pink amylase-sensitive paper to detect the location of saliva stains on objects [10,59].

More recently crime scene analysts from various police agencies and others have investigated the use of alternative light sources, such as ultraviolet lights [60], mercury vapor lights and carbon dioxide, neodymium YAG, and argon ion lasers [61] to isolate and identify latent fingerprints, body fluid stains, and other trace biological evidence. These search modalities are based on the inherent fluorescence of biological evidence. This technology has revolutionized the detection of salivary stains on human skin because it enables the investigator to locate a saliva stain caused by sucking, biting, or kissing, even in the absence of marks from teeth.

3.3 Stability of Saliva

Numerous enzymes from a variety of sources are present in whole saliva. Carbohydrases, esterases, transferases, proteolytic enzymes (e.g., proteinases, peptidases, and ureases), and other catabolic enzymes are produced by the salivary glands, oral micro-organisms, and leukocytes or by a combination of these sources [62].

All of these enzymes and other factors, such as temperature, humidity, time, ambient environment, etc., may have a harmful effect on biological evidence through autolytic or climatic processes [63]. But results from both experimental studies and actual casework confirm that significant conclusions can be obtained from saliva recovered under adverse conditions or samples subjected to potentially detrimental laboratory conditions. For example:

1. Blood group antigens in body fluid stains are often damaged by inclement ambient conditions, making their detection difficult by conventional methods. But saliva stains tested after a period of 2 years were correctly identified in all cases using a dipstick immunoassay method to detect A and B blood group antigens [64].

2. The stability of thiocyanate concentration in saliva is of concern to researchers studying cigarette smoking and to forensic analysts. Callas *et al.* studied the possible evaporation of saliva and the deterioration of salivary thiocyanate concentration over a period of 1 year. Foulds *et al.* in 1994 undertook a similar study. In each case, it was concluded that thiocyanate is stable over short storage intervals. For example, it is stable at room temperature up to 72 hours, frozen at $-18°C$ in airtight containers for 14 days, and for a period of 1 week in the mail in transit to a laboratory [65,66].

3. Adams *et al.* studied bloodstains contaminated with other body fluids using restriction fragment length polymorphism (RFLP) analysis. Whole oral swabs were taken from a set of female subjects and were mixed with aliquots of 3 μL and 10 μL of semen in an attempt to contaminate the saliva samples [67]. The mixed stains on the swabs were allowed to air-dry at room temperature for 5 days prior to analysis. RFLP patterns were identified to each subject, which indicates that saliva did not undergo significant degradation under these conditions.

4. Walsh *et al.* conducted extensive tests to recover DNA from fresh saliva and from mixed samples containing saliva subjected to varying storage conditions. DNA band patterns from saliva stored at $-20°C$ for up to 3 weeks were virtually indistinguishable from the patterns obtained from fresh isolates. In fact, RFLP band patterns were developed from mixed stains of saliva and semen stored at $-20°C$ for as long as 2.5 years [18].

5. The same authors [18] also reported preliminary results from studies using cotton swabs containing saliva stored at 4°C and 20°C, under both dry and humid conditions, for a period of 1 week. Apparently these storage conditions had no effect on the ability to develop DNA patterns from the saliva samples. But samples stored at 37°C for as little as 4 days failed to yield a definitive result.

4.   RECOVERY OF SALIVA

Stains from saliva, semen, vaginal secretions, and blood are usually found on clothing and objects at the crime scene. These stains are analyzed in the laboratory after an investigator has recovered the stained exhibit and transported it for analysis. In these cases, a sample of the actual exhibit material (e.g., cloth) is placed in extraction solvents for processing. This results in almost complete recovery of the biological evidence. When the stained exhibit cannot be recovered and submitted for analysis, a representative sample of it must be collected.

Many diverse methods to collect salivary evidence have been reported [4,10,46,68–73]. Until the mid-1990s forensic odontologists recommended, with varying degrees of success, the use of sterile gauze, moist cigarette papers, or a wet sterile cotton swab to recover saliva from bitemarks. The aim of these methods was to collect blood group data from the site, so a control sample from an adjacent area was always required in addition to the swab directly from the site.

In a landmark study, Sweet *et al.* developed a new method of recovery called the double swab technique that used a combination of wet and dry sterile cotton swabs to increase the yield of DNA for analysis [74]. The potential problem of contamination of the sample with DNA arising from epithelial cells sloughed from the skin of the recipient of the bitemark was acknowledged as the most important potential problem but the double swab collection method was shown to reduce this contamination risk significantly. The double swab method is the recommended saliva collection method for stains on skin. It has also been accepted for wider use, including for blood and semen stains on both animate and inanimate substrates.

Following is a description of the double swab method [74] of collecting stains of saliva and other body fluids from human skin and other substrates.

4.1. Supplies

Two sterile cotton swabs (no preservatives)
3 mL of sterile, distilled water
Fitzpak swab box (holds 2 swabs) (Cat. No. F06129; Invitro Sciences Inc., Welland, Ontario, Canada: invitro.sciences@sympatico.ca)

4.2. Method

Dip the head of one sterile cotton swab in sterile, distilled water to thoroughly moisten the tip ($\approx$10 sec). Roll the swab head over the saliva stain using circular motions and medium pressure to wash the stain from the surface. Place this swab in the evidence box to thoroughly air-dry ($\geq$30 min).

Within 10 sec of completing the first swab procedure, roll the tip of the other dry sterile cotton swab over the area of skin that is now wet from the first swab. Use circular motions with light pressure to absorb the moisture from the skin on to the swab head. Place this swab in the evidence box to thoroughly air dry ($\geq$30 min).

Since the two swabs come from the same site, they can be considered a single exhibit. Both swabs can be placed in the same swab box, marked with evidence continuity details and submitted to the laboratory. No control swabs from an adjacent site are needed.

4.3. DNA Sample from Recipient of the Bitemark

A DNA reference sample is collected from the recipient of the bitemark to allow interpretation of possible mixtures. This DNA sample can be in the form of a whole blood sample, buccal swab, small section of tissue from the autopsy incision, etc. (Any sample that will provide a DNA profile of the recipient of the bitemark for comparison purposes.) Expedited submission of this sample and the saliva swabs to the laboratory for analysis is recommended.

4.4. Storage and Transportation

The swabs and reference sample should be submitted for analysis as soon as possible. If they are submitted within a few hours of collection, storage and transportation at room temperature is adequate. If the time to submission is longer than several hours, frozen storage ($-20°C$) and cold transportation (dry ice or frozen packs) are recommended.

5. DNA ANALYSIS

The primary objective of the odontologist should be to subject bitemark evidence to a complete range of tests in order to reach conclusions that can be used to identify a criminal. Conclusions from physical comparison tests are necessarily conditional since a high level of certainty is not possible using such tests, which are subjective.

Since it is possible to identify a specific individual using the uniqueness of the DNA molecule, the application of molecular biological comparison tests to saliva stains recovered from the injury are recommended as adjunctive and corroborative examinations. Using DNA analysis, it is possible to report the likelihood that a suspect is either implicated by the evidence or should be excluded from further consideration with a much higher degree of confidence than through physical comparison alone.

Forensic scientists have a number of DNA testing methods that reveal either length-specific or sequence-specific variations in DNA. The method of choice largely depends on the quality and quantity of DNA extracted from the sample and the DNA reference source available for comparison. Analysis of nuclear (genomic) DNA using PCR-based amplification techniques is the most widely used.

5.1. Polymerase Chain Reaction

From time to time, a new laboratory technique appears that has a revolutionary impact on a field of science. Such was the case with Southern blotting in 1975, and this also appears to be the case with the polymerase chain reaction (PCR) method, which was formally introduced in 1986 by Mullis *et al.* The PCR permits a minute quantity of DNA to be amplified by the same basic replication machinery that a cell uses prior to normal mitotic cell division [75–77].

The amplification of DNA fragments in an automated system has truly changed the detection of DNA sequence variation and the study of the human genome. Using this method, a specific human DNA fragment can be selectively amplified in a test tube using a bacterial polymerase rather than within the actual bacterial host [78,79].

The technique has two important benefits: First, analysis is possible from very small amounts of DNA. This allows information to be obtained from evidence samples such as a hair follicle, an invisible semen stain [80], swabbings from bitemarks, and similar minute biological samples. Second, amplification is possible from very old material or from degraded DNA. From a practical point of view, the technique is relatively simple to perform and results can be obtained within a short period of time, often within 24–48 hours.

For forensic purposes analysts focus on minisatellite and microsatellite loci [81–84]. Minisatellite loci range in length from 100 to 1500 nucleotide base pairs [85,86]. The microsatellite loci, called *short tandem repeats* (STRs), are 100–350 bp in length with a core repeat unit of 2–5 bp. These loci are the current focus of forensic analysis methods. The PCR products generated during this type of analysis are separated and visualized using (1) conventional polyacrylamide gel electrophoresis methods [77,87], or (2) automated robotic gene sequencers. They can also be detected by dot-blot systems.

5.2. Postmortem Stability of DNA

As the body decomposes after death, the DNA molecules in all parts of the body are presumably degraded by nucleases (enzymes that specifically attack nucleic acids). It is presumed that these nucleases are released with other hydrolytic enzymes as cellular and subcellular membranes lose their integrity [88].

Experiments have demonstrated that DNA that is contained in a test sample incubated in low humidity conditions will degrade more slowly than a sample in high-humidity conditions. Variations in temperature also have an effect on the degradation rate; high temperatures appear to accelerate decomposition and degradation [88,89]. Environmental studies conducted by McNally *et al.* in 1989 showed that dried bloodstains exposed to conditions of varying humidity, temperature, and ultraviolet light for periods up to 5 days did not alter the integrity of the DNA and significantly impact on the ability to analyze the samples [90].

6. SUMMARY

Data obtained through the analysis of DNA are objective, and if the analysis methodology has been correctly performed, the resulting conclusions are difficult to dispute. The analysis of DNA extracted from saliva deposited on human skin by biting or other types of aggressive oral behavior has the potential to identify the biter. Through DNA analysis, results can exclude or include the biter in the events of the crime.

There is absolute certainty associated with a DNA result that produces an exclusion of the biter. If the genotype of the saliva does not match the biter's genotype, the evidence did not originate from the biter. On the other hand, a result producing an inclusion of the biter is expressed in terms of a calculated probability of a positive match. This probability depends on the relative rarity of this genotype in the population.

Interpretation of DNA typing tests should be included with probabilities derived from collateral tests of other evidence from a given case. Investigative efforts should not be focused solely on DNA evidence for two reasons. First, the results or probabilities may not be conclusive. Second, in some situations positive results cannot be interpreted correctly without significant additional information. For example, a stain of saliva may be identified as originating from a specific biter; however, this saliva may have been deposited on the skin with the consent of the victim.

7. CASE EXAMPLES

7.1 Salivary DNA from a Submerged Body

In October 1995, the nude body of a female homicide victim was found ∼ 5.5 hours after it was deposited in a slow-moving river. A human bitemark was found on the victim's right breast. The injury recorded sufficient detail to allow physical comparison of the pattern of the teethmarks to the teeth of several suspects. Standard bitemark evidence collection protocols were closely followed, including photographs, impressions, saliva collection, and dental impressions from the recipient of the bitemark. The saliva collection method was the traditional (one wet swab) serological method in common use at the time. Four swabbings were made to collect saliva deposited on the bite site. Other potential DNA evidence recovered at autopsy included postcoital swabs containing epithelial and sperm cells.

Over a period of several months numerous suspects were found and attempts were made to connect the physical and biological evidence to them. All were excluded eventually, although the respective analysts did not know the physical comparison conclusions or the DNA results until later. Eventually a suspect was arrested who was found to be in possession of certain information that was not released by the police. Comparisons of the available physical evidence to this suspect identified him as the probable biter.

The DNA extracted from the bitemark swabs was low in volume so the extracts were combined into one sample. Using PCR-based analysis, a DNA profile from the saliva evidence was determined to be a mixture of two persons. The major contributor to the mixture was shown to be the recipient of the bitemark. The suspect identified as the probable biter through physical comparisons was identified as the minor DNA contributor [20]. Additionally, this suspect was identified as the origin of the semen sample taken from the postcoital swab. The DNA profile

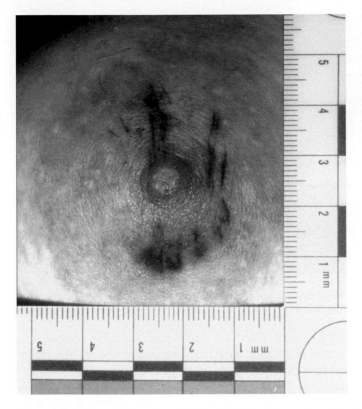

Figure 5 Bitemark found on right breast of submerged recipient of the bitemark showing physical evidence that was combined at trial with conclusions from biological evidence in the form of DNA from saliva.

from the saliva on the bitemark and the male component of the postcoital swab were shown to be the same, so the suspect was identified as the person who had sex with the victim and as the depositor of the saliva. The importance of this case is that a DNA profile was produced from the saliva despite submersion of the body in fresh water > 5 hours (Fig. 5).

7.2. Victim Bites Kidnapper Through Clothing

On her way to school one morning in 1995, a 12-year-old girl was pulled through the driver's side window of a car and abducted. While being pulled into the car the victim bit the male abductor through a dark purple T-shirt. The girl was driven to a remote location where she was sexually assaulted. The victim survived the attack and was able to provide investigators with details of her attacker's physical description and of his clothing and car.

A rape kit was recovered from the girl and no semen was found, but a pubic hair that exhibited a small bloodstain on the shaft was found during the examination. A DNA profile was obtained from the blood and hair. A car fitting the vehicle description was located later the same day parked at a residence. A man fitting the general description of the suspect walked out of the residence to speak to the police officer when the car was being examined. The man's clothing fit the description given by the victim. Later the suspect was arrested and examined.

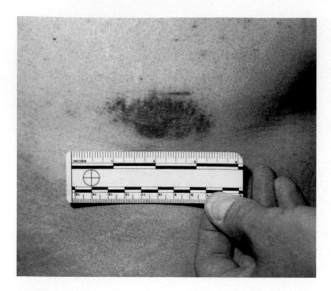

Figure 6　Bruise found on suspect's body that corresponded to location of bitemark described by victim.

A bruise was found under the right armpit in the location of the bitemark described by the victim (Fig. 6). A purple T-shirt was seized from the laundry basket at the residence.

　　Examination of the right side of the T-shirt revealed a white substance present on the cloth in the form of a bitemark pattern. This pattern was photographed and tested for the presence of amylase and DNA. An odontologist examined the photographs and determined that the pattern was consistent with a bitemark (Fig. 7), but the physical comparison of the pattern to the victim's teeth was inconclusive.

Figure 7　Bitemark pattern present on dark purple T-shirt worn by abductor when victim was abducted.

DNA results from the root end of the pubic hair produced a mixed profile that showed contributions from both the suspect and the victim. Results from the bloodstain on the hair shaft area produced a profile that matched the victim. DNA results from the bitemark on the T-shirt showed the victim's profile (Fig. 8). The importance of this case lies in the demonstrated need for the odontologist to consider the opportunity to use salivary evidence to assist in identifying the origin of a bitemark.

7.3 Saliva from Bites Corroborates Conclusions from Physical Comparison

The body of a 31-year-old Hispanic female was discovered in 1996 slumped across the front seat of a parked car. The victim died of asphyxia due to neck compression. Autopsy confirmed that she had been sexually assaulted and beaten. Patterned injuries consistent with marks from teeth were found on both breasts, three areas of the abdomen, the lower lip (self-inflicted), left pubic region, and right forearm. Forensic evidence was collected using current recovery methods. A criminalist used the double swab technique to collect saliva at each of the following patterned injury sites: right breast, left breast, and lower left abdomen. An odontologist photographed the wounds extensively. It was determined that most of the wounds did not show well-defined patterns, but the bitemark on the right breast became the focus of attention because it recorded the most detail.

A suspect was apprehended and forensic physical and biological comparisons were completed. The odontologist concluded that the teeth of the suspect were the probable cause of the bite injury (Fig. 9). DNA analysis using the polymarker system, a dot-blot analysis method, could not exclude the suspect as the contributor of the saliva on the right breast and abdomen. The significance of this case is the additive effects of the conclusions from both the physical evidence and the biological evidence.

7.4 DNA from a Bitemark in Cheddar Cheese

Two suspects were found and arrested the day after a home invasion robbery. They were charged with possession of property stolen from the residence. Investigators found no evidence to link the suspects to the scene of the crime that could be used to increase the charges. Along with the homeowners, police discovered a block of cheddar cheese that was deposited in the living room during the home invasion. One bite had been taken from the piece of cheese before it was discarded. Police officers stored the cheese at $-15°C$ until it was submitted to the laboratory 10 days later.

High-quality physical evidence of the biter's teeth was recorded in the cheese (Fig. 10). It was apparent that the biter exhibited a Class II, Div. II malocclusion. Attention was focused on one suspect who appeared to have such a malocclusion. The cheese was swabbed using the double swab technique in an attempt to recover saliva where it was contacted by the lips and tongue. But it was thought that this evidence would not be needed since (1) the physical evidence was so good, and (2) previous attempts to produce a DNA profile from biological evidence on cheeses had been unsuccessful.

A warrant to seize dental exemplars from the primary suspect was obtained but the warrant could not be executed because the suspect was not able to contact legal counsel for advice during the time that the warrant was active. Plans to obtain the dental exemplars were abandoned. This is because it was expected that since the suspect was informed that exemplars were required for comparison purposes, he would attempt to alter his teeth prior to the police obtaining another warrant. The laboratory recovered DNA from the double swabs and took measures to adequately purify the sample. A full DNA profile was obtained. This was compared to a known DNA sample (blood) that was obtained under the provisions of a DNA warrant. The suspect's genotype

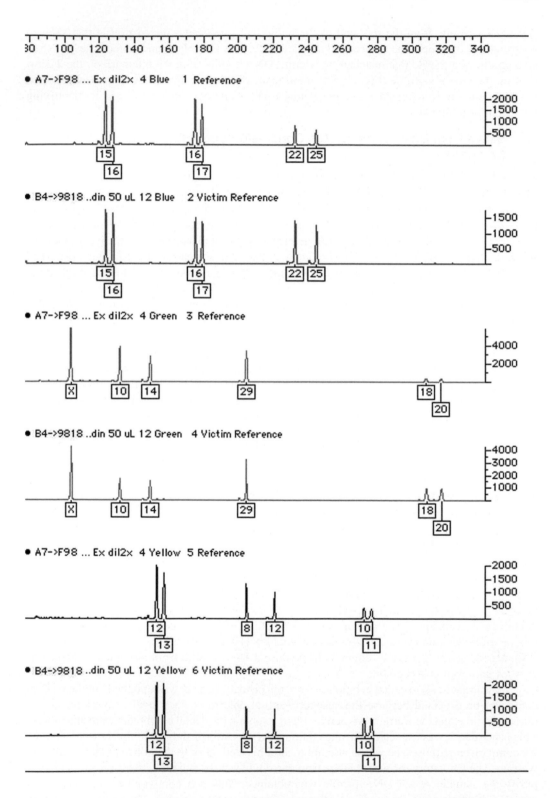

Figure 8   DNA profile of victim (known reference sample) compared to DNA profile from saliva stain on purple T-shirt worn by suspect.

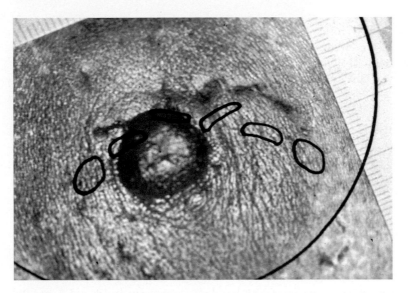

Figure 9 Physical comparison of teeth of suspect to marks from teeth on breast of victim found in car.

matched the genotype from the saliva deposited on the cheese. This identified the suspect as the biter and put him at the crime scene [19]. The charges were increased to break-and-enter.

The case illustrates an important willingness by the police officers to attempt DNA testing in such unusual cases or with unusual evidence samples. It is difficult or impossible to predict if a DNA result can be obtained since it can be influenced by so many factors. Despite this, it is still very important to attempt to produce a profile.

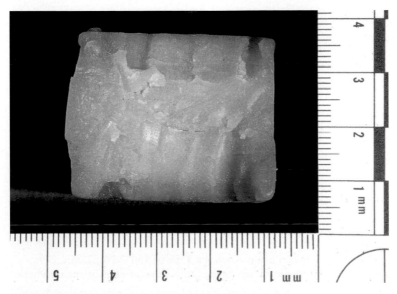

Figure 10 Single bitemark in block of cheddar cheese recovered from living room after home invasion robbery.

ACKNOWLEDGMENTS

The valuable assistance of the following collaborators is gratefully acknowledged: Robert E. Wood, Forensic Odontologist, Toronto, Ontario; Greggory S. LaBerge and Ted A. Davelis, Denver Police Department Crime Laboratory, Denver, CO; Gerald L. Vale, Cathy A. Law, and Gregory S. Golden, Forensic Odontologists, California; and detective Lyle Simpson, Abbotsford Police Department, British Columbia.

REFERENCES

1. Gaensslen RE. Sourcebook in Forensic Serology, Immunology and Biochemistry. Washington. DC: National Institute of Justice, 1983.
2. DeForest PR, Gaensslen RE, Lee HC. Forensic Science—An Introduction to Criminalistics. New York: McGraw-Hill, 1983.
3. Nickolls LC. The Scientific Investigation of Crime. London: Butterworth, 1956.
4. Clift A, Lamont CM. Saliva in forensic odontology. J Forens Sci Soc 1974; 14:241–245.
5. Johnson LT, Cadle D. Bite mark evidence: recognition, preservation, analysis and courtroom presentation. NY State Dent J 1989; 55:38–41.
6. Rutter EA, Whitehead PH. The fractionation of ABH blood group substances in saliva. J Forens Sci Soc 1977; 16:241–246.
7. Sperber ND. Identification of children and adults through federal and state dental identification systems: recognition of human bite marks. Forens Sci Int 1986; 30:187–193.
8. Kipps AE, Quarmby VE, Whitehead PH. The detection of mixtures of blood and other body secretions in stains. J Forens Sci Soc 1978; 18:189–191.
9. Rushton C, Kipps A, Quarmby V, Whitehead PH. The distribution and significance of amylase-containing stains on clothing. J Forens Sci Soc 1979; 19:53–58.
10. Whitehead PH, Kipps AE. A test paper for detecting saliva stains. J Forens Sci Soc 1975; 15:39–42.
11. Willott GM. An improved test for the detection of salivary amylase in stains. J Forens Sci Soc 1974; 14:341–344.
12. Nishi K, Ito N, Hirota T, Fechner G, Rand S, Brinkmann B. Different expression of blood group A antigen in the secretory cells of salivary glands from German and Japanese nonsecretor individuals. In Polesky HF, Mayr WR, Eds. Advances in Haemogenetics 3. Berlin: Springer-Verlag, 1990:177–179.
13. Ballantyne J, Sensabaugh G, Witkowski J. DNA technology and forensic science. In: Banbury Reports. Cold Spring Harbor. NY: Cold Spring Harbor Laboratory Press, 1989.
14. Sweet DJ, Lorente JA, Lorente M, Valenzuela A, Villanueva E. Forensic identification using DNA recovered from saliva on human skin. Adv Forens Haemogen 1996; 6:325–327.
15. Gill P, Jeffreys AJ, Werret DJ. Forens applications of DNA fingerprints. Nature 1985; 318:577–579.
16. Giusti A, Baird M, Pasquale S, Balazs I, Glassberg J. Application of deoxyribonucleic acid (DNA) polymorphisms to the analysis of DNA recovered from sperm. J Forens Sci 1986; 31:409–417.
17. Hopkins B, Morten JEN, Smith JC, Markham AF. The development of methods for the analysis of DNA extracted from Forens samples. Technique 1989; 1:96–102.
18. Walsh DJ, Corey AC, Cotton RW, Forman L, Herrin GL, Word CJ, Garner DD. Isolation of deoxyribonucleic acid (DNA) from saliva and Forensic science samples containing saliva. J Forens Sci 1992; 37:387–395.
19. Sweet DJ, Hildebrand DP. Saliva from cheese bite yields DNA profile of burglar. Int J Legal Med 1999; 112:201–203.
20. Sweet DJ, Shutler GG. Analysis of salivary DNA evidence from a bite mark on a submerged body. J Forens Sci 1999; 44:1069–1072.
21. Dawes C. Rhythms in salivary flow rate and composition. Int J Chronobiol 1974; 2:253–279.
22. Dawes C, Jenkins GN. The effects of different stimuli on the composition of saliva in man. J Physiol (Lond) 1964; 170:86–100.
23. Schneyer LH, Levin LK. Rate of secretion by individual salivary gland pairs of man under conditions of reduced exogenous stimulation. Appl Physiol 1955; 7:508–512.

24. Selkurt EE. Physiology. Boston: Little, Brown and Company, 1971.

25. Grant DA, Stern IB, Everett FG. Orban's Periodontics, A Concept—Theory and Practice. Saint Louis: C.V. Mosby, 1972.

26. Dawes C. Factors influencing salivary flow rate and composition. Consensus Workshop on Saliva and Dental Health. British Dental Association: County Mayo, 1990:1–18.

27. Heintze U, Birkhed D, Björn H. Secretion rate and buffer effect of resting and stimulated whole saliva as a function of age and sex. Swedish Dent J 1983; 7:227–238.

28. Shannon IL. Physiologic baselines for total protein in human parotid fluid collected without exogenous stimulation. Oral Med 1967; 22:75–82.

29. Shannon IL, Frome WJ. Enhancement of salivary flow rate and buffering capacity. J Can Dent Assoc 1973; 39:177–181.

30. Dawes C. Physiological factors affecting salivary flow rate, oral sugar clearance and the sensation of dry mouth in man. J Dent Res 1987; 66:648–653.

31. Ericson S, Hedin M, Wiberg A. Variability of the submandibular flow rate in man with special reference to the size of the gland. Odontol Rev 1972; 2:411–420.

32. Mason DK, Chisholm DM. Salivary Glands in Health and Disease. London: W.B. Saunders, Company, 1975.

33. Guyton AC. Textbook of Medical Physiology. Philadelphia: W.B. Saunders, 1981.

34. Mitchell DF, Standish SM, Fast TB. Oral Diagnosis, Oral Medicine. Philadelphia: Lea & Febiger, 1978.

35. Spouge JD. Oral Pathology. St. Louis: C.V. Mosby, 1973.

36. Rates A-M, Calonius PEB. The modified Millipore technique for the study of oral leukocytes. Scand J Dent Res 1971; 79:327–332.

37. Klinkhamer JM. Quantitative evaluation of gingivitis and periodontal disease. II. The mobile mucus phase of oral secretions. Perio 1968; 6:253–256.

38. Watanabe T, Ohata N, Morishita M, Iwamoto Y. Correlation between the protease activities and the number of epithelial cells in human saliva. J Dent Res 1981; 60:1039–1044.

39. Wilton JMA, Curtis MA, Gillett IR, Griffiths GS, Maiden MFJ, Stern JAC, Wilson DT, Johnson NW. Detection of high-risk groups and individuals for periodontal diseases: laboratory markers from analysis of saliva. Clin Perio 1989; 16:475–483.

40. Raeste A-M. Lysozyme (muramidase) activity of leukocytes and exfoliated epithelial cells in the oral cavity. Scand J Dent Res 1972; 80:1–6.

41. Calonius PEB. The leukocyte count in saliva. Oral Surg 1958; 11:43–46.

42. Gilkerson SW, Brown HS, Rovelstad GH. Microscopic study of saliva sediment. Research Report NM 750126.06.01. Bainbridge. MD: Dental Research Laboratory, U.S. Naval Training Center, 1958.

43. Wright DE, Jenkins GN. The differential leukocyte count in human saliva. Arch Oral Biol 1968; 13: 1159–1161.

44. Raeste A-M. Morphological changes and lysozyme activity of neutrophil polymorphonuclear leukocytes in the human dentulous oral cavity. Masters Thesis, University of Helsinki, Finland, 1972.

45. Lange D, Schröder HE. Cytochemistry and ultrastructure of gingival sulcus cells. Helv Odontol Acta Suppl 1971; 6:65–68.

46. Berlin YA, Kazazian H. Rapid preparation of genomic DNA from dried blood and saliva spots for polymerase chain reaction. Hum Mutat 1992; 1:260–261.

47. Comey CT, Budowle B. Validation studies on the analysis of the HLA DQA1 locus using the polymerase chain reaction. J Forens Sci 1991; 36:1633–1648.

48. Eriksen B, Svensmark O. DNA-profiling of stains in criminal cases: analysis of measurement errors and band-shift. Discussion of match criteria. Forens Sci Int 1993; 61:21–34.

49. Kauffman DL, Kelle PJ, Bennick A, Blum M. Alignment of amino acid and DNA sequences of human proline-rich proteins. Crit Rev Oral Biol Med 1993; 4:287–292.

50. Kloosterman AD, Budowle B, Daselaar P. PCR-amplification and detection of the human D1S80 VNTR locus. Amplification conditions, population genetics and application in forensic analysis. Int J Legal Med 1993; 105:257–264.

51. Kojima T, Uchihi R, Yamamoto T, Tamaki K, Katsumata Y. DNA typing of the three HLA-class II loci from saliva stains [in Japanese]. Jpn J Legal Med 1993; 47:380–386.

52. Ovchinnikov IV, Gavrilov DK, Nosikov VV, Debabov VG. Use of the polymerase chain reaction for typing allelic variants of the human HLA-DQA1 by hybridization with oligonucleotide probes, specific for specific alleles [in Russian]. Molekulyarnaya Biologiya 1991; 25:1266–1272.

53. Ohashi A, Aoki T, Matsugo S, Simasaki C. PCR-based typing of human buccal cell's DNA extracted from whole saliva and saliva stains [in Japanese]. Jpn J Legal Med 1993; 47:108–118.

54. Hochmeister MN, Budowle B, Jung J, Borer UV, Comey CT, Dirnhofer R. PCR-based typing of DNA extracted from cigarette butts. Int J Legal Med 1991; 104:229–233.

55. Allen M, Saldeen T, Gyllensten U. PCR-based typing of saliva on stamps and envelopes. BioTech 1994; 17:546–552.

56. Sweet DJ, Lorente M, Lorente JA, Valenzuela A, Alvarez JC. Increasing DNA extraction yield from saliva stains with a modified chelex method. Forens Sci Int 1997; 83:167–177.

57. Sweet DJ, Lorente JA, Lorente M, Valenzuela A, Villanueva E. PCR-based typing of DNA from saliva recovered from human skin. J Forensic Sci 1997; 42(3):447–451.

58. Maximov AA, Bloom W. Textbook of Histology. Philadelphia: W.B. Saunders, 1970.

59. Sax SM, Bridgwater AB, Moore JJ. Determination of serum and urine amylase with use of procion brilliant red M-2BS amylopectin. Clin Chem 1971; 17:311–315.

60. Wilkinson DA, Misner AH. A comparison of thenoyl europium chelate with ardrox and rhodamine 6G for the fluorescent detection of cyanoacrylate prints. J Forens Ident 1994; 44:387–402.

61. Auvdel MJ. Comparison of laser and high-intensity quartz arc tubes in the detection of body secretions. J Forens Sci 1988; 33:929–945.

62. Glickman I. Clinical Periodontology. Philadelphia: W.B. Saunders, 1972.

63. Masters R, Schlein F. Factors affecting the deterioration of dried bloodstains. J Forens Sci 1958; 3: 288–302.

64. Rao DV, Kashyap VK. A simple dipstick immunoassay for detection of A and B antigens. J Immunoassay 1992; 13:15–30.

65. Callas PW, Haugh LD, Flynn BS. Effects of long-term storage on salivary thiocyanate concentration. Addict Behav 1989; 14:643–648.

66. Foulds J, Bryant A, Stapleton J, Jarvis MJ, Russell MAH. The stability of cotinine in unfrozen saliva mailed to the laboratory. Am J Public Health 1994; 84:1182–1183.

67. Adams DE, Presley LA, Baumstark AL, Hensley KW, Campbell PA, McLaughlin CM, Budowle B, Giusti AM, Smerick JB, Baechtel FS. Deoxyribonucleic acid (DNA) analysis by restriction fragment length polymorphisms of blood and other body fluid stains subjected to contamination and environmental insults. J Forens Sci 1991; 36:1284–1298.

68. Clark DH. Practical Forensic Odontology. Oxford: Wright, 1992.

69. Cooke CW. A Practical Guide to Physical Evidence. Springfield. IL: Charles C. Thomas, 1984.

70. Lundquist F. Methods of Forensic Science. New York: Interscience Publishers, 1962.

71. Mittleman RE, Stuver WC, Souviron R. Obtaining saliva samples from bite mark evidence. Law Enforcement Bull 1980:1–4.

72. Nickolls LC, Pereira M. A study of modern methods of grouping dried bloodstains. Med Sci Law 1962; 2:172.

73. Rothwell TJ. Studies on the blood group substances in saliva. J Forens Sci Soc 1979; 19:301.

74. Sweet DJ, Lorente JA, Lorente M, Valenzuela A, Villanueva E. An improved method to recover saliva from human skin: the double swab technique. J Forens Sci 1997; 42:320–322.

75. Mullis K, Faloona F, Scharf S, Saiki R, Horn G, Erlich H. Specific enzymatic amplification of DNA in vitro: the polymerase chain reaction. The 51st Meeting of Quantitative Biology. Cold Spring Harbor. NY: Cold Spring Harbor Laboratory Press, 1986:263–273.

76. Mullis KB, Ferré F, Gibbs RA. The Polymerase Chain Reaction. Boston: Birkhäuser, 1994.

77. Smith BC, Sweet DJ, Holland MM, DiZinno J. DNA and the forensic odontologist. In Bowers CM, Bell GL, Eds. Manual of Forensic Odontology. Colorado Springs. CO: American Society of Forensic Odontology, 1995:283–299.

78. Saiki RK, Scharf S, Faloona F, Mullis KB, Horn GT, Erlich HA. Enzymatic amplification of beta-globulin genomic sequences and restriction site analysis for diagnosis of sickle cell anemia. Science 1985; 23:1350–1354.

79. Saiki RK, Walsh PS, Levenson CH, Erlich HA. Genetic analysis of amplified DNA with immobilized sequence-specific oligonucleotide probes. Proc Nat Acad Sci USA 1989:6230–6234.

80. Hegele RA. Molecular forensics: applications, implications and limitations. J Can Med Assoc 1989; 141:668–672.

81. Edwards A, Civitello A, Hammond HA, Caskey CT. DNA typing and genetic mapping with trimeric and tetrameric tandem repeats. Am J Hum Genet 1991; 49:746–756.

82. Edwards A, Hammond HA, Jin L, Caskey CT, Chakraborty R. Genetic variation at five trimeric and tetrameric tandem repeat loci in four human population groups. Genomics 1992; 12:241–253.

83. Boerwinkle E, Xiong WJ, Fourest E. Rapid typing of tandemly repeated hypervariable loci by the polymerase chain reaction: application to the apolipoprotein B 3′ hypervariable region. Proc Nat Acad Sci USA 1989; 86:212–216.

84. Kasai K, Nakamura Y, White R. Amplification of a variable number of tandem repeats (VNTR) locus (pMCT118) by the polymerase chain reaction (PCR) and its application to forensic science. J Forens Sci 1990; 35:1196–1200.

85. Budowle B, Chakraborty R, Giusti AM, Eisenberg AJ, Allen RC. Analysis of the VNTR locus D1S80 by the PCR followed by high-resolution PAGE. Am J Hum Genet 1991; 48:137–144.

86. Frégeau CJ, Fourney RM. DNA typing with fluorescently tagged short tandem repeats: a sensitive and accurate approach to human identification. BioTech 1993; 15:100–119.

87. Budowle B, Baechtel FS, Adams DE. Validation with regard to environmental insults of the RFLP procedure for forensic purposes. In Farley MA, Harrington JJ, Eds. Forensic DNA Technology. Chelsea: Lewis Publishers, 1991:83–91.

88. Perry WL, Bass WM, Riggsby WS, Sirotkin K. The autodegradation of deoxyribonucleic acid (DNA) in human rib bone and its relationship to the time interval since death. J Forens Sci 1988; 33:144–153.

89. Rodriguez WC, Bass WM. Decomposition of buried bodies and methods that may aid in their location. J Forens Sci 1985; 30:836–852.

90. McNally L, Shaler RC, Baird M, Balazs I, DeForest P, Kobilinsky L. Evaluation of deoxyribonucleic acid (DNA) isolated From human bloodstains exposed to ultraviolet light, heat, humidity and soil contamination. J Forens Sci 1989; 34:1059–1069.

10
Bitemark Impressions
NONINVASIVE ANALYSES

Robert B. J. Dorion
Laboratoire de sciences judiciaires et de médecine légale,
Ministry of Public Security for the Province of Quebec,
Montreal, Quebec, Canada

1. INTRODUCTION

The report on bitemark evidence [1] listed the common impression materials used for bitemark impressions in 1977. They included alginate, rubber base, silicone, and hydrocolloid, none of which are in use today for forensic purposes. Other materials employed at the time include plaster of Paris, casting stone, and Silcoset [2]. Various authors have described the different techniques utilized for bitemark impressions on the body [3–6]. The American Board of Forensic Odontology (ABFO) recommends taking dental impressions of the bite site in its guidelines.

Photography and salivary swabbing precede impression taking in the bitemark protocol. Normally the body would be cleaned of contaminants such as sand, soil, and blood prior to the third/fourth set of photographs (crime scene, at the morgue prior to autopsy, undressed, cleaned) and impression taking. The bitemark impression should therefore contain no contaminants. On the other hand, there might be trace residual DNA present in the bitemark impression, which might be transferred to the stone model. Odontologists should be mindful of this possibility.

2. MATERIALS

Specifications for dental materials are regulated and approved by the American Dental Association (ADA). Materials listed under ADA specification 19, Type 1 (low viscosity), and Type 3 (low consistency), ISO specification 4823-1992 include vinyl polysiloxanes (VPS). Commercial brands such as Water Mark (Jeneric/Pentron), Correct (Jeneric/Pentron), 3M Express (3M), Supersil (Bosworth), Aquasil and Reprosil (Densply), Mirror-3 (Kerr), President (Coltene), and Splash (Discus Dental) are among a plethora of dental materials available. Approved for intraoral use, they have also been adopted by a number of forensic disciplines as impression materials of choice. They are employed for shoe and tire prints, for reproducing/capturing tool marks in bone and on cartilage (knife wounds, saw marks, bullet holes, etc.) and inanimate objects (wood, metal, etc.) and for impressions on a variety of other substrates including skin.

Impression materials have a limited shelf life. It is important to monitor and register both batch (serial) number and expiry date of the material used. The manufacturer's instructions in manipulating the material and recommendations on storage should be followed. Models should not be poured before the recommended time.

The dental stone's trade and brand name and the manufacturer's instructions on water/powder ratio and on pouring should be noted. The initial pour master model should be identified, preserved, and stored in a secure area in a specific container (such as orthodontic boxes) for court presentation. Duplicate models can be poured for examination, analysis, and testing purposes.

3. TECHNIQUES

Light body vinyl polysiloxane (VPS) is injected without pressure from a central point to at least 2 cm beyond the bitemark periphery. A sufficient quantity (1 cm plus) heavy body vinyl polysiloxane is then applied to the 5-mm-thick set light body material. Some authors have suggested imbedding paper clips in the heavy body material to increase retention between it and the backing material.

Currently, Tak Hydroplastic has replaced Hygon as this author's material of choice for both impression backing and ring construction. The beads (white, pink, yellow, or blue) are heated in a beaker of water to a temperature of 165–175° in a microwave. The individual beads coalesce becoming transparent when the appropriate temperature has been attained. The blob of material is then manipulated with wet rubber gloves and shaped to form a covering for the set impression material. The hydroplastic hardens in 5–10 min in cooling. Hardening can be hastened with the application of a bag of frozen peas. Backing material has also included different acrylics, stone, mesh wire, and custom tray material [7].

Easy Tray custom tray impression material by Kerr is another current material in use. The thermoplastic wafers are immersed in hot water for 15–30 sec. The water temperature must be 170°F (77°C) or greater, which is easily achieved in a microwave. Wafers will adhere to each other and can be shaped to obtain the desired contour. The material is reusable, is not adversely affected by repeated heating, and has an indefinite shelf life. The manufacturer claims the material is 100% dimensionally stable. A method for using the material is described by Dailey et al. [8].

Whatever backing material used, it should contain some identification (Fig. 1) such as case number, relationship to anatomical site, date, or other pertinent information. Impressions might contain intricate details of lacerations, indentations or perforations of the skin associated with the bitemark or other source of trauma, as well as body hair.

A vibrator should be used to minimize/eliminate air bubbles when pouring models from bitemark impressions. The die stone or other hard stone should be poured following the manufacturer's instructions on water/powder ratio. The initial pour master model should remain pristine for the court. Duplicate models may be made for study, analytical, and testing purposes. All bitemark models are identified, boxed in an appropriate container, registered for date of fabrication (and other pertinent information on the fabrication process), and for chain of possession with the requesting agency, and secured in an appropriate place.

Materials other than stone have been used for models of impressions. One such material is S.S. White's Melotte's Moldine, a fusible metal melting at 260°F (97°C). The silver-colored material was initially used for making dies and counterdies in dentistry. The material is heated with a Bunsen burner or other source of heat in a crucible, then poured directly on to the impression material. Figure 2 depicts three photographs of a Moldine casting depicting tooth prints on the nose. Various acrylics have also been used in the production of models over the years.

4. STORAGE

Manufacturers of impression materials usually recommend delaying pouring of models for a specific period of time. This allows for the material to regain its original shape particularly when undercuts are present. Additionally, the material may not be completely set, providing

Figure 1 Bitemark on breast (top), impression (middle), and excision ring (bottom).

additional time for the process. Manufacturers do not usually indicate the number of pours that can be made from an impression. Presumably, the fewer the undercuts, the more times an impression may be poured.

On the other hand, impression materials were not designed with a postmixing shelf life in mind. There are no recommendations from manufacturers for the storage of set impression materials. What happens to the material over time? How should the material be stored? At what

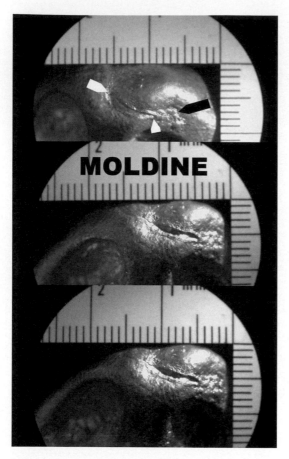

Figure 2   Three views of a Moldine casting of a bitemark on the nose.

temperatures and under what conditions? Questions that can only be answered by the experienced forensic odontologist.

Long-term storage of set dental impression materials may lead to serious complications, as this author can attest. In the early 1970s, rubber base was a material of choice for bitemark impressions. At that time, the set impression material was placed in a box in contact with its stone model. Over time, the set rubber base impression material deteriorated significantly becoming a ''tacky'' adherent mass enveloping the stone models (Fig. 3). Both the impression material and stone models were rendered useless. As a result, this author recommends that each impression be identified, placed in separate sealable plastic bags, and stored separately from its stone models in a container such as an orthodontic box. Should the impression material deteriorate, it would not adversely affect the stone models or other materials stored within the container. Should the long-term stability of the current set impression materials deteriorate, duplicate impressions could then be made using the casting (stone model). This may prove necessary when duplicate or additional stone models may be required for study, analysis, additional tests or to send to colleagues.

Figure 3 Disintegrating rubber base impression material (black and white arrows).

REFERENCES

1. Dorion RBJ. Chairman, Committee for Recommended Methods. Odontology Section, American Academy of Forensic Sciences, February 1977.
2. Harvey WH. Dental Identification and Forensic Odontology. London: Henry Kimpton, 1976:165–166.
3. Benson BW, Cottone JA, Blomberg TJ, Sperber ND. Bite mark impressions: a review of techniques and materials. J Forens Sci 1988; 33(5):1238–1243.
4. Vale GL. Discussion of ''Bite mark impressions: a review of techniques and materials''. J Forens Sci 1989; 34(4):805–807.
5. Sperber ND. Further discussion on discussions of ''Bite mark impressions: a review of techniques and materials''. J Forens Sci 1990; 35(4):777–778.
6. Dorion RBJ. Impressions of the bite site. In Bowers CM, Bell GL, Eds. Manual of Forensic Odontology. 3rd ed.: American Society of Forensic Odontology, 1995:170–171.
7. McNamee AH, Sweet D. Adherence of forensic odontologists to the ABFO Guidelines for Victim Evidence Collection. J Forens Sci 2003; 48(2):382–385.
8. Dailey JC, Shernoff AF, Gelles JHW. An improved technique for bite mark impressions. In Bowers CM, Bell GL, Eds. Manual of Forensic Odontology. 3rd ed.: American Society of Forensic Odontology, 1995:174–177.

11

Scanning Electron Microscopy

NONINVASIVE ANALYSES

Thomas J. David
Medical Examiner's Office
Atlanta, Georgia

1. RATIONALE FOR USAGE

The scanning electron microscope can accentuate three-dimensional (3D) characteristics occasionally present in bitemarks. The analysis focuses on individual rather than class characteristics (arch size; tooth size and shape). When present, particularities of the bitemark and of a suspect dentition can be evaluated and compared for differences and similarities [1]. By contrast, the more common the set of class characteristics, the less likely that one individual can be linked to a particular bitemark [2]. The scanning electron microscope (SEM) (Fig. 1) examination is not intended to replace traditional methods of bitemark analysis [3]. Rather, it is used as an adjunct to traditional analysis that might otherwise yield inconclusive results. SEM examination could potentially identify a biter on the basis of individual characteristics.

2. MATERIALS AND METHODS

SEM analysis requires the production of bitemark and tooth exemplars. The exemplars are fabricated in acrylics or epoxies rather than dental stone. The SEM stage is available in a variety of interchangeable sizes that can accommodate exemplars measuring 1 mm to 1 foot in diameter [4]. The stage most commonly utilized in bitemark analysis measures 8 cm^2 (Fig. 2).

3. BITEMARK TISSUE PREPARATION AND IMPRESSION

The bitemark impression should be taken in situ following the traditional photography and DNA collection protocols. Alternatively, an impression can be taken of the excised specimen. In either case, surface contaminants must first be removed with a sable brush saturated with isopropyl alcohol. An impression is then made, using one of the methods described in Chapter 10, first pouring models in dental stone, for study and court exhibits, then in acrylic or epoxy.

4. BITEMARK EXEMPLAR FABRICATION

Certain epoxy resins are resistant to carbon coating essential for the conductance of the electron beam in the SEM (Fig. 3). For this reason, acrylics (Lang's Jet Acrylic, Ortho Acrylic, or Duralay) are preferred. The bitemark impression is trimmed and its surface brushed with isopropyl alcohol,

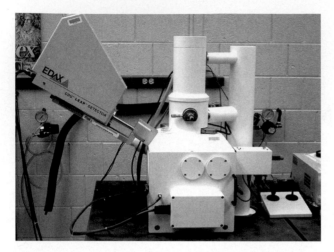

Figure 1 Scanning electron microscope (SEM).

then coated in acrylic monomer (liquid). Acrylic polymer (powder) is then added to the excess monomer until absorbed. The process is repeated in "salt and pepper" fashion, until the thickness of acrylic measures 6–10 mm. The bitemark impression is retained as a court exhibit and duplicate exemplars are poured as needed.

5. DENTAL EXEMPLAR FABRICATION

Using polyether or polyvinylsiloxane, an impression is taken of the original cast of the suspect dentition. The internal surface of the impression is brushed with isopropyl alcohol and poured in acrylic. The new dental impression is retained for duplicate exemplars as needed.

Figure 2 Scanning electron microscope stage.

Figure 3 Scanning electron microscope carbon coater.

6. EXEMPLAR PREPARATION FOR ANALYSIS

All acrylic exemplars are trimmed for stability on the SEM stage [4]. The exemplars are then placed in a vacuum chamber and coated with carbon or gold to facilitate conductivity of the electron beam [4]. Small segments of orthodontic wire (1–2 mm in length) are attached to the bitemark exemplar with cyanoacrylate glue (Fig. 4). These segments are placed at different

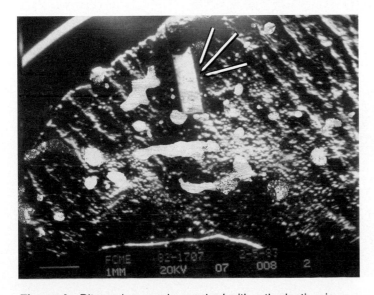

Figure 4 Bitemark exemplar marked with orthodontic wire.

angles in close proximity to the bitemark to facilitate orientation as the field of vision is reduced by magnification.

7. EXEMPLAR ANALYSIS

Optimal magnification for SEM bitemark analysis should be in the range of 13–15 times normal. Greater magnification precludes visualization of the monitored tooth. Comparing 3D bitemark detail to incisal edge details is the goal as individual characteristics are analyzed (Fig. 5) [5].

8. TEETH

Dental exemplars are viewed for class and individual characteristics [6]. While dental class characteristics are usually represented by various geometric patterns, individual characteristics are not necessarily geometric in shape, but rather deviations from these patterns (Fig. 6, top). All configurations should be noted, along with the sequence in which they occur. This is done to facilitate comparison with characteristics found on the bitemark exemplar.

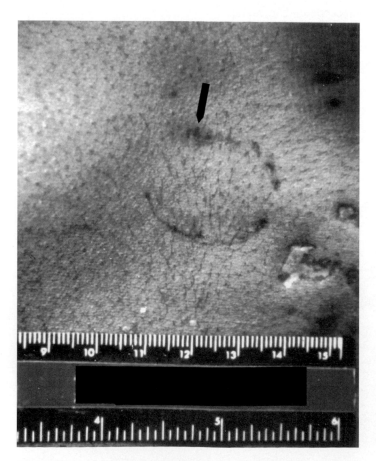

Figure 5   Individual bitemark characteristic. (Courtesy ASTM.)

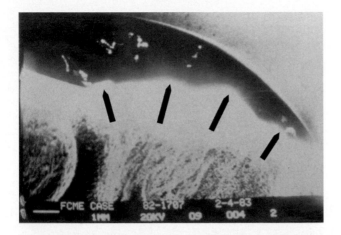

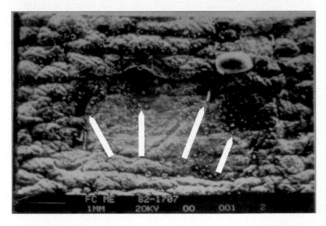

Figure 6   Individual dental characteristics on SEM photograph.

9.   BITEMARK TISSUE

The 3D characteristics found on the exemplar are viewed with specific attention to individual shapes found within the overall bitemark pattern. It should be noted whether the shapes within the bitemark are geometric or nongeometric (Fig. 6, bottom). As with the dental exemplar, the specific configuration of each shape should be documented along with the sequence in which the configurations occur. This process avoids confusing class characteristics with individual characteristics.

10.   DOCUMENTATION

A camera is mounted on the SEM to document what is visualized on the monitor. Newer SEMs relay their images directly to a computer monitor without having to mount a camera. The monitor's bottom left corner integrates a 1-mm scale (Fig. 7) that provides dimensional reference regardless of image magnification. The two-dimensional photographs capture elusive third dimensional characteristics.

Figure 7   Monitor's 1-mm scale. (Courtesy ASTM.)

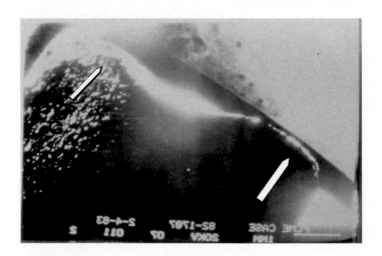

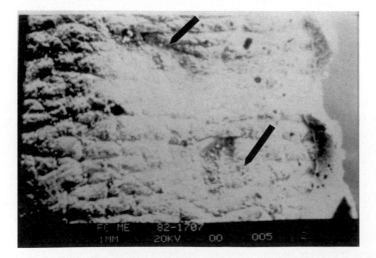

Figure 8   Individual dental characteristics on SEM photograph. (Courtesy ASTM.)

11. INTERPRETATION OF ANALYSIS

The amount of correlation between class and individual characteristics in comparative exemplars can influence the strength of an opinion. Specific attention should be focused on whether configurations represent class or individual characteristics [3]. Special significance is given to the presence of any individual characteristics found in bitemark, teeth, or both (Fig. 8), and whether the configurations found correspond as to shape and sequence (Fig. 6). If both bitemark and suspect dentition contain highly specific characteristics, it is suggestive of a common origin. This evidence should not conflict with other evidence gathered in conventional analysis [5]. Exemplar inaccuracies and interpretation can be sources of conflict. When used appropriately, SEM examination can be a useful adjunct in bitemark analysis.

REFERENCES

1. Beckstead JW, Rawson RD, Giles WS. Review of bite mark evidence. JADA 1979; 99:70.
2. Sognnaes RF, Rawson RD, Gratt BM, Nguyen NBT. Computer comparison of bite mark patterns in identical twins. JADA 1982; 105:449.
3. Sognnaes RF. Forensic bite mark measurements. Dent Survey, April 34, 1970.
4. Sognnaes RF. Forensic identifications aided by scanning electron microscopy of silicone-epoxy microreplicas of calcified and cornified structures, Proceedings of the 33rd Annual Meeting of the Electron Microscopy Society of America, Las Vegas, 1975:678.
5. Vale GL, Sognnaes RF, Felando GN, Noguchi TT. Unusual three-dimensional bite mark evidence in a homicide case. J Forens Sci 1976; 21(3):642.
6. Cottone JA, Standish MS. Outline of Forensic Dentistry, Year Book Medical Publishers. 1982:118.

12

Nonperishables and Perishables

NONINVASIVE ANALYSES

Robert B. J. Dorion
Laboratoire de sciences judiciaires et de médecine légale,
Ministry of Public Security for the Province of Quebec,
Montreal, Quebec, Canada

1. BITEMARKS ON NON-PERISHABLES

Personal identifiers on nonperishables can be analyzed for DNA, fingerprints, and bitemarks. The bitemark quality deposited on these objects will largely depend on the substrate. Impressions left in a solid substrate will give better results than those left in a porous one.

The defendant was arrested during a police raid on his home attempting to chew and ingest a block of hashish (Fig. 1). The suspect presented with no anterior teeth, and a positive impression was made of the imprinted hashish. The three-dimensional dental characteristics were compared to the suspect's dentition for a positive identification. Although this case predates the use of DNA, it vividly demonstrates the application of three-dimensional objects in comparative analysis, despite the fact that few teeth are present. Conversely, the suspect's dental casts can also be directly applied to the block of hashish for a positive match since the substrate retained its original shape.

Styrofoam comes in many thicknesses, shapes, and colors. Teeth will usually imprint fairly accurately in Styrofoam, recording both class and individual characteristics. Coffee/cold drink cups are the most common form of Styrofoam bitten object (Fig. 2). This author reported on the use of Styrofoam as an impression media for registering and analyzing a suspect dentition [1].

Bitemarks are not always associated with criminal acts. The following case illustrates a forensic dentist's contribution in solving a cause of death. A healthy 6-month-old female was found dead in her crib. The autopsy revealed the cause of death as asphyxia and the manner as accidental. The detached distal portion of the synthetic rubber pacifier (Fig. 3, top) was found completely obstructing the trachea. The middle photograph depicts an end view of the handle portion of the pacifier, while the bottom photograph shows a lateral view of the distal end of the pacifier. A pair of adjacent curved patterns each measuring ~ 6 mm can be seen on the rubber. These imprints were consistent with the mesiodistal dimension of the child's two only teeth. Authorities questioned the mother, who revealed that the pacifier had been boiled repeatedly despite the manufacturer's packaged instructions on limiting the procedure. The synthetic rubber had deteriorated upon repeated boiling and a child had bitten/torn off the end of the pacifier. The tragedy could have been averted had the manufacturer's instructions been followed.

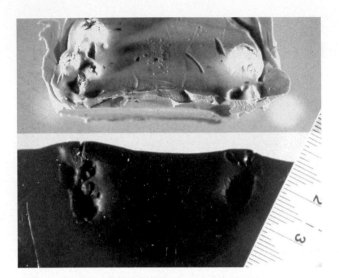

Figure 1   Block of hashish with dental imprints.

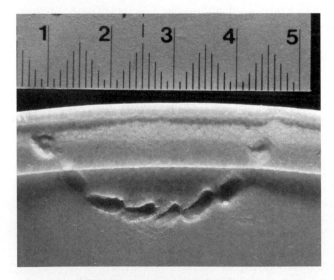

Figure 2   Bitemark on Styrofoam coffee cup.

Figure 3 Two toothprints on a pacifier.

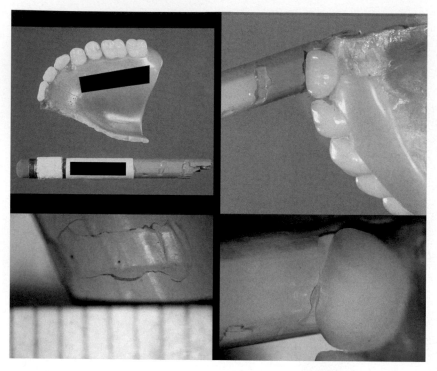

Figure 4 Fragment of complete denture and tooth imprints on a broken pencil.

The following case illustrates that bitemarks left on objects at a crime scene can be valuable evidence for the prosecution. Figure 4 (upper left photo) reveals a portion of a complete upper denture and broken pencil found at a "break and entering" and robbery of an automobile dealership. A suspect was later apprehended with the complementary fragments in the stolen car.

While the match of individual fragments (denture/denture and pencil/pencil) was relatively straightforward, it was interesting to speculate on how the event occurred. If the fracture of pencil and denture occurred simultaneously, it is hypothesized that a left-handed individual placed the pencil in the mouth and bit twice. The uneventful first bite produced the distal notching of the pencil. The second fractured the previously repaired denture and pencil simultaneously (upper right photo). The lower natural teeth (not seen in the photographs) also marked the pencil's underside at the fracture site.

In an unrelated case, a complete upper denture was left at the crime scene. The male homicide victim, a taxi driver, had a full complement of natural teeth. An edentulous suspect was eventually identified as the owner of the denture based on palatal rugae (convolutions on the anterior roof of the palate) comparison. What links the two stories? Is important to remember that personal identifiers, such as complete or partial dentures, lost-discarded at crime scenes must be identified as to ownership.

2. FACTORS AFFECTING BITEMARKS IN PERISHABLES

Bitemarks in perishables present specific problems for the odontologist. Some of the factors affecting bitemarks in perishables have a commonality with those affecting bitemarks on skin.

Webster [2] suggested a method of classification of bitemarks on foodstuff: Type 1 on materials such as chocolate that readily fracture with a limited depth of tooth penetration; Type 2 on materials such as apples where the bitten piece is removed by fracturing it from the main material; Type 3 on materials such as cheese which show the same features as in Type 2 and where there are extensive scrape marks. A commendable classification, but it is too general and does not take into account the many variables outlined in Figure 5.

Dense, semihard chocolate is probably one of the better bitemark impression perishables. Figure 6 demonstrates the three-dimensional dental characteristics recorded in chocolate recovered from a crime scene. Not only is this evidence three-dimensionally stable, but an astute odontologist can direct investigators to the suspect's dental profile. The effect of this diagnosis is immediate and concise. One cannot obtain the perpetrator's physical profile from a fingerprint nor from DNA.

Figure 6 illustrates impressions obtained from chocolate left at the crime scene. Regardless of the analyses, it is important to remember that each specialty should contribute where and how it can. Just as important is the order in which the analysis takes place. Generally speaking, one should go from nondestructive analysis, saving the more invasive and destructive to the last.

FACTORS AFFECTING BITEMARKS IN PERISHABLES*

PERPETRATOR	OBJECT BITTEN	RECORDING	OTHER FACTORS
. MOVEMENT	. AGE OF OBJECT	. ACCURACY IN PHOTOGRAPHY	. EVIDENCE COLLECTION
. FORCE OF BITE	. SIZE	. ACCURACY OF IMPRESSION	. PRESERVATION
. DENTITION:	. WEIGHT	. SEM	. STORAGE
NATURAL	. VOLUME		. TRANSPORTATION
NATURAL AND SYNTHETIC	. NUMBER OF BITES		. ELAPSE OF TIME
SYNTHETIC	. DEPTH OF PENETRATION		. EXTRINSIC FACTORS:
. CLASS CHARACTERISTIC	. AVULSION		CHEMICALS
. INDIVIDUAL CHARATERISTIC	. TYPE OF MATERIAL:		ARTIFACTS
. OCCLUSION	SOLID		CONTAMINATION
. HORIZONTAL INCISAL RELATIONSHIP	SEMI-SOLID		. ENVIRONMENTAL FACTORS:
. DENTAL FRACTURES	POROUS		TEMPERATURE
. DENTAL ANOMALIES	. SURFACE AREA EXPOSED		HUMIDITY
. SINGLE BITE			VENTILATION
. MULTIPLE BITES (OVERLAP)			BACTERIA
. CALCULUS			WATER
. ORAL FLORA			FOREIGN MATERIAL
. FINGERPRINTS			. ENTOMOLOGICAL ACTIVITY
. DNA			. RODENT ACTIVITY

*Modified version of a table first published in the Journal of the Canadian Dental Association and reprinted with kind permission.
RBJ Dorion. Bite mark evidence, JCDA 48:12:795-798, 1982.

Figure 5 Factors affecting bitemarks in perishables.

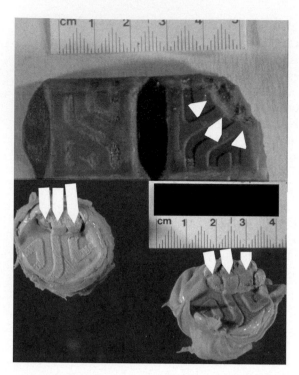

Figure 6   Bitemark in (top), and impressions of the chocolat (bottom).

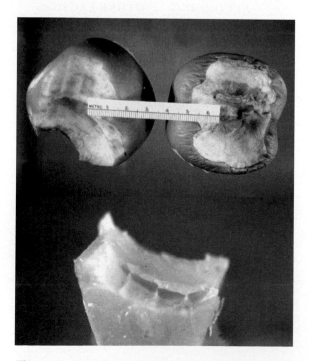

Figure 7   Bitemarks in apples and cheese.

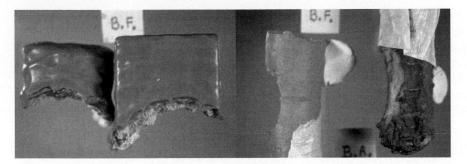

Figure 8 Bitemarks in chocolate and carrots under various experimental conditions.

3. PRESERVATION, STORAGE, AND TRANSPORTATION OF PERISHABLES

The 45 contributors to the bitemark survey of the American Academy of Forensic Sciences, Odontology Section, in 1977 [3] listed only 13 cases of bitemarks on inanimate objects. Of those, only one case had gone to court. The bitemarks on inanimate objects were found in the following materials: cheese, apple, sandwich, candy, chewing gum, wood, leather jacket, and baked clay. The report's conclusion: "the amount of information received was insufficient to form reliable conclusions for evaluating procedural and technical methods employed." This author [4,5] has since reported on the results of experiments on the variables of refrigeration/ nonrefrigeration, bitten/pristine/aging foodstuff, in sealed/unsealed containers over a 7-day period. The food items included apples (Fig. 7), carrots (Fig. 8), cheese (Fig. 7), and a variety of chocolate bars (Fig. 8). The study also included a discussion on the collection of fingerprints, salivary evidence predating DNA evidence, impression techniques, and model production.

4. CONCLUSIONS

In summary, the conclusions were predictable. Bitemarks in perishables, particularly fruits and vegetables, were adversely affected. The greater the number of bitemarks, the more quickly the produce dehydrated and the bitemarks distorted. Dehydration of the perishable and distortion of the bitemark occurred more slowly when the material was placed in a sealable plastic bag. The deterioration was further slowed by placement of the plastic bag in the refrigerator.

As a result, transportation of perishables from crime scene to lab should involve a protocol that requires sealable plastic bags for both contamination/cross-contamination and conservation/ preservation issues. In addition, the specimens should be transported within a Styrofoam container to protect them from temperature changes. Multiple specimens within the Styrofoam container should be separated by packing material (plastic bubbles).

Rudland [6] considered the dimensional stability of bitemarks in apples after long-term storage in a fixative, while Stoddart [7] in a dated study concentrated on a method of producing permanent models from bitemarks in perishable substances. Jarvie and Harvey [8] focused on the preparation of models of teeth and bitemarks in food.

David, et al. [9] considered the dimensional change in bitten foodstuff and methods of preservation under variable conditions over a 1-month period. The materials studied included apples, cheese, chewing gum, and candy bars. The materials were frozen, refrigerated, immersed in glycerin or exposed to the air with/without being sealed in Ziploc bags.

In conclusion, it would be fair to say that few bitemark cases on perishables and nonperishables materials have been reported in the literature. There has been little research in the field, possibly owing to the fact that bitemarks in perishables have the disadvantage of rapid and potentially extreme distortion of bitemark and substrate. In addition, other means of identification can be obtained from the material, notably fingerprints and DNA. In cases where bitemark identification is an issue, the type and quality of the substrate will influence the investigator's ability to arrive at a conclusion.

REFERENCES

1. Dorion RBJ. Styrofoam as an impression material. Presented at American Academy of Forensic Sciences, Las Vegas, Feb. 13–18, 1989.
2. Webster G. A suggested classification of bite marks in foodstuffs in forensic dental analysis. Forens Sci Int 1982; 20:45–52.
3. Dorion RBJ. Chairman, Committee for Recommended Methods, AAFS, Odontology Section. February 1977.
4. Dorion RBJ. Conclusions to research projects in forensic odontology: preservation and transportation of foodstuff with bite mark evidence. AAFS, odontology section, Washington, Feb 16–20, 1976.
5. Dorion RBJ. Preservation in bite mark evidence: inanimate objects, foodstuff and human tissues. AAFS, Odontology Section, Las Vegas, Feb 12, 1985.
6. Rudland M. The dimensional stability of bite marks in apples after long-term storage in a fixative. Med Sci Law 1982; 22:47–50.
7. Stoddart TJ. Bite marks in perishable substances. A method of producing permanent models. Dr. Dent J 1973; 135:285–287.
8. Jarvie JK, Harvey W. The preparation of models of teeth and bite marks in food and on bodies. In: Dental Identification and Forensic Odontology. The Criminologist. London: Kimpton, 1976.
9. David TJ, Haugseth RM, Hauptle MB. A comparative study of methods of preservation of bitemarks in foodstuffs. AAFS, Odontology Section, Seattle, Feb 22, 2001.

13

Tissue Specimens
INVASIVE ANALYSES

Robert B. J. Dorion
*Laboratoire de sciences judiciaires et de médecine légale,
Ministry of Public Security for the Province of Quebec,
Montreal, Quebec, Canada*

1. INTRODUCTION

A pathologist determines whether tissues are normal, abnormal, or diseased. The pathologist's postmortem duty is to examine and excise tissues in order to diagnose disease processes. A forensic pathologist's principal duty is not diagnosing disease processes, but rather deciphering the cause and manner of death. In diagnosing for cause and manner of death, the forensic pathologist might encounter the problem of bitemark recognition.

In a like manner, a dentist's duty is not the same as a forensic dentist's duty. The latter's principal functions are those of confirming identities of the presumed/unknowns, as well as bitemark recognition, diagnosis, interpretation, and comparison. Unless the forensic pathologist also holds a dental degree, it would be a wise and prudent decision for the forensic pathologist to consult with a board-certified forensic dentist. With anyone less educated, knowledgeable, and experienced than a board-certified forensic pathologist performing the initial examination and diagnosis of a bitemark, the greater is the need for consultation with a board-certified forensic dentist. The same principles apply to the dental identification of an unknown/presumed identity even in the most obvious of cases. Failure to perform basic requirements for a dental identification can lead to disaster.

Noninvasive bitemark techniques should always precede the invasive forms. Invasive bitemark techniques should normally be performed on the deceased only. Prior to 1981 pathologists excised bitemarks for two major reasons: confirming the presence/absence of hemorrhage, and to analyze the cellular components for the "timing" of the bitemark. In Figure 1 the unsupported excised and transected specimens highlight distortion and hemorrhage.

Failure to preserve the tissue in its original three-dimensional form (Fig. 2) eliminates the possibility of (1) additional or future and direct analysis of the bitemark; (2) analysis of the relationship among the skin abrasions, erosions, perforations, etc., and the underlying tissue, the inflammatory response, subcutaneous hemorrhage; and (3) direct comparison of the suspect dentition (dental casts) to the bitemark. This last point may be particularly significant if a potential suspect is later detained.

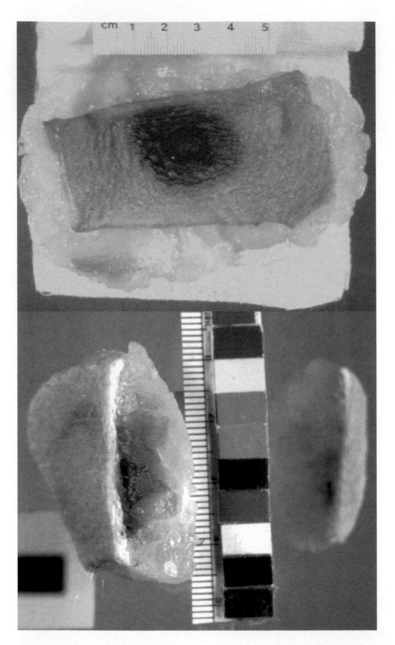

Figure 1 Unsupported excised breast tissue and transected bitemark from an arm.

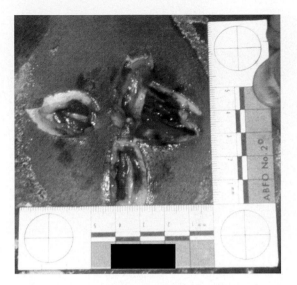

Figure 2   Excised tissue from a bitemark. (Photo courtesy of Dr. Richard Souviron.)

2. SKIN WETNESS

When a body is recovered from an aquatic environment, the skin is wet (hydrated). If recovered from a snow bank it may not only be hydrated but also frozen. Allowing the body to attain room temperature and to "dry out" may reveal important information that might otherwise be imperceptible. The body "wetness" may conceal abrasions including bitemarks. As a body dries, the contrast between abraded and nonabraded skin becomes more apparent. Figure 3 reveals the "wet" breast of the female homicide victim retrieved from a river. As the breast dries (bottom photo), the surface markings become more apparent. One should then further distinguish the surface markings as abrasions from skin creasing/wrinkling/cellulites. The following chapter has an example of skin abrasions on the neck.

3. SKIN DEHYDRATION

Postmortem desiccation is a serious complication in patterned injury assessment. Skin can change color, texture, and shape. The breast configuration and trauma (Fig. 4) cannot readily be visualized or identified. The deceased had been wrapped in a rug for several days in an abandoned apartment. At autopsy the breast was excised using the Dorion technique (Type 2) and rehydrated in a 50% solution of water and glycerin for 1 week.

Following rehydration the specimen had partially regained its color, texture, and shape before insertion into a standard fixative. The breast was rephotographed normally and microscopically. Prior to treatment, it was thought that the indentations and abrasions could have resulted from tooth imprints. That evaluation was quickly dismissed when the treated specimen was viewed with the microscope. The cause of the repetitive, linear, fine, parallel abrasions was ascribed to a razor blade.

4. RING TECHNIQUE AND TISSUE EXCISION

Bitemarks and other patterned injuries are often removed as part of an autopsy protocol. Sopher, the medical examiner/pathologist and dentist, remarked in 1993 that it is the responsibility of

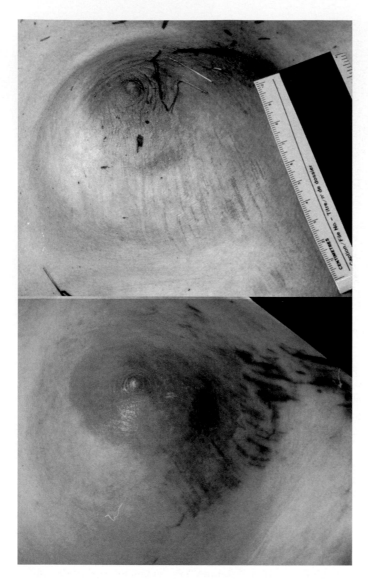

Figure 3 Wet female breast (top) and dried breast (bottom).

the pathologist to recognize a patterned injury as a bitemark, to immediately notify the dental consultant, to use the proper procedures regarding the bitten tissue or substance, and to recover possible secretor substances coating the bitten tissue [1].

The judgment to excise suspected bitten tissue is the forensic dentist's decision to make, and the coroner/medical examiner/pathologist's to approve. Since the coroner/medical examiner/pathologist is the person ultimately responsible for approving excision, it should be noted that failure to grant permission to excise might be considered by the courts, licensing/certifying body, or specialty as professional misconduct, negligence, or incompetence—to say nothing of the potential loss of information that could have ultimately lead to the conviction of the bitemark perpetrator. In a recent article McNamee and Sweet [2] report that 87.5% of diplomates of the American Board of Forensic Odontology excise the bite site.

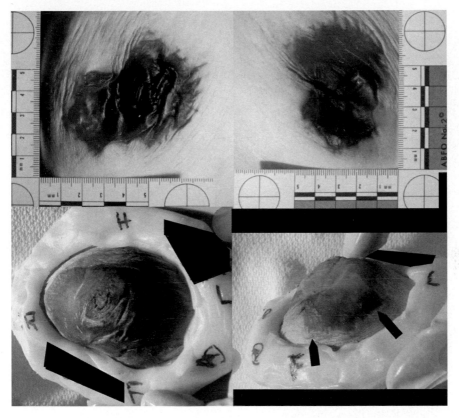

Figure 4 The breast before (top photos) and after (bottom photos) rehydration.

It is known and well documented by forensic pathologist/dentist that unsupported excised tissue may shrink by as much as 50% or more (Fig. 5). In 1981 a method was developed fixing a ring to the excised tissue. The hypothesis being that the ring would support the tissue, acting as an exoskeleton, thus minimize/eliminate tissue distortion [3–7]. The malleable plastic ring Hygon®, formed by mixing powder and monomer liquid, hardened by exothermic reaction. Hygon® is a dental material used in the fabrication of individual trays for dental impressions in prosthodontics. When the ring was formed, cyanoacrylate Krazy Glue® was applied to the ring facing the skin, a technique that became known as the Dorion (Type I) technique. When fixed, the ring was marked for orientation and identification purposes and the tissue excised with the ring. Identification information included the case number, the date, the examiner's initials, and the orientation of the specimen to the body as examples (Fig. 6).

A variety of specimens of known dimension were collected, including tattoos. They were photographed, excised with ring, fixed, stored, and periodically monitored for dimensional change/stability. Other skin specimens collected included those containing stab wounds, ballistic injuries, tire marks, and bitemarks. The pre/postexcision/fixed bitemark was monitored by direct measurement of the specimen, using scaled photograph comparisons, and/or by bitemark impression comparisons. Examples of ring placement on the throat (top of photo), breast (top right photo), pubis (bottom right photo), and shoulder (bottom left photo) are displayed in Figure 6.

TAK® Hydroplastic has replaced Hygon® as the material of choice for ring fabrication. TAK® is a thermoplastic that softens in hot water (145–180°F). The 4- to 5-mm beads come

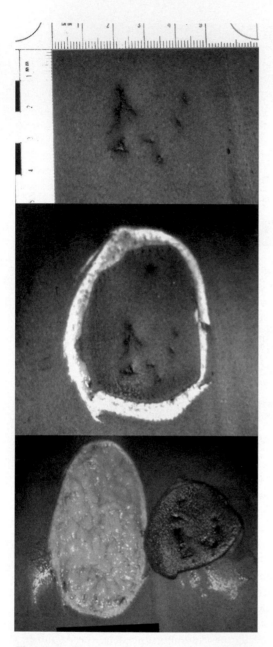

Figure 5 Unsupported excised skin. (Photos courtesy of Dr. Richard Souviron.)

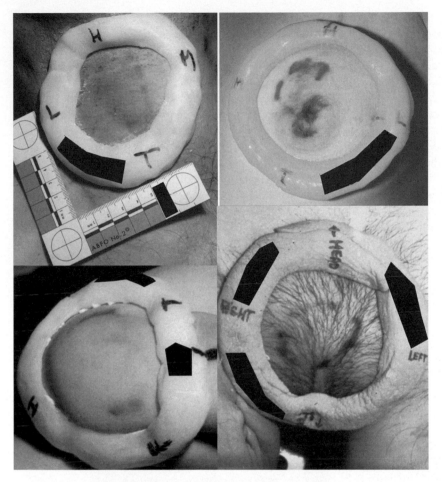

Figure 6 Ring placement on the throat (top left), breast (top right), pubic area (bottom right), and shoulder (bottom left).

in a variety of colors: white, yellow, pink, and blue. The water is microwaved in a beaker until the opaque beads coalesce to become semitransparent. The hydroplastic rehardens in 5–10 min with <1% shrinkage. Maximum rigidity is obtained at 4- to 5-mm thickness, well below the recommended thickness for ring fabrication.

TAK® Hydroplastic is also used as a backing for bitemark impressions. The reader is referred to Chapter 10 for additional reading on the subject. Vinyl polysiloxanes, polyethers, and rubbers are better retained with the adhesive supplied by TAK® Hydroplastic. The advantages of Hydroplastic over Hygon® are:

1. TAK® is self-contained.
2. No mixing of powder and monomer.
3. No exothermic reaction.
4. No smell.
5. Can be remolded and reused.

Ring placement and tissue excision from the shoulder (left photos), arm, and elbow (right photos) are depicted in Figure 7. No specimen is too small, too large, or too tortuous for the ring technique. A modified ring technique has recently been developed making use of Hexcelite® orthopedic tape. Hexcelite® is cut in the form of a ring, water-heated in a microwave, and adapted to the required shape encircling the bitemark. One of the disadvantages of Hexcelite® tape is that it distorts when cooling. The material must be reheated and recooled several times to attain the desired shape to conform to the tissue outline. When the proper form and curvature is achieved, Krazy Glue Gel®, rather than plain Krazy Glue®, is used to fix the Hexcelite® to skin. The adherence is verified making sure that the entire meshwork is attached. Krazy Glue® is reapplied as necessary. A previously prepared TAK® Hydroplastic ring is slightly reheated and applied to the fixed Hexcelite®. Once the ring has hardened, adherence is verified. Krazy Glue Gel® may be reapplied where necessary. The advantage of this technique over the former is that mechanical and chemical bonds are established between orthopedic tape and ring. Since the adhesion of the orthopedic tape to the skin had been previously verified, there is less chance of ring detachment. Since the technique is relatively new, time will reveal whether the additional mechanical/chemical bond is beneficial in retaining ring to skin.

Another application for Hexcelite® orthopedic tape involves its use for large specimens that centrally sag owing to either thinness or bulk. Examples include a massive breast or a large but thin skin specimen from a child's abdomen. Following ring construction with TAK®, Hexcelite®, and Krazy Glue Gel®, additional tape is cut to form a matrix (meshwork) supporting the skin side of the ring. The tape is shaped in the usual manner and temporarily bound to the

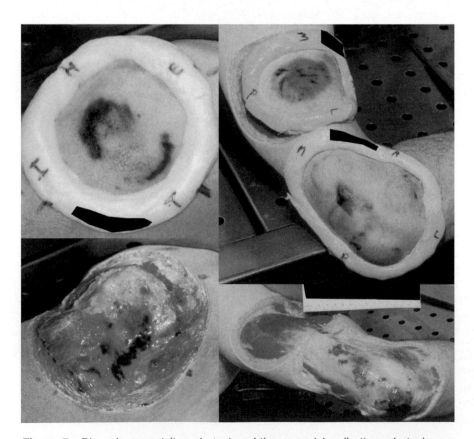

Figure 7   Ring placement (top photos) and tissue excision (bottom photos).

ring and/or the skin with an adhesive that does not contain cyanoacrylate. The additional mesh-work support is then removed after fixation.

Another proposal for ring fabrication makes use of acrylonitrile-butadiene-styrene (ABS) rather than acrylic [8]. Unfortunately, ABS is a difficult material to manipulate, is limited in the number of sizes available, and does not easily achieve the desired contours of the specimen to be excised. This is particularly significant for bitemarks on highly curved surfaces. Additionally, there are no long- or short-term studies on the dimensional stability of the material for use as an excision ring material. There is, however, anywhere between 1 year and 22 years of experience with different acrylics.

Tissue excision should incorporate the entire layer of fat below the skin. If there is bleeding within the muscle, it should be noted and photographed. If the excised specimen contains muscle fiber, it should be removed. Inflammatory response in the form of a vessel engorgement and/ or hemorrhage in the fat should be noted, transilluminated, and photographed. If the layer of fat is thick, gradual layer removal should be achieved until vessel engorgement and/or hemorrhage is observed, noted, transilluminated [9], and photographed. The absence of vessel engorgement and/or hemorrhage should also be noted.

Figure 8 depicts a tattoo excised/fixed (left photo) in 1981 and photographed in 2002. The ring is still attached to the tattooed specimen, and there is virtually no dimensional change in 22 years. Not all supported excised specimens experience the same fate, however. Some rings have detached (Fig. 8, right photo) from the skin. Why do they detach?

Ring detachment can be attributed to three principal factors: temperature, humidity, and the cyanoacrylate itself. Removal of a body from a refrigerated unit necessitates that it attain room temperature before ring fabrication. Complete removal of humidity/condensation/wetness from the skin to be excised is another important attribute. Finally, the cyanoacrylate must be "fresh," which means opening a new tube of material and discarding the unused portion. Other cyanoacrylates such as The Gripper® and Avdel Bond 2® have been used with similar success. Krazy Glue Gel® is currently the adhesive of choice as it can spread more easily and evenly on both skin and ring. Although the manufacturer does not suggest there is a limited shelf life,

Figure 8 Tattoo excised/fixed in 1981 and photographed in 2002 (left). Breast specimen 5 years after excision/fixation is depicted on the right.

it is preferably stored in the freezer or refrigerator and brought to room temperature prior to use. When a bitemark case presents itself, it is not the time to scrounge for the required material. It is important to keep an appropriate supply and to periodically verify the expiry date when it exists.

Some authors suggest suturing ring to skin as an additional means of retention. The technique may inadvertently create distortion of the excised tissue as some sutures may be more tightly drawn than others. It would not matter whether single or continuous sutures are used if distortion results. There have not been long-term studies on the effects of the sutured ring technique.

Rothwell and Thien [10] studied the dimensional stability of excised tissue utilizing a prefabricated template approximating bitemarks in Hanford pigs. The sutured acrylic ring specimens glued with cyanoacrylate were stored in 10% formalin, and measurements were taken for 38 days. The data confirmed this author's findings that a wide range of distortion is expected from dimensionally stable to contraction and expansion of specimens. This author questions, however, the conclusions drawn from the study that "it appears that standard techniques for storage and preservation of bite mark samples does not produce reliable dimensional accuracy." The dimensional stability of the acrylic ring material (Formatray) used in the study is untested as well as the effects of suturing. The removal of the underlying subdermal tissue before fixation is not what is recommended in standard technique. Figure 1 of the article [10] demonstrates that the pig has already been sectioned in various parts of the body before the stamp and acrylic ring had been applied. What were the effects of this preexisting sectioning, rigor mortis, tension lines, etc., on the results? Was the experimental animal refrigerated, frozen, etc.? The authors point out that "other distortion factors in the indentations themselves and changes in skin coloration made measurements difficult and in some cases were virtually impossible," and that "the experimental 'bites' made in this study are not directly analogous to those seen in the majority of cases investigated in human skin bite marks."

Dimensional stability of ringed excised specimens is influenced, in part, by the following factors:

1. The temperature and humidity of the specimen prior to excision
2. The size of the excised specimen (width and thickness)
3. The size of defect(s) if the skin is punctured
4. The dimensional stability of the ring
5. The type and the "age" of the adhesive
6. Adherence of the ring to skin (without suturing)
7. The fixative
8. The time allotted for fixation
9. The storage conditions
10. Postfixation storage conditions.

When the preceding factors are controlled, minimal distortion can be expected in most instances of tissue excision [11–14].

Is tissue excision ever contraindicated? The ring technique of excision may be contraindicated under very few circumstances. These may include the following rare conditions/circumstances:

1. If the specimen is to difficult to access
2. If placement of the ring is impossible or impractical
3. If the body part to be excised is too large

4. If the resulting facial mutilation is a genuine aesthetic concern when the body is to be exposed
5. If sample bitemark(s) is/are excised in a multiple bitemark case, and the perpetrator(s) can be shown to be the same animal or person(s) responsible for the other bites.

The commonest reasons cited for failing to excise bitemarks on the deceased are:

1. Fear of potential lawsuits and/or family or political repercussions
2. Tissue shrinkage
3. There is no forensic dentist in the jurisdiction
4. Economic/financial issues
5. Never had a bitemark case in the jurisdiction.

A bitemark is an important piece of evidence that may solve a crime. It should be treated as such and dealt with accordingly. Failure to take appropriate measures might be interpreted as obstruction to justice, professional negligence/malpractice, and/or incompetence.

5. TISSUE FIXATION

Following excision and prior to fixation, photographs are taken when the transilluminated specimen reveals blood vessel engorgement or subcutaneous bleeding. Generally speaking, a specimen is fixed for at least 1 week depending on tissue thickness and size. Larger specimens needing additional support should float freely in the formaldehyde bath. The skin side of the specimen should be facing but not touching the bottom of the container. Should specimen support be required, one is devised that will contact the ring rather than the tissue. Plastic autopsy containers have been cut transversely, forming rings of various sizes as a means of additional support.

The fixative used at the Laboratoire de sciences judiciaires et de médecine légale for bitemark specimens is either: (1) 4% formaldehyde by volume. "Formalin" is 40% formaldehyde in water. Ten percent formalin is equal to one part formalin in nine parts water; or (2) a solution of 5 mL 40% formaldehyde, 5 mL 99.8% glacial acetic acid, and 90 mL 70% ethanol.

The fixed specimen is removed from the bath of formaldehyde the following week to assess dimensional stability and adherence to the ring. It may be rephotographed before placement in a sealed plastic container (or bag) properly identified and stored in a refrigerated room (or refrigerator) in a secure area. The specimen should be rephotographed as necessary over time.

In addition to tissue distortion resulting from excision of unsupported tissue, fixation itself can also contribute to shrinkage. Distortion due to fixation of supported "ringed" tissue varies depending on circumstance. Dorion reported [15] a postfixation dimensional stability of $< + 0.81\%$ but $> - 3.23\%$ in an 11-year study. This means that some of specimens might have "shrunk" by as much as 3.23% while others might have "expanded" by as much as 0.81%. The latter is the result of the tissue sagging in the central portion of the excised specimen. The specimens collected between 1981 and 1991 were of various sizes and shapes and included facial and head specimens, ear, thorax, arm, breast, pubis, thigh, and calf. They exhibited injury patterns from gunshot, knife, and saw wounds; tire tract injuries; and bitemarks. "Open" injuries from gunshot, knife, and saw wounds were different in shrinkage from those having "closed" injuries with tire marks and bitemarks. As a whole, tissue shrinkage/expansion was minimized when using the ring and cyanoacrylate technique.

Brzozowski et al. [16] studied the comparison of dimensional stability of excised patterned injuries using various fixatives in a preliminary study and the following year [17] focused on a comparative study of materials and methods used for collecting, stabilizing, and preserving excised tissue. In the preliminary study the fixatives used where: (1) neutral 10% buffered formalin; (2) modified Millonigs solution (formaldehyde 37%, distilled water, sodium phosphate monobasic, and sodium hydroxide); (3) Prefer, a biodegradable fixative made of glyoxal, 20% ethanol, and a buffer (designed to replace formalin and zinc formalin as a fixative for histology and surgical pathology). Prefer is available from Anatech Ltd., 1020 Harts Lake Road, Battle Creek, MI 49015 (800-ANATECH or 616-964-6450).

A 2-inch square rubber stamp divided into quarter-inch grades with a centrally located circle of 1-inch diameter. The pattern was stamped on postmortem porcine skin then excised to the dermal layer with a PVC ring support, eight 3–0 silk black sutures, and cyanoacrylate glue. Samples were stored at room temperature with color photographs taken preincision, postexcision, and postfixation. Measurements were taken with a dial Vernier caliper at weekly intervals for the first 6 weeks and then at monthly intervals thereafter. P values, standard deviations, and variances for each of the materials and fixatives used are being evaluated. At the time of writing there appears to be no significant difference among the fixatives: Millonigs, formalin, and Prefer. Most tissue dimensional change occurs at the excisional stage with more changes occurring on curved excised tissue than on flat surfaces. All samples remained stable after fixation over a 12-month period.

This author in an attempt to further minimize shrinkage devised a variety of experiments. In one experiment, the skin was completely covered with impression material within the supporting ring prior to excision. Following fixation, the impression material was removed only to find the skin had completely wrinkled (Fig. 9). The wrinkling was probably due to an uneven fixation rate between the exposed fatty side and the protected skin side.

Another aggravating problem involves the written information or identification markers placed on the supporting ring. Over time, the fixative has removed some of the written informa-

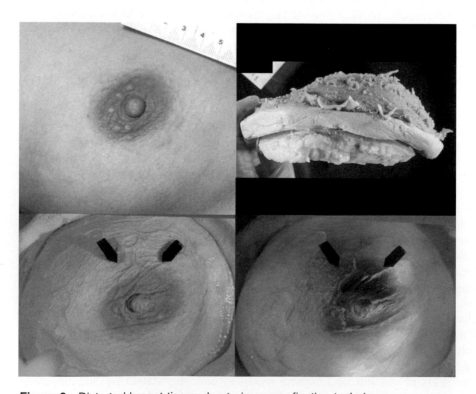

Figure 9 Distorted breast tissue due to improper fixation technique.

tion. A variety of markers have been tested including pencils, ink and indelible pens, and grease pencils. The most effective, long-lasting markings were made with a grease pencil.

6. TISSUE STORAGE

As previously mentioned, the fixed supported "ringed" excised specimen is placed in an identified sealed plastic container such as Tupperware® or a sealed bag preferably in a refrigerated unit, or otherwise at room temperature. When the specimen is initially placed in a refrigerated unit, it has the effect of slowing the fixation rate to further minimize distortion. Twenty-two years of postfixation storage favors permanent formaldehyde emersion of the excised ringed tissue in a sealed plastic container such as Tupperware® and placed in a refrigerated unit over bagging.

Several methods of bagging have been experimented with. The bagged specimen has been in contact with or without gauze-impregnated formaldehyde and placed in a refrigerated unit or at room temperature. Leaving the postfixation specimen in a sealed plastic bag without impregnated formaldehyde gauze at room temperature lead to a combination of dehydration, shrinkage, and/or detachment of the ring over time.

7. TRANSPORTATION

Should displacement of the specimen become necessary, it should be transported in an additional container, preferably made out of Styrofoam. This latter material is strong, light, and tolerates environmental and temperature changes.

8. TRANSILLUMINATION

Transillumination is a technique whereby light is transmitted through an excised specimen. Transillumination is paramount when skin indentations or abrasions are present, and/or the identity of the causative agent is to be confirmed or is unknown. If the tissue specimen exhibits an inflammatory response notably vascular engorgement or subcutaneous hemorrhage it can readily be observed. The equipment setup for transillumination includes (Fig. 10 top photo):

1. X-ray film illuminator model 188 with variable rheostat made by S. &. S. X-Ray Products, Inc.
2. A 5-mm-thick round glass plate (15 cm in diameter) mounted on the x-ray film illuminator
3. A 75 watt soft light bulb
4. Sheets of Styrofoam: 1.25 cm thick perforated in the center to various diameters
5. Photographic equipment: standard camera, digital camera, video digital camera
6. A photographic mounting table
7. Side-mounted variable-intensity photoflood lamps.

The additional benefits of conserving supported excised fixed tissue and the use of transillumination include:

1. The possibility of performing three-dimensional analysis of the patterned injury
2. To confirm the presence/absence of the inflammatory response (blood vessel engorgement and/or subcutaneous bleeding) without having to cut through the specimen
3. The ability to analyze the relationship between the skin trauma (indentations, abrasions, etc.) and the inflammatory response

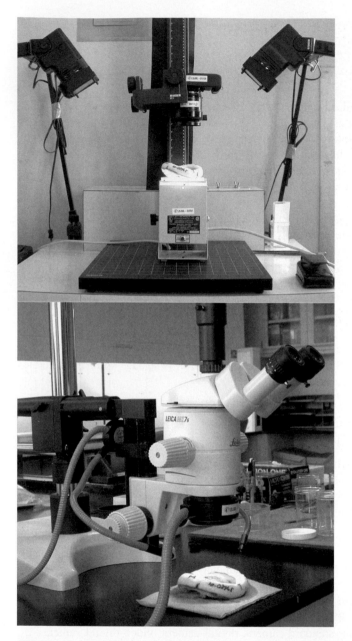

Figure 10 Illuminator/camera stand setup (top) and microscope/camera/fiber optic setup (bottom).

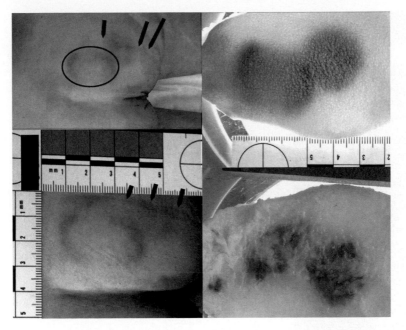

Figure 11 Diaper indentation (arrows) adjacent to bitemark (oval) and a bruise. Transilluminated bitemark and bruise (right photos).

4. A means for an eventual direct and/or indirect three-dimensional comparison of the patterned injury to the causative agent (tire, knife, dentition, or other objects etc.).

Blood vessel engorgement and subcutaneous bleeding (hemorrhage) is an affirmation of antemortem trauma. Figure 11 exhibits bruising, a bitemark (within the oval in the upper left photo), and diaper indentations (marked by the black arrows) on the buttocks of the deceased child. Both the bruising and bitemark were hemorrhagic rather than blood vessel engorgement. The photos (Fig. 11on the right) depict the transilluminated specimen, skin side and underside.

Bitemarks can involve one or two teeth only, if the biter was almost edentulous, for example. The dental imprints can be on one side of the body with the antagonist imprints on the opposite side. Figure 12 depicts over five superimposed bitemarks on the anterior and lateral surface of a child's thigh. The individual bitemarks appear more like bruises on the thigh, but are clearly identified as bitemarks in the transilluminated tissue.

Figure 13 depicts a bitemark on the right thigh of a female homicide victim and the excised and transilluminated specimen. Figure 14 represents various views of a transilluminated bitemark from the shoulder while Figure 15 depicts a bitemark on the pubis of a female homicide victim. One arch can be identified while the opposing arch is somewhat obscured.

9. THE MICROSCOPE

The microscope setup can be used with or without (Fig. 10, bottom photo) the equipment used for transillumination:

1. A Leica MZ 75 microscope
2. A Volpi Intralux 6000–1 fiber optic lamp with variable rheostat

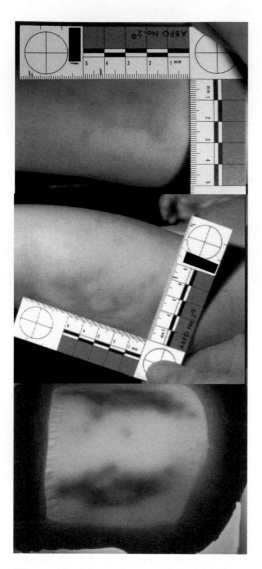

Figure 12   Bitemarks on child's thigh (top, middle) and transilluminated specimen (bottom).

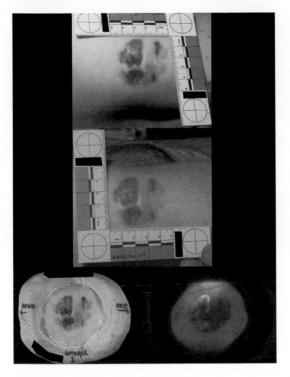

Figure 13 Bitemark on an adult female thigh, excised and transilluminated specimen. Also see color photograph insert section.

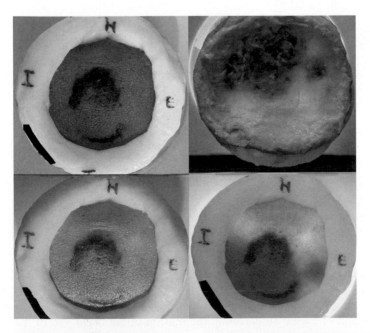

Figure 14 Different views of excised and transilluminated bitemark on a shoulder. Also see color photograph insert section.

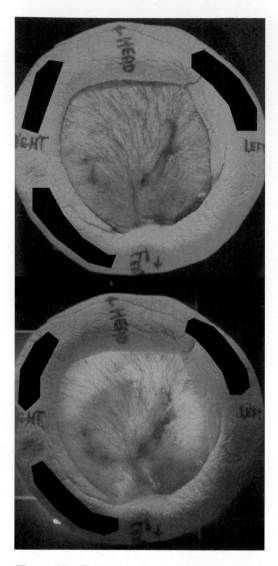

Figure 15 Excised and transilluminated bitemark on the pubis.

3. Side-mounted fiber optic lamps
4. Various adapters for the microscope
5. The equipment setup for transillumination.

Figure 16 illustrates a bitemark on the shoulder where both class and individual dental characteristics can be observed. The arrows on the lower right photograph outline barely perceptible
contusions attributable to two additional lower teeth. Also note the tooth rotation adjacent to
the barely perceptible contusions.

Figure 17 is a magnification of Figure 16 depicting the imprint of the upper and of the
lower teeth. Note the parallel striations within the bitemark representing the T-shirt fibers being
compressed and dragged on the skin by the perpetrator's teeth.

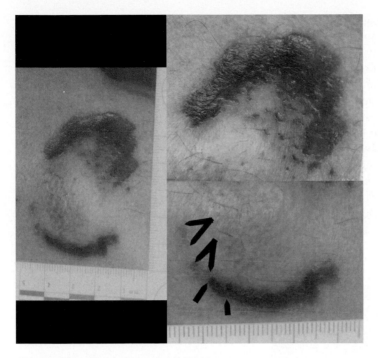

Figure 16 Bitemark on a shoulder.

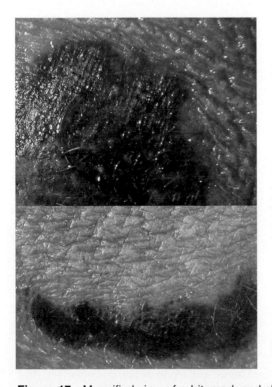

Figure 17 Magnified view of a bitemark and clothing imprint.

Figure 18 depicts various magnifications of the bitemark produced by the perpetrator's upper teeth. Note the creasing of skin immediately adjacent to the incisors' impact. The blood vessels are clearly engorged in the absence of subcutaneous bleeding. There are three phenomena occurring simultaneously: (1) compression of tissue by the upper and lower dental arches; (2) compression of the T-shirt into the bitemark; and (3) dragging of the upper dental arch. This is an unusual bitemark since the upper teeth are dragged. This could have resulted from victim movement rather than jaw closure. Normally the lower teeth are dragged as a result of jaw closure. In other cases both upper and lower teeth are dragged. Figures 17–19 required a combination of off-angle lightning from above and transillumination from below the specimen to view the striations and the blood vessel engorgement.

Blood vessel engorgement and subcutaneous bleeding/hemorrhage are vital tissue responses that can only occur if the recipient is alive at the time of trauma. Placing the bitemark perpetrator at the crime scene and being able to evaluate the amount of pain suffered by the recipient (e.g., perforated tissue) may be critical in a capital case. The presence of DNA does

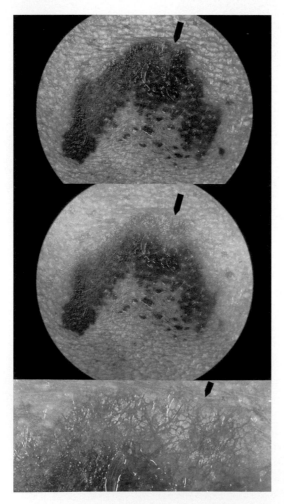

Figure 18   Microscopic view of bitemark, transillumination, and blood vessel engorgement. Also see color photograph insert section.

Figure 19 Magnified view of bitemark, blood vessel engorgement, and clothing imprint. Also see color photograph insert section.

not indicate the timing of the incident, or if there was any clothing at the bite site, or the degree of force applied, or the perpetrator's intent. The bitemark can.

The presence/lack of inflammatory response coupled with the presence of indented or perforated tissue can give an indication of the timing of the bitemark. A total absence of the inflammatory response (vascular engorgement or hemorrhage) coupled with tissue indentations and perforations attributable to the dentition would indicate the bitemark was inflicted postmortem (Fig. 22).

Figure 20 (top photos) illustrates imprints from the upper central incisors photographed normally and transilluminated. Note the absence of subcutaneous hemorrhage and the barely perceptible blood vessel engorgement. The bottom photos view abrasions of unknown etiology on the nipple with neither blood vessel engorgement nor subcutaneous hemorrhage.

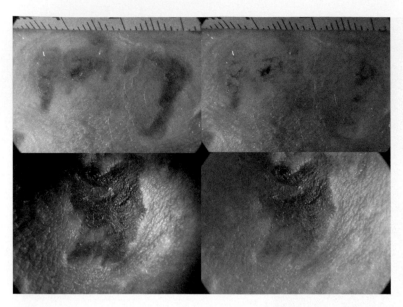

Figure 20   Imprints of upper centrals and transilluminated tissue (top photos). Abrasions of unknown etiology on the nipple (bottom photos). Also see color photograph insert section.

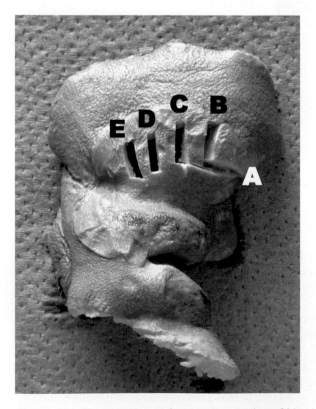

Figure 21   Five tissue cuts for the preparation of histology slides.

10. HISTOLOGY

Histology will be dealt with at length in the following chapter. Suffice it to say that histology examination is the last of the invasive techniques. All of the previous noninvasive and invasive techniques should have been considered if not implemented prior to making histology sections. Once histology sections have been obtained, the excised specimen is rendered useless for bitemark analysis and comparison.

Figures 21 and 22 illustrates various cuts, ''A'' through ''E'', of indentations on the skin from which histological sections were made. The transilluminated tissue (middle photo in Fig. 22)

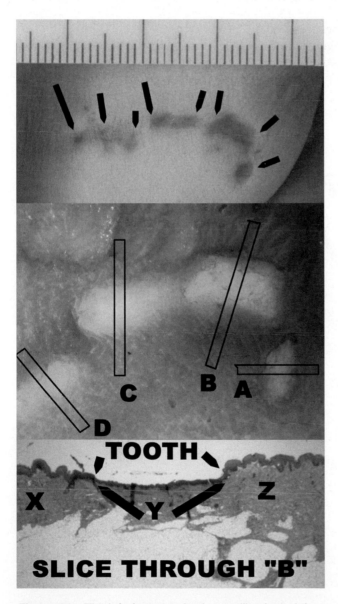

Figure 22   Thigh indentation (top), transilluminated tissue (middle), histology slide (bottom).

shows neither blood vessel engorgement nor subcutaneous hemorrhage. It is important when cutting and subsequently reading histological sections that the areas adjacent to the tooth impact be examined for tissue changes including blood vessel engorgement and subcutaneous hemorrhage. Figure 22 bottom photograph illustrates the necessity of examining areas denoted by X, Y, and Z. It should also be noted in the same example, if areas A, B, C, D, and E represent sections through individual tooth imprints, the sections not represented adjacent to the tooth imprints could contain an inflammatory response as a result of the pinching action between the teeth but would not be seen in the histology slide selection.

Blood vessel engorgement and/or hemorrhagic patterns are associated with:

1. The incisal/occlusal/lingual surfaces of teeth or a combination thereof (e.g., Figure 18)
2. Tissue being "pinched" between teeth
3. A form of blunt trauma injury, adjacent to the site of impact produced by individual teeth (e.g., Fig. 29 in the color insert section, black arrows)
4. Produced by the crushing/compression of tissue between the dental arches (example of Figure 14) and
5. Produced by a negative pressure on the tissue (sucking).

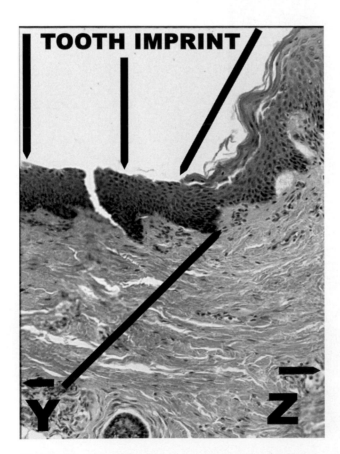

Figure 23   Histology slide of a tooth imprint showing no vessel engorgement or hemorrhage.

11. POSTFIXATION AND STORAGE

Figure 24 depicts two excised bitemarks and the transilluminated tissue. The freshly excised bitemark on an arm on the left and the 2-year-old excised breast on the right clearly show different characteristics of the bitemark. The arm bitemark is basically a compression injury whereas the breast specimen shows no hemorrhage with slight vascular engorgement in the indentations created by the central incisors.

Figure 25 delineates four bitemarks on a male homicide victim's elbow (left photos), and a bitemark on a female homicide victim's shoulder. The hemorrhagic patterns on the elbow are attributed to the dentition whereas the one on the shoulder is a compression injury resulting from the crushing and pulling of tissue between the dental arches as well as by the individual teeth. The shoulder specimen had been excised and fixed 6 years previously. The specimen has remained dimensionally stable since the autopsy despite its curvature. This can be verified through photographic, impression, and tissue comparison.

Figure 26 represents the same bitemark on the shoulder and transilluminated one year later (7 years since excision) while Fig. 27 is a magnified version of the former showing the upper anterior teeth imprints (abrasions) and contusions.

Figure 28 depicts a transilluminated bitemark photographed following the autopsy and 3 years later. What has happened to the blood vessel engorgement/subcutaneous hemorrhage? It appears to have disappeared! This phenomenon was first reported at the American Academy of Forensic Sciences annual meeting in 1992 [15]. At the time, it was attributed to dilution of the red blood cells (RBC) in the fixative or to RBC blanching. Whatever the reason(s), the importance

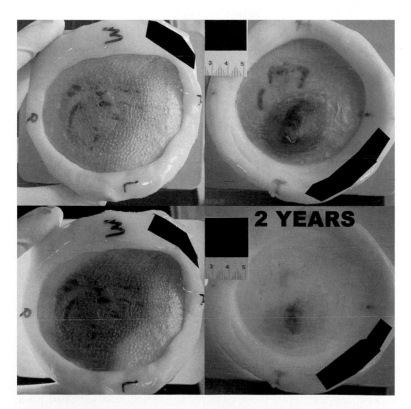

Figure 24 Excised and transilluminated bitemarks on arm (left) and breast (right).

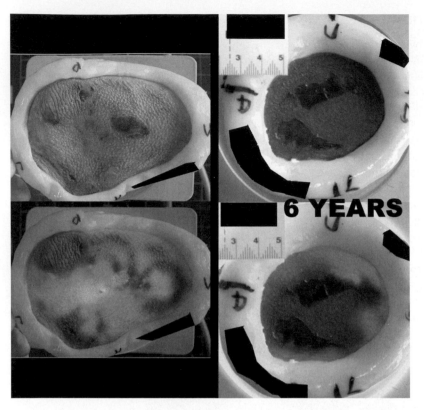

Figure 25 Excised and transilluminated tissue: arm/elbow (left), shoulder (right). Also see color photograph insert section.

of photographing the specimen upon excision and prior to fixation particularly when blood vessel engorgement/subcutaneous hemorrhage exists cannot be overemphasized.

Figure 29 (top photo) displays two sets of indented bruises at right angles to each other superior to the navel on a child's abdomen. At first glance, the suspicious marks lack both class and individual characteristics to classify them as bitemarks. Excision and transillumination of the tissue (bottom photo) clearly demonstrate that the indentations represent sets of maxillary deciduous central incisors. There are, in fact, two bitemarks at right angles to each other. Blunt trauma injury, a well-known principle in forensic pathology, can be observed from the impact of the left central maxillary incisor (see color insert section). The hemorrhagic pattern surrounds the dental imprint from the left incisor. There is no corresponding blood vessel engorgement or hemorrhage associated with the adjacent incisor. This photograph is an excellent example of the potential of transillumination. Not only was transillumination essential to the diagnosis and confirmation of bitemarks, but also clearly identifies the perpetrator's dentition as a child's. Transillumination also serves to indicate where to excise the tissue for ulterior histological analysis. There are other advantages for the forensic dentist. This type of injury lends itself to the study of indentations and its association with the hemorrhage by ''layering'' in computer analysis.

Lastly, Figure 30 demonstrates once again the need to photograph the excised tissue prior to fixation. The specimen has ''lost'' its hemorrhage over the years.

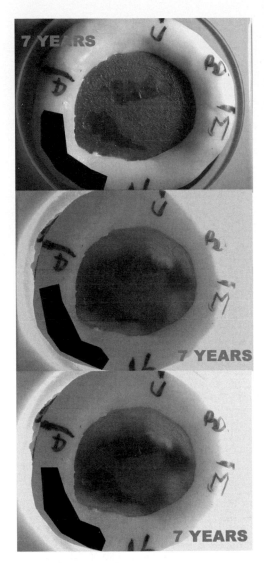

Figure 26 Transilluminated bitemark on the shoulder 7 years postexcision. Also see color photograph insert section.

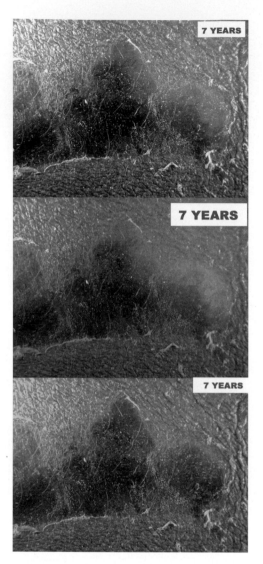

Figure 27 Closeup transilluminated bitemark on the shoulder 7 years postexcision. Also see color photograph insert section.

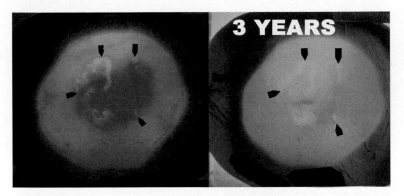

Figure 28 Transilluminated bitemark at autopsy (left) and 3 years later (right).

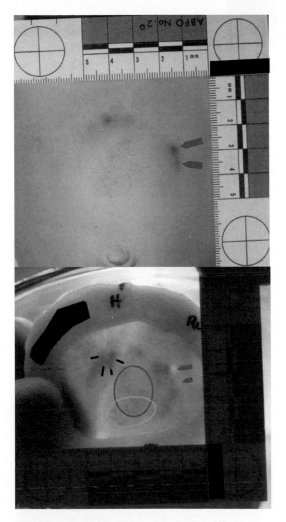

Figure 29 Suspicious marks on abdomen and transilluminated specimen. Also see color photograph insert section.

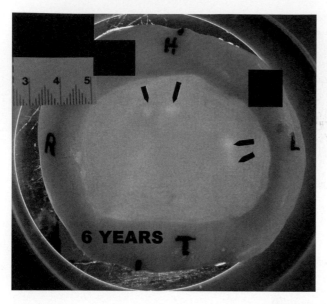

Figure 30 Transilluminated tissue 6 years postexcision/fixation.

REFERENCES

1. Sopher IM. In Spitz WU, Ed. Medical Legal Investigation of Death: Guidelines for the Application of Pathology to Crime Investigation. 3rd ed.. Springfield. IL: Charles C. Thomas, 1993:127.
2. McNamee AH, Sweet D. Adherence of forensic odontologists to the ABFO guidelines for victim evidence collection. J Forens Sci 2003; 48(2):382–385.
3. Dorion RBJ. Preliminary research on the preservation of traumatic injury patterns. Can Soc Forens Sci., Hamilton, ON, 1981.
4. Dorion RBJ. Preliminary research on the preservation of traumatic injury patterns. AAFS. Orlando. FL, Feb. 1982.
5. Dorion RBJ. Preservation and fixation of skin for ulterior scientific evaluation and courtroom presentation. J Can Dent Assoc 1984; 50(2):129–130.
6. Dorion RBJ, Preservation of and transillumination in bite mark evidence AAFS meeting, odontology section, Anaheim, Feb. 21–25, 1984.
7. Dorion RBJ. Preservation of bitemark evidence: inanimate objects, foodstuffs and human tissues. American Society of Forensic Odontology, Las Vegas, Feb. 12, 1985.
8. Sweet DJ, Bastien RB. Use of an acrylonitrile-butadiene-styrene (ABS) plastic ring as a matrix in the recovery of bite mark evidence. J Forens Sci 1991; 36(5):1565–1571.
9. Dorion RBJ. Transillumination in bite mark evidence. J Forens Sci 1987; 32(3):690–697.
10. Rothwell BR, Thien AV. Analysis of distortion in preserved bite mark skin. J Forens Sci 2001; 46(3): 573–576.
11. Dorion RBJ. Bite mark recovery, preservation and forensic aspects of physical evidence. Council on Dental Practice, ADA, Chicago, March 26, 1999.
12. Dorion RBJ. Bitemarks in life and in death. Detection and recovery of human remains. Child Abduction and Serial Killer Unit, Evidence Recovery Team (ERT), FBI Quantico May 21, 1999.
13. Dorion RBJ. Forensic dentistry overview and bitemark evidence. Regional Organized Crime Information Center. Lexington. KY, June 8, 1999.
14. Dorion RBJ. Pitfalls in documenting and preserving bitemark evidence in pediatric deaths, American AAFS meeting, odontology section, Seattle, 2001.

15. Dorion RBJ. Lifting, preserving, storing and transporting skin: an eleven year study, AAFS meeting, odontology section, New Orleans, Feb 22, 1992.
16. Brzozowski CC, Nawrocki LA, Friedman BK. A comparison of dimensional stability of excised patterned injuries using various fixatives: a preliminary study, AAFS meeting, odontology section, Feb. 1999.
17. Brzozowski CC, Nawrocki LA, Friedman BK. A comparative study of materials and methods used for collecting, stabilizing, and preserving excised tissue, AAFS meeting, odontology section, Reno, Feb. 26, 2000.

14

Histology and Timing of Injury

INVASIVE ANALYSES

Joseph H. Davis
Medical Examiner Department, Miami-Dade County
Florida, U.S.A.

1. DID A BITE OCCUR AND IF SO, WHEN?

Bitemarks may occur on any surface of the body, including the tongue. Bitemarks may be self-inflicted or inflicted by some other person or animal, including insects. Documentation and interpretation of a bitemark are complex and raise many questions. One such question may pertain to the temporal relation of the bite. Bitemark infliction may have occurred before, at the time of, or after death. In life, the patient may or may not be able to provide an accurate history of the event. It is incumbent upon investigators to gather all circumstantial data and attempt to verify the victim's account.

2. TIMING OF BRUISES; TEXTBOOK DISCORDANCE

The healing response of tissue to injury applies only to the living. Conversely, bitemark injury occurring at or after death cannot produce this response. When healing reaction is evident, it may assist in estimating the approximate time of injury. Many variables affect the precision of such estimates, especially those concerning the histopathology of bruising. Spitz discusses color changes over time and opines that microscopic examination is "considerably more reliable" than color changes [1]. DiMaio and DiMaio opine that histology "can be disposed of very rapidly" because consistent microscopic dating is impossible [2]. In neither text does there appear a detailed justification for the expressed opinions.

3. COMPONENTS OF A BITEMARK—GROSS

The gross appearance of an acute bitemark reveals combinations of abrasions, contusions, sometimes laceration from breaking of skin, or intradermal capillary hemorrhages. Variables of site, variables of skin tissue thickness and health, variables of positional relationships, variables of interposed clothing, variables of forces and dynamics, all serve to alter the type and appearance of injury and reactions to the injuries. The microscopic findings add to this spectrum as noted below.

4. ABRASION

The most prominent visible part of a bitemark pattern is abrasion. As commonly used by pathologists, an abrasion is a loss of epidermis by scraping, exposing the dermis. However, what

257

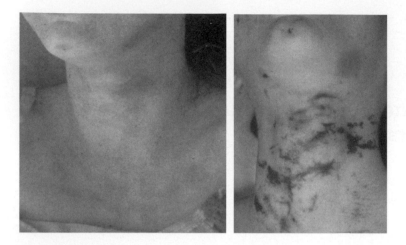

Figure 1 Strangled woman found in water. Undiscerned neck abrasions when wet, revealed when dry. Also see color photograph insert section.

grossly appears as a scrape abrasion may be a compression of the epidermis when viewed microscopically. Hence the terminology of a gross abrasion may allude to two different histological patterns—compression and scraping. A scrape abrasion may be superficial or deep. A deep abrasion may result in some damage to the capillaries in the dermis and result in leakage of erythrocytes and plasma which create a crust during a healing process. Abrasions become firm as they dry. If moisture is present, an abrasion may not be visible.

Figure 1 illustrates a female victim of manual strangulation who was found in a canal. Initial photographs of the damp skin of the throat revealed almost no evidence of abnormality. After drying in the morgue refrigerator, the anterolateral neck region contained a mass of irregular abrasions. These were present earlier but were obscured by dampness. A body found in the rain or removed from water may have a bitemark that is overlooked at the scene but becomes visible at the morgue. The longer it dries, the more intense becomes the contrast between abraded and nonabraded skin. That may also lead to confusion as to its time relation to death.

5.   CONTUSION/BRUISE

A contusion is an escape of blood from damaged capillaries into surrounding tissue. The contusion portion of a bitemark is variable depending on the forces applied and the nature of the tissue. Skin and subcutaneous tissue vary widely over the body of a person. The highly vascular loose tissue near the orbits on the face is different in bruising capability from the tight skin over the cartilage of the ear. A bruise may be superficial or deep. It may be a more or less obvious component of a visible bitemark.

When blood escapes into soft tissue, it infiltrates and tends to follow lines of least resistance. Spread is affected by the amount of vascular injury, vital pressure in the arteries, and the nature of the tissue. Blood may track for long distances under unique circumstances. This author has incurred a minor tear of a deep gluteal muscle during a minor fall. No local surface coloration occurred, but blue discoloration of the toes became apparent 1 week later. One mitigating factor may have been the use of cardioprotective low-dose maintenance aspirin.

Can a body bruise after death? Certainly, if the forces applied are sufficient, blood is still fluid and tissue is still loose enough to permit gravitational ooze of blood. A man bludgeoned his wife to death, then shot himself in the temple with a handgun and was found in a sitting position back to the wall. His face appeared normal. Two hours later the attendants stretched him out on the floor. A large swollen black eye rapidly arose caused by gravitational oozing of blood into the orbit whose roof was fractured by the intracranial forces associate with the bullet. Similar prominent hemorrhages of the eyelids, mainly upper, can occur following post-mortem removal of the eyes. These examples serve to indicate the variables of flow of blood during and after-death. With a bitemark, the chances are that the amount of contusion is too small to yield dramatic variations. However, a dependent postmortem position assures additional after death leakage of blood into the initial contusion.

6. LACERATION

A laceration is an actual break through the skin into deeper tissue. Some bitemarks include a laceration component that should be readily apparent. Avulsion, the tearing away of tissue, may occur with severe biting.

7. AGING OF A BRUISE

Estimation of the duration of an injury may become an issue during legal proceedings. A defendant may admit to biting but may claim that it was consensual and occurred long before death. Careful documentation of physical characteristics of the wound, both macroscopic and microscopic, is indicated. The gross documentation includes photography with linear and color balance scales and proper lighting. Highlights from flash photography should be avoided. A careful documentation of the presence or absence of skin indentations should be made. In life, indentations of skin are ephemeral, lasting only several minutes. After death, without vital circulation in the tissues, they may persist until decomposition occurs. Artifacts of postmortem drying, insect activity, especially ants, or decomposition should be documented. Proper documentation has another value. A bite that leaves permanent scarring in the living victim may be just cause for a criminal charge of aggravated battery.

Healing processes are one avenue to estimate the duration of an injury in a living person but only if healing processes may be demonstrated. The absence of reaction may not be as valuable as the presence of a healing reaction. Reaction varies depending on the size and location of the wound as well as the physical status of the victim.

In the living, color changes of contusion blood may indicate a time frame as the bruise changes from blue to yellow-green to yellow and finally fades from view. Bruises vary from case to case in their color change. Also, observers differ from one another in their ability to notice color changes. Ambient light affects color estimates. Observers do not see things in a uniform manner [3]. Cultural differences affect our perception of color. In the Kalahari Desert of Botswana, with an almost perpetual blue sky and rare rainfall, a single Setswana word exists for green and blue, whereas nearly a dozen exist for shades of brown, the color of foliage, ground, and cattle, which represent wealth (B. Davis, personal communication, 2003). An artist may note color shifts in photographs unnoticed by the nonartist. Human variables of perception may detract from the use of color change as a factor in time estimation.

Bitemark bruises tend to be small and obscured by overlying abrasions. Color changes would be less prominent than in an uncomplicated larger bruise elsewhere. Textbook and literature reports concerned with color change over time are based on bruises much larger than a bitemark. The variables in color pattern determination make this an unreliable time indicator other than to offer broad estimates—fresh, not fresh, older, and healed. Such estimates must be proffered within the total context of the investigation.

8. HISTOPATHOLOGY

8.1. Bruise

During the late 19th and early 20th centuries the histological patterns of sterile wound healing was extensively studied. Most references concerned open wounds. Forensic pathology texts defined different types of wounds, including contusions (bruises). Moritz [4], in his 1954 forensic pathology text, offers descriptions of contusion components. If neutrophils have disintegrated, erythrocytes have lost their normal staining characteristics, and hemosiderin is present, the bruise is over 24 hours of age, even in the absence of neutrophilic reaction. This author recalls his discomfiture as a fledgling forensic pathologist trying to age bruises using these limited reference points. Simpson [5], in discussing the dating of injuries, advises caution for ''bruises are spreading, moving things.'' He focuses on color change and affords little space to histological changes, which may represent a lack of support for histological studies in his jurisdiction. Perper and Wecht [6], in a text devoted to microscopy in forensic pathology, caution the precision of a bruise age estimate. They mention that early neutrophilic infiltration is histologically demonstrable about 4 hours after injury. Unfortunately, they omit reference to the report of Robertson and Mansfield [7], who published a key article, often overlooked, that demonstrates critical elements of tissue reaction. Extravasated blood, by itself, is bland. Their Figure 5 is a photomicrograph of the edge of a 5-day-old bruise that cannot be differentiated from a fresh bruise. No inflammatory healing reaction is evident. The overlooked point by prior and subsequent authors is that tissue crush, with cellular damage, creates the stimulus for neutrophilic reaction usually cited as evidence of time since injury infliction. A series of bruises, inflicted at the same time, may result in different cellular healing reactions depending on the presence or absence of crushed tissue cells.

The tiny bitemark bruise may not present histological time changes of value. Absence of reaction may only reflect simple extravasation of blood. However, one should look carefully for disrupted or crushed tissue cells during the microscopic examination. These cells, with altered eosinophilic staining, may indicate that neutrophilic reaction might have been expected if life had continued after the injury.

8.2. Abrasion

Bitemarks usually possess a surface abrasion component. Bruises may have associated surface abrasion trauma. Robertson and Hodge studied the histopathology of abrasions as an aid to determining the aging of associated bruises [8]. Their study materials were derived from automobile trauma where postinjury survival time was known. They divided their abrasions into two types—a tangential scrape with loss of epidermis and stratum papillaris, and a right-angle blow by a hard object to the skin with crush of the epidermis. In either case, the healing changes are similar except that the right-angle blow results in a crushed devitalized epidermis and stratum reticularis that become incorporated into the crust (scab). The results of the study indicate:

1. Scab formation consists of damaged epithelium and collagen, infiltrating neutrophils coagulated blood and fibrin. From the time aspect, neutrophils were clearly visible at 4–6 hours.

Mention is made of an infrequent earlier appearance of neutrophils, but associated circumstances are not described. At about 8 hours the zone of neutrophils is a dense layer. At 12 hours the zone of neutrophils is intense with an outer surface layer of erythrocytes and fibrin, or crushed epithelium if present in the first place. The neutrophilic zone has degenerating neutrophils and a deeper zone of abnormally stained collagen of the zona reticularis. Neutrophilic infiltration continues in the deeper zone at 48 hours, this being the total scab that will be shed.

2. Epithelial regeneration is visible at 48 hours extending beneath the scab at the margins.

3. Subepidermal granulation, consisting of blood vessels and fibroblasts, occurs after the surface is epithelialized and is well formed during days 5–8.

4. After 12 days a stage of regression of cellular activity occurs with a basement membrane beneath an atrophic epithelium. Weeks later a few lymphocytes may yet be present about vessels.

Robertson and Hodge mention that not all abrasions are deep and intense. Some are quite superficial, and epithelial growth may be demonstrated in 30 hours. In small abrasions, complete epithelialization has occurred in as little as day 4 or 5. They found, in blind studies, that predictions were most accurate when survival exceeded 4 days. The surface abrasions are most useful in assessing the age of the underlying bruise. A single victim with multiple abrasions may run the gamut from faint and superficial to deep and intense, all from the same time period. The viewer of a bitemark should realize that Robertson and Hodges did not study bitemarks. Also, the degree of skin damage may vary from one part of a bitemark compared with another part of the same bite.

8.3. Literature Reviews

Vanezis assessed and reviewed in great detail the interpretation of bruises at necropsy [9]. His is an omnibus review of all things with bruises and includes listing of all coagulopathies that affect bruising, considerations apart from aging, use of light sources and spectrophotometry in assessing color, aspects of healing of tissues, and histochemical and immunochemical assessments. His bibliography omits reference to the two works of Robertson but is otherwise wide ranging. A difficulty is separating the changes of healing of open wounds from those factors dealing strictly with bruises. In fact, most of the literature on timing of wounds is based on studies of open wounds, not bruises. That is why the Robertson papers are most valuable.

9. HISTOCHEMICAL/BIOCHEMICAL—LITERATURE REVIEWS

As for histochemical studies and time related changes, most of the methods would seem to have little application in daily forensic practice. The text by McMinn is detailed up to its time, 1969 [10]. The most current with potential for forensic applications is by Raekallio dealing with aging of wounds by histochemical and biochemical methods [11]. It deals mainly with open wounds and is not very applicable to aging of bruises. From the forensic standpoint, Raekallio is proper in emphasis of the importance of correlation of all data including the death scene information. Determination of serotonin and histamine in neck tissues has been used to demonstrate a neck hanging of a body suffocated earlier in order to simulate a suicide. Hanging after death would be expected to result in the same concentrations of these substances at the hanging groove and control tissues elsewhere because the vital changes caused by injury would be absent. In a vital injury the histamine and serotonin would rise, resulting in a variance between the injured tissue and control tissue nearby. This is a potentially valuable tool because conventional wisdom in forensic pathology, dating back a half century, was that it is not possible to tell the difference between the person suffocated and hanged later (homicide) and a victim of self-hanging (suicide). However, the applicability of histochemical and biochemical methods to bitemarks remains for the future.

10. LITERATURE REVIEWS—CRITIQUE

Literature reviews fall into three broad categories. The first, and quite rare, is that which is critical. The author has specific expertise in the field and is capable of rendering a critical analysis of all referenced literature citations. The second is the most common and involves a noncritical literature summary of bibliographic references. A third combines some personal experience in the methodologies being reviewed but summarizes other publications without critical analysis. Vanezis' article is of that type [10]. He has experimented with instruments to measure and analyze light and color in the study of bruises but also reviewed a diverse array of literature covering the field of bruises in general. A two-page report on histological studies of bitemarks by Millington does not present full details or illustrations [15]. Literature review citations do not concern bitemarks and can be misleading as to histopathological characteristics of bitemarks.

11. AGING OF BITEMARKS

Dailey and Bowers have specifically addressed the topic of bitemarks and their aging [12,13]. Theirs is a noncritical review containing summaries of some key references discussed above. They also mention three appellate court cases in which dental experts opined as to the age of a bitemark. The courts did not address the qualifications of the experts to so opine. The purpose of their review was the "hope of distilling the facts related to this controversial subject." A certainty from their review is that estimating an age of the bruise from color is problematic.

12. THE VALUE OF MICROSCOPIC STUDY

One factor that detracts from microscopic study is cost. Many large-volume death investigative agencies limit microscopic sections or frequently omit them, relying on formaldehyde tissue retention for a finite time in the event of a later need for microscopic slides. In Miami-Dade County the Medical Examiner Department has a policy of taking routine sections from each autopsy which average 5.2 slides, some with more than one tissue sample, for each of the 2213 autopsies performed during fiscal year ending in 2002. Routine agency habits may affect the use of microscopic slides in bitemarks.

Why bother to prepare microscopic sections upon a bitemark? Despite limitations of precision, microscopic evaluations of bitemarks are useful. Slides increase understanding of the complex processes of the bite. They furnish a permanent documentation of the characteristics of the bitemark. If omitted, allegations of insufficient investigation may arise in court. Full documentation is always proper. One may anticipate a defense allegation that the bitemark was consensual and not associated with the time of death. The forensic odontologist should orchestrate the slide preparation procedure. The characteristics of the bitemark must be documented first, before any alteration by removal of tissue blocks. When the odontological studies are complete, the pathologist may then prepare the slides and render an interpretation. The dissection

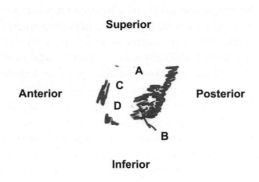

Figure 2 Plastic overlay bitemark tracing. Letters represent tissue block sites chosen for microscopic study.

procedure should be photographically documented so that the completed microscopic slide may be later matched with a specific site in the bitemark. Alternatively a clear plastic overlay may be prepared with indications of which microscopic section pertains to a specific portion of the bitemark pattern (Fig. 2). The pathologist should carefully detail the microscopic findings of surface and deeper features.

A forensic pathologist is not expected to possess the skill of a competent forensic odontologist but should be able to recognize the bitemark and its significance. When the odontologist has decided that the specimen may be incised (Editor's note: see Chapter 13) for transillumination and later microscopic study, the pathologist should work together with the odontologist. The first step for the pathologist is to carefully document the changes of skin and underlying tissue from the slide. False-positive neutrophil reactions may occur. During the initial bleeding a neutrophil may accompany an erythrocyte. That is not time dependent. When blood settles in a test tube, or after death in a vein within the body, it may separate with the erythrocytes being covered with a thin layer of white cells, the buffy coat. Rarely a microscopic section may include a small vein containing a buffy coat, a finding expected to mislead an unwary pathologist because healing changes may be subtle. Pathologist estimates of healing should be correlated with the gross appearance plus the circumstances.

13. THE REPORT

A careful description of details within each microscopic slide should be prepared. As to a specific time estimate, it is well to opine only evidence of vital reaction, meaning that the bitemark antedated the death. One should be conservative about the determination of lack of histopathological vital reaction in the bruises. One should not always expect to find clear patterns of healing, as demonstrated by Robertson and Hodges [8]. Should additional information arise concerning specific times, that may be addressed later. Initial expression of a finite time range without consideration of all the circumstances may result in discrepancies harmful to the case investigation.

14. FREQUENCY OF BITEMARKS

Bitemarks constitute an infrequent component of a busy medical examiner or coroner practice. During the 12-year period 1992 through 2002, Miami-Dade County, population, 2.3 million, sustained 3343 homicides. Only five homicide investigations involved a fresh bitemark as part of the criminal activity. Also within this group of homicides were noted three healed bitemarks, one in the healing process, and one pseudo-bitemark pattern secondary to abrasions from shattered window glass. A 12-year study from the Southern California area revealed a total of 92 bitemark examinations of all types [14]. Forty-two of these concerned deaths from Los Angeles County, an average of 3.5 per year as compared to only 0.4 per year in Miami-Dade County. Los Angeles County has five times the homicides than Miami-Dade County (www.losangeles-almanac.com).

Because histopathology studies of bitemarks are not frequent in any one institution, a registry might to be considered where duplicates of slides and reports may be stored for study. Local odontologists could coordinate the submission to the registry. The American Board of Forensic Odontology or the American Society of Forensic Odontology might initiate such an endeavor. Only with a carefully analyzed large series may the full value of bitemark histopathology patterns and aging patterns be appreciated. A registry could also coordinate the use of histochemical and biochemical methodology to the examination of bitemarks.

15. ACUTE BITEMARK HISTOPATHOLOGY IS UNIQUE

Acute bitemark histopathological patterns present unique patterns not found in skin wounds from other forces. Outstanding are compression of epidermis and dermis in some zones. In marked contrast are very acute edematous changes of epidermis and dermis that may occur in the same bite. Microscopic slides from three acute cases were available. The bitemark paraffin blocks were recut and carefully stained with hematoxylin and eosin. They were studied with $10\times$ and $40\times$ objective lenses. Best detail was revealed with the $40\times$ objective lenses. Representative fields were chosen for photomicrography.

Case I is a sexually assaulted housewife murdered by multiple stab wounds. Death had occurred during the prior night hours. Two bite injuries were noted, a full bitemark on the right forearm and a partial bite arch on the dorsum of the right hand. They appeared fresh, as were the stab wounds. Two sections of the forearm bitemark were available. An abrupt transition of normal epidermis to a compressed form was noted. Cells were flattened with pyknotic nuclei (Fig. 3). The compression zone gave way to a scraped section with only bits of basal cells remaining until the end of the scraped area revealed an abrupt resumption of normal epidermis

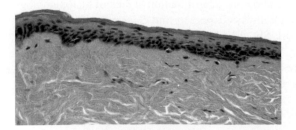

Figure 3 Compression of skin. Epidermal cells are flattened and pyknotic. Reticular dermis is dense with collagen fibers pressed together.

Figure 4 Scraped zone with intact epidermis on the right.

(Fig. 4). The dermis beneath the compressed and scraped epidermis was condensed with fibroblast nuclei becoming pyknotic and elongated. The compressed dermis extended to the subdermal fat layer. No extravasated erythrocytes were noted in the superficial reticular dermis. The other forearm section was similar except for a much smaller zone of scraped epidermis. Within deep underlying fat, bleeding without neutrophilic reaction was present. The hand slide contained two portions of tissue. One had a scraped loss of a thick stratum corneum with residual compressed epidermis remaining in place. The edge of the remaining corneum remained but had separated from the epidermis (Fig. 5). The dermis was compressed and dense. No extravasated erythrocytes were in the superficial dermis. The other piece of tissue had a small zone of corneum loss with compression of the residual epidermis and the underlying dermis. Some hemorrhage was present at the junction with underlying fat. In summary, case I had evidence of both compression of skin with focal loss of the stratum corneum.

Case II is a man found alongside a dirt road shot multiple times in the torso. Beneath a short-sleeved shirt was found a fresh bitemark of his left posterior axillary fold (Fig. 5 in Chapter 3). A plastic overlay sketch was prepared with indications of four microscopic sections, A, B, C, D (Fig. 2).

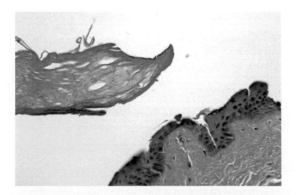

Figure 5 Stratum corneum scraped loose from compressed epidermis.

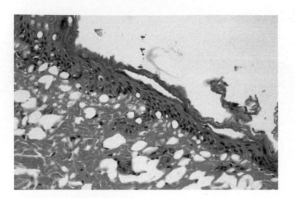

Figure 6 Edema and compression of epidermis. Edema vacuoles in deeper epidermis and underlying reticular dermis.

    Patterns varied among the four skin sections. At one end of section A was a zone of dense
compression of epidermis and dermis. Toward the other end of the section small vacuoles of
dermal papilla suggested slight edema. A scant amount of hemorrhage was present within deeper
fat with some fat cells being ruptured. Section B had a zone of compression of epidermis and
dermis at one margin. That gave way to a pronounced degree of intracellular vacuolization of
epidermal cells and underlying edematous spaces of superficial reticular dermis. This pattern
continued to the end of the tissue section. No deep hemorrhage was present. Section C had
dense compression at one edge plus a small scraped area. Beyond this was a zone of edematous
vacuolization of epidermis and dermis (Fig. 6). Within superficial reticular dermis were noted
a few extravasated erythrocytes, some of which were fragmented. Section C also had a deep
zone of hemorrhagic fat with rupture and coalescence of fat cells (Fig. 7). Section D had a
pronounced degree of edema of epidermis and dermis with some extravasated partially fragmented erythrocytes within papilla. At the opposite end of the section was compression of
epidermis with a small scrape plus compression of thick dermis extending to underlying fat.
    In summary, Case II demonstrates both compression distortion of full skin thickness plus
edema of epidermis and superficial dermis elsewhere. Traumatically fragmented extravasated

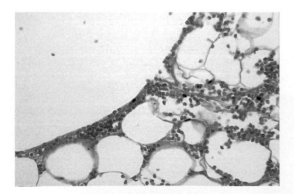

Figure 7 Coalescence of fat plus adjacent hemorrhage. At this site the hemorrhage was slight,
but fat cells had been ruptured.

erythrocytes are consistent with the forces that crushed deep fat cells, resulting in coalescence of fat.

Case III is a man who was shot in the head during a close physical altercation with two men. He had been wearing a shirt which was torn at the bite location. Below the right scapula was a bitemark with demonstrable indentations of the skin. Sections of skin and underlying tissue were excised at 3 o'clock, 6 o'clock, 9 o'clock, and 12 o'clock.

Section 3 had no zone of dermal compression but did exhibit a zone of edema of epidermis and dermis. Intracellular vacuolization was confined to the deeper layers of the epidermis. Dermal edema vacuoles were more prominent in the papillary dermis and adjacent most superficial reticular dermis. Beneath the thick deeper dermal collagen was hemorrhage in the fat. Section 6 had a zone of compression of epidermis but less prominent in the underlying dermis. Elsewhere was a minimal zone of vacuolization of epidermal cells and edema of dermis yet deep hemorrhage with fat droplets in the blood were present. Section 9 had scant edema of epidermis and papillary dermis (Fig. 8) and little deep fat hemorrhage. Section 12 had a continuous edema end to end with vacuolization of epidermis and dermis. Occasional tiny areas of epidermis were suggestive of some compressive pyknosis. In summary, Case III demonstrates the variability of compressive force increasing the epidermal and dermal density while within the same tissues edematous changes are evident. Deep fat hemorrhage is variable with evidence of rupture of deep fat cells.

It is clear from review of these three cases of fresh bitemarks that the complexity of bitemarks creates variable epidermal patterns of compression, scraping, and edematous intracellular vacuolization. The reticular dermis may likewise be densely compressed along with the epidermis or may exhibit edematous changes along with the epidermis. Deep fat hemorrhage may also include fat cell rupture and coalescence of fat into large globules.

The compression changes are those of a crushing force yielding dense compressed tissues. The removal of circulation from the dense tissue results in no edema reaction. Elsewhere, without dense compression, very acute edematous reactions of epidermis and dermis have occurred. Edema may be considered an initial vital reaction of tissue. Most biting episodes are not documented with a specific time line. How many minutes took place before the reaction ceased is not determinable. It is expected that the edematous reaction is a function of the applied disrupting forces plus the short postinjury survival time. What is quite evident is that histological patterns

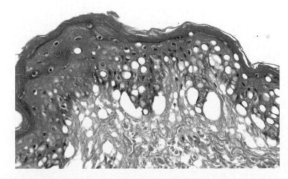

Figure 8 Focal edema of epidermis and dermal papilla. A few epidermal cells appear compressed; others, not.

of fresh bitemarks are variable and cannot be unthinkingly extrapolated from the published literature which is based on tissue reaction to other injury types. Bitemark histopathological characteristics are those of bitemarks, not automobile trauma. A thorough understanding of acute bitemark histopathology is essential before consideration of later healing phases.

Had any of the above victims survived a matter of days, the histopathological patterns would have changed. Each edematous site would have reached its maximum edema. Bleeding would have reached its maximum. Some edematous epidermis may or may not become necrotic depending upon the force damage. The compressed epidermis and dermis would have become necrotic depending upon the degree of irreversible damage. Those areas of irreversible damage would be expected to undergo the formation of a crust (scab) and heal according to the phases described by Robertson and Hodges [8]. However, until a collection of bitemarks in various stages of healing have been properly documented, one may not forecast with exactitude what should be seen with light microscopy.

15.1. Artifacts

Initial study of microscopic slides on file were complicated by variants of staining technique and fading. Recutting and staining were a necessary part of the review. Portions of some tissue blocks had not been placed at right angles in the cassettes. This results in local areas of pseudo-thickening of epidermis, shifting of location of vacuolated cells, or even loss of portions of epidermis where interpretation of scraping loss is being sought. Lymphocyte infiltration as a reaction to the healing process is of concern. But what is the significance of lymphocyte infiltrates in the dermis beneath a bitemark? Not much if it were present before the bite occurred and is not a reaction to the bite. In two of the three cases chance occurrence of lymphocyte foci were noted in the affected and nonaffected zones (Fig. 9).

15.2. Interpretation

The complexities of a bitemark, with multiple variations of pressure distortion, result in nonuniform tissue patterns. In the above case examples patterns of epidermis and dermis reaction vary. The not grossly apparent, yet microscopically demonstrable, patterns of pressure distortion of

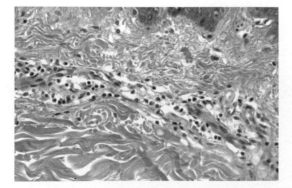

Figure 9   Perivascular lymphocytic infiltration. Dermal infiltrates in nonaffected as well as affected zones, plus no other signs of healing, indicate prior presence.

epidermis and dermis along with dermal edema and overlying epidermal vacuoles was not described in the reviewed literature. Errors of interpretation may occur when dissimilar and separate processes are considered as one. Because skin may contain preexisting small foci of dermal lymphocytes, their presence as indicators of inflammatory reaction to the bitemark must not be assumed in the absence of other corroboration.

The pathologist should document precisely the variable changes in epidermis, dermis, and subdermis for each microscopic slide. Representative slides from different portions of the bitemark should be technically perfect. Interpretation should be performed with exquisite care and only in the light of the totality of the case investigation.

During the review for this chapter, a "healing bitemark" opinion in one autopsy report was discovered to be erroneous, Case III. It was not only fresh but had retained skin indentations.

16. HEALING BITEMARK

The single true healing bitemark was not initially subject to histological study although it had been excised and retained in formalin solution. Case IV was a 32-year-old white female killed by a gunshot to the head. Above the right breast was noted a bitemark pattern "surrounded by a rim of purplish green-yellow contusion" (Fig. 10). After processing by the forensic odontologist, it was excised and preserved in formaldehyde (Fig. 11). Eight and one-half years later the author retrieved it and prepared five sections. Each was excised, placed atop the specimen, and photographed for orientation (Fig. 12). Each tissue block was processed and sections stained with H&E plus iron stains.

The residual of a fresh bitemark pattern with additional changes wrought by healing was expected. Crush defects, residual epidermal edema, and residual hemorrhage altered by the

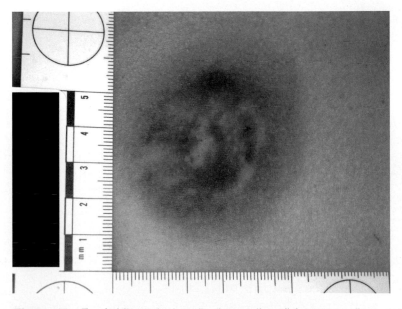

Figure 10 Fresh bitemark described as a "purplish green-yellow contusion." Also see color photograph insert section.

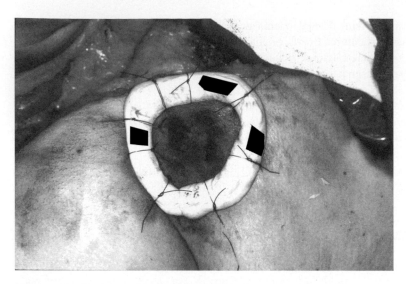

Figure 11 Excision of bitemark. Black is fingerprint powder.

healing processes were noted. These varied within the five sections. Prominent were infiltration by polymorphonuclear leucocytes in looser tissue (Fig. 13) but not yet within the dense compacted dermal collagen. Many of the polys had dense nuclei and dense pink cytoplasm. A few were undergoing disintegration. In the subcutaneous fat, erythrocytes had variable decrease in staining. A few zones of fibrin exudate admixed with erythrocytes and polys were also noted in the subcutis. Epidermal changes were variable depending on the acute change that had been

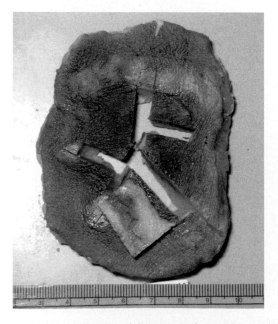

Figure 12 Preserved tissue specimen after excision of tissue blocks for microscopic study. Block E is atop the specimen.

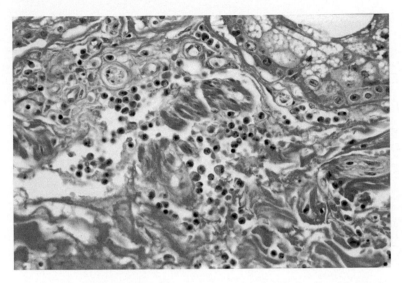

Figure 13 Polymorphonuclear leucocyte infiltration in deeper dermis.

present, simple compression or acute edema where residual effects remained (Fig. 14). Commonly noted beneath the stratum corneum were necrotic epidermal cell debris zones, some thin (Fig. 15) and some thick (Fig. 16). Prussian Blue stains for hemosiderin were negative.

The key concern with histological aging of a bitemark is whether it can be shown to antedate the time of death by the presence of unequivocal healing reaction, a life process. If a time frame is to be considered, it should be expressed in terms of the total evidence including

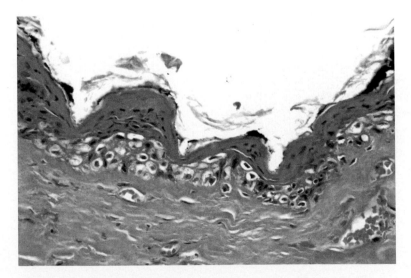

Figure 14 Compressed epidermis with residual edema vacuoles.

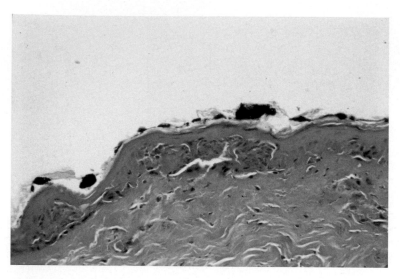

Figure 15 Compressed epidermis containing a thin zone of necrotic epidermal cells. Black surface material is fingerprint powder.

circumstances and odontology review. Findings within each mode of investigation must be compared with the others before rendering final opinions. As for opinions, they fall into two types—investigative and evidentiary. The former is knowingly based on incomplete data and is subject to change as newer data are received. Investigative opinion is used to assist others in their investigations. When the investigation is complete, a final assessment will result in evidentiary opinion, that which may be expressed in court.

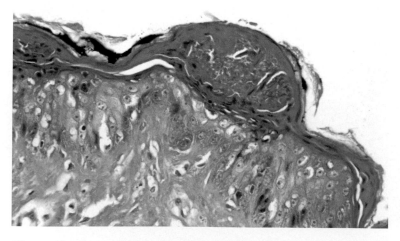

Figure 16 Compressed epidermis containing a thick zone of necrotic epidermal cells.

17. SUMMARY

Published texts and literature are not uniform in their applicability to the histopathological aging of bitemarks. Two popular forensic pathology textbooks lack concordance. Published literature on microscopic evidence of tissue healing for the most part is based upon en wounds not representative of the usual closed wound of a human bitemark. Although a literature review dealing specifically with bitemark histopathology exists, it is not based on bitemark histopathological study [12,13]. Bitemark histopathologic findings are those of bitemarks, not other forms of injury upon which literature reviews are based.

Bitemarks are not frequent. Local histolopathological experience is limited. It is suggested that a national bitemark histopathological registry be created under the auspices of the American Board of Forensic Odontology or the American Society of Forensic Odontology. ABFO and ASFO members could coordinate the submission of case material when consulting with their local death investigative agencies.

REFERENCES

1. Spitz WU. Spitz & Fisher's Medicolegal Investigation of Death. 3rd ed.. Springfield. IL: Charles C. Thomas, 1993:202.
2. DiMaio VJ, DiMaio D. Forensic Pathology. 2nd ed.. Boca Raton. FL: CRC Press, 2001:101.
3. Munang LA, Leonard PA, Mok JYQ. Lack of agreement on colour description between clinicians examining childhood bruising. J Clin Forens Med 2002; 9(4):171–174.
4. Moritz AR. The Pathology of Trauma. Philadelphia: Lea & Febiger, 1954:35.
5. Simpson K, Ed. Taylor's Principles and Practice of Medical Jurisprudence. 12th ed.. Vol. I. Boston: Little, Brown, 1965:188.
6. Perper JA, Wecht CH. Microscopic Diagnosis In Forensic Pathology. Springfield. IL: Charles C. Thomas, 1980.
7. Robertson I, Mansfield RA. Ante-mortem and post-mortem bruises of the skin, their differentiation. J Forens Med 1957; 4(1):2–10.
8. Robertson I, Hodge PR. Histopathology of healing abrasions. Forens sci 1972; 1:17–25.
9. Vanezis P. Interpreting bruises at necropsy. J Clin Pathol 2001; 54:348–355.
10. McMinn RMH. Tissue Repair. New York: Academic Press, 1969.
11. Raekallio J. Determination of the age of wounds by histochemical and biochemical methods. Forens Sci 1972; 1:3–16.
12. Dailey JC, Bowers CM. Aging of bitemarks: a literature review. J Forens Sci 1997; 42(5):792–795.
13. Dailey JC, Bowers CM. Aging of bitemarks: a literature review. In Bowers CM, Bell G, Eds. Manual of Forensic Odontology. 3rd ed.. Montpelier. VT: Printing Specialists, 1995.
14. Vale GH, Noguchi TT. Anatomical distribution of human bite marks in a series of 67 cases. J Forens Sci 1983; 28(1):61–69.
15. Millington PF. Histological studies of skin carrying bite marks. J Forens Sci Soc 1974; 14:239–240.

V
Bitemark Variables and Cases

15
Animal Bites

Richard R. Souviron
Medical Examiner Department, Miami-Dade County
Florida, U.S.A.

> "Thorough documentation and thoughtful interpretation are essential prerequisites if justice
> is to be done."—J.H. Davis, M.D.

1. GENERAL CONSIDERATION

Man and animal have interacted from prehistoric times. Man evolved from hunter to domesticator
of animals. Domesticated animals provide food, companionship, labor, recreation, and entertainment for humans. Wild animals, on the other hand, view humans as threatening rivals or as a
food source. With increasing interaction between humans and wild animals, death often results.

2. AQUATIC ANIMAL BITES

The oldest living aquatic predator, the shark, is master of his domain. Man's increased presence
(swimming, surfing, spear fishing, diving, etc.) has led to a corresponding increase in the number
of shark attacks [1,2]. The remarkable predator/scavenger will attack and feed on just about
anything, living or dead.

2.1. Nonfatal Aquatic Animal Bites

In most nonfatal fish bites the victim/witnesses description of the event and the pattern of injury
is generally self-evident. Figure 1 depicts a healed shark bite on the lower leg. A spear fisherman
aroused a Carribean reef shark with a "bang stick." The startled shark attacked the diver, who
was then rescued by companions.

A witnessed and videotaped barracuda bite resulted in a severe laceration of a diver's
index finger (Fig. 2). The diver was feeding fish using a Ballyhoo (a needle-shaped bait fish)
at a depth 80 feet. A 4-foot barracuda took the bait and index finger, leaving a scalpellike
laceration. Nonfatal alligator bites on humans are on the increase in the Southeastern United
States. Figure 3 depicts an alligator bite received while attempting to wake the startled reptile
by "stomping on its head."

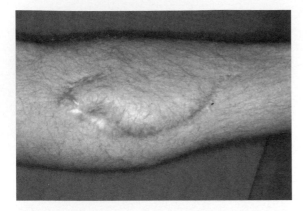

Figure 1 Healed Caribbean reef shark bite.

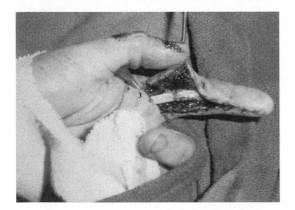

Figure 2 Lacerated index finger from a barracuda bite.

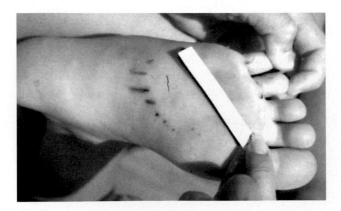

Figure 3 Nonfatal alligator bite.

2.2. Fatal Aquatic Animal Bites

There are basically four questions to be answered in a fatal human aquatic attack: (1) what is the victim's identity; (2) was the victim alive or dead when attacked; (3) what is the cause of death; and (4) what was the manner of death.

The pathologist should be able to determine whether the victim was alive or dead when attacked. The third and fourth questions are more difficult to answer. Did the swimmer die of a heart attack or drown? Was the homicide victim dumped, then scavenged? Were the sharks "frenzied" into killing as the victim was tossed overboard? Did the victim slip, hit his head as he went overboard? Was he pushed?

The forensic dentist, although not involved in the cause or manner of death, might provide useful assistance in identifying of the deceased and in evaluating the patterned injuries and identifying predator species and fish size. Other aquatic scavengers, including the crocodile and the alligator, have the same ability as the shark of replacing lost teeth. Although the bitemark may only be secondary to the cause and manner of death, it is an important factor in accessing the total picture.

The recognition/differentiation/interpretation of fish bites are the shared responsibility of police investigators, coroner/medical examiner, pathologist, odontologist, and other experienced specialist such as an ichthyologist and marine biologist (Figs. 4, 5).

The great white shark is responsible for more fatal human attacks than any other shark species. The majority of these occur off the shores of Australia, while Florida's bull, tiger, and hammerhead sharks are also bitemark contributors. The following example illustrates a shark bite, most likely produced by a bull shark, over 10 feet long (Fig. 6).

Circumstantial and eyewitness accounts determined the cause of death as shark attack (nondescript) and the manner as accidental. In another case, a scuba diver in South Florida disappeared in approximately 40 feet of water.

His mutilated body was found 36 hours later with large shark bites and missing flesh [3]. The witnessed manner of death was accidental, but the cause was greatly debated: air embolism, exanguanation, drowning, etc. (Fig. 7). A last case involves retrieval of partial human remains

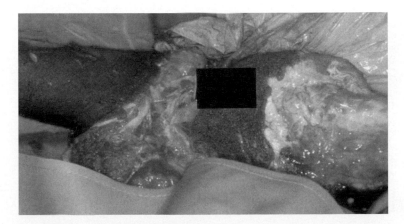

Figure 4 Leg avulsion shark bite.

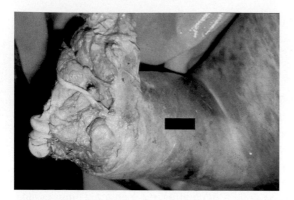

Figure 5 Homicide victim scavenged by alligator.

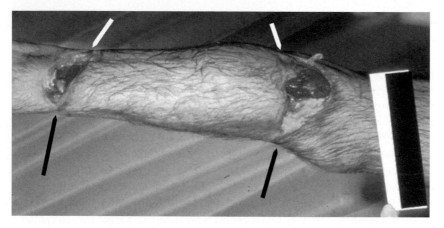

Figure 6 Fatal shark attack. Width of bitemark suggests an estimated shark length of over 10 feet.

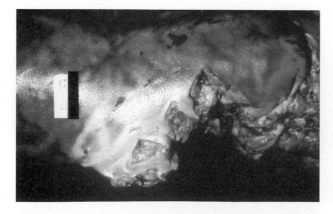

Figure 7 Shreaded body from shark attack.

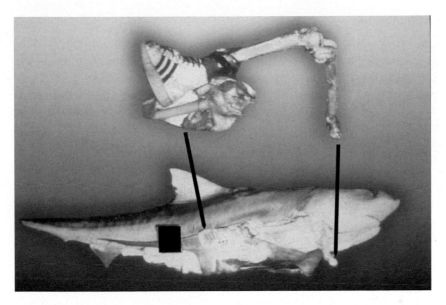

Figure 8 Leg with tennis shoe found in tiger shark stomach.

found in a large tiger shark (Fig. 8). Unfortunately the remains were never identified nor was it possible to determine the cause or manner of death.

3. CARNIVORES

The carnivore's dental anatomy and biting dynamics are important features in interpreting the species. (Editor's note: see Chapter 5 for the carnivore dental formula.) Carnivore teeth vary greatly in size and arrangement (Fig. 9).

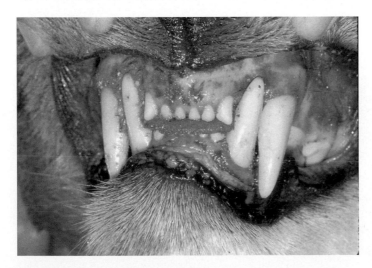

Figure 9 Mountain lion dentition.

3.1. Nonfatal Animal Bites

In most cases of nonfatal animal bites, the victim simply describes the circumstance and identifies the animal. There are exceptions. An 11-year-old white, mute, mentally retarded, paraplegic with congenital spina bifida was left unattended and attacked by two German shepard family pets with no previous history of violence [4]. The mother awoke to discover her daughter's night clothing shredded, injuries including claw marks, a bruised forearm, and avulsion of the daughter's mons pubis (Fig. 10).

The pattern of injuries was initially correctly interpretated by police and family as dog inflicted. Later, a child protection team nurse opined in sworn deposition, "I don't know what caused the injury but it was not dogs." The statement seemed ludicrous in light of the circumstances of lack of blood or tissue at the scene. No one had bothered evaluating the dogs, verifying the gastric or fecal content, or swabbed the victim for animal DNA.

The court seized the child, and the mother was charged with felony child abuse. Subsequently the public defender acquired the assistance of three experienced forensic experts: pathologist, odontologist, and veterinarian. One year of litigation resulted in the state dropping the charges against the mother [5].

The odontologist made dental casts of the sedated dogs employing vinyl-polysiloxane rather than alginate impression material. The latter does not produce an accurate impression of the anterior teeth. In addition, a series of models were poured from the vinyl-polysiloxane impression. Casts should be poured in plastic (Fig. 11) rather than stone since the anterior teeth are varied in size, relatively short and conical. Bubbles, dental and model fractures are more likely to occur with stone models.

The tragedy of this case is that a nurse familiar with human-inflicted injuries rendered an opinion outside her field of expertise. The lack of familiarity with circumstance, the scene, and lack of consultation with experts familiar with dog-inflicted injuries led to a protracted miscarriage of justice. Since criminal and or civil litigation might result from animal bites, it might be wise for the inexperienced diagnostician (emergency response personnel/nurse/physician/ pediatrician/dentist/social worker) to consult rather than misdirect an investigation. In certain cases consultation with veterinarians, wild life officers, forensic pathologist, odontologist, and anthropologists might prevent/reduce/correct misinterpretation of animal bites. A team approach provides the best opportunity for thorough documentation of circumstance, scene analysis, and proper photographic documentation.

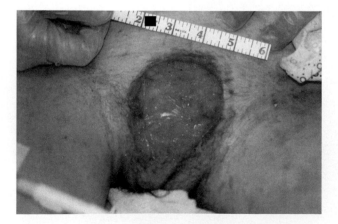

Figure 10 Tissue avulsion in nonfatal dog attack.

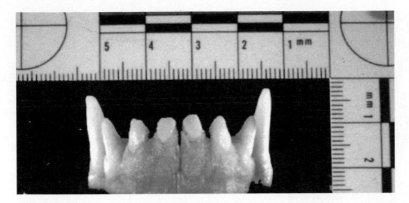

Figure 11 Plastic cast reproducing dental detail without bubbles or fractures.

In 1985 the New York City Department of Health reported 9807 dog bite cases and 1591 human bite cases (man on man). Interestingly, forensic odontologists are consulted far more often on human bites (man on man) than on dog bites [6–8]. Most nonfatal dog bite cases are resolved by personal testimony as the following example attests.

A defendant charged in the homicide death of a dog owner claimed self-defense as the Doberman Pincher was ordered to attack. The defendant's claim was that he accidentally shot the owner instead of the dog. The prosecution claimed that the defendant's leg pattern injuries were self-inflicted fork wounds administered following incarceration rather than dog bites contended by defense pathologist and odontologist. There was no evaluation of the injuries at the time of arrest and the only evidence consisted of a few rulerless photographs. The defendant was tried for murder, and the state lost the case. The lesson: Forensic consultation should be the rule when pattern injuries are present.

3.2. Fatal Animal Bites

The mountain lion and brown, black, and grizzly bears are the most dangerous wild animals to humans in North America. More mountain lion attacks have been reported in the previous 20 years than had been reported in the previous 100 years. The reason: The mountain lion habitat is shrinking (Fig. 12).

Grizzly bear and mountain lion bitemarks are similar in appearance, yet species specific. Paw prints, on the other hand, are quite characteristic [9,10]. Differentiating animals within a species is more difficult. Drs. Curtis Rollins (medical examiner for Sacramento, CA) and Duane Spencer (forensic dental consultant) were able to determine the mountain lion's sex, a female, based on the bitemark arch dimension (Fig. 13). A professional hunter was used to locate the animal, and the teeth matched the bitemarks (Fig. 14). The victim's DNA was recovered from the mountain lion's claws [11–13].

Fatal bites from zoo animals are usually the result of mishandling safety procedures. An unsecured gate led to the tragic death of a Florida zoo handler attacked by a white Bengal tiger. The bitemark included an imbedded lower canine in the victim's cheek (Fig. 15). The tiger was not destroyed and required endodontic treatment (Fig. 15).

The forensic dentist does not normally visit the crime scene, nor is he always initially privy to the details of an investigation. Crime scene investigators, on the other hand, are trained at processing crime scenes. Photography, videography, and topographic drawings are used to record the event. The odontologist should familiarize himself with these findings and the circum-

Figure 12   Victim of mountain lion attack California. (Photo courtesy of Drs. Curtis Rollins and Duane Spencer.)

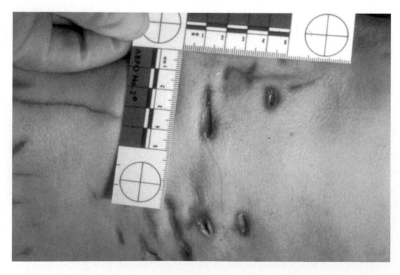

Figure 13   Mountain lion bitemark.

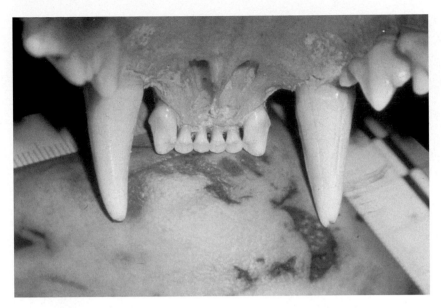

Figure 14 Mountain lion teeth over bitemark. (Photo courtesy of Drs. Curtis Rollins and Duane Spencer.)

stances of the event preferably before the autopsy, but certainly before rendering an opinion regarding the origin of the pattern injury [14].

It is the role of the medical examiner/pathologist/coroner to diagnose and consult with the forensic dentist where patterned injuries consistent with bitemarks of human or animal origin are suspected. The forensic dentist will examine, record, document (Fig. 16), and preserve the pattern injury as needed.

Black-and-white, color, alternate light photographs, and video documentation are but a few of the means of documenting the condition. In the presence of multiple animal bites, it is difficult if not impossible to apply a bitemark protocol that would record each and every wound individually, take impressions, and remove all of the affected tissue. Selective tissue impression/excision/preservation (Fig. 17) and direct tissue comparison may be more appropriate under certain circumstances (Fig. 18).

Claw marks, drag marks, and tissue avulsion present specific interpretation issues (Fig. 19). Canines, premolars, and molars in larger dogs and cats can produce a pattern injury that may be misinterpreted as stab wounds by the unsuspecting or inexperienced (Figs. 20, 21). Careful macroscopic and microscopic examination will differentiate stab wounds from animal bites. (Editor's note: see Chapter 16.)

The American Veterinary Medical Association (AVMA), the American Society of Plastic Surgeons (ASPS), and the Centers for Disease Control and Prevention (CDC) sponsor National Dog Bite Prevention Week in May. A 20-year review of fatal dog attacks in the United States (238 cases) revealed that about half involved pitbulls or Rottweillers. In Miami-Dade County, Florida, it is illegal to own a pitbull and if caught is punishable by a fine of $500.00. In spite of the fine, some dogs are raised for combat while others are illegally kept. A recent case from central Florida depicts a deceased 5-year-old white girl found in a backyard adjoining a lake. Family members claimed the child, while playing with three family pitbulls, was attacked by an alligator. Florida Game, Fish and Wildlife, and Sheriff's Department personnel opined that

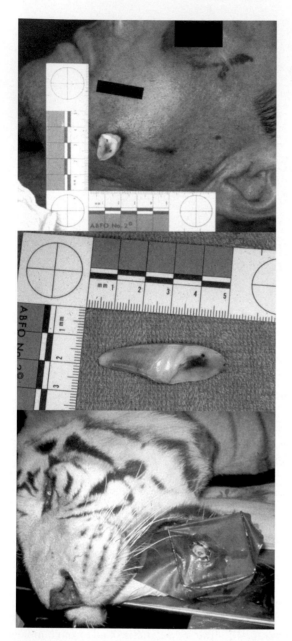

Figure 15 Bengal tiger tooth imbedded in jaw, tiger tooth, and endodontic treatment.

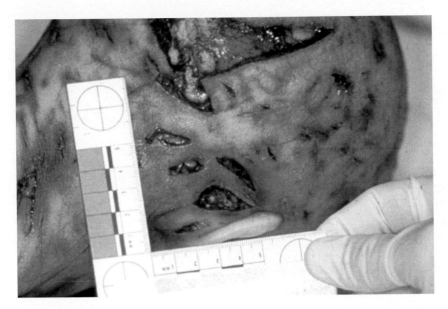

Figure 16 Placement of ABFO No. 2 scale for photography.

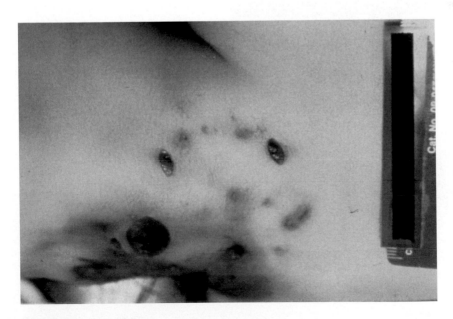

Figure 17 A dog bite.

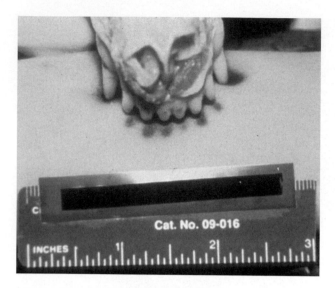

Figure 18   Direct dental comparison.

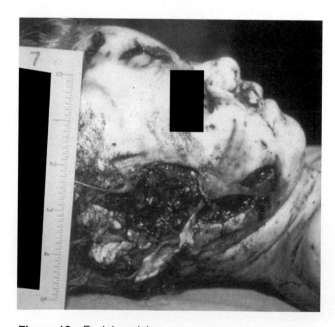

Figure 19   Facial avulsion.

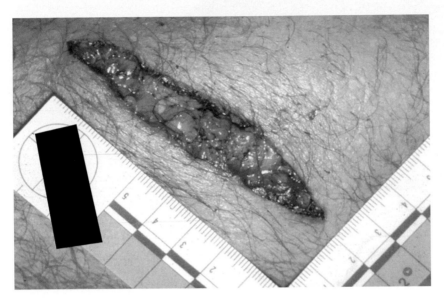

Figure 20   Tiger canine laceration.

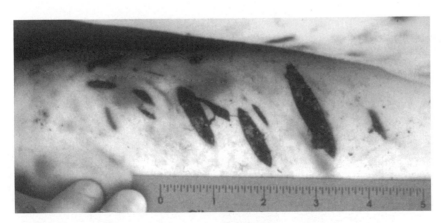

Figure 21   Leg lacerations in a fatal pitbull attack.

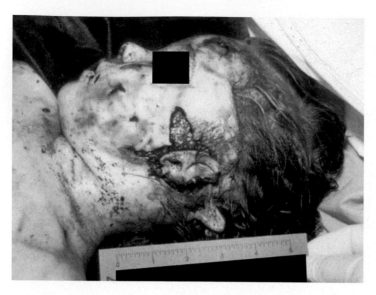

Figure 22 Fatal pitbull attack.

the bites resulted from dogs, not alligator. Scene photographs were critical in assessing the situation as the child's toys and torn, bitten clothing were scattered. The forensic dentist arrived at the same conclusion: dog bites, not alligator (Fig. 22).

The alligator's (Fig. 23) primary food source is fish, small animals, and the occasional child. Death usually results from drowning, and the victim is eaten later. The following example illustrates a case of a child seized by an alligator. Several hours later the captured "gator" still had the child in its mouth (Fig. 24).

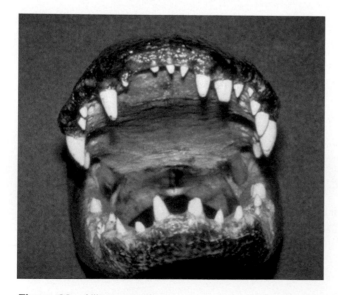

Figure 23 Alligator teeth.

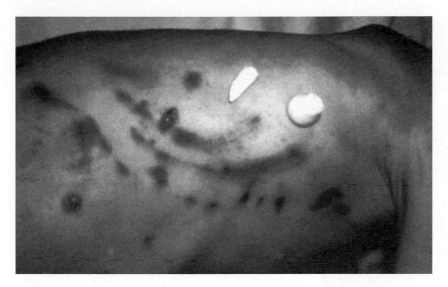

Figure 24 Alligator bitemarks with imbedded teeth.

4. ANIMAL BITE PROTOCOL

The suggested protocol is valid for all land animals but particularly applicable to domesticated dogs.

1. Examine the animal for blood and visible transfer of evidence from the victim.
2. Gather the victim's DNA from the animal's claws.
3. Immediately take the animal to a veterinary to induce vomiting.
4. Strain the contents and preserve tissue and cloth fragments or other foreign bodies found in the vomitus for comparison with victim and clothing.
5. Quarantine the animal for collection of feces, and compare the evidence of hair, tissue, bone, and clothing.
6. Take dental impressions of the suspect animal; create and pour models in plastic.
7. Do a rabies test on both victim and animal since the animal's owner may later claim that the animal, unknown to him, may have been rabid.

5. ANIMAL BITE VICTIM EVIDENCE

1. Swab for animal saliva, DNA left on the victim.
2. Retain the victim's clothing for DNA analysis.
3. Analyze the clothing for teethmarks.
4. Follow ABFO guidelines for preservation of bitemark evidence

6. POSTMORTEM ANIMAL BITES

Identification and interpretation of bitemarks on the deceased, especially the decomposing, is difficult [15]. Rodent, cat, small dog, or wild animal bites may be difficult to differentiate yet contribute to the problem. Scene evaluation and circumstance are important factors in pattern injury interpretation particularly if the body has been found outdoors or in the presence of

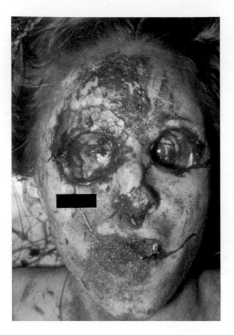

Figure 25 Opposum feeding on homicide victim.

animals, insects, etc. In the following instance, pattern injuries on a homicide victim found in a wooded area were attributed to witnessed opossum bites (Fig. 25). Crime scene personnel can best evaluate ant and roach attribution (Fig. 26).

Alan R. Moritz, M.D., is quoted as saying, "If evidence has been properly gathered and preserved, a mistake in interpretation may always be corrected. If the facts required for a correct interpretation are not preserved, the mistake is irreversible."

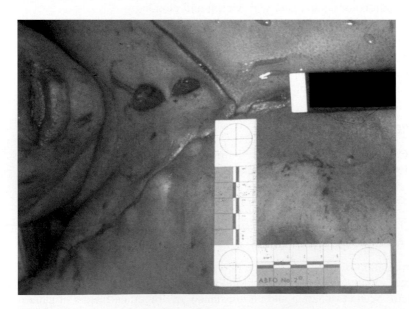

Figure 26 Insect activity mimicking single-arch bitemark.

REFERENCES

1. Matthews R. The Deep—Shark Bites, Nightmares of Nature, The Book of the BBC, TV Series, 1995.
2. Gilbert PW. Sharks and Survival. Boston. D.C. Health, 1963:510–567.
3. Davis JH. Injuries due to animals. In: The Pathology of Trauma. 2nd ed. Mason JK, Ed, 1993. Hodder Stoughton, Ltd, dist. by Little, Brown & Co. Boston, MA.
4. Foote T. That is not a bad dog—that's a splendid dog. Smithsonian, 1992.
5. Reigger MH, Guntzelman J. Prevention and amelioration of stress and consequences of interaction between children and dogs. J Am Vet Assoc 1990; 196:1781–1785.
6. Lauridson JR, Myers L. Evaluation of fatal dog bites: the view of the medical examiner and animal behaviorist. J Forens Sci 1993; 38(3):726 731.
7. Borchelt P, Lockwood R, Beck A, Voith V. Attacks by packs of dogs involving predation on human beings. Public Health Rep 1983; 98:57–66.
8. Sacks J, Sattin RW, Bonzo SE. Dog bite related fatalities from 1979 through 1988. JAMA 1989; 262(11):1489–1492.
9. Tough SC, Butt JC. A review of fatal bear maulings in Alberta. Am J Forens Med Pathol 1992.
10. Matthews R. Maneaters—Bears, Nightmares of Nature, The Book of the BBC, TV Series, 1995.
11. Rollins CE, Spencer DE. A fatality and the American mountain lion: bite mark analysis and profile of the offending lion. J Forens Sci 1995; 40(3):486–489.
12. Cohle SD, Harlan CW, Harlan G. Fatal big cat attacks. Am J Forens Med Pathol 1990; II(3):208–212.
13. Matthews R. Maneaters—Large Cats, Nightmares of Nature, The Book of the BBC, TV Series, 1995.
14. Nordby JJ. Can we believe what we see, if we see what we believe? Expert Disagreement. J Forens Sci 1992; 37(4):1115–1124.
15. Clark MA, Sandusky GE, Hawley DA, Pless PM, Tate LR. Fatal and near-fatal animal bite injuries. J Forens Sci 1991; 36(4):1256–1261.

16
Dog Bitemarks

Robert B. J. Dorion
Laboratoire de sciences judiciaires et de médecine légale,
Ministry of Public Security Province of Quebec,
Montreal, Quebec, Canada

1. INTRODUCTION

Between 1979 and 1994 the Center for Disease Control and Prevention (CDC) reported almost 300 deaths attributed to dogs in the United States [1]. In addition, 4.7 million persons sustained dog bites in 1994, some 800,000 of them requiring medical attention.

An attacking animal will attempt to immobilize its subject by striking the limbs. Once the subject has been ''brought down,'' it will attack any body part to ultimately strike the throat, neck, or skull. If the attack persists, death will ultimately result from asphyxiation, exsanguination, broken neck, or fractured skull or its complications. Dog bites will vary in size and pattern of injury depending on the animal and the surface bitten. The appearance will be totally different on a skull from on the arm, leg (Fig. 1), back, or neck.

2. CANINE DENTITION

The American Staffordshire pitbull terrier is by far the most fearsome and dangerous canine to humans. The incisal horizontal height of the pitbull's posterior teeth is uneven (Fig. 2). When teeth are in occlusion, the lower canines are set anterior to the upper canines. The anterior teeth are interlocking while the posterior teeth are not in contact.

The human dentition has six anterior teeth while the dog has eight. The size, shape, and horizontal height of the anterior teeth vary. The third tooth from the midline is usually longer than the first two. The shape of the first three teeth is not necessarily conical (Fig. 3). By far the largest and longest tooth is the canine. Of any puncture mark attributed to a dog's dentition, the canine would be the most penetrating.

Tooth alignment along the dental arch from canine to the last molar does not follow a straight path (Fig. 4). If a dog grabs hold of a person's limb with its back teeth, the dentition penetrates unevenly as a result of different sizes of teeth, different horizontal heights of teeth, and the uneven anteroposterior alignment of teeth. The bites attributed to the maxillary teeth on one side of the limb would be different in appearance from those attributed to the mandibular teeth on the opposite side of the limb. Couple this with the dog's shaking movement causes a ripping and shredding of skin and muscle tissue.

Trauma resulting from a dog bitemark on the scalp (round surface) or on the person's back (flat surface) is entirely different in appearance from that seen on the arm or the leg. For

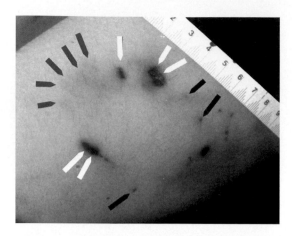

Figure 1 Contusion, laceration, and puncture marks from a dog bitemark.

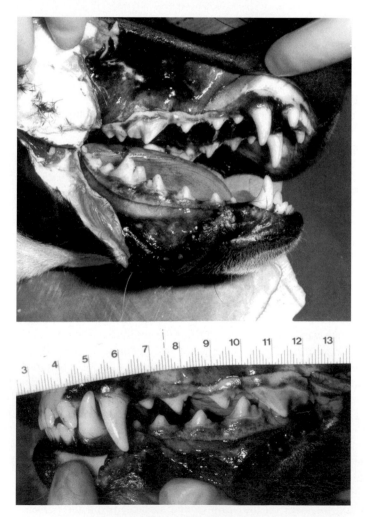

Figure 2 Lateral view of the pitbull dentition.

294

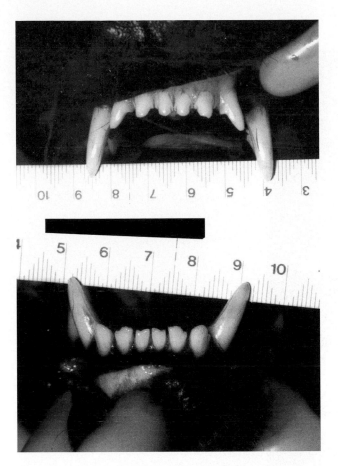

Figure 3 Frontal view of a pitbull dentition.

this reason there are probably more variations in appearance of dog-inflicted bitemarks than there are in human-inflicted bitemarks.

The pit bull has by far the most powerful jaws among canines.

1. Pitbull   1350 lb/in^2
2. Rottweller   750 lb/in^2
3. German Shepherd   575 lb/in^2

3. NONFATAL CANINE ATTACK

A mentally challenged 13-year-old female was found at home in the state of shock hemorrhaging from partial scalping. The parents claimed to have found a child in this condition upon returning from a shopping trip. Authorities were concerned that the parents/intruder may have beaten or stabbed the adolescent.

Fortunately, the adolescent did not have neurological implications, and the medical emergency was restricted to numerous scalp sutures (Fig. 5). Numbers 1, 2, and 3 represent slippage of the dog's lower right canine. Numbers 3 and 10 indicate where the lower canines engaged

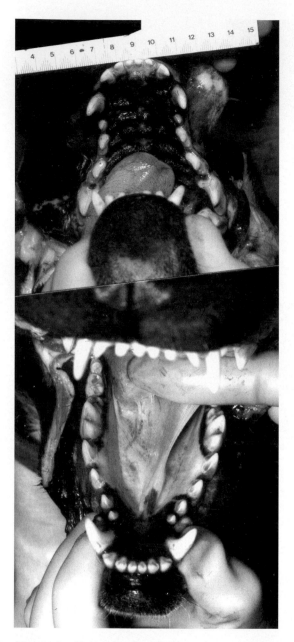

Figure 4 Occlusal views of the pitbull dentition.

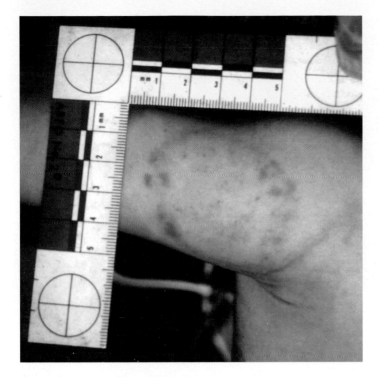

Figure 2.2 Bitemark on an arm.

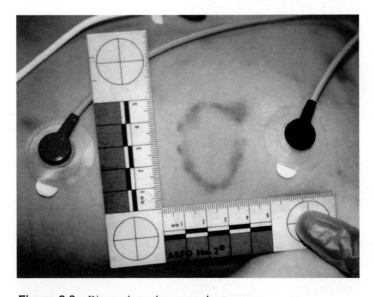

Figure 2.3 Bitemark on the upper chest.

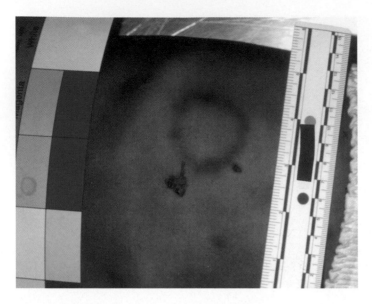

Figure 2.4 Diffuse bitemark on the abdomen.

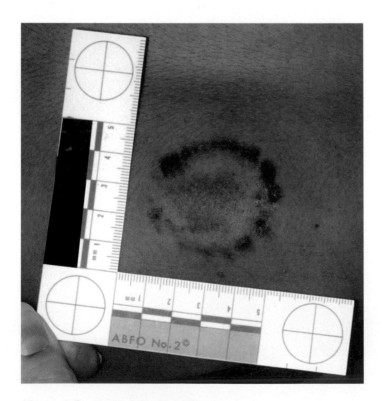

Figure 2.7 Bitemark on the back.

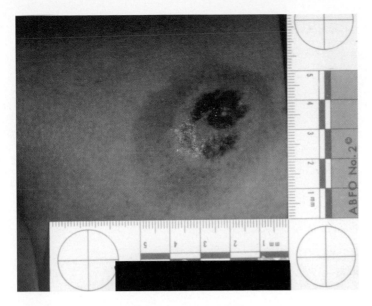

Figure 2.8 Bitemark on the upper right chest.

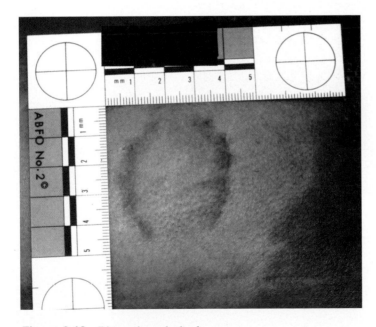

Figure 2.12 Bitemark on the back.

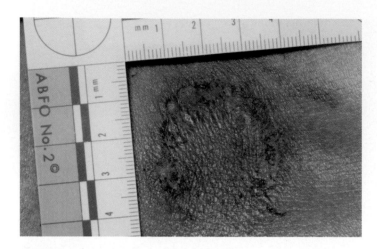

Figure 2.14 Bitemark on the upper chest.

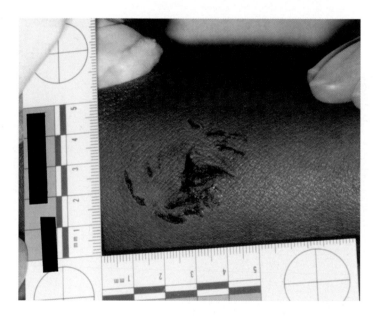

Figure 2.15 Bitemark on the arm.

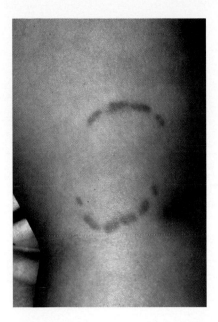

Figure 5.3 Typical bitemark from a child showing small, spaced teeth.

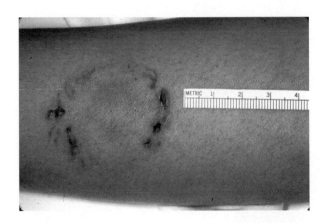

Figure 5.4 Bitemark showing central contusion with pale area from tongue thrusting. Note continuous ring due to approximation of maxillary and mandibular arches.

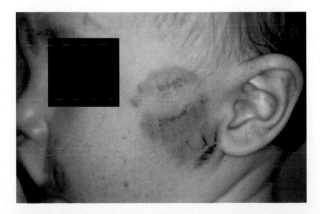

Figure 5.5 Drag marks left by mandibular teeth scraping across face.

Figure 5.6 Three drag marks in a bitemark made by mandibular left teeth.

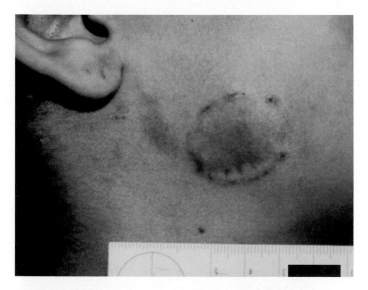

Figure 5.7 Lingual markings formed when pressure from mandibular cingula prevented spread of central contusion. (From ABFO Bitemark Workshop).

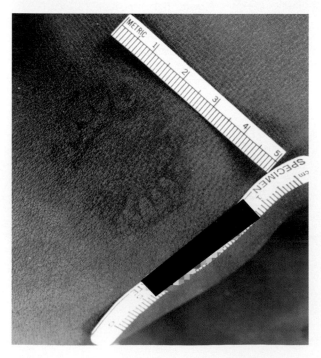

Figure 5.8 Five maxillary and five mandibular teeth recorded as lingual markings.

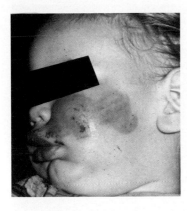

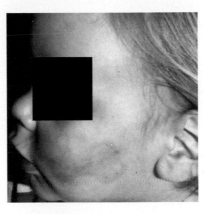

Figure 5.9 Acute inflammation and swelling account for solid appearance of bitemarks.

Figure 5.10 Same bitemarks as Fig. 5.9 photographed a day later when subsiding inflammation revealed the ring pattern of arches.

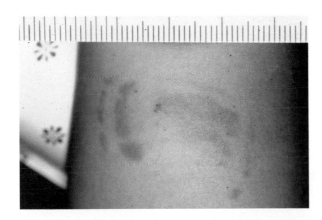

Figure 5.12 "Double bite" occurring as teeth slipped, followed by re-application of force, creating concentric duplication of pattern.

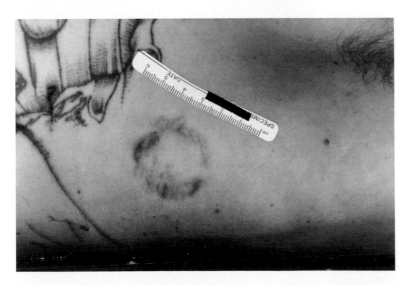

Figure 5.15 Close-up of bitemark inferior to axilla in Fig. 5.13. showing repetition and improvement of pattern seen in Fig. 5.14. Note severe labial crowding and rotation of No. 27, overlapping of 26, 25, and 24 (Universal System), and drag marks of entire anterior maxillary arch.

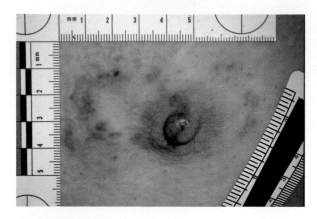

Figure 5.16 Two superimposed bites converging at the nipple.

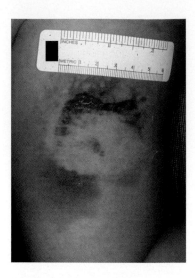

Figure 5.18 Excessive hemorrhage surrounding bitemark. Courtesy of Dr. William Smock.

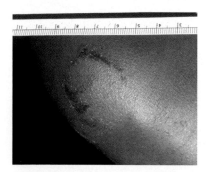

Figure 5.19 Partial bitemark created by left maxillary and mandibular arch. Courtesy of Dr. William Smock.

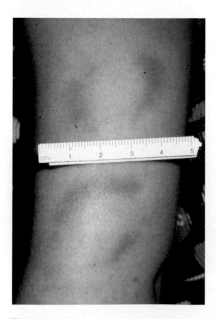

Figure 5.22 Toothless bitemarks showing only arch form and size as class characteristics.

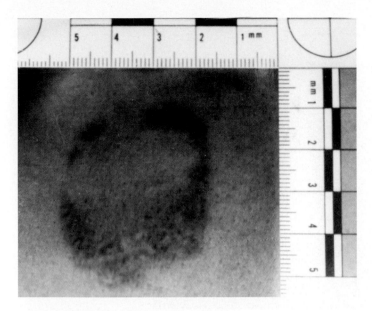

Figure 5.24 Old healed bitemark showing post-lesional pigmentation. Photograph courtesy of Dr. Richard Souviron.

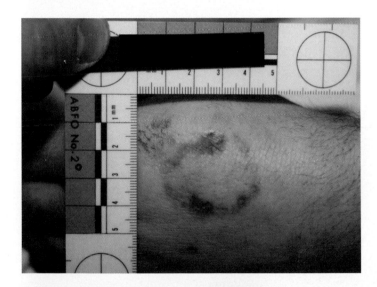

Figure 7.2 Typical color photograph of bitemark on hand.

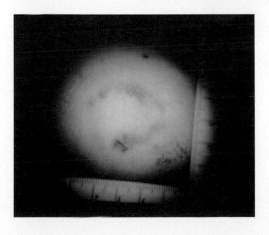

Figure 7.6 Same bitemark on hand as in Fig. 7.2, in alternate light imaging (ALI) photograph.

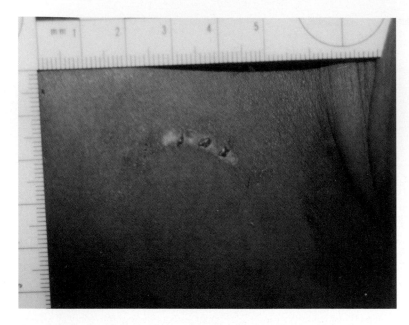

Figure 7.8   Single arch bitemark on shoulder in color photograph.

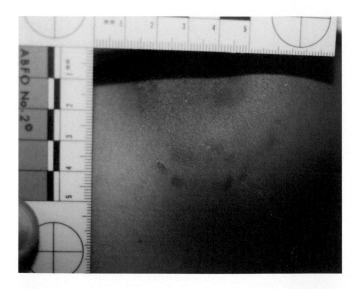

Figure 7.10   Color photograph of bitemark on shoulder taken the day of the incident.

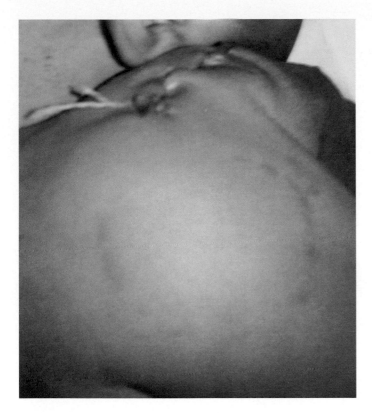

Figure 7.13 ALI photograph of Fig. 7.12.

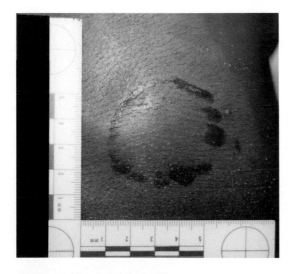

Figure 7.15 Color photograph of a bitemark on the neck on the day of the homicide.

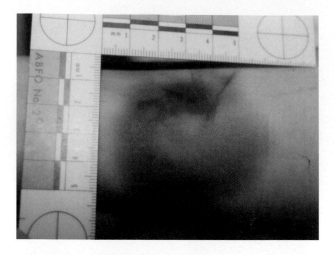

Figure 7.19 Color photograph of poor-quality bitemark on an arm.

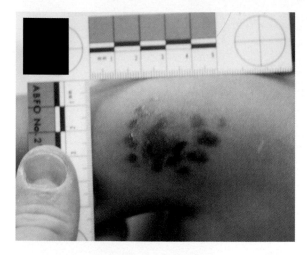

Figure 7.32 Color close-up with scale in place.

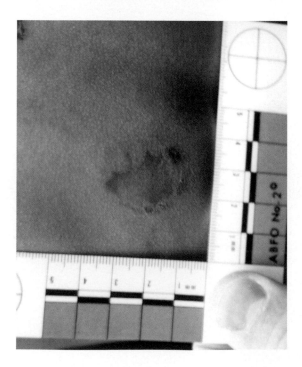

Figure 7.35 Color photograph of bitemark on the back.

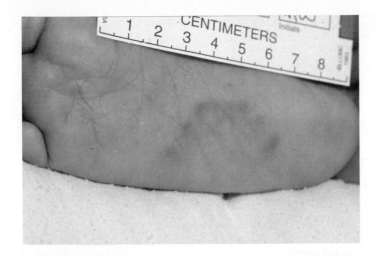

Figure 7.48 Un-retouched color image scanned from a slide.

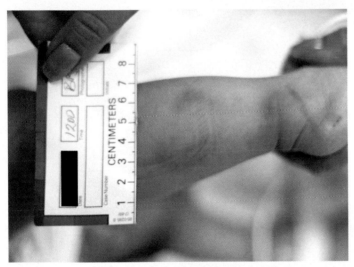

Figure 7.50 Scanned from original color slide with no modifications.

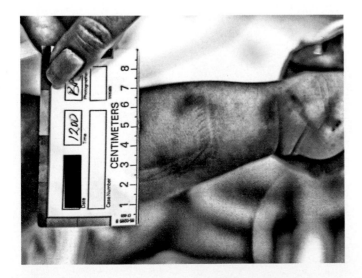

Figure 7.51 Same photo after enhancement with LucisPro.

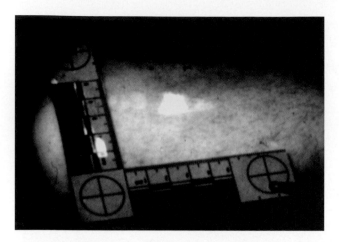

Figure 7.56 Leg close-up with ALI showing presence of fluorescing semen.

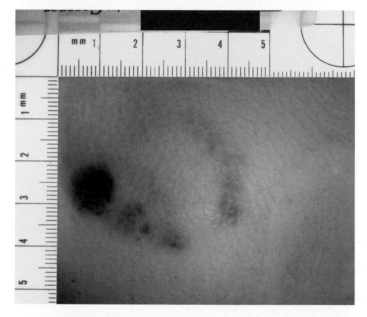

Figure 7.58 Same bite as Fig. 7.57 taken with ALI.

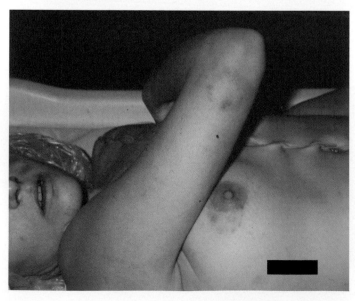

Figure 7.59 Orientation photo: Note bitemarks near right elbow, breast and left cheek.

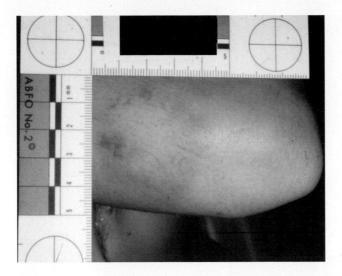

Figure 7.60   Close-up of right elbow, normal light.

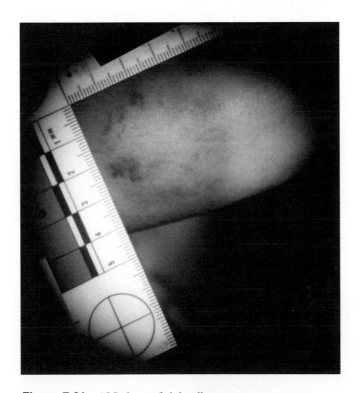

Figure 7.61   ALI photo of right elbow.

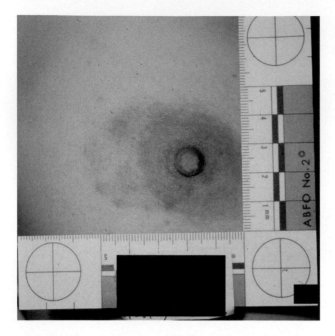

Figure 7.62 Color flash photo of bitemark on right breast.

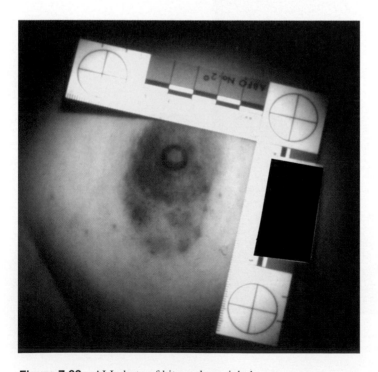

Figure 7.63 ALI photo of bitemark on right breast.

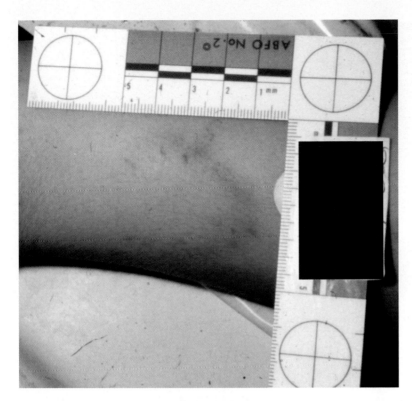

Figure 7.65 Close-up of bitemark on left bicep.

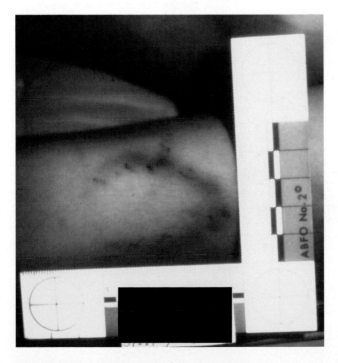

Figure 7.66 ALI photo of bitemark on left bicep.

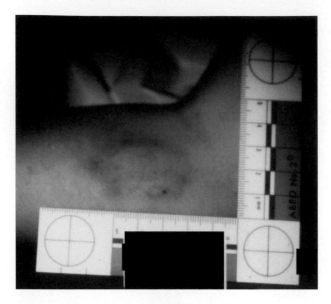

Figure 7.68 ALI photo of bitemark on right forearm.

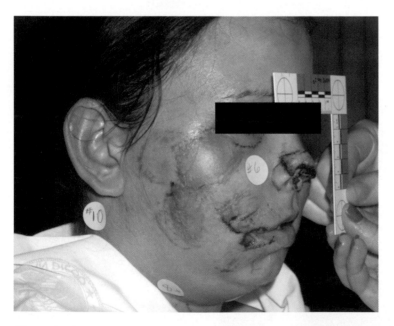

Figure 7.69 Orientation photo. Note numerous overlying bites on face, avulsed bite to nose.

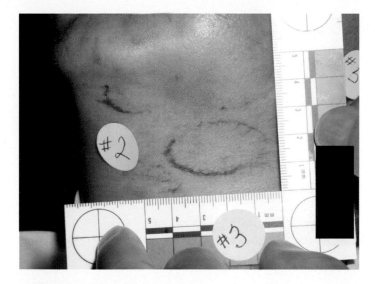

Figure 7.72 Color photo of the bite on the neck.

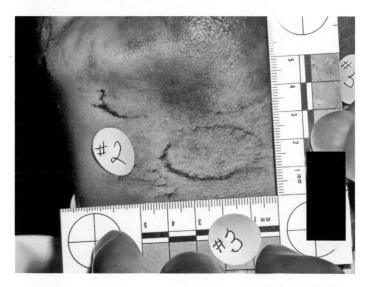

Figure 7.73 LucisPro enhanced image.

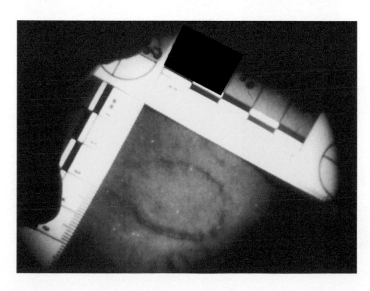

Figure 7.75 ALI photo of same bite on the neck as Fig. 7.74.

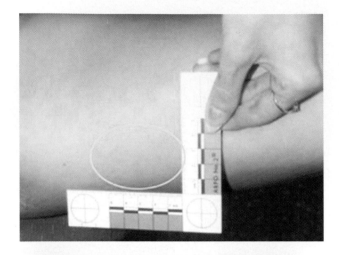

Figure 7.81 Color photograph of same area 20 months after the assault.

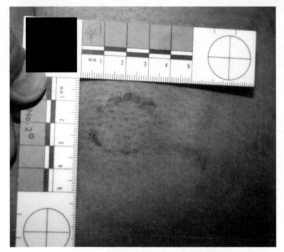

Figure 7.97 Color photograph on the abdomen on the day of the incident.

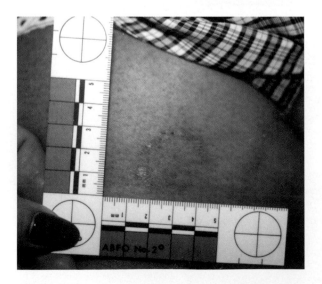

Figure 7.98 Color photograph on the eighth day.

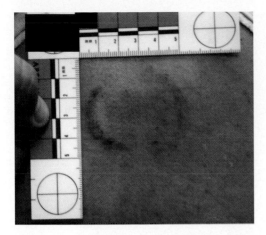

Figure 7.104 Color photograph of the bitemark on the back on the day of incident.

Figure 7.105 Color photograph on the eighth day.

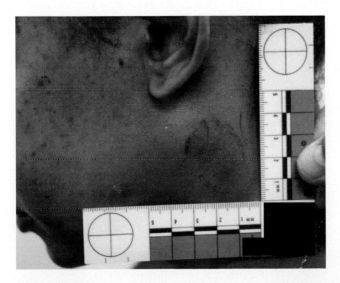

Figure 7.111 Color photograph on the neck on the day of the incident.

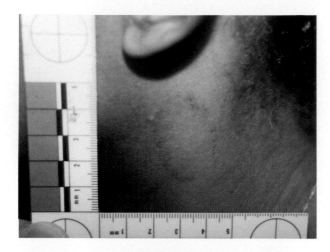

Figure 7.112 Color photograph on the eighth day.

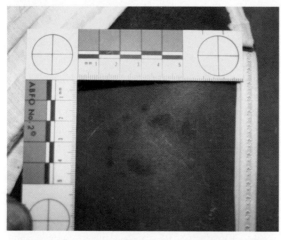

Figure 7.123 Color photograph of a bitemark on the back taken on the day of the incident.

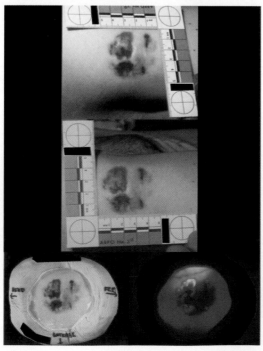

Figure 13.13 Bitemark on an adult female thigh, excised and transilluminated specimen.

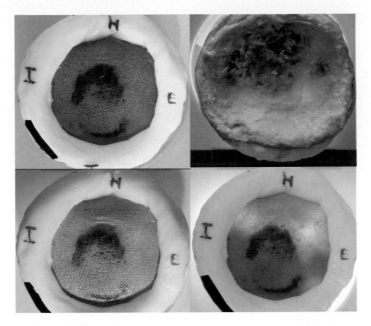

Figure 13.14 Different views of excised and transilluminated bitemark on a shoulder.

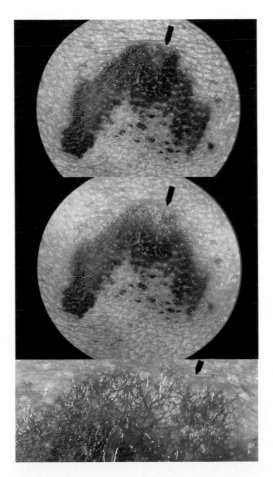

Figure 13.18 Microscopic view of bitemark, transillumination, and blood vessel engorgement.

Figure 13.19 Magnified view of bitemark, blood vessel engorgement, and clothing imprint.

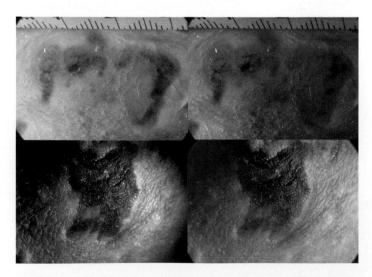

Figure 13.20 Imprints of upper centrals and transilluminated tissue (top photos). Abrasions of unknown etiology on the nipple (bottom photos).

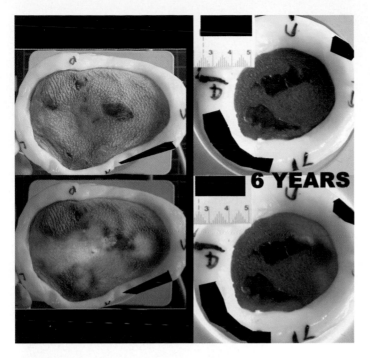

Figure 13.25 Excised and transilluminated tissue: arm/elbow (left), shoulder (right).

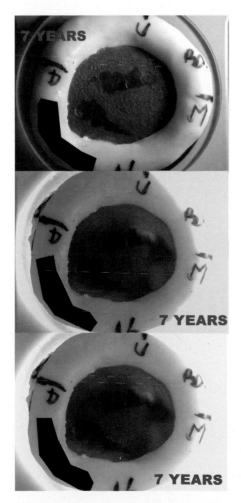

Figure 13.26 Transilluminated bitemark on the shoulder 7 years post-excision.

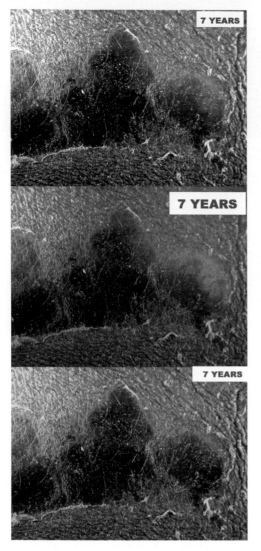

Figure 13.27 Close-up transilluminated bitemark on the shoulder 7 years post-excision.

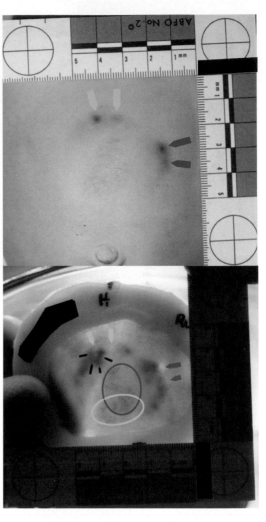

Figure 13.29 Suspicious marks on abdomen and transilluminated specimen.

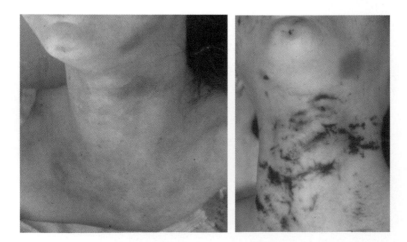

Figure 14.1 Strangled woman found in water. Undiscerned neck abrasions when wet, revealed when dry.

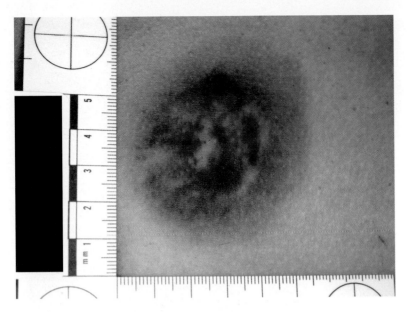

Figure 14.10   Fresh bitemark described as a "purplish green-yellow contusion".

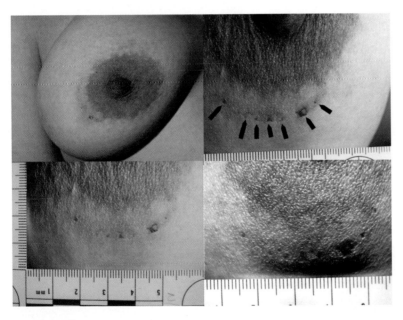

Figure 17.11   Breast abrasion and contusions.

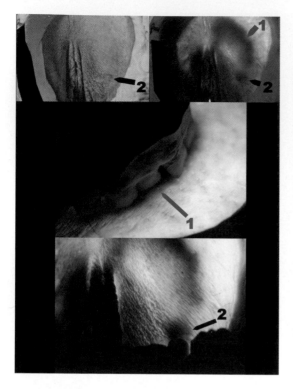

Figure 17.18 Excised and transilluminated pubis and external genitalia and dental comparison.

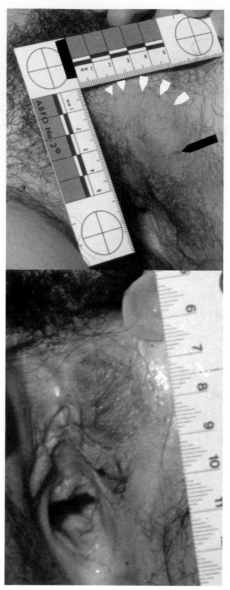

Figure 17.22 Bitemarks on the genitals.

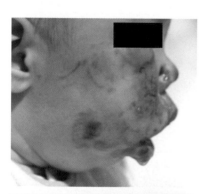

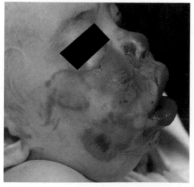

Figure 17.37 Multiple bitemarks on the face photographed 24 hours apart.

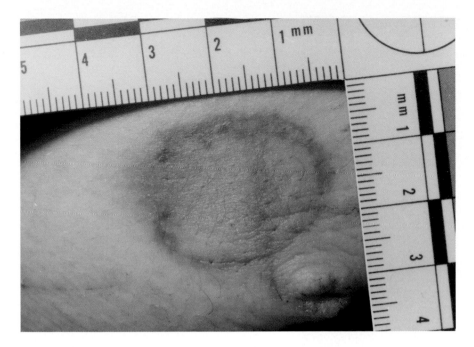

Figure 17.54 Diffuse bitemark on the breast.

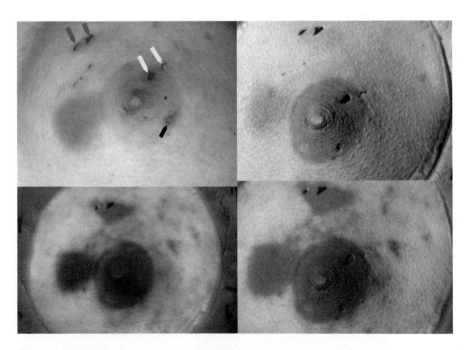

Figure 17.63 Breast (TL), excised (TR), and transilluminated (B) specimen.

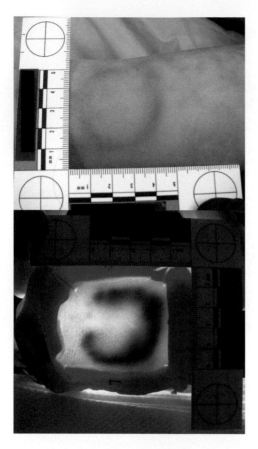

Figure 17.71 Excised supported bitemark (top) and transilluminated specimen (bottom). Photograph courtesy of Dr. Bryan Chrz.

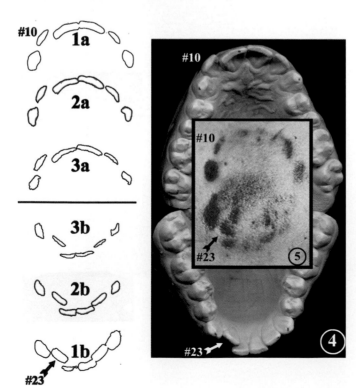

Figure 20.22 Comparison of the three methods of transparent bitemark overlay fabrication with the biter's dental models and the photograph of the bitemark. All three methods are more accurate than the bitemark, yet the correlation of all three to patterned injury is quite high and easily recognized.

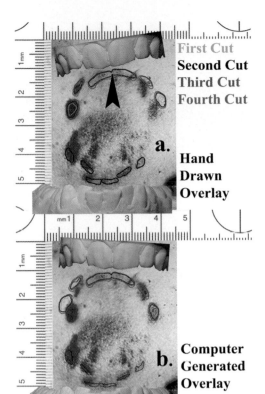

First Cut
Second Cut
Third Cut
Fourth Cut

a. Hand Drawn Overlay

b. Computer Generated Overlay

Figure 20.23 Maxillary Topographic Overlay a) and b) with a mandibular overlay produced using the Photocopy Technique in a) and the Computer Generated Technique in b).

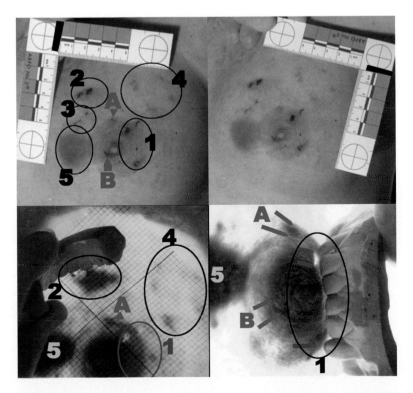

Figure 29.16 Bitemarks on breast (top), and dental comparison of transilluminated specimen.

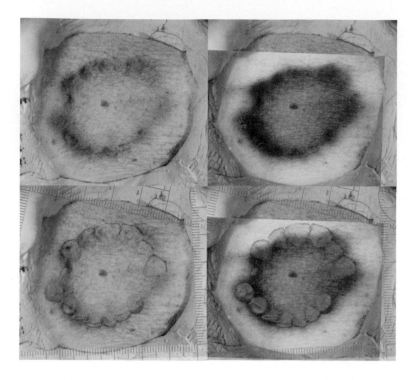

Figure 29.20   Bitemark comparison technique and transillumination.

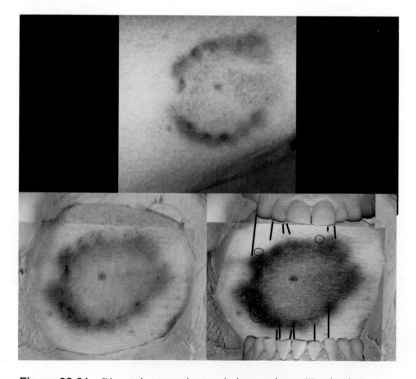

Figure 29.21   Bitemark comparison technique and transillumination.

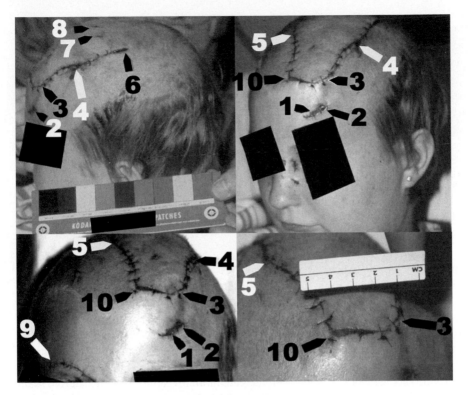

Figure 5 Bitemark produced by a Great Dane.

the skull. Maximum contact of the dog's eight lower anterior teeth with the skull was achieved and formed a crescent-shaped contusion. The upper right canine engaged the skull at 6. As the animal closed the upper jaw, two shorter upper anterior teeth grazed the skull, producing parallel marks [7 and 8] to the upper canines. Note the absence of a crescent-shaped pattern on top of the skull. As the lower anterior teeth penetrated the scalp, closure of the lower jaw produced a loose flap of tissue extending from 3–10 to 4–5. The upper and lower canines approximated one another in jaw closure at 4 and 5. The anterior view depicts the wider track produced by the upper canines. Tracts 3–4 and 5–10 should not be confused with teeth alignment of the lower jaw. The tracts represent the canines' trajectories in jaw closure. The dog's posterior teeth are not involved in any part of this bitemark. Number 9 represents a claw mark. The family pet was a Great Dane.

4. FATAL CANINE ATTACK

Fatal canine attack have been reported by numerous authors [2–13]. The following case highlights facial wounds, partial scalping, and a fractured skull from a fatal Husky attack (Fig. 6). The dog's anterior maxillary dental arch alignment is represented by the white arrows encircling No. 3. A second bite produced a flap of tissue (tissue held by hemostat). The canine tooth penetrated and fractured the skull in a third bite (No. 4). Numbers 1 and 2 represent canine tracks from the Husky's opposite jaw. Note track No. 1 extending from below the mandible throughout the right cheek to the inferior medial aspect of the right eye.

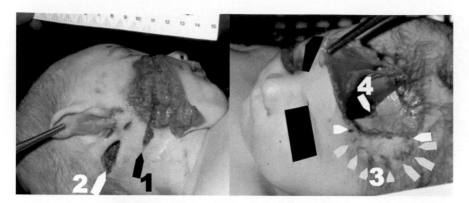

Figure 6 Fatal Husky attack: facial, scalp, and skull trauma.

In an unrelated case, a 2-year-old white male was found dead in a Husky enclosure. Bitemarks were found on the head, neck, and trunk. It is interesting to compare the scalp injuries in Figures 5–8. They are different in appearance as a result of the particular dog's dentition, the animal's head and paw position and movement, and the victim's head position and movement. In the latter two photographs there is no clear indication of paired incised wounds attributable to the canine teeth from the same dental arch. Moreover, there is little indication of an alignment of contusions forming a semicrescent shape that would indicate the dog's eight anterior teeth.

The underlying subcutaneous scalp hemorrhages are more revealing than the external scalp injuries. The same observation can be made of the underlying neck and thoracic injuries (Figs. 7–10). Note the single incised wound on the scalp (Fig. 7) and on the back to the skull

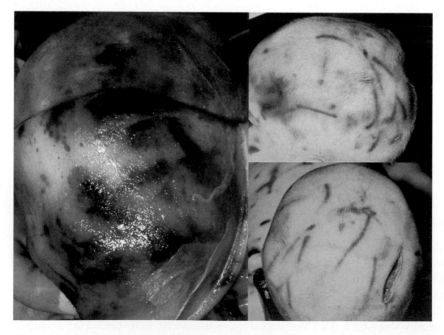

Figure 7 Scalp and underlying tissue damage.

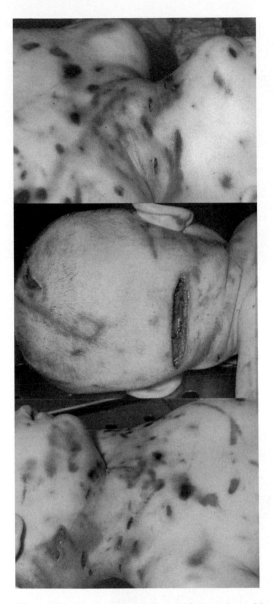

Figure 8 Husky bitemarks on the neck and head.

(Fig. 8). Both of these wounds are caused by a canine tooth. The cause of death was attributed to internal and external hemorrhage including perforation of the left jugular vein (Figs. 8, 9) secondary to multiple dog bites.

The following case illustrates the participation of a German Shepherd and pitbull in a homicide. The pregnant female victim had received over 50 dog bites at the direction of the owner. In addition, she was tied, beaten, and scalded; underwent an attempted hanging; was stabbed seven times in the chest; and was placed nude in a steamer trunk and discarded in −20°F weather.

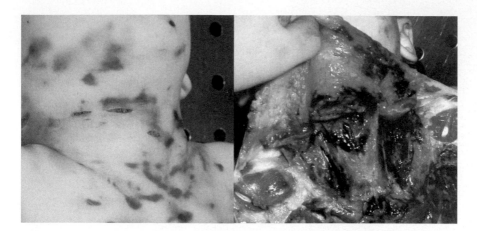

Figure 9 Closeup of Husky bitemarks on neck, and internal damage.

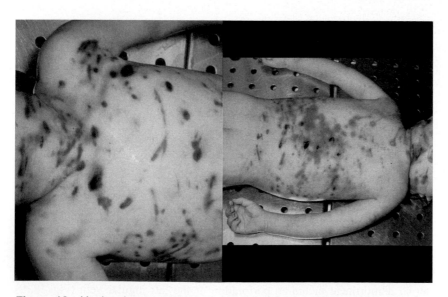

Figure 10 Husky claw and bitemarks on the thorax and back.

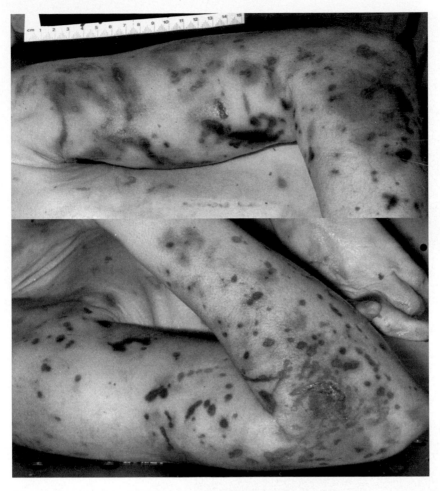

Figure 11 Multiple dog bitemarks on the arms and forearms.

The accused, a pastor of the Universal Life Church of Enlightened Reason, claimed the victim was a witch possessed by the devil. He claimed that he was performing an exorcism on his former secretary.

The dog bites, principally inflicted by the pitbull, were on the arms, forearms (Fig. 11), and legs (Fig. 12). Of the over 50 bites, 27 were individually identifiable. Part of the leg was avulsed (Fig. 12). The primary cause of death was attributed to the seven stab wounds and hemorrhagic shock as result of blood loss. The lungs were punctured, the bronchial tubes severed, and the liver and kidney also affected by the knife wounds.

Both dogs were destroyed by authorities, autopsied, and tested for rabies. The latter was performed in the event the accused had later claimed the dogs were rabid and that he had no control over them. The dogs were not rabid.

5. FORENSIC NIGHTMARE—MISDIAGNOSIS

A 7-year-old white female was found dead and mutilated in her basement. Laser analysis was conducted on the victim's body and no fingerprints were found. No DNA other than the victim's was found in fingernail clippings. The victim was not sexually molested.

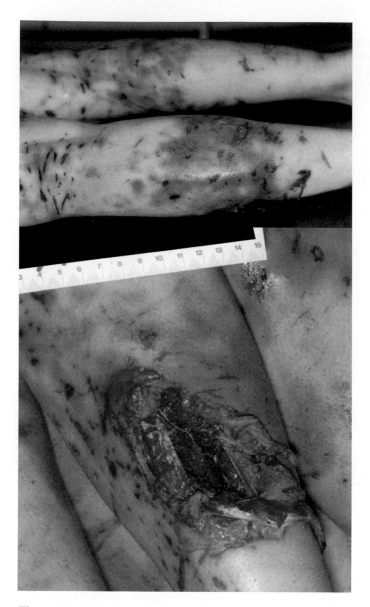

Figure 12   Multiple dog bitemarks on the legs with avulsion.

A pathologist performed an autopsy and concluded that there were (1) multiple cutaneous abrasions and contusions, (2) exsanguination, and (3) excision of the scalp (with a pair of scissors).

He attributed the cause of death to more than 80 stab wounds created by scissors and/or knives. The child's blood was not found on any clothing elsewhere in the house, nor was there blood found on any knives or scissors. The single mother was charged with second-degree murder 11 days later. She was refused bail and was placed in isolation for her own protection as social services took custody of her other children.

Although the pathologist was aware of the presence of a pitbull in the victim's basement at the time of death, a forensic dentist was not summoned at autopsy. The pitbull's owner, a friend of the mother's, told police that the dog had a ''reddish'' substance on him when summoned from the basement prior to the discovery of the body. The victim's blood was later found on the shaved dog hair and dog collar. The dog's owner also told police that the dog feces subsequently contained hair.

The pitbull owner had the dog destroyed 2 months later for a ''nipping and biting'' incident. During all of this time, authorities (police, veterinarian, pathologist, odontologist) failed to isolate, examine, and take the dog's dental impressions. When testing for rabies the dog's head was destroyed and was no longer available. The odontologist concluded:

> The marks found on the (autopsy) photographs are completely inconsistent with dog bite marks be they either domestic or wild. I base this conclusion on the following findings: the markings are the wrong shape to be dog bite marks. The markings on the deceased are linear incisions rather than conical punctures which are typical of dog bite marks. ⋯ In summary I can say without equivocation that the markings seen on the deceased are not dog bite marks.

The odontologist's report preceded the pathologist's by 2 weeks.

Defense counsel consulted an odontologist and a pathologist. Available reports were reviewed and crime scene/autopsy photographs assessed, and both defense experts attributed the injuries to animal bitemarks.

The following month, the prosecution's pathologist testified at the preliminary hearing and under cross-examination professed that it ''was absurd to think that the marks on the body could be attributed to a dog'' and ''as absurd as it is to think that a polar bear attacked (the victim), so is it equally absurd that it's a dog wound.'' The defense informed the prosecution of its experts' conclusions.

The accused, a welfare recipient, fired her lawyer and obtained the services of a new one.

The prosecution made an application for an order to have the child's body exhumed and halted judicial proceedings pending the results of a second autopsy. Twenty-five months following the alleged homicide, defense counsel made a new application for bail, this time unopposed by the prosecution. As part of her condition for release to a halfway house, the accused was not permitted to contact either her children or any of the witnesses in the case. She literally remained under house arrest and was escorted on outings.

A new pathologist performed an autopsy of the exhumed remains. Present were the original pathologist and odontologist and the like experts representing the defense's interest. The body was poorly preserved. The right humerus, some vertebrae, skull, and mandible were kept for ulterior examination.

The new conclusions: A dog was responsible for at least some of the injuries without naming their location or numbers. In addition, ''the possibility that a weapon was also involved in the infliction of the injuries is not excluded by the second autopsy,'' again without naming the location, type of weapon, or number of injuries that might have been produced by this (these) unnamed mysterious weapon(s). Oddly enough, the examination of the retained bony specimens was deferred to the odontologist who had failed to correctly identify the soft tissue injuries as bitemarks in the first place. The reports date 2 years and 3 months after the alleged homicide.

The judge ordered the original pathologist to write a second report in light of the second autopsy results. His new conclusion: ''Because death resulted not from a single injury but the combined effect of numerous injuries, it is not possible along morphological grounds alone to determine the relative responsibilities of the noncanine versus the canine like injuries in causing the death.''

Despite the admitted presence of the dog bites, the prosecution claimed that there was sufficient evidence to proceed with a trial despite the fact that (a) weapon(s) was/were never found. The alleged motive for the murder was that the mother was angry at the child for having head lice.

> On the basis of all the evidence in the case, there is a reasonable prospect of conviction. Therefore, the Crown [prosecution] has no intention of withdrawing the charges. I wish to make that clear, since you have made at least three requests so far for withdrawal, and I do not want you to be under the mistaken impression that this is a possibility.

The prosecution was now claiming that the dog simply ''interfered'' with the body.

The prosecution consulted many other experts including fiber, entolomologist, animal behaviorist, bloodstain pattern analyst, and toxicologist. Three months before trial the prosecution consulted an anthropologist who examined the skull and vertebrae. The conclusions: The marks on the skeletal remains were caused by dog bites except for eight or nine marks on the skull. Of these markings, some were described as incisions along the skull caused by a scalpel or a very sharp knife. The cutting instruments seized by the police were all excluded as being the cause of the marks on the skull. The last sentence of the report concludes, ''While osteological analysis is important in a case like this, the best analysis of trauma is conducted using skin and bone. Skin is more accurate in recording trauma, while bone is more permanent. It is only with the combination of the pathological and anthropological examination (of) the whole body, that accurate assessments can be reached.'' Ironically, the anthropologist was mistaken in at least one conclusion because the crime scene/autopsy photographs were not presented for his examination.

The prosecution dropped all charges the week before trial ''since it no longer has proof that this death was caused by stab wounds.'' The accused spent almost 4 years awaiting trial for a murder that never occurred, grieved over the death of a child, lost custody of her other children, and became a social outcast.

The following week a $7 million lawsuit was launched against the original pathologist, the odontologist, the police, and the prosecutor's office for malicious prosecution, false imprisonment, and gross negligence.

5.1. Pattern Distribution on the Arm

Spitz [14] defines blunt trauma injury as one of three basic types: contusion, abrasion, or laceration. A contusion (bruise) signifies hemorrhage into the skin, the tissues under the skin, or both. An abrasion is a scraping and removal of the superficial layers of the skin. A laceration is a tear produced by blunt trauma. Sharp force injury such as a standalone results from penetration of a pointed instrument into the depth of the body, causing a wound that is deeper than its length on the skin.

Figure 13 depicts the pattern distribution on the victim's right arm. Bruising and lacerations are more apparent on the inner aspect of the arm (bottom photo), while penetrating wounds abound on the outer surface.

5.2 Wound Patterning on the Neck

The neck trauma is illustrated in Figure 14. Note the similarity in pattern distribution and injury on the neck and scalp produced in the fatal pitbull attack to those produced in a fatal bear attack (Fig. 15). A bitemark pattern on the neck may vary greatly in size and shape depending on the victim's head and neck movement (flexion, extension, rotation, etc.), the animal's dentition, and head and neck movements. The cause of death of the victim of the fatal bear attack depicted in Fig. 15 was perforation and fracture of the third and fourth cervical vertebrae and exsanguination.

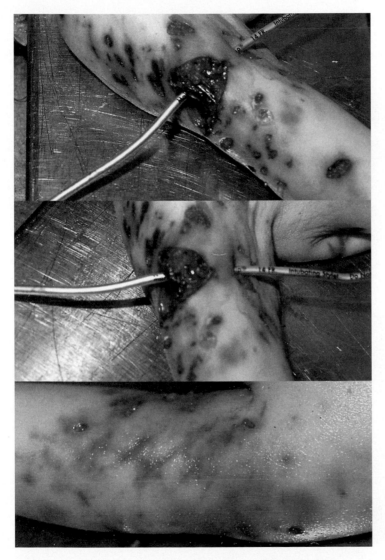

Figure 13 Different views of pitbull bites on the right arm.

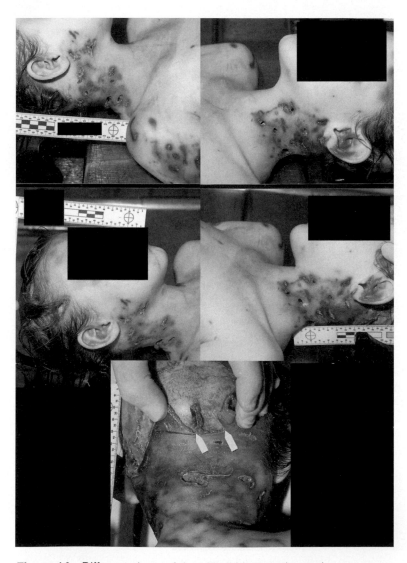

Figure 14   Different views of the pitbull bites on the neck.

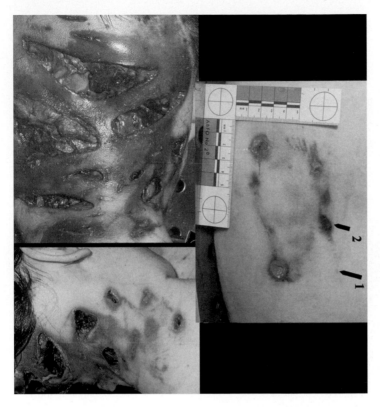

Figure 15   Bear bites on the skull (top left), neck (bottom left), and thigh (right).

5.3.   Direction of Wound Patterning on the Neck

Figure 16 depicts a closeup view of pitbull bitemarks on the neck. All of the neck wounds are sloping perpendicular to the neck and oriented in an anteroposterior direction.

5.4.   Bitemarks on the Back

The original overexposed photograph Figure 17 of the back (top photo) and ''corrected'' image (bottom photo) reveals a wealth of information. The original overexposed color photograph was digitized, gray-scaled, and corrected for brightness and contrast. The dark gray areas represent dried blood. The imprint of five lower anterior teeth can be seen at the tip of the black arrows. These contusions were evidently inflicted when the victim was alive since they represent an inflammatory response. Given that the back is a relatively flat surface, a dog is unable to open its jaw sufficiently wide to obtain contact of the canines to skin. The bitemark pattern is markedly different from those on the arm, the neck, and the skull. Tracing a path from the five contusions toward the right shoulder, a region devoid of blood can be observed. This is the result of the dog dragging its chin along the child's back. The white arrows represent claw marks. Within the white ellipse are intersecting bitemark/claw marks. Another bitemark is present on the left scapula (within the square). Note the absence of the canine teeth in this bitemark also.

Despite the fact that an ABFO No. 2 scale was used in two of the initial autopsy photographs, neither pathologist nor odontologist diagnosed the dog bitemarks (Fig. 18). The photo-

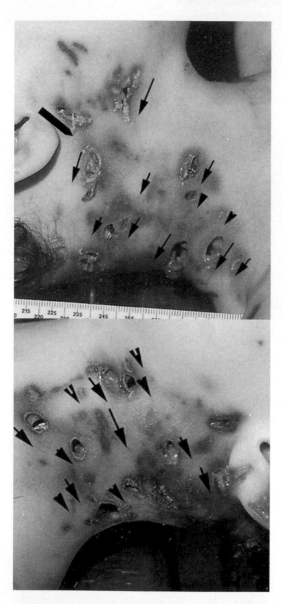

Figure 16 Neck trauma from a pitbull dentition.

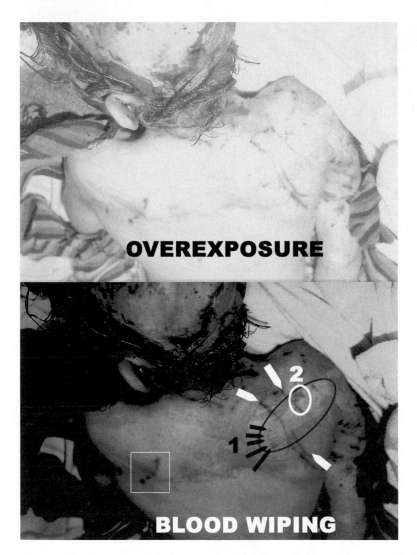

Figure 17 Overexposed photograph of the back (top) and "corrected" photograph (bottom).

graph on the left depicts five contusions representing five anterior teeth. The right photograph presents a similar pattern with an intersecting claw mark (Figs. 17, 18).

5.5. Clothing

The relationship between torn clothing and underlying tissue trauma cannot be overemphasized (Fig. 19). The prosecution's fabric specialist claimed that R2 may have been caused either by normal wear-and-tear or by a pointed blunt instrument. R3 resulted from a dull bladed instrument and suggests that the bladed instrument may have penetrated and more than once. R4 was a very clean cut "L" shape produced by a sharp instrument and created by the pathologist cutting the garment from the body. If a bladed instrument is the cause of the tears in the T-shirt, where are the corresponding skin lesions (Figs. 17, 18)? Where are the corresponding T-shirt perforations over the right arm from the alleged stab wounds (Fig. 13)?

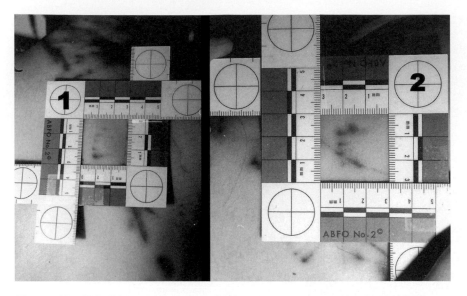

Figure 18   Pitbull bitemark on back (left) and an intersected bitemark (right).

5.6.   The Humerus

The defense's forensic odontologist and the prosecution's anthropologist arrived at the same conclusions regarding the humerus. The humerus demonstrated shallow U-shaped parallel striations consistent with the carnivore dentition. There were no signs of sharp instrument markings from knife or scissors. Moreover, there were no penetrating injuries to the bone representing the tips of either knife or scissors.

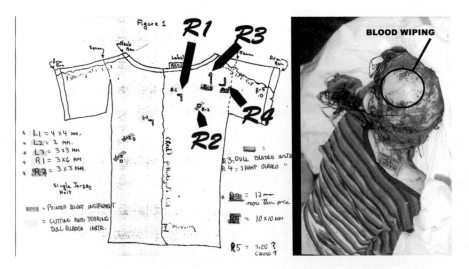

Figure 19   Diagram of clothing (left), and clothed victim (right).

5.7.   The Mandible

The original pathologist described the mandibular injury as follows: "The right jugular and sternocleidomastoid region bore penetrating stab and incised injuries with one penetrating injury also present at the inferior angle of the right mandible and others more superficially over the right mandibular skin." That was the extent of the mandibular examination.

Not a single prosecution expert witness (two pathologists, an odontologist, and an anthropologist) examined and described the injury to the retained mandible from the second autopsy. There were, after all, six separate reports from these experts.

The fracture at the angle of the right mandible was examined on the dried specimen by the defense odontologist. The compression fracture was consistent with what would have been produced by a dog's canine tooth and not as the result of a sharp instrument blow such as a knife or scissors. The overlying soft tissue injury can be observed in Figures 14 and 16.

5.8.   The Skull and Cervical Vertebra: Holes and Bitemarks

There was a round puncture mark in the midsquamous area just left of the midline occipital which measured 4.6 mm in diameter (Fig. 20 right photos). A second oval puncture on the left temporal bone above the external auditory meatus in the squamous area of bone measured 4.8 mm vertically and 7.6 mm horizontally (Fig. 20 left photos). According to the autopsy report, the occipital and temporal perforations were beveled on the inner table but did not open directly into the cranial cavity. A third puncture over the left mastoid region broke through the outer table only and measured roughly 9 × mm. The distance, from center to center, between the

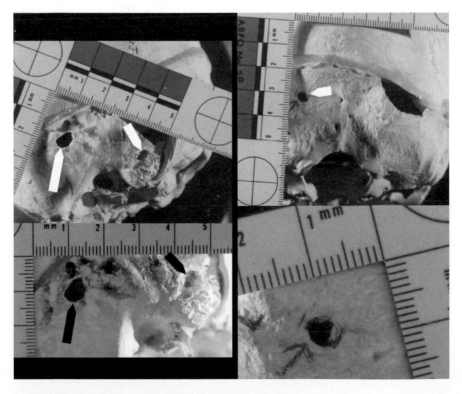

Figure 20   Location of the three skull perforations.

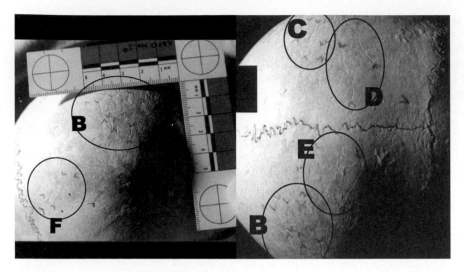

Figure 21 Various indentations on the skull.

latter two defects was 34 mm. The shape, size, and distance between these two perforations are consistent with a dog's canine teeth within the same dental arch. Figures 21–23 depict numerous parallel indented U-shaped striations on the skull consistent with the carnivore dentition.

One area of interest that involved the use of a sharp instrument on the skull was in the posterior right lateral region. The three sharp parallel marks highlighted between the arrows (Fig. 24) were made with an implement similar to the one used to produce a fourth test mark between the two dots—namely, a scalpel blade. The three parallel scalpel marks coincide with a region of remaining scalp that would have been reflected during the first autopsy (Fig. 14). The

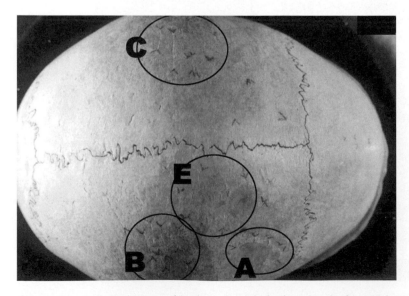

Figure 22 Indentations on the skull. Oval A depicts the dog's anterior tooth alignment.

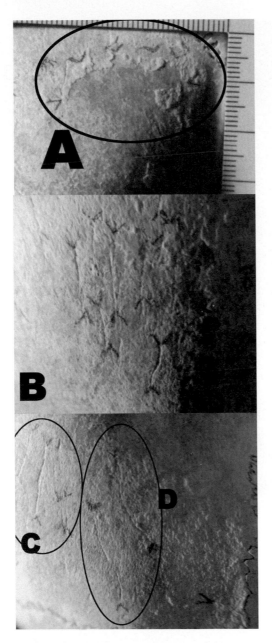

Figure 23 Various indentations on skull. Oval A depicts dog's anterior tooth alignment.

prosecution implied the marks were produced by the unfound murder weapon. It is interesting to note that the entire periphery of missing scalp on the skull was devoid of similar markings. Would it have been so had the scalp been removed by scissors and or knife? Would there not be the tip of the knife and or scissors implant somewhere on the skull surface?

The second cervical anterior body (vertebra) contained a small defect left of the midline measuring 8.9 mm horizontally by 2.5 mm vertically. The shape was dissimilar to what would have been produced by either scissors or knives.

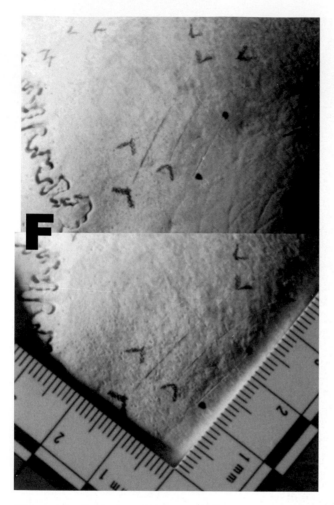

Figure 24 Scalpel markings on skull.

5.9. "Blood Wiping" on the Skull

There is "blood wiping" along the back (Fig. 17) as well as the top left-hand side of the skull (Fig. 19).

5.10. Impressions and X-Rays

During the first autopsy the pathologist took an impression of the perforations of the skull. There was mention of neither the protocol followed nor the materials utilized, nor the results obtained in the autopsy report. There was no mention either of the odontologist's examination of the impression. The impression was introduced as evidence at the 14-day preliminary hearing and returned to the pathologist for safekeeping. That impression has never since been located. The original autopsy radiographs have also been misplaced.

5.11. The Avulsed Scalp

The blood-soaked scalp was never swabbed for the presence of animal DNA at the original autopsy. Despite the 2.5-year custody, the initial pathologist had yet to shave the avulsed scalp to observe the presence/absence of lacerations, abrasions, etc., on the external surface of the scalp and to associate/disassociate any corresponding subcutaneous hemorrhage and scalp perforations.

The fixed scalp was shaved during the second autopsy and viewed against an autopsy light. The transilluminated scalp confirmed the presence of bitemarks of animal origin. In addition to the abrasions and perforations attributed to a dog dentition, the corresponding associated hemorrhage was observed. This clearly indicated scalp removal during life.

Despite this finding, the second pathologist's cursory examination simply reported: ''The scalp is distorted by fixation and shows areas of postmortem sectioning. There are also several defects, which invariably penetrate the scalp.''

The prosecution's odontologist submitted a report on the examination of the retained skull from the second autopsy, but he also failed to examine/analyze/correlate the findings to the available scalp. In fact, he had failed to examine and analyze the scalp's evidentiary value for his first report.

A dog bite pattern on the scalp will be markedly different in appearance from those found on other areas of the body. The scalp is relatively fixed, large, and curved. The physical characteristics of the scalp is different when detached. A single wound produced by a canine tooth must be distinguished from a claw mark, for example.

5.12. Size of Defect on the Skull Versus Avulsed Scalp

The perimeter of the missing scalp should have been measured on the skull at the first autopsy. This measure should have been compared to the perimeter of the avulsed scalp. This could have been determined if any of the avulsed scalp was missing/lost or could have been ingested by the dog. When comparing size and shape of the avulsed scalp to the missing scalp on the skull, it would appear from photographic evidence that a portion of the avulsed scalp is missing. This would be consistent with the dog's having eaten part of the scalp and a dog owner's statement of finding hair in the dog feces. The periphery of the missing scalp on the skull and periphery of the avulsed scalp can best be measured by aligning string along its outer border.

Figures 25–27 show different views of the skull and missing scalp. The photo in Figure 27 demonstrates the relationship between the three skull perforations and remaining scalp tissue. As the prosecution's anthropologist points out, ''While osteological analysis is important in a case like this, the best analysis of trauma is conducted using skin and bone.'' The canine perforations 2 and 3 from the same dental arch are 3.4 cm apart. A line drawn perpendicular to the midpoint orients toward the back of the skull. Perforation 1 and the remaining soft tissue

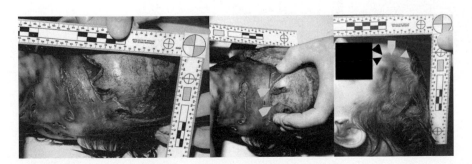

Figure 25 Skull views with missing scalp from a fatal pitbull attack.

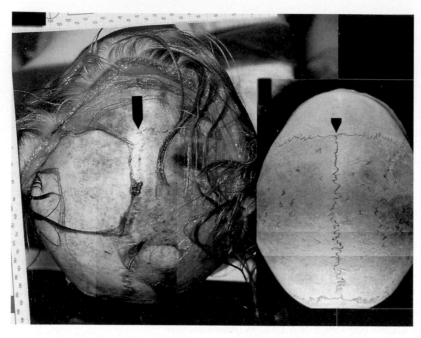

Figure 26 Missing scalp on the skull (left) and dry skull (insert).

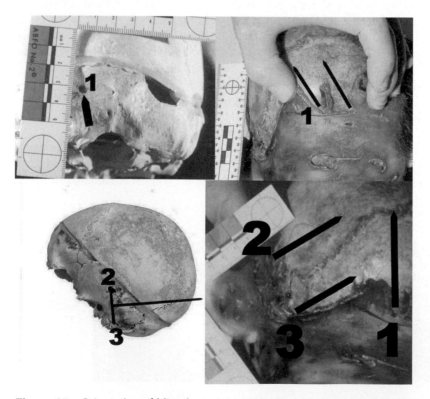

Figure 27 Orientation of bites based on perforation alignment and residual tissue.

(top photos) orients toward the top left of the skull. In addition, the distance between perforations 1 and 3 is too large to have been produced by a single bite (opening diameter).

5.13. Size and Location of Perforations on Scalp

The size, location, and orientation of perforations on the scalp can indicate the direction of removal of the scalp. This can be associated and compared to the skull tooth markings. The size of the missing scalp from the skull, together with the aforementioned factors, suggests a minimum of four bites would have been needed for scalp avulsion.

Even though the avulsed scalp had been fixed for over 2 years, it is interesting to note that the intercanine distance had been relatively well preserved with minimal shrinkage of the tissue (Fig. 28). The base measurement utilized to compare scalp shrinkage was 3.4 cm, the distance between the perforations on the skull. To demonstrate intercanine distance and the relationship of the other six anterior teeth, dental models were made of another dog (the suspect dog having been destroyed) and compared to the avulsed scalp (Fig. 29).

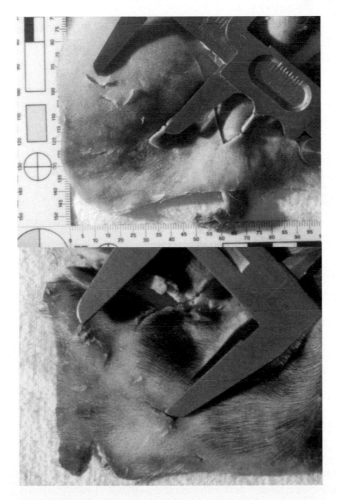

Figure 28 Caliper measurements of perforations on avulsed scalp.

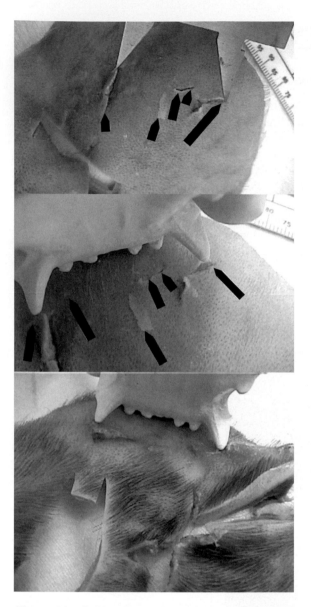

Figure 29   Canine bitemark comparison on avulsed scalp.

5.14.   Tissue Vitality and Transillumination

Blood vessel engorgement and subcutaneous hemorrhage can be visualized in transilluminated tissue when they exist. Both phenomenan are the result of the inflammatory process, which by definition can only take place in the living.

Figure 30 shows three views of the avulsed scalp. The photograph on the left is the avulsed scalp at the first autopsy prior to fixation. The middle photograph depicts the fixed transilluminated scalp after shaving at the second autopsy. Lastly, the right photo shows the entire shaved resected fixed scalp. Contusions, lacerations, perforations, and associated subcutaneous bleeding are evident (Figs. 29, 30).

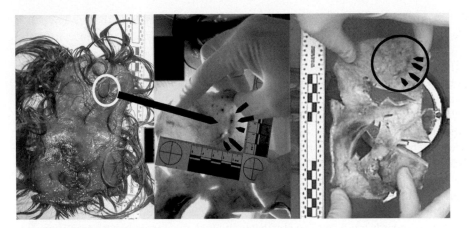

Figure 30   Three views of the avulsed scalp.

5.15.   Failures of the First Autopsy

It would be futile to critique a case without learning from it. Were there system failures? How can these failures be prevented in the future? Who is ultimately responsible? What are the forensic lessons to be learned? The last question is better answered by the failures in the autopsy protocol. They can simply be listed as follows:

1. Failure to take DNA swabs of the body/wounds, clothing, and avulsed scalp for the presence of animal DNA
2. Failure to recognize the patterned injuries as bitemarks
3. Failure to request the presence of the forensic dentist at autopsy
4. Failure to interpret blood smear with the patterned injuries of the back and the skull
5. Failure to analyze and associate marks on the clothing to the patterned injuries
6. Failure to take adequate impressions of the bitemarks and the perforated skull
7. Failure to measure the peripheral dimension of the avulsed scalp
8. Failure to measure the peripheral dimension of the missing scalp on the skull
9. Failure to shave and analyze the abrasions, contusions, etc., and the pattern distribution on surface of the avulsed scalp
10. Failure to correlate the latter to the markings on the skull
11. Failure to transilluminate the avulsed scalp
12. Failure to analyze the marks on bone (humerus, skull, jaw, and vertebra)
13. Failure to recommend, seize, quarantine, examine, take impressions of the dog's dentition, and have a rabies test performed.

The forensic pathologist's principal duty is to diagnose and arrive at conclusions for the cause and manner of death. The misdiagnosis of bitemarks for stab wounds changed the manner of death from accidental to homicide. In turn, this led police up an erroneous investigative path. This does not excuse investigators since the factual evidence did not match the thesis of homicide. When motive is reduced to the presence of hair lice, and a weapon cannot be found despite the limited time between the discovery of the body and the alleged homicide, one needs to question oneself. When the victim's blood cannot be found on any of the accused's clothing despite the fact that she had not changed her clothes, one needs to question the thesis of a knife/scissors homicide.

When there are known facts that are completely disregarded such as the presence of a dog at the death scene, one can expect trouble. Failure to obtain physical evidence from the suspect dog for comparison with victim evidence is substandard protocol.

When a defense lawyer can differentiate dog bites from stab wounds and a pathologist and odontologist cannot, one needs to question the expert's education, knowledge, training, experience, and credentials.

When the court declares a person an expert witness and that person is not board certified in that specific forensic discipline, one needs to question the system. While it is true that in certain jurisdictions board certification in forensic disciplines is unavailable or does not exist, international boards in that specific discipline may exist. The designation "forensic pathologist" and "forensic dentist" has no academic basis. Any pathologist or dentist can claim to be a forensic expert. Board certification in a forensic discipline assures the trier of fact of basic knowledge, education, experience, and training of the expert in that forensic discipline. More-over, certain ethical standards are maintained by that individual, the person can be peer reviewed, and he must keep current in knowledge, standards, and procedures of the discipline, and must be recertified on a timely basis.

5.16. Failures of the First Autopsy Report

Aside from the misdiagnosis of cause and manner of death, the first autopsy report failed in other respects. It should have reported the following:

1. The names of persons present at the first viewing
2. The names of persons present at autopsy (2 days later)
3. The name(s) of the person(s) taking the autopsy photographs
4. The name of the person performing the dissections (denar or pathologist)
5. Listing what was performed at the initial viewing separate from the autopsy
6. Test ordered and/or recommended other than toxicology
7. A description of the chain of possession of various exhibits.

5.17. Forensic Lessons to be Learned

The death of this child and subsequent murder charges against the mother underlie important issues concerning medical/dental expert witnesses: accountability; coordinating/integrating all factual and forensic elements in the case; and board certification.

Crime scene investigators and the pathologist set the tone for a police investigation. In this case, the manner of death was established as homicide; it should have been accidental. The cause of death was established as stab wounds by knife/scissors; it should have been dog bites.

Forensic conferences periodically debate the theme: How much factual/related information should a forensic expert receive before undertaking a case? Failure to obtain as much factual information as possible prior to autopsy can prove disastrous. Moreover, having different experts examine individual exhibits separately without having factual knowledge of the case, can lead to wrongful conclusions. The evidence must match the facts, and vice versa. In this case, the erroneous conclusions of both pathologist and odontologist "fit" into the investigative theme of homicide despite an incredibly flimsy motive and lack of weapon.

A forensic expert's background, training, education, skill, and experience are at issue. An opinion is to an expert witness what a diagnosis is to a physician/dentist. An erroneous opinion is potentially catastrophic. Liability may result from such opinions.

Board certification may soon become a prerequisite to testimony in North American courts for all forensic disciplines. Today anyone with a dental degree/pathology certificate can call himself or herself a forensic dentist/pathologist. The term is nonrestrictive, denoting neither the claimant's forensic background, forensic education, forensic knowledge, forensic training, forensic skill, nor forensic experience. There are relatively few forensic dentists/pathologists practicing in North America, and virtually all reside/travel to metropolitan areas where forensic autopsies are performed. Their forensic education, training, knowledge, skill, and experience vary greatly from one jurisdiction to another. The limited number of dentists/pathologists actively involved in the practice of forensic dentistry/pathology precludes the viability of certifying boards in the different provinces/states. As a result this author and seven colleagues founded the American Board Forensic Odontology in 1976. It is the certifying body in forensic dentistry for North America.

> The objective of the Board was to establish, enhance, and revise as necessary, standards of qualification for those who practice forensic odontology, and to certify as qualified specialists those voluntary applicants who comply with the requirements of the Board. In this way, the Board aims to make available a practical and equitable system for readily identifying those persons professing to be specialists in forensic odontology who possess the requisite qualifications and competence. Certification is based upon the candidate's personal and professional record of education, training, experience and achievement, as well as the results of a formal examination [15].

REFERENCES

1. Centers for Disease Control and Prevention. Dog bite related fatalities in the United States in 1995–1996. JAMA 1997; 278(4):278–279.
2. Lauridson JR, Myers L. Evaluation of fatal dog bites: the view of the medical examiner and animal behaviorist. J Forens Sci 1993; 38(3):726–731.
3. Sacks JJ, Lockwood R, Hornreich J, Sattin RW. Fatal dog attacks, 1989–1994. Pediatrics 1996; 97(6):891–895.
4. Avis SP. Dog pack attack: hunting humans. Am J Forens Med Pathol 1999; 20(3):243–246.
5. Sacks JJ, Sinclair L, Gilchrist J, Golab GC, Lockwood R. Breeds of dogs involved in fatal human attacks in the United States between 1979 and 1998. J Am Vet Med Assoc 2000; 217(6):836–840.
6. Calkins CM, Bensard DD, Patrick DA, Karrer FM. Life-threatening dog attacks: a devastating combination of penetrating and blunt injuries. J Pediatr Surg 2001; 36(8):1115–1117.
7. de Munnynck K, Van de Voorde W. Forensic approach of fatal dog attacks: a case report and literature review. Int J Legal Med 2002; 116(5):295–300.
8. Dorion RBJ. Pattern injuries on the deceased, AAFS meeting, Odontology Section, Seattle, Feb. 23, 2001.
9. Dorion RBJ. Pitfalls in documenting and preserving bitemark evidence in pediatric death, AAFS meeting, Odontology Section, Seattle, Feb. 23, 2001.
10. Dorion RBJ. The Sharon Reynolds case, AAFS meeting, Odontology Section, Atlanta, Feb. 14, 2002.
11. Klim-Lemann JW, Golden GS. Bitemark analysis in the mauling death of child: a case study, AAFS, Odontology Section, Chicago, Feb. 21, 2003.
12. Sur AKY. What drives a dog to bite, AAFS, Odontology Section, Chicago, Feb. 21, 2003.
13. Winter DM, Biggs C. Christopher Wilson: unintentional second-degree murder conviction for a killing committed by dogs, AAFS, Odontology Section, Chicago, Feb. 21, 2003.
14. Spitz WU, Ed. Medical legal investigation of death: guidelines for the application of pathology to crime investigation. 3rd ed.. Springfield. IL: Charles C. Thomas, 1993:199–310.
15. Background, Functions and Purposes of the American Board of Forensic Odontology, Inc.

17
Human Bitemarks

Robert B. J. Dorion
Laboratoire de sciences judiciaires et de médecine légale,
Ministry of Public Security for the Province of Quebec,
Montreal, Quebec, Canada

1. INTRODUCTION

Class characteristics (Fig. 1) distinguish bitemarks from other patterned injuries. Rectangular and circular contusions and/or depressions are aligned to form a round to oval pattern representing maxillary and mandibular tooth arrangements. The size, arrangements, and overall diameter distinguish adult from child dentitions. The difference between animal and human bitemarks are even more dramatic.

Individual characteristics (Fig. 2), on the other hand, are features or patterns that present individual variation within a defined group. These features include rotation, notching, misalignment, and fractures, as examples.

2. FACTORS AFFECTING BITEMARK DYNAMICS

There are many factors (Fig. 3) affecting bitemark dynamics. Some are associated with the victim; others, with the assailant, the recording, and the preservation of the evidence as well as miscellaneous factors. One of the many problems involved with experimental bitemark replication is that the circumstances and the factors involved can never be duplicated precisely. Every bitemark is unique. There are over 90 factors listed in Figure 3, and controlling for each and every factor experimentally would be impossible.

The present chapter will attempt to explain the influence of some of the factors involved with bitemark evidence by case demonstration. When a specific factor is implicated, it is not at the exclusion of others.

Pretty and Sweet [1] reported on the distribution of 148 human bitemarks was as follows: breast 33%; arm 19%; genitalia 8%; back 7%; face and thigh 6% each; leg and hand 5% each; neck 4%; shoulder 3%; abdomen and buttocks, 2% each. This closely approximates Vale and Noguchi's earlier report on 67 bitemark cases [2].

Figure 4 demonstrates two cases of contusions around the areolas. Neither case is specific enough to demonstrate class characteristics associated with the aggressors' dentition. This does not imply that proper examination and recording of these findings are unnecessary; quite the contrary. Supported tissue excision, transillumination, and histological examination of the specimen might give additional information not available from external examination alone. Figure 29 in Chapter 13 and others in this text illustrate this point very clearly.

CLASS CHARACTERISTICS

➤ OVAL TO ROUND SHAPE
➤ ARCHES OPPOSING EACH OTHER
➤ MAX / MAN ARCH DIMENSION
➤ HUMAN / ANIMAL
➤ ADULT / CHILD
➤RECTANGULAR CONTUSION OF CENTRALS AND LATERALS

Figure 1 Class characteristics of the bitemark.

Figure 5, on the other hand, demonstrates not only class characteristics but individual characteristics. Even though the class characteristics are not numerous, they are clearly those associated with an adult human dentition. Are there sufficient numbers of individual characteristics to be able to identify the perpetrator? This would depend on the case. If exclusive opportunity is at issue, where the parents are the undisputed and exclusive suspects and one of the pair is edentulous, a case might be made if the dental characteristics of the bitemark matched the other parent's dentition. In terms of the general population, the dental characteristics seen in the bitemark might not be sufficiently specific to identify the perpetrator. On the other hand, a live victim could identify the perpetrator, and the saliva deposited at the bitemark site might confirm the perpetrator's identify through DNA.

Figure 6 demonstrates four different views of a healing bitemark on an alleged rape victim. There are both class and individual characteristics decipherable from the patterned injury. The

INDIVIDUAL CHARACTERISTICS

A FEATURE, TRAIT OR PATTERN THAT REPRESENTS AN INDIVIDUAL VARIATION WITHIN A DEFINED GROUP:
❖ ROTATION
❖ NOTCHING
❖ MISALIGNMENT
❖ FRACTURE

Figure 2 Individual characteristics of the bitemark.

FIGURE 17.3

FACTORS AFFECTING BITEMARK DYNAMICS*

PERPETRATOR	RECIPIENT	RECORDING/ PRESERVING	OTHER FACTORS
. physical strengh	. alive	. accuracy in	. extrinsic factors:
. emotional/mental	. twilight zone	photography	clothing
state	. deceased	. accuracy of	elapse of time
. selectivity of tissue	. intrinsic factors:	impression	postmortem trauma
. head position	general health	. collection	chemicals
. movement	fatness	. lifting	water
. force of bite	capillary fragility	. fixing	tissue distortion
. sucking (negative pressure)	skin diseases	. preserving	artifacts
. pinching (positive pressure)	blood disorders	.distortion	embalming
. dentition:	melanin	.transportating	evidence collection
natural	fluid imbalances	.transillumination	contamination
natural and synthetic	salt imbalances	. histology	.environmental factors:
synthetic	systemic diseases	. SEM	temperature
. class characteristic	tissue tonus		humidity
. individual charateristic	tension lines		soil type
. occlusion	drugs		burial condition
. horizontal incisal	. antemortem bite		bacteria
relationship	. perimortem bite		water
. mouth props	. postmortem bite		. entomological activity
. dental fractures	. self-inflicted bite		. rodent activity
. dental anomalies	. race:		. carnivore activity
. single bite	caucasoid		. taphonomic changes
. multiple bites (overlap)	negroid		. transportation, victim:
. calculus	mongaloid		antemortem
. oral flora	. sex		perimortem
. fingerprints	male		postmortem
. DNA	female		
	. age:		
	child		
	adolescent		
	adult		
	. tissue type		
	. underlying tissue		
	. position		
	. movement		
	. physical state :		
	passive		
	struggling		
	. state of body or corpse		
	. depth of penetration		
	. avulsion/amputation		

*MODIFIED VERSION OF A TABLE FIRST PUBLISHED IN THE JOURNAL OF THE CANADIAN DENTAL ASSOCIATION AND REPRINTED WITH KIND PERMISSION. RBJ DORION. BITE MARK EVIDENCE, JCDA 48:12:795-798, 1982.

Figure 3 Factors affecting bitemark dynamics.

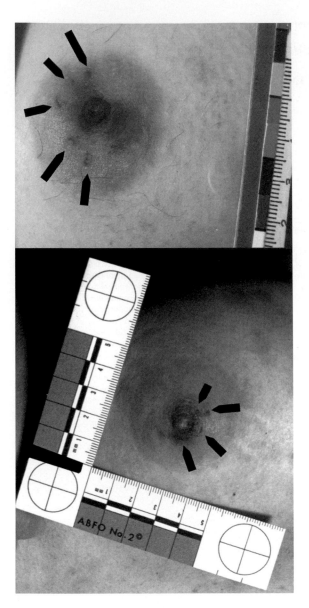

Figure 4   Minor contusions on the areolas.

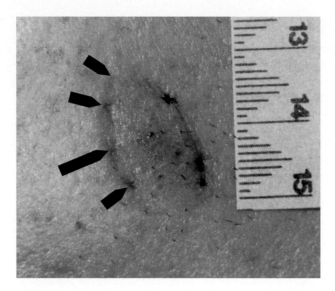

Figure 5 Bitemark on the cheek.

bitemarks are relatively ''fresh'' with scab formation. The bitemark originates from an adult dentition. The next question to be asked is whether it a self-inflicted bitemark. Analysis of the bitemark's location on the body, the bitemark orientation, and the analysis of the victim's dentition should resolve the issue of whether the alleged victim is also the bitemark perpetrator. There is also the possibility of DNA analysis of the bite site assuming the alleged victim has not washed the area.

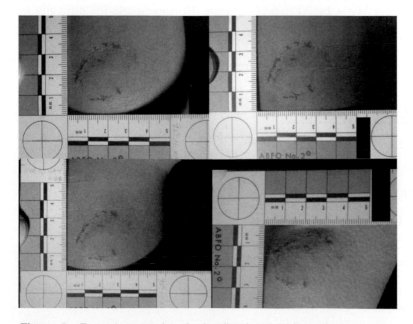

Figure 6 Four photographs of a healing human bitemark on an arm.

3. RECIPIENT OF THE BITEMARK ALIVE

Figure 7 lists types of persons predisposed to human bitemarks. These include but are not limited to the very young and very old, senile, amnesics, the unconscious, the drugged, and the siblings and victims of crime. The recipient's general health and intrinsic factors such as medication, capillary fragility, body fat, skin diseases, blood disorders, melanin pigmentation, fluid and salt imbalances, tissue tonus, tension lines, and other factors contribute to the varied appearance of a bitemark (Fig. 3).

A bitemark recipient can be alive or dead, and the bitemark, self-inflicted or not. The bitemark perpetrator can be alive or dead. The bitemark perpetrator can die during the commission of the crime or because he/she was not apprehended at the time the bitemark was inflicted.

3.1. Child

What are the classical signs of a battered child? The A-to-H rule is an easy guide to remember. They are: Abrasions; Burns and Bitemarks [3,4]; Contusions; Dental neglect; Ecchymosis; Fractures old/new, osseous/dental; General health neglect; Hematoma (Fig. 8). It is incumbent upon all health practitioners, whether in the public or private sector, to be able to diagnose the classic signs of the battered child.

In the living child one of the prime considerations in the recording and the analysis of bitemarks is the healing process. Figure 9 depicts multiple bitemarks on a child's face. Healing proceeds at a much faster rate in the child than in the adult. Figure 37 illustrates the same bitemarks photographed 24 hours apart. The ''vanishing'' bitemarks accentuate the necessity for capturing the trauma on film when initially observed. Serial photography, taken 24 hours apart for example, could furnish information regarding that particular child's healing rate. In addition, it might help in assessing similar patterned injuries in other children of equal stature and health within the same family. It is not uncommon to have a favored twin inflict bitemarks on the lesser fortunate rival.

A single bitemark produced by an adult dentition on the cheek (left) and multiple primary dentition bitemarks on the eyebrow/eyelid (right) in Figure 10 demonstrate the difficulty in

LIVE PERSONS

VERY YOUNG / OLD
SENILE / AMNESIC
UNCONCIOUS / DRUGGED
SIBLING RIVALRY
COMMISION OF CRIME

Figure 7   Persons predisposed to human bitemarks.

> # <u>WHAT TO LOOK FOR</u>
>
> <u>A</u>BRASIONS   <u>E</u>CCHYMOSIS
>
> <u>B</u>URNS AND B.M.   <u>F</u>RACTURES
>
> <u>C</u>ONTUSIONS   <u>G</u>ENERAL HEALTH
>
> <u>D</u>ENTAL   <u>H</u>EMATOMA

Figure 8 Battered child signs, A-to-H rule.

interpreting multiple overlapping bitemarks as compared to a single bitemark. Adding the healing factor renders the task appreciably more difficult.

Multiple overlapping bitemarks are often found in cases of sibling rivalry. It is not unusual, however, to find overlapping bitemarks on the breast and genital area in sexual assault cases.

3.2. Adult

The adult heals at a much slower rate than the child. Add factors such as medication, blood disorders, a variety of other health issues, nutrition, age, and the healing pattern may vary dramatically from one adult to the other. It is important when assessing bitemark evidence to get as much pertinent information from the bitemark recipient when possible. It is incumbent upon first responders, nursing, medical, and dental personnel to be able to evaluate the situation. Once primary emergency treatment has been rendered and the patient has been stabilized, forensic evaluation can be undertaken. The types of crime usually associated with bitemark evidence

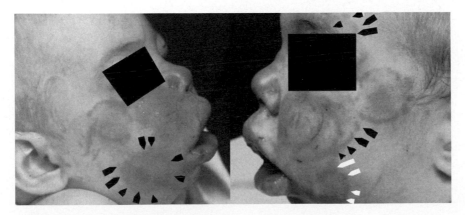

Figure 9 Multiple facial bitemarks.

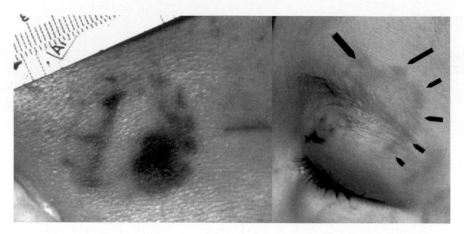

Figure 10   Single bitemark on cheek and overlapping bitemarks eyebrow/eyelid.

in the living adult include rape, abduction, and battering. Elder abuse and neglect is not confined to mental or psychiatric institutions but can take place in the home of potential victims.

Figure 11 depicts four photographs of a healing bitemark on a living adult female breast. The coloration of the surrounding tissue is yellow. Assessing the timing of a bitemark based strictly on color changes to the tissue is not recommended in light of the variables that affect healing. Fortunately, in the living victim an assessment can be made to corroborate or negate the victim's version of the event. Knowing the patient's medical history and other pertinent factors (Fig. 3) would be valuable information, if not a requirement.

In Figure 12 there are multiple healing bitemarks on the live female victim's back. According to the patient, she was repeatedly abused and raped over months. Some of the bitemarks

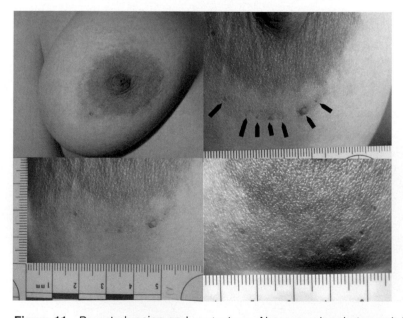

Figure 11   Breast abrasion and contusions. Also see color photograph insert section.

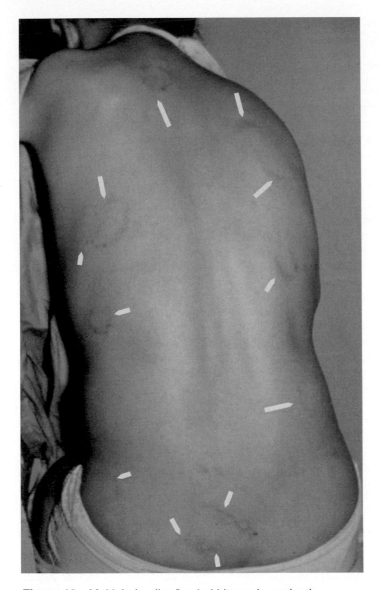

Figure 12   Multiple healing/healed bitemarks on back.

had scar tissue associated with the assaults. Figure 25 shows multiple human adult bitemarks on the legs, thighs, and amputation of the chin by a human bite.

3.3. Specialized Hospital Centers

In the author's jurisdiction there are specialized centers for the care and management of rape and child-abuse victims. Competent personnel in various fields of health and social services staff these centers. Minors are cared for in specialized centers within children's hospitals, for example. Nurses, pediatricians, dentists, psychologists, psychiatrists, social service personnel, specialized units of child protection agencies, and law enforcement form part of the team approach to the problem. It is incumbent upon the institution that cares for these victims to have competent and well-trained staff that can diagnose and follow not only the medical but the forensic protocol including photography. Some institutions might call on the services of police identification personnel for the forensic photographic requirements in a specific case.

The forensic kits include a detailed questionnaire and different sterile containers for the collection of bodily fluids, hair, and a variety of other samples. When all the information and evidence has been collected it is forwarded to the forensic laboratory for analysis.

4. RECIPIENT OF THE BITEMARK IN THE TWILIGHT ZONE

For the purposes of this book, the "twilight zone" refers to a comatose dying patient on a life-support system. Death can occur within hours, days, or years later. Figure 57 depicts a comatose child who was admitted to hospital with multiple old and new fractures of the long bones and rib cage, and with multiple bitemarks and a fractured skull. She survived 7 days.

Figure 34 depicts the same victim with several bitemarks on the calf, thigh, and leg inflicted by the same perpetrator. Note the appearance of the bitemarks is different. Even though the patient was on a life-support system and administered anti-inflammatory drugs, it is interesting to note that the bitemarks were still present and interpretable 7 days later. Serial photographs were taken from the day of admission to hospital, throughout the week, at autopsy, and 3 days thereafter. The ring technique for excision of tissue (Dorion type I) and transillumination was demonstrated for the first time by means of posters during the 1984 trial (Figs. 1, 2 in Chapter 25).

5. RECIPIENT OF THE BITEMARK DECEASED

Figure 13 depicts a bitemark with minimal contusion inflicted by an adult human dentition. Can one diagnose the timing of the bitemark in relationship to the death from this picture alone? This homicide case is an excellent example where proper protocol for excision of tissue, transillumination, and histological analysis can confirm the timing of the bitemark. One of the classic signs of bitemark infliction after death is the presence of teethmarks, indentations, and skin perforations in the absence of the inflammatory response (blood vessel engorgement and/or subcutaneous hemorrhage).

Figures 22, 23 in chapter 13 and 55 depicts a postmortem bitemark. Figure 62 in chapter 17 and 16 in chapter 29 depict (see color photograph insert section) a combination of antemortem and postmortem bitemarks.

6. BITEMARK DISTORTIONS

Bitemark distortions can result from movement of either the recipient or the perpetrator of the bitemark during infliction. Clothing and improper photographic techniques can also contribute to bitemark distortions.

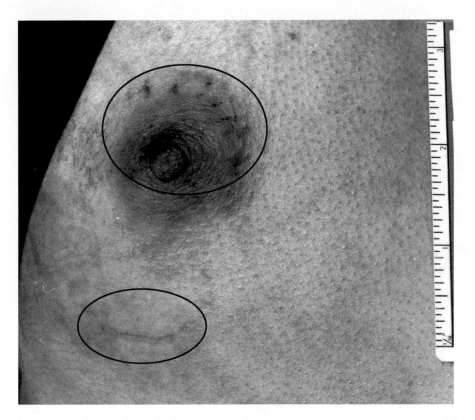

Figure 13 Bitemark on the breast.

Figure 14 illustrates deformation resulting from improper autopsy technique/manipulation. Most bitemarks on the deceased should be excised following an established protocol for ring excision, discussed in a previous chapter.

It is important to demonstrate by photographic means the bitemark when first observed at the crime scene, at autopsy, at the time of excision, during transillumination, and even postfixation. If the consultant forensic odontologist was not present at autopsy and only given the bottom photograph (Fig. 14), an improper conclusion could result. It is extremely important that the odontologist obtain all of the crime scene photographs of the victim. This author has seen displacement of body, body position changes, clothing displacement and removal, etc., perpetrated by crime scene investigators and seen on crime scene photographs. Failure to obtain such photographs can lead to improper conclusions. The odontologist should also obtain copies of the autopsy photographs regardless of type or source.

Figure 15 illustrates three victims with breast bitemarks. All three photographs demonstrate breast manipulation and improper photographic technique. An odontologist neither was present nor directed photographic efforts in all three cases. It is incumbent upon those who first see/diagnose the bitemarks to be fully aware of the bitemark protocol including proper photographic technique or to contact appropriate experts. Failure to follow an appropriate protocol binds the investigation and limits interpretation and conclusions.

Figure 16 illustrates the use of the ABFO No. 2 scale in bitemark photographs. The three circles should be clearly seen in the overview photograph. In closeup photography it would be preferable, but might prove impractical, to visualize all three circles.

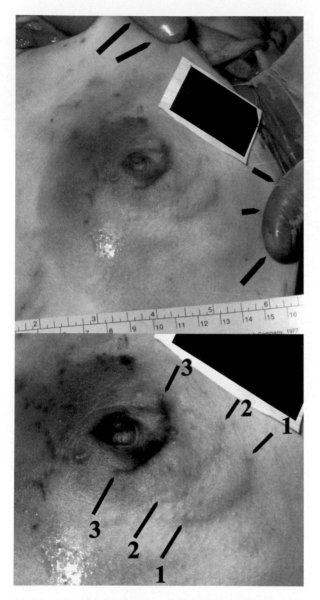

Figure 14 Distorted bitemark due to improper autopsy technique. Note stretching of the breast tissue.

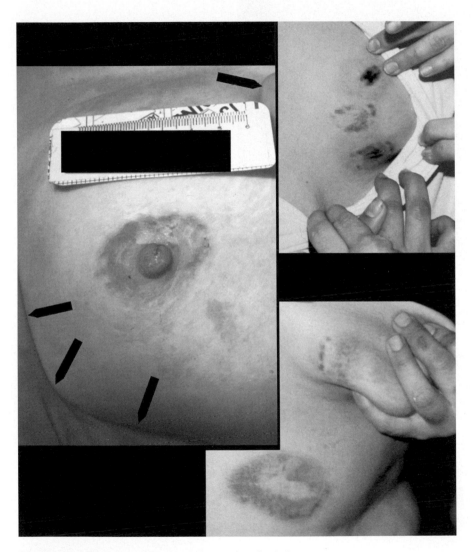

Figure 15 Bitemark distortions due to manipulation.

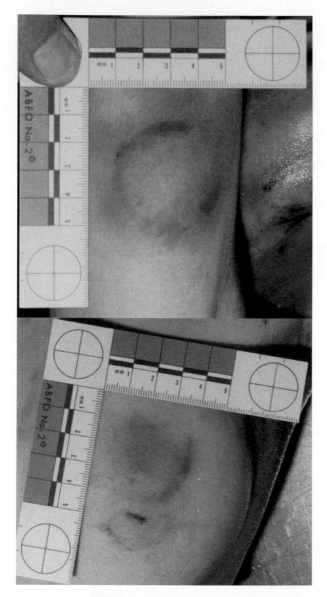

Figure 16 Diffuse bitemark on the arm and the breast.

7. HAIR

Hair-covered skin should always be carefully examined. This includes but is not restricted to the head, pubic, genital, and axillary regions. When bitemarks are suspected, the area should be shaved preceded by the prescribed protocol for DNA collection. Figures 17, 18, 22 in this chapter, 5 in chapter 2, and 2 in chapter 3 illustrate several cases of bitemarks on the adult female pubis and genitalia where shaving was required to properly evaluate the bitemark. In Figure 19 the mons pubis was not shaved because of the scarcity of hair, but that did not influence the interpretation of the bitemark or that of the transilluminated tissue (Fig. 15 in Chapter 13).

Figure 22 reveals several barely perceptible abrasions on a homicide victim's pubis. Care must be taken to ensure that shaving does not result in artificial abrasions. The inner aspect of

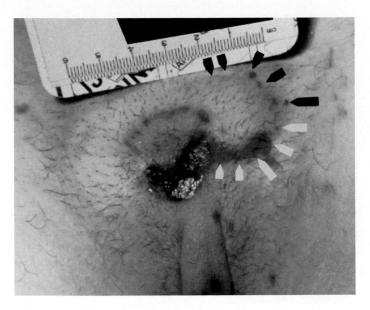

Figure 17 Bitemarks on mons pubis.

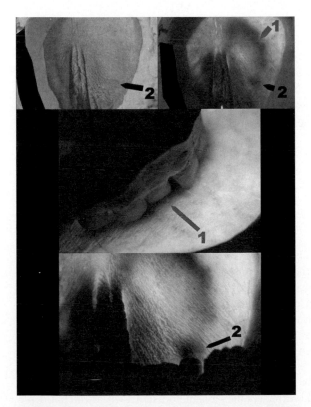

Figure 18 Excised and transilluminated pubis and external genitalia and dental comparison. Also see color photograph insert section.

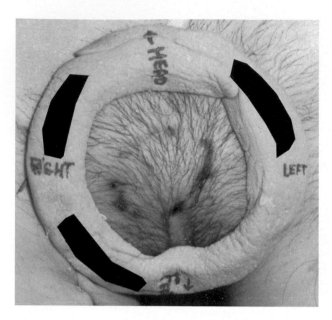

Figure 19   Excision ring circumscribing bitemark on pubis.

the major lips shows some tissue redness (also see color photograph insert section Figures 18 and 22). Figure 18 illustrates the excised and transilluminated pubis and the relationship between the bitemark, the subcutaneous hemorrhage, and the perpetrator's dentition. This case once again clearly illustrates that, without proper ring excision and transillumination of tissue, one could not conclusively confirm the presence of a bitemark even if the perpetrator's DNA were present. Note the relationship between the subcutaneous hemorrhage and the protruded lower right canine (identified by No. 2) and the palatal position of the upper right lateral incisor (identified by No. 1) of the suspect's dental casts.

The bitemarks can also be found on the head, a unique site with special characteristics found nowhere else on the body. The reader is referred to Chapter 16 and Section 12 of this chapter for information.

8.   ORIFICES

There are seven natural orifices to the body: the nose (2), the ears (2), the mouth (1), the anus (1), and urethra/vagina (1). Attention to these areas can reveal hidden bitemarks.

While Figure 20 displays natural creasing of both upper and lower lips, Figure 21 reveals an arched depression on the inner aspect of the upper lip. This depression was caused by an adult human dentition. The U-shaped arch faces outwardly, eliminating the possibility of a self-inflicted injury. It should also be noted that there is little trauma to the outer lip/nose area, where the opposing dental arch might have rested. Was clothing involved, some other interference, or is it a single arch bite?

Figure 22 illustrates recent erosions and discreet ecchymosis on the anterior part of the vulva and clitoral region and on the internal surface of the labia majora of a 14-year-old homicide victim. Moderate hyperemia of the vulva is apparent. The cause of death was asphyxia by strangulation. On the internal aspect of the left labia majora, a bitemark was identified. The

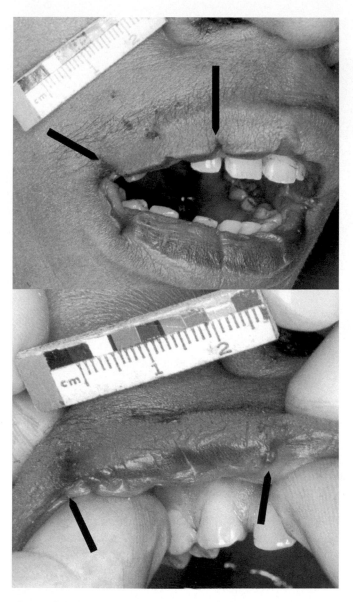

Figure 20   Bitemark on lip. Note the indentations on the lip border.

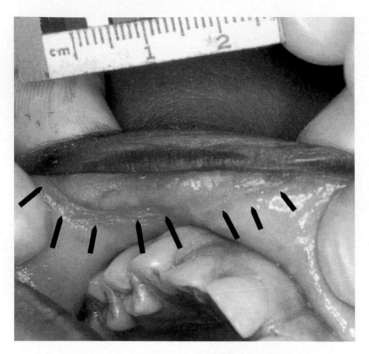

Figure 21   Bitemark on inner lip. Note arch orientation (bitemark is not self-inflicted).

entire pubic area was excised and transilluminated to reveal the presence of a vital human adult bitemark (Fig. 18).

9.   AMPUTATION/AVULSION

Virtually any part of the body can be amputated during a criminal act. Amputation of the nose (Fig. 19 in Chapter 18) and thumb (Figs. 14, 15 in Chapter 18) by a sharp instrument is illustrated in the following chapter. Body parts have been amputated by a variety of wild and domesticated animals. The human dentition has also been known to perform partial or complete amputations [5–9] and beyond. In fiction there is Hannibal Lecter, and in real life there are Andrei Chokatilo and Jeffrey Dahmer, the cannibals. There are those who perform amputations in sport (Mike Tyson) or in self-defense.

Figure 23 depicts a clean external cut to the ear. The multiple neck stab wounds would lead one to believe that a knife was probably the instrument of amputation. Examination of the medial aspect of the attached ear clearly shows a semicircular amputation of tissue (bottom photograph). Crime scene investigators were asked to return to the scene, where they recovered the missing segment (Fig. 24). The perpetrator's dental imprints can be clearly seen on both the inner and outer surfaces. The ear was literally torn from its base.

Figure 25 illustrates multiple new and old (scar tissue) bitemarks on a abused female victim's legs. The inset photograph depicts a partial amputation of the chin by a human bite.

Lovemaking, self-defense, and aggression have been cited as reasons for having bitemarks on a body. In a homicide case, the prosecutor attempts to associate the homicide with the bitemark. The importance of establishing the timing of the bitemark is critical to the investigation and subsequent prosecution of the case.

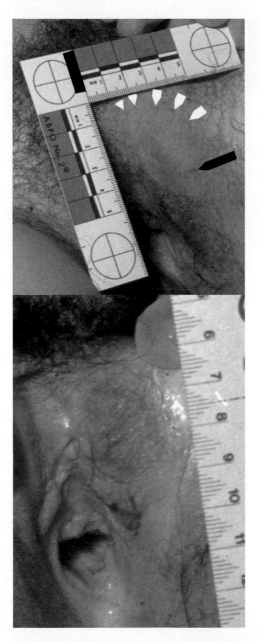

Figure 22 Bitemarks on the genitals. Also see color photograph insert section.

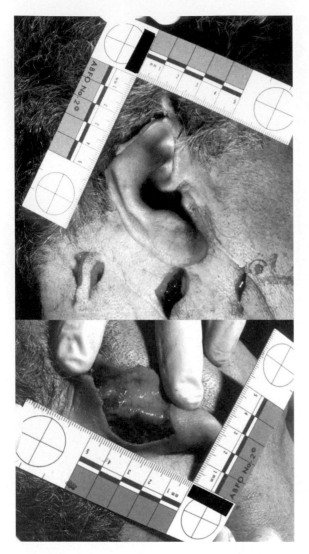

Figure 23   Ear amputated by a human bite.

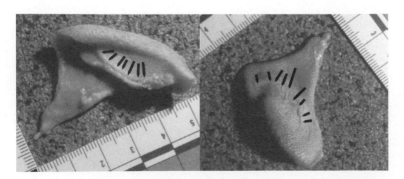

Figure 24   Recovered amputated ear.

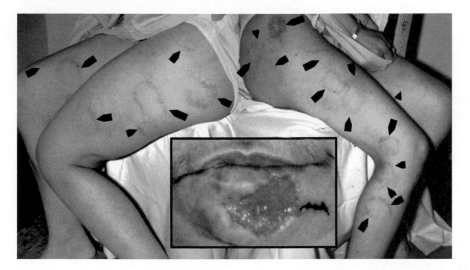

Figure 25 Multiple human bitemarks on legs and thighs; chin amputation.

In extremely rare cases, the bitemark will signal the cause and the manner of death. Consider the following; a female was found without tongue. The first question to be answered: Is it automutilation? Figure 26 illustrates the convexity of the dental arch faces outward. This is not a case of tongue self-amputation resulting from an epileptic seizure or accidental self-amputation. The cause of death is exsanguination and the manner is homicide. The bitemark perpetrator and aggressor bit off the victim's tongue. To this author's knowledge, this is the first such reported case in the scientific literature.

Figure 26 illustrates two attempts at tongue amputation. The dorsal surface shows one arch while the ventral surface shows two distinct bites from the aggressor's lower dentition. The primary bite, closest to the tip of the tongue, was inflicted while the aggressor's jaw was in a normal position. In order to bite off the tongue the aggressor had to slide the lower jaw

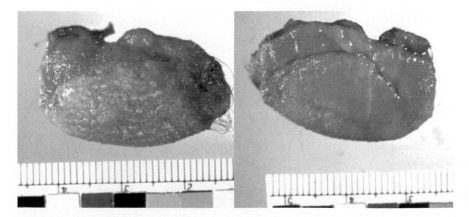

Figure 26 Victim's amputated tongue.

into an edge-to-edge tooth position. Did the victim cooperate by placing the tongue in the aggressor's mouth? Doubtful. The victim was probably unconscious as a result of other trauma, and the aggressor could have pulled out the tongue or the tongue could have been out already.

Such mutilation is rare, for the most common cause of an amputated tongue is accidental. People may fall or receive some other form of trauma and bite off part of the tongue. Epileptic seizure is another cause. In both instances the dental arch imprint would be facing inward rather than outward.

10. FOREIGN OBJECTS

Foreign objects can interfere with the appearance of bitemarks. On the other hand, they may mimic the appearance of a bitemark (Chapter 18). One of the classic circumstances of bitemark misinterpretation results from emergency medical treatments. The injuries on the victim's cheeks (Fig. 27) is not the result of bitemarks but rather is artifact produced by the tubing and the tape.

In another case, the hand injury (Fig. 28) is a healing bitemark and is not associated with the needle insertion nor the tape.

A last case (Fig. 29) depicts a healing bitemark beginning at the throat area with the suspect's lower teeth sliding lateroposterosuperiorly toward the angle of the mandible. The adult perpetrator's upper teeth were in contact with the child's right cheek. This and other healing

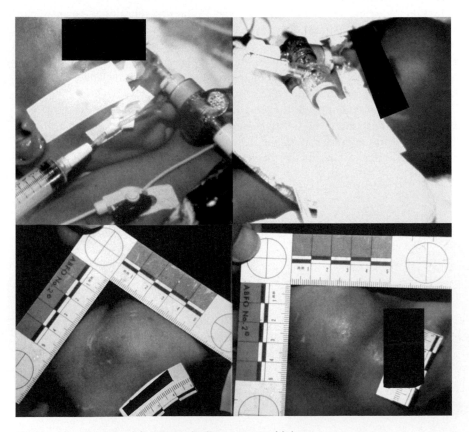

Figure 27   Equipment/tape producing patterned injury.

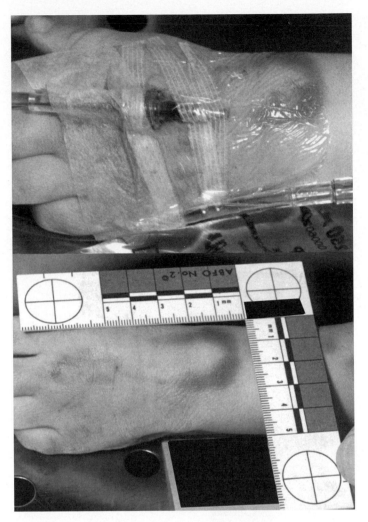

Figure 28 Aged bitemark on the wrist complicated by the presence of tape and needle.

bitemarks, and fractures, demonstrated a history of aggression. Note the white arrows outlining the tape's position. Compare the illustrated case in Figure 27 to 29.

11. DENTITION

The morphological traits of alignment, rotations, incisal fractures, chipping, etc., can be transferred to the bitten object. Keyes [10] conducted a pre- and posttrial examination of over 1000 casts in an attempt to find six lower anterior teeth resembling the alignment of a defendant's teeth without success. The accused was successfully prosecuted based on the uniqueness of the alignment of these teeth in a case involving a bitemark on a deceased's arm. Sognnaes et al. [11] studied computer comparison of bitemark patterns in identical twins with interesting results.

Dental morphological traits can vary with the dental condition. A 4.5-year-old white female spent 6 days on the life-support system in hospital. Multiple self-inflicted bitemarks were found on the victim's hands and arms, while the mother's lover had inflicted four bitemarks on the

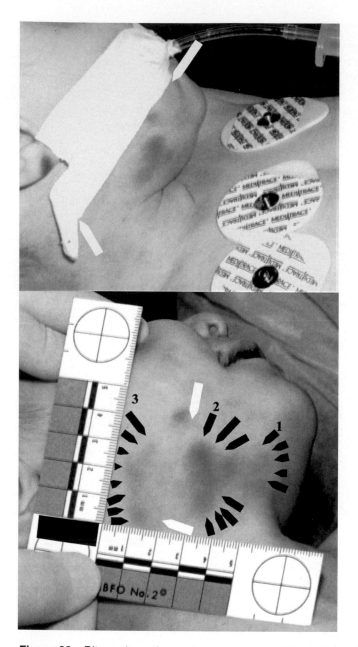

Figure 29 Bitemark on the neck, over the mandible and the cheek area.

legs. The child had seven unreported old fractures of the ribs, sternum, and leg, was deprived of basic necessities, and was psychologically tortured. Despite the fact that free dental care was available, it was not provided. The child had chronic carious lesions with multiple abscesses in the upper teeth (Fig. 30). The self-inflicted bitemarks on the arms appeared as scratch marks produced by the jagged remnants of the upper teeth (Figs. 57 and 58).

Differentiating the adult from the deciduous dentition in a bitemark is usually uncomplicated when both upper and lower arches can be identified [12]. Differentiation becomes more complicated in a single-arch bitemark produced by the lower teeth. Not surprisingly, the lower intercanine distance is remarkably similar to that of the permanent dentition in the late deciduous dentition stage. Differentiation becomes even more difficult when specific dental characteristics are absent in the bitemark as a result of nonregistration or if the bitemark is diffuse and healing.

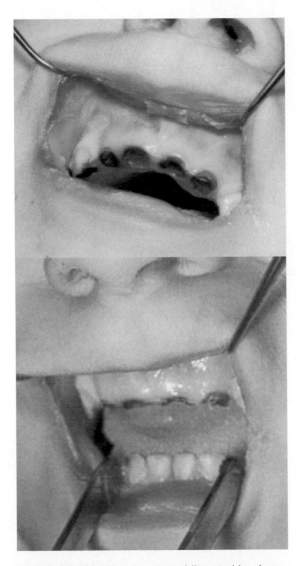

Figure 30 Maxillary crowns obliterated by decay.

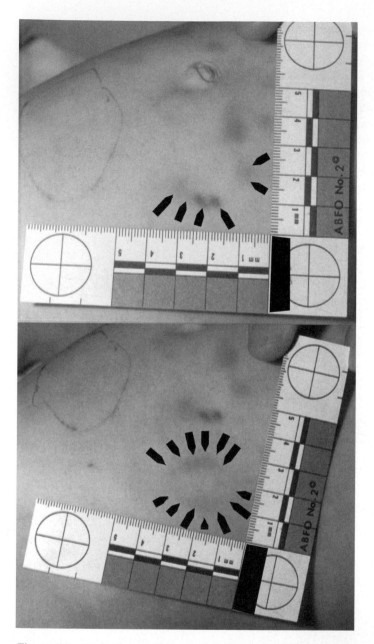

Figure 31 Illustrates multiple healing bitemarks inflicted by the primary dentition.

Not all of the teeth within a given arch are necessarily recorded in a bitemark despite its oral presence. The horizontal height discrepancy or alignment of adjacent teeth may account for its nonregistration in the bitemark.

Figure 32 depicts a permanent dentition with uneven incisal heights (horizontal plane). The lower teeth most likely to register in a bitemark, in the present example, would be the left central and lateral incisors and the right lateral incisor. The right central incisor is out of alignment and at a lower level on the horizontal plane. The canines and more particularly the first bicuspids are below the level of the four incisors. The peculiarities can be recorded in the bitemark. Specific teeth may be involved with more intense markings, lacerations, or hemorrhaging as a result of the horizontal alignment. Notwithstanding, it is important to consider the other factors that contribute to bitemark dynamics (Fig. 3).

A black male child was admitted to hospital emergency room with contusions of recent origin to the legs, arms, abdomen, chest, back, neck, and left and right cheeks. He also had a mildly displaced midshaft fracture of the right clavicle and was diagnosed with multiple nondepressed comminuted bilateral skull fractures. The child survived 3 days. A contusion of the external aspect of the left foot was noted on admission to the hospital. The single bitemark was unusual in that it did not include all of the six anterior teeth of either arch. Five adults had contact with the child during the week. The last persons to have contact with the child were the godmother and her boyfriend. All but the boyfriend consented to providing dental impressions. The specific characteristics of the bitemark and of the dental casts permitted the exclusion of all suspects but the boyfriend. This was the first infanticide case with bitemark evidence in the jurisdiction in question. The criminal code of that jurisdiction had no provisions for the

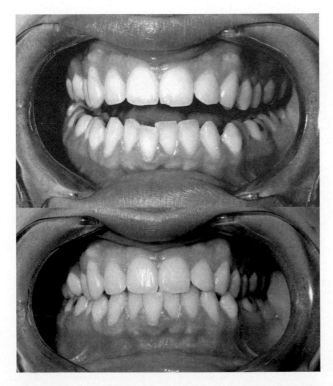

Figure 32 Frontal views of dentition: in and out of occlusion.

taking of dental impressions from an uncooperative suspect, and as a result it was unclear whether the court could order that such a procedure be taken.

The defense in an unusual tactic produced its forensic dental expert's opinion prior to trial. The expert witness for the defense relied solely on digitized images of the casts in the comparison. The defense expert also had the boyfriend's dental casts, which were not provided to the prosecution. The defense expert concluded that the boyfriend could not be eliminated as the bitemark suspect but potentially implicated other persons as its source. The Crown was satisfied with this admission since it was confident that the two other named suspects in the expert's report could be eliminated as the bitemark source. The defense changed its plea to guilty the day the trial was to begin.

Although the bitemark was correctly identified at the child's hospital admission and at autopsy, the odontological analysis was hampered by a lack of properly scaled bitemark photographs (despite the availability and non-use of an ABFO No. 2 scale), the lack of bitemark impressions, and the unsuitability of the excised bitemark specimen.

As for the marks on the cheek that the defense's expert opined as a bitemark, the readers are referred to Figures 27, 33, Section 10; and Chapter 18, Section 4.2.

Figure 34 illustrates three unscaled bitemarks on the calf, thigh, and ankle (top to bottom photographs) inflicted by the same perpetrator. The variations in the appearance of the bitemark are the result of different bitemark dynamics (Fig. 3). In the middle picture, the presence of buccal and lingual cusp registration in the bitemark from both the upper and the lower bicuspids is unusual. Normally, the upper bicuspids are more likely to register buccal and lingual cusps in a bitemark. The lingual cusps are the usual holding cusps in the maxillary arch and are more prominent than the mandibular counterparts. In the three photographs, the absence of a reference scale and the improper photographic technique of the bitemarks render interpretation difficult for the forensic dentist.

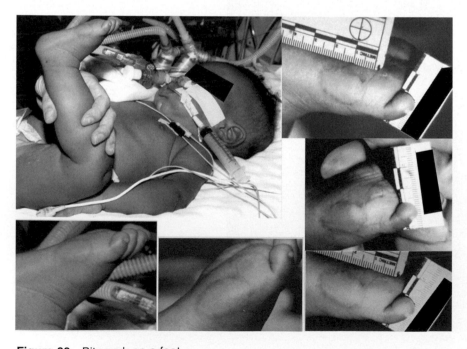

Figure 33 Bitemark on a foot.

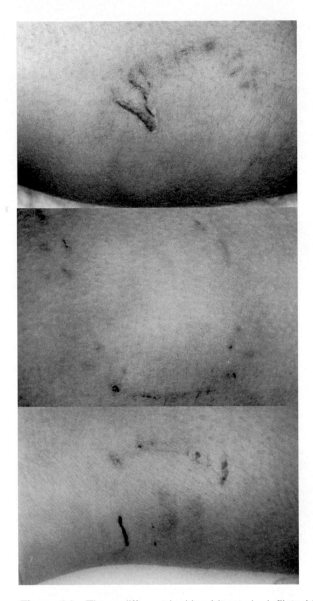

Figure 34 Three different-looking bitemarks inflicted by the same dentition.

12. IMMOBILE TISSUE

A woman found her 14-month-old son lifeless in bed. The child was pronounced dead and his body embalmed. Suspecting child abuse, burial was halted and an autopsy ordered. The autopsy attributed death to asphyxia by suffocation despite a lack of the trauma to the hyoid and thyroid regions.

The pathologist noted multiple blunt trauma injuries to the head, trunk, and extremities in various stages of healing. The right humerus and left tibia were fractured, and there was edema of the cerebrum and occipital lobe. Most of the anterior teeth had erupted, and the lips, cheeks, and frenulum were bruised.

Head shaving revealed contusions over several areas of the head (Fig. 35). Retraction of the scalp confirmed the presence of arch-shaped hemorrhages consistent with bitemarks of human origin from an adult dentition (Fig. 36).

Improperly scaled photographs, lack of bitemark impressions, embalming procedures, and burial of the tissue rendered the analysis of this case much more difficult than it should have been.

The scalp is the only skin tissue of the body that is relatively immobile, with little fat or muscle support, is highly convex, and is mostly supported by bone. Bitemarks from an adult dentition unto an adult scalp are less likely to be distorted as a result of skin movement than on any other skin surface. On the other hand, a bitemark is less likely to include the upper and the lower dental arches. In fact, it is more likely that only a portion of one or the other arch

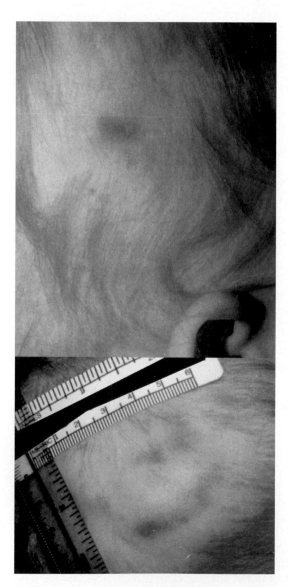

Figure 35   Contusions on the scalp.

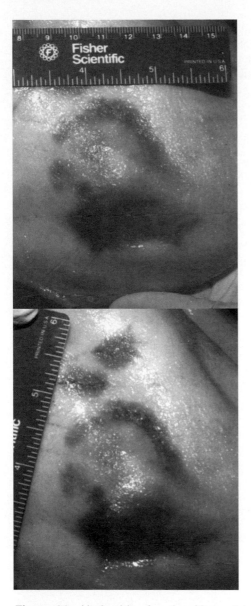

Figure 36   Underside of scalp with semicircular bruising.

will be registered in a human bitemark. One to three teeth are normally registered in a bitemark rather than the ideal six to eight teeth per arch. The reasons are the convexity of the adult skull and the limitation of the opening diameter of the human jaw. It would be exceptional to find more than two or three teeth from either the upper or the lower jaw registering in an adult scalp bitemark. For this reason, the trauma produced by an adult human dentition on an adult scalp might be misinterpreted as one produced by an instrument, such as a screwdriver.

A human bitemark from an adult dentition unto an adult scalp will not be semicircular or oval in appearance when there are more than one to three teeth registered. The bitemark will have less of a curvature than the dental arch that produced it. To produce more than one to three teeth in the bitemark, the victim and/or aggressor would need to rotate the head(s).

On the other hand, bitemarks in the facial area adjacent to the orbits, the cheeks, the ears, the nose and the lips are more than likely to record the perpetrator's upper and lower dental arches.

13. BITE OVERLAP

Figure 37 depicts single and overlapping bitemarks on the child's face inflicted by an older jealous sibling. The photographs, taken 24 hours apart, demonstrate the importance of recording the trauma on film at the earliest possible moment. Note that the bitemark adjacent to the eye has considerably faded 24 hours later.

Five overlapping semicircular ecchymosis on both the anterior and lateral aspect of the left thigh of a 9-month-old deceased white male can be observed in the excised and transilluminated tissue (Fig. 12 in Chapter 13). The cause of death was cardiopulmonary arrest, and the manner of death remained undetermined for this case. Additional examples of overlapping bitemarks can also be seen in Figures 12, 14, and 17 and in Figure 25 of Chapter 13.

14. PIGMENTATION

The reader is referred to Chapter 7 for guidance in the photographic techniques employed in capturing trauma on highly pigmented skin in the living. Figure 38 illustrates a bitemark on a

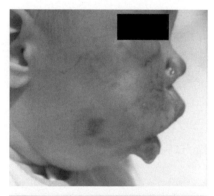

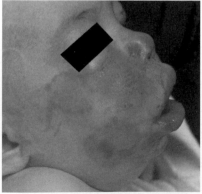

Figure 37   Multiple bitemarks on the face photographed 24 hours apart. Also see color photograph insert section.

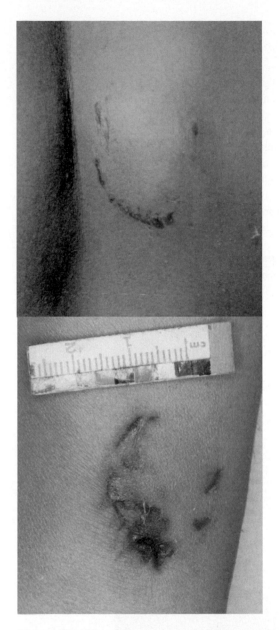

Figure 38 Bitemarks on scapula (Black male) and arm (Black female).

black homicide suspect's back (top photo), and an unrelated black homicide victim's arm (bottom photo). The appearance of the bitemark on the back can dramatically change depending upon the suspect's body position (sitting, standing, bending, twisting, etc.). Additional examples of bitemarks on lesser pigmented individuals, such as North American Indians, are illustrated in Figures 6, 11, 12, and 25.

In deceased highly pigmented individuals, transillumination is extremely useful in visualizing and diagnosing an inflammatory response (blood vessel engorgement/subcutaneous hemorrhage) (Figures 26, 27 in Chapter 13).

15. PHOTOGRAPHIC PERSPECTIVES

The American Board of Forensic Odontology officially endorsed the ABFO No. 2 scale, codesigned by the late Dr. Tom Krauss, as the recommended ruler for use in bitemark photography. The scale is basically two rulers at right angles to each other and three equidistant circles (see Figure 34 in Chapter 7). The circles are used as reference points to correct angular distortion. The importance of having the scale in contact with the tissue and parallel to the plane of the film cannot be overemphasized. On a highly curved surface, such as a breast or shoulder, the importance of having pictures from several angles is essential. In addition, the ruler's gray scale can be used as reference for color correction.

Figure 39 depicts photographs of two highly convex surfaces, a breast (top photo) and the shoulder (bottom photo). The photographs were purposefully taken at extreme angles to display specific points of interest. The former illustrates a partially sectioned nipple observable

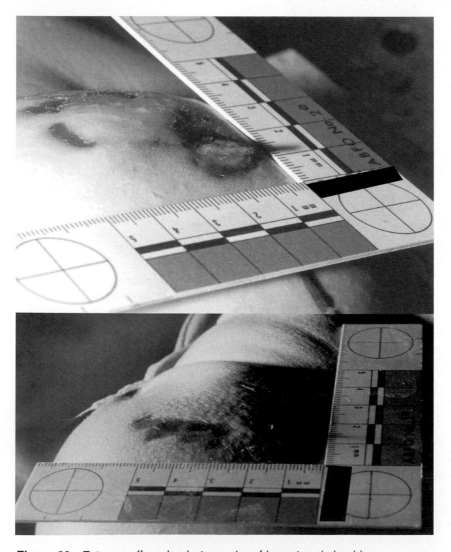

Figure 39 Extreme off angle photographs of breast and shoulder.

from the projected shadow on the scale. The latter was photographed to demonstrate the convexity of the shoulder in relationship to the bitemark. Note that angle of photography and photographic lighting even accentuate the dust on the scale. Both of these photographs would be of little use without an appropriate scale as reference. The photographs depicted in Figure 40 are of the same shoulder as seen in Figure 39.

Figure 41 shows a human bitemark on the highly curved surface, the tip of the nose. Compare these photographs to those in Figures 3–7 in Chapter 1 and Figure 2 in Chapter 10. Generally speaking, bitemarks on highly curved surfaces require more photographs than those on flat surfaces. Figure 42 reveals three bitemark photographs on a cheekbone. Note the change in

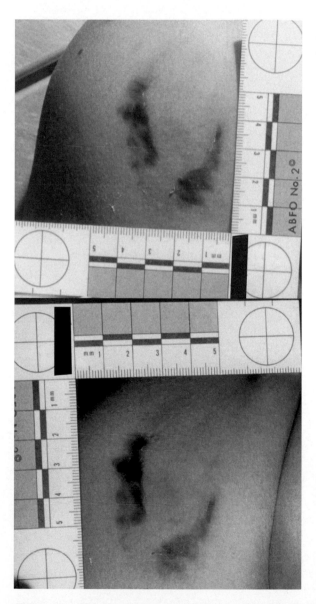

Figure 40 Bitemark on shoulder photographed from different angles.

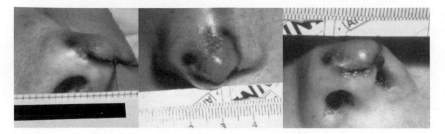

Figure 41   Nose bitemark photographed from different views.

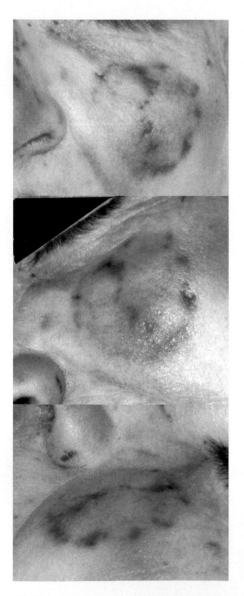

Figure 42   Bitemark on cheek seen from different angles.

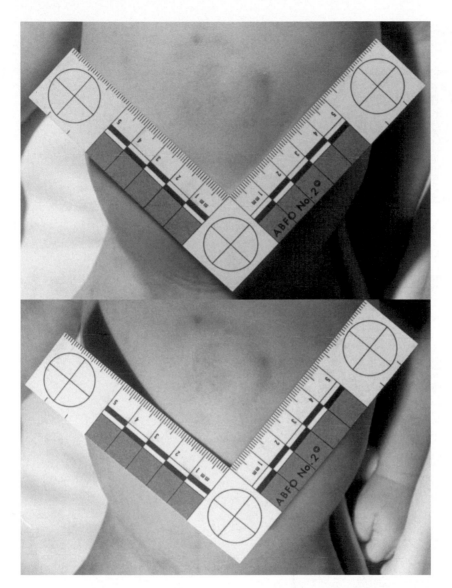

Figure 43 Change in the incidence of light from normal overhead (top) to off-angle (bottom).

angulation and photographic perspective. Figures 43 and 44 demonstrate the same photographic perspective but with different lighting conditions.

Figure 45 shows two views of a bitemark that lack both class and individual characteristics. Transillumination may be of great benefit in distinguishing individual dental characteristics not seen on the skin surface. Skin slippage, perpetrator/victim movement, clothing, shoulder convexity, and/or underlying tissue may have contributed to the lack of dental specificity in the bitemark (Fig. 3).

16. HEALING/OLD BITEMARKS

The inflammatory response begins as soon as trauma has been inflicted in the living. Figure 46, top photograph, depicts a bitemark on 7-year-old's buttock. The bottom photograph depicts the

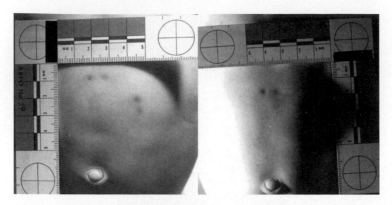

Figure 44   Off-angle (left) and extreme off angle (right) lighting of abdomen.

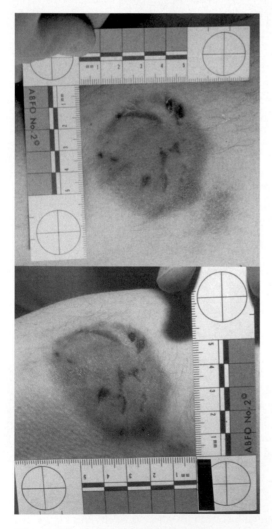

Figure 45   Two views of a bitemark on an arm.

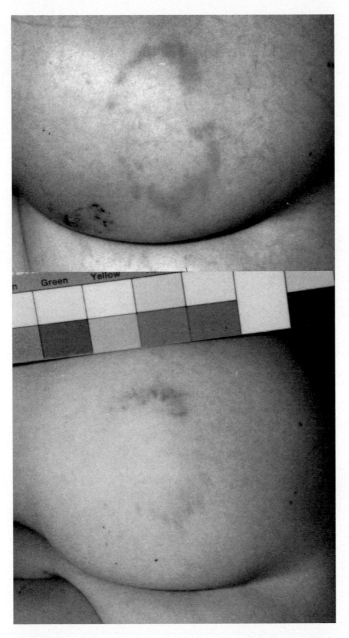

Figure 46 Bitemark on buttock. Photos taken 24 hours (top) and 51 hours (bottom) after assault.

same bitemark 27 hours later. Serial photography in the living records two phenomena: the healing process and color changes over time. Because of the many factors involved in bitemark dynamics (Fig. 3), one should not exclusively depend on color changes for the timing of the bitemark [13]. This point has also been emphasized elsewhere in this textbook.

Figure 47 illustrates a bitemark on the lower abdominal wall and on the child's scrotum. A known pedophile was captured 24 hours after the kidnapping, and his dentition was found to be responsible for the bitemarks. Note that the ''healing rates'' in Figures 46 and 47 appear to be different. This discrepancy is not accounted for by the ''healing rate'', but rather by the biting dynamics (Fig. 3).

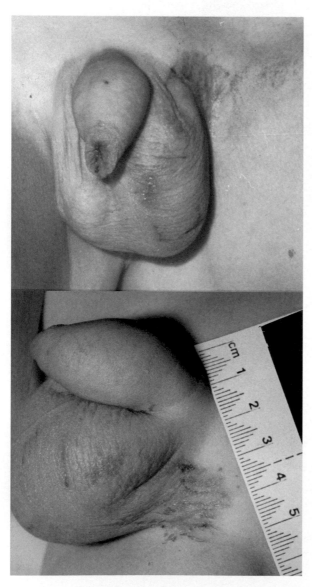

Figure 47 Bitemark on genitals. Photos taken 24 hours (top) and 51 hours (bottom) after the assault.

Figure 48 are photographs of multiple healing bitemarks on the arm and a single bitemark on a leg of a 6-month-old male admitted to the hospital. Figure 59 is a photograph of the same victim taken 48 hours previously, while Figure 60 was taken eight days later. The healing process in children is both rapid and dramatic. Any and all injuries should be immediately photographed with an ABFO No. 2 scale. It is incumbent upon all health professionals, caregivers, teachers, and parents to signal any such trauma to competent authorities for proper evaluation and diagnosis.

Figure 49 illustrates opposing semicircular bruises on a rib cage. There is sufficient information to suggest that the pattern is consistent with the human dentition. Is it from an adult or a child's dentition? The dimensions of the top arc would represent only two maxillary adult teeth (18–20 mm), more if it was the deciduous dentition. The clue that distinguishes the culprit lies in the linear distance between the center point of the top hemorrhagic arc to the center point of the bottom hemorrhagic arc (32 mm). The linear distance between the farthest point of the top hemorrhagic arc to the farthest point of the bottom hemorrhagic arc measures 39 mm. The

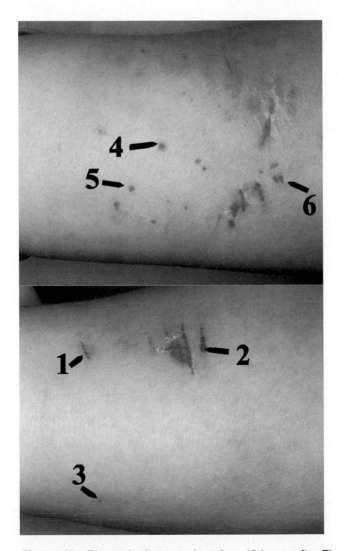

Figure 48 Bitemark photographs taken 48 hours after Fig. 59; arm (top), leg (bottom).

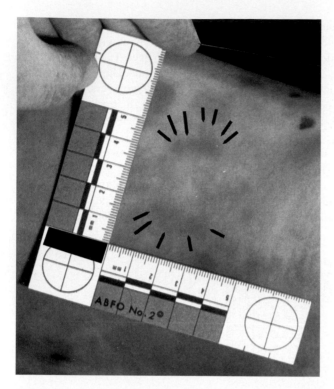

Figure 49   Two arched bruises facing each other on the lateral aspect of the rib cage.

skin on a child's rib cage has little fat and is a relatively immobile other than for the expansion/ contraction of breathing in life. In other words, there is little predictable bitemark distortion in this specific case for this particular area. The culprit would, therefore, have an opening diameter between 32 and 39 mm. Can a child open that wide?

Even though many authors have commented on the relative inaccuracies of timing bitemark injuries on bruise coloration alone, it should be stated that "relative" timing might be the issue at hand. Aggravated assault as opposed to simple assault might be at issue. If a child's death has resulted from inflicted trauma, it might be significant to display repeated assaults that have led to the child's death. This, in combination with additional injuries such as healing/old fractures, dental, oral, and other facial injuries can be used to display the aggressor's intent. The child's past medical and dental history should be carefully evaluated. It is incumbent upon health professionals and forensic experts to seek any and all medical/dental files that might be found in various health clinics, hospitals, social services, and dental offices. It is also important to realize that the child's parents/guardians might have been living in other jurisdictions prior to the latest aggression. A last partner background check in a single-parent family is often telling. This author's experience has shown that the new live-in boyfriend is more than the likely, but not exclusively, source of the trauma and battering.

Figure 50 and Figure 17 from Chapter 29 outline semicircular bruises on the right arm. These bruises as well as those depicted in Figures 51 and 52 are human bitemarks that differ considerably in appearance one from the other. The female child survived 7 days in the hospital on life-support systems and eventually died of complications as a result of a fractured skull. Figure 52 illustrates photographs taken 8 days apart. The top photograph was taken upon admission to hospital.

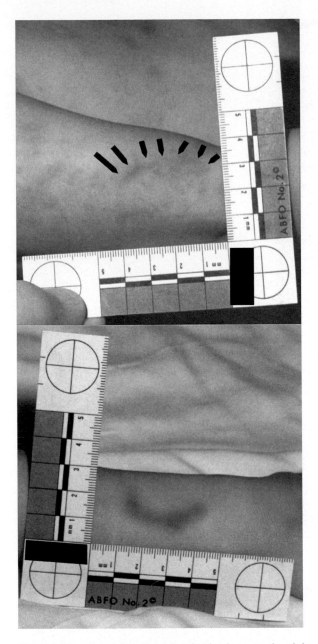

Figure 50 Opposing semicircular bruises on the right arm.

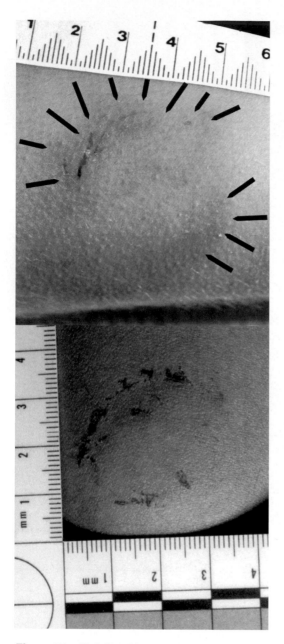

Figure 51   Ill-defined healing bitemark on calf (top) and well-defined healing bitemark on an arm (bottom).

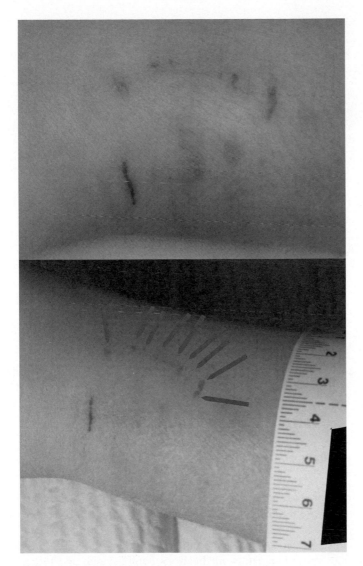

Figure 52 Bitemark on medial aspect of lower leg below the calf. Photos taken 8 days apart.

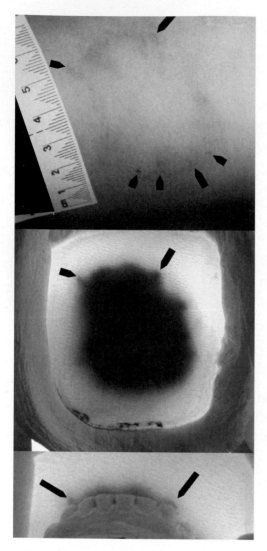

Figure 53 Bitemark, transilluminated bitemark, and suspect dentition.

Even though the bitemark in Figure 53 does not present with clear evidence of class and individual dental characteristics, the transilluminated tissue clearly demonstrates subcutaneous hemorrhage, which is compared to the suspect dentition (bottom photo). This case is unusual in that little resorption of the hemorrhage has occurred in the interim 7 days. This is partially due to her medical condition, to the anti-inflammatory medications administered, and to her dependency on the life-support system.

Some bitemarks in the living may leave permanent scars that can lead to aesthetic complications, civil as well as criminal litigation.

17. ANTEMORTEM/PERIMORTEM BITEMARKS

The laws of nature are such that when sufficient trauma is inflicted in life, an inflammatory response results (blood vessel engorgement and /or subcutaneous hemorrhage). Figure 54 illustrates a contused oval bitemark inflicted before the victim's death.

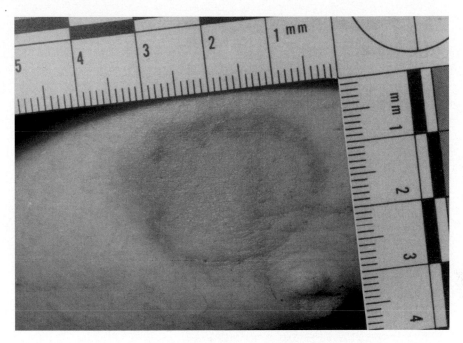

Figure 54 Diffuse bitemark on the breast. Also see color photograph insert section.

18. POSTMORTEM TRAUMA

A 3-month-old white female was found dead in her crib. On the vulva and buttocks were lesions due to chronic diaper rash. The left thigh also presented with five pale brownish irregular erosions that when taken together formed a semicircular pattern suggestive of a single-arch bitemark. An impression was made and the tissue was excised, fixed, and transilluminated. There was an absence of any other marks of violence on the deceased. The cause of death was not determined. Five microscopic sections were made of the area through and around the depressions. There was neither hemorrhagic infiltration nor any acute inflammatory reaction in the five sections examined. It is important to note that the histological specimens incorporated both the depressions and the area immediately adjacent to the depressions (Figs. 21–23 in Chapter 13). The depressions were attributed to adult human teeth having considered and eliminated the rough edges of a plastic diaper as a possible source of the depressions. Note that the depressions are on the left inner thigh only (Fig. 55). While it is certain that the presence of subcutaneous bleeding would indicate antemortem injury, sufficient force must be applied to cause blood vessel engorgement and/or subcutaneous hemorrhage. If sufficient force was applied, as indicated by skin perforations, for example, in the absence of blood vessel engorgement and/or subcutaneous hemorrhage, the biting would have taken place at the time of death (perimortem) or after death (postmortem).

Can one tell if a bitemark has been inflicted antemortem, perimortem or postmortem by looking at a photograph alone (Figure 3 Chapter 8, and Figure 13 from this chapter)? In the absence of an inflammatory response, it would be impossible to tell from a color or black-and-white photograph alone whether the bitemark was inflicted antemortem, perimortem, or postmortem. One would need additional information such as infrared, ultraviolet, or ALI photography; excision of tissue; transillumination; and/or histological sections to determine the timing of the bitemark.

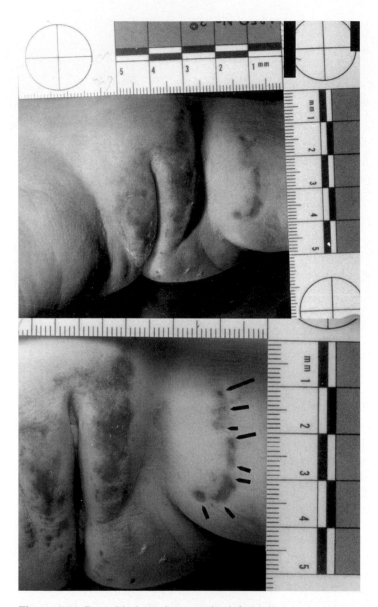

Figure 55   Dental indentations on the left thigh.

19. CLOTHING

Figure 56 depicts a bitemark on the abdomen of a female rape victim admitted to hospital. The unavailability of an ABFO No. 2 scale led the photographer to place two plastic rulers perpendicular to each other and to incorporate three quarters as reference points. Bitemark interpretation was further hampered by the presence of clothing when the bite was inflicted [1,2] and cellulites [3].

Consult Figures 17 in Chapter 5; 50, 51 in Chapter 7; 14, 16–19 in Chapter 13; and 18, 19 in Chapter 16 for additional photographs of the appearance of bitemarks through clothing.

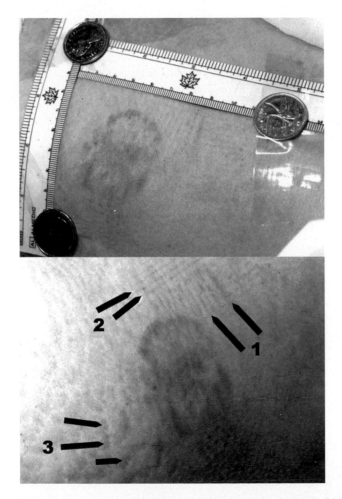

Figure 56   Nonstandard scale, clothing imprint, and cellulitis complicating bitemark interpretation.

20. TISSUE PRESERVATION

Case examples in Chapters 13, 14, and 17 underline the importance and the significance of proper tissue excision, fixation, preservation, storage, and transportation in the analysis of bitemark evidence. Failure to maintain an adequate protocol in these matters minimizes the expert's ability to arrive at proper conclusions.

21. SELF-INFLICTED BITEMARKS

Self-inflicted bitemarks are common to the literature [14–16]. There are two categories of self-inflicted bitemarks—voluntary and involuntary. Voluntary self-inflicted bitemarks are intentional whereas involuntary bitemarks are categorized as accidental, medical, or third-party induced.

Voluntary self-inflicted bitemarks occur for variety of reasons from suppression of pain (Fig. 57), to self-esteem issues, to intentionally and wrongfully accusing a third party for the bitemark or simulated bitemark (Fig. 5 in Chapter 18). Anderson and Hudson describe that battered children occasionally bite themselves to stifle crying or to mask intense pain [14].

Accidental self-inflicted bitemarks might result from a fall (slippery or wet surface, ice) causing lip and/or tongue laceration, or partial or complete amputation. A self-inflicted bitemark might also result from a medical condition such as loss of consciousness resulting in a fall, an epileptic seizure, neurological disorders, or in a drug-induced seizure producing bitemarks on the lip, tongue, arms, hands, or fingers. Any area of the body other than the head and neck, upper thorax (except large female breasts), the back, and buttocks is a suspect area for self-inflicted bitemarks.

The following case illustrates voluntary self-inflicted bitemarks to suppress pain. A comatose child was admitted to the hospital with a fractured skull and older healing and untreated fractures of the leg and rib cage. The victim survived 8 days on a life-support system. The child was regularly beaten and, in order to prevent herself from screaming, bit herself on the arms (Fig. 57). Four additional bitemarks inflicted by her tormentor are seen on the thigh, leg, calf, and ankle areas.

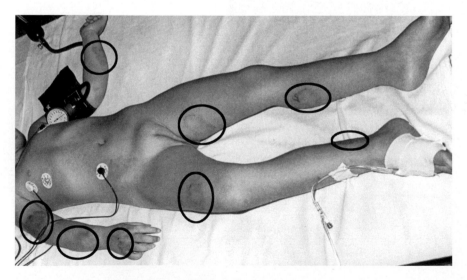

Figure 57 Bitemarks on the arms and the legs.

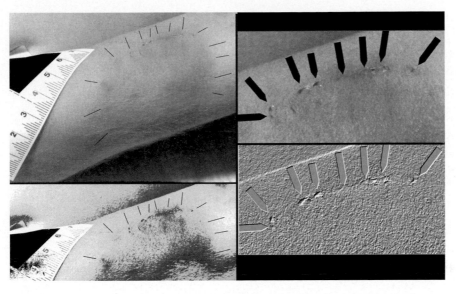

Figure 58 Gray-scale, solarized, and embossed photos of self-inflicted bitemark on the arm.

The photographs depicted in Figure 58 illustrate a self-inflicted bitemark on the arm also seen in Figure 57. Readers are referred to Section 11 for the biter's dental description.

An involuntary, third-party-induced, self-inflicted bitemark is illustrated in Figure 65. The inner lip abrasions are the result of the perpetrator's action to muzzle the victim to prevent him/her from screaming. In more serious cases, the lip abrasions can be associated to manual or object suffocation (pillow, etc.).

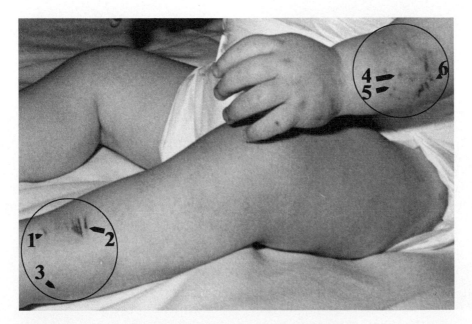

Figure 59 Single bitemark on the leg and superimposed bitemarks on the arm.

22. MULTIPLE BITEMARKS

Photographs in Figures 9, 10, 12, 14, 17, and 25 exhibit multiple overlapping bitemarks. (See also Figures 13,14,16 in Chapter 5, and 12 in Chapter 13.) There are many examples throughout this book that illustrate multiple bitemarks on the same victim. Suffice it to say that from a statistical point of view if one bitemark is found on a body, it is more than likely others are present.

Figures 59 and 60 depict single and overlapping bitemarks in various stages of healing. Readers are referred to Section 16 for an explanation of these illustrations.

In an unrelated case, Figure 61 illustrates multiple healing bitemarks on a child's back. Note the appearance of the bitemarks differs with location. Some lesions look like scratch marks; others, a dermatological condition. Readers are referred to Figure 15 in Chapter 29 for an illustration of a hand-drawn overlay of the suspect's deciduous dentition and one of these bitemarks.

23. MUSCLE

In extremely rare cases, the three-dimensional class and individual characteristics of the offending dentition is imprinted in muscle (Fig. 62). This phenomenon defies explanation since, in

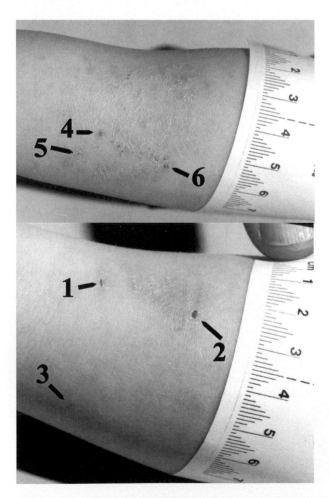

Figure 60   Bitemark photographs taken 8 days after those in Fig. 59; arm (top), leg (bottom).

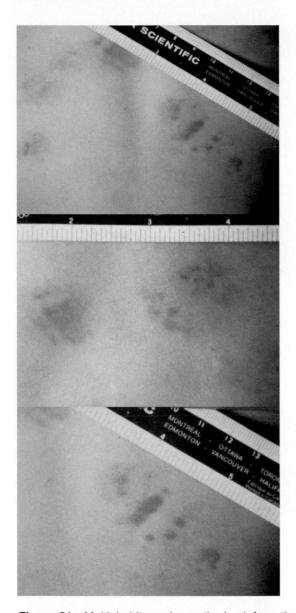

Figure 61   Multiple bitemarks on the back from the deciduous dentition.

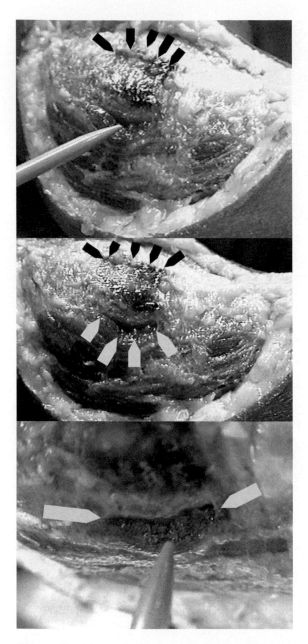

Figure 62　Three-dimensional dental imprints in muscle.

this case, the epidermis is not perforated (Figs. 39, bottom, and 40; and 26,27 in Chapter 13). Moreover, the bitemark was inflicted while the victim was alive, as witnessed by the intramuscular and subcutaneous hemorrhage. Why did the muscle not regain its natural shape? This author has yet to see this phenomenon on bites inflicted postmortem.

24. DIGITS

Bitemarks on digits are not rare but are difficult to interpret because few of the offending teeth are normally registered. Bitemarks on fingers may be willfully or accidentally inflicted during the commission of a crime. A victim might inadvertently place fingers in the aggressor's mouth to ward off attack. Conversely, the victim might bite the aggressor's fingers in self-defense. The aggressor might attempt to muzzle the victim in order to prevent him/her from screaming or in an attempt to suffocate the victim. Any other of the aggressor's body parts can be bitten, but the fingers are commonly involved.

Readers are referred to Figures 14–16 in Chapter 18 for a differential diagnosis of bitemarks versus another potential cause.

25. DNA

A bitemark was discovered on a homicide victim's breast. The principal suspect, her boyfriend, admitted to having ''sucked'' the breasts but denied having bitten or having had sexual intercourse with her. His dentition excluded him as the perpetrator of the bitemark. He remained under suspicion pending DNA results. Months later, the presence of the boyfriend's DNA at the bite site was confirmed as well as that of another person's. There was an absence of DNA on the raped victim's mons pubis and genital, vaginal, and rectal areas. Empty packages of condoms littered the student's residence, but condoms were not found. Imagine the dire consequences had bitemark analysis not been performed.

The presence of DNA at a bite site does not necessarily associate it to the bitemark. In the former case, the boyfriend's DNA at the bite site was confirmed. Had the bitemark been inflicted through clothing, the perpetrator's DNA would have been absent on the breast. If the body was subsequently dumped elsewhere without clothing and bitemark analysis not performed, any DNA bitemark association would have been erroneous. There must be a proven association between the DNA and the perpetrator's bitemark.

While the presence and identification of a biological substrate such as saliva, blood, semen, or hair may be confirmed by DNA analysis, it does not provide for the timing of the event, or how the biological substrate got there in the first place (could have been deposited by a third party).

A bitemark can confirm the identification of the person who made it, the timing and the aging of the bitemark, its temporal relation to the event (kidnapping, infanticide/homicide, etc.), an estimate on the amount of force applied and pain suffered, and physical descriptors of the perpetrator's dentition. DNA cannot establish any of these parameters. All of these issues are critical in an infanticide/homicide case. The importance of a bitemark should never be underestimated.

The question arises as to how many cases may have been prosecuted/overturned by the courts on DNA results when the presence of bitemarks has been improperly evaluated, overlooked, or disregarded. How difficult would it be to contaminate the victim's clothing with DNA evidence even years following the homicide? DNA is but a fragment of the puzzle, not its sole solution.

26. NEW EVIDENCE

Twenty-year-old Gail Miller, a nursing assistant, died of stab wounds to the chest on January 31, 1969, in Saskatoon, Saskatchewan. Sixteen-year-old David Milgaard was convicted of the sex slaying and was released 23 years later following a Canadian Supreme Court decision to set aside the conviction. The Saskatchewan government awarded Milgaard $10 million dollars for wrongful conviction, the largest compensation package in Canadian history.

On July 25, 1997, another person was charged with Gail Miller's murder. It was then the prosecution's contention that the pathologist failed to diagnose a bitemark at autopsy 31 years earlier. The crown's forensic dental expert submitted four reports. The defense's forensic dental expert examined the crime scene and autopsy negatives and prints. There was at least one critical print (photograph) that had been inverted in printing in the set of photographs submitted by the crown during the Milgaard trial in 1969 and subsequently at the more recent pretrial hearing in 2000.

It was the defense expert's opinion that the patterned injury above the breast was not a bitemark, lacking both class and individual dental characteristics. In addition, the maxillary intercanine distance was around 26–28 mm according to the Crown's defense expert, far less than the accused's intercanine measurement (less also than what would be considered normal for an adult white male). The judge reviewed and ruled on the admissibility of the ''new bitemark'' and also on the results from DNA analysis of semen found on Miller's clothing 31 years after the homicide. After listening to opposing forensic dental experts, he ruled that he did not believe in the prosecution's ''bitemark theory'' and ruled it inadmissible for trial, while the DNA results were admitted.

How could the nonswollen, noninflamed, circular, centrally depressed patterned injury be explained? On the coat there was a missing button. The button was too large to leave such a mark. Could it be the base or the end of the flashlight found in David Millgaard's possession at the time of his arrest? This was also too large a diameter. The nursing insignia found on the victim's discarded dress? Too small. What could have caused the patterned skin depression? Her nude body, draped only by a coat, was found lying face down with folded arms and watch facing the chest. The only major exhibit not retained by the prosecution for 31 years was the victim's watch.

27. BLUNT TRAUMA INJURY

Figure 29 (bottom photograph) in Chapter 13 depicts blunt trauma injury produced by a single tooth. Note that the blood vessel engorgement/hemorrhagic pattern surrounds the tooth's impact site. Also see the color photograph insert section Figure 13.29.

28. SINGLE-ARCH BITE

Bitemarks do not always involve both dental arches (Figs. 21, 66; Fig. 20 in Chapter 5). This may be due to factors such as the presence of clothing, victim or suspect movement, partial anodontia, the removal of one of the set of complete dentures, the convexity of the bitten tissue, etc. (Fig. 3). A single-arch bite occurs more frequently on flat surfaces such as the back or highly curved surfaces such as the scalp. Quite simply, the human jaw is limited in its opening diameter. The importance of photographing and analyzing crime scene photographs and informing the odontologist on factual matters regarding the investigation cannot be overemphasized.

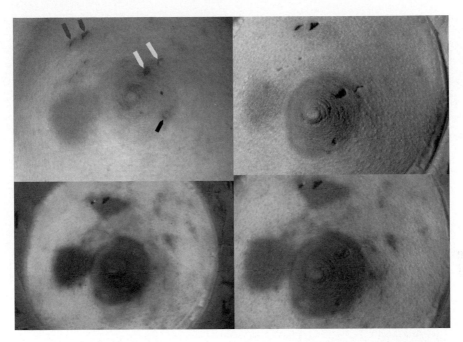

Figure 63 Breast (top left), excised (top right), and transilluminated (bottom) specimen. Also see color photograph insert section.

In a multiple-bitemark case one looks for similarity in patterns. The blue arrows situate two skin puncture marks that closely resemble two other puncture marks depicted by the yellow arrows in Figure 17.63 in the color photograph insert section. These puncture marks are similar in size, orientation, and distance from each other. Could they have a common origin? The excised, fixed, and transilluminated specimen clearly illustrates an inflammatory response related to the puncture marks (blue arrows), and the absence of hemorrhage related to the puncture marks depicted by the yellow arrows. A word of caution is in order. Pigmentation in the form of freckles, the areola, or the nipple should not be misinterpreted as inflammatory response (blood vessel engorgement and/or hemorrhage) in transilluminated tissue. The bruise to the left of the areola does not have puncture marks.

From the same case, photographs in Figure 29.16 in the color photograph insert section demonstrate a direct comparative technique between the excised transilluminated tissue and a suspect dentition. The peculiar V-shaped skin puncture mark was produced by a morphologically atypical extruded canine. Three single-arch bitemarks were attributed to the lower arch. Note the absence of an upper arch registration.

29. CIRCUMFERENTIAL VERSUS LINEAR DISTANCE

Readers are referred to the Chapter 8 for an explanation of the differences between circumferential and linear distances. Figures 4 through 7 in Chapter 8 are photographs depicting circumferential and linear distances.

30. ERECTILE TISSUE

By its very nature erectile tissue will change shape, and it could be extremely difficult to recognize bitemark injury. Figure 64 demonstrates two adjacent imprints reminiscent of the

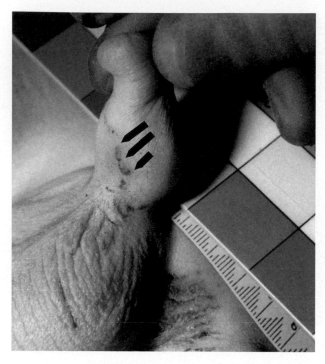

Figure 64 Marks on penis suggestive of tooth imprints.

human dentition on the shaft of a child's penis. The size of the individual imprints will change depending on when the bite was inflicted, namely during an erection or not. It is imperative to recognize not only class characteristics but individual characteristics that might associate the trauma to the perpetrator. Tooth rotations, misalignments, fractures, and other specific character-istics would be significant in either eliminating or implicating a suspect. Dental characteristics could also be sought on the opposite side of the penis. It is imperative that any and all trauma be photographed in a timely manner. The marks on the penis could not be seen the following day.

31. EXTERNAL PRESSURE BITEMARK

Involuntary bitemarks are categorized as accidental, medical, or third-party induced. Figure 65 demonstrates a third-party-induced self-inflicted bitemark resulting from the aggressor pressing and holding the child's lips against the teeth. In certain cases the lips, the oral mucosa, and the frenula can be lacerated or torn. Under exceptionally violent circumstances there might be fractures of the teeth and/or jaws. The cause of death in the present example was asphyxia by suffocation; the manner, homicide. Other classic signs accompanied the oral manifestation of asphyxia.

Readers are referred to Section 21 for other forms of self-inflicted bitemarks.

32. POSITIONAL CHANGES

Figure 66 demonstrates a positional change of the aggressor's dentition from the top of the shoulder toward the clavicle. This positional change can also be due to jaw closure, slippage,

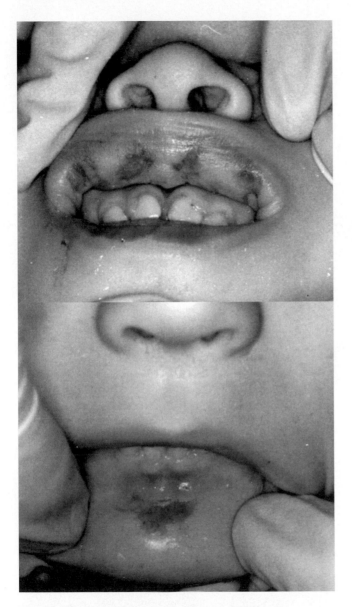

Figure 65   Teeth imprints on upper and lower lips.

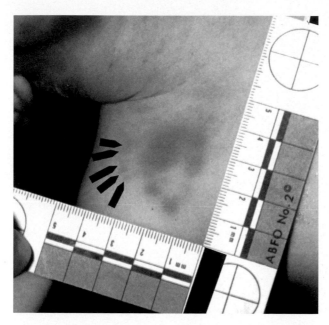

Figure 66 Bitemark dynamics (sliding lower jaw on a curved surface).

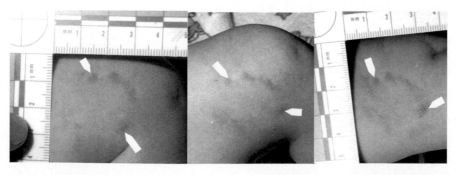

Figure 67 Dimensional change of bitemark with positional change of the leg.

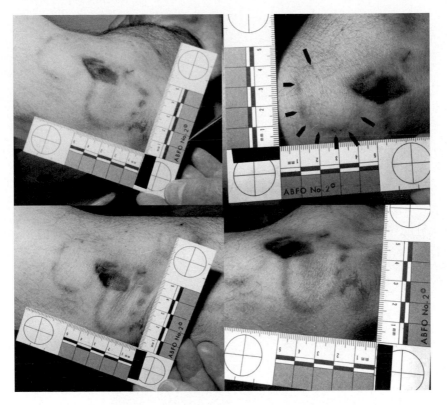

Figure 68   Dimensional change of bitemark with positional change of the arm.

convexity of tissue, aggressor/perpetrator movement, etc. (Fig. 3). Readers are referred to Figure 29 for another example of positional change.

Figure 67 illustrates bitemark on the inner aspect of the upper/lower leg near the knee joint. Note the changes in shape that result from flexion/extension of the leg. This type of bitemark is very difficult to evaluate because of the changing nature of the bitemark. Unless there are other bitemarks from the same perpetrator on the body, it would be difficult to place the leg in the exact position when the bitemark was inflicted.

Figure 68 depicts multiple bitemarks near the elbow joint. The shape of the dental arches that contributed to the bitemark changes with the extension/flexion/rotation of the arm. Readers are directed to Figure 5 in Chapter 3 for another example of flexion/extension of the arm/forearm. Positional changes resulting from joint movement render bitemark analysis/interpretation and perpetrator identification more difficult.

33. OPPOSITE SIDES

Figures 69 and 70 illustrate bitemarks on the inner aspect of the arm/elbow and the front/back of the shoulder, respectively. It might be difficult to demonstrate both the upper and the lower dental arch that contributed to the bitemark in one overall photograph. As mentioned in other chapters, each arch should be photographed independently under these circumstances. Photographs should be taken with the plane of the film parallel to the bitemark or as close to it as possible.

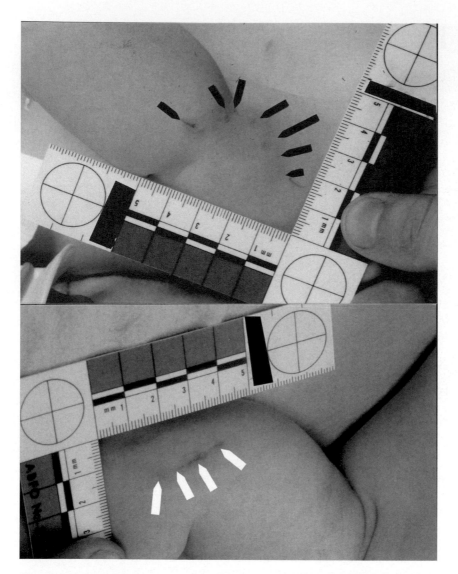

Figure 69 Bitemark at the junction of the arm/forearm and elbow.

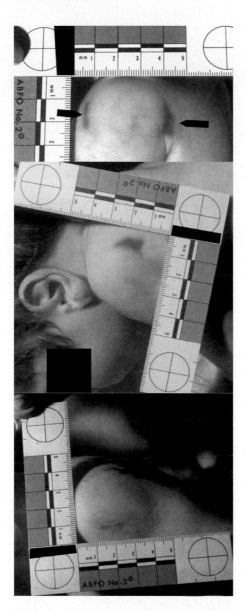

Figure 70 Bitemark in the front and in back of the shoulder.

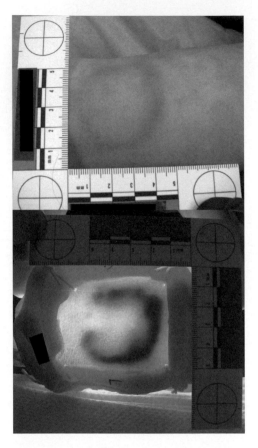

Figure 71 Excised supported bitemark (top) and transilluminated specimen (bottom). (Photo courtesy of Dr. Bryan Chrz.) Also see color photograph insert section.

34. ONE-SIDED BITE

Some bitemarks are more one-sided than others (Fig. 71). There are many factors that can contribute to this phenomenon, including access and convexity of the bitten tissue, slippage, aggressor/victim movement, whether a joint is involved (arm or leg), etc. (Fig. 3).

REFERENCES

1. Pretty IA, Sweet D. Anatomical location of bitemarks and associated findings in 101 cases from the United States. J Forens Sci 2000; 45(4):812–814.
2. Vale GL, Noguchi T. Anatomical distribution of human bite marks in a series of 67 cases. J Forens Sci 1983; 28(1):61–9.
3. Sims BG, Grant JH, Cameron JM. Bite-marks in the "battered baby syndrome". Med Sci Law 1973; 13(3):207–210.
4. Dorion RBJ. Recognition of child abuse, special session, Anthrop/Path/Bio/General. Atlanta: AAFS, Feb 16, 2002.
5. Govindah RBJ. Traumatic amputation of a finger as a result of a human bite. J Forens Sci 1972; 1(445).

6. Pantanowitz L, Berk M. Auto-amputation of the tongue associated with flupenthixol induced extrapyramidal symptoms. Int Clin Psychopharmacol 1999; 14(2):129–31.
7. Dahlin PA, Van Buskirk NE, Novotny RW, Hollis IR, George J. Self-biting with multiple finger amputations following spinal cord injury. Paraplegia 1985; 23(5):306–18.
8. Robey KL, Reck JF, Giacomini KD, Barabas G, Eddey GE. Modes and patterns of self-mutilation in persons with Lesch-Nyhan disease. Dev Med Child Neurol. 2003; 45(3):167–71.
9. Shimoyama T, Horie N, Kato T, Nasu D, Kaneko T. Tourette's syndrome with rapid deterioration by self-mutilation of the upper lip. J Clin Pediatr Dent 2003; 27(2):177–80.
10. Keyes FA. Teeth marks on the skin as evidence in establishing identity. Dental Cosmos 1925; 67: 1165–1167.
11. Sognnaes RF, Rawson RD, Gratt BM, Nauyen BN. Computer comparison of bite mark patterns in identical twins. J. Am. Dent. Assoc. 1982; 105:449–452.
12. Barsley RE, Lancaster DM. Measurement of arch widths in a human population: relation of anticipated bitemarks. J Forens Sci 1987; 32(4):975–982.
13. Dailey JC, Bowers CM. Aging of bitemarks: A literature review. J Forens Sci 1997; 42(5):792–795.
14. Anderson WR, Hudson RP. Self-inflicted bite marks in battered child syndrome. J Forens Sci 1976; 7:71–74.
15. Sobel MN, Perper JA. Self-inflicted bite mark on the breast of a suicide victim. Am J Forens Med Pathol 1985; 6(4):336–339.
16. Warnick AJ, Biedrzycki L, Russanow G. Not all bite marks are associated with abuse, sexual activities, or homicides: a case study of a self-inflicted bite mark. J Forens Sci 1987; 32(3):788–92.

18

Patterns, Lesions, and Trauma-Mimicking Bitemarks

Robert B. J. Dorion
*Laboratoire de sciences judiciaires et de médecine légale,
Ministry of Public Security for the Province of Quebec,
Montreal, Quebec, Canada*

Richard R. Souviron
*Miami-Dade County Medical Examiner's Office
Miami, Florida, U.S.A.*

1. GENERAL CONSIDERATION

A patterned injury is imprinted when a hard object is pressed into skin over a period of time. The tissue compression may be active or passive, such as lying on an object. The period of time and amount of compression may vary considerably. Great force applied over a short period of time, hitting a person with a baseball bat, for example is referred to as blunt trauma injury. Certain objects can leave impressions similar to the human dentition. This chapter illustrates patterns, lesions, and trauma that might be misinterpreted as bitemarks, and vice versa.

2. HEALING LESIONS

Fresh compression injuries on the living are analyzed by photographic record supported by the injured party's statement. Victim testimony is not always available. Children may be too young, or a person may be mentally handicapped, amnesic, unconscious, comatose, senile, have Alzheimer's, or be uncooperative. Figures 1–3 are patterned injuries the circumstances of which are victim described. The force applied to produce the injury in the first example was insufficient to cause lacerations.

The degree of force applied can, in itself, account for the differences in appearance between Figure 1 and Figure 2. The potential for misdiagnosing patterned injuries is depicted in Figure 3. The class and individual characteristics of the offending instrument, not unlike those of the human dentition, produce repetitive and similar patterns. The end of a steel pipe produced the lesions on the back. Compare the healing injuries on the back inflicted by the end of a pipe in Figure 3 to those of bitemarks on the back depicted in the preceding chapter.

The lesions (Fig. 4) on the external genetalia of a 17-month-old female were misdiagnosed as human bites and "matched" to a suspect dentition. Second opinions obtained from forensic odontologists corrected the misdiagnosis to dermatitis.

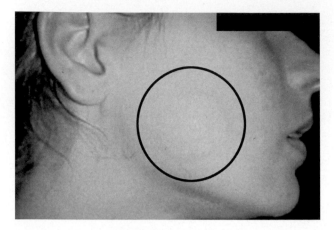

Figure 1 Victim-attested bitemark less than 24 hours old. (Photo courtesy of Dr. Richard Souviron.)

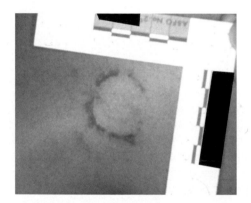

Figure 2 Bitemark on shoulder less than 24 hours old. (Photo courtesy of Dr. Richard Souviron.)

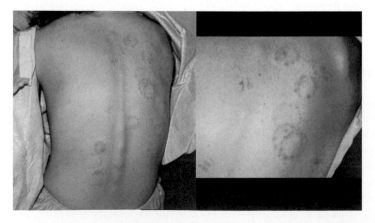

Figure 3 Patterned injuries on the back resembling human bitemarks. (Photos courtesy of Dr. Richard Souviron.)

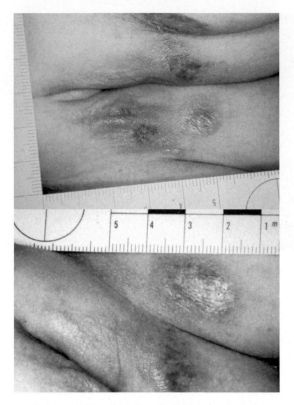

Figure 4 Dermatitis on the external genitalia of a 17-month-old female. (Photos courtesy of Dr. Richard Souviron.)

As previously mentioned, victim testimony is not always available in the living; nor, on the other hand, is it necessarily reliable. In the following example, the alleged victim claimed she was sexually assaulted, cut with a razor blade, burned with a cigar, and bitten on the breast. The victim's background investigation, not to mention the pattern interpretation, cast doubt on the alleged attack. The alleged cigar burn is actually one resulting from the application of a heated penny on the breast. Lincoln's outline is observable in the burn (Fig. 5). The ''victim'' and a friend wanted to publicly humiliate the intended accused in a racially and politically motivated misdeed. The other patterned injury on the breast is devoid of class, and individual characteristics typically present in a ''fresh'' bitemark. There are exceptions to this general statement, however. The color of the lesions adjacent to the penny burn is yellow/green/blue. The dimension of the alleged bitemark in relationship to the penny impression is somewhat large.

Mincer (H. Mincer, personal communication with R. Dorion, 2003) describes the case of a young child with healing crusty patterned injuries on the hands and arms. These burns were produced by an electrical heat hair setting device known as a ''hot comb'' (Fig. 6).

3. HEALED LESIONS

As mentioned, the victim and/or witness account often confirms the diagnosis for the cause of the patterned injury. Pattern injuries including bitemarks usually disappear within a few hours

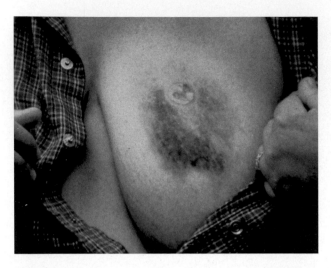

Figure 5 Patterned injury from a penny with adjacent burn. (Photo courtesy of Dr. Richard Souviron).

and in more serious cases within 7–14 days provided the tissue is not amputated. Lacerations and deep compression wounds heal to form scar tissue. While the preceding chapter outlined factors affecting bitemark dynamics, Figure 7 illustrates an unusual 1-year-old bitemark. Imagine the potential misdiagnosis in the timing of the injury if excision, transillumination, and histological analysis had not been performed had the victim been deceased. In law, scaring may be considered a permanent disability and subject not only to criminal but civil litigation under specific circumstances.

Healed injuries often create an indistinct pattern that is difficult to analyze. Figure 8 depicts a victim-confirmed 2-year-old scar from a denture bite. During the altercation the victim pulled his arm from the biter's mouth. The laceration was seen, documented, and sutured by a hospital emergency room physician. Within 24 hours the victim returned with an acute infection, swelling, and bacteremia. The lesion was reopened and allowed to drain. A complete upper denture, particularly against lower natural teeth, can produce bitemarks and, under the proper circumstances, tearing or laceration of the skin in addition to serious and even life-threatening infections.

4. PATTERN INJURIES ON THE DECEASED

Postmortem insect activity is the most common form of patterned injury (Fig 9) on bodies collected outdoors. Insect activity begins within minutes of death and is influenced by temperature, humidity, wind, soil, bacteria, body disposition, circumstance, and other factors. In rare cases, it has been misdiagnosed as human bitemarks and, even worse, "matched" to a suspect dentition by the uninformed, unwary, inexperienced investigator. Figure 10 displays a case where the investigator "matched" a suspect dentition, upper teeth only, to over 20 patterns thought to be bitemarks. It should be remembered that a single-arch bite is the exception and not the rule. Moreover, it would be improbable to have a single-arch bite over 20 times on the same body. Insects caused the patterned injuries. Scene investigation and proper autopsy protocol would have promptly resolved the issue.

The second most common cause of patterned injuries on the deceased is the result of animal predation. Figure 11 illustrates the tragic case of a young child discovered floating in a

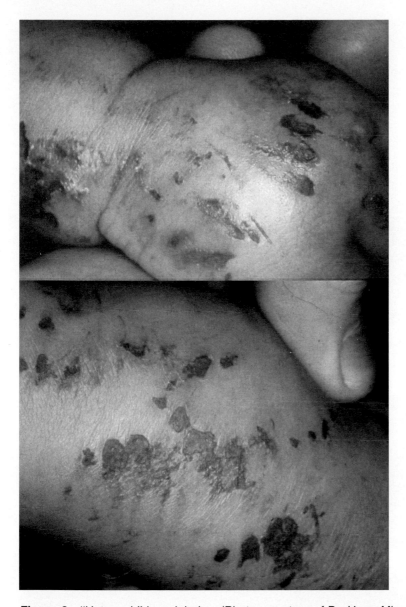

Figure 6 "Hot comb" burn injuries. (Photos courtesy of Dr. Harry Mincer.)

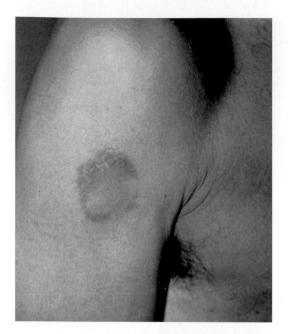

Figure 7   Documented bitemark over 1 year old. (Photo courtesy of Dr. Richard Souviron.)

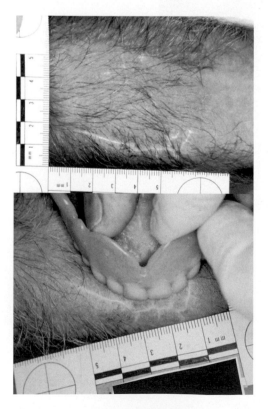

Figure 8   Scar tissue produced by a full upper denture. (Photos courtesy of Dr. Richard Souviron.)

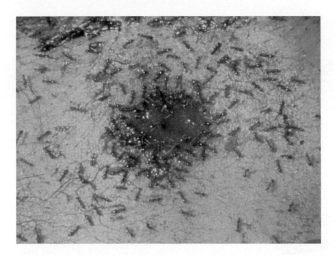

Figure 9 Ant predation. (Photo courtesy of Dr. Richard Souviron.)

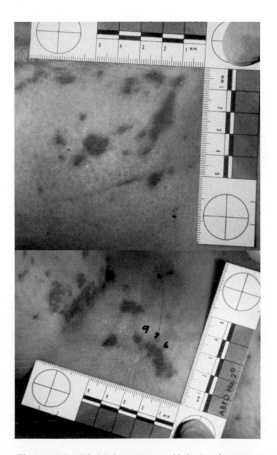

Figure 10 Multiple patterned injuries from insect bites. (Photos courtesy of Dr. Richard Souviron.)

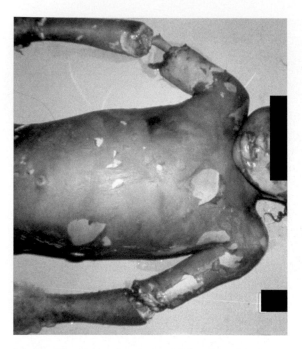

Figure 11   Body of a young child retrieved from a pond. (Photo courtesy of Dr. Richard Souviron.)

pond. While the child had obvious signs of predation, some patterns were erroneously interpreted as human bitemarks and matched to a suspect dentition (Fig. 12).

Figure 12 demonstrates an attempt by the investigator to ''match the suspect dentition'' to the marks on the body. Notice the ''match'' allegedly coincides with the single-arch bite. Note the desquamation in Figure 11. Readers are reminded that a single-arch bite is highly unusual and not the rule. The presence of multiple single-arched bites is even less common.

Tissue sectioning is one method used to differentiate between insect activity, surface abrasion, and postmortem artifact (Fig. 13). The pathologist consulted the odontologist for interpretation of the lesions found on an amputated thumb (Fig. 14) and hand (Fig. 15) of a strangled male homicide victim. The victim also had perforated eyes and had been disemboweled. The

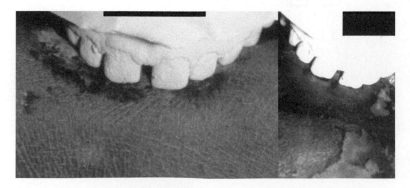

Figure 12   Alleged bitemark and suspect dentition. (Photos courtesy of Dr. Richard Souviron.)

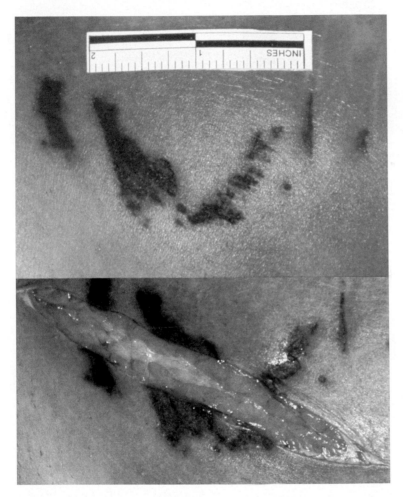

Figure 13   Tissue sectioning through surface abrasion. (Photos courtesy of Dr. Richard Souviron.)

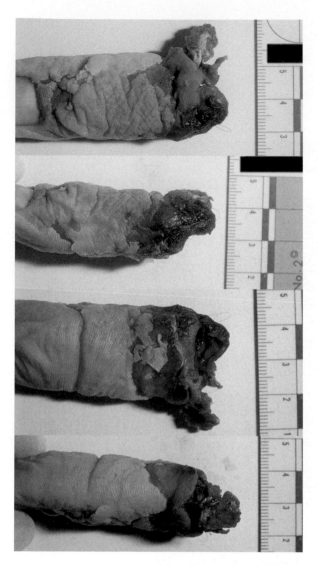

Figure 14 Thumb amputation. (Photos courtesy of Dr. Robert Dorion.)

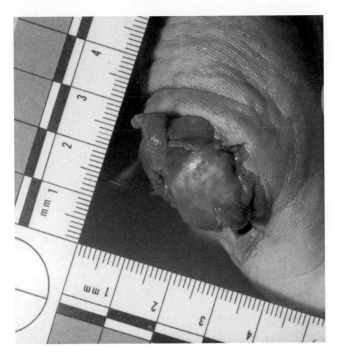

Figure 15 Distal end of the phalange. (Photo courtesy of Dr. Robert Dorion.)

male suspect was the only other prisoner in the cell. It was initially thought that the amputated thumb could have been bitten off. Examination of the tissues revealed "clean" cuts with skin shredding. It was determined that a razor blade was the instrument of amputation rather than the human dentition. The eyes were perforated with pens, and the broken pens, were also used in skin mutilation. Figure 16 reveals the incised and shredded wounds of the right index finger on the same victim. Presumably the suspect had insufficient time to amputate the index finger.

The pathologist consulted the odontologist for interpretation of the lesions found on the scalp of the male infant homicide victim. The semicircular hemorrhagic patterns under the scalp (Fig. 17) measure almost 4 cm across and trails off toward one end. The scalp is the only bodily tissue that is, for all practical purposes, relatively immobile. The result is that the instrument that produces the patterned injury will be more accurately recorded on the scalp than on any other bodily tissue. Generally speaking, there will be very little distortion of the pattern. In the present case, it would be impossible to produce a single-arch 4-cm-diameter human bite that also records posterior teeth. The unidentified causative instrument was never recovered. Compare this patterned injury to a similar patterned injury under the scalp in the preceding chapter.

The examining pathologist consulted the odontologist regarding a partially excised nipple of a female homicide victim. Other markings were found at the base of the breast and the areola (Fig. 18). The edges of the wound on the nipple were very "clean" and sharp. The continuous incised wound almost encircled the nipple. The excision was perpendicular, not parallel, to the markings at the base of the breast. The curved pattern at the base of the breast measured 4 cm end to end and was attributed to support wiring and the bra cloth. The partial excision of the nipple was credited to a sharp instrument, probably a knife. The causative instrument was never recovered.

Examination revealed an amputated nose tip (Fig. 19) in a male homicide victim. Unlike the nose bitemarks described in previous chapters, the edges of the excised tissue are extremely

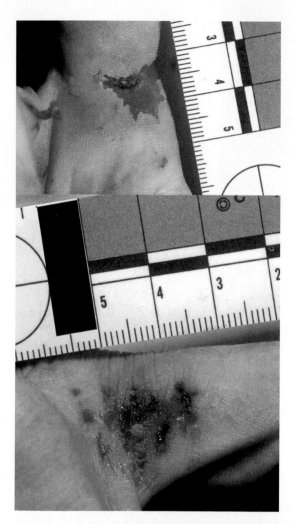

Figure 16 Incised and shredded wounds of the right index finger. (Photos courtesy of Dr. Robert Dorion.)

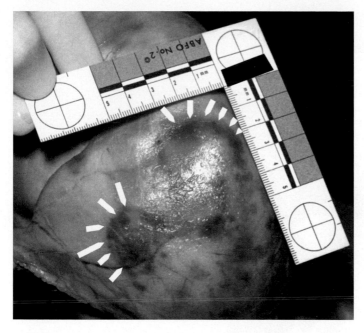

Figure 17 Hemorrhagic pattern on the underside of the scalp. (Photo courtesy of Dr. Robert Dorion.)

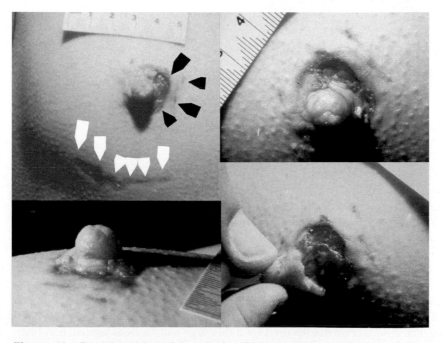

Figure 18 Partial excision of the nipple. (Photos courtesy of Dr. Robert Dorion.)

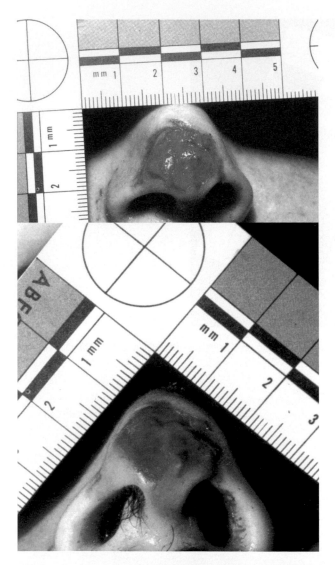

Figure 19 Partial nose amputation. (Photos courtesy of Dr. Robert Dorion.)

sharp and "clean." There are no "indentations" at the edge of the amputated tissue or in the cartilage. The nose tip was removed with a razor blade.

Vale (G. Vale, personal communication with R. Dorion, 2003) reports on a patterned injury that appears remarkably similar to a human bitemark despite the marked differences between the human and canine dentitions (Fig. 20). The child died as a result of a witnessed dog attack. The forensic odontologist was privileged in this instance to see the injuries on the basis of educational opportunity rather than forensic need. When this photograph was inserted in a bitemark exercise, it was not always correctly identified as an animal bite by the examinees. The 4-cm-plus distance between opposite teeth in the same arch should be a clue as to its nonhuman origin. The case accentuates the need for a thorough and cautious approach in interpreting bitemark evidence.

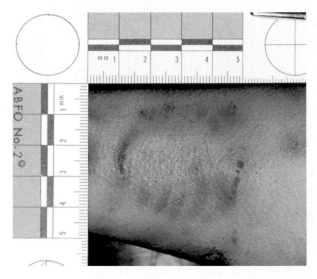

Figure 20 Patterned injury on the arm. (Photo courtesy of Dr. Gerald Vale.)

Figure 21 shows linear parallel abrasions-contusion measuring approximately 13 mm by 23 mm, anterior to the hairline of the temple. The linear parallel abrasions were produced by a comb. Patterned injuries on the deceased may or may not have been witnessed. If witnessed and revealed exclusively by the perpetrator, a healthy skepticism as to cause and circumstance of the injury is a prudent tactic to adopt. If the event is witnessed and revealed by independent uninvolved parties, the integrity of the observers and the veracity of the information is less likely to be questioned.

Figure 22 illustrates a patterned injury on the scalp of a female homicide victim. The pathologist initially questioned the unusual starburst pattern. The philosophy adopted by most experienced, knowledgeable forensic pathologists is to err on the side of caution, rather than to side with imprudence, negligence, or stupidity. The bitemark hypothesis was eliminated by the odontologist. The second instrument suspected was the base of a Molson beer mug. Although

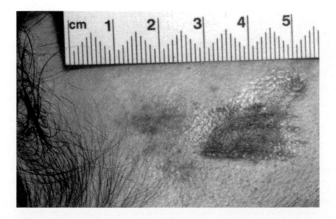

Figure 21 Linear parallel abrasions-contusion. (Photo courtesy of Dr. Robert Dorion.)

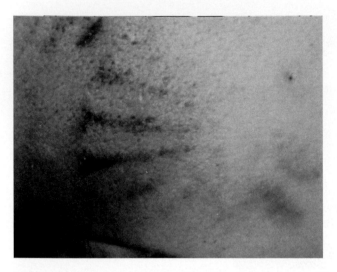

Figure 22   Patterned injury with starburst appearance. (Photo courtesy of Dr. Robert Dorion.)

the base of the beer mug had a central starburst pattern, it also was eliminated. Lastly, another implement was analyzed and found to be the causative agent, the base of an ashtray.

Figure 23 reveals contusions of the nipple, areola, and breast tissue, as well as a lateral aspect of the breast (chest wall). The contusions around the nipple and areola are nonspecific and lack both class and individual characteristics. The contusions on the lateral aspect of the breast measures 33 mm end to end but lacks curvature. In addition, the distance between the

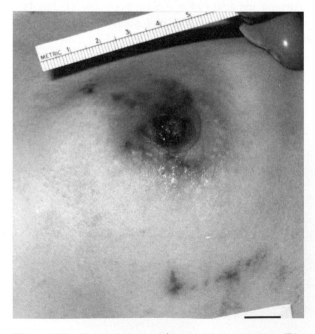

Figure 23   Contusions on chest wall and breast. (Photo courtesy of Dr. Robert Dorion.)

midpoint of this curvature and the nipple measures 53 mm. The breast is relatively flat (little mass/curvature), minimizing the possibility for tissue distortion. A photograph taken at the scene of the body disposal revealed a displaced bra. The partially clad female homicide victim was found face down in snow in −20°F weather. The contusions on the lateral aspect of the thoracic cage were attributed to bra wiring. This case predates DNA analysis that could have resolved the issues of identification and of ''oral'' contact (saliva) at both sites, nipple and thoracic cage. The presence of DNA would not have resolved the issues of ''tooth'' contact and/or ''biting.''

4.1. Passive Compression

Pattern development occurs from trauma or passive compression (lying on an object). Figure 24 reveals a patterned injury on the lateral aspect of the abdomen that resembles, in many aspects, a human bitemark. The deceased was recovered lying on the open end of a pipe.

Figure 25 represents an oval patterned injury found below the right ear lobe of a transvestite homicide victim. There are both class and individual characteristics to the patterned injury. The class and individual characteristics are not, however, associated with the human dentition. The victim was found lying on a round braided metal earring through the pierced ear. Note the shape of the mark is oval and not round, an excellent example of tissue distortion.

Objects can imprint strange patterns, such as the one recorded in Figure 26. To the unwary the pattern might resemble a contused bitemark or a lip print on the inner aspect of a lower leg. The pattern is due to neither. It is a leaf print.

4.2. Medical Conditions, Treatment, Autopsy Trauma, and Other Objects

Caution should prevail when crime scene photographs are unavailable and/or the person autopsied has received medical attention. Individuals who receive emergency medical care may present with

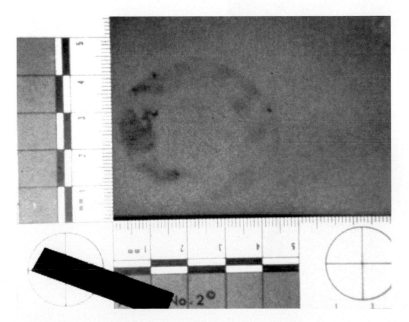

Figure 24 Patterned injury resembling a human bitemark. (Photo courtesy of Dr. Richard Souviron.)

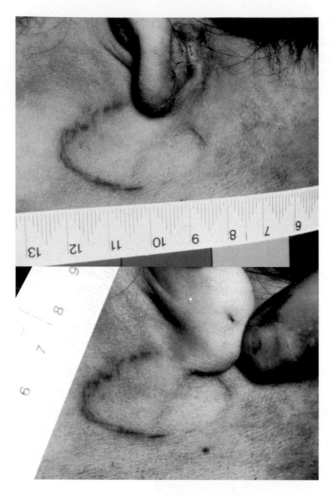

Figure 25   Oval pattern below the ear. (Photos courtesy of Dr. Robert Dorion.)

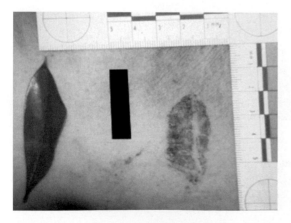

Figure 26   Pattern on the leg resembling a contused bitemark or a lip print. (Photo courtesy of Dr. Richard Souviron.)

traumatic lesions/patterns resulting from treatment. Accurate information of events leading to autopsy will prevent patterned injury misinterpretation. The reader is referred to the preceding chapter for additional examples and related problems.

In the following example the initial analysis of the patterned injury on the leg ruled out a human bitemark. The pattern was correctly interpreted as the receptacle for a Foley catheter (Fig. 27).

There are reported cases of artifactual injury from cardiac defibrillators simulating bitemarks in the literature [1]. Vale (G. Vale, personal communication with R. Dorion, 2003) reports having examined the upper left chest of an adult male decedent (Fig. 28, top photo). The wound was consistent with a human bitemark in several respects. It consisted of two arched injuries facing each other, and each arch had an interrupted pattern suggestive of individual toothmarks. However, the injury had a yellowish brown color. This was inconsistent with the deep red or blue to purple color usually associated with a recent antemortem contusion on light-colored skin. The odontologist photographed the injury and requested a consultation. When two forensic odontologists saw the injury the following evening, it had changed appearance considerably, with substantial necrosis and sloughing of tissue (Fig. 28, bottom photo). Such dramatic change in a body refrigerated for 24 hours would be quite unusual if this was a contused injury.

Since the injury was located in an area where electrocardiograph (EKG) monitor pads are commonly placed, an inquiry was made of the deceased's emergency medical treatment. Emergency personnel had repotedly placed EKG monitor pads during resuscitation efforts. Careful evaluation shows a faint but visible smooth, curved mark extending downward from the ''dental arch'' on the right side. This would be incompatible with a bitemark, but compatible with an EKG pad mark. An EKG monitor pad was then compared to the injury. The size was similar, but the pad was circular, while the injury was ovoid. This apparent discrepancy was easily reconciled when the location of the injury was taken into account. The axillary region is one of the areas that change shape markedly as the result of body position, such as raising or lowering the arm. This is easily demonstrated by drawing a circular mark on one's own body or by moving the arm in an actual

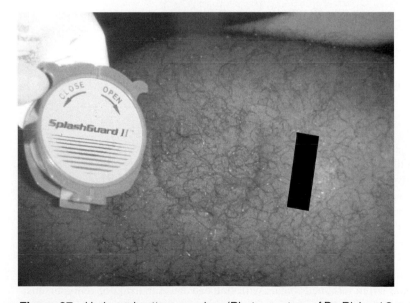

Figure 27 U-shaped pattern on a leg. (Photo courtesy of Dr. Richard Souviron.)

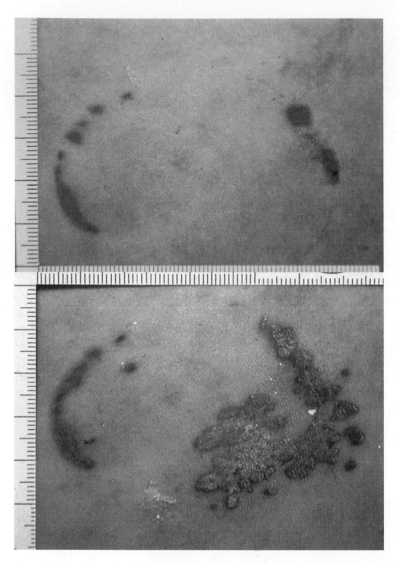

Figure 28 Patterned injury on chest wall Photographed 24 hours apart. (Photos courtesy of Dr. Gerald Vale.)

case. It was concluded that the injury was a surface abrasion caused by the removal of the EKG monitor pad rather than a contused injury caused by a human bite. The sloughing may have been related to refrigeration and dehydration of the abraded tissue.

There are a number of wounds and natural diseases that share class characteristics with bitemarks and must be ruled out before ascribing a particular patterned injury to biting. Bernstein reports (M. Bernstein, personal communication with R. Dorion, 2003) that the round paddles of a defibrillator can create a circular patterned injury of compatible size to mimic a bitemark on the torso [1]. These represent burns occurring when inadequate lubricant is applied to the paddles. Similarly, EKG electrodes left in sustained contact with skin can cause an irritation or hypersensitivity reaction that outlines the circular pattern of the contacting ring (Figs. 29, 30). If suspected,

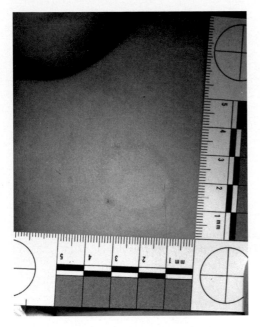

Figure 29 Ring-shaped mark simulating toothless bitemark, created by an EKG electrode left on skin. (Photo courtesy of Dr. Mark L. Bernstein.)

these diagnoses are easily confirmed by medical history. Animal hoof marks (horses, cows) can create rounded bruises resembling bitemarks. Heel marks sustained in stomping injuries can closely resemble bitemarks [2], particularly if the heel has elevations that might simulate toothmarks. Circular jewelry, particularly rings, belt buckles, flashlight handles, and children's toys can produce circular patterns [3–5] (Figs 31, 32).

Some natural diseases produce erosive or erythematous annular or circinate lesions that can be mistaken for bitemarks. Tenia circinata (ringworm), impetigo, erythema multiforme, erythema

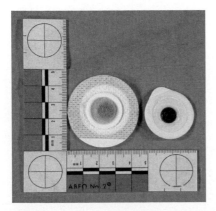

Figure 30 Two EKG electrodes having peripheral adhesive rings that cause skin irritation as seen in Figure 29. (Photo courtesy of Dr. Mark L. Bernstein.)

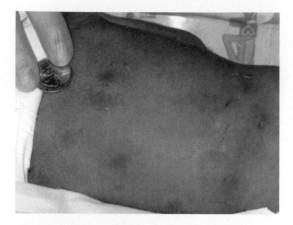

Figure 31 Multiple circular ring-like patterned injuries simulating continuous arched bitemarks. Note central contusion surrounded by aligned "toothmarks." (Photo courtesy of Dr. Mark L. Bernstein.)

Figure 32 A ring with peripheral prongs that could create the injuries seen in Figure 34. (Photo courtesy of Dr. Mark L. Bernstein.)

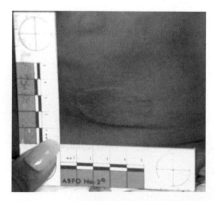

Figure 33 Ringworm in right abdomen, simulating a toothless bitemark. (Photo courtesy of Dr. Mark L. Bernstein.)

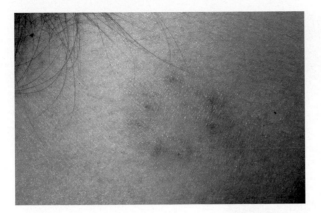

Figure 34 Annular pattern of vesicles caused by herpes simplex virus simulating a bitemark in the neck. (Photo courtesy of Dr. Mark L. Bernstein.)

annulare, granuloma annulare, pityriasis rosea annular lichen planus, contact allergy, urticaria, and herpes are some examples [1,6,7] (Figs. 33, 34).

The Southeast Asian custom of *cao gio* (coining) uses coins heated with oil to mark the skin. The folklore ritual is designed to ward off evil spirits. The heated coins produce ringlike burns.

4.3. Unspecified Marks and Lesions

Postmortem patterned injuries can be caused by a variety of devices. Some are more difficult than others to identify, and some remain unresolved as to source. Figure 35 depicts a pattern on the right shoulder of an exhumed and embalmed body. The investigator determined the pattern on the

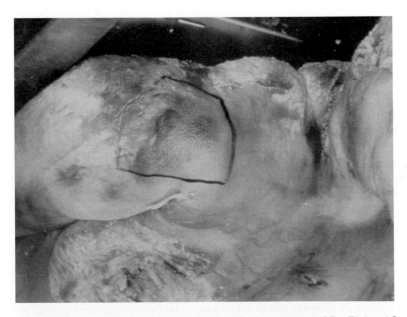

Figure 35 Shoulder of exhumed body. (Photo courtesy of Dr. Richard Souviron.)

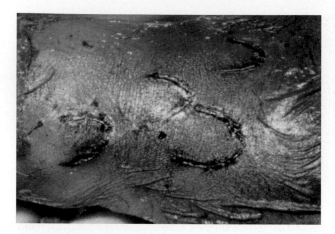

Figure 36 Unknown cause for the patterned injury. (Photo courtesy of Dr. Robert Dorion.)

shoulder to be a three-tooth single-arch bitemark, two lower bicuspids, and a canine. As mentioned several times in this text, single-arch bites are rare. A three-tooth single-arch bite from posterior teeth is improbable. What appears to be tissue excision is in fact demarcation of the area with a marking pen. The analysis in this case was based solely on an unscaled photographic interpretation without the benefit of bitemark impressions, tissue preservation, transillumination, or histology. The need to adhere to a bitemark protocol as outlined in this book would have resolved the issue in the scientific manner.

Figure 36 illustrates several patterned injuries on a decomposing hand. The elderly person living alone was found with several bitemarks from a pet cat that had not been fed in several days. The patterned injuries on the hand, however, could not be attributed to the feline dentition and remains unresolved.

5. SUMMARY

Proper determination of the origin of the patterned injury in life or death is critical. In the living, one can usually benefit from the victim's explanation, whether truthful or not. In death investigation, witness reports may or may not serve to reinforce autopsy findings. Regardless of witness reports, proper autopsy protocol and analysis of the patterned injury will minimize the chances of pattern misdiagnosis. It is important when analyzing a patterned injury that the investigator obtains scene photographs and be well informed of the circumstances leading to the death. Without full knowledge and other pertinent information relating to the patterned injury, including the medical history, misinterpretation can result.

Alan R. Moritz, M.D., is credited with the saying: ''If the evidence has been properly gathered and preserved, a mistake in interpretation may always be corrected. If the facts required to correct the interpretation are not preserved, a mistake is irreversible.''

REFERENCES

1. Grey TC. Defibrillator injury suggesting bite mark. Am J Forens Med Pathol 1989; 10(2):144–145.
2. Harvey W. Dental Identification and Forensic Odontology. London: Henry Kimpton Publishers, 1976: 88–140.

3. Stimson PG, Mertz CA. Bite mark techniques and terminology. In Stinson PG, Mertz CA, Eds. Forensic Dentisry. Boca Raton. FL: CRC Press, 1997:137–159.

4. Clark DH. Practical Forensic Odontology. Oxford: Wright, 1992:128–205.

5. Rawson RD. Child abuse identification. Can Dent Assoc J 1986; 14(3):21–25.

6. Pillsbury DM. Principles of clinical diagnosis. In Moschella SL, Allsbury DM, Hurley HJ, Eds. Dermatology. Philadelphia: W.B. Saunders:189–190.

7. Habif TP. Clinical Dermatology: Color Guide to Diagnosis and Therapy. St. Louis: C.V. Mosby, 1985: 86–100.

VI
Collection of Evidence from the Suspect

19
The Suspect

L. Thomas Johnson
Milwaukee County Medical Examiner's Office
Milwaukee, Wisconsin, U.S.A.

1. COURT ORDER/INFORMED CONSENT

In 1984 the American Board of Forensic Odontology (ABFO) established guidelines covering the subject of bitemark analysis. It has subsequently updated these guidelines from time to time to include the collection of evidence from the suspect. The guidelines are available on the ABFO's website www.abfo.org and are outlined in Appendix I of this book.

Before collecting evidence from a suspect, the requesting agency should obtain a search warrant, court order, or informed consent. The forensic odontologist should discuss with appropriate authorities and list all procedures required under the warrant for the collection of evidence from a suspect, prior to submission to a court for approval. Once approved, the odontologist should retain a copy of the search warrant. The document should be read carefully before proceeding, to assure that the requested collection of evidence is clearly specified in the document. This is an essential component to admissibility of the evidence in court. Motions filed by opposing counsel may later challenge any warrant shortcomings or the collection of unspecified material.

In most jurisdictions the warrant applicant (officer or detective) is present for its execution. In practice, it is also advisable to have the law enforcement case investigator present even when informed consent has been obtained. It is also good practice to have the session videorecorded to demonstrate exactly what was done and when, who was present, and the demeanor of all parties present.

As a precautionary measure, the odontologist should monitor his actions with a checklist. This serves at least two purposes: it assures that the mandated procedures are followed and no more, and it provides a detailed recording of a myriad of other information. Details such as the date, time, location, and the names and titles of those present/affected/witnessing/assisting in the procedure should always be documented. All of these details will ultimately serve in report writing and as a refresher for ultimate court testimony.

2. DENTAL HISTORY

The suspect's complete dental history, including recent dental treatment, periodontal disease, and other pathology, should be documented. The maximum extent of jaw opening, the degree of lateral excursions, and the ability to protrude the mandible may be crucial to the analysis.

415

Mobility, missing, supernumerary, or damaged teeth should be charted. The subject's present and past dental records should be subpoenaed to establish the dental condition at the time of bitemark infliction. This is particularly important if there has been an extended period of time from infliction of the bite to examination of the suspect. Additional photographic (smiling photographs) and radiographic records (medical, orthodontic, etc.) and casts might be important for this purpose. Consult Appendix II checklist.

3. STANDARD PHOTOGRAPHY

A protocol should be established before beginning dental and suspect photographs. Conducting the photographic documentation in the same orderly fashion each time avoids unintentional omissions and reduces the time allotment.

It is desirable for the odontologist to have an assistant when executing the collection of evidence. Since the odontologist will be wearing personal protective gear, it would be otherwise necessary to remove the gloves to avoid contamination of the camera and accessory equipment. Having a competent assistant or, even better, a professional photographer set up the camera and expose the film alleviates this problem. The odontologist should guide the placement of the camera, determining the views required. Since there will generally be only one opportunity to document the subject, it is advisable to bracket each exposure [1].

This author suggests the use of a 35-mm single-lens reflex camera with normal and macrolens with full manual capability as the ideal photographic armamentarium for the collection of evidence from a suspect. An alternative zoom lens is suggested with focal length from medium-wide angle (28–35 mm) to medium telephoto (70–135 mm) [1]. Closeup capability with a minimum of 1:4 magnifications is advantageous [1]. Zoom lens, or a noncalibrated system, poses a problem for 1:1 intraoral photographs of occlusal surfaces. A camera with interchangeable lenses is most desirable. A ring light, detachable hot shoe flash, PC connector, cheek retractors, and a quality front surface intraoral mirror are advantageous. A medium-format camera for extraoral photographs is also desirable. Even more desirable is a large-format camera capable of 1:1 images. The author utilizes a Polaroid CU-5 camera with the dental accessory kit for 1:1 and 2:1 images. This camera is capable of accepting either a Polaroid Model 545i, 4×5″ film holder with Polacolor ER, type 59 professional 4 × 5″ sheet film, or a 4 × 5″ negative film holder with Kodak Porta NC (100 ISO). There are at least two advantages in using this camera: the Polaroid exposures serve as test images and thereby provide instant working photographs, and the exposure values for the negative film are very similar. Since the camera produces 4 × 5″ prints with the intraoral kit, captured images are approximately 1:1, making enlargements unnecessary.

Begin with full-face, midrange photographs for identification of the suspect. To avoid distortion, if a medium-format camera is unavailable, use a long lens. Remember that your identification of the subject of a workup, at trial, might be delayed for months or, in unusual cases, years. Some photographers also expose right and left lateral subject profiles. Autofocus cameras must allow for full manual override, or at least offer aperture and shutter priority. Using cheek retractors, closeup photographs of the dentition should be made both with the teeth in occlusion (Fig. 1) and also at maximum opening (Fig. 2).

Photographing the biting surfaces of the teeth requires specialized equipment. An intraoral, front surface mirror and ring light is recommended for documenting the incisal/occlusal surfaces (Fig. 3). Be aware, though, that images of the tooth surfaces taken with an intraoral mirror must be reversed when printed. To avoid fogging of the mirror, request the subject to hold his/her breath momentarily while the mirror is inserted into the mouth and the exposure is made.

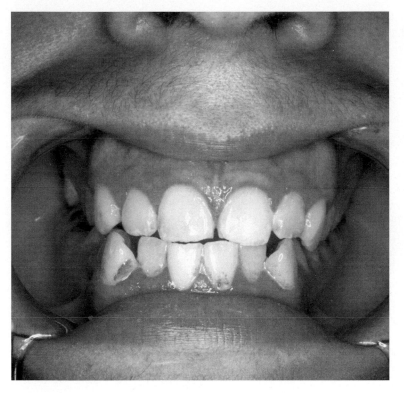

Figure 1 Frontal view of the dentition in occlusion.

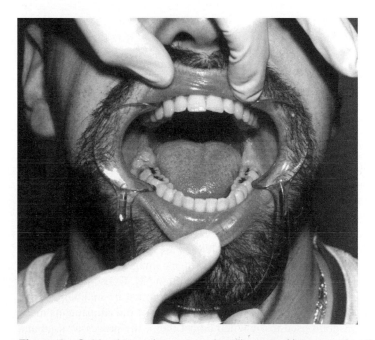

Figure 2 Subject's maximum opening diameter. Note use of self-retaining cheek retractor.

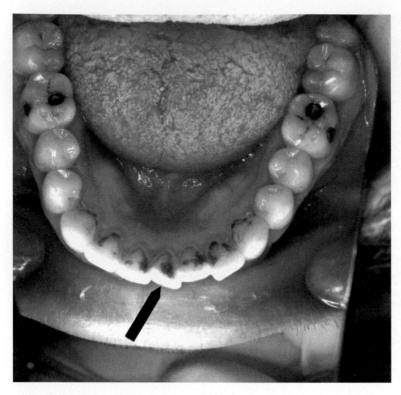

Figure 3   Note the presence of a rotated, supernumerary incisor in the midline. The photograph was taken with an intraoral mirror, requiring reversal printing.

Increasingly, digital photography is replacing standard photography. There are some advantages to digital photography; expensive, high-end, megapixel equipment, however, is necessary to create high-quality enlargements. Consider also that full manual capability is required for the desired goal. The effects of long-term storage of digital images have yet to be demonstrated, whereas negatives can be archived indefinitely. Digital files are also subject to being accidentally deleted or corrupted.

The FBI's Scientific Working Group on Imaging Technologies (SWGIT) states that digital imaging processing is an accepted practice in forensic science. (Editor's note: see Chapter 8 for more information on SWGIT.) However, to be acceptable, any changes made to an image must meet the following criteria: the original image is preserved; the processing steps are logged; the end result is presented as a processed image which may be reproduced by applying the logged procedures; and the recommendations of the SWGIT Guidelines are followed [2]. In practice, the original images are placed in a separate directory called primary images, and the properties are changed to read-only, making it more difficult to overwrite them [3]. Consequently, if the odontologist uses digital photography, the original digital image file must be maintained, and only copies should be used to make adjustments. By maintaining a log of the adjustments made to the copies and the computer program used to view and adjust them, the processes used and results obtained are reproducible. Although the term image ''enhancement'' is commonly used,

SWGIT prefers the term "processed" image, and this author prefers "adjusted" image. Interestingly, for viewing raw and processed images, the courts have yet to require supplying the appropriate software to opposing counsel.

4. EXTRAORAL EXAMINATION

The examiner should observe and record any significant factors that could influence the subject's ability to bite, e.g., facial asymmetry, the classification of occlusion, any deviations of the jaws in opening and also in lateral excursions [4]. Complaints of joint clicking or joint pain should be evaluated and recorded. Record the presence of facial hair, e.g., moustache or beard. This also is a time to record the subject's demeanor and any other information that may be pertinent.

5. INTRAORAL EXAMINATION

Approach the intraoral examination as a complete oral/dental workup for any new patient. When possible, an assistant can chart the findings as dictated. This avoids chart contamination and saves time. The examiner should record all virgin, unerupted, missing, decayed, and restored teeth, prosthetic replacements, periodontal health, mobility, and overall oral health. A graphic representation of existing restorations and other dental conditions should be placed on an odontogram. The subject's tongue size and functionality should be recorded, (e.g., ankyloglossia [4]).

Buccal swabs should be taken if enumerated in the search warrant or court order. Depending on the laboratory preference, swabs might need premoistening with sterile distilled water or saline solution. Be aware of the laboratory preference. The laboratory might require air-drying the swabs before packaging and returning them to the DNA unit. It is important to avoid cross-contaminating the swabs with other DNA.

6. IMPRESSIONS

Full-arch dental impressions should be made with an American Dental Association–accepted dental impression material, following the manufacturers' directions. An elastomeric, accurate, and stable material (e.g., vinyl polysiloxane) is recommended. If it is at all possible, and depending on the warrant mandate, a second set of impressions might prove beneficial. Record the type, manufacturer, and expiration date of the material used. Consult Appendix II checklist.

Water-based impression materials such as alginates are not recommended, since they are not dimensionally stable, must be poured immediately, and the impressions cannot be preserved undistorted. The impression trays and/or the containers in which they are held should be immediately marked with case number, date, and personal identifiers such as initials.

Along with the full-arch dental impressions, sample bites can be taken in an appropriate material to record the subject's bite pattern. This author uses a horseshoe-shaped wax wafer, called CoprWax, manufactured by the Surgident Corporation (Fig. 4). This is a valuable three-dimensional adjunct to dental casts and two-dimensional photographs. By using at least three separate registrations at progressive depths, a three-dimensional representation of the dental characteristics is produced. The variation in patterns resulting from differences in incisal heights that can be seen in the bitemark is then more readily apparent.

7. STUDY CASTS

Casts should be poured in an ADA-approved dental material such as Type II dental stone (Fig. 5) and prepared in accordance with the manufacturer's instructions. Common dental plaster

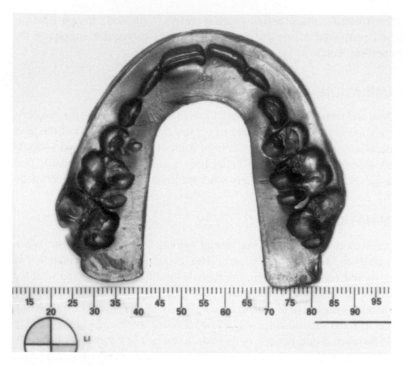

Figure 4   Example of progressive depth of closure into a softened wax wafer.

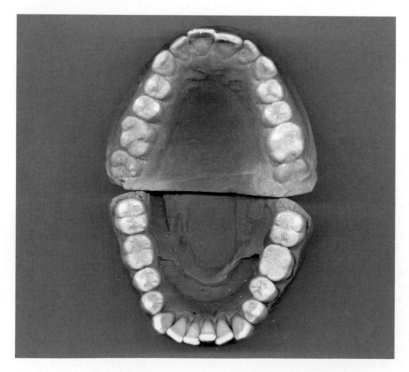

Figure 5   Dental casts poured in Type II beige dental die stone.

is not recommended, nor is white die stone, since the latter is difficult to photograph and the former, too weak. Teeth or adjacent soft tissue on casts should not be altered, trimmed, or marked [4]. Casts should be identified at their base by case number and other personal identifiers. Models should be stored in identified boxes or containers as orthodontic casts would be in the dental office. Additional, working duplicates of the master cast may be made using accepted duplication procedures and marked as duplicates.

Warrant or court-ordered collected specimens, whether biologic, photographic, impressionistic, poured, or duplicated, may all be considered evidence. Some jurisdictions consider only the photographic negatives and impressions as evidence. The photographic prints and poured models in those instances are considered work product. It is vital that the odontologist become thoroughly familiar with the legal concept of evidence in the jurisdiction in which he or she is working and the necessity for maintaining a chain of custody or possession. The integrity of evidence must be protected from damage, alteration, and loss. It must be stored in a secure area, accessible only to those entitled to use or view it.

REFERENCES

1. Groffy RL. Criminal Investigation Photography, unpublished monograph, Wisconsin Department of Justice, Crime Laboratory Bureau., 1998:1–2.
2. Recommendations and Guidelines for the Use of Digital Imaging Processing in the Criminal Justice System, Proceedings of the Scientific Working Group on Imaging Technologies (SWGIT), Ver. 1.2, June 2002.
3. Cadle DE. Imaging specialist, Wisconsin Department of Justice, Crime Laboratory Bureau. personal communication. 2003.
4. Bell GL, Ed. ABFO Bitemark Analysis Guidelines, Diplomate Reference Manual: American Board of Forensic Odontology, 2002:25–31.

VII
Methods of Comparison

20
The Comparison

Jon Curtis Dailey
Dental Corps, U.S. Army*
4504 Guilford Court, Evans, GA, J0809

1. INTRODUCTION

A meticulous bitemark examination will profile the arrangement of the perpetrator's teeth. This assessment may in turn assist investigators in developing a potential suspect. When authorities have identified the potential biter, his/her dental records provide the basis for comparison with the bitemark known as bitemark analysis. The results from this comparison culminate with the forensic dentist's opinion of a possible, probable, positive, or negative correlation.

Ideally, the suspect's dental models, frequently called dental casts, would be directly compared to the tooth-created indentations in the patterned injury on the skin. This is an extremely rare occurrence, as the elastic rebound of skin renders tooth indentations fleeting. When tooth indentations are present, they should be recorded and preserved with an accurate impression material. A three-dimensional replica of the bitemark is made using this impression.

A more likely scenario for a direct comparison exists with bitemarks in foodstuff or other inanimate objects. Figure 1 reveals a bitemark left in a piece of cheese.

In a large number of bitemark cases the only evidence collected are photographs, a two-dimensional representation of a three-dimensional object. The photographic evidence is usually compared to the three-dimensional models of a suspect's teeth. The models may be used to produce sample bites on a volunteer's skin or on various materials serving as tissue substitutes. Alternatively, two-dimensional transparent acetate overlays, photocopies, computer scans, and other forms of recording tooth edges are employed.

2. TEST BITES

Test bites or sample bites are produced on various materials. The goal is to visualize the pattern produced by the biting edges of the teeth in a position that simulates the bitemark injury. While direct comparison of the dental model to the bitemark might seem more logical, the process often obstructs the examiner's view, making it less practical. The issue has been addressed by the fabrication of clear dental models made of urethane dimethacrylate (Triad Clear Colorless

---

* ''This is the work of the author and does not reflect the views of the U.S. Army or the U.S. Government.''

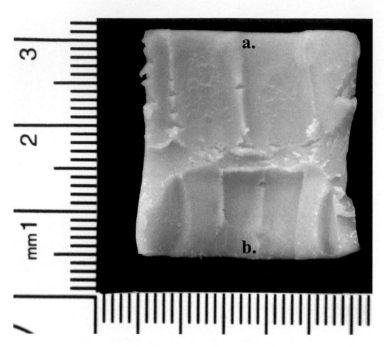

Figure 1 Bitemark in cheese exhibiting maxillary (a) and mandibular (b) teeth imprints.

Gel from Dentsply International, York, PA), crystal-clear epoxy resin (Marglass 658 from Acme Chemicals and Insulation Co., New Haven, CT), and acrylic resin (Leocryl from Leone Orthodontics, Beaconsfield, NSW, Australia) [1,2]. The author considers Triad insufficiently transparent and recommends the other materials [1]. Figure 2 depicts a clear model on a bitemark photograph.

2.1. Static Test Bites

Static test bites represent a recording of the biting edges of the maxillary or mandibular teeth at one depth, at one moment in time, and without recording movement of the edges in the bitten substrate.

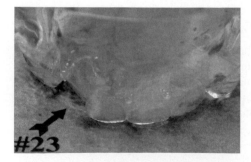

Figure 2 A clear acrylic resin study model on a bitemark photograph. (Note: #ns23 Universal System of Nomenclature.)

2.2. Wax

Numerous types of waxes have been used over the years. Currently, Aluwax (Aluwax Dental Products Company, Grand Rapids, MI) remains very popular owing to its physical properties. This material is sold as U-shaped wafers in which a cloth base is sandwiched between layers of wax. The material is semirigid at room temperature, but can be softened in a variety of ways. Aluwax wafers were used to record the test bites in Figure 3.

    The quandaries with wax lie in the questions of how far should the examiner push the tooth edges into the wax; if some teeth lie outside the plane of the anterior bite, how much should the wax be forced to bend in order to cause such malpositioned teeth to register their mark; and does this introduce significant distortion into the test bite that is discrepant from the bitemark pattern? Bending of the wax is evident in Figure 4.

2.3. Styrofoam

Numerous illustrations from published literature demonstrate test bites made into Styrofoam. Recently, the limitations of Styrofoam as a test bite material have been discussed and illustrated [3]. In 1984, the American Board of Forensic Odontology (ABFO) published their Bitemark Analysis Guidelines. Guidelines are suggested procedures, and these recommended the use of American Dental Association (ADA)-approved materials for impression making and for the fabrication of dental models made from those impressions [4]. These suggestions were designed to ensure the greatest accuracy at each step in the bitemark analysis process. Logically, it follows that odontologists would apply this goal for accuracy to every material and method. In 1994, the ABFO surveyed their diplomates to see what analytical methods they used in the comparison of bitemark evidence. The results of this survey were published as findings, not as recommendations [5]. Styrofoam was one material found to be in the analytical armamentarium of the time. Applying the principals for obtaining accuracy at every step, the only acceptable use for this material today should be as a preliminary mechanism for recording the biting edges of teeth in

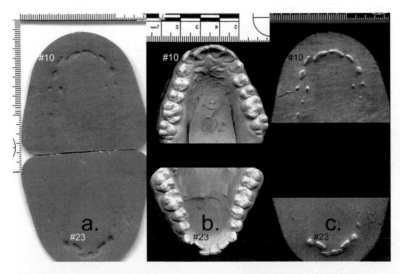

Figure 3 Static test bites in Aluwax (a). The suspected biter's dental models (b) have been flipped horizontally to align with the pattern they created. (c) The Aluwax image has been digitized and "inverted" using Adobe Photoshop.

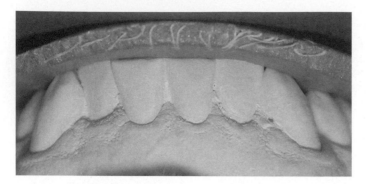

Figure 4 Wax distortion created when the misaligned mandibular tooth biting edges are brought in contact at a uniform depth.

the absence of other, more accurate, widely accepted materials and techniques. Styrofoam is not a dental material and does not meet the quality standards set forth by the ABFO Standards for Bitemark Analytical Methods [6]. Standards are methods of practice that have met the scrutiny of scientific study and verification.

2.4. Dental Impression Materials

When the bitemark is avulsive or involves inanimate objects, test bites can be created in similar objects for comparison. The goal is to reproduce the anatomical area of the teeth observed in the original bite, using the suspected biter's dental models. The use of a bolus of previously set impression material has been advocated [7]. However, this is not applicable after the final set of rigid impression materials such as polyvinylsiloxanes (PVS) or polyether, which set so hard

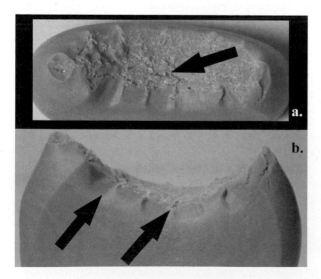

Figure 5 A bitten bolus of setting PVS impression material showing compressive distortion (a) and stretching distortion (b).

they are resistant to being bitten easily. An alginate impression material (irreversible hydrocolloid) would be the material of choice in such situations.

Figure 5 demonstrates the results of the author attempting a bite into a bolus of PVS immediately prior to the final set of the material. The incision of the material at this stage resulted in poorly recorded tooth edges. The author was barely able to generate enough biting force with his natural dentition to create a bite into the material, and attempts to do so with stone models proved futile.

2.5. Identical Substances

Numerous scientific papers have been published in the forensic odontology literature concerning foodstuffs and other inanimate objects bearing tooth marks. Pieces of cheese [8–11], soft cake [12], chocolate [13], chewing gum [14], a sandwich [15], and soap [16] have been collected as evidence and presented as case reports. Test bites into similar pieces of cheese, fruit, or other foodstuffs should be attempted if the examiner is analyzing a bite into such substances. Care should be taken to use a duplicate set of dental models for this purpose, as the foodstuffs being bitten may have a deleterious effect on them. These models can be protected to some degree by coating them with an air-thinned layer of cyanoacrylate, or painting them with a layer of liquid floor wax. Most of these cases, chewing gum being the primary exception, represent incisive bites, where a piece of the original object was bitten off by the biter. In such cases, the facial configuration (outline or profile) of the teeth is usually recorded, rather than the biting edges. With chewing gum, the occlusal, or chewing surface, of the posterior teeth is usually captured in the evidence.

With all of these substances, a replica can be created using an impression made of the original object. These are considered the negative representations of the biting teeth. From the negative, a model of the positive profiles of the labial surfaces of teeth that created the bite can be fabricated. This positive profile model can be sliced through to create a demonstration model for comparison with the negative profile left by the bite into the bitten object, and with the profile of the suspect's dentition. Figure 6 illustrates the profile comparison technique.

Making a stone model of chewing gum would create a model of the chewing surfaces of the teeth recorded in the gum, for a side-by-side comparison to the same posterior teeth of the suspect's dentition.

2.6. Animal Skin

Porcine (pig) skin has seen limited use as a substitute for human skin when creating test bites [17,18]. Such studies generally use the pigskin after the animal has been sacrificed and the tissue resected, rather than making the test bite on the living animal and removing it later. Therefore, these test bites differ little from the other forms of static test bites.

2.7. Dynamic Test Bites on a Voluteer

A test bite created on a human volunteer is considered a dynamic test bite owing to the interplay of tissue and teeth that can be demonstrated, and the potential for the observation of subsequent tissue healing if the test bite can be made with enough force to injure the tissue. The goal is to create a representative facsimile of the original bitemark-patterned injury for comparative study.

The most common method of creating these test bites uses the suspect biter's models attached to a set of pliers, or mounted on a dental articulator, to ''bite'' the volunteer's skin to the maximum degree of tolerance by the subject. Using this technique, the resultant bitemarks are usually short-lived, and evidence of tissue damage/bruising is quite minimal if present at all. Harvey discusses the creation of test bites on volunteers who were bitten while under general anesthesia in an operating room [19]. In their study, the biters used their own natural dentition to create the bitemarks. Even when goaded to make a more severe mark, the biters could not

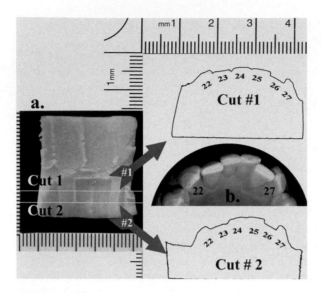

Figure 6 Cheese bite with the negative shapes of the biting teeth (a), the positive profiles created with horizontal slices through the positive profile model (Cuts #ns1 and #ns2), and the suspect biter's dentition. (From Ref. 6.).

generate tissue damage to the extent commonly seen with real bitemarks. Harvey related this finding to the psychological state of the criminal biter and any simultaneous response by their victim, at the moment of the injury.

When creating test bites on a volunteer's skin, it is important to consider the influence of the complex bouillabaisse of variables that affect the appearance of any injury created. Most of the variables that contributed to the original bitemark pattern injury are unknown. With test bites, the applicable variables can only be correlated to each individual bite being inflicted on that volunteer, at that anatomic location, at that moment in time, and by the individual researcher creating the marks. Dailey and Bowers published a literature review paper enumerating the variables affecting the appearance of bruises, and a comparison chart of the previously published time-related color changes observed with healing bruises [20].

The processes of wound healing are poorly understood. Any or all of the 19 published variables involved in the evolution and appearance of patterned injuries may be in play for each bitemark, and even vary among multiple bitemarks on the same victim. Furthermore, quantifiable conclusions related to the appearance of such injuries are examiner dependent, since color discrimination is widely variable among the members of the human race. Figure 7 demonstrates the difference in the appearance of a bruise on a shoulder before and after 4 days of healing. The color change is minimal, yet the expansion, or migration, of the bruise is significant. Since no scientific ruler had been included in the photos, the author used triangulation of the anatomically stable nevi to establish and confirm accurate sizing between the two photos.

As would be expected, the direct comparison of static test bites with dynamic test bites yields similar and discrepant findings. It has been demonstrated that transparent bitemark overlays made from test bites of the same dental model in wax, in Styrofoam, and on skin will not be identical [21]. This is primarily due to the flat configuration and rigid nature of the two former static test materials versus the near-infinite possible configuration of the skin's surface in combination with its elasticity and compressibility during dynamic test bites.

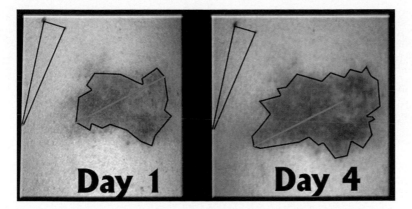

Figure 7 The migration and expansion of a bruise as observed over 4 days.

3. DIRECT COMPARISON

3.1. Suspect Biter and the Excised Tissue

Using the technique advanced by Dorion (Chapter 13), the tissue specimen containing the bitemark and a peripheral area are preserved by resection in preparation for direct comparison studies and the capture of transillumination images. As seen in Figure 8, once the tissue specimen has been dissected and preserved, a comparison of the suspected biter's dentition directly to the tissue can be performed. Additionally, the comparison of the models to the tissue can be videotaped or photographed to create exemplars for courtroom presentation. Photographs made of the transillumination of the tissue injury often produce images that have evidentiary value for comparison using conventional overlay techniques.

4.2. Suspect Biter and the Bitemark Impression

When impressions have been made of the tissue injury, the replicas made from such impressions can be compared directly to the stone models of the suspected biter's dentition. Where significant

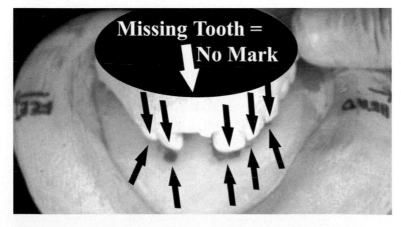

Figure 8 The biter's stone dental model compared directly to the excised bitemark. (Photo courtesy of Dr. Robert Dorion.)

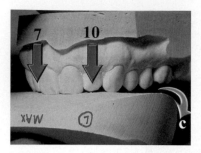

Figure 9 Teeth #7 and #10 are above the horizontal plane of the other anterior teeth and do not approximate the indentations they created in the original bitemark as recorded in the stone model. The curvature of the bitten surface (an arm) is demonstrated at (c).

tooth indentations are present in the bitemark, the incisal edges of the stone teeth can oftentimes be fitted directly into their corresponding negative configuration on the replica of the bitemark.

When several tooth edges can be fitted accurately into their indentations simultaneously, the evidence is quite compelling. However, as shown in Figure 9, even with dramatic tissue indenting, the biting edges of any teeth that are positioned above the anterior incisal plane may be distant to their stone receptacle. This is easily explained when considering the surface of the elastic and compressible tissue was captured in one position while the impression was made, and the stone cannot be similarly compressed.

5. DENTAL NOMENCLATURE

Authorities should routinely collect the suspected biter's prior dental information. The possibility exists those dental records will be documented with a tooth numbering system unfamiliar to the examining odontologist. This is commonplace during mass disaster identification efforts, especially those involving commercial aircraft. Consequently, it behooves the examiner to be cognizant of such possibilities and have ready access to information explaining the various tooth numbering systems in use around the world.

6. INVERTING CAST (FLIP HORIZONTAL) FOR COMPARISON

One of the most difficult concepts for health professionals, as well as the trier of fact and the jury, to grasp when first looking at bitemark evidence is that of sidedness. That is, when looking at a bitemark, being cognizant of which side of the biter's dentition created the left and right side of the mark they are viewing. While this point may seem ridiculous at first reading, during their careers dental health professionals must learn to think in reverse when dealing with a patient's dentition. When they examine a patient, dental professionals see the right side of the patient's dentition on their left, and vice versa. However, when looking at a bitemark, they must consciously remind themselves that the left-side tooth marks observed in the bitemark were created by the left-side teeth of the biter. The tendency for the neophyte is to see the bitemark as they see their patients, which reverses the sidedness of the injury and subsequent interpretations related to the causative teeth. If the investigator thinks of it as though he is the creator of the mark, as if placing his own teeth in the tissue, then sidedness on photos or replicas of the bitemark will not be an issue.

The use of a transparent bitemark overlay, a clear acetate sheet with the biting edges of the teeth outlined or shaded in to some degree, is the most common method of comparing the biting edges of teeth with photographs of bitemarks. Without a mechanism for recording the correct sidedness on the overlay, it can be quite difficult to determine right versus left when the tooth arrangement is fairly symmetrical. The only solution to avoid such confusion is to clearly mark the left and/or right side of the suspected biter's dentition on the overlay. These overlays are commonly created using photocopiers, flatbed scanners, or digital cameras to capture the image of the tooth biting edges from the dental models. Regardless of the technique used to make the overlay, an unwritten convention has developed among forensic odontologists. Since the use of a two-legged or L-shaped ruler is now the standard, it has become commonplace to put the ruler in a position that forms an L on the left side of the dental models. This position can be carried forward during each step of the overlay fabrication process.

There are other ways of maintaining the proper orientation throughout an analysis. Another technique takes advantage of the large depth of field created by photocopiers and scanners. As shown in Figure 10, the letters L and R can be drawn on areas of a dental model away from the pertinent dental structures, yet these will be clearly readable in the captured images. Additionally, photographs can be made of the dental structures as they are reflected into a mirror. Figure 11 illustrates the reversal of sidedness with this technique.

Without proper image labeling, it is easy to become confused, during the stress of testimony in a court of law, about sidedness while attempting to demonstrate the relationship of transparent overlays to photographs of bitemarks. Additionally, the exemplars of the evidence the expert will leave with the court should enable, not confuse, the members of the jury during their deliberations. Successful analysis and presentation of bitemark evidence can be assured when small but significant steps are taken to prevent confusion over sidedness.

7. OVERLAYS

7.1. Simple Overlays

Historically, the most common method of recording bitemark evidence is through two-dimensional photographs. A straightforward method to relate the biting edges of a suspected biter's dentition to the bitemark photograph is with an overlay. These are generally colorless transparent acetate sheets containing information transferred by the examiner from the dental models. The goal of the various overlay techniques is to capture the biting edges of the teeth as objectively as possible. Overlays can be made to demonstrate the outlined edges of the teeth (hollow-volume overlays), or the edges can be filled in (filled-volume overlay). Additionally, the actual tooth image, either solid or semitransparent, can be captured within the outline (compound overlay). These three types of overlays are seen in Figure 12.

Early on, acetate sheets were placed directly on the edges of the dental models of the suspected biter's teeth, and the examiner hand-marked the position of the edges on the acetate sheet using indelible ink to create the overlay. This overlay was laid onto the bitemark photographs and the comparison initiated. From this very unsophisticated and subjective beginning, odontologists have continually sought to improve their methodology toward greater accuracy, total objectivity, and operator reproducibility, the hallmarks of the scientific method.

Numerous overlay methods have been published in the scientific literature, and many more have been presented at scientific meetings or taught as part of forensic odontology seminars. Techniques utilizing radiographic plates made by placing amalgam powder, barium sulfate, or other radiopaque substances into indentations created by tooth edges in wax, plaster, or other materials; and the inking of tooth edges in order to imprint them on various materials are all easily accomplished and unburdened by multiple steps, expensive materials, or advanced technology requirements. At the opposite extreme is a photographic techniques that is time and labor intensive [22] a technique that utilizes computer tomography (CT) scans [23]; and the

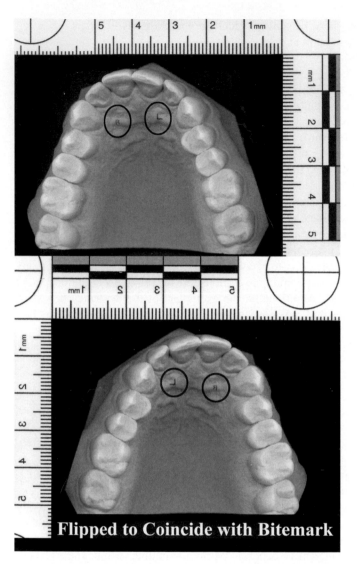

Figure 10   Scanned image of a maxillary model where left (L) and right (R) are indicated on the model, and the image is flipped to place the toothmarks on the correct side of the bitemark pattern they created.

ongoing search for applicable CAD-CAM hardware and software that will recreate both real and virtual reality models of the suspected biter's dentition, as well as have the capability to generate slices through the teeth a various levels for horizontal profile views. The technology for the latter method exists, but these commercial proprietary systems are unavailable for forensic odontological study.

When Dailey published his photocopy technique for bitemark overlay fabrication [24], the ubiquitous photocopy machine was employed to produce a quick, accurate, and inexpensive image of the dental models of the suspected biter. This image is placed image side down onto a radiograph viewing box to illuminate the image of the tooth edges from below. The examiner traces the edge outlines. This side of the paper, now containing the outlined biting edges of the

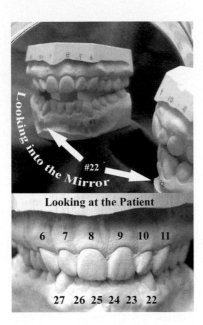

Figure 11 The upper image is a view of dental models (foreground on the right side) with the Universal Numbering System designations placed on the model, and shown reversed in the mirror image. The lower image is the normal patient view and tooth numbering that health care professionals have foremost in their minds.

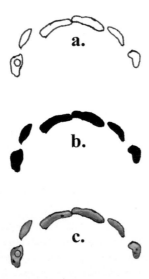

Figure 12 Hollow volume overlay (a), filled volume overlay (b), and compound overlay (c).

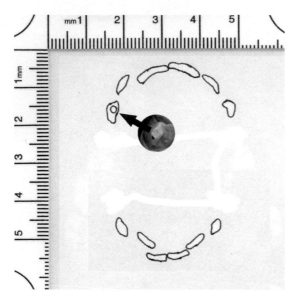

Figure 13 A transparent bitemark comparison overlay created using the original Photocopy Technique of Dailey, and demonstrating an observed wear facet at the incisal edge of tooth #11 (enlarged inset).

teeth, is turned over and placed against the glass platen of the photocopy machine. The tooth edge outline image is then photocopied and printed onto a clear acetate sheet that has been loaded into the paper tray of the copy machine. To ensure sidedness and accuracy at each step, the ruler's image is transferred along with the teeth image. The finished product is the final hollow-volume overlay.

An example of this type of overlay is shown as Figure 13. In the illustration, a small circle is visible within the traced outline of the left canine, tooth 11. This is the traced periphery of a wear facet that penetrated the enamel into the dentine at the incisal edge. Such unique and not so subtle characteristics cannot be captured or demonstrated following the published methodology for creating the computer-generated overlays that will be presented in the next section. While the photocopy technique is often cited as the first overlay technique designed to eliminate subjectivity during overlay fabrication, it still involves the selection of the tooth edges by the examiner, a process that is neither totally objective nor without a small degree interoperator and intraoperator unreliability.

7.2. Computer-Generated Overlays

The search for the holy grail of objectivity moved from the photocopy machine to the home computer as forensic odontologists discovered graphic arts software programs that had applicability to image enhancement and bitemark overlay fabrication. While there are numerous programs available that have various digital tools for accomplishing the fabrication of overlays, the program Adobe Photoshop (Adobe Systems Incorporated, Seattle, WA, Version 7.0) will be the program discussed since it is the program used by a large majority of odontologists who make computer-generated overlays. Additionally, there are more instructional and informational manuals published for this program than for any other.

When using graphic arts programs, better results are obtained if graphic arts hardware tools are employed as well. A graphics tablet is one such tool that facilitates greater operator control over the software tools in Photoshop, ensures economy of motion, and provides for proper operator ergonomics. With these tablets, a pen is used as a substitute for the conventional roller mouse so often used with desktop computers, and the finger mouse pad or miniature joystick mouse commonly seen on laptop computers. The pen controls can be customized by the operator, allowing these devices to be more precise than the conventional alternatives. The significance of quick and precise pixel selection with such devices is easily apparent from their first use.

Numerous computer-generated overlays used as illustrations in the published forensic odontology literature often demonstrate the outlines of the biting edges of teeth as irregularly pixelated shapes that barely look like the tooth edges they are purported to represent. All the while the authors of these papers tout the accuracy of this type of overlay when discussing the technique's ability to represent the tooth edges that will be compared to the bitemark patterned injury. Figure 14 demonstrates a computer-generated overlay.

Naru and Dykes [25,26] introduced the fabrication of computer generated overlays to forensic odontology in 1996. While innovative, this method required the examiner to adjust the brightness and contrast (a subjective visual interpretation process) of the image in order to facilitate selection of tooth edges by a technique known as "edge detection." The selected edges were then printed onto clear acetate sheets as the overlay. In their first paper, theses authors describe a very small-scale investigation they conducted to test the reproducibility of this method

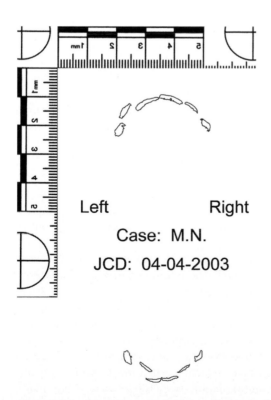

Figure 14 A transparent computer-generated overlay for bitemark comparison showing the pixelated appearance of the tooth outlines.

between operators. However, when discussing the methodology of this study, they state they provided identical images to each test candidate. From the images provided, the candidates were able to generate what the authors said were identical overlays. It is important to understand that the completed overlays should be identical. The test began at the last step in a series of steps that were all subjective in nature to this point (i.e., the recording of the image of the dental models, and the adjustment of brightness and contrast were completed for the candidates before they started their test). The candidates then used the computer to select the edges from those identical images. Finally, in their conclusions the authors discuss a reduction in subjectivity using this technique, but not its elimination.

In various combinations and independently, several authors have published, lectured, and conducted numerous seminars related to the fabrication of computer generated overlays using Photoshop [27–30]. However, there is disagreement among these authors concerning the degree of subjectivity for this technique. The primary issue concerns the gradual selection of the biting edges of the teeth using the Magic Wand Selection Tool (MWST) resident in the Photoshop software. After establishing the settings to be used with this tool, the examiner touches the tool to the image of the dental models and, while holding down the SHIFT key, continues to make similar pixel selections from within the confines of each tooth until he or she is satisfied they have selected all of the biting edges of the teeth in question. The decisions of where to select and when to stop selecting pixels are subjective decisions. This process often involves dozens of keystrokes.

Because of variations in the quality and temperature of each image imported from numerous types of scanners into Photoshop, the examiner must frequently adjust the brightness and contrast before the MWST process can begin. This is another subjective decision.

The issue with the MWST subjectivity highlights the lack of interoperator and intraoperator reproducibility. The avocation of the use of the History Palate in Photoshop is presented as a method of archiving the steps taken by an examiner while enhancing an image. While this is necessary, the use of this tool is fraught with problems for several reasons. The history palate information exists only as long as the image is open; that is, the history information is discarded when the image file is closed. Therefore, in order to save/archive the history list of operations done to an image, or ''states,'' as operations are called, the list of history states must be recorded elsewhere by the examiner. Additionally, the examiner must establish a preference setting in the program to tell Photoshop how many history states to record. If the programs default of 20 is used, then when the 21st state is created, the first state (operation No. 1) will be eliminated from the top of the list. This is easily corrected since the examiner is allowed to create a preference setting up to 1000 saved history states if he/she wishes. More history states require more memory, so if computer temporary memory, or RAM, is minimal, a much smaller number of history states will be the rule.

Undoubtedly, the most significant point to discuss about the History Palate concerns what is actually being recorded with each operation performed. The information recorded concerns only what the keystroke did, such as inverting the image, making a selection with the MWST, and so on. With selections made by the MWST, the actual pixel selected at that moment is not recorded. This strikes to the heart of the reproducibility issue concerning this type of overlay. In order to be reproducible, every overlay must have the exact pixels selected every time, by every operator. For this to happen between two examiners would require an astronomical degree of luck. Figure 15 demonstrates the difference in pixel selection when the MWST is moved only one pixel apart during the selection process. In (a), the life size (100%) view of the image is seen on the computer screen to demonstrate the minute size of the two adjacent pixels that are bounded in black.

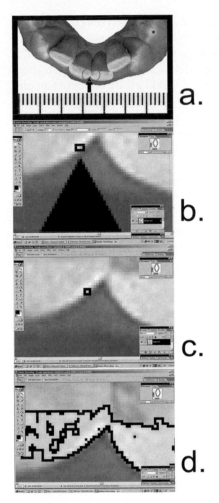

Figure 15 A demonstration of the variability of the results created by the MWST in Adobe®
Photoshop® when two adjacent pixels are selected.

When the examiner is using the MWST with the life-size image or even the 200% image
(twice life-size), the size of the tool on the screen actually blocks which pixel is being selected
from the examiner's view. In (b) the image has been enlarged to the maximum size possible
(1600%) in Photoshop to show the two pixels. When the MWST is touched to the right-side
pixel (c), that one keystroke selected only the one chosen pixel. When the left-side pixel was
touched with the MWST, hundreds of pixels across two tooth edges were chosen (d). This is
easily illustrated at the 1600% magnification possible in Photoshop; however, when the image
is that large the examiner loses his perspective and orientation to the whole photo. There is no
happy median. Through this demonstration, it is easy to see that while the computer generated
overlay technique is purported to increase interoperator and intraoperator reliability/reproducibil-
ity, it does neither.

    If one now reconsiders the discussion of Naru and Dykes' original small study of operator
variability, the issue previously raised concerning test subjects receiving nearly completed images and achieving nearly identical results becomes significant when reconsidered in a different

light. If a technique were developed that was accurate and reproducible at each step; that allowed a permanent record to be made of each step that could be passed between experts, similar to the passing of photographic and dental model evidence as is currently done; and the computer generated overlay could be created with only one selection click of the MWST in Photoshop, regardless of where on a group of teeth the tool was placed, would all of the criticism and discussion of subjectivity disappear? The answer should be yes. What follows is such a technique.

A technique has been developed that allows stone dental models of the suspected biter's dentition to be enveloped in a contrasting color dental stone [31]. This technique was originally developed to facilitate the total elimination of subjectivity from the process of using the MWST when selecting the biting edges of teeth.

As shown in Figure 16, the anterior incisal plane of the dental model is recorded with a red dot on each of the three points on the tooth edges that create that plane in space. A flat-plane denture tooth setting plate is affixed to the model at the three red points. The model and plate are placed in a retaining receptacle, and an enveloping layer of a contrasting color stone is poured around the original model (Flowstone, Whip Mix Dental Product, Louisville, KY).

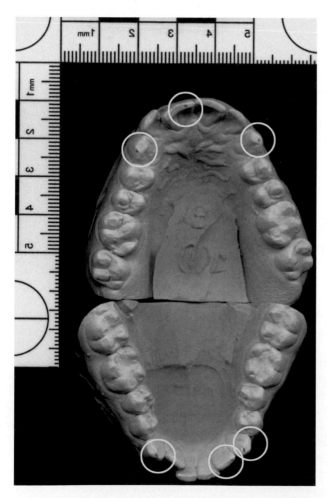

Figure 16   The anterior plane was created by the three teeth in each dental arch that are marked with a red dot.

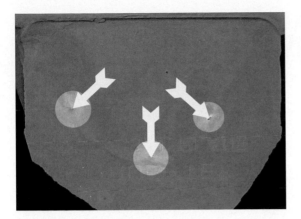

Figure 17 The three red dots are evident at the surface of the anterior plane recorded in the enveloping stone layer.

When the enveloping stone is set and the flat-plane plate is removed, the three red dots will be seen at the surface of the stone, as shown in Figure 17. Next, the opposite side of the model is cut parallel to this incisal plane on an orthodontic model trimmer. With the base now parallel to the anterior plane, the model is turned toward the cutting wheel of the model trimmer and sequential 1-mm cuts are made into the anterior teeth. The models are dried after each cut, then scanned into Adobe Photoshop. Once in Photoshop, the tooth edges are selected as discussed above, with one major exception: because of the contrasting colors between tooth edges and enveloping layer, all tooth edges can be selected simultaneously with a single keystroke of the MWST. This one-keystroke selection is demonstrated on the History Palate in the image captured as Figure 18. Figure 19 presents the final Envelopment Overlay.

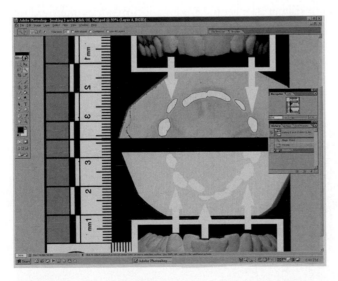

Figure 18 The History Palate (small box on the right) shown in this screen-save from Adobe® Photoshop® demonstrates that only one click of the MWST was needed to select the outlines of all six maxillary anterior teeth presented by this cut into the enveloped model. Only one click would then be required to select the six mandibular tooth edges.

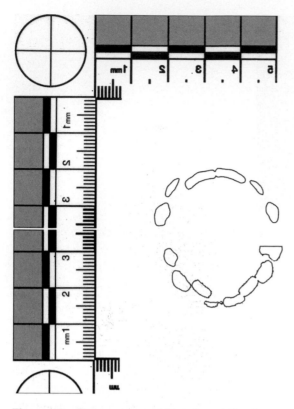

Figure 19 The transparent Enveloped Overlay.

As often happens with scientific research, a tangential finding occurred that improved on the original premise. The author discovered that when one or more anterior teeth were positioned well above or below the anterior plane of occlusion, several cuts into the enveloped model were required before those edges were reached and exposed for scanning. Figure 20 shows how a V-shaped notch in a tooth was revealed to the examiner during a cut into the enveloped model,

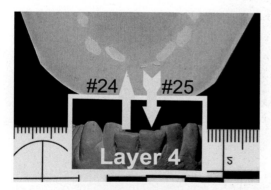

Figure 20 A v-shaped notch on the edge of tooth #25 is clearly demonstrated by this cut into the enveloped model, while tooth #24 is not yet visible (see also Fig. 24).

while the adjacent incisor is at a level well below the anterior plane (see also Fig. 24). When these sequential cuts were stacked upon each other in Photoshop, a topographic map of the teeth was created. This has also been referred to as a pseudo-CT (computed tomography) technique. A completed Topographic Overlay is presented in Figure 21.

If several duplicated models were simultaneously enveloped using this technique and each was cut 1 mm deeper than the previous model, the entire sequential series of models could then be transferred from one examiner to the next, thus allowing all to examiners to make one-keystroke overlays that are identical at every layer. This should end any debate over inter- and intraoperator reproducibility.

Fabricating an accurate and objectively produced overlay representative of the biting surfaces of the suspected biter's teeth is the goal. As demonstrated, there are several methods for creating accurate overlays. Figure 22 demonstrates the Envelopment Technique (1a and 1b), the Photocopy Technique (2a and 2b), and the Computer-Generated Technique (3a and 3b). Also, these are compared to the dental models used (4), and the bitemark photograph they will be compared to (5) during the analysis process. Until now, the degree of subjectivity between tooth edge selection techniques has been a topic for debate. With the development of a technique that allows all examiners to analyze the same objectively created evidence that has been recorded in stone, the debates over variations (on the order of magnitude of fractions of a millimeter) between overlay fabrication techniques should subside, and the direction of future research should be more aggressively related to analyses of tissue healing dynamics, and the gleaning of additional evidence from photographs of bitemarks not currently being recognized by current technology and analysis methodologies.

Of great concern is the comparison of these very accurate overlays to the less accurate recordings, in human tissue, of the tooth edges that created the bitemark patterned injury being

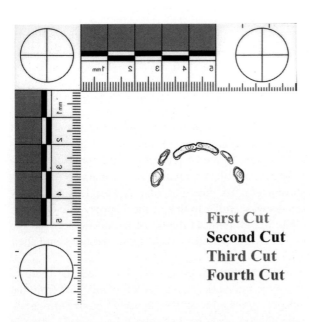

Figure 21   The maxillary Topographic Overlay.

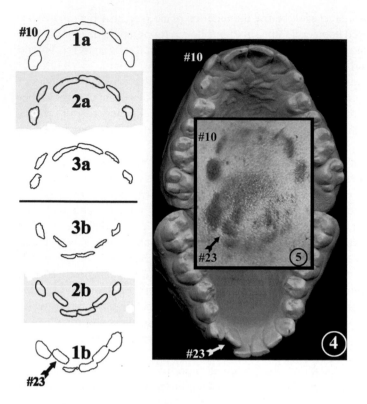

Figure 22 Comparison of the three methods of transparent bitemark overlay fabrication with the biter's dental models and the photograph of the bitemark. All three methods are more accurate than the bitemark, yet the correlation of all three to patterned injury is quite high and easily recognized. Also see color photograph insert section.

analyzed. Much research has been directed at truly objective overlays. However, owing to the quality of skin as an impression material, the accuracy of recording tooth edges in skin is less than that of the overlays they are being compared to. This factor remains out of the control of odontologists. Importantly, this does not preclude an analytical comparison of the overlay to the patterned injury. Figure 23 demonstrates a high degree of accuracy in the tissue recording of the mandibular teeth that created the bitemark, and the correlation of the mark to two types of overlays made of the biting edges of those teeth. The maxillary marks were less accurately recorded in the tissue and the fit of all overlays was similar to that of the Topographic Overlay. However, rotation of the overlay around the fulcrum point at the tip of the arrow between the central incisors aligns teeth Nos. 11–8 in (a) and 9–6 in (b). Such demonstrations and their explanations allow the trier of fact to decide the weight of the evidence.

Concomitant with the various methods of comparison previously discussed, the forensic odontologist will perform a metric analysis of the bitemark related evidence collected from the recipient of the bitemark and from the evidence collected from the suspected biter. Ultimately, a comparison of the totality of the evidence will be made between these two groups, and the expert will render an opinion as to the degree of probability that the suspect caused the bitemark in question.

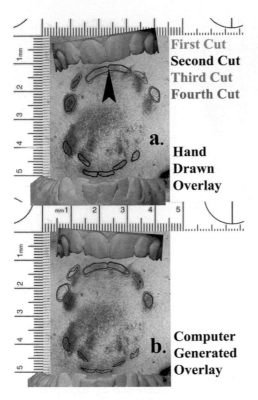

First Cut
Second Cut
Third Cut
Fourth Cut

a.

**Hand
Drawn
Overlay**

b.

**Computer
Generated
Overlay**

Figure 23   Maxillary Topographic Overlay (a) and (b) with a mandibular overlay produced using the Photocopy Technique in (a) and the Computer Generated Technique in (b). Also see color photograph insert section.

8.   METRIC ANALYSIS

A metric analysis is performed of the bitemark injury and of the dentition of all suspected biters. These analyses are done independently of one another. The goal of the metric analysis is to ascertain as much quantitative information about each tooth represented in the patterned injury and in the dentition that might have created that injury. Of concern is the size, or metric measurement, of each tooth and its position (i.e., spatial relationship or geometric position in relation to a uniform axis) within the dental arch complex. The relationship of each tooth within the collection of teeth contributes to the collective descriptors of the pattern as a whole.

For the bitemark evidence recorded, the maxillary and mandibular dental arches will first be identified. Then the individual teeth within each arch will be identified. Finally, the mesial-to-distal width and degree of rotation from the x-axis or y-axis will be recorded for each of these teeth.

For the evidence collected from the suspected biter, or biters, this same metric analysis will be performed. This can be done directly from the stone dental models or from sample bites created by the examiner using any or all of the methods previously presented. Additionally, from the models of the teeth, measurements in the third plane can be recorded. As shown in Figure 24, these measurements would relate the biting edges of the teeth to the anterior plane of occlusion.

Historically, odontologists using scientific calipers, rulers, compasses, protractors, and other instruments with great success have performed the various measurements that make up the

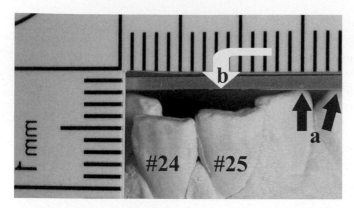

Figure 24 (a) Two of the three teeth used to first determine the anterior plane shown as (b), while the three-dimensional nature of tooth biting edge relationships to that plane is recognized and recorded.

metric analysis. Recently, digital metric analysis utilizing readily available commercial computer software programs has made such analyses less time-consuming, without any sacrifice in accuracy. While computers are pervasive in today's world, there can exist a form of what Dr. Thomas R. O'Connor calls "digital divide" between some members of the older generation of odontologists and the rest of this specialty who have made computers part of their forensic armamentarium [32]. The manual methods of metric analysis are tried and true, and these old ways still work well.

9. DIGITAL ANALYSES

The digital tools available in Adobe Photoshop allow the forensic odontologist to measure tooth width and angulation accurately and easily. Figure 25 demonstrates the digital metric analyses from the dental models and from the scanned and inverted digital image of the wax bite made from the models. While the angles of the teeth to the x-axis were the same for both, the mesiodistal widths were different. This finding relates to the earlier discussion concerning the quandary faced by forensic odontologists over the depth of recording, when imbedding the biting edges into test bite materials.

Additionally, with the click of a mouse, in milliseconds the images being examined can be enhanced or converted to other formats that allow the investigator to view details in the evidence that previously required time- and labor-intensive darkroom techniques, if possible at all. Looking at a color image of a bitemark, it is possible to view the information of an individual color channel independently of the other channels; images are easily converted from color to grayscale; inverting images from positive to negative or vice versa is a one-keystroke operation; changing the brightness or contrast of an image is done using a simple sliding-scale tool; and many other techniques can be easily performed by the examiner. It is important to stress that while these varied functions are being performed, at any point an image state can be captured and saved; and until the image is actually closed, the original starting image can be restored with a single keystroke. It is imperative that an untouched archival copy of all original images be stored in a permanent format such as on CD-ROM or on DVD.

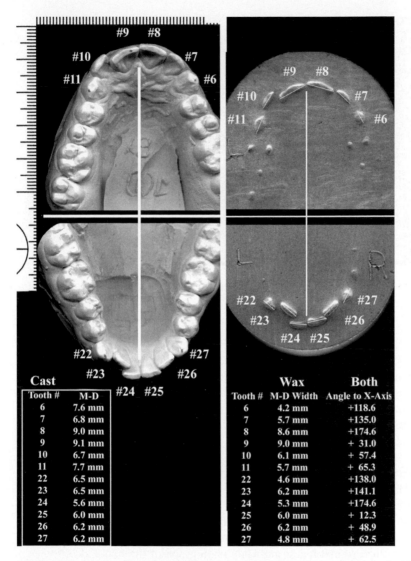

Cast	
Tooth #	M-D
6	7.6 mm
7	6.8 mm
8	9.0 mm
9	9.1 mm
10	6.7 mm
11	7.7 mm
22	6.5 mm
23	6.5 mm
24	5.6 mm
25	6.0 mm
26	6.2 mm
27	6.2 mm

Wax		Both
Tooth #	M-D Width	Angle to X-Axis
6	4.2 mm	+118.6
7	5.7 mm	+135.0
8	8.6 mm	+174.6
9	9.0 mm	+ 31.0
10	6.1 mm	+ 57.4
11	5.7 mm	+ 65.3
22	4.6 mm	+138.0
23	6.2 mm	+141.1
24	5.3 mm	+174.6
25	6.0 mm	+ 12.3
26	6.2 mm	+ 48.9
27	4.8 mm	+ 62.5

Figure 25 The metric information for the anterior teeth can be recorded from the dental models (left image) or their wax bite (on the right). It can be measured manually from the cast or wax, or digitally from their images in Adobe® Photoshop®.

10. OTHER COMPARISON TECHNIQUES

10.1. Pattern Analysis in Three-Dimensions

Pretty [33] has stated, ''Indeed, it could be argued that most biologic features are unique if measured with sufficient resolution.'' This statement seems validated when one reviews the SEM images of the incisal edges of teeth as recorded in selected bitemark cases (see Chapter 11). True three-dimensional comparisons such as this and direct dental cast comparisons to the tissue, or model of the tissue, are infrequent for the reasons discussed throughout this textbook.

Pseudo-three-dimensional computer image visualization software is changing the way forensic scientists are seeing their evidence. Methods that display evidence as a pseudo-three-

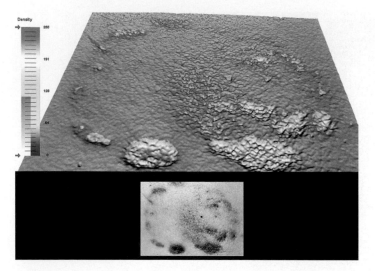

Figure 26 The pseudo-three-dimensional image created from the grayscale original using the MICS software.

dimensional image are being used by other forensic disciplines such as questioned document examiners and fingerprint examiners. Odontologists are constantly looking for new or emerging technologies, methods, and materials to improve their ability to analyze evidence. Many of the imaging software programs are rather expensive at this time, but as with all new technology, time will correct this issue. One such emerging technology software program is MICS from Limbic Systems (Bellingham, WA). MICS, or Measurement of Internal Consistencies Software, displays all 256 shades of gray recorded in a radiograph or photographic image. This provides the human eye with access to what it could not see, via traditional forensic analysis methods, in an original image. The average human visual system perceives less than 50 shades of gray when one views an image; therefore, a significant amount of the available photographic evidence goes unrecognized. With MICS, these data are made available for the human examiner, allowing two-dimensional images to be viewed as pseudo-three-dimensional images. Figure 26 is a MICS enhancement compared to the original black-and-white photograph of the bitemark.

10.2. Videotape

The use of videotape in an attempt to demonstrate the dynamics of the biting event has been published in the forensic odontology literature [34]. Such reenactments should be kept as simple as possible and limited only to the obvious facts as recorded in the evidence. Videotape is also a useful way for the expert to demonstrate to the trier of fact the sequence of steps taken during the various comparison techniques utilized during the bitemark analysis process.

10.3. Ink Imersion Technique

Another technique to aid in the visualization of the sequence of tooth edge contacts with tissue during the biting event is an ink immersion technique. Being used by the faculty at the University of Queensland, this technique involves placing a stone dental model into a bowl or other receptacle. Black ink is slowly poured into the receptacle while videotaping is used to record the ink slowly covering the teeth until all tooth edges disappear. The video is then viewed in reverse

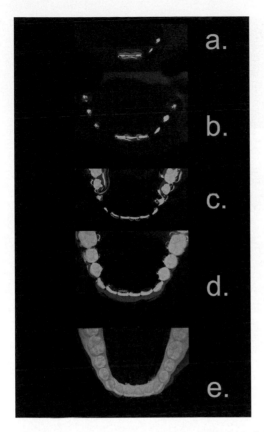

Figure 27   A still-photograph modification of the original ink immersion videotaping technique is an attempt to demonstrate the successive tooth contacts as they might occur during the creation of the bitemark.

to simulate first tooth edge contact to last tooth edge contact. This is claimed to be relatable to the premise that the earlier the contact the greater the extent of the subsequent injury observed in the bitemark injury.

　　While this approach seems logical, there is not yet any scientific proof to substantiate the validity of this hypothesis. Also, the interexaminer and intraexaminer reproducibility required of such techniques has not yet been demonstrated. Figure 27 is a photographic representation of this technique. In the images, the teeth in (a) would strike the tissue first, and sequentially more teeth would be brought into play by (e).

10.4.   Other Methods of Computer-Aided Visualization

In Figure 28 the maxillary wax wafer sample bite, shown in the center of the image, has been layered atop the bitemark photograph and the inverted bitemark image in Photoshop. The opacity of the image of the wax wafer has been lowered to allow the bitemark to show through from below. Varying the opacity is accomplished with a slider control that allows the results to be visualized instantaneously. The ability to demonstrate evidence using computerization appears to be limited only by the investigator's imagination.

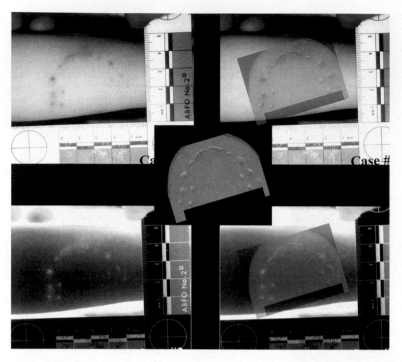

Figure 28 This composite image presents a bitemark photograph and the negative image, or inverted image, with and without the semi-transparent wax test bite wafer on top for comparison purposes.

11. CONCLUSION

There are advantages and disadvantages for each method of comparison during the bitemark analysis process. At this time, there is not one all-encompassing method for the comparison of bitemark patterned injury evidence with that from a suspected biter. The standard among forensic odontologists is to use two methods of comparison in the analysis process. Owing to the generally heinous nature of crimes that produce bitemark evidence and the concomitant severity of the punishment to be metered out with a guilty verdict, two methods of comparison should be considered the minimum for the analysis of such cases rather than the recommended requirement.

Currently, looking at a photograph of a bitemark injury is analogous to looking at a photograph of a home run being hit during the World Series or the running of the bulls in Pamplona, Spain. That is, an event that occurs over a period of time, in a known spatial location, and in three-dimensions is captured as a single frozen moment in time of extremely short duration, and reduced to a two-dimensional photograph. While the picture may tell a very compelling story and reveal a wealth of information about the event it depicts, it cannot reveal everything related to the circumstances that were occurring before, during, and after the moment the photograph was made. An important point is raised by this analogy. Forensic odontologists know there is often a wealth of information available within each piece of evidence that goes unrecognized or unused because the techniques or technology have yet to be discovered to allow its utilization. It is a fact that we are not yet able to use all of the available evidence recorded in the patterned injury.

Critics claim that bitemark patterned injury analysis is not yet founded on adequate scientific research. It is important to remember that pattern recognition is something the human brain is genetically wired to do thousands, if not millions, of times per day. During the reading of this book, each word is recorded as an image by the eyes and transmitted to the brain where they are recognized first as a printed word, not as an image of a flower, an animal, a glass of wine, or a loved one; the exact word is then recalled; and finally its meaning and the context are registered in the conscious mind of each individual. Additionally, most images in this textbook have short, one- or two-sentence, legends, yet the readers are capable of discerning many additional facts from those images. The readers will undoubtedly formulate opinions related to the image quality (such as clarity, contrast, and adequate size of the area of concern in that photo), as well as appropriateness for inclusion as an illustration of the point being presented by the author. Finally, they will search the images for information unrelated to the discussion at hand.

Humans are, by nature, good at solving puzzles. Most readers have had some experience at putting together jigsaw puzzles. They have been able to look at the photograph of the soon to be completed image on the box cover; review the work in progress before them; formulate a mental image of the shape, or pattern, of the next piece to be searched for; and then scan across dozens, or even hundreds, of puzzle pieces scattered at random on the tabletop to successfully find the needed piece and slip it into place.

With rapidly advancing information technology delivery systems invading every aspect of human life, most people have observed video images from surveillance cameras recording a crime in progress at a bank, convenience store, or other crime scene. While the quality of these images is poor compared with well-focused photographic images, associations with the perpetrators of the crimes are usually quite easily made by individuals trained to recognize the facial patterns and other telltale characteristics of humans. It is important that such associations are oftentimes made just as easily by the untrained watching these videos on television or via the Internet.

There is validity to the discussion that the experience and training of the examiner of a bitemark patterned injury is crucial to the successful outcome of the analysis, as well as the convention that it is better to be conservative in the approach to an analysis and the final opinions rendered concerning the value of the bitemark evidence and the correlation with any suspected biters. What is not valid is the argument that bitemark analysis is totally subjective and does not belong in a court of law. As long as the bitemark evidence recovered from the victim is of high quality and the examiner is thorough in his/her analysis and conservative in his/her conclusions, such analysis is a valuable tool for the courts. If such evidence and the analysis is obvious, logical, and understandable to the trier of fact, it should be admissible and the appropriate weight given to that evidence.

A common recurring question in this arena asks if bitemark patterned injuries are unique enough to allow individualization (segregation) of the causative dentition from among the pool of suspected biters developed by the investigating authorities. Importantly, research in this direction is beginning to take place in the field of forensic odontology. Admissions of guilt by suspected biters, concurrent DNA evidence, observed biting, and other means of authenticating ''gold standard'' (i.e., ''known'') bitemarks validate many successful bitemark analyses.

Another area of frequent discussion involves the accuracy of the evidence when the events surrounding the moment of the bite are unknown. Unless the recipient of the bite survives his/her assault and can duplicate, via demonstration, the exact spatial position of the bitten area of their anatomy at the moment of the bite, the examiner will never know the true circumstances surrounding the event. Therefore, when recording the bite evidence in all other situations, the photographs and impressions of the patterned injury will be captured with the tissue in a position most likely discrepant from that at the moment of injury infliction. When discussing experimental human bitemarks in his textbook, published over a quarter of a century ago and apparently forgotten by a new generation of forensic scientists, Harvey stated that while discrepancies created by positional changes of the body do occur, unique characteristics that exist within the pattern, "which can be clearly recognized throughout changes in posture," would still be clearly ascertainable to the examiner [35]. Harvey also states that while "superimposition is negated, it is also superfluous." This is the fundamental principle that will ensure the viability of bitemark pattern injury analysis in our legal system. It seems illogical that controversy should exist if the quality of the evidence is high, the pattern demonstrates unique characteristics that can be correlated to a suspect biter's dentition, and the conclusions derived from the bitemark analysis are conservative.

REFERENCES

1. McKinstry RE. Resin dental models as an aid in bite mark identification. J Forens Sci 1995; 40: 300–302.
2. McKenna CJ, Haron MI, Taylor JA. Evaluation of a bitemark using clear acrylic replicas of the suspect's dentition—a case report. J Forens Odont 1999; 17:40–43.
3. Wright FD, Dailey JC. Human bite marks in forensic dentistry. Dent Clin North Am 2001; 45: 365–397.
4. American Board of Forensic Odontology. ABFO guidelines and standards. In Bowers CM, Bell GL, Eds. Manual of Forensic Odontology. 3rd ed. Colorado Springs. CO: American Society of Forensic Odontology, 1997:338–341.
5. American Board of Forensic Odontology. ABFO guidelines and standards. In Bowers CM, Bell GL, Eds. Manual of Forensic Odontology. 3rd ed. Colorado Springs: American Society of Forensic Odontology, 1997:337.
6. American Board of Forensic Odontology, Inc. ABFO guidelines and standards. In Bowers CM, Bell GL, Eds. Manual of Forensic Odontology. 3rd ed. Colorado Springs: American Society of Forensic Odontology, 1997:338.
7. Wright FD, Dailey JC. Human bite marks in forensic dentistry. Dent Clin North Am 2001; 45: 365–397.
8. Layton JJ. Identification from a bite mark in cheese. J Foren Sci Soc 1966; 6:76–80.
9. Sweet D, Hildebrand D. Saliva from cheese bite yields DNA profile of burglar: a case report. Int J Legal Med 1999; 112:201–203.
10. Bernitz H, Piper SE, Solheim T, Van. Niekerk PJ, Swart JP. Comparison of bitemarks left in foodstuffs with models of the suspects' dentitions as a means of identifying a perpetrator. J Forens Odont 2000; 18:27–31.
11. Bernitz H, Kloppers BA. Comparison microscope identification of a cheese bitemark: a case report. J Forens Odont 2002; 20:13–16.
12. Aboshi H, Taylor JA, Takei T, Brown KA. Comparison of bitemarks in foodstuffs by computer imaging: a case report. J Forens Odont 1994; 2:41–44.
13. McKenna CJ, Haron MI, Brown KA, Jones AJ. Bitemarks in chocolate: a case report. J Forens Odont 2000; 18:10–14.
14. Nambiar P, Carson G, Taylor JA, Brown KA. Identification from a bitemark in a wad of chewing gum. J Forens Odont 2001; 19:5–8.
15. Simon A, Jordan H, Pforte K. Successful Identification of a bite mark in a sandwich. Int J Forens Dent 1974; 2:17–21.
16. Corbett ME, Spence D. A forensic Investigation of teeth marks in soap. Br Dent J 1984; 157:270–271.
17. Whittaker DK. Some laboratory studies on the accuracy of bite mark comparison. Int Dent J 1975; 25:166–171.
18. Rothwell BR, Thien AV. Analysis of distortion in preserved bite mark skin. J Forens Sci 2001; 46: 573–576.
19. Harvey W, Millington P, Barbenel JC, Evans JH. Experimental bite-marks. In Harvey W, Ed. Dental Identification and Forensic Odontology. London: Henry Kimpton, 1975:124–135.

20. Dailey JC, Bowers CM. Aging of bitemarks: a literature review. J Forens Sci 1997; 42:792–795.

21. West MH, Barsley RE, Frair J, Seal MD. The use of human skin in the fabrication of a bite mark template: two case reports. J Forens Sci 35:1477–1485.

22. Robinson E, Wentzel J. Toneline bite mark photography. J Forens Sci 1992; 37:195–207.

23. Ferrell WL, Rawson RD, Steffens RS, Stephens D. Computerized axial tomography as an aid in bite mark analysis: a case report. J Forens Sci 1987; 32:266–272.

24. Dailey JC. A practical technique for the fabrication of transparent bite mark overlays. J Forens Sci 36:565–570.

25. Naru AS, Dykes E. The use of a digital imaging technique to aid bite mark analysis. Sci Justice 1996; 36:47–50.

26. Naru SA, Dykes E. Digital image cross-correlation technique for bite mark investigations. Sci Justice 1997; 37:251–258.

27. Sweet D, Parhar M, Wood RE. Computer-based production of bite mark comparison overlays. J Forens Sci 1998; 43:1050–1055.

28. Pretty IA, Sweet D. Digital bite mark overlays-an analysis of effectiveness. J Forens Sci 2001; 46: 1385–1391.

29. Sweet D, Bowers CM. Accuracy of bite mark overlays: a comparison of five common methods to produce exemplars from a suspect's dentition. J Forens Sci 1998; 43:362–367.

30. Bowers CM, Johansen RJ. Digital Analysis of Bitemark Evidence. Santa Barbara. CA: Forensic Imaging Services, 2000:59–76.

31. Dailey JC. The topographic mapping of teeth for overlay production in bite mark analysis. Proceedings of the American Academy of Forensic Sciences, Atlanta, 2002:158–159.

32. O'Connor TR. http://faculty.ncwc.edu/toconnor/425/425lect16.htm.

33. Pretty IH, Turnbull MD. Lack of uniqueness between two bite mark suspects. J Forens Sci 2001; 46:1487–1491.

34. West MH, Frair J. The use of videotape to demonstrate the dynamics of bite marks. J Forens Sci 1989; 34:88–95.

35. Harvey W, Millington P, Barbenel JC, Evans JH. Experimental bite-marks. In Harvey W, Ed. Dental Identification and Forensic Odontology. London: Henry Kimpton, 1975:134.

VIII
Reports

21
Bitemark Report

Mark L. Bernstein
University of Louisville School of Dentistry
Louisville, Kentucky, U.S.A.

1. GOAL OF THE FORENSIC REPORT

The goal of any forensic report is to communicate the expert's conclusion. For the conclusion to be valid, it must reflect an objective evaluation and interpretation of complete and accurate information.

2. OBJECTIVES OF THE FORENSIC REPORT

The forensic report, as an accounting of a medicolegal investigation, has three objectives: documentation, education, and communication. The report identifies the case and records the observations, studies, and results on which opinions are based. It also accounts for the disposition of evidence. As such, the report itself becomes evidence that can be scrutinized in court and for which the author is accountable. Additionally, it serves to refresh the memory of the author, who might be summoned to defend opinions years after the report was completed. Forensic reports are prepared by those with special knowledge in a particular aspect of a case. It is the author's obligation to educate the other medical and legal personnel who rely on this information. The report must convey the investigator's opinions in clear and simple language. The odontologist must be mindful that professional terminology is erudite and must be explained to nondentists.

3. BASIC QUALITIES OF THE FORENSIC REPORT

The style, length, and specific content of a report will vary with the author, the case, and the purpose for which the report is intended [1]. Regardless of these variables, all forensic reports must express valid conclusions. To this end, it is desirable that reports reflect four basic qualities that help safeguard validity: (1) The report should be complete in that it includes all relevant data, whether or not they support the investigator's opinion. (2) The data must be accurate to the extent that they can be verified. (3) The third quality, objectivity, signifies that complete and accurate data have been evaluated in an unbiased manner with a commitment to the tenets of scientific methodology and professional ethics. Although objectivity is not necessarily expressed in a report, it is a contentious area in trials. When assurances of objectivity can be contained in forensic reports, the expert's opinion is more credible. Table 1 lists examples of

Table 1   Measures to Maintain Objectivity

1. Following complete analysis of a bitemark, profile the biter's dentition (if possible) in the report prior to the examination of the suspect's teeth.
2. Refrain from verbalizing conclusions based on early speculation and unsubstantiated preliminary opinions until the report is written.
3. Evaluate suspect evidence in a blinded fashion (collected by another dentist including nonsuspect controls and submitted as coded unknowns).
4. Evaluate all suspects in a case (if possible).
5. Report any factors that complicate analysis.
6. Attribute statements made by others to their sources or as alleged facts rather than as uncontested facts.
7. List literature or references that were used to aid analysis.
8. Formulate conclusions independent of other influences such as DNA analysis, statements, or reports made by others.
9. Before reporting a level of confidence in perpetrator identification, test the distinctiveness of the bitemark against other dentitions.
10. Obtain a second opinion.

procedures that support objective analysis and can be embodied within the report. (4) Lastly, the conclusions expressed in a report must be logically derived from the analysis. Their wording must be unambiguous, using prescribed terminology or explaining terms that could be misconstrued. Other qualities desirable in forensic reports include organization and proper use of language. Reports should be concise — not necessarily short, but prepared with economy of words. Finnegan advises that attorneys may request brief reports listing only demographic identifiers and the expert's conclusions, omitting details and analysis. In this situation, the investigator should maintain complete notes and thorough analysis in anticipation of future testimony [1].

4. BITEMARK REPORT

The foregoing text provided goals, objectives and qualities generally applicable to all forensic reports. The remainder of the chapter focuses on the specific construction of the bitemark report.

4.1. Preparation

The final report can only be as complete and accurate as the investigation on which it is based. The typical bitemark case is an emergent situation requiring an immediate response. During the chaos, it is possible to overlook certain aspects of evidence collection. Experienced odontologists often prepare for such events by maintaining a standard protocol to help document and sequence evidence collection. In this way, a checklist of prescribed procedures prompts the investigator so that nothing is omitted.

The American Board of Forensic Odontology (ABFO) provides Bitemark Methodology Guidelines [2] to help the odontologist customize a worksheet that conforms to his or her practice. The bitemark report is finalized upon completion of the case, often months after it has begun. In order to guarantee a thorough and meticulous report, it is desirable to make notes as the case progresses. Observations and communications promptly recorded tend to be more accurate than recollections made afterward.

As mentioned, reports may vary depending on the case. Table 2 illustrates some of the factors that may influence the organization or length of the report. In some cases, the odontologist may wish to make two separate reports; one issued to the agency that requested the examination

Table 2 Factors that Influence Length and Style of the
Bitemark Report

1. Living or deceased victim
2. Bitten individual—victim or crime suspect?
3. Nature of pattern injury (adult, child, or animal bitemark or not identifiable as a bitemark)
4. Cutaneous bitemark or bitemark in substrate
5. Number of bitemarks
6. Number of suspects
7. Evidence collected by author or received from another source
8. Primary report or second opinion

and documentation of injuries and a second, issued sometime later, incorporating the details of the first report with the comparative studies and analysis made on suspect evidence.

4.2. Contents of a Bitemark Report

In his abstract presented at the AAFS annual meeting in 2001, Finnegan listed elements to be included in a standard anthropological report. In similar fashion, the ABFO has suggested guidelines for writing standard bitemark reports [3]. These have been modified for this chapter and are summarized in Table 3. These guidelines are further detailed below. As guidelines they are comprehensive and cover most circumstances. All are not mandatory, and only individual cases determine which of these components are applicable.

4.3. Victim of Injury Data

4.3.1. Demographics/History

This serves to identify, file, and locate the case and to describe the odontologist's initial involvement. It includes the full name of the injured person, including maiden name and aliases, date

Table 3 Suggested Components of a Standard
Bitemark Report

1. Injury data
   a. Chronology (demographics/history)
   b. Collection and description of injury evidence
   c. Evaluation of injury/evidentiary value
2. Suspect data
   a. Demographics/history
   b. Collection of evidence
3. Comparison
   a. Methods
   b. Results
4. Conclusion and its basis.
   a. Analysis
   b. Opinion
   c. Scientific basis
   d. Critique of other expert opinions (if applicable)
5. Inventory and disposition of evidence
6. Name, title, signature of odontologist, and date sent

of birth, gender, race, and case number (ME/coroner, police, court case, etc.). Also included is the notification and response of the odontologist — date and time contacted, by whom, the requested task, as well as the arrival time of the odontologist, location and parties present.

4.3.2. Collection of Evidence

This includes any consent or court order (on living bitten persons) and the order and details of evidence collection. Initial photographs, swabs, sketches, narrative description of injuries, making of critical photographs, history of injury (on living patients), impressions, excision of injuries, and examination and impressions of victim's dentition would be described and detailed in this section. In cases where the odontologist was not directly involved with evidence collection, the evidence should be inventoried and described.

4.3.3. Analysis of Evidence

The odontologist determines the nature of the injury using established criteria and terminology, such as ABFO Bitemark Terminology Guidelines [4], then indicates a level of confidence that the injury represents a bitemark. It may also be desirable to profile the biter's dentition from the bitemark and comment on quality of the bitemark and its anticipated value as evidence in the case.

4.4. Suspect Data

4.4.1. Demographics/History

This would include a synopsis of communications between the odontologist and legal authorities to direct collection of suspect evidence (informed consent, court order, appointment date to collect evidence, instructions to others who might collect evidence).

4.4.2. Collection of Evidence

Included here are the details of the oral examination, photographs, impressions and models, bite registrations, buccal swabs (if appropriate) and procedures used to maintain objectivity.

4.5. Comparison

This section lists the procedures used for comparison and records the results.

4.6. Conclusion

The results of comparative analysis are interpreted. Using ABFO Bitemark Terminology Guidelines [4], a conclusion is formulated that accurately communicates the level of confidence regarding the origin of the bitemark and the scientific basis for the conclusion. If another odontologist's report was submitted as evidence, it should be critiqued.

4.7. Disposition of Evidence

An inventory of all evidence and its disposition, along with chain of custody information, should accompany the report. The use of imbedded and annotated images is easily accomplished with computer software programs, as suggested in ABFO Forensic Report Writing Guidelines [3]. Certainly, images are helpful in illustrating the descriptions and techniques used. However, if a written report is collected as trial evidence, it becomes public record, which can be problematic if it violates privacy laws. Some odontologists prefer to keep photographs and diagrams separate from formal reports.

4.8. Investigator Information

Finally, the report should include the name, title, address, phone number, and signature of the odontologist and date sent. This may conclude the report or appear as a letterhead.

5. PERSPECTIVE

The odontologist must always assume that, as a potential expert witness, his/her techniques, findings, and opinions are going to be challenged. The report, as a discoverable and unalterable expression of his/her work, becomes a target of the challenge. If a report reflects a valid opinion derived from reasonable analysis of accurate data, then the challenge will be footloose, based on irrelevant protests or, perhaps, a less competent analysis from an opposing expert. A challenge can also be based on perceived shortcomings in a report, such as errors, omissions, unsubstantiated conclusions, or overzealous opinions. In order to construct a report that is essentially unassailable, the forensic odontologist should place it aside for a few days and then reexamine it with the perspective of an opposing expert or attorney. How might an attack be launched? What errors, such as incorrect tooth numbers or right/left orientation, were overlooked in proofreading? What could have been stated more accurately? What oversight can be exploited? What assurances of objectivity have been provided? What conclusion is vague in meaning, allowing a possible misinterpretation? What opinion is worded in noncompliance with ABFO guidelines that can garner a challenge? Having addressed these considerations, the report can be submitted with confidence.

6. SECURITY

The only recipient of a bitemark report is the agent who requested the services of the odontologist or designee. Reports should be posted, faxed, emailed, or hand delivered to the intended recipient in a manner that will guarantee confidentiality. Any other requests for a copy should have written approval of the primary solicitor or a court order.

REFERENCES

1. Finnegan M. What should be in a forensic anthropological report? Abstract H35, Proceedings of American Academcy of Forensic Sciences, Annual Meeting, Feb. 19–24, 2001.
2. ABFO Bitemark Methodology Guidelines. American Board of Forensic Odontology, 1994.
3. ABFO Report Writing Guidelines, American Board of Forensic Odontology, 1999.
4. ABFO Bitemark Terminology Guidelines, American Board of Forensic Odontology, 1995.

IX
Prevention and Contamination

22
Precautionary Measures

Paul G. Stimson

Odontology Consultant, Harris County Medical Examiner
Houston, Texas, U.S.A.

1. INTRODUCTION

This chapter proposes means and methods of protecting the forensic examiner/assistant from contamination or infection emanating from the living/deceased individual. Every examinee should be considered potentially chemically, virally, or bacterially contaminated or infectious, particularly since the era of terrorism. There is also the possibility of radioisotope contamination from the use of a "dirty bomb." The simple act of photographing or recording a person/body's condition can lead to contamination issues. Airborne pathogens such as anthrax or those causing severe acute respiratory syndrome (SARS) can be transferred from examinee to equipment to ultimately be inhaled or absorbed by third parties. Hepatitis B and C, human immunodeficiency viruses (HIV), and other pathogenic diseases can be present with no obvious outward signs. Suggestions incorporating decontamination measures for various tools/equipment required in forensic procedures are discussed. Self-protection is a prime consideration in the examination. The ultimate goal is to obtain the necessary information, photographs, examination, specimen, etc., free of contamination and infection. Prevention of cross-contamination is another objective. In case of an exposure to nuclear materials from a dirty bomb, the site would have to be secured and the resultant casualties decontaminated prior to being brought to either a morgue or a hospital. If the morgue is in the area of exposure or is heavily exposed to nuclear material, a temporary morgue would have to be set up in an uncontaminated area. Proper procedures for decontamination of facilities, personnel, and bodies must be followed and procedures should be in place for these procedures.

2. PERSONNEL

Strict personal sanitation habits must be observed by anyone dealing with a living or deceased individual. One problem quickly encountered is that of hand-washing. It has been shown by Rotter [1] that the use of nonaqueous ethanol or propanols offers many advantages with either unmedicated or medicated soap in both hygienic and surgical hand disinfection: "Alcohols exert the strongest and fastest activity against a wide spectrum of bacteria and fungi (but not bacterial spores) as well as enveloped (but less so against non-enveloped) viruses, being little influenced by interfering substances." In other words, self-protection can be achieved in any contamination situation by the use of alcohol-type hand-washing material. Alcohol materials are easily obtained and should be a part of the kit that a forensic individual carries. Alcohol-based antiseptic agents are available in gels, foams, or rinses that do not require the use of water. According to studies summarized in the present CDC guideline [2], the waterless, alcohol-based products are more effective at reducing microbial flora on the health care worker hands than a plain soap or antimicrobial handwash. The use and method of application are simple and easy to accomplish when sinks may not be available.

Nosocomial infections are a problem in intensive care units. One study showed a 30% increase in handwashing compliance using the alcohol-based hand rub [3]. The authors state that the less time-consuming hand-rubbing might replace standard hand-washing and overcome the barrier of time constraints in intensive care units. This technique is ideal for the forensic scientist in a situation where hand-washing and hygiene have been compromised. When gloves are worn, hands can quickly be cleaned before and after use. Alcohol-based hand rub can be used when gloves are punctured by a variety of sharp objects present in the environment, the equipment, or the oral cavity. Thicker gloves can be used to overcome this problem; however, there is a decrease in tactile sense.

Alcohol-type hand-washing preparations should not be used on visibly soiled hands. These products cannot ever fully replace the need for sinks or other hand-washing hygiene in a health care or forensic setting. Dispensing the proper amount of material is critical. After frequent use, drying occurs unless the formula contains emollients or other skin-conditioning materials. It is also important to realize that alcohol-based materials are flammable and must be stored away from high temperatures or flames. Soaps and alcohol preparations with additives (e.g., fragrance or preservatives) may cause allergic skin conditions. Allergies to natural rubber latex (NRL) affect between 8% and 25% of healthcare workers. Methods of treatment and prevention are covered in the article by Mills [4].

The use of protective clothing is a key element and essential to infection control and prevention. Anyone likely to be exposed to potential infection should approach each contact, living or deceased, as contaminated. The protective clothing must be accessible and worn prior to contact. Many items of protective clothing are incorporated within the concept of universal precautions; that is, those precautions necessary to reduce exposure to blood or body fluids (Centers for Disease Control and Prevention, 1987) [5]. Gowns, aprons, lab coats, clinic jackets, or similar outer garments, either reusable or disposable, must be worn when clothing or skin is likely to be exposed to blood or body fluids or contaminated materials. A forensic kit should be assembled and ready to use when needed. Many disposable products are available that can be safely and easily discarded. If biohazard bags are not provided, heavy plastic bags may be used for disposal of soiled materials and clothing. Clothing to be washed after removal must also be placed in heavy plastic bags [6].

3. IN THE LIVING

When called to examine or perform a forensic procedure, obtain a clinical briefing of case and circumstance. The more questions asked, the better prepared. Where will the examination be done? Under whose authority will it be done? Where is the written authorization, warrant, or court order? You must know the full extent of the hazards present or potentially present before you start the work. Prevention is worth a pound of cure for yourself and for those who assist you. Is the examined individual incarcerated, unconscious, etc.? A checklist will be helpful to ascertain the above questions and other inquiries for a particular case. Caution is the advice for any practicing dentist who chooses to use his own office for forensic work. An escorted AIDS-tubercular detainee in chains strolling through your office during normal business hours may not be appreciated. A forensic examination kit and protocol should be preassembled. The kit may contain equipment, instruments, impression trays, etc., specific to forensic examinations. Be prepared to answer questions that may be raised about your forensic endeavors. This makes good business, forensic, and preventive sense.

4. AT AUTOPSY

The same rules apply for the clinical briefing of case and circumstance prior to autopsy. Written authorization should always be obtained. Most medical examiner offices and hospital morgues have protocols that dictate the use of proper clothing, aprons, gloves, hair covering, masks, etc. Shoe coverings or separate forensic footwear (disposable or not) is highly recommended. Nolte et al. point out that an autopsy may subject prosectors and others forensic examiners to a wide variety of infectious agents [7]. These include bloodborne and aerosolized pathogens such as human immunodeficiency virus (HIV), hepatitis B and C viruses, and *Mycobacterium tuberculosis*. They also discuss other hazards such as toxic chemicals (e.g., formalin, cyanide, and organophosphates) and radiation from radionuclides used for patient therapy and diagnosis. These risks will be reduced by proper assessment and appropriate autopsy procedures.

Healing et al. [8] point out that none of the organisms that caused mass death in the past—for example, plague, cholera, typhoid, tuberculosis, anthrax, smallpox—is likely to survive long in buried human remains [9]. Items such as mold spores or lead dust are a much greater risk to those involved in exhumations. However, in the recently deceased, risks include tuberculosis, group A streptococcal infection, gastrointestinal organisms, the agents that cause transmissible spongiform encephalopathies (such as Creutzfeldt-Jakob disease), hepatitis B and C, viruses, HIV, and possibly meningitis and septicemia (especially meningococcal). It is readily apparent that the use of protective clothing and proper morgue protocol is imperative. In addition, individuals in the health and forensic related fields should have an immunization against hepatitis B. Other immunizations might prove beneficial if not necessary following discussions with an infectious disease specialist or family physician.

When doing the examination and procedure(s), protective clothing must be worn. Surgical masks or chin-length plastic face shields are recommended as well as protective eyewear with side shields. Hand or alcohol cleaner washing should be performed before gloving. When working and charting alone, double-gloving is recommended. The first pair of gloves is used for charting while the second is used for work on the deceased. The chance of cross-contamination is minimized.

Surface disinfection can be accomplished with a bleach solution (dilution 1:100 bleach to water). This is extremely effective for most pathogens. Viruses and tuberculosis spores are killed by this solution in about 10 min. High-concentration alcohols (ethyl alcohol or isopropyl of at least 70%) can be used on precleaned surfaces. Any product that is routinely used in a dental office can also be used if the directions and procedures are properly followed.

Clothing storage in a morgue situation presents many problems. If the contaminant on the clothing is a biological agent such as blood or sperm, the clothing can be dried with forced warm air. After drying, clothing can be sealed in plastic wrappings until needed. Gentle drying will preserve blood and sperm, and they can be rehydrated for further testing when needed. If other special tests such as volatile materials, smokeless gunpowder, of trace metals are required, the clothing will have to be processed in a special manner to preserve the element for the test. Some morgues have enough freezer capacity to store wet clothing until needed for testing. The inventory of materials stored must be closely monitored and discarded when no longer needed for testing or other uses.

5. INSTRUMENTS AND EQUIPMENT

All dental instruments should be cleaned, preferably by ultrasonic equipment, to remove adherent materials and organic debris, sterilized (autoclaved or rapid dry heat), and bagged. The bags should be dated as to procedures undergone and stored in a secure area. There are also some FDA-cleared immersion disinfectants and sterilants for instruments that cannot be autoclaved.

Table 1 Enviromental Protection Agency (EPA)-registered surface disinfectants for forensic dentistry.

Category/ active ingredient	Contact[a]	Pros	Cons
Chlorines (sodium hypochlorite diluted in office, chlorine dioxide, commercial preparations of sodium hypochlorite with added surfactants)	2–10 min 20°C or 25°C[b]	Economical; rapid; broad spectrum; tuberculocidal; effective in dilute solution	Diluted solutions must be prepared daily; cannot be reused; corrosive to some metals; may destroy fabrics; may irritate skin and other tissues; chlorine dioxide is a poor cleaner.
Complex phenols ("synthetic phenols" containing multiple phenolic agents)	10 min 20°C or 25°C[b]	Broad-spectrum activity; residual activity; effective cleaner and disinfectant; tuberculocidal; compatible with metal, glass, rubber, and plastic	Extended exposure may degrade some plastics or leave etchings on glass; many preparations are limited to one day of use; may leave a residual film on treated surfaces
Dual/synergized quaternary ammonium compounds (alcohol and multiple quaternary ammonium compounds)	6 or 10 min 20°C[b]	Broad-spectrum activity; tuberculocidal; hydrophilic virus claims; low toxicity; contains detergents for cleaning	Readily inactivated by anionic detergents and organic matter; can damage some materials
Iodophors (iodine, combined with a surfactant)	10 min 20°C	Broad-spectrum activity; tuberculocidal; relatively nontoxic; effective cleaner and disinfectant; residual biocidal action	Unstable at higher temperatures; may discolor some surfaces; inactivated by alcohol and hard water; must be prepared daily; dilution and contact times are critical
Phenol-alcohol combinations (phenolic agent in alcohol base)	10 min 20°C or 25°C[b]	Tuberculocidal; fast acting; residual activity; some inhibit the growth of mold, mildew, and other fungi	May cause porous surfaces to dry and crack; poor cleaning capabilities
Other halogens (sodium bromide and chlorine)	5 min 20°C	Fast acting; tuberculocidal; supplied in tablet form for simple dilution; requires minimal storage space	For use on hard surfaces only; chlorine smell

[a] Contact time/temperatures for tuberculocidal activity.
[b] Varies by active ingredient or disinfectant brand.

Table 2 FDA-approved instrument immersion disinfectants for forensic dentistry.

Category/active ingredient	Classification	Contact timing
Glutaraldehyde 2.4%–3.4% alkaline and acid formulations[a]	Sterilant; high-level disinfectant	6–10 hr at 20°C, 22°C, or 25°C[a]
		20–90 min at 20°C, 22°C, or 25°C[a]
Hydrogen peroxide, 7.3%	Sterilant; high-level disinfectant	6 hr at 20°C
		30 min at 20°C
Ortho-pthalaldehyde, 0.55%	High-level disinfectant	12 min at 20°C
Synergistic solutions		
1.12% glutaraldehyde and 1.93% phenol/phenate	Sterilant; high-level disinfectant	12 hr at 25°C
		20 min at 25°C
7.35% hydrogen peroxide and 0.23% peracetic acid	Sterilant; high-level disinfectant	3 hr at 20°C
		15 min at 20°C

Note: Glutaraldehyde and simple quaternary ammonium should not be used for surface disinfection in dentistry or forensics. High-concentration alcohols (ethyl alcohol or isopropyl alcohol of at least 70%) should be used on precleaned surfaces.

[a] Varies by active ingredient or disinfectant brand.

Examples include all plastic instruments (cheek retractors, etc.) and instruments containing solder (impression trays, etc.). Organization for Safety and Asepesis Procedures [9] (OSAP) charts (Tables 1 and 2) might assist in selecting the best surface and instrument immersion disinfectants for dentistry and forensics. On rare occasions, autopsy instruments are autoclaved when a highly contagious case has been done or is suspected. This procedure is done to ensure the instruments are clean and infectious agent free because of their multiple uses in a morgue situation.

Cameras should be kept in hand or placed in plastic bags or paper towels when in use in the morgue. In extremely hazardous and infectious situations, photographs can be taken with an underwater camera setup, and then the outer surface of the watertight camera case can be wiped with a bleach solution. The photographer should wear disposable gloves and discard them after the photography is completed. Alcohol wipes of 70% or more can be used on the outer surfaces of cameras, but it might effect the outer portions of the camera over time. Care should be taken with alcohol type swabs near camera lenses as this can affect/remove the ultraviolet and other lens coatings.

6. IMPRESSIONS AND CASTS

Bitemark and dental impressions must be disinfected. The American Dental Association (ADA) makes the following recommendations [10]:

> Immersion in disinfectants improves the wettability of polysulfide impression materials but the hydrophilic addition silicone impression materials are somewhat adversely affected by most disinfectants. Agar (alginates) impression materials should be immersed in hypochlorite, iodophor or glutaraldehyde with phenolic buffer. Stone casts may be immersed in iodophor or hypochlorite or alternatively spray disinfectants may be used. Zinc oxide eugenol impression materials may be disinfected by immersion in glutaraldehyde or iodophor. These impression materials are rarely used in a forensic setting, but can be used if nothing else is available or

the usual materials used will not set under the situation being impressed. The use of ADA accepted disinfectants that require no more than 30 minutes for disinfection is preferred. As the impression material/disinfectant compatibility may vary even within the same generic areas, the manufacturers' recommendations for proper disinfection should be followed.

Polysulfides, silicones, and polyethers can be immersed in accepted products. Polysiloxane and the acrylic tray materials used for bitemark impressions can also be immersed in accepted products.

REFERENCES

1. Rotter ML. Arguments for alcoholic hand disinfection. J Hosp Infect 2001; 48(Suppl A):S4–S8.
2. CDC RR. Guidelines for hand hygiene in healthcare settings, April 12, 2004. October 25, 2002; 51(RR16):1–44.
3. Hugonnet S, Perneger TV, Pitter D. Alcohol-based handrub improves compliance with hand hygiene in intensive care units. Arch Intern Med 2002; 162:1037–1043.
4. Mills C. Combatting latex allergies. Infection Control Today 2002; 66:1.
5. CDC RR. Perspectives in disease and health promotion update: Precautions for prevention of transmission of human immunodeficiency virus, Hepatitis B virus, and other bloodborne pathogens in healthcare settings. June 24, 1988; 37(24):377–388.
6. York V. Using protective clothing. Nurs Times 2002; 98:52.
7. Nolte KB, Taylor DG, Richmond JY. Biosafety considerations for autopsy. Am J Forens Med Pathol 2002; 23:107–122.
8. Healing TD, Hoffman PN, Young SE. The infection hazards of human cadavers. Commun Dis Rep CDR Rev 1995; 5:R61–R68.
9. OSAP Chart & Checklist. Infection Control in Practice 1: 5, 2002. Med Pathol 2002; 23:107–122.
10. Fan PL. Disinfection of impressions. J Am Dent Assoc 1991; 122:110.

X
Legal Considerations and the Courtroom

23
Science and the Law

Richard A. Mincer
Hirst and Applegate
P.C. Cheyenne, Wyoming, U.S.A.

Harry H. Mincer
Shelby County Medical Examiner's Office
Tennessee, U.S.A.

1. INTRODUCTION: WHY DO ALMOST HALF OF ALL EXPERTS GET IT WRONG?

According to news reports by the popular media, almost every high-profile courtroom litigation features a parade of key expert witnesses (including forensic odontologists in bitemark cases) who give diametrically opposite opinions. This would indicate that as many as 50% of all scientific opinions offered under oath during legal proceedings are just plain wrong. How is this possible? How can half of the trained and educated scientific experts, utilizing nearly identical methodology derived from the same body of scientific knowledge, and analyzing exactly the same data, get it wrong at such an alarming rate? Certainly, if the *New England Journal of Medicine* had such a dismal track record, there would be wholesale changes in the editorial staff, cries of fraud, and a mass exodus of those who provide financial support to that esteemed publication. One would certainly question the integrity of the contributors and carefully scrutinize both their methodology and their objectivity, not to mention their ability to honestly interpret the data.

The answer to this conundrum may lie in the inherent conflict between true science and a justice system that encourages advocacy to resolve adversarial proceedings. When the scientist turns advocate, objectivity and scientific reliability are often the victims. On the one hand, the expert should utilize effective and persuasive communication skills to help the jury understand the testimony. On the other hand, the expert should not attempt to manipulate the outcome of testing to support a given position. There is a very real difference between effectively communicating the results of an objective and unbiased review of the evidence, and tailoring the testing and methodology to achieve a specific result. The question is whether the rules of the game are different when offering an expert legal opinion as opposed to publishing a conclusion for the scientific community. Shouldn't expert witnesses employ the same level of intellectual rigor in the courtroom as when presenting a paper to their peers or submitting an article to a peer-reviewed publication?

This chapter discusses the interplay (or is it tension?) between science and the law with respect to scientific expert testimony. The following is neither a cookbook to advise experts how to persuade jurors nor a recitation of the relative merits or drawbacks of Daubert [1], Mohan [2], and similar precedent cases. Rather, the purpose of this chapter is to explore a possible explanation for the divergence of expert opinions in legal proceedings and to analyze how experts who cross the line between science and advocacy affect the administration of justice. What role does scientific evidence have in this process that ultimately intends to search for the truth? How does science affect the judicial system? More specifically, what is the proper role of the expert witness offering scientific opinions in a judicial proceeding?

2. THE LEGAL SYSTEM

2.1. Purpose: A Search for the Truth Versus the Administration of Justice

The legal system in civilized countries was designed to settle disputes and is premised, at least ostensibly, on a search for the truth. Whether the dispute is criminal or civil, the legal system is only triggered when the litigants cannot agree among themselves on a just outcome—in other words, cannot agree as to the definition of a just result.

The basic operation of the legal system involves a trier of fact, a judge or a jury, who serves as the ultimate arbiter of factual disputes. The judge also makes threshold determinations regarding the admissibility of evidence based on established rules. These evidentiary rules are generally designed to ensure that the jury only considers reliable evidence. The legal reliability of evidence is typically based on the nature of the evidence, rather than on the content of the evidence, but there are exceptions.

Hearsay evidence is a good example of the possible complexity confronting the judge when deciding admissibility. Hearsay is generally thought to be unreliable evidence. Anyone can say anything, and later that statement may be reported by someone else, so the basic problem with hearsay is that the jury cannot assess the accuracy of the core statement. When B reports what he was told by A, his recall of the statement may be flawless. The question is not B's memory of the conversation, but whether A's statement was accurate in the first place, and if A is not present at the proceedings, this cannot ordinarily be ascertained by the trier of fact. Sometimes, however, hearsay may be judged admissible by virtue of the context in which the statement was made or by the content of the statement. If, for example, the statement is made while observing an event and describes the event, it is more likely to be judged reliable and therefore admissible than a description of the same event made after some time has passed. Similarly, a statement against the declarant's personal interest may also be considered reliable, because people do not normally make statements that can get them into trouble. Thus, if a hearsay statement contains certain recognized indicia of reliability, it may be admitted into evidence, although the jury will ultimately determine whether the statement is true or false.

In addition to admissibility, the judge also determines the law applicable to the facts and instructs the jury, as trier of fact, on the same. Application of the law to the facts yields a result—in criminal cases a determination of guilt or innocence, and in civil cases whether one party is liable to another for damages. If the process works, justice is done; if the process fails, the result is unjust. Obviously, just results promote public confidence in the system. Confidence and respect for the judicial system constitute a bedrock of a civilized society. Should the expert witness concern himself with whether or not the justice system works, and if so, to what extent?

2.2. Justice Versus Truth

Justice is defined as "moral rightness, equity, fairness, or honor" or "the proper administration of laws" that will "render every man his due." Truth, on the other hand, is defined as "reality, actuality or conformity to knowledge, fact, actuality or logic.'' The question becomes whether there can be a ''just'' result in any given case based on something other than ''truth.''

In practice, justice and the truth are not always the same. The legal system acknowledges, at least in a sense, that the two may diverge. While finding the truth is certainly a goal of the administration of justice, a ''just'' result is considered to have been achieved by giving a litigant a fair trial. If a dispute is tried before an impartial tribunal and the litigant has the opportunity to present evidence in his favor and to confront contrary evidence, then the result is looked upon as ''just,'' even if it is flatly contrary to factual truth. Despite this, many scholars have agreed that trial by jury may not be perfect (i.e., it may not always find the truth), but it is deemed better than alternative systems used in other parts of the world.

Other aspects of the difference between truth and justice seem to be heavily dependent on individual points of view. In the civil arena, for example, many plaintiffs' lawyers believe justice is achieved by fully compensating an injured victim, regardless of whether the party held liable is actually to blame for the injuries. If the person truly at fault is absent or, more importantly, incapable of paying a judgment, any available pocket will do as long as the victim (and the attorney) is compensated. Hence, the ''deep-pockets syndrome'' maintains its attractiveness to certain litigants and, unfortunately, to certain judges and jurors.

Similarly, in criminal cases some members of society believe that it may be just to wrong-fully convict the habitual, but as yet unpunished, criminal for a particular crime. Since he has committed other crimes for which he has never been punished, in many people's minds it is not a travesty to convict him for a crime he did not commit since he still deserves punishment for something. Of course, this leaves the subject crime unsolved, thereby depriving the victim of justice.

Again, should expert witnesses concern themselves with whether the justice system works, and if so, to what extent? Should experts seek impartial truth or should they tailor their testimony to support the position of the attorney? More pointedly, should an expert fabricate testimony that might help convict an innocent person or free a guilty criminal? What could possibly motivate an expert to aid and abet such an unjust result?

2.3. The Adversarial System

One explanation for an expert's motivation to further this apparently unseemly cause lies in the fact that attorneys who retain experts are advocates. As an advocate, an attorney is only concerned with representing the best interests of his or her client as long as the claim or defense is cognizable under the law and has some basis in fact. In civil cases, this duty to zealously represent the interests of the client is relatively uncomplicated. In criminal cases, however, many defense attorneys do not want to know whether or not their client actually committed the crime. Rather, the focus is to present the best defense available under the law. In other words, the criminal defense attorney must do everything reasonably possible to see that the client gets his or her day in court and has a fair trial. Again, the attorney's duty to advocate the position of the client is fairly clear-cut. After all, an acquittal certainly serves the best interest of the client, even if the client is truly guilty.

Prosecutors, on the other hand, would seem to have a need to be more concerned with truth. Prosecutors serve the public, that is, all the citizens in the prosecutor's jurisdiction. The citizens are interested in seeing perpetrators of crime punished for their wrongs. Citizens, as ''clients'' of prosecutors, lose when the result at trial does not reflect the truth. Certainly, citizens lose when a guilty man is acquitted. Similarly, citizens' interests are not served when the prosecutor wins a conviction only to jail an honest person. After all, the real perpetrator, who presumably poses a threat to strike again, is still at large despite the prosecutor's apparent victory at trial.

The ideal role of the expert witness is to provide the attorney advice regarding the merits of the case and, ultimately, to help advance the client's cause before a jury through the explanation of scientific or other technical evidence that may not otherwise be understood. A responsible attorney should seek a candid, unbiased opinion from the expert to assist with evaluation of the case. If the client's case is weak, the attorney should seek early resolution of the case through settlement or a plea agreement. Early negotiations, if successful, will ameliorate or avoid risk and uncertainty, not to mention the time and expense of trial. Presumably, such tactics benefit the client who otherwise is unlikely to prevail at trial. By definition, compromise is never a complete victory or a total loss.

Too often, however, the attorney is only interested in advocating the position of the client, and has already evaluated the case before he retains an expert witness. Such an attorney is only interested in an expert who will further the preconceived "cause" of his client. Most attorneys believe that one can find an expert witness to support any position, regardless of how apparently untenable that position may be.

Especially in cases in which the facts indicate a close call on the evidence, the attorney's zeal to advocate his client's position may infect the retained expert. When this occurs, the expert embarks on a course designed to prove a desired result rather than to provide an unbiased opinion based on objective testing. Worse, the expert may attempt to offer an opinion without doing the investigative work necessary to support that opinion. As one U.S. court remarked about an overzealous expert, "[the expert's] affidavit exemplifies everything that is bad about expert witnesses in litigation. It is full of vigorous assertion (much of it legal analysis in the guise of expertise), carefully tailored to support plaintiffs' position but devoid of analysis. [The expert] must have allowed the lawyers to write an affidavit in his name. ⋯ An expert who supplies nothing but a bottom line supplies nothing of value to the judicial process" [3].

Many, if not most, experts, of course, refuse to be so swayed toward advocacy. The conscientious expert will provide an honest and objective evaluation of the issue at hand, regardless of whether the attorney actively seeks such candor. The desirable expert, at least from a responsible lawyer's perspective, will then effectively and, yes, persuasively communicate this opinion to the jury. Unfortunately, communication skills, rather than scientifically valid results, often carry the day with the jury.

2.4. Evidentiary Restrictions

It is important for the expert witness to remember that the threshold ruling on admissibility does not equate to a determination of whether or not the ultimate opinion reflects the truth. Judges merely decide whether the methodology or process utilized by the expert witness to reach a conclusion reflects a reasonable and responsible evaluation of the evidence. Therefore, the key to admissibility is really the same as the key to a valid and reliable opinion—namely, to employ objective and unbiased methodology to analyze all of the relevant evidence and, of equal importance, to consider and analyze contrary theories, which, if proven, will effectively thwart the position of the party retaining the expert. Proving a given theory while simultaneously disproving all contrary theories is powerful and persuasive evidence.

3. SCIENCE—GOOD VERSUS JUNK AND EVERYTHING IN BETWEEN

3.1. The Scientific Method

Courts have recently encouraged use of the scientific method as a prerequisite to the admissibility of scientific expert testimony. The scientific method encompasses the formulation of a theory followed by rigorous testing to either confirm or disprove the theory. Numerous texts address this basic philosophy of science, so the relative merits of these arguments will not be addressed in detail here. Rather, we will point out that reliable scientific testimony entails something more than offering an opinion that is carefully tailored to advocate a given position, but completely devoid of analysis. The theory and the testing should be broad enough to include opposing and contrary theories. It is important that the expert's opinion and testimony emanate from objective testing, as opposed to the expert simply reviewing the facts of the case and the position of the advocate, and then attempting to work backward to manipulate the testing or otherwise craft methodology designed to explain a preconceived opinion solely for the purpose of supporting the retaining party. Moreover, if the testing negates the contrary opinion of the opposing expert, as well as confirming the result, the ultimate conclusion, both from scientific and legal standpoints, will be all the more reliable and persuasive.

3.2. The Importance of Testing

From a legal standpoint, the hallmark of good science is objective testing. Such testing will generally utilize an accepted methodology that faithfully analyzes all the relevant facts of that specific case. Testing that employs questionable methodology or ignores salient facts is the easiest for a judge to rule inadmissible, regardless of the validity of the outcome. If the original testing was performed for scientific rather than legal purposes (in other words, was initially developed for use outside the courtroom), it is all the more persuasive with the trial judge.

Typically, the expert should address the viability of the opinion in both general and specific terms. Most expert testimony deals with the validity of a cause and effect relationship between a set of circumstances and a known condition (did the occurrence of A result in B?) The facts that comprise A are usually known, as is the result defined as B. The typical question for the scientist is whether or not there is causal relationship between the two. This analysis usually requires a two-step inquiry; first, could the occurrence of A ever have caused the occurrence of B and, second, did it actually occur in this specific case? Testing designed to address both general and specific causation should yield the more reliable and persuasive result. In bitemark analysis, the scientific question is simple. Was the condition B (the injury) a result of A (a human bite) (general) caused by the teeth of the suspect (specific)? The most widely accepted testing methodology for the analysis of bitemark evidence is detailed in the Guidelines of the American Board of Forensic Odontology.

3.3. The Importance of Objectivity

Good science demands objectivity. The scientific method is premised on objective testing and assumes that the scientist is searching for the truth, whatever form the truth may take. From both a scientific and a legal standpoint, the objective expert fulfills the role that expert witnesses are expected to play in the search for the truth.

The legal system permits expert witnesses to offer opinions on the ultimate issue of fact precisely because the expert is presumed to be objective. After all, the very reason that experts are allowed to testify is to help the jury understand the evidence based on the expert's specialized knowledge and training. Expert testimony is very powerful. Jurors are apt to cede their fact-finding mission to experts since the nature of the testimony is beyond the ken of the average juror. For this reason, judges act as gatekeepers, whose function is to admit testimony that meets certain indicia of reliability while excluding that based on an incomplete review of the facts or that is the product of unreliable or biased methodology. When it is apparent that an expert is merely saying whatever is necessary to support a party's position at trial, that testimony is usually excluded, provided the opposing party is able to point out such shortcomings.

Judges and juries can usually smell a hired gun. In fact, it is probably fair to say that most judges and many juries expect the retained expert to be a hired gun and begin their review of expert testimony with a certain amount of distrust. The quickest and easiest way to dispel these preconceived notions is to show that the testing, methodology, and, ultimately, the testimony at trial emerged from objectivity and impartiality. This bespeaks the professional integrity of the expert and fosters respect and trust from the jury. Thus, in addition to the other positive properties of objectivity, it is a very powerful tool for persuasion.

4. INTERPLAY/TENSION BETWEEN SCIENCE AND ADVOCACY

4.1. Different Rules for Different Roles

It should be apparent from the foregoing that lawyers and expert witnesses play by different rules as they serve different roles in the administration of justice. Yet, in practice lawyers and experts often do not appreciate or adhere to this distinction, which often leads to both overstepping their respective ethical bounds. Interestingly, each aids and abets the other's unethical behavior.

Lawyers are expected to zealously represent the interests of their clients. However, this responsibility is tempered by the duty to act as a responsible officer of the court, as well as the lawyer's self-interest to earn a satisfactory living while remaining an upright person [4]. In essence, a lawyer as an advocate "has a duty to use legal procedure for the fullest benefit of the client's cause, but also a duty not to abuse the legal procedure" [5]. In that regard, a lawyer may not "make a false statement of material fact or law to a tribunal ⋯ or offer evidence that the lawyer knows to be false" [6]. Furthermore, the lawyer may not counsel a person to falsify evidence or otherwise testify falsely [7].

The function of the expert is to address subject matter that is typically outside the lawyer's scope of knowledge. Therefore, the lawyer relies on the expert to interpret the evidence within the pertinent field, to advise as to how the evidence will influence the outcome of the case, and to present and explain the evidence to the trier of fact at trial. However, an expert's role in the case ends when the evidence is received, while the lawyer must then argue to the jury how they should interpret the evidence and how an application of pertinent law to the facts of the case should result in a verdict in favor of the client. Remember that ascertaining the facts of a given situation is only the first task faced by a jury. Once the facts are determined, the jury must then apply the relevant law as provided by the judge to determine whether a party is guilty, negligent, reckless, or otherwise culpable. After that determination is made, the jury or the judge must then impose a sentence or determine a fair award of damages.

Too often, the lawyer does not communicate to the expert the distinction between their roles. Perhaps the lawyer assumes the expert knows the difference; or perhaps the lawyer would rather not know. On the other hand, the expert may not appreciate his duty to provide an honest evaluation of the evidence and may believe that his job is to do whatever is necessary to support the lawyer's, and, hence, the client's ultimate position in the litigation.

In any event, expert witnesses and lawyers alike have a duty to present truthful evidence. In this respect, the relative duties correspond. Neither has a license to present false testimony or even to argue for the adoption of unreasonable inferences from the evidence, and, certainly, neither is capable of changing the facts of a given case.

Unfortunately, some lawyers cross the line between providing an interpretation of the evidence and attempting to change facts. But in fairness, sometimes the line between advocating reasonable inferences or deductions to be made from the facts, and manufacturing evidence out of whole cloth is amazingly murky. After all, the end result of expert testimony is often "to provide the judge and jury with a ready-made inference which the judge and jury, due to the technical nature of the facts, are unable to formulate'' (8).

Everyone knows that it is a crime to knowingly testify falsely under oath. Why then do we have so many cases with two opposing experts in which one or the other is, by definition, providing false testimony? Is it really possible that neither knows, or at least strongly suspects, that his or her testimony is patently false? How can this be? Perhaps the explanation for this is ignorance of the proper role for experts and confusion between a lawyer's duty to advocate for his client and the expert's duty to provide truthful testimony.

The result-oriented expert may manipulate the data and/or the testing to achieve a desired result by either ignoring certain unsupportive facts or by tailoring the testing or other methodology to yield a given result. In either event, the testing may be valid as far as it goes but not reflect the facts of the specific case. To put it another way, the ultimate result exemplifies the old adage: ''Garbage in, garbage out.'' When either the data or the methodology is inaccurate or suspect, the ultimate opinion of the expert suffers from the same shortcomings. The expert has, therefore, failed in his mission to help the jury understand the evidence since the true evidence is not reflected in the expert's opinion or testimony.

4.2. Choosing Sides

Why would an expert brush aside the product of his training, education, and experience to work backward from a conclusion rather than following the scientific method in which the testing defines the outcome? More importantly, why would an expert, with no stake in the outcome of the litigation, ever gamble with the possibility that an innocent person might be convicted, a criminal might be freed, or assets in a civil litigation might be unjustly reallocated?

One apparent, but decidedly jaded, explanation is money. While many experts disdain any involvement in the legal process, many will participate provided the hourly rate of compensation is much higher than that received for typical work within their field. The expert who builds a reputation of ''loyalty'' to whoever is paying his fees will initially find more work as an expert, but only until this willingness to keep the payor happy backfires in front of a judge and jury and his game is exposed. Nevertheless, it cannot be disputed that monetary gain can certainly have an adverse effect on a person's objectivity.

Competitiveness and a ''desire to win'' may be another explanation for a loss of objectivity. Less experienced experts, particularly, seem to show a tendency to overstate the value of evidence that they have examined, possibly to enhance their reputations.

Additionally, preconceived notions of right and wrong may affect the expert's objectivity. For example, personal views regarding the scope of corporate responsibility may entice an expert witness to slant his assessment of a toxic tort case if he would personally impose duty of care on corporate defendants that is higher than that imposed by law. Similarly, some experts may not be able to stomach testifying in support of a criminal suspect who is a scoundrel, while losing no sleep over the prospect of jailing this scoundrel for a crime he did not commit. More commonly, an expert for the prosecution may be biased toward believing that a defendant is probably guilty just because he is in custody, despite the fact that the evidence does little to support this belief. In this instance, the expert must be careful not to stretch the importance of the evidence toward the cause of the prosecution. Perhaps there are other explanations, but none would suffice to justify an expert's attempt to mislead both the judge and the jury in a process that will have very real implications for the litigants.

4.3. The Court-Appointed Expert: A Solution to All the Problems?

If lawyers blur the lines or even encourage an expert to ignore the need for objectivity, or if experts are easily led astray by lawyers or by extraneous incentives, why not have the court retain a neutral expert or even impanel a collection of experts to render a final and unbiased opinion on matters outside the understanding of the court, the jury, and the attorneys? Would not the strict use of court-appointed experts alleviate the need for the judge to make threshold determinations on the admissibility of expert testimony—an exercise nonscientists are certainly ill-equipped to make in the first place? This would also alleviate the need for lay jurors to decide which of two competing experts has provided the most scientifically valid assessment of a set of facts that they, too, are simply unqualified to assess. Judges certainly have the ability and the procedural mechanisms at their disposal to retain court-appointed experts. Why not take this a step further and substitute a jury of experts for a lay jury to decide cases where a thorough understanding of a technical topic is central to the case?

Undoubtedly, the use of experts in such a manner will often yield results that more closely reflect the truth than would a verdict rendered by lay jurors. This idea is not without ardent supporters. While we will not attempt to treat this complex topic here, suffice it to say that such mechanisms will face an uphill battle to gain widespread support. Certainly, in the United States trial by jury is cherished as a unique and vital characteristic of the legal system. Many citizens, not just lawyers, espouse the belief that while the system is far from perfect, it is better than any alternative. Litigants take comfort in knowing that their dispute will be resolved by a jury of their peers, i.e., a jury of folks just like them, even if the system is imperfect.

Along these lines, the American Board of Forensic Odontology, in an attempt to alleviate expert bias in bitemark cases, has adopted a guideline that recommends that after interpretation by one expert, bitemark evidence should be reviewed independently by a second board-certified odontologist who has no direct interest in the case. Needless to say, this practice has not received universal acceptance among odontologists, attorneys, or the courts.

4.4. What Do Lawyers and Their Clients Really Want—"Hired Guns" or "Straight Shooters"?

Believe it or not, most lawyers, and, more particularly, their clients, really want an honest objective evaluation of the issues presented to the expert for review. Sometimes this may not be readily apparent, but both are best served by hearing both the good news and the bad from the retained expert. Some lawyers may fail to clearly convey this principle when discussing the case with experts, but a review of the consequences of a slanted, biased report reveals otherwise.

When an expert has decided that the position of his side, be it defendant, plaintiff, or prosecution, has significant weaknesses, he must reveal these to the attorney, who will then make the decision whether compromise is appropriate. The opportunity to resolve an untenable case, either civil or criminal, by pretrial settlement will usually save everyone concerned immeasurable time, expense, and discomfort. When a client has lost the opportunity to compromise, he faces whatever the ultimate downside was of losing at trial and, in a civil case, must pay the taxable costs of the other side. In a criminal case (as virtually all bitemark cases are), the prosecution may lose an otherwise winnable case at taxpayers' expense, or the defendant may face a stiff sentence, both of which could have been ameliorated through a pretrial plea agreement. On top of all this, the parties now may face the added expense of an appeal, all because good science was lacking. Also, it is no longer rare for clients or their attorneys to then make claims against experts, spawning even more litigation.

This is not to suggest that bad expert advice is the only reason clients find themselves in such predicaments. Clients and their attorneys make the same bad decisions for a number of reasons, even when an expert has properly advised as to the weaknesses of the client's position. Nevertheless, these illustrations should reveal that the best course of action when serving as an expert witness is to act as a straight shooter rather than a hired gun. Recognizing that your case is weak or even hopeless may be tough medicine to swallow, but it is usually preferable to learning this fact months or years and thousands of dollars later from a jury. Over time, an expert with a reputation as a straight shooter will not only find repeat business, but will also facilitate early resolution of claims because the opposing party will know that the expert's opinions are accurate and will convince juries.

5. EFFECTIVE PRESENTATION VERSUS FACTUAL ADVOCACY

As noted above, sometimes experts confuse the distinction between an effective presentation of their testimony and advocating for a specific result. While there is, arguably, some overlap, expert witnesses must appreciate and adhere to the distinction. There is, after all, a difference between an advocate and a scientist. Lawyers are advocates; you must remain a scientist, despite being hired by an advocate. The expert's objectivity and professionalism greatly enhance the advocate's ability to argue the case and persuade the jury.

This is not to suggest that expert witnesses should ignore the importance of an effective presentation. A witness faithfully serves the role of expert if he or she succeeds in teaching the subject matter to the jury so that at the end of the testimony they have gained at least a working understanding of the evidence. To achieve this, objectivity, professionalism, and an unbiased approach are powerful tools for gaining the jury's trust. Also, the jury must trust the messenger or they will likely ignore the message.

Similarly, organization, thoroughness, visual aids, and effective communication skills all assist to convey the message. Numerous texts and articles provide suggestions about how best to convey the message. Read these articles. If the jury falls asleep or is incapable of following your testimony because you talk over their heads, your message will be lost. Understand, however, that the message should simply be an explanation of the evidence—nothing more, nothing less. The message is not necessarily that the jury should find for the party retaining the expert, although the two are often inextricably intertwined. Regardless, the expert witness should not have an interest in the outcome and should present the evidence in a straightforward and objective manner. Leave the arguing to the attorneys.

6. HOW TO APPROACH SERVING AS AN EXPERT WITNESS IN A BITEMARK CASE

Bitemark evidence is often very important, sometimes vital, in the administration of justice. Incidents in which one human bites another are frequently parts of violent criminal activity, often homicides, and therefore, often result in capital cases or litigation potentially resulting in long prison sentences. Such cases in most American jurisdictions are considered important enough to merit jury trials. However, in most instances the issues are straightforward. Is the skin injury in question the result of a human bite? Was it caused by the teeth of the defendant?

Of course, there are other technical considerations as outlined elsewhere in this text, such as clarity of the bitemark, uniqueness of the purported biter's teeth, degree of certainty, an open versus a closed population of suspects (exclusive opportunity), etc.

The following are suggestions for serving as an expert witness in a bitemark case, as based on the foregoing discussion.

1. As soon as possible after receiving the evidence, give a completely honest appraisal of the evidence to the attorney. Stress the weaknesses and potential downside rather than bolstering the upside. It is best that the attorney knows the case's weaknesses from the start.

2. Understand your role and your limitations. Disclose and discuss these limitations with counsel and make sure your role is clearly defined. Also, discuss any budget considerations

with counsel at the beginning of the relationship. Be certain that you understand any admissibility thresholds in the relevant jurisdiction, discuss these with counsel, and make sure your work on the case satisfies these requirements.

3.   Examine everything available to counsel that could bear on your interpretation of the bitemark evidence, and request additional materials as needed. For example, you should read the opposing experts' reports and depositions, carefully look at all crime scene photographs and reports, and examine the medical examiner's documentation, injury orientation photographs, and diagrams. These can provide valuable information for your analysis, such as, ''Was the bitemark inflicted through clothing, explaining its lack of clarity?'' ''Was the wound distorted by body position?'' ''What was the position of the biter in relation to the victim?'' And ''What was the estimated timing of the bite injury as related to death?'' Remember, however, that your expertise deals only with physical evidence. You do not need to know the criminal record of the suspect, the relationship between the suspect and the victim, or other information that might bias your interpretation. In fact, some authorities go so far as to recommend that to prevent this type of bias, an expert should not meet the suspect until the trial. This would necessitate that some other individual gather evidence from the suspect (dental measurements, oral photographs, dental impressions, etc.).

4.   Research the field. Be totally familiar with the published bitemark literature. Know what others have done before you, particularly when the research was performed, for pure scientific purposes as opposed to litigation. Educate the attorney about the science of bitemark analysis. Most importantly, know what you have said or published on this topic prior to this litigation. Be prepared to address contrary opinions of others or those previously given by you.

5.   Carefully organize and maintain a detailed file in a way that will facilitate its use throughout your work on the case, including depositions and trial. Record the date and time for every activity that you perform in your analysis. Remember that the trial will probably be delayed for several months after your investigation, and you may not remember all the details without adequate notes.

6.   Formulate theories, testing, and methodology designed to find the objective truth. Make sure you understand the contrary theories that may be presented by the opposing party. Incorporate these into your testing and final opinions.

7.   Rigorously test your hypotheses as if you were going to publish the results in a respected, peer-reviewed journal. Do not cut corners, and refrain from the impulse to slant either the data or the methodology.

8.   Meticulously document your testing and the results. It is very damaging to the case to forget why you performed a specific test or, even worse, to forget the results. It is also very unprofessional, not to mention personally embarrassing.

9.   Provide a formal report as described elsewhere in this text. Include the purpose of your work, the evidence reviewed, the testing protocols, the raw data generated by your tests, the results, and your conclusions. Address weaknesses and contrary or inconclusive results. At trial you may be questioned about any part of your reports: therefore, it is a good idea to reference your file so you can easily locate appropriate supporting data when testifying. Confer with counsel to ensure that your testimony and its implications are understood. If counsel assists in drafting your report or authoring your designation, review the final product in detail for accuracy.

10.   You have no obligation before the trial either to meet with the opposing attorney or to volunteer information to him. However, if requested, to prevent the appearance of bias, it is often better to do so.

11.   During cross-examination, answer direct questions from the opposing attorney with concise but polite and complete responses. Admit any weaknesses in the evidence leading to your conclusions. This is often a very effective preemptive strategy, while failure to point out

shortcomings may subject you to effective impeachment that could result in the jury ignoring all of your testimony. Do not spar with the opposing attorney and do not get angry or emotional. Emotionally charged, evasive responses to direct questions can undermine your demeanor of objectivity and professionalism. You may think you have won the battle, but the judge and jury will likely think otherwise.

12.   Maintain your honesty, objectivity, and professional dignity. Treat counsel, the court, and opposing experts with respect. These practices will allow the jury to view you as a messenger of truth.

13.   Have faith in the jury and the system. Believe that if you successfully convey a clear and concise explanation of the evidence, and the attorney coherently explains how the law should be applied to this evidence, justice will prevail.

REFERENCES

1.   Daubert v. Merrell Dow Pharmaceuticals, Inc. 509 U.S. 579, 1993.
2.   Mohan Rv. 2 S.C.R. 9, 1994.
3.   Minasian v. Standard Charter Bank, 109 F.3d 1212, 1216 (7th Cir. 1997).
4.   See generally American Bar Association, Model Rules of Professional Conduct, Preamble: A Lawyer's Responsibilities. See also ABA Model Code of Professional Responsibility, Preamble.
5.   Model Rules 3.1, cmt (1).
6.   Model Rules 3.3(a).
7.   Model Rules 3.4; see also Model Code, EC 7–26 and DR 7–102.

24
Case Law

Robert E. Barsley
Professor and Director, Dental Health Resources LSUHSC School of Dentistry
New Orleans, LA

1. INTRODUCTION

This chapter will guide the reader through a basic understanding of case law as it applies to the field of bitemark evidence. Some cases discussed earlier in the text will be revisited and numerous other cases will be discussed. The reader is referred to Figure 1 for a lesson on understanding the legal citation system. This simple system makes it easy for attorneys and other interested parties to succinctly communicate information about a case. It will be used throughout this chapter.

What is meant by the term "case law"? In American jurisprudence the principle of *stare decisis*, "to stand by that which is decided," establishes the precedent to abide by or adhere to previously decided cases. Under this rule, a point of law, once settled by decision, forms a precedent that is not afterward to be departed from unless a court finds it necessary to overrule a prior case that may have been hastily decided or was decided contrary to principle. Because the legal reporter volumes are filled with such overruled cases, one of the most important obligations of an attorney when researching the law is to be certain that any cases relied upon in making the necessary legal arguments have not been overruled by subsequent cases.

> It is ⋯ a fundamental jurisprudential policy that prior applicable precedent usually must be followed even though the case, if considered anew, might be decided differently by the current justices. This policy ⋯ is based on the assumption that certainty, predictability and stability in the law are the major objectives of the legal system; *i.e.*, that parties should be able to regulate their conduct and enter into relationships with reasonable assurance of the governing rules of law [1].

An appeal court panel is "bound by decisions of prior panels unless an en banc decision, Supreme Court decision, or subsequent legislation undermines those decisions [2]." In the following pages, the phrase "citation omitted" indicates that the court is quoting from an earlier decision in its ruling. The reader is referred to the full text of the decision for the citation.

A considerable amount of case law exists in the area of bitemark evidence in American jurisprudence. A query of the popular legal search engines using the terms "bite mark*," "bitemark*," "bite mark!," or "bitemark!" (depending on the search engine) will return hits in nearly every jurisdiction. Several observers maintain updated listings of appellate court cases containing those terms. Unfortunately, owing to the mechanism of the American legal reporting system, many (perhaps most) of the cases and testimony involving bitemark evidence are not

---

<u>*Daubert v. Merrill Dow Pharmaceuticals, et al (509 US 579, 1993)*</u>
   - the full citation (also called the "style" of the case).

<u>*Daubert v. Merrill Dow Pharmaceuticals, et al*</u>
   - the parties, decisions or cases are often referred to by one of the parties. This decision is
      widely known as "Daubert". Other such cases include the 1973 Roe v. Wade
      which commonly is referred to using both named parties.

<u>*(509 US 579*</u>
   - The reporter name, volume, and starting page number. The decisions of each appellate
      level court in the United States are published in a official text, called a "reporter."
      Today, many are published online by the court as well. The first number (509 in
      this example) refers to the Volume (or book) Number. The reporter name tells in
      which court system or state the case was decided. In this example "US" stands for
      the United States Supreme Court. LA would stand for the Louisiana Supreme
      Court, MS for the Mississippi Supreme Court and so on. Many states have now
      combined to issue their decisions in multi-state volumes such as the So.3d
      meaning the third edition of the Southern Reporter covering states including
      Louisiana, Alabama, and Florida among others. Some cases are reported in more
      than one reporter, for example Daubert is also reported at 113 S.Ct. 2786.
      Finally, the 579 refers to the page upon which the current case report or decision
      begins. Often the case will be cited with a second page also listed (579, 583) in
      which the second number references the page upon which the precise language or
      point at issue can be found.

   Cases that are decided by intermediate level appellate courts will have the name
      (abbreviated) of the court listed prior to the date. For example the case Rinehart
      v. Barnes, 819 So. 2d 564 (Miss. App. 2002) was decided by the Mississippi Court
      of Appeals.

<u>*1993)*</u>
   - The date the decision was issued.

   Additional information about the case may be entered after the date. The words "cert. denied"
   denote that a higher court (usually the state or federal supreme court) has declined to rehear the
   appeal. Similarly the words "rehearing denied" denote that the same court has refused to
   reconsider the case.

   Cases may also be found on web-based reporter systems. While these systems often have their
   own style of citation (most cases are available online well in advance of their actual book
   publication), the official citation and page breaks will be displayed as well.

Figure 1   Abbreviated explanation of the legal citation system.

reported. Only cases that have been argued or heard before an appellate or supreme court on the specific issue of bitemark evidence would be discovered in such a search. Since the prosecution is constitutionally barred from appealing a not guilty verdict in a criminal case, there can exist no appellate decisions for such cases. While the defense or prosecution might have appealed issues concerning admissibility of an expert after a guilty verdict; in every ''not guilty'' case, the gist of the testimony and associated evidentiary issues is lost. Consider for a moment that if Milone had been found not guilty in Illinois in 1976 or Marx in California in 1975, two of the most oft cited appellate decisions about bitemarks would not even exist. It is therefore important to realize that the judge in the courtroom will declare much of the ''law'' involving a particular case. Please see the earlier discussion in this text on Daubert v. Merrell Dow Pharmaceuticals, Inc., 509 U.S. 579 (1993), [2a] and the qualifications of an expert and several subsequent decisions since that case such as *Kumho Tire v. Carmichael*, 526 U.S. 137 (1999), [2b] that declare the judge the gatekeeper for determining the admissibility of expert opinion.

One must also realize that there are parallel systems of laws and courts in America. Each of the 50 states operates an independent court system based upon the laws and constitution of the state. In general, neither the laws nor the court decisions of one state system have any bearing on the legal system of any other state. For the vast majority of legal cases (civil, criminal, and administrative), the decision of the state appellate or supreme court is the final decision. The federal court system adjudicates cases involving violations of federal law, decides disputes between citizens of differing states, and includes numerous specialized courts such as patent, bankruptcy, and military law. The federal Circuit Courts of Appeal and ultimately the United States Supreme Court have final jurisdiction in these cases. Interestingly, while certain state criminal cases may reach the federal courts if violations of federal constitutional law apply, in civil cases in federal court, the federal judiciary often interprets the law of the state in which the case arose.

What, then, can we learn about bitemarks from the case law? To date, no case has been overturned on appeal strictly on the issue of bitemark evidence alone. Similarly, no case has ever held as a matter of law that bitemark evidence is inadmissible; in fact, most courts have readily accepted dental experts (and others) in the field of bitemarks. Additionally, courts have accepted the expert opinion of forensic odontologists in fields of patterned injuries or marks made in human skin by objects other than teeth.

2. FOUNDATION

In order to testify, a forensic dentist must base his or her opinion on an examination and analysis of the materials that comprise the case. How does case law bear on this phase of bitemark evidence? As mentioned in previous chapters, the injury must be compared to the dentition(s) of the suspected biter(s) and other persons. Several constitutional principles are involved here. First, the gathering of this type of evidence must be either voluntarily consented to by the subject, or the provisions of the Fourth Amendment to the U.S. Constitution must be followed — a search warrant is required. To gain a search warrant, the investigating officer must demonstrate to the court probable cause potentially relating the subject (now a suspect) to the crime. It is well established in the American case law that obtaining photographs and dental models of the suspect's dentition does not violate the Fifth Amendment protection against self-incrimination. The surrender of these items is treated as any other exemplar such as handwriting, hair, blood, or DNA samples.

Milone in his first attempt to overturn his murder conviction *Illinois v. Milone*, 356 N.E.2d 1350, IL App. (1976), alleged:

> The pictures of his mouth and the impressions made of his upper and lower teeth, pursuant to a search warrant, were seized in violation of his constitutional rights and that the trial court therefore erred in denying his motion to suppress such evidence. His first argument is that there was an absence of 'probable cause' for the search warrant to issue and says that the affidavits are "so devoid of facts and replete with conclusions that it was impossible for the issuing magistrate to form an independent judgment as to the existence of probable cause." A review of the record shows that the judge was allowed, on the basis of the four affidavits, to determine for himself the persuasiveness of facts relied upon by the affiants and was not forced to rely merely on their conclusions [3].

After discussing the contents of and the circumstances surrounding the production of the affidavits, the Court concludes that "the affidavits attached to the complaint for warrant provided sufficient probable cause for the issuance of the search warrant. Having so held, we need not discuss the defendant's further contention that this dental evidence was the direct result of an unlawful arrest. As the defendant concedes in his brief, the probable cause to search would also establish probable cause to arrest, and so taking the defendant into custody to obtain exemplars of his dentition was proper [4].

Milone continues,

> The defendant also maintains that the techniques employed to obtain the dental evidence amounted to an unconstitutional invasion of his right to privacy and a violation of his privilege against self-incrimination. He relies upon *Rochin v. California* (citation omitted) where the United States Supreme Court found the act of pumping the defendant's stomach against his will to be shocking and repulsive and therefore an invasion of his right to privacy. The situation in the instant case is not analogous. On January 24, 1973, the defendant was taken to a dental office in Wheaton, Illinois, and was asked to sit in a dentist's chair, while photographs and impressions were taken of his teeth. The defendant did not resist, and at no time was the defendant harmed or put in an uncomfortable position. The dentist whose office was being used testified that the police treated the defendant courteously and at no time did he indicate any pain, discomfort or reluctance to have the procedure performed. The techniques used to examine the defendant and to take impressions of his teeth were in accordance with the standard practice, and we cannot find that such procedures were shocking and repulsive. The nature of the procedures and the manner in which they were performed did not invade the defendant's right to privacy [5].

In the Wyoming case, *Seivewright v. State*, 7 P.3d 24, WY (2000), the court when asked by the defense to hold a *Daubert* hearing to bar the testimony of a forensic odontologists stated,

> Because [the] motion for a *Daubert* hearing provided the district court with little reason to hold an evidentiary hearing to analyze [the dentist's] testimony, we find no abuse of discretion in the district court's refusal to hold such a hearing. [The] motion provided the district court neither with authority to establish the methodology or technique being applied was unreliable nor did it assert that another expert would refute reliability. In short, [the request] did nothing more than boldly assert that [the expert's] testimony was unreliable. Under these circumstances, we conclude there was no abuse of discretion in the district court's refusal to hold a *Daubert* hearing. Our conclusion on this issue requires examination of the scientific principle being applied. Bitemark identification is based on the theory of uniqueness. "Identification of a suspect by matching his dentition with a bite mark found on the victim of a crime [or a substance] rests on the theory that each person's dentition is unique."

Here the appellate court cites Giannelli and Imwinkelried [6] and other cases (citations omitted). The court continues,

> Although several methods of bite mark analysis have been reported, "all methods involve three steps: (1) registration of the bite mark and the suspect's dentition, (2) comparison of the dentition and bite mark, and (3) evaluation of the points of similarity or dissimilarity." (citation omitted) [The defense] does not seriously contend that bite mark identification is not a proper subject for expert testimony. Indeed, the courts faced with this question have unanimously concluded that bite mark comparison is a proper subject for expert testimony (citations omitted). While the majority of cases involve flesh bites, courts have also approved bite mark identification in cases involving various foods (citations omitted). Given the wide acceptance of bite mark identification testimony and [the defense's] failure to present evidence challenging the methodology, we find no abuse of discretion in the district court's refusal to hold an evidentiary hearing to analyze [the] testimony. The district court was simply exercising its "discretionary authority ··· to avoid unnecessary 'reliability' proceedings in ordinary cases where the reliability of an expert's methods is properly taken for granted" (citation omitted). While this is not true for all subjects of expert testimony, we are comfortable that it is true under the circumstances of the case at bar [7].

An opposite result was reached by the courts in *Illinois v. Dace*, 506 N.E.2d 332, IL App. (1987), where

> An essential portion of the State's case against the defendant consisted of the testimony of three forensic odontologists who compared the teeth marks on the victim's arm with the teeth of the defendant. Utilizing photographs and impressions of defendant's teeth a comparison was made. The photographs and impressions were obtained by executing a search warrant for them ⋯ on the complaint of Officer Baum of the Joliet police department. The photographs and impressions were taken the following day. The defendant prior to trial moved to suppress this information; however, said motion was denied. The precise question to be determined is whether the defendant's rights under the Federal and State constitutions were violated because the warrant was illegally obtained because of lack of probable cause (citation omitted). An examination of the complaint for search warrant discloses that it contained only two allegations that relate to probable cause. It alleged that the defendant was the last person known to be present with the victim ⋯ while she was still alive ⋯ during the early morning hours of February 21, 1985. The complainant Baum made the further allegation that while interviewing the defendant on February 28, 1985, he was told by the defendant that he in fact was the last person in the club besides the victim and while there he entertained thoughts of having sex with her. The complaint did not indicate the time on February 21, 1985, when the victim's body was found, nor did it attempt to indicate the time of her death. ⋯ That defendant was the last person to be with the victim ⋯ during the early hours of February 21, 1985, may have given the police reason to suspect that he was involved in the homicide. Suspicion, however, does not constitute probable cause (citation omitted). The facts and circumstances within Officer Baum's knowledge would not warrant a man of reasonable caution believing that the defendant committed the offense (citation omitted). We are unaware of any Illinois cases deciding the precise issue of whether probable cause exists where all the knowledge possessed by the police is that the defendant was the last person seen with the victim. A Federal case has held that such minimal knowledge does not support a finding of probable cause (citation omitted). To hold otherwise would be an invasion of constitutionally protected rights. It would permit intrusion upon the constitutional right to privacy and the seizure of fingerprint samples, blood samples, and dental impressions based upon suspicion and probability and not reasonable grounds or probable cause [8].

The search warrant should have at a minimum mentioned the bitemark on the victim.

Another forensic dentist was rebuffed in the recent, as of yet unpublished case *People v. Mostrong*, 2003 Cal App. Unpub. LEXIS 1179, that barred a forensic dentist's expert opinion offered for the defense to establish comparative negligence in an accident. The defense claimed that,

> Welter's genital injuries were bite marks not caused by hitting the dirt after the collision. Defense counsel indicated the testimony was relevant to the defense that the victims ''were not paying attention, were not exercising due care and safety for themselves and ⋯ were the sole cause of the accident.'' The prosecution countered that there was nothing in Welter's medical records indicating the genital injuries were bite marks [9].

The prosecution objected that to admit the offered testimony would be highly prejudicial and countered by eventually dismissing the penalty enhancement on the criminal charge. The court indicated that while it would have allowed the testimony if the enhancement had been claimed,

> reasoning the evidence was relevant and necessary to prove Mostrong did not cause the injuries. The court further indicated the evidence had only minor probative value if Welter's injuries were not going to be considered on the enhancement issue, in light of the other evidence in the case of the victim's contributory negligence and the fact the evidence might

distract the jury. The court ultimately sustained the prosecution's objection on relevancy ⋯ instructing the jury that the enhancement allegations were dismissed. After the court ruled, the defense continued to argue that the proffered evidence revealed Grady and Welter engaged in oral sex, that this explained why the cart lights were off and it mitigated the gross negligence element of the alleged crime. The defense later renewed its request ⋯ offering a letter from [the expert] stating that Welter's genital injuries were bite marks. The court again excluded the evidence, concluding the "misleading confusion" the evidence might have on the jury outweighed its probative value. A trial court has wide discretion in admitting and excluding expert testimony and the exercise of that discretion will not be disturbed on appeal unless it was clearly abused (citation omitted). We conclude the trial court properly excluded the evidence. ⋯ Because the victims' contributory negligence was not a defense, the trial court acted within its discretion when it concluded that the probative nature of the evidence was outweighed by the risk of confusing the issues by focusing the jury's attention on the victims' conduct, rather than on Mostrong's conduct and the elements of the charged offenses. Even if exclusion of the testimony were error, it would not have affected the jury's conclusions in this case because the evidence was merely cumulative. [10]

Canadian forensic dentists have historically faced a more difficult time obtaining suspect dental information and exemplars. The case of *R. V. Stillman*, 37 W.C.B. (2d) 215 (1998):

made the finding that the police had no right to obtain the teeth impressions from the Appellant without his informed consent. The Appellant clearly expressed his refusal to provide bodily samples, yet by threat of force the police obtained the sample. ⋯ They proceed with the lengthy and intrusive process of taking impressions of his teeth. There can be no doubt that the police, by their words and actions, compelled the Appellant to participate in providing the evidence. Equally, there can be no doubt that the evidence of bodily samples constituted conscriptive evidence [11]

In violation of the Charter of Rights and a new trial was ordered. The Canadian Parliament has since enacted a section in the Criminal Code authorizing a justice to issue a warrant to obtain teeth impressions that became effective in June of 1997. In one respect, criminal law in Canada is more uniform than in the United States because, since historically the criminal system in England and its dominions stems from redress of offenses against the Crown, Canada has one set criminal laws for the entire country. Unlike the United States, where each state develops its own criminal law and court system through the sovereign immunity of each state, each Canadian province does not have separate criminal laws. In the Canadian court system there are no individual provincial supreme courts, only one single Supreme Court in Canada.

Questions have also arisen over which type of permission for sample collection is preferred. While voluntary consent can be satisfactory, an argument can always be made that the subject was not fully aware of the gravity of the situation when he or she agreed to the collection and therefore would not have consented had he or she been fully informed. Similarly, the consent may not be adequately drafted to "protect" the "rights" or needs of the prosecution and thus may expose the evidence gathered through it to attack during litigation or trial or on appeal.

The use of the search warrant is also subject to potential problems. A number of forensic dentists have anecdotally reported instances in which evidence collected under a search warrant was disallowed owing to the absence of the named police officer at the site and time when the dental evidence was collected from the subject (although many search warrants use the language "to any law enforcement officer in the state of ————" [or similar words]). A search warrant may be subject to other attacks during trial. Therefore, this author prefers to operate at the command of a court order demanding that the subject present him- or herself to the dentist for the gathering of the specified exemplars.

In the 1978 case of *Vermont v. Howe*, 386 A.2d 1125, VT (1978), the court discussed the case of *United States v. Wade* (citation omitted), stating that the taking of nontestimonial evidence pursuant to court order was not such a "critical stage" at which the defendant has the Sixth Amendment right to the presence of counsel. "Knowledge of the techniques of science and technology is sufficiently available, and the variables in techniques few enough, that the accused has the opportunity for a meaningful confrontation of the Government's case at trial through the ordinary processes of cross-examination ⋯ they are not critical stages since there is minimal risk that his counsel's absence at such stages might derogate from his right to a fair trial" [12].

Although forensic dentists have also stated anecdotally that subjects have been ordered sedated to ensure the collection of dental evidence such as impressions, the author can find no appellate case directly on point. The case of *Winston and Davis v. Lee*, 470 U.S. 753 (1985), held, in a case in which law enforcement officials sought to compel a victim of a crime to undergo surgery to retrieve a bullet that might constitute important evidence in that crime, that:

> The Fourth Amendment is a vital safeguard of the right of the citizen to be free from unreasonable governmental intrusions into any area in which he has a reasonable expectation of privacy. Where the Court has found a lesser expectation of privacy, or where the search involves a minimal intrusion on privacy interests, the Court has held that the Fourth Amendment's protections are correspondingly less stringent. Conversely, however, the Fourth Amendment's command that searches be "reasonable" requires that when the State seeks to intrude upon an area in which our society recognizes a significantly heightened privacy interest, a more substantial justification is required to make the search "reasonable" (citations omitted) [13].

No matter what type of device is selected to obtain dental exemplars, it remains critically important to discuss in advance with the investigating officers the number and types of exemplars that will be needed – two or more impressions of each dental arch, photographs of the teeth and face of the subject, radiographs (if desired), and the taking of a dental and/or medical history in order that all necessary material will be included in either the warrant or court order.

3. QUALIFICATION OF THE EXPERT

What then have courts accepted as bitemark evidence and who has been qualified as experts in these cases? It might surprise many readers to know that the testimony of a dentist is not always required to establish that a bitemark exists. In the seminal bitemark case *Doyle v. State*, 263 S.W.2d 779, TX App (1954), the court appeared to give the greatest weight to testimony from a firearms examiner at the Texas Department of Public Safety who used caliper measurements from a plaster cast of the suspect's exemplar bite into cheese to compare to the bitemark left by the perpetrator in a cheese at the crime scene. The court did note that a local dentist "examined the plaster casts and the photographs and gave his opinion that all were made by the same set of teeth" [14]. In the case *Mobley v. Georgia*, 441 S.E.2d 780, GA App (1994), the defendant at trial objected to

> opinion testimony concerning the bite marks be allowed, as there was no expert witness to testify to it. The State responded that this was a matter for the jury to determine from the evidence, and the court agreed. The police officer later gave the complained-of testimony on direct examination without objection. On cross-examination, the officer referred to the "bite marks," but when defense counsel corrected him by saying "alleged bite marks," the officer agreed. Appellant requested a curative instruction that whether these were in fact bitemarks was for the jury to determine. The court ultimately charged the jury that it judges the facts and is not bound or concluded by the opinion testimony of any witness. This testimony was admissible. It was essentially [the police officer's] way of describing what he saw, so the jury could visualize the same physical condition. "The opinion given by the [witness] was

a conclusion or opinion based upon [his] personal observation of a physical fact and not an [expert] opinion. Description of one's physical observations and opinions logically flowing therefrom have long been admissible in this state (citation omitted)." [Holding in that case] that a lay witness could testify that in her opinion bruises observed by her were caused by a shoe [15].

In a prisoner disciplinary matter, *Hoskins v. McBride*, 2000 U.S. Appeals LEXIS 27398, 7th Cir. (cert. denied), two inmates "were cited for fighting after a disturbance during prison recreation time." According to the report of "two correctional officers ⋯ [one inmate] requested medical attention for injuries he said occurred while playing basketball. When the officers investigated further, they discovered a large quantity of blood on the wall and floor of the recreation area. They also learned that [the inmate] had sustained various injuries, including a bite on his left breast." No expert testimony was required to establish the bona fides of the bitemark and hence the occurrence of the fight (which the inmates later denied ever occurred) [16]. In the case *Louisiana v. Martin*, 645 So.2d 190, LA (1994, rehearing denied) (later upheld at *Martin v. Cain*, 246 F.3d 471, 5th Cir [2001]), the testimony of the defendant's cousin "established that the defendant had a bite mark on his shoulder" [17].

The testimony of a physician may or may not suffice to prove the existence of a bitemark. In an early case, *Rhode Island v. Adams*, 481 A.2d 718, RI (1984),

> It should have been apparent to the trial justice that [a forensic pathologist] was not testifying, to a reasonable degree of medical certainty, that the marks on the victim's wrist were bite marks. Defense counsel had informed the trial justice at side bar that [the doctor] was not an expert in forensic dentistry. Moreover, defense counsel requested that if the prosecutor was going to be allowed to ask the question, then he should be required to answer within a reasonable degree of medical certainty. In light of the fact that he had been clearly forewarned by defense counsel, the trial justice committed error in overruling defense counsel's objection to the question and in denying his motion to strike. This error is illuminated by the fact that [the forensic pathologist] admitted on cross-examination that he could not state with any degree of medical certainty that the marks on the victim's wrist were bite marks. As [he] testified, only an expert in forensic dentistry, which he is not, could testify to that degree of certainty [18].

This particular bitemark testimony not allowed because as the court said, "In a long line of civil cases, this court has required that expert testimony must speak in terms of strong probability, not mere possibility" [19].

Contrast those cases with the unpublished case of *Harris v. Arkansas*, 1992 Ark. App. 728 LEXIS (1992), in which "the state medical examiner, testified that the victim died by strangulation. He also noted the presence of a bite mark above the victim's right breast. [Another] pathologist ⋯ examined the victim's tissue to determine the age of the bite wound in relation to the victim's death. He testified that the injury occurred within ten minutes prior to the cessation of heart activity." After the physicians had established the fact that the injury was a bite mark, the state's "forensic odontologist ⋯ compared photographs of the bite mark and dental impressions taken of appellant's teeth. It was his opinion that appellant's teeth had made the bite marks found on the victim." The defense's forensic dental expert "disputed the opinion of [the state's dental expert] that the bite mark was made by the appellant. However, weighing the evidence, determining credibility, and resolving conflicts in the testimony are matters to be resolved by the fact finder (citation omitted). We cannot say there is no substantial evidence to support appellant's conviction" [20].

4. FORENSIC DENTISTRY AND "DEGREE OF CERTAINTY"

How then does the expert testimony of a dentist figure into this mélange? In an unpublished appellate decision, *Draper v. Adams*, 2000 U.S. App. Lexis 11826, 6th Cir (2000), speaking in an appeal that focused on ineffective assistance of counsel, the court was apparently satisfied with "[a]n expert in forensic dentistry [who] testified that the bite mark on Johnson's back was made by Darian Draper, asserting that he was 90% plus certain of this conclusion" [21]. In another Louisiana case, *Louisiana v. Vital*, 505 So.2d 1006, LA App. (1987), a dentist

> who testified at trial as an expert in the field of forensic dentistry, stated that he took photographs and made impressions of the bite marks left on the victim's breast by the assailant. ⋯ After the dentist thoroughly described the procedure he used in comparing bitemarks, he stated as follows: "The bite on Miss Smothers has a high degree of consistency with that of Mister Vital to the point that I feel I can say that within a reasonable forensic or medical certainty that his teeth would have been able to make that bite mark" [22].

The court was satisfied with that degree of certainty.

In *Illinois v. Queen*, 474 N.E.2d 786, IL App. (1985 rehearing denied) the state's dental expert and the medical examiner

> who performed the autopsy on the victim, testified that he found four bite marks on the victim's body. [He] removed one of these bitemarks by excising the skin containing it; asked why he did not remove the others, he attributed his failure to do so to "stupidity" on his part. [A] dentist trained in forensic dentistry and oral surgery testified that he compared molds made of defendant's dentures with the bitemark on the skin sample excised by [the medical examiner]. After testifying at length regarding his methodology, [the state's dental expert] offered the following conclusion:
>
> Q. And based on what you have testified here today relating to your examination, doctor, your examination of the casts [*sic*] models, the skin specimen, the photographs, did you form an opinion within a reasonable degree of medical, dental certainty?
>
> A. Yes, I did.
>
> Q. Would you tell the ladies and gentlemen of [the] jury what that opinion is?
>
> A. Yes. When I examined this material I came to the conclusion that I could not exclude these dentures as being the mechanism for perpetrating these bite marks.
>
> Q. Why is it? What is it about those dentures that made you come to that conclusion?
>
> A. Well, I feel, when I initially started evaluating this case I went into it with a certain amount of reservance [*sic*] one dealing with some dentures. And I had some questions in my mind whether dentures could perpetrate a mark like this. So, I really strived throughout the entire investigation to exclude these dentures. I felt this was the best approach to take in this particular type of case. If I could find any portion of evidence that would exclude these dentures then I felt as though I would have done my job. When I finally concluded the valuation [*sic*] of the evidence I found nothing that I could definitely exclude these dentures on.
>
> Under re-cross-examination by defense counsel, [the expert] further explained the meaning of his conclusion:
>
> Q. Doctor, the summation of your testimony is that these dentures could have made the bite marks. Is that right?
>
> A. My statement was that I could not exclude these dentures from making the mark.
>
> Q. All right. Does that mean the same thing to you as they could have made the bite mark.
>
> A. That means the same⋯

The court continued,

> Where a verdict of guilty is returned by a jury, it is our duty not only to carefully consider

the evidence, but to reverse the conviction "if the evidence is not sufficient to remove all reasonable doubt of the defendant's guilt and is not sufficient to create an abiding conviction that he is guilty of the crime charged" (citations omitted). Upon careful examination of the record here, we are compelled to conclude that the State failed to prove the defendant guilty beyond a reasonable doubt. ⋯ The forensic dentist who analyzed defendant's dentures and the bite mark on the victim's skin did not say that in his opinion defendant's dentures caused the mark; rather, he could do no more than conclude that they could have done so, and that he could not exclude that possibility. ⋯ The evidence simply does not establish defendant's guilt beyond a reasonable doubt. We therefore reverse the judgment [23].

In the case *Wisconsin v. Stinson*, 397 N.W.2d 136, Wisc. App. (1986), the

jury also heard from two expert witnesses who testified to a reasonable degree of scientific certainty that the multiple bite marks found on the victim's body had been inflicted at or near the time of death. The experts also concluded that Stinson was the only person who could have inflicted the bite marks on the victim. [The first expert] discovered multiple bite marks located on the victim's body ⋯ [and] stated that the availability of bite marks from different parts of the body eliminated the possibility that the impressions obtained may have been distorted. He also testified as to the methods used in preserving and comparing the bite mark evidence gathered. A total of fourteen upper and lower jaw impressions were made from the bite marks found on [the victim's] body. Because of the opportunity to examine so many bites, and the fact that some of the bites were so deep as to be three-dimensional, [the expert] testified he was able to detect a repetition of some particularly unique features in several of the bites. [He] later performed a forensic odontological examination of Stinson ⋯ [that allowed him to note] the following unique features: one of the central incisors was fractured and decayed almost to the gum line; the lateral incisor in the upper jaw was set back from the other teeth; all of the upper front teeth were flared; the lower right lateral incisor was worn to a pointed edge; the right incisor was set out from the other teeth on the lower jaw. [He then] used these features along with the arch of the mouth and the spacing, width, and alignment of the teeth to make comparisons with the bite marks found on the victim. After an exhaustive examination of the photos, models and tissue samples taken from Stinson and the victim, [he] concluded, to a reasonable degree of scientific certainty, that the bite marks on the victim were made by Stinson [24].

Continuing on in Stinson, the second dental expert

concluded, based on the workup ⋯ [already] performed on both the victim and Stinson, that Stinson had inflicted the bite marks on the victim. In [his] opinion the evidence in the case was overwhelming and he stated that "if we have four or five teeth that we are able to examine, then we can say that there is no other set of dentition like that." In this case, [the first expert] was able to identify seventy-five individual tooth marks in various combinations of between five and eleven teeth. Based upon this evidence, we hold that a jury could reasonably conclude beyond a reasonable doubt that Stinson murdered [the victim]. The reliability of the bite mark evidence in this case was sufficient to exclude to a moral certainty every reasonable hypothesis of innocence [25].

The previously discussed case of *Vermont v. Howe*, 386 A.2d 1125, VT (1978), also mentioned the degree of certainty required of an expert. The trial court

allowed the State to cross-examine an expert witness for appellant "on any matters which are material and in issue in this case." This expert, a forensic odontologist, testified on direct examination that contrary to the opinion of the prosecution's expert odontologist it was not possible to determine that a particular person was the maker of a bitemark to the exclusion of all others. The State was allowed on cross-examination to ask the defense expert if he had observed the models of appellant's dentition and the photographs of the bitemarks and if so, whether the expert found the bitemark to be "consistent" with appellant's dentition.

Apparently he agreed that they were and the court accepted "consistent" as the required degree of certainty [26]. As already noted in the previously discussed case *Rhode Island v. Adams*, the court said "this court has required that expert testimony must speak in terms of strong probability, not mere possibility [27]."

The degree of certainty was expressed as a mathematical probability by the forensic dentist in the case *Arizona v. Garrison*, 585 P.2d 563, AZ (1978) "that there is an eight in one million probability that the teeth marks found on the deceased's breasts were not made by appellant. ⋯ [He] obtained the figure of eight in one million not from personal mathematical calculations, but from 'articles written in the journals of the American Academy of Forensic Sciences' and two books, and 'there are articles written throughout the literature that do mention the possibility or the numerical values of finding two [sets of teeth] of the [exact] same[ness].'" The court went on to state, "we do not think the admission of the eight in a million statement is reversible error. Were we to reverse on this ground, it would only result in a retrial at which the same evidence would be admitted since [his] testimony, obtained from published treatises and periodicals would be admissible. ⋯ Courts should not engage in such futile practices" [28].

That same year in a neighboring state, the case *People v. Slone*, 143 Cal. Rptr. 61, Cal. App. (1978), three forensic dentists testified for the prosecution. After describing the tests and processes involved in arriving at their opinions, further testimony elicited from one of them "could not exclude defendant's dentition. ⋯ [He] found a minimum of 10 [ten] points of significant correlation between the bite mark that was on [the] body and defendant's dentition. Of the 414 dentitions culled from thousands of records at the U.C.L.A. clinic, [he] found only three which had any points of similarity to the bite mark; he made wax impressions of these dentitions and studied them further. They were eventually ruled out" [29]. The second expert for the prosecution "also studied the impressions made of the teeth of [five] other males who had seen [her] on December 19, 1975. By the use of slides as evidentiary exhibits, [he] concluded that these individual dentitions could not be matched positively with the bite mark on the victim. He testified concerning the three most similar models found at the U.C.L.A. Dental Clinic — and pointed out their essential dissimilarity with the bite mark replica" [30]. The Court also ruled,

> There is no merit to defendant's corollary contention that by employing screening of thousands of cases at the U.C.L.A. Dental Clinic, the experts were attempting to impose mathematical probability statistics or odds on the fact-finding process, an evidentiary principle rejected by the California Supreme Court (citation omitted). The experts in the instant case were simply attempting to negate the potential disapproval of their scientific method in the area of specificity — the problem posed by the defense counsel, who inquired whether the experts could testify that no other human being on the planet could have bit the victim on the thigh. The expert witnesses were careful to say that they could not. There is a probability factor in even the most carefully structured scientific inquiry; seldom is it possible to exclude all possible chance for error in human endeavor. But there is no requirement in our law that the admissibility of scientific-test evidence must be predicated on a 100 percent degree of accuracy [31].

5. BATTLING EXPERTS

The issue of "hotly contested" bitemarks has frequently arisen in bitemark cases. First with dental experts who have a fundamental disagreement — whether or not the injury in question even represents a bitemark at all. A second area that is subject to vigorous argument surrounds the certainty of any linkage between the suspected biter (often the criminal defendant) and the injured party. Several recent cases demonstrate these types of disagreement and the courts' resolution of bitemark evidence issues. In *State v. Duncan*, 802 So.2d 533, LA (2001, cert. denied), the court was faced with the defendant's appellate argument that the trial judge erred in prohibiting his expert "from showing the jury photographs depicting 'actual' bite marks. The 'actual' bite mark pictures, depicting bite marks made by unknown biters on the bodies of various unknown victims, were part of a booklet prepared by defendant's expert." Additionally, this booklet included several pages of written materials explaining the characteristics of bite marks along with several pictures of the victim in the case [32].

In *Duncan*, the questions on appeal were did the trial judge err in ruling the booklet itself could not be used as demonstrative evidence. The second issue was "whether the judge erred in ruling the 'actual' bite mark pictures [from the booklet] could not be used. ··· At trial, the issue of whether certain wounds on the victim's body were bite marks was hotly contested." The odontologist who testified on behalf of the state claimed "that several marks on the victim's body were bite marks that with varying degrees of certainty matched defendant's dentition." The defense relied on two bitemark experts, one a forensic pathologist and the other a forensic odontologist. "Both defense experts testified that these marks on the victim's body were not bite marks" at all. During the direct examination of their forensic odontological expert, "the defense sought to distribute to the jury the booklet ··· prepared to 'educate' them about what genuine bite marks look like." The expert summarized the contents as follows:

> Generally the material is what I was given in 1996, on this case and it contains reprints from the odontology information on bite mark evaluation, terminology and standards for bite marks. It also has a section in there that has a series of bite marks of cases that I have done to show Juries what a real bite mark looks like and then a little demonstrative part in there to show them when we talk about how we identify people and what bite marks look like and how we can identify people by the class and individual characteristics.

The booklet contained 23 pages, the first 10 of which discuss bitemark analysis generally and five photographs of bite marks from other, unrelated cases. The remaining pages contained various photographs of the victim [33].

The *Duncan* decision echoed the trial judge's sustaining the prosecution's objection to the use of the booklet, ruling the testimony "needed to be restricted to evidence that has been presented in the case ··· [and that the] trial judge clearly was entitled to prohibit the defense's expert from turning his courtroom into a classroom." The defense odontologist's testimony that none of the markings on the victim's body were bite marks was premised, at least in part, on the fact that all of these marks were single arches; *i.e.*, they lacked the corresponding other arch's teeth prints, and his opinion was that such single-arch bitemarks are rare.

> In disallowing the photographs of bite marks on others (not the victim), the trial judge reasoned that it was the circumstantial use of such photographs that he found objectionable, stating: "if you're going to use a picture now, look here's a bite mark made on so and so over her[e] just look at the difference? Now, how is that fair?" The implication, the judge stated, is "that all bite marks have got to be like this. Now, the picture of [the victim] doesn't look like that so that's not a bite mark." Still further, the judge reasoned that while [the doctor] could voice his opinion that there were no bite marks based on photographs of the victim "I don't want him to show a picture of somebody else that's bitten almost all the way through or more pronounced bite and say now here's a bite mark, that's not a bite mark"[34].

In *Duncan* the appellate court concluded that the defense was not precluded from "presenting a defense; rather, the trial judge allowed [the defense expert] to testify fully as to why he opined the marks on the victim's body were not bite marks." Additionally, the decision discusses other effective ways to educate jurors about bitemarks, such as having them bite themselves or taking "the mold of defendant's dentition and [using] it to bite things like an apple, or people" [35].

Contrast that result with the outcome in a neighboring state when a similar dilemma was presented to the appeals court. In *Kinney v. State of Arkansas*, 868 S.W.2d 463, AR (1994), the odontologist for the state sought to introduce into evidence a photograph of another child's penis (not the victim in the case) "to demonstrate bite marks on a penis" for the jury that "was instructed that the pictures were from another case and not the present victim." The defense alleged the picture was irrelevant and was used to inflame the jury and that if there were any relevancy to this picture, it was outweighed by unfair prejudice under the rules of evidence. The trial judge heard in-chambers arguments regarding the photograph. The state's expert "explained to the judge that he used his previous experience, the photograph in question being one of those cases, to determine the origin of bite marks. The questioned photograph was known to be that of bite marks on an infant's penis because the perpetrator in that case admitted to doing so. The trial judge admitted the photograph for demonstrative purposes only, and the jury was informed that this photograph was not of the victim." The appeals court held that the "admissibility of photographs is a matter within the sound discretion of the trial court, and we do not reverse its rulings unless it abused its discretion (citation omitted). Even inflammatory photographs are admissible if they tend to shed light on an issue, enable a witness to better describe the objects portrayed, or enable the jury to better understand the testimony (citation omitted)" [36]. In the Duncan case above, it was the state arguing that the photographs in question were prejudicial and that their probative value was greatly outweighed by their potential to confuse or mislead the jury.

A court in the state of Washington was faced with the question of whether or not a photograph of the defendant in *Washington v. Kendrick*, 736 P.2d 1079, Wash. App. (1987), with dental retractors in place to expose his teeth and gums was gruesome. The defendant characterized the pose as "vampire-like." The court ruled that it

> is clear that ··· [the photograph's] probative value outweighed any unfair prejudicial impact. The photograph of Kendrick's teeth was offered in connection with the testimony of an odontologist who opined that Kendrick's bite mark was consistent with the bite mark on [the victim's] breast. The photographs aided the witness in explaining a rather complex theory. Moreover, the jury was told both why the photograph was necessary and why the dental retractors were employed in the taking of the photograph. It was therefore within the court's discretion to admit the challenged photographs [37].

An often more hotly contested area of disagreement between forensic odontologists concerns the linkage of a particular suspect's teeth to a bite injury. Perhaps the most discussed and quoted case is that of Richard Milone, convicted in 1973 in a bench trial (no jury) of the murder of Sally Kandell, *Illinois v. Milone*, 356 N.E.2d 1350, Ill App (1976).

> The [trial] record contains over 1300 pages of dental testimony and numerous exhibits including photographs and impressions which were admitted into evidence at trial. Briefly, this evidence included the testimony of three State expert witnesses who asserted that, in their opinion, Richard Milone was without a doubt the perpetrator of the bite on the victim's thigh. The defendant, on the other hand, presented four expert witnesses who concluded that no positive correlation could be made between the defendant's dentition and the bite mark in question.

The body was found in a state of extreme rigor mortis and taken to the morgue where the bitemark was observed and photographed. An "impression of the bite mark was made and clear plastic overlays were placed on the wound and the markings were traced on the plastic. These exhibits, along with the pictures and casts of the defendant's teeth, provided the basis for the comparison made by all of the experts. There was ample testimony that because of the advanced state of rigor mortis, the victim's leg was immobile and thus there could be no distortion of the bite mark resulting from movement of the leg.'' The

> State's leading expert testified that, in terms of quality for comparison purposes, the bite mark on the victim's thigh was an excellent specimen. The marks were clear, the quality of the marks was good, and because the victim was already deceased when the bite was inflicted, the skin and underlying tissue provided an unchanging medium for the marks. As the most experienced of the expert witnesses, [he] testified that in the course of his work as a dentist and instructor in forensic dentistry he had seen between 200 and 300 bite marks in human skin and had been called upon to give his opinion in five bite-mark cases. In comparing the defendant's dentition to the bite mark in the instant case, [he] enumerated 29 points of comparison between the marks and the defendant's dentition which led him to identify positively the defendant as the perpetrator of the bite. In addition, [he] was able to produce an explanation for the distortion which appeared in one segment of the bite mark by inflicting bite marks on human skin, with casts of defendant's teeth [38].

In *Milone*, a second expert for the state,

> an orthodontist for 20 years and chairman of the Department of Orthodontics at Northwestern Dental School, testified that he had seen over 40,000 casts of teeth in his work and that in his opinion, every individual's dentition is as distinct as his fingerprints. He concurred with the positive identification made by [the first state's expert] and pointed out that less than 1% of the population would have a fracture of the left central incisor as was observed in the casts of the defendant's teeth and the bite mark on the victim. He stated that this correlation, along with a number of other outstanding characteristics present in both the mark and the defendant's dentition, could leave no doubt that defendant had inflicted the bite [39].

In this case the third state's expert, a dentist and forensic pathologist, ''testified that, compared to numerous bite marks he had seen on human bodies or read about in forensic literature, the bite mark in question was good in terms of definity of points, clarity, lack of distortion, and lack of decompositional change. He also found numerous unique and specific points of identification which enabled him to concur with the other State experts in their positive identification of Richard Milone as the perpetrator of the bite [40].''
In contrast to the prosecution,

> The four forensic odontologists called by the defendant testified that it is far easier to exclude a suspect through bite-mark comparison than to positively identify a subject through the marks left by his teeth. All four pointed out areas of inconsistency between the bite mark and the moulds of defendant's teeth, and for this reason either denied that a positive identification could be made, or specifically ruled out the defendant as the person responsible for the tooth marks on the victim [41].

''In rebuttal, the State witnesses explained why the inconsistencies pointed out by the defense experts existed, and steadfastly held that defendant's teeth made the impression on the victim's thigh.'' The court in its discussion of the dental evidence commented ''that the record in this case reflects the utmost diligence and care in preparation by the investigating police, the State's Attorney, and counsel for the defendant. It must be realized that our synopsis of the dental testimony hardly does justice to the 1300 pages of intense examination which took place at trial, and, without the painstaking care exercised in preserving evidence; none of the dental testimony would have been available. Had the quality of the scientific or legal preparation been less thorough, we might have given less credence to this entire area of inquiry [42].''
Milone's counsel contends that the ''State should have been precluded from introducing such evidence to identify him as the perpetrator of the bite mark because under the then prevailing

Frye Test he claimed that bite-mark identification as a science has not 'gained general acceptance in the particular field in which it belongs,' and therefore should not be admissible in a court of law.'' Offering statements made by four forensic odontologists to support this contention that downplayed the ability of bite marks to link a biter and a bite, the court stated that the statements relied upon were not dispositive in the case at bar.

> A lack of complete unanimity in the medical profession as to the reliability of certain scientific testimony does not mean that such testimony fails to satisfy the requirements of Frye. ⋯ Bite-mark comparison ⋯ involves only a visual comparison between the wound and the dentition of the defendant. The great care taken to preserve and gather the physical evidence in this case precludes any problems arising in regard to the quality of the exhibits being compared. For this reason, the testimony of the experts serves only to lend assistance to the trial court in interpreting physical evidence not within the ken of the average trial judge's knowledge. There is no intermediate mechanical stage in which reliability may be questioned. Such evidence is more analogous to footprint, fingerprint, and hair, comparisons which are made for purposes of identification. ⋯ The court differentiated between the interpretation of mechanical measurements such as print-outs from a polygraph, and testimony based upon direct observation of physical characteristics such as the characteristics of a bite mark and the known dentition of a suspect [43].

The *Milone* court, citing the earlier Illinois case of *People v. Mattox,* 237 N.E.2d 845, Ill. App. (1968), in which the court stated,

> Although a question of first impression in this State, it cannot be seriously disputed that a dental structure may constitute a means of identifying a deceased person, otherwise unrecognizable, where there is some dental record of that person with which the structure may be compared. Comparison of dental structures falls within the category of circumstantial evidence and involves the question of weight and credibility, rather than that of competency [44].

Having thus taken judicial notice that the unique quality of an individual's dentition had already been recognized for purposes of body identification, the court *Milone* reasoned that ''[t]he concept of identifying a suspect by matching his dentition to a bite mark found at the scene of a crime is a logical extension of the accepted principle that each person's dentition is unique'' [45]. The court went on to cite numerous cases in other jurisdictions along with articles in scientific and legal journals to show that

> the trial judge was correct in allowing expert testimony to aid his comparison between the bite mark on Sally Kandel's thigh and the dentition of the defendant. The weight given this testimony was within the province of the court, and nothing in the record indicates that the trial judge abused his discretion in allowing the testimony. Keeping in mind the excellent quality of the dental evidence introduced at trial, we conclude and hold that it was properly admitted [46].

Ten years later, in an appeal in the federal court system, *Milone v. Camp,* 22 F.2d 693, 2nd Cir. (1994, cert. denied),

> Milone raises several issues in his habeas petition that were not presented to any state court. He wishes the Court to excuse his failure to exhaust all of his state remedies on the ground that it would constitute a miscarriage of justice, due to his innocence of the murder, not to entertain his petition. In support of his claim of actual innocence Milone makes the following points:
>
> 1) The evidence presented at his trial that linked his dentition to the bite mark found on Sally's thigh was unreliable. First, it failed both the *Frye* and the *Daubert* tests of admissibility of scientific evidence because the science of ''forensic odontology'' was in its infancy at the

time of his 1973 trial. Second, expert testimony is now available (and is reliable because the science of forensic odontology has advanced considerably in the past 20 years) tending to show that Milone could not have made the mark found on Sally's thigh. Indeed, the mark on Sally's thigh can now be shown to match the dentition of a known serial murderer, Richard Macek.

2) Richard Macek confessed to the murder of Sally Kandel several times before committing suicide in his jail cell in 1987. (The parties dispute whether Macek also recanted these confessions.)

The federal appeals court continued,

[the] admissibility of evidence is generally a matter of state law (citations omitted). In this case, the Illinois Appellate Court held that the state's expert testimony was admissible. Absent a showing that the admission of the evidence violated a specific constitutional guarantee, a federal court can issue a writ of habeas corpus on the basis of a state court evidentiary ruling only when that ruling violated the defendant's right to due process by denying him a fundamentally fair trial. The standard, then, is not whether the testimony satisfied the *Frye* or *Daubert* tests neither of which purports to set a constitutional floor on the admissibility of scientific evidence but rather is whether the probative value of the state's evidence was so greatly outweighed by its prejudice to Milone that its admission denied him a fundamentally fair trial. It is clear that the probative value of the odontology evidence presented by the state was not so outweighed by its prejudice to Milone as to deny him a fundamentally fair trial. With respect to its probative value, while the science of forensic odontology might have been in its infancy at the time of trial, as Milone asserts, certainly there is some probative value to comparing an accused's dentition to bite marks found on the victim. With respect to the prejudice to Milone caused by the admission of what he claims was unreliable evidence, he had ample opportunity to persuade the trial judge to discount the testimony of the state's expert: Milone was able to cross-examine the state's expert both in regard to his credentials and in regard to the general reliability of the science of bite mark identification, and Milone presented several experts of his own to testify that he could not have made the mark found on Sally's thigh. Accordingly, it was not constitutional error for Illinois to have allowed the admission of the bite mark evidence. ⋯ [T]he evidence adduced against Milone at trial reveals that there was sufficient evidence to support his conviction. He had an opportunity to commit the crime, he was linked to the murder weapon, and evidence was introduced from which a reasonable finder of fact could conclude that Milone was observed near the scene of the murder and that his dentition was linked to the bite mark found on the victim [47].

6. QUALIFYING TO TESTIFY, PARTICULARLY THE FIRST TIME FOR AN EXPERT

How, then, does the dentist initially get into court? The following cases describe the reasoning of various courts when facing forensic dentists who were making their first foray into the courtroom, either in general or as an expert in bite marks. In the 1977 case *Niehaus v. Indiana*, 359 N.E.2d 513, IN (1977), the state's expert

acknowledged that the identification of suspects by this manner of comparison between marks in human tissue and the teeth of suspects was a relatively new procedure and had not yet been extensively used. He further acknowledged that this was the first occasion of his having personally undertaken such a determination. From this, the defendant contends that the field is not sufficiently recognized for reliability as to qualify as an area of expertise and that [the doctor] was not sufficiently experienced in the area to qualify as an expert. ⋯ [T]he defendant relies upon holdings excluding evidence of polygraph test results as not being sufficiently reliable. ⋯ The method of identification utilized here, however, is simply a matter of comparison of items of physical evidence to determine if they are reciprocal. The methods for making such comparisons are indeed complex and require skilled technicians to perform, but they consist of standardized procedures known to procure accurate models and measurements. We see no reason why such evidence should be rejected as unreliable, simply because it has thus far had limited application. As for the qualifications of [the expert], we deem it unnecessary to go into great detail. His testimony revealed that he was a graduate dentist with some thirty years of practice and teaching experience. He had become interested in this subject several years earlier, had attended twelve to fifteen lectures and read thirty to forty articles upon the subject by others experienced in the field. The determination of whether a witness is qualified to testify as an expert lies in the sound discretion of the trial court and may not be set aside unless there is manifest abuse of discretion (citations omitted) [48].

Three years later, in Kansas, another court held in *Kansas v. Peoples*, 605 P.2d 135, KS (1980), a case in which the admissibility of expert testimony on bitemark identification was a matter of first impression in Kansas and also citing the language of the *Niehaus* case,

We think bite-mark identification by an expert witness is sufficiently reliable and can be a valuable aid to a jury in understanding and interpreting evidence in a criminal case. When the witness has the requisite skill and experience, and demonstrates the accuracy and reliability of his models, photographs, X-rays and supporting exhibits in bite-mark identification, the trial court in the exercise of its power of discretion may properly admit the opinion testimony of the expert witness [49].

The defendant also challenged the admission of the state's dental expert opinion testimony,

claiming that an inadequate foundation was presented to qualify [him] as an expert, and that the exhibits and models were inaccurate. [The state's expert] described himself as a general dentist, specializing in forensic odontology. He was a ⋯ graduate of Northwestern University, and served five years in the military before entering private practice. He is a certified diplomat of the American Board of Forensic Odontology [*sic*], a fellow in the American Academy of Forensic Sciences, and a member of the American Society of Forensic Odontology. He teaches forensic odontology to senior students and provides continuing education courses for graduate dentists at the University of Colorado School of Dentistry ⋯ [and] has been a consultant for various law enforcement agencies, including the Kansas and Colorado Bureaus of Investigation. He has attended many lectures and seminars on forensic odontology and is acquainted with the major literature and experts in the field of bite-mark identification. [He] testified at length about the various procedures and practices underlying bite-mark identification. The testimony spans more than 150 pages in the record. He discussed the manner of comparing dental casts, wax impressions, and photographs. He also testified to the numerous factors that are considered in bite-mark identification. In comparing the appellant's dentition with the bite marks ⋯ us[ing] casts and photos of the appellant's teeth and compar[ing] those to the bite marks shown in the photographs of the victim ⋯ [and] several photographic enlargements of the bite marks, the cast of the appellant's teeth, and the wax imprints to illustrate the many shared characteristics of the teeth and the bite marks. All of these exhibits and models were admitted into evidence. After explaining the procedure he used to develop the exhibits and identify the many important points of comparison, [he] gave his opinion. He testified that in his opinion it was highly probable that the appellant had bitten the left breast of [the victim] [50].

The appellate court continued, "After carefully reviewing the detailed testimony ⋯ we find no error in the trial court's admission of his testimony. [The doctor] was sufficiently qualified to be an expert witness and provided an adequate foundation for his testimony. He was shown to have special skill and expertise in the field of forensic odontology, and was qualified to impart this otherwise unavailable knowledge to the jury (citation omitted)." The appellant specifically challenges "the use and admission of a set of dental casts and several enlarged photographs. [The state's expert] testified to the origin and production of those exhibits and stated he found them reliable and acceptable for his use. The trial court did not abuse its discretion in admitting those exhibits. Any discrepancies go to the weight of that evidence, and the testimony based upon it, and are properly a matter for the jury (citations omitted) [51]."

Six years later, the Supreme Court of Massachusetts in *Commonwealth v. Cifizzari*, 492 N.E.2d 356, MA (1986), in another case of first impression "summarize[d] the experts' testimony in some detail because the major issue raised in this appeal is the admissibility of their opinions" [52]. The court stated that the

> admissibility of expert dental witnesses' testimony does not depend on meeting the Frye test. The experts' testimony merely aided the jury in comparing the photographs of the bite marks with the defendant's dental impressions. The [trial] judge, in expressing his position that perhaps expert testimony was not necessary on the subject, reached the core issue which is that bite mark evidence is merely a valuable tool to the jury in understanding and interpreting the evidence [53].

The court went on to note, "Other jurisdictions that generally follow the principles of the Frye test have reached the same conclusion that we have concerning the admissibility of expert testimony concerning bite marks (citations omitted)." The court then cited the California case of Marx holding "that the determination of general acceptance of bite mark identification in the scientific community goes to the weight rather than admissibility of the evidence. ⋯ It was open to defense counsel to impeach the doctors as to the methods used. Defense counsel raised the issue that skin elasticity, blood pressure, and plane variations, as affecting the photographs, could have some effect on the reliability of the doctor's ultimate conclusions" [54].

Fourteen years later, a court in the Louisiana case *Louisiana v. Wommack*, 770 So.2d 365, LA App. (2000), discussed a defense attack on the testimony from two experts, one an oral surgeon and the other a forensic pathologist.

> Before accepting the testimony of the experts, the trial court conducted a hearing pursuant to *Daubert v. Merrell Dow Pharmaceuticals, Inc.* (citation omitted). Commenting on *Daubert* and its applicability in Louisiana cases, a panel of this court has explained:

> In *Daubert*, the Supreme Court suggested that the trial court should consider four factors in determining whether expert scientific evidence is reliable: (1) whether the theory or technique can be, and has been, tested; (2) whether it has been subjected to peer review and publication; (3) the known or potential rate of error of the theory or technique; and (4) whether the theory or technique is generally accepted in the scientific community. ⋯ The [State] relies upon La. Code of Evidence Article 702, which states: If scientific, technical, or other specialized knowledge will assist the trier of fact to understand the evidence or to determine a fact in issue, a witness qualified as an expert by knowledge, skill, experience, training, or education, may testify thereto in the form of an opinion or otherwise [55].

The court continued saying,

> Although the trial court considered the expert testimony in a separate hearing, the Daubert standards do not appear to be readily applicable to the present case. Neither expert used complex testing in identifying the wound found on Wommack's arm. In simplest terms, [the oral surgeon] made his determinations after inspecting the wound within days of the offense and [the pathologist] reached his opinion after looking at pictures of it. Expert opinion testimony based upon personal observation and experience is admissible (citation omitted). [The oral surgeon's] testimony at the *Daubert* hearing revealed his significant background in various aspects of dentistry and oral surgery [56].

After conducting an extensive *Daubert* hearing, the trial court concluded that [the oral surgeon] had sufficient experience and training to identify Wommack's wound as a human bite-mark. The court further ruled that [he] would not be allowed to testify regarding the age of the mark, or to identify it as matching the victim's dental pattern. In view of [his] extensive experience, we conclude that the lower court did not abuse its discretion in accepting him as an expert. The other expert who testified about the bite ··· did not personally examine the defendant. Rather, he viewed photographs of the wound the week prior to trial. At the *Daubert* hearing, [he] testified that he had no special training in bite-mark identification and had never given testimony on the subject. Although he works as a forensic pathologist, [he] is not board certified. He noted that along with being the coroner for Calcasieu Parish, he is the jail physician ··· [and] stated that he has seen human bite-marks and is familiar with their appearance. He sees bite-marks from jail fights once or twice per year. He reviewed the photographs of Wommack's wound and formed the opinion that it resulted from a human bite. ··· [H]e could testify whether or not the wound was consistent with a human bite. On cross-examination, he estimated his error rate would be approximately forty-nine percent. He used the same figure at trial, but on redirect placed the error rate closer to ten percent [57].

Considering the transcript of the hearing, we do not find that the lower court abused its discretion in accepting [the pathologist] as an expert. Further, even if [his] testimony regarding Wommack's wound should have been excluded, we find any such error harmless. As discussed above ··· an oral-maxillofacial surgeon presented strong credentials and testified the wound was a human bite-mark. The jury was also presented with numerous photographs of the wound found on the defendant's arm. These assignments [of error] have no merit [58].

In the previously discussed case *Seivewright v. State*, 7 P.3d 24, WY (2000), the court was faced with another challenge to a dentist testifying about a bitemark. In answering the defense's contention that the expert was not "board certified" the appellate court responded,

[The] chief complaint is that [he] was not qualified to offer expert testimony because he is not certified by the American Board of Forensic Odontologists [*sic*] (ABFO), which has established standards for qualification to testify as an expert in the field of forensic odontology. [The defense] directs us to no authority establishing that ABFO certification is a prerequisite to testifying as an expert in the field of forensic odontology. Indeed, an expert need only have sufficient "knowledge, skill, experience, training, or education" to qualify as an expert (citation omitted). Therefore, the question is simply whether [he] was qualified to testify despite his lack of ABFO certification. The record establishes that [he] has been a practicing orthodontist for nearly 20 years. In addition to being a board certified orthodontist with a master's degree in the field, he previously qualified to testify as an expert. He has also worked in the field of forensic odontology, for the local coroner, since 1980 and has completed numerous courses in that field. Given these credentials, we can find no abuse of discretion in permitting [him] to testify despite his lack of ABFO certification (citation omitted, "An expert need only have experience and knowledge which is not common to the world.").

The decision continues,

[The defense] also complains [the dentist] was not qualified to testify because of admissions the doctor made under cross-examination. In addition to admitting he was not an expert, but "most qualified," [the dentist] stated that, without training as a dentist or orthodontist, even ··· trial counsel could have rendered an opinion on whether a particular person took a bite of a piece of cheese. It is, however, the function of the jury to sort out the weaknesses and the strengths of expert testimony (citations omitted "Vigorous cross-examination, presentation of contrary evidence, and careful instruction on the burden of proof are the traditional and appropriate means of attacking shaky but admissible evidence.") ··· and we conclude [his] statements go to the weight to be given his testimony, and not to admissibility. Finally, [the complained-of] testimony was more involved than his admission under cross-examination would indicate and thus helpful to the trier of fact. Not only did he make the impressions of the cheese and [the defendant's] teeth, [the dentist] performed a more thorough examination than the naked-eye analysis suggested by defense counsel ⋯ [explaining] how he measured the teeth spacings in reaching his conclusions, explain[ing] in detail the peculiar idiosyncracies [*sic*] found in [the defendant's] dentition, and ultimately concluded that [the defendant] had bitten the cheese. The testimony was thus helpful to the trier of fact, and we find no abuse of discretion in its admission [59].

7. ADMISSION VERSUS WEIGHT OF THE EXPERT'S TESTIMONY AND OPINION

An interesting case from Illinois describes the court's findings when the state's expert dentist was challenged by the defense upon changing his expert opinion. In *Illinois v. Holmes*, 601 N.E.2d 985, IL App (1992), the first forensic dental report attributed different teeth of the same suspect to several bite injuries. In addition, the state's expert was allowed to testify as to his opinion on the manipulation of the injured area that must have occurred in order for the bites have to have attained their size and shape as well as why certain teeth made no marks. The discovery of an additional photograph of the injured area taken by the medical examiner's office but not originally furnished to him, allowed him to reissue an amended report linking different teeth of the same suspect to the injured areas. A second state's forensic dentist agreed with the testimony [60]. The first defense forensic dentist

testified that the injuries found on the victim's body were not bite marks at all. With respect to the injuries on the victim's jaw, [he] said he had difficulty analyzing how the bite marks could have been inflicted in the direction that these marks made in the absence of a drag pattern ⋯ he noticed that the drag patterns went in the opposite direction of the alleged bite mark ⋯ [and he] explained that it would have been physically impossible for defendant to have inflicted the mark because his head would have been in the way. He reached this conclusion after attempting unsuccessfully to place a model of a head in such a position that a bite mark could have been inflicted [61].

The second defense expert "stated that the injuries on the right side of the victim's jaw were not bite marks. He explained that he saw a series of different types of injuries in that area and that they lacked the pattern of a bite mark." The court concluded that,

With regard to defendant's argument that the State's experts assumed facts not in evidence, the State maintains that [the state's expert's] opinion that defendant's teeth caught on the victim's T-shirt was a plausible explanation for the lack of lower teeth marks and that his opinion was supported by evidence which showed that the victim was wearing a T-shirt which was pulled up near her breast. Although it appears that [the state's expert] was speculating that defendant's teeth may have caught on the victim's shirt in order to explain the lack of a corresponding set of marks on the clavicle injury, and assuming that the court erred in admitting such testimony, its ruling should not be reversed absent a clear showing that the trial court abused its discretion to the manifest prejudice of the defendant (citation omitted). Moreover, regarding defendant's argument that the State's experts' testimony was impeached, as the State points out, the credibility of an expert is a matter for the trier of fact to determine (citation omitted), and if expert testimony is conflicting, the reviewing court should not substitute its judgment for that of the trier of fact (citation omitted). We note further that the ultimate issue is for the court and not the expert to decide (citation omitted) [62].

In a 1996 federal appeal of his 1985 murder conviction *Spence v. Scott*, 80 F.3d 989, 5th Cir. (1996, cert. denied), the defendant complains that the district court erred in not holding a hearing on his challenge to the admission of testimony by the State's forensic odontologist ⋯ Spence contends that, because he submitted materials challenging [the expert's] methodology and conclusions, the district court should have held a hearing to determine whether the admission of [that] testimony violated the Eight Amendment's requirement of "heightened reliability" under *Johnson v. Mississippi* (citation omitted). *Johnson* is, however, inapplicable to the instant case. In *Johnson*, the Supreme Court vacated the death sentence because the jury had been allowed to consider evidence that was false [63].

In a footnote, the Court stated that the false evidence was "the sole piece of documentary evidence of any relevance to [the State's] sentencing decision. In the instant case, much other evidence demonstrated Spence's guilt" [64]. The decision goes on to state that "Spence does not raise a question over whether [the forensic dentist's] testimony is false, but rather over what weight the jury should have accorded his testimony. Spence's argument that [the expert] had misidentified the remains of another woman likewise does not expose his testimony against Spence as false [65]."

The court concluded,

Spence is simply trying to re-litigate this aspect of his defense eleven years too late. At trial, Spence introduced his own forensic odontologist ⋯ a leading expert in the field [who] spiritedly criticized [the state's expert's] methodology and conclusions, although, critically, [he] admitted he could not rule out Spence's teeth as the source of the bite marks. Because this evidentiary issue was fully and competently aired in the state courts, no violation of fundamental fairness under the due process clause has been shown (citation omitted). Alternatively, Spence argues that the federal district court erred in excluding reports from five other expert odontologists who concluded that [the state's expert's] testimony was unreliable. But because Spence filed these reports after the district court's discovery deadline, without explanation for his untimely filing, the district court did not abuse his discretion in refusing to admit the reports.

The conviction was upheld [66].

The 1978 case from the U.S. Military Justice System, *U.S. v. Martin*, 9 M.J. 731, USNCMR (1978) (later overturned on other grounds as *Monk v. Zelez*, 901 F.2d 885, 10th Cir. (1990) [67] was another of first impression for military courts. The Court noted,

The record unquestionably established that ⋯ is an expert in the field of bite-mark identification. He was so recognized at trial by ⋯ a witness for the appellant, another expert in this very limited field of about 30 individuals nationwide. There were, as might be expected, differences of opinion in this case between the expert for the Government and the expert for the defense, but these differences go to the weight rather than to the admissibility (citation omitted). ⋯ These gentlemen both displayed impressive qualifications, training, and experience in their field of expertise and both ably acquitted themselves during direct and cross-examination. The members of the [jury] no doubt fully considered and weighed the content of the expert testimony and opinions in reaching a verdict in this case. ⋯ We find no merit to this assignment of error [68].

8. BEYOND LINKAGE

Several courts have recognized that a bitemark is an indication of a violent interaction between two individuals. In a long-running attempt to overturn his conviction for a second murder within a dozen years, a Virginia prisoner has challenged his conviction on numerous occasions. In *Tuggle v. Nederland*, 79 F.3d 1386, 4th Cir. (1996) [original conviction appealed as *Tuggle v. Virginia*, 334 S.E.2d 838 VA (1985, cert. denied 1986)], the medical examiner testified that both the bite mark on the breast and the bruising around the vagina occurred while [the victim] was alive. ⋯ A forensic odontologist testified that he examined the bite mark on the victim's right breast. He compared the mark with models of Tuggle's teeth and concluded "with all medical certainty these marks on the body of [the victim] were made by the teeth of Mr. Tuggle." He further opined that [the victim] was alive and moving when she was bitten [69].

The court agreed that such evidence was an "aggravating circumstance, and the murder in this case was unquestionably vile. The murder involved rape and sodomy, and Tuggle bit [the victim] on the breast before shooting her in the chest" [70]. These findings contributed to the imposition of the sentence of death.

In the previously discussed *Hoskins* [71] case from 2000, the presence of the bitemark was presumptive proof that a fight rather than an accident was the root cause for the altercation. Similarly, in the *Martin* [72] case discussed above, the bitemark on the suspect was part of a triad of injuries that the court accepted as evidence of aggravated rape. In the recent case of *Gilliam v. Florida*, 817 So.2d 768 FL (2002, rehearing denied), "an expert in forensic dentistry testified that the pattern of bite marks on the victim's breast indicated that she was more than likely moving at the time the injury was inflicted." In combination with testimony from the medical examiner that the victim did not lose consciousness during the commission of the crime, this evidence was sufficient to enhance the penalty levied as a heinous, atrocious, or cruel (HAC) finding under Florida law [73]. In another case from 2002, *U.S.A. v. Kills in Water*, 293 F.3d 432, 8th Cir (2002), "the district court did not automatically apply the serious bodily injury enhancement. Instead, the district court specifically relied on the victim's bitemarks, her physical trauma to the vaginal and perianal areas, her continued psychological problems such as recurring nightmares and attempted suicide, and her ongoing need for psychological counseling, as the basis for concluding that the victim suffered serious bodily injury" [74]. In a footnote to this case, "Defendant argues that the bite marks should not be considered in assessing his sentence because the co-defendant, not he, actually bit the victim during the rape. However, we agree with the district court's conclusion that defendant's participation in the biting by holding the victim down while his co-defendant bit her is sufficient to render defendant liable for the resultant bite marks during sentencing" [75].

9. LINKAGE TO OBJECTS OTHER THAN TEETH

In an unpublished 1992 Illinois case, *People v. Cumbee* [76], a forensic dentist after ruling out the presence of any bite injuries on the victim was called upon by the state to testify as a layman regarding the interpretation and classification of the victim's blunt trauma wounds. The judge ordered a hearing to assess the dentist's fitness to testify in these matters, at which the dentist readily admitted that he was not a pathologist, that he was not regularly consulted in such matters, and that he had never previously been qualified to testify in a court of law concerning blunt trauma wounds not caused by teeth. In spite of those admissions, the dentist was allowed to testify. The appellate court found that the trial court abused its discretion an allowing the testimony because his qualifications were in fact not sufficient. In *Cumbee v. Nygren*, 2000 U.S. App LEXIS 3148 (7th Cir., 2000), the federal appellate court notes "that the trial court both failed to properly instruct the jury regarding the prosecution's burden to prove venue and also admitted improper evidence, a state appellate court reversed his conviction and ordered that Cumbee be retried" [77].

In a very recent decision by the Mississippi Supreme Court, not only was the testimony of a forensic dentist as to the bitemark injuries on the victim accepted, but also a much broader range of opinion testimony was allowed. In *Stubbs and Vance v. Mississippi*, 845 So.2d 656,

MS (2003, rehearings denied), the appellate court upheld convictions for numerous criminal acts committed by the defendants.

> The State next called ⋯ a forensic odontologist to testify as to bite marks discovered on [the victim's] hip. Over the objection of the defense, [he] was qualified as an expert in the fields of forensic odontology and bite mark identification ⋯ [and] testified that on March 10, 2000, he was contacted by the district attorney's office concerning a woman who had been sexually abused. ⋯ [He] testified that upon his examination of [the victim's] injuries that same day, he noticed swollen and bruised nipples, substantial trauma to the vaginal area and what appeared to be a bite mark on her right thigh. He immediately informed the district attorney's office of the bite mark and asked for dental molds of any possible suspects. After he received the dental molds of [four individuals, he] returned to the hospital on March 15, 2000, to compare the molds to the actual bitemark. One of his testing procedures was to press the dental molds literally into [the living victim's] skin. After numerous tests, [he testified he] could not exclude Stubbs as being the person who caused the bite mark on [the victim] ⋯ [and] was able to state the other three molds did not match the bite mark.

The case becomes more interesting when the dentist then testified that

> "he was also informed by the medical staff that [the victim] additionally suffered from head injuries. He took pictures of the injuries and informed Det. Jones of the newly discovered injuries. While ⋯ with Det. Jones, he was able to view the surveillance video tape from the night the [female suspects] checked into the Comfort Inn. [The dentist] testified that after numerous video enhancements, he was able to determine that Stubbs removed [the victim] from the toolbox and carried her inside the motel room. [He] also noticed the latch on the toolbox was similar [in shape] to the injuries on [the victim's] head and lower thigh. He measured the distance between the two latches and the distance between [her] injuries. Both distances were thirty-seven [37] inches apart. Using his assistants, [he] was able to determine that a woman of [the victim's] size could be placed into the tool box and then removed by another woman" [78].

> "The defense called their own expert witness ⋯ to refute the claim of [the forensic dentist] that the mark on [the victim's] hip was a bite mark. [The defense expert], a forensic pathologist, testified [the victim] could not have fit in the tool box. He also stated [that the victim] could not have sustained her head injuries from the tool box because the tool box was aluminum and the hinges do not allow the box to be closed with enough force. He did agree the thirty-seven inches coincided with the latches on the toolbox and [the victim's] injuries. [The pathologist] also testified there were many objects, other than teeth, that could have left the appearance of the half moon or semicircle marks found on [the victim's] hip, such as a flashlight or the heel of a shoe. He stated when he first saw the video of the bite mark, he did think it could be an animal bite, but that was before he realized [the forensic dentist] had pressed the dental mold into the skin to compare the mold to the mark. In order to preserve the actual mark, [the pathologist] testified he would have performed the test to compare the molds to the bite mark differently ⋯" [79].

The defense argued that the forensic dentist's

testimony should have been excluded because it was clearly beyond his field of expertise ⋯ [contending] the opinion ⋯ regarding the teeth impressions of Stubbs was not an expert opinion ⋯ [because] "he could not find enough details in the mark to give it his highest opinion as an expert." Vance argues [the] testimony was prejudicial because it concluded a question of fact; he was not able to testify to a reasonable degree of certainty; and, it did not help the jury clearly resolve an issue of fact.

The defense also argued that although the forensic odontologist

was never qualified as an expert in video enhancement, he was allowed to offer testimony as to a videotape which he believed depicted [the victim] being carried out of Stubbs's truck into the hotel. Vance contends that [the dental expert] was also allowed to offer lay opinion testimony regarding alleged cigarette burns on [the victim] by holding a cigarette next to the wounds to conclude they matched. Vance also strongly contends [the expert] tampered with evidence by taking a dental mold of Stubbs and pressing it against [the victim's] leg and creating a bite mark that was not present before his procedure.

The State responded that

the trial court did not abuse its discretion in accepting ⋯ or in allowing [him] to testify at trial. The State argues this Court has previously recognized odontology as an acceptable area of professional and forensic expertise. The State contends that [he] followed the proper procedures for bite mark testimony, that the appearance of bite marks was testified to by others before [he] was called to consult on the case, and that exhibits also clearly showed the evidence of bite marks on [the victim] prior to ⋯ conducting his test regarding the dental molds of Stubbs.

Furthermore, the defense pathologist "did agree that the marks on [the victim] resembled bite marks" [80].
The court ruled,

With regard to the contention that [the forensic dentist] testified outside the area of his expertise, the State argues that the record shows this was not the basis of the objections made at trial; that the objection regarding the cigarettes was only to [his] testifying to "the history of cigarettes," not to using a cigarette to point to alleged cigarette burns; that the objection regarding the surveillance tape photographs was only to [his] using the term "blow" as well as a Rule 403 objection; that the objection was not regarding the video enhancement showing a body being carried into the hotel room; and, that the Miss. R. Evid. 403 objection was repeated when [the victim herself] was brought in before the jury to demonstrate the distance between the injuries on her head and side.

Continuing, on the court also held, "Regarding the alleged tampering of evidence by [the forensic dentist], the State argues [he] clearly explained his procedure to the jury. Although [the pathologist] testified he would have used a different procedure, he did not testify that [the dentist] employed an improper medical or forensic procedure" [81].
The court concluded with two cautionary statements;

There is little consensus in the scientific community on the number of points which must match before any positive identification can be announced (citation omitted). Because the opinions concerning the methods of comparison employed in a particular case may differ, it is certainly open to defense counsel to attack the qualifications of the expert, the methods and data used to compare the bite marks to persons other than the defendant, and the factual and logical bases of the expert's opinions. Also, where such expert testimony is allowed by the trial court, it should be open to the defendant to present evidence challenging the reliability of the field of bite-mark comparisons (citation omitted). Although Stubbs and Vance both objected to [the dentist] being qualified as an expert, they were each given the opportunity to challenge the reliability of the bite mark evidence as required [82].

Secondly, the court noted,

The defense failed to object to [the dentist] testifying outside the area which he had been qualified as an expert except as to narcotics. The trial court found [his] testimony, including testimony regarding bite marks, [the victim's] injuries, and video enhancement, to be relevant and more probative than prejudicial. Because of the extensive record before this Court, because of the trial court's permitting extensive cross-examination of [the dentist] by defense counsel, and because the defense called its own expert ⋯ to rebut [the dentist's] testimony, we cannot say that the trial court abused its discretion in admitting the testimony. ⋯ While, as noted above, this Court ⋯ made an affirmative statement that bite-mark identification is clearly admissible in our state trial courts, we in no way implied that [this dentist] was given carte blanche to testify to anything and everything he so desired. From our cases wherein [he] has been involved, he has primarily been recognized by this Court to have been appropriately declared by the trial courts to be an expert in the field of forensic odontology. This does not mean that [he] can indiscriminately offer so-called expert testimony in other areas in which he not even remotely meets the Miss. R. Evid. 702 criteria. ⋯ A different record in this case could have brought about different results [83].

In a footnote to a Florida murder case *Ramirez v. Florida*, 810 So.2d 836, FL (2001, rehearing denied), that was overturned (for the third time) on grounds other than the forensic dental evidence, the court alluded to dental testimony that bears on the case discussed above. In the original 1983 trial of Ramirez the "State presented the live testimony of ⋯ a dentist and consultant in forensic odontology ⋯ who testified that use of hard casts is generally accepted in the field as a method of analyzing wounds made in human tissue." In Ramirez the use of a knife mark identification "[f]or the first time in the history of the Florida courts" was ruled inadmissible [84].

10. EVEN FURTHER BEYOND LINKAGE

In *Arizona v.Tankersly*, 956 P.2d 486, AZ (1998), "a forensic odontologist testified it was 'highly probable' that defendant had bitten the victim's left breast, and another said that his teeth 'matched' the bite marks" [85]. In affirming the conviction, the court also noted the following testimony adduced at trial, "Finally, evidence presented at trial established that [an alternate suspect] had no teeth and that his dentures had been destroyed in a fire years before the murder. Expert testimony demonstrated that the bite marks found on the victim's body could not have been made by someone without teeth or [by someone] with dentures" [86].

After a jogger was attacked and killed by dogs running lose from their owner's property in the case *North Carolina v. Powell*, 446 S.E.2d 26, NC (1994), the court on appeal accepted the testimony of "[a] forensic odontologist ⋯ that dental impressions taken from Bruno and Woody [the 'accused' dogs] were compatible with some of the lacerations in the wounds pictured in scale photographs of [the victim's] body" [87]. There have since been numerous animal bite cases litigated, but no others were discovered in the appellate records.

Fingernails linked to scratch marks found on the back of the neck of a murder victim take center stage in the case of *Pennsylvania v. Graves*, 456 A.2d 561, PA Super. (1983). Three forensic dentists and a criminalist participated for the state. The primary forensic dental investigator testifying that he

made an impression or cast of one of those scratch marks, using a compound of the same general type as dentists use in making impressions of teeth. He then compared that impression with an impression made from the nail on appellant's fourth (left) finger, using among other things, a comparison microscope. On the basis of these comparisons he testified that: "it was highly likely that the nail of the fourth finger, left hand, of Bennie Graves had made the mark in the neck of [the victim]" [88].

The second dentist then

testified based upon his examination of finger nail clippings, photographs, slides and [the] impression, testified to a "fractured edge" on the impression of appellant's finger nail, and to his opinion that "it is highly probable" that appellant's finger nails made the mark on the neck of [the victim]; and that it was "very unlikely" that "some person other than Bennie Graves ⋯ made these marks" [89].

The third dentist,

utilizing photographs and slides of the decedent's body and finger nail clippings of appellant, testified to his opinion "that the left-little finger and the left-ring finger (of appellant) were consistent with the injury patterns shown in the photographs" of the deceased; that there was "a high degree of certainty in this case," and finally that there was "[a]n extremely high degree of probability to the point of practical impossibility of finding two other nails on two fingers adjacent to each other that would make these marks" [90].

In *Graves*, interestingly the criminalist was much less strident, testifying that he

characteriz[ed] a fingernail mark in the skin as "a tool mark," based upon an examination of the impression made by [the first forensic dentist], and of a wax impression of appellant's left little finger, again using the comparison microscope concluded that: "the fingernail impression as seen on the wax mold had the same class characteristics as the fingernail." He testified further that "there is probably a fair degree of probability that this nail or any nail of this shape made this kind of mark. ⋯" Over appellant's objection, he was later permitted to say that "this would be one (case) of high probability," although the nail could not be characterized as "unique" [91].

The original conviction was affirmed.

In the case *Washington v. Oklahoma*, 836 P.2d 673, OK Crim. App. (1992), one judge dissents from the majority holding that failure to provide funding for defense experts is harmless error. In his dissent he outlines the basis for the evidence offered by the state's forensic dental expert.

Regarding the first expert, the State relied upon the testimony of a forensic odontologist to establish that appellant was the perpetrator of the bitemark found on the murder victim. The State's expert testified that he used two types of analyses to identify appellant as the assailant: bitemark/dentition comparison and a comparison of microorganisms found in the wound and in appellant's mouth. The doctor placed primary identification emphasis on the microorganism "aspergillus" [*sic*] being present in both the bitemark and in appellant's mouth. At trial, the doctor testified that aspergillus would be found in the mouths of only "one in a billion people." Although the doctor claimed that his tests were "accepted," he admitted that he was aware of no other persons who either used or advocated the use of microbiological analysis in bitemark comparisons. I agree with the trial court's conclusion that without an expert odontologist, the defense was unable to determine the reliability of the comparison techniques used by the State's expert or the accuracy of the conclusions he reached [92].

Your author would also concur with the dissenting judge.

Another voyage into the fringes of forensic odontology would appear to have occurred in the case *Henry v. Horn*, 218 F.Supp.2d 671, E.D.PA (2002), in which a convicted murderer seeks relief in the federal courts, claiming that

he was denied a fair trial and due process by the prosecution's presentation of false, inadmissible, unreliable and misleading testimony during both the guilt and penalty phases of trial. Specifically, he claims that the testimony of ⋯ [a forensic dentist] that he could determine the mental state of the attacker from a bite mark, was false, unreliable and misleading. Henry alleges that the prosecution either knew or should have known that this testimony was false and that it knowingly utilized this false testimony to obtain both the conviction of first-degree murder and the resulting death sentence.

The court denied the requested relief, finding

that "the present case, however, does not involve the knowing use of false evidence ⋯ simply because Henry's experts disagree with the Commonwealth's experts does not mean that the Commonwealth knowingly presented false evidence in violation of Henry's due process rights.'' The evidence before the Pennsylvania Supreme Court when it decided this claim included no affidavits from either the prosecutor or the witnesses whose testimony was challenged. (''The foundation for Henry's claim that the Commonwealth presented false evidence is the testimony of his experts ⋯ at the ⋯ hearing. These experts disputed the validity of the scientific theories on which [the forensic odontologist] based [his] testimony.'') Henry simply presented opposing experts who criticized government's expert witnesses and the bases of their testimony. As this evidence falls far short of the affidavits of false testimony that the Supreme Court has consistently required for such claims, the Pennsylvania Supreme Court did not unreasonably [deny] him relief [93].

11. EXPERT FOR THE PROSECUTION BUT NOT THE DEFENSE

A number of appeals have arisen discussing the issue of the defendant in a criminal case not having access to a forensic dental expert to analyze and possibly controvert the testimony and opinion of the state's expert. Perhaps the best known of these cases is *Wilhoit v. Oklahoma*, 816 P.2d 545, OK Crim. App. (1991), in which the central issue was the allegation of ineffective assistance by counsel during trial. As a basis for ruling that defendant Wilhoit had not received adequate representation, the court stated in its order demanding a new trial that

> the Oklahoma Bar Association had found counsel's ability to function as a lawyer was noticeably impaired by alcohol during the time he was representing appellant. Trial counsel even stated in an affidavit that there was no strategic reason for his not pursuing the bite-mark evidence nor for not using a bite-mark expert. This omission is even less excusable in light of the fact that the Wilhoit family had hired a forensic odontologist who was available to examine the bite-mark evidence. Judge Pearman found that because of his failure to investigate the bite-mark evidence, appellant's counsel was deficient and that there is a reasonable probability that the result of the trial would have been different had the defense used an expert. The omission of this evidence cannot be considered a strategic defense tactic [94].

In a case that arose in the Eastern District of Louisiana, *Jackson v. Day*, 1996 U.S. Dist. LEXIS 7001, a federal district judge granted a writ of habeas corpus stating that counsel's

> failure to move the trial court for a declaration of indigency and funds to retain an odontologist was not a strategic decision but rather a legal mistake. Despite the plethora of decisions on this topic in the 1980's, [the defense counsel] actually testified that it was not until 1992 that the ''Supreme Court [held] that a person has a constitutional right to have his expert witnesses funded if he was indigent'' (Transcript, p. 68). An odontologist was a ''crucial'' safeguard to W. Jackson's ''ability to marshal his defense and, thus, ensure an accurate result.'' Therefore, all reasonable trial strategy in W. Jackson's case as testified to by [counsel] mandated the retention, or at least attempted retention, of an odontologist [95].

However, in an unpublished decision, *Jackson v. Day*, 121 F.3d 705 (1997), the U.S. Fifth Circuit Court of Appeals reversed finding ''no constitutional error,'' citing overwhelming evidence against the defendant, and further commenting that had the defense hired a forensic odontologist ''that there is no reasonable probability that 'a battle of the experts' would have been sufficient to raise a reasonable doubt [as to guilt]'' [96]. In 1998 the U.S. Supreme Court at 523 U.S. 1006 refused to grant certiorari.

In *Missouri v. Fleer*, 851 S.W.2d 582, MO App. (1993), the prosecution offered testimony from a forensic dentist to refute a claim concerning a possible bitemark on the victim's genitals. Although the primary issue on appeal was the late entry of the forensic dentist as a witness, the court's holding does address the issue of the defense not rebutting the opinion with an independent forensic dental opinion. The state's forensic odontologist

> stated that marks found on Howlett's penis were not caused by human teeth. Fleer argues that this testimony was fundamentally unfair to him since he intended to argue that: (1) Howlett murdered Price after Price resisted his sexual advances, as evidenced by the clenched teeth marks on Howlett's penis; and (2) Howlett murdered Tyler because Tyler could have identified him. Although Fleer did not waive his objection to [the state's expert's] testimony, he failed to show that the State intended surprise or acted deceptively or in bad faith with intention to disadvantage him. Moreover, Fleer has failed to show that he was surprised or that [the complained of] testimony might not have been contemplated. Since Fleer intended to argue that the marks on Howlett's penis were caused by Price's teeth, Fleer could expect that the State would attempt to foreclose this theory by presenting evidence which would negate this hypothesis. Moreover, we are unable to conclude that the admission of [the dental] testimony resulted in fundamental unfairness to Fleer, for four reasons. First, defense counsel opened the door to rebuttal testimony regarding the marks on Howlett's penis when he asked [the medical examiner]: (1) whether the marks on Howlett's penis could be consistent with any number of things; (2) whether the marks were applied when Howlett had an erection; and (3) whether he had any means of telling what caused Howlett's wound. Second, defense counsel, apparently, did not depose [the state's forensic dental expert] before trial. Third, defense counsel did not find a rebuttal witness, although they had thirteen days to do so. Fourth, defense counsel did not seek a continuance after having been notified that [the forensic dentist] would testify. For these reasons ⋯ [his claim] is denied [97].

12. TESTING THE EXPERT

On occasion courts have devised their own method of qualifying a would-be expert. In the 1983 case *Louisiana v. Stokes*, 433 So.2d 96, LA (1983), the trial judge responded to the prosecution's request

> to compel the defendant to submit to the taking of an impression of his upper and lower teeth ⋯ in order to compare the defendant's teeth with the marks found on the victim. After a hearing on the matter, the trial court granted the state's motion. Out of fairness to the defendant, however, the trial court structured the test as follows: The teeth impression[s] of five different persons would be sent to the state's expert for analysis. Four of the impressions would be from male Caucasians within ten years of the defendant's age. The defense and state would each select two of the persons giving the impressions. The fifth impression sample would be that of the defendant. The identity of the five persons submitting impressions would not be disclosed to the expert. This would insure that the test would be conducted in a non-suggestive manner. The five impressions were made and sent to the state's expert ⋯ [dentist] ⋯ for comparison with photographs taken of the bite-marks on the victim. [The expert's report] concludes that there was not enough evidence to positively identify the suspect. He also states that he could not exclude any of the persons submitting impressions from consideration as having produced the bite-marks on the victim. A copy of this report was presented by the prosecutor to the defense counsel on the day of trial. ⋯ [D]efense counsel notified the trial court that it wanted to introduce [the] report into evidence during the trial. The trial judge stated that he had no intention of allowing the report into evidence without the testimony of [the expert] when the latter was available for subpoena. ⋯ After the state rested its case, the defendant again sought to introduce the report ⋯ without the testimony of the doctor. He argued that the report should be allowed in evidence under the business records exception to the hearsay rule. He also contended that he would be prejudiced by the fact that he would be required to call [the expert] on direct examination [rather than have the ability to cross-examine him]. The trial judge refused to admit the report into evidence due to the fact that

[the doctor] was available for testimony. ⋯ [The] document itself may not be reliable. Without the testimony of the doctor, it would be difficult to assess the validity of the test upon which the opinions of the doctor expressed in the report were based. Furthermore, we find no merit to the defendant's contention that he would be prejudiced by calling [the expert] on direct. In effect, the defendant is willing to vouch for the credibility of the doctor's conclusions included in his report. Yet, he refuses to vouch for the credibility of the doctor's testimony which would explain how he arrived at his conclusions [98].

13. CONCLUSIONS

As stated in the beginning of this chapter, not all cases involving bitemark evidence are available for review and comment. The law on any given subject, bitemark evidence included, is constantly evolving from case to case and from state to state as both the scientific underpinnings of forensic odontology gain a firmer (hopefully not a weaker) foundation and as the defense bar hones its skills in contesting the evidence. As this chapter is being written, new cases on the emerging field of expert witness liability, of the impact of DNA and other tissue/cell typing, and the very state of "identification science" itself are being litigated in numerous courts throughout the United States and other nations. It would be presumptuous of the author as well as the reader to expect that any treatise could provide a deep and broad enough background to safely navigate the legal waters of forensic odontology. Constant study of the case law, the methodology, and the parallel forensic disciplines is required. Perhaps the single best piece of advice that could be gleaned from the case law is look to the past to see where the future lies. Rereading the testimony of some of the pioneers in the field reveals their abiding commitment to forensic odontology and their great reluctance to overstep the bounds of their expertise. The author is concerned that names such as Krone, Burke, Morris, Brewer, and Keko may become better known in forensic circles than those of the many cases cited above. Without constant attention to the foundations and continual improvement in the underlying science of odontology, it may come to pass, as Risinger and Loop state in their Cardozo Law Review article of 2000 entitled Three Card Monty, Monty Hall, Modus Operandi, and "Offender Profiling": Some Lessons of Modern Cognitive Science for the Law of Evidence, "[i]t is becoming increasingly clear that, as a general proposition, bitemark identification is shockingly untrustworthy" [99]. The author does not believe that such is true, but only the future testimony of forensic dentists can prevent it.

REFERENCES

1. Moradi-Shalal v. Fireman's Fund Ins. Companies, 46 Cal.3d 287, (1988) at page 296.
2. *United States v. Washington*, 872 F.2d 874, (9th Cir. 1989) at page 880.
2a. Daubert v. Merrell Dow, 509 U.S. (1993) at page 595.
2b. Kumho Tire v. Carmichael, 526 U.S. 137 (1999) at page 157.
3. *Illinois v. Milone*, 356 N.E.2d 1350, IL App. (1976) at page 1353.
4. *Illinois v. Milone*, 356 N.E.2d 1350, IL App. (1976) at page 1354.
5. *Illinois v. Milone*, 356 N.E.2d 1350, IL App. (1976) at page 1354.
6. Giannelli PC, Imwinkelried EJ. Scientific Evidence. 3rd ed.>. Miarnisburg. OH: Lexis Law Publishing, 1999:583.
7. *Seivewright v. State*, 7 P.3d 24, WY (2000) at page 30.
8. *Illinois v. Dace*, 506 N.E.2d 332, IL App. (1987) beginning at page 335.
9. *People v. Mostrong*, 2003 Cal App. Unpub. LEXIS 1179 at page 4.
10. *People v. Mostrong*, 2003 Cal App. Unpub. LEXIS 1179 beginning at page 4.
11. *R. V. Stillman*, 37 W.C.B. (2d) 215 (1998) at page 2 in the printout and page 4 in the original.

12. *Vermont v. Howe*, 386 A.2d 1125, VT (1978) at page 1131.
13. *Winston and Davis v. Lee*, 470 U.S. 753 (1985) at page 767.
14. *Doyle v. State*, 263 S.W.2d 779, TX App (1954) at page 779.
15. *Mobley v. Georgia*, 441 S.E.2d 780, GA App (1994) at page 782.
16. *Hoskins v. McBride*, 2000 U.S. Appeals LEXIS 27398, 7th Cir. (cert. denied) at page 2.
17. *Louisiana v. Martin*, 645 So.2d 190, 204, LA (1994, rehearing denied) in J. Calagero's concurrence at page 204. This case was later upheld at *Martin v. Cain*, 246 F.3d 471, 5th Cir (2001).
18. *Rhode Island v. Adams*, 481 A.2d 718, RI (1984) beginning at page 727.
19. *Rhode Island v. Adams*, 481 A.2d 718, RI (1984) at page 727.
20. *Harris v. Arkansas*, 1992 Ark. App. 728 LEXIS (1992) beginning at page 4.
21. *Draper v. Adams*, 2000 U.S. App. Lexis 11826, 6th Cir (2000) at page 3.
22. *Louisiana v. Vital*, 505 So.2d 1006, LA App. (1987) beginning at page 1007.
23. *Illinois v. Queen*, 474 N.E.2d 786, IL App. (1985 rehearing denied) beginning at page 787.
24. *Wisconsin v. Stinson*, 397 N.W.2d 136, Wisc. App. (1986) beginning at page 141.
25. *Wisconsin v. Stinson*, 397 N.W.2d 136, Wisc. App. (1986) at page 142.
26. *Vermont v. Howe*, 386 A.2d 1125, VT (1978) at page 1132.
27. *Rhode Island v. Adams*, 481 A.2d 718, RI (1984) at page 727.
28. *Arizona v. Garrison*, 585 P.2d 563, AZ (1978) at page 566.
29. *People v. Slone*, 143 Cal. Rptr. 61, Cal. App. (1978) at page 67.
30. *People v. Slone*, 143 Cal. Rptr. 61, Cal. App. (1978) at page 68.
31. *People v. Slone*, 143 Cal. Rptr. 61, Cal. App. (1978) at page 70.
32. *State v. Duncan*, 802 So.2d 533, LA (2001, cert. denied) at page 553.
33. *State v. Duncan*, 802 So.2d 533, LA (2001, cert. denied) at page 553 including Note 20.
34. *State v. Duncan*, 802 So.2d 533, LA (2001, cert. denied) beginning at page 554.
35. *State v. Duncan*, 802 So.2d 533, LA (2001, cert. denied) beginning at page 557 including Note 25.
36. *Kinney v. State of Arkansas*, 868 S.W.2d 463, AR (1994) at page 465.
37. *Washington v. Kendrick*, 736 P.2d 1079, Wash. App. (1987) at page 1082.
38. *Illinois v. Milone*, 356 N.E.2d 1350, Ill App (1976) beginning at page 1355.
39. *Illinois v. Milone*, 356 N.E.2d 1350, Ill App (1976) at page 1356.
40. *Illinois v. Milone*, 356 N.E.2d 1350, Ill App (1976) at page 1356.
41. *Illinois v. Milone*, 356 N.E.2d 1350, Ill App (1976) at page 1356.
42. *Illinois v. Milone*, 356 N.E.2d 1350, Ill App (1976) at page 1357.
43. *Illinois v. Milone*, 356 N.E.2d 1350, Ill App (1976) beginning at page 1356.
44. *People v. Mattox*, 237 N.E.2d 845, Ill. App. (1968) at page 846.
45. *Illinois v. Milone*, 356 N.E.2d 1350, Ill App (1976) at page 1358.
46. *Illinois v. Milone*, 356 N.E.2d 1350, Ill App (1976) at page 1360.
47. *Milone v. Camp*, 22 F.2d 693, 2nd Cir. (1994, cert. denied) beginning at page 700.
48. *Niehaus v. Indiana*, 359 N.E.2d 513, IN (1977) at page 516.
49. *Kansas v. Peoples*, 605 P.2d 135, KS (1980) at page 139.
50. *Kansas v. Peoples*, 605 P.2d 135, KS (1980) beginning at page 139.
51. *Kansas v. Peoples*, 605 P.2d 135, KS (1980) at page 140.
52. *Commonwealth v. Cifizzari*, 492 N.E.2d 357, MA (1986) at page 360.
53. *Commonwealth v. Cifizzari*, 492 N.E.2d 357, MA (1986) at page 363.
54. *Commonwealth v. Cifizzari*, 492 N.E.2d 357, MA (1986) beginning at page 363.
55. *Louisiana v. Wommack*, 770 So.2d 365, LA App. (2000) beginning at page 373.
56. *Louisiana v. Wommack*, 770 So.2d 365, LA App. (2000) at page 374.
57. *Louisiana v. Wommack*, 770 So.2d 365, LA App. (2000) beginning at page 375.
58. *Louisiana v. Wommack*, 770 So.2d 365, LA App. (2000) at page 376.
59. *Seivewright v. State*, 7 P.3d 24, WY (2000) beginning at page 30.
60. *Illinois v. Holmes*, 601 N.E.2d 985, IL App (1992) at page 991.
61. *Illinois v. Holmes*, 601 N.E.2d 985, IL App (1992) beginning at page 992.
62. *Illinois v. Holmes*, 601 N.E.2d 985, IL App (1992) beginning at page 993.
63. *Spence v. Scott*, 80 F.3d 989, 5th Cir. (1996, cert. denied) at page 1000.

64. *Spence v. Scott*, 80 F.3d 989, 5th Cir. (1996, cert. denied) at page 1000 Note 8.

65. *Spence v. Scott*, 80 F.3d 989, 5th Cir. (1996, cert. denied) at page 1000.

66. *Spence v. Scott*, 80 F.3d 989, 5th Cir. (1996, cert. denied) at page 1000.

67. *Monk v. Zelez*, 901 F.2d 885, 10th Cir. (1990).

68. *U.S. v. Martin*, 9 M.J. 731, USNCMR (1978) at page 738.

69. *Tuggle v. Nederland*, 79 F.3d 1386, 4th Cir. (1996) beginning at page 1388.

70. *Tuggle v. Nederland*, 79 F.3d 1386, 4th Cir. (1996) beginning at page 1393.

71. *Hoskins v. McBride*, 2000 U.S. Appeals LEXIS 27398 (cert. denied) at page 2.

72. *U.S. v. Martin*, 9 M.J. 731, USNCMR (1978) at page 738.

73. *Gilliam v. Florida*, 817 So.2d 768, FL (2002, rehearing denied) at page 779.

74. *U.S.A. v. Kills in Water*, 293 F.3d 432, 8th Cir (2002) beginning at page 434.

75. *U.S.A. v. Kills in Water*, 293 F.3d 432, 8th Cir (2002) at page 436 Note 5.

76. *People v. Cumbee*, Rule 23 Order, Nov 15, 1995, 2nd District Appellate Court, appeal from Circuit Court McHenry County, Illinois, N0. 92-CF-676.

77. *Cumbee v. Nygren*, 2000 U.S. App LEXIS 3148 (7th Cir., 2000) at page 1.

78. *Stubbs and Vance v. Mississippi*, 845 So.2d 656, MS (2003, rehearings denied) beginning at page 661.

79. *Stubbs and Vance v. Mississippi*, 845 So.2d 656, MS (2003, rehearings denied) beginning at page 662.

80. *Stubbs and Vance v. Mississippi*, 845 So.2d 656, MS (2003, rehearings denied) at page 668.

81. *Stubbs and Vance v. Mississippi*, 845 So.2d 656, MS (2003, rehearings denied) beginning at page 668.

82. *Stubbs and Vance v. Mississippi*, 845 So.2d 656, MS (2003, rehearings denied) at page 669.

83. *Stubbs and Vance v. Mississippi*, 845 So.2d 656, MS (2003, rehearings denied) at page 670.

84. *Ramirez v. Florida*, 810 So.2d 836, FL (2001, rehearing denied) at page 848 Note 31.

85. *Arizona v. Tankersly*, 956 P.2d 486, AZ (1998) at page 489.

86. *Arizona v. Tankersly*, 956 P.2d 486, AZ (1998) at page 497.

87. *North Carolina v. Powell*, 446 S.E.2d 26, NC (1994) beginning at page 27.

88. *Pennsylvania v. Graves*, 456 A.2d 561, PA Super. (1983) at page 565.

89. *Pennsylvania v. Graves*, 456 A.2d 561, PA Super. (1983) beginning at page 565.

90. *Pennsylvania v. Graves*, 456 A.2d 561, PA Super. (1983) at page 566.

91. *Pennsylvania v. Graves*, 456 A.2d 561, PA Super. (1983) at page 565.

92. *Washington v. Oklahoma*, 836 P.2d 673, OK Crim. App. (1992) Judge Lumpkin in dissent at page 678.

93. *Henry v. Horn*, 218 F.Supp.2d 671, E.D.PA (2002) beginning at page 699.

94. *Wilhoit v. Oklahoma*, 816 P.2d 545, OK Crim. App. (1991) at page 546.

95. *Jackson v. Day*, 1996 U.S. Dist. LEXIS 7001, E.D.LA beginning at page 8.

96. *Jackson v. Day*, 121 F.3d 705 (1997) unpublished opinion 96-30563 beginning at page 6.

97. *Missouri v. Fleer*, 851 S.W.2d 582, MO App. (1993) beginning at page 591.

98. *Louisiana v. Stokes*, 433 So.2d 96, LA (1983) beginning at page 102.

99. Risinger DM, Loop JL. Three card monty, Monty Hall, modus operandi, and "offender profiling": some lessons of modern cognitive science for the law of evidence. Cardozo L Rev 2002 at Note 194; 24:193-285.

25
Courtroom Aids in Bitemark Evidence

John P. Kenney
Deputy Coroner and Director of Identification Services, Du Page County, Illinois

1. INTRODUCTION

The use of courtroom visual aids is very significant in bitemark cases. As dentist/odontologist, the special skill in discerning three-dimensional spatial relationships is a professional requirement. That skill coupled with the forensic expertise permits the odontologist to envision the class and individual characteristics of the offending dentition that inflicted the injury(ies), and hopefully to communicate these findings clearly to the trier of fact, be it judge, jury or both.

This chapter will present a number of methods of evidence presentation gleaned from respected and experienced American Board of Forensic Odontology (ABFO) colleagues. It is important to remember that each bitemark case is different, with evidence presenting on the body, on foodstuff or on inanimate objects. Each case may require some creative thinking to present the evidence clearly, to make it understandable, and to demonstrate it well. While some jurisdictions may have technical assistance available to produce courtroom aids, it usually falls to the odontologist to produce their own.

2. THE PROBLEM

The average jurist may at best adjudicate one or possibly two bitemark cases during an entire career on the bench (H Pitluck, R Barsley, G Vale, personal communication, 2003). The average juror has a high-school education. Bitemarks on humans usually involve a heinous and violent crime. By the time the odontologist testifies, the trial will have likely run a number of days, and the juror has already seen and heard very disturbing evidence. The forensic dental expert understands the nuances of the evidence, how it was analyzed, and how to visualize the conclusions. It is up to that expert to convey the information in as simple and straightforward a manner as possible. The purpose is to inform and educate the judge/jury on the derivation of the expert's conclusions. Perhaps the classic case of courtroom blunder from the prosecution's perspective is the O.J. Simpson trial, where the jury was overwhelmed by the scientific evidence and likely discounted much of it.

3. THE EXPERT WITNESS

A good courtroom presentation for the prosecution begins with the methods used in evidence recovery, collection, and preservation—in other words, the chain of possession or custody of the material evidence. Each collected item may eventually find its way into court, either as primary evidence or as part of an analysis (work product) that allows a forensic specialist to come to a conclusion. Like a house of cards, unless the chain of custody is preserved, it may topple. The introduction of the material at trial by the prosecution or expert will come under intense scrutiny by the defense team, namely, lawyer and expert witness. In addition of course, the opposing expert witness focuses on the methodology, analysis, and conclusions of his counterpart. Defense will question the qualifications of the expert in *voir dire* in an attempt to ''kill the messenger, if you can't kill the message.'' When a budget allows, a second odontologist might approach the case by different means or presentation yet arrived at the same conclusion, thus reinforcing the client(s)/attorney(s)/agency's case. Alternate light imaging [1–3] and SEM analysis [4] are fields where a second odontologist could be utilized.

A defense expert does not have to disclose either the report or the opinion in the case unless called to do so in cross-examination. On the other hand, defense counsel knowing the expert's opinion will not place the expert on the stand unless it benefits the client. Depending on the jurisdiction, a work product may not be discoverable. A work product might be considered to be materials used in arriving at a conclusion or personal notes made during the analysis of a case.

In each of the methods described, the expert witness must carefully document, demonstrate, and explain the methodology used in the analysis and comparison for the trier of fact. One or several posters/diagrams or a video might be used as an aid for this purpose. The credibility of the expert witness might well hinge upon his/her ability to communicate the information.

Unfortunately, the communication skills of the expert witness are not always at fault. This author has experienced the dozing juror that led to a ''hung jury'' despite the compelling bitemark evidence. The outcome even surprised the defense. The second trial resulted in a conviction of first-degree murder. The best method of conveying testimony is by looking at the trier of fact, be it judge or jury. Eye contact is important. Is the jury attentive? Is the information pertinent? Is the information understandable? In direct testimony the experienced expert witness is normally unstressed. In cross-examination the expert might feel resentment, conflict, aggression, mistrust, or trepidation, bordering on hate for the opposing attorney. This is the adversarial component of the trial. The expert witness must understand this principle and must detach his personal feelings to concentrate on the message he or she is attempting to convey. The expert witness must appear impartial on cross examination despite the fact that the conclusion favors the opposing side.

4. THE MATERIAL

The type of evidence a forensic dentist might utilize includes photographs, dental and bitemark impressions and casts, personal notes, and the official agency report. If the victim is deceased, perhaps resected and preserved tissue, but more likely photographs thereof may be permitted by the judge. From the suspect/accused, facial and oral photographs, an odontogram, dental impressions, bite registration, measurement of maximum bite opening, and a checklist record of evidence are collected [5]. In addition, dental records from both/either victim or suspect might be required. For specifics on these items see the appropriate chapter(s) in this textbook.

Each item of evidence will be introduced individually in court. The collective regrouping of evidence for demonstrative purposes will be introduced separately. For example, if incorporating given photographs within a chart, diagram, poster (Figs. 1 and 2), or video, a duplicate will need to first be introduced as a court exhibit. Opposing counsel might attempt to block its introduction, or its use as part of the composite (group) demonstrative aids. A favorable ruling by the judge will be needed to introduce the material at trial.

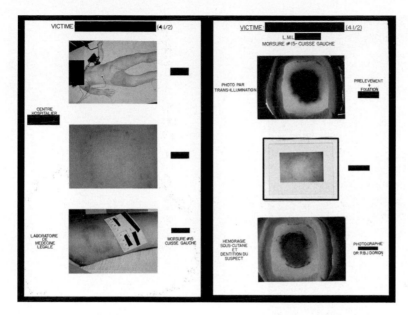

Figure 1   Photographs mounted on posters for court presentation. (Courtesy of Dr. Robert Dorion.)

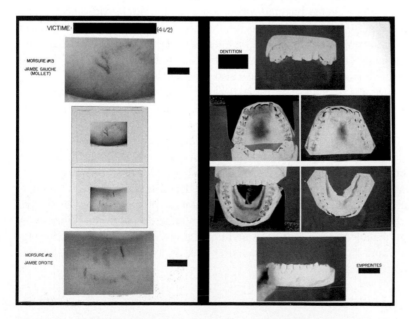

Figure 2   Photographs mounted on posters for court presentation. (Courtesy of Dr. Robert Dorion.)

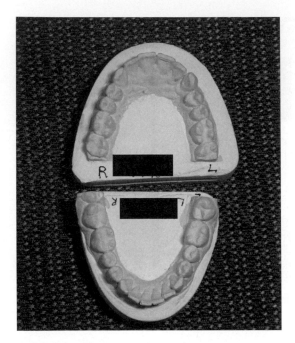

Figure 3 Contrasting-color die stone.

Dorion reports (personal communication, 2003) on a series of four posters presented in a 1984 homicide trial. The color posters measured approximately three feet by two feet with imbedded black-and-white and color photographs. The smallest photographs were in a 1:1 ratio in black-and-white. The posters depicted bitemark photographs of the thigh, calf, and leg of a female infanticide victim (Figs. 1 and 2), and the accused's dental casts in standard and mirror images. A fourth poster demonstrated the Dorion techniques of excision, fixation, and transillumination of bitemarks for the first time. The comparative technique of using the accused's incisal overlays to the subcutaneous hemorrhage pattern was also used for the first time.

Be prepared for any eventuality in the courtroom, because it can and will happen. Opposing attorneys have been known to ''accidentally'' damage evidence, such as dropping dental casts or separating overlays from photographs.

Dental cast should be as neatly trimmed as would be ideal orthodontic models. There is nothing more unprofessional than dental casts that look like quick-pour study models. To improve the visibility of dental models, they can be poured in a contrasting color die stone (e.g., Green Die Keen, Kerr Dental Mfg.), and its base in a yellow or white dental stone (Fig. 3). All models and other evidence should be clearly labeled for identification purposes. If a model box or container is available, the items therein can additionally be numbered as group evidence. A supply of Ziploc bags and bubble wrap can serve as additional protection in preserving/storing/ transporting the various impressions and models to court. Wax or styrofoam bite registrations should also be properly preserved and stored.

5. COURTROOM AIDS

The earliest courtroom aids for bitemark evidence relied on hand-drawn transparent acetate overlays produced from either wax bite incisal/occlusal impressions or incisal outlines of dental casts. The life-size overlays were then placed on top of the bitemark photograph for visual comparison. A one-to-one scale overlay/bitemark photograph was difficult for the expert/judge/jury to appreciate, so multiple times life-size props were created. Charts and drawings with arrows and other markings (Fig. 4) were used on easels or overhead projectors.

In an attempt to move from hand-drawn acetate overlays to a more precise analytical method, Rawson [6] mentions radiographic duplication of the incisal image by placing a radio-paque powder such as barium sulfate, or amalgam filings and acrylic into the wax bite registration, irradiating the bite registration and underlying x-ray film, and then comparing it to the photographs of the injury. By reverse-printing the radiographic image, hollow volume overlays were produced for comparison [7]. Later, analog photographs created black-and-white transparencies in various magnifications ($1\times$, $2\times$, $3\times$, etc), which were compared to analog photographs of the bitemark at the same magnification. Other methods utilized copying machines [8] for the production of overlays. This involved the blackening of incisal edges of dental casts and photocopying the models on acetate rather than paper. Sweet [9,10] first described a method of comparison by computer scanning dental models and bitemark photographs using Adobe PhotoShop. Currently digital images can be captured directly rather than having to scan standard photographs.

As overlay techniques have changed, so have courtroom aids progressed. Stone models have been replaced by multicolored or clear [11] acrylics. Models can be articulated using simple hinge articulators or the more sophisticated ones such as Whip Mix or Hanau (Fig. 5). It should be noted, however, that mounting dental models on an expensive articulator might not be a wise business decision, unless reimbursement has been prearranged with the hiring party. Moreover, a personal articulator would not be returned until the end of trial at the very earliest, or until all appeals have been exhausted.

A cheaper technique of mounting stone or acrylic dental casts employs the Vise Grip sheet metal plier (Fig. 6) [12]. In one court testimony, the "dramatic" effect was not lost on the jurors, who proceeded to "bite" themselves both in the jury box and room, much to the dismay

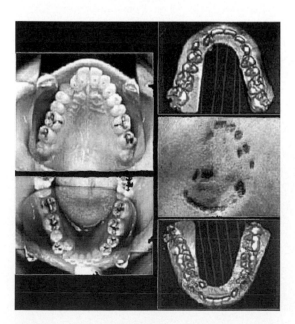

Figure 4 Poster of perpetrator's dentition, Aluwax, and bitemark.

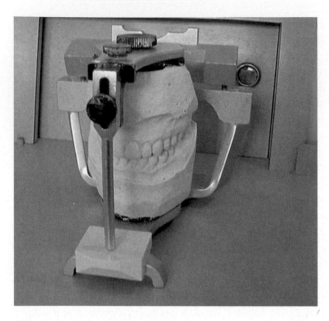

Figure 5 Hanau articulator.

of opposing attorneys. More sophisticated and adjustable pliers were developed but failed to gain general acceptance because of excessive cost.

This author has used a pediatric Dentek dental form (Fig. 7) restored with multiple stainless-steel crowns and multisurface restorations as present in the plaintiff's oral cavity for demonstration in a malpractice case. The axiom is to think creatively while preserving good taste and science.

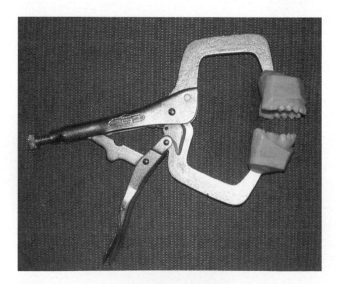

Figure 6 Vise Grip sheet metal pliers.

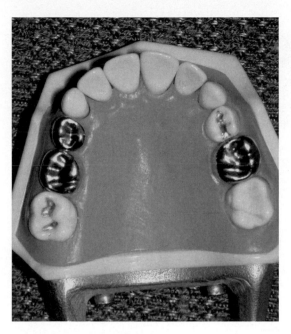

Figure 7 A pediatric Dentek dental form.

One of the first examples of video presentation of evidence was done by Rawson in the mid-1980s [6]. Two cameras and a video mixer were used to wipe and fade the image of the dentition over the injury. At the time, the equipment was costly and confined to institutions with audiovisual/television production capabilities. Various adaptations of video superimposition techniques were carried out by Dorion and Gould (personal communication, 2002) and Kenney (Figs. 8, 9), among others, over the past 15 years. Each item of evidence was recorded and a step-by-step "storyboard" created. Video lends itself to a compelling, direct, and dynamic presentation of the comparison, by moving the model or overlay over the photograph of the injury. Alternatively, the model can be "moved" over the polyvinylsiloxane replica of the injured tissue or against the resected supported (ringed) tissue itself. As home video editing equipment became more sophisticated and reasonably priced, it became easier to produce court-room presentations on videotape adding labels, arrows, and other diagrammatic aids. Wiping between overlaid images or fading in and out demonstrated the comparison/exclusion of the suspect/accused's dentition to the bitemark. The same superimposition technique (also called approximation) utilizes an antemortem photograph of a known person comparing it to the un-known's skull. A refinement of the technique compares the dentition in a like manner (G. Gould, personal communication, 2003). Lastly, the superimposition technique has successfully been used in tool mark, tire print, shoe print, knife, print and ballistic comparison, although depending on the jurisdiction an odontologist's testimony in these matters may or may not be permitted at trial or upheld on appeal.

To give a trier of fact evidence that could not be damaged, Stimson (P. Stimson, personal communication, 2003) in the mid-1970s initially had orthodontic wire contour the buccal surfaces of the teeth, then approximated it to the bitemark photograph as an overlay (Fig. 10). After the exhibit was physically distorted by a defense attorney during trial, chrome cobalt castings (Fig. 11) replaced the wire. Occlusal rests placed on posterior teeth stabilized the appliance.

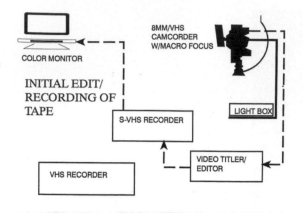

Figure 8 Initial edit/recording of tape flow chart.

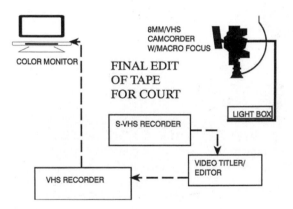

Figure 9 Final tape-editing flow chart.

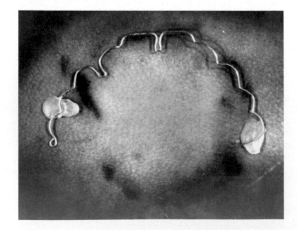

Figure 10 Orthodontic wire outlining bitemark. (Photo courtesy of Dr. Paul G.Stimson.)

Figure 11 Chrome cobalt casting outlining bitemark on cast. (Photo courtesy of Dr. Paul G.Stimson.)

Stimson (personal communication, 2003) also suggests the following method to index overlays, be they photographic, xerographic, or computer generated. The occlusal table of a posterior tooth such as a first bicuspid on only one side of the arch is blackened, so it is duplicated on the overlay as well as the model. Marking right and left as well makes it easier for the jurors to determine which ''side is up'' when watching the demonstration, and later attempting to duplicate it in the jury room. Another method used by this author is to color code the incisal edges of the teeth on the overlays. Red is always the right front tooth, green the left front tooth etc. (Figs. 12 and 13) working outward to the cuspids. In this way the jury can be instructed to view the ''green tooth'' or the ''red tooth,'' or whatever tooth/color is significant, rather than confusing them further with tooth numbers or names such as central or lateral incisor, cuspid, etc.

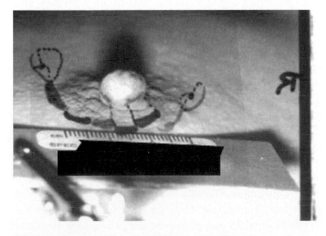

Figure 12 Overlay on bitemark photograph.

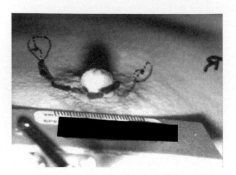

Figure 13   Overlay on bitemark photograph.

The use of computers, scanning devices, and digital photographs are in current usage. Manipulating digital images is facilitated by the presence of the ABFO No. 2 scale used to orient dental casts and bitemarks in comparison techniques. The scale/ruler associated with the dental casts will be ''flipped'' if in the wrong orientation.

Golden (Golden, personal communication, 2003) prepares sequential working images of the bite and the overlays in various positions for comparisons. He suggests an Epson printer that has a 60″-wide format, and uses continuous roll photo paper for length, to create poster size exemplars. The evidence unit of a large police department or county sheriff/district attorney/ state's attorney may have such a printer available. Another option would be a local quick print franchise; however, if they are open 24 hours it would be wise to choose a low traffic time such as 2–3 AM, to do this kind of work.

Scanning electron microscopy (SEM) presents its own set of problems because of the ''shades of gray'' in the created images. It is necessary to clearly explain to the jury what SEM is, how it creates the image, and how the comparisons are made. Fade-in/fade-out and wiping the blended images can all work to demonstrate the techniques to the jury. Sometimes the simpler method of ''poster and arrows'' will adequately convey the correspondence between the perpetrator's dentition and the bitemark. David (personal communication, 2003) suggests that the overlay technique is as good a method as any in demonstrating to the jury how the injury was inflicted.

Courtroom presentations have undergone development in the past quarter century and are more sophisticated. Today, PowerPoint presentations are commonplace. High-resolution projectors and large-screen HDTV are equipment necessities.

According to a protocol suggested by Wright (personal communication, 2003), a copy of the CD/DVD should be provided the court, as well as 1200-dpi prints of each slide in the program that are authenticated. Wright (personal communication, 2003) and Averill are developing a ''streaming video'' for use in PowerPoint presentations. Pixelization of the image can be problematic, particularly if you are attempting to show a dynamic bitemark comparison at macro focus via PowerPoint.

Digital analysis of bitemark evidence is state of the art. The best ''cookbook'' is Bowers and Johansen's text Digital Analysis of Bite Mark Evidence [13], which covers step-by-step procedures to follow. Some legal problems have arisen regarding digitalization and implied manipulation of evidence to ''make it fit.'' This author digitally enlarged and printed standard bitemark photographs to life-size for court use. The public defender called into question the technique and authenticity of the photos. The original 35-mm negatives and prints were available to refute the public defender's misguided queries. If the ''history'' palette within Photoshop is ''logged,'' the step-by-step changes from the original scanned image can be traced, duplicated, and printed. This still does not preclude the defense from arguing that the image was otherwise manipulated by addition or subtraction to make it fit. Wright (personal communication, 2003) further suggests that images be scanned and printed, not just cut and pasted on the computer so that the jury can take the evidence into the jury room and do their own testing.

A word on courtroom demeanor should be added. Being well prepared, neatly and conservatively dressed in a dark suit or sport-coat with tie will add to one's credibility. In unfamiliar jurisdictions, the client attorney can serve as guide. Look at the jurors while testifying. Likewise, in a bench trial, attention should be directed to the judge, the trier of fact, decision maker, and verdict renderer. Provide a business card for the court reporter, perhaps with a glossary of terms to be used. It is also helpful to spell out unfamiliar words (odontology is probably first on the list) for the court.

6. CONCLUSION

In conclusion, the expert should present the scientific evidence creatively and understandably. He should educate the judge and jury on the relevant evidence to which he has been called to testify in a simple and straightforward manner. The expert should guide his audience from collection, to analysis and comparison of evidence with precision and humility be it for prosecution or for the defense.

REFERENCES

1. Krauss TC, Warlen SC. The forensic science use of reflective ultraviolet photography. J Forens Sci 1985; 30(1):262–268.
2. David TJ, Sobel MN. Recapturing a five-month-old bite mark by means of reflective ultraviolet photography. J Forens Sci 1994; 39(6):1560–1567.
3. Golden GS. Alternative light source illumination in bite mark photography. J Forens Sci 1994; 39(3): 815–823.
4. David TJ. Adjunctive use of scanning electron microscopy in bite mark analysis: a three dimensional study. J Forens Sci 1986; 31(3):1126–1134.
5. Vale GL. Los Angeles County Coroner's Office Forms 21 and 21A.
6. Rawson RL. Northwestern Universtiy bitemark update course, 1985.
7. Rawson RL, Ommen RK, Kinard G, Johnson J, Yflantis A. Statistical evidence for the individuality of the human dentition. J Forens Sci 1984; 29(1):245–253.
8. Dailey JC. A practical technique for the fabrication of transparent bite mark overlays. J Forens Sci 1991; 26(2):565–570.
9. Sweet D, Parhar M, Wood RE. A computer-based production of bite mark comparison overlays. J Forens Sci 1998; 43(5):1050–1055.
10. Sweet D, Bowers CM. Accuracy of bite mark overlays: a comparisoin of five common methods to produce exemplars from a suspect's dentition. J Forens Sci 1998; 43(2):362–367.
11. McKinstrey RE. Resin dental casts as an aid in bite mark identification. J Forens Sci 1995; 40(2): 300–302.
12. Smith ES. Northwestern University bitemark update course. 1985.
13. Bowers CM, Johansen RJ. Digital Analysis of Bitemark Evidence, Forensic Imaging Services. 2000.

26
Legal Liability of an Expert Witness

Haskell M. Pitluck
Crystal Lake, Illinois

1. REASONING BEHIND ABSOLUTE IMMUNITY

The concept of witness immunity stemmed from the old English common law to encourage witnesses to participate in litigation without fear of retaliating lawsuits from unhappy participants. In the case of Briscoe v. LaHue [1], the United States Supreme Court held that trial witnesses are entitled to absolute immunity for their trial testimony. The Court noted that ignoring liability for testimony in a judicial proceeding could have the effect of inducing two types of self-censorship: "First, witnesses might be reluctant to come forward to testify. And once a witness is on the stand, his testimony might be distorted by the fear of subsequent liability. ⋯ A witness who knows that he might be forced to defend a subsequent lawsuit, and perhaps, to pay damages, might be inclined to shade his testimony in favor of the potential plaintiff, to magnify uncertainties, and thus to deprive the finder of fact of candid, objective and undistorted evidence" [2].

Witness immunity has also been held to extend to pretrial statements and opinions offered in deposition testimony and advisory reports prepared in the course of litigation [3]. This is a logical extension to include those items the witness has to prepare leading up to his or her testimony.

Expert witnesses have enjoyed almost universal immunity from liability as a result of their court testimony. Within the Past few years, however, this immunity is being eroded to the point that experts should, and rightly so, be cautious, careful, and confident when expressing their opinions.

As recently as November 2000, Mark Hansen, in an article in the American Bar Association Journal, wrote that up to that point, only eight states courts had addressed the issue of expert witness immunity [4]. To that time, no court had allowed an expert witness to be sued by an adverse party over testimony [5]. However, lawsuits against friendly experts are increasing [6].

2. CHANGING CONCEPTS REGARDING ABSOLUTE IMMUNITY

To give the reader an idea of how suits against experts are progressing, a brief history and evolution of some of the pertinent cases follow.

On July 20, 1989, the Supreme Court of Washington, in the case of Bruce v. Byrne-Stevens & Associates Engineers Inc [7] held that an engineer who testified as an expert witness, on behalf of the people suing him, at a previous trial, was entitled to absolute immunity from suit based on his testimony. The defendant miscalculated the cost of the amount of damages necessary to stabilize the plaintiffs' property that resulted in the plaintiff getting a judgment for about half of the necessary actual cost. This is an interesting case decision as four judges concurred in the majority opinion, one judge concurred in the result only, and four judges dissented. So, although it was a close 5–4 decision, the defendant was granted absolute immunity. However, with close decisions such as this one, you look for a possible change of the law in the future.

While the law in Washington has not changed relative to the absolute immunity from testimony, the case of Deatherage v. State of Washington Examining Board of Psychology [8] decided by the Supreme Court of Washington on December 24, 1997, held that such immunity cannot be raised as a defense to a state licensing board's initiation of a professional disciplinary proceeding. In other words, although the expert was not subject to liability, he could still lose his license to practice.

On April 9, 1992, the California Court of Appeal decided Mattco Forge Inc v. Arthur Young & Co. [9] and held that the litigation privilege does not shield a party's own witness from an action by the party arising from the expert's negligence and breach of contract. Several months later, on November 24, 1992, The Supreme Court of Missouri, in the case of Murphy v. AA Mathews [10] held that witness immunity does not bar negligence suits against professional experts who agree to provide litigation-related service for compensation if the professional is negligent in providing the agreed services.

Opposite to this ruling, the Pennsylvania Supreme Court held in the case of Panitz v. Behrend [11] on October 13, 1993, that Panitz was immune from civil liability even though on cross-examination, she failed to support the position she had earlier informed the law firm she would take.

On December 7, 1993, the Court of Appeals of Nebraska in Central Ice Machine Company v. Cole [12] held "in the absence of a statute imposing civil liability, we believe the better policy to be to grant witnesses immunity from civil liability for damages resulting from statements made by them as such, and to leave the matter of liability for perjury to the criminal law" [13].

In Tyner v. State of Washington [14], the Court of Appeals in Washington, on September 28, 1998, denied the State the shield of expert witness immunity wherein the Plaintiff was suing the State for negligent investigation, not for negligence in providing expert testimony [15].

The Colorado Court of Appeals in the case of Dalton v. Miller [16] held on April 29, 1999, that the defendant psychiatrist was entitled to absolute immunity from civil liability for statements he made in an evidence deposition and for the contents of the report he prepared for counsel [17]. It is interesting to note that the court stated, "In so holding, we note that the liability of expert witnesses to the party or parties employing them is not at issue in this case. Our holding here is limited to suits against witnesses by parties who are adverse to those who employed the witness" [18]. The matter was remanded for trail on other issues.

In LLMD of Michigan Inc v. Jackson-Cross Company [19], the Supreme Court of Pennsylvania on October 20, 1999, distinguished the case of Panitz [20] in not extending the witness immunity doctrine to professional negligence actions that are brought against an expert witness when the allegations of negligence are not premised on the substance of the expert's opinion [21]. There was a dissent filed that stated that the distinction was unworkable and a radical departure from their accepted law regarding witness immunity [22].

In a case of first impression, the Superior Court of Connecticut, Judicial District of New Haven, on May 17, 2000, held in the case of Pollock v. Panjabi [23] that claims in connection with an expert's alleged failure to provide adequate support services were not barred by witness immunity.

Shortly after that decision, in the case of Rohrer v. Connelly [24], the Court of Common Pleas of Pennsylvania, Dauphin County on July 21, 2000, citing the Pennsylvania Supreme Court in LLMD of Michigan Inc v. Jackson-Cross Co [25], to be directly on point in illustrating the distinction between unfavorable expert testimony and professional negligence in the preparation of an expert report [26] and denied the defendant's claim for immunity from plaintiff's claim for professional negligence. The Court stated, "The sound public policies afforded by the immunities granted to lay witnesses — and even non-negligent expert testimony — will not be undermined by holding experts to the same standard of care in preparing for litigation as they would in their routine professional practice" [27].

Less than a year later, on April 12, 2001, the United State Court of Appeals for the Fifth Circuit, on an appeal from the U.S. District Court for the Eastern District of Louisiana, in the case of Marrogi v. Howard [28], certified the following questions for decision to the Louisiana Supreme Court: "Under Louisiana law, does witness immunity bar a claim against a retained expert witness, asserted by a party who in prior litigation retained that expert, which claim arises from the expert's allegedly deficient performance of his duties to provide litigation services, such as the formulation of opinions and recommendations, and to give opinion testimony before or during trial?" [29].

The Louisiana Supreme Court answered that question in the negative on January 15, 2002, and furthermore held that, as a matter of first impression under Louisiana law, witness immunity did not bar a claim against a retained expert witness, asserted by a party who in prior litigation retained that expert, which claims arose from the expert's allegedly deficient performance of his duties to provide litigation services [30].

Also in a case of first impression, the Supreme Court of Massachusetts, on October 31, 2001, in the case of Boyes-Bogie v. Horwitz [31] denied the Defendant's motion for summary judgment and held that the doctrine of witness immunity does not bar a claim for negligence against an expert privately retained to provide litigation support services by the party who retained the expert in the circumstances of this case [32], which dealt with business evaluation in a divorce case.

On April 26, 2002, the Supreme Court of Appeals of West Virginia in the case of Davis et al v. Wallace et al [33] filed a most interesting opinion. The plaintiff, Davis, an incarcerated felon, sued many experts who were witnesses for the State in her criminal trial. She alleged that the experts negligently performed tests, negligently prepared for testimony, negligently testified, and otherwise failed to meet the "standards of science and medicine as it existed at that time" [34].

The Circuit Court granted the defendants' motion to dismiss and allowed sanctions in the amount of $8500 for attorney fees against Davis, her next friend, and their attorney, finding the claims frivolous in nature with no evidentiary support, and that the appellants filed the lawsuit with a vexatious, wanton, or oppressive intent to intimidate the appellees regarding their testimony at any post trial hearing in the criminal case, or to seek to punish them for their testimony at the criminal trial [35].

The appellants appealed the awarding of sanctions. The Appellate Court reversed the sanctions in stating that some jurisdictions held expert witnesses liable in some circumstances and that while West Virginia law is not settled in the area of expert witness immunity, and that at this time, they were not addressing the issue of witness immunity. The appellate court stated they were only addressing whether a trial judge abused his discretion by sanctioning a litigant and her attorney for expounding a novel cause of action that is not currently recognized in West Virginia [36].

Further, the appellate court stated that "since there is a plurality of opinions in other jurisdictions, the appellants' claim cannot be found to be in bad faith as an assertion that cannot support a good faith argument for the application, extension, modification, or reversal of existing law'' [37].

The Chief Justice filed a vigorous dissent and another justice filed a concurring opinion, criticizing the dissent: "The unnecessarily harsh dissent is but a lengthy essay on the issue of whether there exists in West Virginia a cause of action for negligence or malpractice against forensic experts. The majority opinion clearly acknowledges that there is not a cause of action for suing an opposing party's expert witness in West Virginia ···'' [38].

The concurring opinion goes on to say,

> The majority merely acknowledges that there is an emerging body of case law and scholarly work that have begun to question the granting of absolute immunity to expert witnesses, often known in legal circles as "hired guns" for their in-court testimony and out-of-court preparations. Several law review articles and courts have begun to argue that it is not unreasonable to expect that expert witnesses should be held to standards of their profession both in and outside of the courtroom, and several jurisdictions have permitted such lawsuits. Considering the developing trend, the appellants' suit against the State's expert witnesses should not be seen as frivolous. Thus this Court was within its authority to find that the trial court erred in levying sanctions [39].

3. EXPERT WITNESS IMMUNITY SPECIFIC TO DENTISTS

There are also two cases regarding immunity of expert witnesses that are of specific interest to dentists, regarding bitemarks.

The first is Anthony Otero v. Allan J. Warnick, D.D.S. [40], decided by the Michigan Court of Appeals on May 12, 2000. The plaintiff, a former suspect in a murder case, appealed from the Circuit Court's order granting summary disposition in favor of defendant Allen J. Warnick, D.D.S., the chief forensic odontologist for the Wayne County Medical Examiner's Office.

> In October 1994, Virginia Airasolo was sexually assaulted and murdered. Defendant performed an examination and concluded that wound pattern injuries on the body were consistent with human bitemarks. Following plaintiff's arrest in connection with the murder, he consented to a search and allowed defendant to take impressions of his teeth and to review his dental records. In his written report to the Detroit Police Department, defendant opined that some of the bitemarks on Airasolo's body matched plaintiff's dentition. A warrant was issued charging plaintiff with first-degree murder and felony murder, and he was arrested and incarcerated. During plaintiff's preliminary examination on December 13, 1994, defendant testified regarding his findings, suggesting that plaintiff was the only person in the world who could have inflicted the bitemarks on Airasolo's body.
>
> On January 30, 1995, the Detroit Police Crime laboratory released a supplemental report that concluded that plaintiff was excluded as a possible source of DNA obtained from vaginal and rectal swabs taken from Airasolo's body. In April 1995, following the issuance of a favorable DNA report, plaintiff — who by that time had spent five months in jail — was released after posing a $60,000 cash bond. At about the same time, plaintiff obtained his release from jail, defendant solicited a second opinion from forensic odontologist Richard Souviron of Dade County, Florida. Souviron issued a report concluding that, while the injury patterns on Airasolo's body were consistent with human bitemarks, the details of the injuries were too indistinct to be used to include or exclude any suspect. As a result of this second opinion, the charges against plaintiff were dismissed. Plaintiff subsequently sued defendant, alleging gross negligence [41].

"As a government employee, Warnick was immune from tort liability, while engaged in governmental functions if he was acting, or reasonable believed he was acting, within the scope of his authority, unless his conduct amounted to gross negligence that was the proximate cause of the plaintiff's injury or damage'' [42].

Warnick ''moved for summary disposition arguing that he was entitled to absolute witness immunity; that, pursuant to the public-duty doctrine, he owed no duty to plaintiff; and that plaintiff's claim was barred by the statute of limitations. The circuit court granted the motion, concluding that the public-duty doctrine was applicable and the defendant, therefore, owed plaintiff no duty of care'' [43].

The Court stated,

> The statute specifically authorizes county medical examiners to employ non-licensed physicians to assist in the investigation of deaths if the medical examiner determines that persons with specialized qualifications and knowledge are needed to assist in that investigation. Considering this legislative scheme, we see no reason to limit the analysis ⋯ simply to the appointed county medical examiner. To the contrary, the logic ⋯ would apply to any person duly authorized by the examiner to assist in an investigation authorized and, in fact, required by the statute. ⋯ We conclude that the protection afforded a county medical examiner extends to persons employed by the medical examiner to assist in the investigation of a death. The county medical examiner here employed defendant, an odontologist, to assist in the investigation of a crime where the victim had bitemarks that might have helped establish identify of the assailant. Having been authorized by the medical examiner to assist in the investigation because of the special knowledge and experience he brought to the case, defendant's only duty was to the medical examiner and to the state, and defendant fulfilled that duty by providing his expert opinion and testimony to aid in the investigation of the offense. Thus, under the medical examiner's statute, defendant owed no duty to plaintiff [44].

The court went on to say that no duty was owed to plaintiff for a separate and independent reason as well. ''Defendant's role in the investigation was plainly adversarial to plaintiff's interests and defendant's duty as a witness at the preliminary examination was owed to the court, not to plaintiff. ⋯ We conclude that defendant would have owed plaintiff no duty even if the medical examiner's statute was inapplicable'' [45].

With regard to witness immunity, the Court stated:

> Finally, to the extent that plaintiff's claim is based on the theory that defendant was grossly negligent in testifying against him at his preliminary examination, summary disposition was also proper. ⋯ Because defendant was a witness testifying during the course of judicial proceedings, his statements were absolutely privileged, provided they were relevant, material or pertinent to the issue being tried. ⋯ This quasi-judicial immunity applies even though defendant's examination was performed, and his opinion developed, out of court [46].

The Appellate Court affirmed the dismissal of the plaintiff's case. However, their conclusion in the opinion contains language that no expert witness likes to see, and is included here only as an instructional caution for future behavior.

> Accepting as true the allegations in plaintiff's complaint, it is apparent that defendant performed his tasks with respect to the Airasolo murder in an incompetent, if not reprehensible, manner. Plaintiff ends his brief to us with an impassioned plea:

> Defendant Warnick, for whatever reason, crossed the line between prosecution and persecution, turning a system of justice into a system of oppression. In so doing, he trampled upon the rights of Plaintiff and caused him enormous, horrific harm. Plaintiff now turns to you jurists, simply seeking and demanding a fair trial in his quest for a measure of justice. No self-respecting system of justice would deny him access to the courts and to our cherished jury system [47].

In response the Appellate Court stated: "We sympathize with plaintiff but conclude that regardless of how badly defendant performed his investigation and the harm that resulted, plaintiff's claims are so clearly unenforceable as a matter of law that they cannot go to a jury" [48]. How long this will remain the law in Michigan remains to be seen.

The second case is an opinion filed January 8, 2003, by the United States court of Appeals for the Fifth Circuit (Eastern District) of Louisiana in the case of Anthony G. Keko v. I.F. Hingle et al. [49]. Two interlocutory appeals were brought from the district court's decision in a 42 U.S.C 1983 action filed by Tony Keko "to redress his overturned conviction of the 1991 murder of his estranged wife Louise. Keko appeals the court's rendition of a Rule 54(b)–certified summary judgment in favor of two sheriffs and several law enforcement and prosecutorial personnel involved in obtaining the conviction. Dr. Michael H. West, whose tainted expert testimony led to the overturning of Keko's conviction, appeals from the denial of absolute immunity. We affirm the appeal of the latter judgment" [50].

Keko argued on appeal that the other defendants (Appellees) contributed to a constitutionally defective search warrant that, when approved by a state court judge, authorized, among other things, the taking of Keko's dental impressions. "The dental impressions, according to Dr. West, ⋯ corresponded with bite marks found on Louise's exhumed body. Dr. West's evidence provided the only direct evidentiary link at trial connecting Keko to the crime" [51].

The judgment in favor of Dr. West's codefendants was affirmed. The Court stated, however, "Dr. West's appeal of the denial of absolute immunity is more problematic" [52]. He was not an employee of the Parish or of any state or local government agency.

The court went on to say,

Dr. West has not contested the legal sufficiency of the claims against him. Nor has Dr. West challenged the district court's ruling that he might be entitled to qualified immunity, but fact issues preclude its being granted at this time.

Instead, and more boldly, Dr. West asserts that he is entitled to absolute immunity (a) for the expert witness report he authored, which was offered at a probable cause hearing to obtain an arrest warrant for Keko, and (b) for the research and investigative work that led to preparation of the expert report. ⋯ Dr. West argues, not without force, that the protection of absolute immunity is lost if an expert witness, whose testimonial competence derives solely from the application of his expertise to an investigation conducted by the state, may be sued for the activity that spawned his testimony [53].

The Court, however, pointed out that absolute immunity applies only "within the precise confines of adversarial judicial proceedings" [54] and since the testimony in question here was not West's trial testimony, but an ex parte probable cause hearing—not the type of judicial proceeding for which a witness's testimony would require the full shield of absolute immunity [55]. The court determined that the case presents a question of fact as to the degree of Dr. West's participation in the prosecution that could not be resolved on summary judgment based on the record.

The Court stated:

West may not have been a formal member of the prosecutorial team or responsible for final prosecutorial decisions, but his report stated that "indeed and without doubt," the bitemarks he observed on the exhumed body of Louise Keko matched Tony's dental impressions. Further, according to the state court, his report was critical to obtaining probable cause to arrest, he examined only Tony Keko's dental impressions and not those of any other potential suspect, and he performed his function at the behest of the sheriff's office to assist in "identifying" the attacker. The complaining witness doctrine thus offers no defense as a matter of law to Dr. West [56].

The Court concluded,

> The doctor also seeks absolute immunity for his pre-testimonial activities in examining Mrs. Keko's body, obtaining and examining Keko's dental impressions and writing a report, ··· to the extent Dr. West's pre-testimonial activities were investigative, his immunity ought to correlate with the merely qualified immunity granted to the police for comparable activities. Thus, if, as alleged, Dr. West used shoddy and unscientific research techniques that resulted in a report critical to a baseless murder prosecution of Keko, there is no obvious reason why Dr. West should enjoy immunity greater than that of other investigators. By holding that absolute immunity does not shield Dr. West, we do not imply any opinion on the strength of his qualified immunity defense or the ultimate validity of Keko's conspiracy allegations [57].

The Court is, in effect, saying that Dr. West may have immunity but not absolute immunity, and that a determination will have to be made on a factual basis.

This case also is not one that an expert likes to see, and is also included as an instructional caution for future behavior. Whatever the outcome, the time, trouble, and monetary expense is something with which no one would like to be involved. This case was settled after the Court's ruling. Thus, no further appeal or hearing will take place.

4. WHAT DOES IT MEAN FOR THE EXPERT?

It is easy to see from the chronicled cases that the law is changing. Absolute immunity for expert witnesses is no longer a sure thing. Experts should be aware of this and conduct themselves accordingly.

There are arguments both for and against expert immunity. The primary argument for allowing expert immunity is as set forth in the Briscoe case earlier [58]—i.e., to encourage witnesses to come forward with candid testimony without fear of reprisal. Bear in mind, however, there are literally thousands of expert witnesses who are being paid for their testimony. Although, in theory, they are to aid the court in understanding the evidence, in fact, they are hired by one of the parties, and in some cases, the Court itself, to propound that party's portion of the case. If their testimony or opinion is not favorable to the party who hires them, they will probably not be called to testify. There is also some concern that by allowing experts to be sued, litigation will increase.

The primary argument against witness immunity is also logical in that it alleges that the threat of liability will encourage experts to be more careful and accurate in their preparation and testimony. Experts are hired professionals and are paid for their work. They should be held to the same standards as anyone else. If their work is not competent, they should be held responsible. There is an excellent law review article on this subject, ''Witness Immunity Under Attack: Disarming 'Hired Guns,''' by Randall K. Hanson in the Wake Forest Law Review [59].

It is easy to see that the law is changing when it comes to absolute immunity for expert witnesses. Although absolute immunity for experts is no longer a certain thing, it is also very important to remember that even if you have immunity from liability, you can still be subject to disciplinary proceedings within your state or professional organization's licensing boards. You could lose your license to practice, even if you are not civilly liable. You could also be subject to perjury or contempt of court.

Even if an expert witness is not civilly liable monetarily, the expert witness can still be sued. Even if the expert wins, the accompanying cost in time, trouble and financial cost is not a pleasant experience. In this day and age, no one should be involved as an expert witness without malpractice insurance. Expert witnesses should check with their insurance carrier to discuss the type of insurance coverage most appropriate for their work, and remember that it may not be enough to be insured by the government agency that hires you.

The cases previously discussed are by no means an exhaustive list of cases regarding liability of expert witnesses. They are only selected examples to alert the reader that the law is changing and that expert witnesses should be careful, conscientious, and competent.

REFERENCES

1. Briscoe v. LaHue 460 US 325, 103 S.Ct 1108, (March 7, 1984).
2. Briscoe v LaHue 460 US 325 at page 333 (1984).
3. Moses v McWilliams 379 Pa Sup Ct 150 at 166 (1988).
4. Hansen M. Experts Are Liable Too, ABA Journal, Nov. 2000.
5. Hansen M. Experts Are Liable Too, ABA Journal, Nov. 2000.
6. California, Connecticut, Missouri, Pennsylvania, Texas have allowed litigation to proceed against friendly experts. Louisiana and Washington had held that friendly experts were absolutely immune from liability. New Jersey held that even a court-appointed expert is not immune from deviating from the accepted standards applicable to his or her profession.
7. 113 Wash. 2d 123, 776 P. 2d 666 (1989).
8. 134 Wash. 2d 131, 948 P.2d 828 (1997).
9. 5 Cal. App 4th 392 (1992).
10. 841 S.W. 2d 671 (1992).
11. 429 Pa. Super. 273, 632 A.2d 562 (1993).
12. 2 Neb. App. 282, 509 N.W. 2d 229 (1993).
13. 2 Neb. App. 282 at 288 (1993).
14. 92 Wash. App. 504, 963 P.2d 215 (1998).
15. 92 Wash. App. 504 at 513 (1998).
16. 984 P.2d. 666 (1999).
17. 984 P.2d 666 at 669 (1999).
18. 984 P.2d 666 at 669 (1999).
19. 559 Pa. 297, 740 A. 2d 186 (1999).
20. 429 Pa. Super 273, 632 A. 2d 562 (1993).
21. 559 Pa. 297 at 306 (1999).
22. 559 Pa. 297 at 308 (1999).
23. 47 Conn. Sup. 179, 781 A.2d 518 (2000).
24. 48 Pa. D. & C. 4th 76 (2000).
25. 559 Pa. 297, 740 A.2d 186 (1999).
26. 48 Pa. D. & C. 4th 76 at 83 (2000).
27. 48 Pa. D. & C. 4th 76 at 85 (2000).
28. 248 F. 3d 382 (2001).
29. 248 F. 3d 382 (2001).
30. 2001 – CQ-1006 (La. 1/15/02), 805 S. 2d 1118 (2002).
31. 2001 WL 1771989 (Mass. Super.), 14 Mass L.Rptr 208 (2001).
32. 2001 WL 1771989 (Mass. Super.), 14 Mass L.Rptr 208 (2001).
33. 211 W. Va. 264, 565 S.E. 2d 386 (2002).
34. 211 W. Va. 264, 565 S.E. 2d 388 (2002). On September 15, 1997, Marybeth Davis was convicted of the attempted poisoning by insulin of her son and the murder of her daughter by caffeine. State v Davis, 205 W. Va. 569, 519 S.E. 2d 852 (1999).
35. 565 S.E. 386 at 388 (2002).
36. 565 S.E. 386 at 391 (2002).
37. 565 S.E. 386 at 391 (2002).
38. 565 S.E. 386 at 398 (2002).
39. 565 S.E. 386 at 388, 399 (2002).

40. 241 Mich. App. 143, 614 N.W. 2d 177 (2000). Appeal denied by Michigan Supreme Court 463 Mich. 903, 618 N.W. 2d 771 (2000).
41. 614 N. W. 2d 177 at 178–179 (2000).
42. 614 N. W. 2d 177 at 179 (2000).
43. 614 N. W. 2d 177 at 179 (2000).
44. 614 N. W. 2d 177 at 181–182 (2000).
45. 614 N. W. 2d 177 at 182 (2000).
46. 614 N. W. 2d 177 at 182 (2000).
47. 614 N. W. 2d 177 at 182 (2000).
48. 614 N. W. 2d 177 at 182 (2000).
49. 318 F. 3d 639 (2003).
50. 318 F. 3d 639 at 641 (2003).
51. 318 F. 3d 639 at 641 (2003).
52. 318 F. 3d 639 at 642 (2003).
53. 318 F. 3d 639 at 642 (2003).
54. 318 F. 3d 639 at 642–643 (2003).
55. 318 F. 3d 639 at 643 (2003).
56. 318 F. 3d 639 at 643–644 (2003).
57. 318 F. 3d 639 at 644 (2003).
58. Briscoe v. LaHue 460 US 325, 103 S. Ct. 1108 (1984).
59. 31 Wake Forest L. Rev. 497. (1996).

XI
Contentious Issues

27
Reliability of Bitemark Evidence

Iain A. Pretty
Lecturer in Restorative Dentistry,
The University of Manchester

1. INTRODUCTION

The detection, observation, collection, and analysis of bitemarks have been thoroughly described in the previous chapters of this volume. Guidelines exist for both the novice and expert to ensure that protocols are followed and that a uniformity of approach is achieved [1,2]. However, the analysis of bitemarks, following, and assuming, good evidence collection is the sole responsibility of the odontologist. He must select an analysis technique, which he believes to be accurate, and apply this, using his prior knowledge, to the materials in front of him [3,4]. The results of these analyses form the basis of the conclusions contained within the written report.

Within the modern judicial system, the previously blind acceptance of science has evolved into an equally sceptical view, and scientists of all disciplines, who present evidence within the judicial system, must be prepared to defend their techniques and demonstrate the sound scientific principles upon which they are based [5–8]. Nowhere is this the case more so than the United States, where specific legislation, in the form of the Daubert ruling, has enlisted the Judge as a scientific ''gatekeeper'' whose function is to assess the scientific integrity of the evidence (rather than the individual presenting that evidence) and determine if it should be heard. While the U.S. judiciary has taken the lead in this area, examples can be found within Commonwealth and European law mirroring the spirit of the Daubert philosophy.

In brief, Daubert states that individuals presenting scientific evidence, based on the application of tests, assessments, or other analyses, should be able to prove, preferably by citing peer-reviewed research, the validity, reliability, and accuracy of such examinations. By doing so, the trier-of-fact (normally the jury) is able to afford the testimony the appropriate weight. Indeed, should a particular test or system prove to be too unreliable, or have a hiatus of supporting research demonstrating efficacy, it is possible that evidence based on such tests may not be admissible in Court. A common example of such science would be the polygraph test.

The purpose of this section is; firstly, to define the terms used when assessing efficacy of tests, and secondly, to demonstrate and appraise some of the research that has been conducted to satisfy the requirements of Daubert for bitemark analysis.

2. WHAT IS RELIABILITY? STATISTICAL DEFINITIONS

There are a number of terms and definitions that are commonly used when describing the effectiveness of tests, many of which are incorrect. It is therefore worthwhile briefly defining some of the terms we will encounter in this section.

2.1. Reliability

Synonymous terms would be reproducibility or agreement. If a test is performed 100 times, will it give the same result on each occasion? The extent of the differences in the results is a measure of reliability. When considering bitemarks, there are two types of reliability that we can consider. The first is interexaminer reliability (or agreement). This is a measure of the examiners reliability. If the same individual examined the same bitemarks 100 times, would he arrive at the same conclusion? The second is intraexaminer reliability; this measures the reliability of the test in the hands of several individuals—i.e., if we presented the same case to 100 odontologists would they all arrive at the same result? [9].

2.2. Validity

This is often misunderstood as accuracy. Validity is simply defined as, ''Is the test measuring what it claims to measure?'' This is of particular importance when considering indirect measurements — for example, the detection of caries from dental radiographs is an indirect measurement. It has been established that an increase in radiographic translucency is a *valid* measure of demineralization and hence radiographs are suitable tests for the diagnosis of caries. Within bitemarks, validity is associated with the analysis technique. For example, Are the biting edges of the teeth represented on transparent overlays a valid means of assessing an injury? [9]

2.3. Accuracy

This is very simply defined as the percentage correct results from any given test. Accuracy is usually presented in this way; Dr. Smith was 90% accurate when he assessed 100 bitemark cases. Accuracy is a somewhat crude measurement of a tests performance, and hence it is usual to include data on sensitivity and specificity [9].

2.4. Sensitivity and Specificity

Sensitivity and specificity are measures of a test's validity, i.e., its ability to correctly identify those individuals with and without the questioned disease, or a test's ability to identify correctly those responsible or not responsible for creating a bite injury. In a diagnostic situation, there can be two outcomes; the person has the disease, or the person does not have the disease; or the suspect is responsible for the bite, or the suspect is excluded as a possible biter. When the results of an examined test are compared to a gold standard, there can be four possibilities:

   1. True positive (TP): The test results indicate that an individual has the disease and this is confirmed by the gold standard.

   2. False positive (FP): The test result indicates that an individual has the disease, but this is not confirmed by the gold standard that finds the individual is disease free.

   3. False negative (FN): The test result indicates that an individual is not suffering from the disease but the gold standard indicates that the disease is present.

   True negative (TN): Both the test result and the gold standard agree that the individual does not have the examined disease.

   The gold standard can be either an established test (e.g., radiographs for dental caries) or a confirmatory standard (e.g., histology sections for dental caries) [9]. Figure 1 illustrates the application of these principles in a 2 × 2 contingency table that permits a clearer view of the system. These tables are commonly used to present the results of such comparisons.

   The sensitivity of a test is its ability to detect correctly people who have the disease, i.e., the percentage of diseased people who are correctly diagnosed. A test that is 100% sensitive will identify every guilty biter; an insensitive test will lead to missed biters. A sensitive test

Gold Standard			
		Positive	Negative	Total
Test Result	Positive	True positive (TP)	False positive (FP)	TP + FP
	Negative	False negative (FN)	True negative (TN)	FN + TN
	Total	TP + FN	FP + TN	FN + TN + FP + TP

Figure 1 A 2×2 contingency table illustrating the outcomes of a comparison between a diagnostic test and a gold standard.

results in very few false-negative results. Diagnostic tests that have a high degree of sensitivity are used in situations where the consequences of a false negative result are serious. An example of this is the screening of donated blood for HIV. Such highly sensitive tests are used for screening or ruling out disease; if the result of a highly sensitive test is negative, it allows the disease to be ruled out with confidence [10].

The specificity of a diagnostic test is the percentage of disease-free individuals who are diagnosed correctly. A test that is always negative for innocent suspects will have a specificity of 100%. A highly specific test produces few false-positive results. Tests that exhibit a high degree of specificity are used in situations where the consequences of a false-positive diagnosis are serious [11]. Examples include where a positive diagnosis leads to the initiation of complex and painful surgery, such as where it may cause an individual to make irreversible life decisions (Alzheimer's). Other examples include where a diagnosis could result in someone being stigmatized with an incorrect label (schizophrenia). Very specific tests are used for confirming the existence of a disease [11]. If a highly specific test is positive, the disease is almost certainly present, or the suspect is almost certainly the biter.

With many diagnostic tests, sensitivity and specificity are inversely related: an increase in one will cause a reduction in the other. Figure 2 shows a diagrammatic representation of a diagnostic test that has a specificity and sensitivity of 100%. The test results of the biters and non-biters subjects show no overlap, and so the threshold level for a diagnosis is between these distributions. If the test result is higher than the threshold, then the test is positive; if below, then the test is negative. All the biters and nonbiters have been correctly identified [12,13].

Figure 3 demonstrates a more realistic situation, one in which the suspect's bitemark analysis results overlap each other rather than forming two separate groups. It is apparent that the use of this (fictious) test to identify biters will require the imposition of a cut-off or threshold point that will determine the sensitivity and specificity of the test [12,13]—i.e., at what certainty levels will the suspect be either excluded or implicated as the biter?

If we use the cut-off point of 5, the test would be 100% sensitive, i.e., correctly identifying all the suspects who were responsible for biting. However, this threshold choice would cause a reduction in specificity, producing a large number of false-positive results, i.e., innocent individuals who would be branded as biters. This demonstrates the inverse relationship between sensitivity and specificity [14,15]. If the threshold point was moved to the right along the x-axis to cut-off point 1, the specificity would be 100%, but the test would become highly insensitive [12,13]. This would result in a large number of guilty suspects being incorrectly assessed as nonbiters.

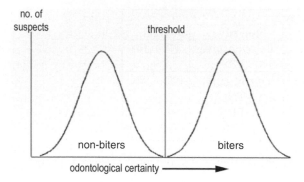

Figure 2   The probability distributions of the results of a perfect diagnostic test. In this example all of the biters have been correctly identified and the non-biters excluded. There is no crossover of the populations of suspects.

From this example, it is clear that a test can only be 100% sensitive and specific when there is no overlap between the biters and nonbiters, or between diseased and nondiseased individuals. Within medical diagnostics this is a rare circumstance and when it does occur, the presence of disease is often so obvious that no diagnostic testing is required. There is no reason to believe that bitemark analyses would differ from these logical rules [16].

2.5   Receiver Operator Characteristics

Sensitivity and specificity describe the results of a procedure in a dichotomous way; a procedure result is either positive or negative [16]. This can be replicated in clinical practice [17]. For example, should we extract a given tooth or not? Should we place this restoration or not? Is this individual a biter or not? However, many clinical procedures are not dichotomous, such as probing of periodontal pockets, or assessment of radiographs for caries where a range of features

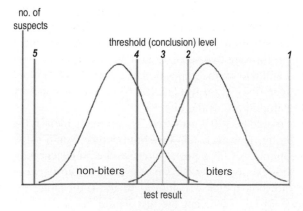

Figure 3   A more realistic situation, one in which the bitemark analysis results overlap each other rather than forming two separate groups.

are examined to produce a certainty regarding the presence or absence of disease. Indeed bitemark assessments, as guided by the ABFO, should be presented using one of a range of possible conclusions, not a dichotomous positive/negative. Is it possible to assess the effectiveness of these tests, without simply imposing an arbitrary threshold? A test known as Receiver Operator Characteristics, or ROC, provides such a technique [14,15].

The use of ROC analyses has increased rapidly over the past 20 years, in particular following the publication of Swets and Pickett's landmark textbook [18]. Many of the early applications of ROC were in the field of radiology, where subjective results are recorded on a rating scale. The expansion of ROC into the evaluation of diagnostic/management procedures that yield numerical results indicates the acceptance of its use and validity [14,15]. ROC analysis is a graphical representation of the reciprocal relationship between sensitivity and specificity calculated from all possible threshold values. ROC analysis can be performed for procedures that provide either continuous data or rating-scale data [16,17,19,20]. The graphical nature of ROC is shown in Figure 4.

Each of the threshold values shown in Figure 3 corresponds to an operating point on the ROC curve of Figure 3 (values 1, 2, 3, 4, and 5). When a high threshold is used (point 1), all suspects are determined to be nonbiters, resulting in both a true-positive fraction (TPF) of zero and a false-positive fraction (FPF) of zero. This situation connotes high specificity (100%). This example relates to the operating point in the lower left-hand corner of the ROC curve. Using a very low threshold (point 5), it can be seen that the TPF and FPF are both 1, with a specificity of 0% and an operating point on the upper right-hand corner of the curve. This means that all the suspects are determined to be biters. The other threshold values represent intermediate points of specificity and sensitivity between the two extremes described [16,17,19,20].

An ROC curve represents the relationship of sensitivity and specificity (and hence is a test used to determine these values) when odontologists are allowed to indicate a degree of uncertainty in their decision-making not afforded when making dichotomous decisions [21].

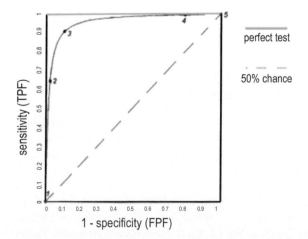

Figure 4 Receiver Operator Characteristics (ROC) curve of the data shown in Figure 3. Each point on the ROC curve relates to one of the thresholds. This method allows a continuous assessment of specificity and sensitivity without imposition of thresholds.

The discriminative ability of any diagnostic test is defined by the distribution of diseased and nondiseased patients or biters and nonbiters. The overlap of these groups determines the shape and position of the ROC curve. A straight line from the lower-left corner to the upper-right corner (shown red in Figure 4) describes a procedure in which the diseased and non-diseased distributions overlap completely and the TPF and FPF are equal at any threshold. This procedure has no discriminative value and is worthless—i.e., no better than a chance allocation of biter/nonbiter to each suspect. A perfect procedure has no overlap between the distributions of biters and non-biters, and would result in the straight along the top of Figure 3.

2.6. Area Under the Curve

The area under the ROC curve (AUC) is a measure of the diagnostic accuracy of a procedure, and is frequently used to permit comparisons between procedures or observers. Using statistical software, the AUC can easily be computed and tested for significant differences using z-scores (univariate). In the example illustrated in Figure 4, the AUC for the procedure that yields no discriminative value (represented by the diagonal hashed line) has an area of 0.5, or 50%. It is no better than a random allocation of positive and negative results (e.g., flipping a coin). The perfect ROC line, represented in solid form, has an AUC of 1.0 or 100%. The results from diagnostic/management procedures used in real life fall within these two extremes of the range. The closer an AUC is to 100%, or 1.0, the more accurate the procedure.

2.7. Positive and Negative Predictive Values

A number of articles have recently been published that describe the positive and negative predictive values of bitemark analysis techniques [22]. When such terms are used in diagnostic medicine, the calculations require a value for the prevalence of the disease within the tested population. When considering bitemarks it would be necessary to apply this in order to arrive at a meaningful value. Ordinarily there is only one biter, but there may be many suspects considered, or individuals with access to the victim. For example, in a case of child abuse where only four individuals had access to the nonambulatory child, the prevalence could be calculated with ease, 1 in 4. However, for the murder victim found by an interstate highway, the possible biters are almost limitless. In such a case it would be impossible to calculate an accurate prevalence. For this reason, it is not recommended that positive and negative predictive values be used to describe the effectiveness of bitemark assessments [11].

3. RELIABILITY, DAUBERT, AND OTHER JUDICIAL RULINGS — THE NEW GATEKEEPERS OF FORENSIC SCIENCE?

The terms Frye, Daubert, and Kumho are well known to those individuals who concern themselves with the acceptance of expert opinion evidence within the U.S. courts. However, the spirit behind these rulings is likely to influence Commonwealth and European law, and thus odontologists the world over should be interested in the admissibility guidelines that have been developed through these judgements.

Daubert was a liability case surrounding the antinausea drug Bendectin (manufactured by Merrell Dow) that, in 1700 actions, was claimed to cause birth defects. The manufacturer asked for summary judgment in the court, stating that a wealth of scientific evidence published in the literature, involving over 130,000 patients, had found no evidence that the drug was capable of causing birth defects. The plaintiffs presented eight experts of their own who had conducted a number of in vitro and in vivo (animal) studies that they claimed proved that the drug caused the defects seen in the two minors, Jason Daubert and Eric Schuller. These experts had also reanalyzed the original research and claimed to have found errors.

The evidence of these experts was not accepted under the Frye standard, in which expert testimony has to be generally accepted. It was decided that epidemiological studies were the accepted form of detecting birth defects and therefore the additional experiments conducted by the plaintiff's experts could not be admitted. Their reanalysis of the original epidemiological studies, while acceptable among the medical field, had not been published or reviewed by peers and therefore was not of a sufficient standard. Merrell Dow's motion was therefore granted.

The Supreme Court reviewed Daubert to resolve the "sharp divisions regarding the proper standard for admission of expert testimony." They developed guidelines for courts to excise their function as gatekeepers of scientific evidence admissibility. A keystone of their advice was that any proffered theory or technique, such as bitemark evidence, can be and has been tested and that the science underlying such techniques has been published in the peer-reviewed literature. Further clarification stated that publication was not necessary a prerequisite, it doesn't guarantee reliability, but that studies that had been exposed to such inquiry supported admission as common errors would be detected. Courts admitting such evidence should also, it was advised, avail themselves of any studies indicating known error rates and the general acceptance of the technique within that particular field. A court would be justifiably sceptical of techniques that held only cursory support or credence within the scientific literature.

It is important to note that the Supreme Court emphasized the importance of flexibility within the guidelines for admissibility. The use of vigorous cross-examination, jury direction, and other judicial tools can assist the trier-of-fact to assign appropriate weight to evidence presented, but that might not have the firmest scientific background. This relates to earlier decisions in which "evidence that is helpful to the Court" would be sufficient for admissibility.

There has been much discussion within both the legal and forensic communities about the likely impact of the Daubert ruling. However, within forensic dentistry, and bitemarks in particular there has been little attention paid to satisfying some of the requirements extolled by the Supreme Court. The case of State v. Hodgson [23] is significant as it was the first appeal case to examine bitemark evidence in the light of the Daubert ruling. Convicted of two counts of first-degree murder, Hodgson appealed the admissibility of the odontological evidence linking a bitemark on his arm to one of the decedents. Arguing that bitemark evidence was not generally accepted he claimed that the science did not meet the requirements of Frye. The Court disagreed with Hodgson stating that Daubert and FRE 702 had superseded Frye and that they were satisfied that bitemark evidence by an accepted expert was neither novel nor an emerging science and thus was admitted correctly. Following Marx [24] and Hodgson, no bitemark evidence has been refused admission due to arguments regarding Frye, FRE, or Daubert.

Despite the Hodgson case, the discipline should still strive to produce research that develops error rates and that properly assess the reliability of the techniques employed. Indeed, there is a great deal of emphasis on the development of new and novel techniques, especially in the area of pattern association analysis, yet there appears to be a reluctance to subsequently test these techniques to develop the data that would produce the variables described previously—validity, reliability, and indications of specificity and sensitivity. A vigorous and robust approach to establishing a sound basis for bitemark analysis is essential.

4. THE RESEARCH

There are four published studies examining the reliability of bitemark analysis, each with very different methodologies. A further study has examined the use of statistics within forensic bitemark analysis in an attempt to gauge the impact of the evidence and the extent to which it assists the trier-of-fact to reach a conclusion on guilt.

5. WHITTAKER, 1975

Published in both the International Dental Journal and the International Journal of Forensic Dentistry [25], this study was the first to empirically test the validity of bitemark analyses and is frequently cited as supporting evidence for the use of the technique.

In this study two examiners were employed to examine bites recorded on wax and pigskin, and also photographs. In each case dental study models were used as comparisons, overlays were not employed, although the examiners were able to use metric analysis. The results from the study were initially encouraging. The two examiners were able to correctly identify 98.8% of the impressions in wax to the appropriate study model, with a similar accuracy achieved when comparing the stone models produced from the wax bites. The comparison method was

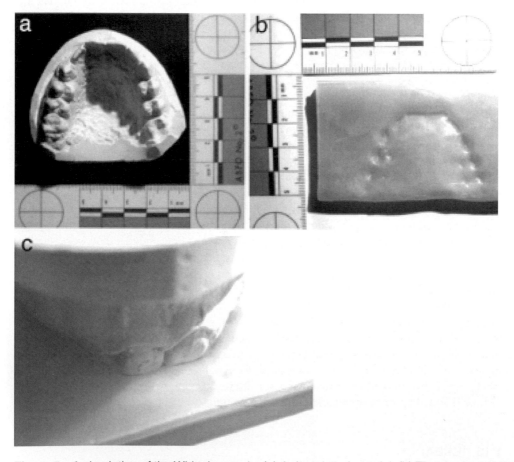

Figure 5   A simulation of the Whittaker study. (a) A dental study model. (b) The resultant "bitemark" impressed in dental wax. (c) The "docking" and comparison of the study model with the three dimensional bitemark.

undertaken by trying to fit the study model into the wax record. When photographs were employed the accuracy decreased slightly to 96% when measurements were taken, and when using only a visual assessment, it fell again to 67.5%. When the pigskin was assessed, this resulted in accurate assessments in 63.7% of attempts, but when photographs of the pigskin 24 hours after biting were used, this fell to 16%.

The study clearly identifies difficulties with bitemark analyses. The ability to match study models to wax bites is, as suggested by the study, a simple matter. This is a reflection of the properties of softened dental wax to register tooth impressions. Wax is an excellent material for bite registrations; indeed, it is used clinically for this very purpose (see Fig. 5). However, it is very dissimilar to human skin, which can be regarded as a poor registration material. This is endorsed by the results from the pigskin study which, with increasing time since biting, resulted in a dramatic drop in accuracy.

The ability of odontologists to identify suspects from pigskin was investigated in a recent study.

6. PRETTY AND SWEET, 2001

This study employed digital bitemark overlays and simulated bites in pigskin [26]. A series of 10 postmortem bites were created in pigskin using dental casts mounted in a vise grip. Each of the bites was photographed according to ABFO guidelines. Two suspects were associated with each case, although in two of the cases, neither of the suspects supplied to the examiners was responsible for the bite. The examiners were provided with photographs of the bites, the suspect's study models, and transparent overlays of each suspect. The examiners were asked to reach a conclusion regarding each suspect, and report their conclusions using the ABFO conclusions for bitemark analyses. The examiners conducted their examinations twice, following a washout period of 3 months to determine values for both intra- and inter-examiner reliability.

While a number of different groups took part in the experiment, only the results of the Diplomates of the ABFO will be discussed here. The results were encouraging. The accuracy scores, when measured using ROC analysis, was an AUC of 80.5%. Sensitivity and specificity scores, for each level of conclusion, again measured by ROC, are shown in Figure 6. If a forced decision model was used, i.e., the odontologists could only indicate "biter" or "nonbiter," the accuracy was 83.2%, which is rated as substantial agreement. However, it is important to note that the range of scores was wide, from 65% to 100%, indicating that some odontologists performed significantly better than others [26].

The interexaminer scores, i.e., how much the odontologists agreed with each other, were rated as only moderate, and the intraexaminer agreement, as fair. This was a surprise finding,

CONCLUSION LEVEL	SENSITIVITY % (SD)	SPECIFICITY % (SD)	YOUDEN'S INDEX
Reasonable medical certainty	27.5 (±24.1)	98.3 (±5.2)	0.26
Probable	57.5 (±26.5)	94.9 (±11.0)	0.52
Possible	81.3 (±22.2)	55.3 (±30.0)	0.40
Exclusion	88.8 (±19.1)	47.7 (±24.0)	0.36
Inconclusive	100.0 (±0.0)	0.0 (±0.0)	0.00

Figure 6 Data from the Diplomates' responses in the Pretty and Sweet study.

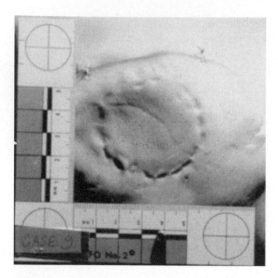

Figure 7   An example of the bitemarks in pigskin used by Pretty and Sweet. Note that this would be regarded as a bitemark of extremely high forensic significance despite the fact that it has been created postmortem.

as a reliable technique should demonstrate substantial agreements when employed by examiners of similar experience and training. In summary, the study found that, in the hands of certain odontologists, bitemark overlays were a reliable and accurate method of identifying biters. However, the wide range of accuracy and reliability scores suggested that individual odontologists should engage in self-proficiency testing so that error rates for each expert would be available for scrutiny. Indeed, in the United Kingdom, individual surgeons are required to publish their success rates for each procedure they undertake [26].

Like all studies, this work had its compromises which must be discussed so that the results can be placed in context. First, the bites were in pigskin, which although a good analog for human skin, is still only a model. Second, the bites were created postmortem, and as such none of the bruising or perimortem effects were present. An example of a bitemark from the study is shown in Figure 7, demonstrating that the bites employed were on the higher end of the scale of forensic significance. An important limitation of this study is that only overlays were studied. Odontological assessment of a bite injury will, usually, involve a number of different techniques before a conclusion is reached. A study in which authentic forensic cases and materials were employed was conducted by the ABFO.

7.   THE ABFO BITEMARK WORKSHOP, ARHEART AND PRETTY, 2001

The ABFO has been instrumental in the development of guidelines for bitemark analysis and for furthering the study of the discipline in order to determine the validity of bitemark comparisons [27]. Further to this, the ABFO conducted a bitemark workshop where 32 Diplomates assessed a total of four bitemark cases and seven potential suspects. Unlike the previous study, all seven suspects were to be assessed for all four cases, rather than an association between a number of suspects and an individual case. Three of the four cases were authentic cases, in which a bitemark was present on the skin of a deceased individual and had been previously investigated and litigated. The fourth case was a bitemark in cheese created specifically for the study. Fig. 8 demonstrates examples from each of the cases assessed [27].

The Diplomates were provided with a seven-point scale to rate their confidence in their conclusions for each case; (1) reasonable medical certainty; (2) probable; (3) possible; (4) improbable; (5) incompatible; (6) inconclusive; and (7) nondiagnostic (insufficient forensic detail). To analyze these data, ROC was again employed and the curve that was produced is shown in Figure 9. The mean AUC, the curve, the measure of diagnostic accuracy, was 0.86. This is similar to that obtained by the previous study. The study also published, anonymously, the range of ROC AUC data for each of the 32 examiners to demonstrate the spread of ability. This ranged from an AUC of 0.52–1.00. An interpretation of these results is that the poorest-performing odontologist (on these cases) scored little better than a random allocation of biters and nonbiters while the best performers correctly identified every biter [27].

This result is similar to that of the previous study, i.e., that the mean scores reflect a test, or methodology, that is reliable and accurate, but that belies the range of scores with a significant spread of abilities. One must exercise caution in the interpretation of these results. When the Diplomates undertook the study, it was not as a proficiency test, and therefore the amount of

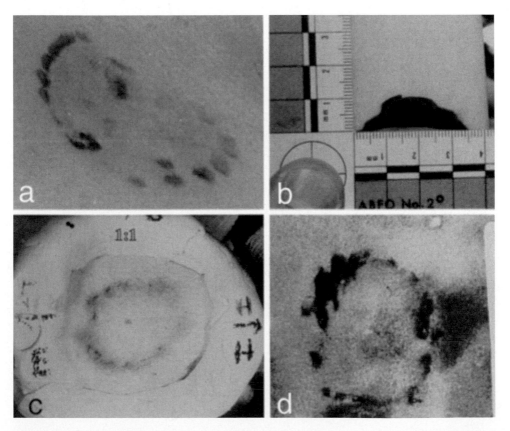

Figure 8 An example from each of the four cases (a-d) presented to the ABFO Diplomates in the 1999 Bitemark Workshop.

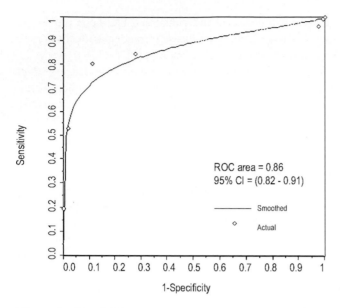

Figure 9 The ROC curve from the 1999 ABFO Bitemark Workshop data.

time, or effort given, to the cases may not have been equal among the examiners. Similarly, the conditions were not standardized; only a small number of cases were examined, with some Diplomates stating that the forensic significance of the cases, in general, was low [27]. Another factor is that of experience. Although all the examiners were Diplomates, current ABFO requirements state that only two bitemark cases must be undertaken to satisfy the requirements for eligibility. It is therefore likely that the group still represented a wide spread of experience in the assessment of bitemarks [27].

8. DORION AND ROBERTS, 2001

This study reported in Chapter 29, Section 4, involved the examination of dental casts of 50 orthodontic patients, both pre- and posttreatment [28]. Experimental bitemarks were made in Styrofoam, and then an inexperienced examiner, using hollow volume overlays, compared each of these in an attempt to identify the biter. They found that, when the preorthodontic bitemarks were assessed, the examiner scored 100%, positively identifying all 50 biters. However, following orthodontic treatment, when the casts were more similar to each other, the score was reduced to 78%. The study demonstrated that, with highly unique features, bitemarks can be more easily identified. Care must be taken in extrapolating the high scores obtained; the bitemarks were produced in Styrofoam, which will result in simulated injuries of high definition. The skin is a poor material for the registration of bitemarks, and hence one would not expect such a high accuracy rate in studies using this as the bitten substrate [28].

9. STATISTICS AND BITEMARKS

The statistics provided previously are descriptive statistics; i.e., they help us understand the value of bitemark analysis as a diagnostic test [4]. However, there have been several forays into bitemark evidence quantification, i.e., attempts to provide a numerical value to represent confidence within a conclusion. Some experts have attempted to provide population statistics; There is only a 1-in-120,000 chance that an individual other than the defendant caused this bitemark. Such statements should be avoided; there is no quantitative base for bitemarks analysis, and this is reviewed in greater detail in the next section [4]. There has, however, been a great deal of interest in the application of Bayesian statistics to the discipline of bitemark analysis. This is a complex topic and is discussed in an excellent paper from researchers in New Zealand [29].

The basic premise is that the jury should be able to measure the impact of bitemark evidence in a quantitative manner and thus be properly able to assess the likelihood of the accused being guilty. The authors of the study, after a thorough discussion, quite correctly conclude that bitemark analysis is an inherently qualitative discipline lacking the required population data to support a more quantitative approach. They further argue that the application of statistics, be it Bayesian or otherwise, is fundamentally incorrect and is more likely to confuse, confound, and bemuse than to assist the trier-of-fact to appropriate correct weight to the bitemark evidence supplied [29].

It is an attractive proposition to attach grand mathematical statements to bitemarks. They are comforting to judges and juries, and are perhaps the last thing heard and retained from testimony. However, despite their appealing nature, forensic dentists should refrain from such statistics; instead, a concentration on the proven research should provide a basis for the justification of opinions. A working knowledge of the descriptive statistical methods described within this chapter should equip any forensic dentist with the skills to present his findings with appropriate reliability data and be able to describe, and justify, the research upon which they are based [29].

10. SUMMARY

The research suggests that bitemark evidence, at least that which is used to identify biters, is a potentially valid and reliable methodology. It is generally accepted within the scientific community, although the basis of this acceptance within the peer-reviewed literature is thin. Only three studies have examined the ability of odontologists to utilise bitemarks for the identification of biters, and only two studies have been performed in what could be considered a contemporary framework of attitudes and techniques [4].

Data from these studies tend to suggest that odontologists can achieve near-perfect results utilizing bitemark overlays on both artificial and forensically authentic material. However, they also suggest that the range of ability is wide, which indicates that the tests are still subjective, with a poor rate of interexaminer agreement. Such results may provide the justification for individual odontologists taking part in self-proficiency tests so that they can place their performance within the wide range already described.

Further research is required to assess the impact of case experience, teaching and learning effects, and other factors that may influence the ability of odontologists to improve their accuracy and reproducibility scores. How do the bitemark data compare to other forensic disciplines? Both footprint and fingerprint comparisons share similarities with bitemark identification in that each technique is involved, in some part, with the comparisons of patterns and the associations between them. A study was conducted comparing the examinations of 23 footwear experts on two cases [30]. There was a high degree of disagreement among the experts, with scientists within the same laboratory reaching polarized conclusions on the likely identification [30]. Similarly, a study of fingerprint experts in 1996 found wide-ranging disagreement [31]. If one

TEST	SENSITIVITY %	SPECIFICITY %	AUTHOR
Caries			
Clinical examination	13	94	Verdonschot, 1992
Fibre-optics	13	99	Verdonschot, 1992
Radiographs	58	66	Verdonschot, 1992
Fissure discoloration	74	45	Verdonschot, 1992
Electrical resistance	96	71	Verdonschot, 1992
Bite-wing radiographs	73	97	Mileman, 1985
Probe and look	58	94	Mileman, 1985
Periodontics			
Bleeding on probing	29	88	Lange, 1991
PMN gelatinase	79	88	Teng, 1992
Bone loss	91	96	Jeffcoat, 1992
Beta glucuronidase	89	89	Lamster, 1988
Temperature	83	83	Kung, 1990
Gingival redness	27	67	Haffajee, 1983
Plaque	47	65	Haffajee, 1983
Antibody assay	65	80	Hujoel, 1990
Bitemarks			
Overlays	71.8	81.5	Pretty, 2001
Any technique	77.2	86.0	Arheart, 2001

Figure 10 A range of dental diagnostic tests, comparing their effectiveness with that of bitemark analysis.

considers bitemark analysis compared to other diagnostic tests in clinical dentistry (upon which decision to initiate treatment are based), the data compare favorably (Fig. 10).

This section commenced with a discussion of the Daubert ruling and its role as an instigated of evidence based research within forensic science. Has the odontological community satisfied the principles extolled by the ruling? The answer is not clear. Certainly forensic odontologists have been shown to embrace research and have been prepared to publish results of their performance. Further work is required to answer the Daubert question in its entirety, but initial results are promising. With further research to answer the questions regarding spread of ability, bitemark analysis should be presented in court with a sound scientific backing.

REFERENCES

1. Guidelines for bite mark analysis. American Board of Forensic Odontology. J Am Dent Assoc 1986; 112(3):383–6.
2. Pretty IA, Sweet D. Adherence of forensic odontologists to the ABFO bite mark guidelines for suspect evidence collection. J Forens Sci 2001; 46(5):1152–8.
3. Atsu SS, Gokdemir K, Kedici PS. Human dentinal structure as an indicator of age. J Forens Odontostomatol 1998; 16(2):27–9.
4. Pretty IA, Sweet D. The scientific basis for human bitemark analyses—a critical review. Sci Justice 2001; 41(2):85–92.
5. Pretty IA, Sweet D. A comprehensive examination of bitemark evidence in the American legal system, American Academy of Forensic Science. 2000.
6. Sweet D, Pretty IA. A look at forensic dentistry—Part 2: teeth as weapons of violence—identification of bitemark perpetrators. Br Dent J 2001; 190(8):415–8.

7. Wright FD, Dailey JC. Human bite marks in forensic dentistry. Dent Clin North Am 2001; 45(2): 365–97.

8. Woolridge ED. Legal aspects of forensic medicine and dentistry. Dent Clin North Am 1977; 21(1): 19–32.

9. Brunette D. Critical Thinking, London: Quintessence Books, 1998.

10. Landis JR, Koch GG. The measurement of observer agreement for categorical data. Biometrics 1977; 33(1):159–74.

11. Glaser AN. High-Yield Bio-Statistics. Baltimore: Williams and Wilkins, 1995.

12. Dunn G, Everitt B. Clinical Bio-Statistics — An Introduction to Evidence-Based Medicine. London: Edward Arnold, 1995.

13. Everitt BS. Statistical Methods for Medical Investigators. London: Edward Arnold, 1989.

14. Hanley JA. Receiver operating characteristic (ROC) methodology: the state of the art. Crit Rev Diagn Imaging 1989; 29(3):307–35.

15. Swets JA, Pickerr RM. Evaluation of Diagnostic Systems: Methods from Signal Detection Theory. New York: Academic Press, 1982.

16. van Erkel AR, Pattynama PM. Receiver operating characteristic (ROC) analysis: basic principles and applications in radiology. Eur J Radiol 1998; 27(2):88–94.

17. Hildebolt CF, Vannier MW, Shrout MK, Pilgram TK. ROC analysis of observer-response subjective rating data—application to periodontal radiograph assessment. Am J Phys Anthropol 1991; 84(3): 351–61.

18. Your help is needed. Dent Tech 1988; 41(4):2.

19. Swaving M, van Houwelingen H, Ottes FP, Steerneman T. Statistical comparison of ROC curves from multiple readers. Med Decis Making 1996; 16(2):143–52.

20. Hanley JA, McNeil BJ. The meaning and use of the area under a receiver operating characteristic (ROC) curve. Radiology 1982; 143(1):29–36.

21. Identity sought. Can Dent Assoc J 1988; 16(9):61.

22. Bowers CM, Johansen RJ. Bitemark evidence. In. Modern Scientific Evidence Saks MJ, Ed. New York: West Publishing, 2002.

23. State v. Hodgson, 512 N.W. 2d 95.

24. People V Marx, 54 Cal. App.3d 100, 126 Cal. 350.

25. Whittaker DK. Some laboratory studies on the accuracy of bite mark comparisons. Int Dent J 1975; 25(3):166–71.

26. Pretty IA, Sweet D. Digital bitemark overlays — an analysis of effectiveness. J Forens Sci 2001; 46(6):1385–91.

27. Arheart KL, Pretty IA. Results of the 4th ABFO Bitemark Workshop—1999. Forensic Sci Int 2001; 124(2–3):104–11.

28. Dorion RBJ, Roberts JD. Bitemark project 2000 — objectivity. Seattle: AAFS, 2001.

29. Kittleson JM, Kieser JA, Buckingham DM, Herbison GP. Weighing evidence: quantitative measures of the importance of bitemark evidence. J Forens Odontostomatol 2003:(in Press).

30. Shor Y, Weisner S. A survey on the conclusions drawn on the same footwear marks obtained in actual cases by several experts throughout the world. J Forens Sci 1999; 44(380–84).

31. Evett IW, Williams RL. A review of the sixteem points fingerprint standard in England and Wales. J Forens Ident 1996; 46(1285–93).

28
Unresolved Issues in Bitemark Analysis

Iain A. Pretty
Lecturer in Restorative Dentistry,
The University of Manchester

1. INTRODUCTION

Within medicine and dentistry there is a movement toward an evidence-based approach to treatment, diagnosis, and management [1]. While some authors have argued that the evidence-based approach is fundamentally flawed (mainly citing the nature of the studies that are published within the literature and the reluctance to publish negative results), many have agreed that an evidence-informed or research-based philosophy is a sound premise [1]. Forensic science should aspire to no lesser a goal. The decisions that are made by the judicial system, informed partly by evidence resulting from scientific tests, have implications that can be at least as serious as those facing the medical profession.

A number of authors have reviewed the research supporting the practice of bitemark analysis, although few of these could be considered as critical reviews [2–4]. It could be argued that there is a cyclical justification for bitemark analysis, with very few empirical studies examining the underlying science of the comparative process [5].

2. THE EVIDENCE

The author has previously conducted an assessment of the bitemark literature, conducted in 1998, and it seems timely to reassess and update this information [5]. The original literature review found 1508 articles concerning forensic dentistry of which 120 were English-language papers related to bitemark research. The same search performed today produced a total of 1703 papers with 151 of these specifically related to bitemarks (Fig. 1). One of the findings of the original study was that the vast majority of the articles were case reports. Figure 2 demonstrates the classification of papers, and it demonstrates that this has not changed since the original comment [5].

As a general rule, case reports add little to the scientific knowledge base, and therefore, if these, along with noncritical reviews, are discarded, very little new empirical evidence has been developed in the past 5 years [6,7]. Several explanations have been postulated for this.

One of these is the employment status of odontologists themselves. The vast majority of practicing odontologists in both North America and Europe are general dental practitioners. Very few hold substantive academic posts within dental departments of universities, and fewer still hold those posts as forensic odontologists [8,9]. For many, odontological work is a part-time pursuit, ensuring that time is spent on casework rather than research.

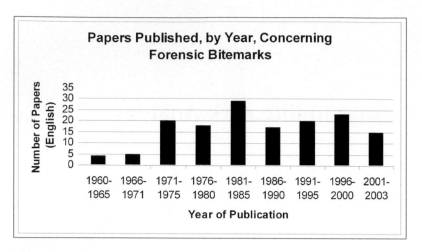

Figure 1   Number of papers concerning forensic bitemarks published in English between 1960 and 2003. Papers sourced from MedLine, ISI Web of Science, and Forensic Abstracts.

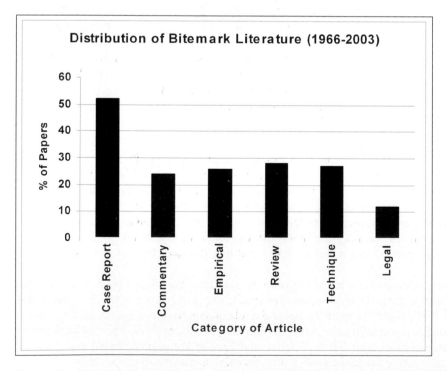

Figure 2   Categorical assessment of bitemark publication type from 1960 to 2003.

Another explanation for the hiatus of empirical research is the nature of bitemark research. Without access to complex laboratory equipment or the use of animal models or human volunteers, bitemark research is difficult. The use of authentic forensic materials for research is also limited, as the average bitemark caseload for individual practitioners has been shown to be minimal [5]. Indeed, a recent study showed that of 37 respondents with forensic training, only one conducted more than 11 bitemark cases per year [10]. Perhaps, given these constraints, the volume of research that is conducted should be applauded.

An assessment of the articles, and from the abstracts published in the odontology section of the annual meeting of the American Academy of Forensic Sciences, a number of contentious areas within bitemark practice can be identified. These are: (1) human skin as bite registration material; (2) methods of analysis; (3) the use of bitemark analysis as purely exculpatory evidence, levels of conclusion; and (4) the uniqueness of the human dentition. Each of these issues is addressed in turn, examining the research base to determine if conclusions can be drawn.

3. HUMAN SKIN AS A BITE REGISTRATION MATERIAL

Throughout the pages of this book it is apparent that there is a wide variation in the appearance of bitemarks upon skin, which has led to its accuracy as a bite registration (or recording) material being questioned. It is important to point out that bitemarks can occur on a number of other substrates such as cheese [11–13], apples [12,14], sandwiches [15], and soap [16], but it is the issue surrounding human skin that has been examined most within the literature.

Skin is a poor registration material [17] since it is highly variable in terms of anatomical location, underlying musculature, fat, curvature, and looseness or adherence to underlying tissues [18]. Skin is highly viscoelastic, which allows stretching to occur during either the biting process or when evidence is collected. This is due to elastic fibers in the dermis, distorting under pressure and then recoiling back to their original position. The degree to which this occurs depends on a number of factors including age and anatomical location [19]. It has been argued that any bitemark on skin will have some degree of distortion, due to edema, recoil, or other factor. This was well demonstrated by a study conducted in 1971 by DeVore [20]. The experiment involved the inking of human skin (living volunteers, typically on the arm) using a stamp with two concentrically placed circles with intersecting lines. Photographs of the inked skin were taken before and after movement, and the distortion was measured.

Following the analysis of the photographs it was found that in all cases there was an expansion or shrinkage of the inked mark, with a maximum linear expansion of 60% at one location [20]. The design of the stamp permitted the investigators to examine the distortion in both size and direction (Fig. 3). DeVore concluded that, owing to the level of distortion found, photographic images of a bitemark in comparative analysis should be used only if the exact position of the body can be replicated [20]. Clearly this is an almost impossible task. If one considers that most bitemarks are examined in a morgue environment, then the body has most certainly been moved. Even if the bitemark is examined at the crime scene, the position of the body at the time of biting is usually unknown. An exception to this is in the case of living victim, who, if conscious at the time of biting, may be able to recall the position.

Clearly, some anatomical positions are less prone to distortion than others (Fig. 4). Typically areas that have small amounts of subcutaneous fat, and areas that are not distorted by movement are less prone to the effects that DeVore describes [4,5]. Such areas include the dorsum of the hand and foot, the midregions of the arm, and the scalp. However, if one examines the anatomical positions where bitemarks are most frequently found, it is more likely than not that a bitemark will be located in an unfavourable position in relation to skin distortion [21,22]. When assessing DeVore's work it is important to note that the skin was simply impressed with

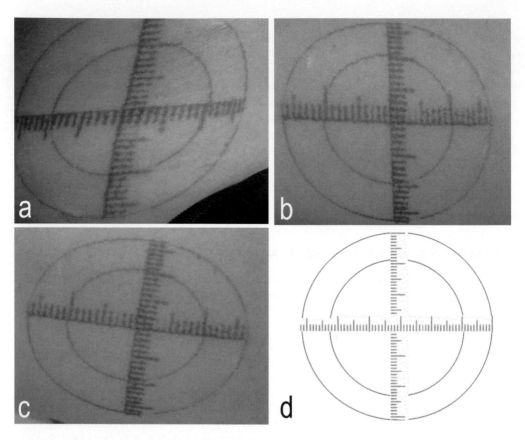

Figure 3 The DeVore experiment revisited. (a, b, c) An inked area of the dorsal midforearm demonstrating the dimensional (postural) changes achieved by arm flexion. (d) The original ink stamp.

an inked stamp; there was no force used. It could be extrapolated that, with the additional force component necessary to create a bitemark, the distortion effect could be even greater.

In 1974, researchers from the Bioengineering Unit of the University of Strathclyde examined the features of the biting process likely to impact upon the appearance of bitemarks on human skin [17]. They described the differing characteristics of skin from a variety of anatomical locations; e.g., Langer's lines represent directional differences in the degree of extensibility of skin. Like DeVore, they emphasised the importance of body location during biting as the directional variations or tension lines will alter with movement. Their report also described distortion that can occur in skin after biting [17]. The edematous response of skin to trauma is likely to stiffen the area, rendering it more stable. However, the subsequent resorption of this fluid will cause a large amount of distortion. They concluded that the changes in bitemark appearance are likely to be greater as the injury grows older. This was found equally applicable to living and dead victims. The article concluded that forensic odontologists where "still ignorant ⋯ of the conditions during normal biting ⋯ considerable research is required" [17,23].

Provisional results from the Strathclyde study and others were described in one of the major forensic dental texts [24]. Chapter 13 of Harvey's book concentrates on a number of studies in which experimental bites were produced on a living volunteer. As well as photographic

Anatomical Location	VALE AND NOGUCHI		HARVEY		PRETTY AND SWEET	
	Number of Bitemarks	Percent of 164 Marks	Number of Bitemarks	Percent of 71 Marks	Number of Bitemarks	Percent of 144 Marks
Abdomen	12	7.3	10	14.1	3	2.1
Arms	32	19.5	5	7.0	27	18.8
Back	20	12.2	0	0.0	10	6.9
Breasts	17	10.4	23	32.4	45	31.3
Buttocks	8	4.9	3	4.2	3	2.1
Chest	7	4.3	0	0.0	4	2.7
Ears	1	0.6	1	1.4	1	0.7
Face/Head	13	7.9	12	16.9	7	4.9
Feet	2	1.2	0	0.0	0	0.0
Genitalia	9	5.5	3	4.2	11	7.6
Hand/Finger	4	2.4	5	7.0	8	5.5
Legs	23	14.0	1	1.4	19	13.1
Neck	5	3.0	1	1.4	1	0.7
Nose	3	1.8	1	1.4	1	0.7
Shoulder	8	4.9	6	8.4	4	2.7
	164		71		144	

Figure 4 Data from three studies examining the anatomical location of bitemarks. The anatomical positions most frequently bitten are often those sites most susceptible to postural distortion.

studies, histological samples obtained via biopsies were undertaken. A total of five bites were produced on a variety of anatomical positions and biopsies taken immediately and on five consecutive days. Photographs were taken immediately and then each day for 5 days.

When examining the photographic data, Harvey found that there was considerable change in bitemark appearance after 24 hours, which continued, at a slower rate, for the remaining 5 days. He noted that, although the biter had attempted to use similar force at each anatomical location, each bite appeared to be quite different. Bites on the thorax and shoulder displayed clear teethmarks but little bruising or hemorrhage, while those on the abdomen appeared more severe. These results demonstrate the effect of anatomical variation on bitemark appearance and its likely impact on forensic significance [24].

The histological study demonstrated that the stress applied to the skin during biting is sufficient to produce a histochemcial change in the collagen fibers and that this change may be of value in assessing and describing bitemarks. The influence of collagen in the presentation of bitemarks also supports the data on the varied appearance of bitemarks in differing anatomical locations [24].

The most recent comment on skin distortion and bitemarks comes from Sheasby and MacDonald, who have divided distortion in bitemarks into two separate areas [19]. Primary distortion is that caused at the time of biting; its two main components are that of the dynamics of the biting process and detailed features of the bitten surface. The study describes these as dynamic distortion and tissue distortion, respectively. The two processes are intrinsically linked and typically occur simultaneously. The degree of dynamic distortion can vary dramatically from almost nil in a static bitemark to a very considerable amount in bites that demonstrate scrape marks. Sheasby comments that the dynamic distortive process is a unique occurrence depending on movements of both victim and suspect, and as such it is possible that the same biter may leave marks of differing appearance on the same victim [19].

Secondary distortion is described as comprising three elements; time, posture, and photography. Time distortion is described as those changes that occur in the appearance of the injury from the time it occurred until it was examined. These changes could be due to contraction—for example, healing artifacts in a case of a laceration or abrasion that can significantly alter the dimensions and appearance of a bite injury. Indeed, it is possible for injuries to contract up to 50% in the absence of treatment (Fig. 5). Similarly, in the case of a bruise, healing can cause diffusion and possible movement of the bruise [19]. Posture distortion is that which was described in DeVore's study — namely, that the position of the body when bitten may be different from that when the evidence is recorded (Fig. 6). Photographic distortion has also been described in detail in other chapters of this book. Briefly, if the bitemark is not recorded at 90°, then photographic distortion can occur. The use of the ABFO No. 2 scale and numerous angled shots should (1) prevent photographic distortion occurring, and (2) enable detection and corrections when it does [25].

It can be stated that distortion in skin following biting is inevitable. The helpful descriptions of Sheasby and McDonald help us to identify the type of distortion present [19]. There is little

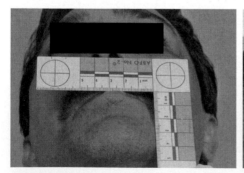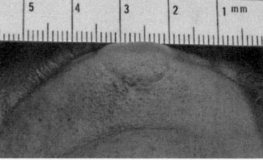

Figure 5   An example of bite wound contraction. Here the victim was bitten on the lower lip, with class characteristics of lower anterior teeth clearly visible. However, the bite wound is only 15 mm across, demonstrating significant contraction. A large fibrous area has developed in the center. Odontological evidence combined with the statement of a plastic surgeon secured a confession of biting from the suspect. The plastic surgeon stated that contraction of 30–50% could have occurred.

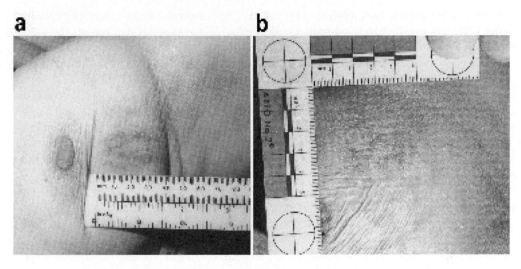

Figure 6 An example of postural and photographic distortion in bite photography. (a) Original bitemark photograph. Postural effects from both the manual manipulation of the breast and the placement of the (inappropriate) scale have produced a significant distortion that led one odontologist to believe that this wound was a bitemark. When examined in the mortuary and correctly photographed it was clear that this was not a bitemark, and that the marks were postmortem changes associate with skin striae.

that can be done to correct or prevent primary distortion, and therefore it is essential that steps are taken to minimize secondary distortion. In either event, the forensic odontologist must be aware of the nature of both, and their likely impact on the injury. Metric analyses, in which, for example, intercanine distances are measured to a millimeter or less, are perhaps flawed as the distortion that has occurred can never be quantified in such resolution. A thorough assessment of the appearance of the injury, taking into account the anatomical position, is essential [26].

The research is unclear as to the significance of distortion. DeVore stated that unless the body position of a victim could be precisely replicated, no attempt at bitemark analysis should be undertaken. Bernstein has stated that distortion occurring in the recording and analysis of bitemarks, while serious, should not preclude analysis [23,27]. It is unlikely that further research will assist us in the handling of primary distortion; the variability of biter and victim is so great any attempt to quantify these changes would be flawed [23,27]. However, further research examining, for example, the effect of time on bruise distortion, could be illuminating. It is recommended that within any bitemark report an indication of the likely distortion and its effect on the strength of the conclusion be described in detail [26].

4. METHODS OF ANALYSIS

4.1. Physical Comparisons

An essential component of the determination of the validity of bitemark analysis is that the techniques used in the physical comparison between suspect dentition and physical injury have been assessed and found valid. One of the fundamental problems with this task is the wide variety of techniques that have been described in the literature [5]. Techniques using confocal [28], reflex, and scanning electron microscopes [12,29,30]; complex computer systems [31,32], typing of oral bacteria (Glass, 1980 #1794); special light sources [33,34]; fingerprint dusting powder [35]; and overlays have all been reported [36–42]. Despite this, the use of transparent overlays to perform a pattern comparison is the emerging dominant technique, although the lack of direction from the forensic dental organisations, both European and North American, complicates this matter [43]. The American Board of Forensic Odontology (ABFO) has reported advice and guidance on many aspects of bitemarks, and yet one of the most pivotal questions, i.e., what is the best comparison technique to use, has not been addressed [26]. Should a court wish to review the literature to ensure that a testifying expert is using generally accepted techniques, they would find the task daunting and ultimately unrevealing. Yet, Daubert and other rulings suggest that this should be the case — i.e., that empirical evidence should exist supporting the use of techniques employed [5].

An example of research undertaken in this area is that of Sweet and Bowers [37]. This paper compared five common techniques of producing transparent overlays; radiographic, Xerox, hand-drawn (directly from casts or from wax bites), and computer generated. The study employed 30 randomly selected study casts to examine the accuracy of overlays produced from each of the five techniques concerning tooth rotation and surface area. The computer-generated overlays were the gold standard. From the results, it was determined that the computer technique represented the most accurate fabrication method with respect to representation of rotation and area of the biting edge [37]. The authors of the paper concluded that the fabrication methods that utilised the subjective process of hand tracing should not be used in favour of techniques that are more objective. Despite this sound research, a review of the proceedings of the American Academy of Forensic Sciences since 1998 suggests that a number of techniques are still used [5,42].

The issue is further complicated in that there are a number of techniques for the fabrication of overlays using computers. There is somewhat of a European/North American divide in the overlay fabrication system used. For example, many U.S. odontologists will employ the Sweet technique [38], while a modification of the Naru system is popular in the United Kingdom (Fig. 7) [41]. One of the highlighted difficulties with the computer-assisted systems is that the subjectivity of the process is still relatively high. Within the Sweet technique, a threshold value must be set prior to the selection of the biting surfaces of the scanned dental cast. This threshold value can affect the appearance of the overlay; the skill of the odontologists, and their subjective judgment, is required to ensure that the biting surfaces are selected accurately (Fig. 8). The effect of tooth wear, resulting in teeth lying below the occlusal plane, is difficult to reflect in the overlay [42].

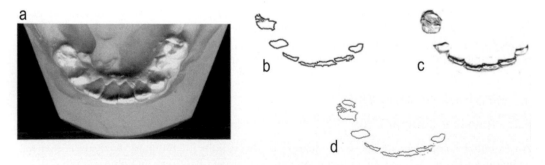

Figure 7 Examples of overlay production techniques. (a) A mandibular cast from a bitemark suspect. An overlay produced using the Sweet technique, (b) using the Naru technique, and (c) using a new contour technique (d).

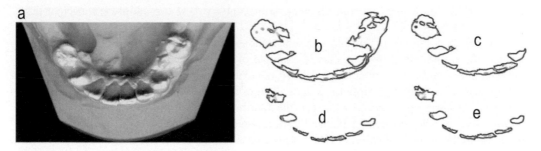

Figure 8 Example of the effect of thresholding on overlay appearance. (a) A mandibular cast from a bitemark suspect. (b, c, d, and e) Overlays produced using the Sweet technique with decreasing threshold levels set within the image analysis software.

An attempt has been made to analyze bitemarks entirely within a computer system; i.e., the cast and photograph are simply scanned into the software, and the remainder of the analysis is automated without input from the odontologist [44]. The use of representative correlation coefficients was proposed to identify the most likely biter. Despite the promising nature of the project, when it was applied to a real bitemark case, the incorrect biter (based upon a court decision) was implicated by the system. In his discussion of these results, Naru stated that the skin may simply not record the dentition accurately enough to enable analysis. The pathological record of the bite on skin is subject to many variables, such as the distortion and colour changes described previously that confound computer systems [44]. Naru recommended that further work would be required to modify the algorithms to contend with these variations. Since this work there has been no further attempts to employ computer systems to objectively analyse bitemarks [44].

4.2. Molecular Biological Techniques

Fully described in Chapter 9 of this book, and included here for completeness, the use of salivary DNA to analyze bitemarks was proposed by Sweet [45,46]. Indeed, this is a highly objective system and offers a solution to the difficulties surrounding physical comparisons. However, the techniques are expensive and are subject to a number of variables, including the presence of sufficient DNA and the time since biting. A number of environmental assaults can affect the quality of such evidence, and the collection of this evidence has so far been relatively poor [47]. Nonetheless, DNA evidence from bitemarks may present the most judicially acceptable methodology of bitemark analysis, particularly as there is a wealth of supporting peer-reviewed materials concerning DNA techniques. Such empirical support is either lacking or less than fully endorsees the physical comparative techniques [5].

5. BITEMARKS AS EXCULPATORY EVIDENCE

To address some of the inherent complications concerning bitemark physical comparisons, a number of authors have suggested that bitemark evidence should only be employed in the exclusion of a suspect [5]. The theory behind this proposal is sound. If a bitemark is observed in which, for example, six anterior maxillary teeth are clearly observed, yet the suspect possesses only three anterior maxillary teeth (and wears no dental prosthesis), it is a simple matter to exclude that suspect as a biter. Complications of skin distortion, photographic artifacts, skin registration, occlusal wear, and bite force are irrelevant — there are simply insufficient teeth to produce such a mark.

There are a number of instances in which the exclusion of biters can be of assistance in implicating an individual [48]. A classic example of this is the child abuse case in which a nonambulatory child has exposure to a closed population of individuals—e.g., mother, father, sibling, and sitter. If it is possible to exclude three of these individuals, then, if the assumption that this is a closed population is correct, the fourth must be responsible for the bite injury. Another example is provided in Figure 9. An argument therefore exists that the use of such evidence, in the absence of salivary DNA, should be restricted to the exclusion of suspects. The difficulty with the application of this seemingly commonsense approach is the nature of bitemark case presentation. In an audit of bitemark cases it was found that only 18% presented with more than one bitemark suspect; in 73% of cases the bitemark was the only physical evidence available, and 84% of the crimes were rated as serious assaults or higher [49]. In none of the cases assessed was DNA either available, correctly collected, or permission given to obtain suspect samples [49].

It is likely that this audit is typical of a forensic odontological casework. The investigative services look to odontologists for assistance when more traditional techniques have failed. It is clearly a desirable situation to have bitemark evidence supplied as just one aspect of a multifaceted case against a suspect in which a number of forensic tests, eye-witnesses, and a clear motive are presented to the court [50]. However, this is rarely the case, and often bitemarks are the only forensic evidence available to the jury. Because of this, there is a perceived reluctance

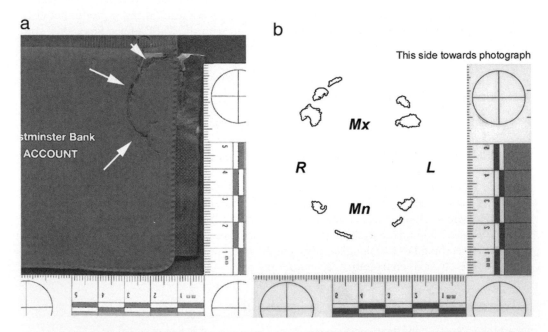

Figure 9 An example of the value of suspect exclusion in bitemark cases. In this case, a bank was robbed. During the robbery one of the suspects held this bank deposit book between his teeth. (a) The arrows indicate the area of the bite, demonstrating an individual with at least six anterior teeth, either upper or lower. (b) An overlay from one of the suspects. It is a simple matter to exclude this individual as a possible biter in this case, he simply has insufficient teeth to produce the mark shown in (a).

among the odontological community to restrict bitemark evidence to exclusions only. Indeed a recent survey of 72 U.S. odontologists, 38% of whom were ABFO diplomates, when asked if bitemarks should only be used to exclude suspects, 22% of the total respondents stated yes, although only 6% of diplomates expressed this view [49]. It seems that the use of bitemarks to positively identify biters is to continue; however, it is important to realize that the empirical evidence to support this is thin; never more so than when the uniqueness of the human dentition is considered.

6. UNIQUENESS OF THE HUMAN DENTITION

Bitemark analysis is based on two postulates: the dental characteristics of anterior teeth involved in biting are unique among individuals, and this asserted uniqueness is transferred and recorded in the injury [3]. A distinction must be drawn from the ability of a forensic dentist to identify an individual from their dentition by using radiographs and dental records and the science of bitemark analysis. Dental identification, as opposed to bitemark identification, utilizes the number, shape, type, and placement of dental restorations, root canal therapies, unusual pathoses, root morphology, trabecular bone pattern, and sinus morphology [51].

The debate over the uniqueness of human teeth is probably one of the fiercest in current forensic dental discourse, and perhaps the most significant [43]. Many forensic dentists, appellants, and lawyers have questioned this fact and demand to know from testifying experts the relative frequency of dental features identified in bitemarks. An examination of the literature divulges the scientific evidence for this commonly held belief [50].

The first article to consider the statistical nature of dental uniqueness was published by MacFarlane and Sutherland in 1974 [52]. The authors began by differentiating between ''positive'' and ''negative'' features of the dentition. A positive feature was described as the presence of a tooth with a certain rotation or other individualising feature. A negative feature was the absence of a tooth. This study concentrated on the positive features that occurred on the anterior teeth (canine to canine, maxillary, and mandibular). Patients were selected from an outpatient clinic; in total, 200 study casts (maxillary and mandibular) were produced. The authors only studied the dental casts, not bitemarks that would have been produced by such casts. This is a crucial aspect of most of the research that has been conducted in this topic — i.e., the uniqueness of the dentition rather than any pattern or wound that such teeth would produce [52].

The investigators noted the number and shape of each tooth, the presence of any incisal restoration, relationship of teeth to arch form, and tooth rotation (four categories). The study did not examine the presence or absence of spacing between teeth. The assessments of each cast were entirely subjective. Disappointingly, the authors elected not to publish a table of results; rather, they presented images of typical casts and calculated, using their data, the frequency of the traits shown. The authors noted that certain characteristics were not interrelated, so the products of their incidences could be used to indicate an overall frequency. However, certain features, such as mesiopalatal rotation of the upper central incisors were interrelated with a significance of $P<.001$. The authors stated that mesiopalatal rotation of the maxillary central incisors should therefore be taken as a single feature. This demonstrated that the true frequency of such features was almost four times greater than the frequency when the rotations were considered as individual variables [52].

In an example, MacFarlane concluded that a particular dentition would only be seen in eight people in 100,000 of the population with natural teeth. This figure was introduced in a U.S. trial to much debate [53]. The authors concluded that they had not confirmed the individuality of the human anterior teeth, nor had they considered the impact or representation of any of the features examined on a bitemark in human skin. The highly subjective examination of the casts by multiple examiners and lack of tabulated results make this study weak, especially in light of the increased scientific scrutiny required by recent court rulings. However, a large (N = 200) sample was used of a defined population, and efforts were made to ensure that this sampling was randomized [52].

The next paper to address the issue of individuality of human teeth was published in 1982. Authors frequently cite it as conclusive evidence for dental individuality [54]. The premise of the paper was to examine the dentitions of five pairs of monozygotic (identical) twins and, should individualization among the pairs be established, to extrapolate this finding to the general population. The twins were selected from another, unrelated study—the authors state that no selection based on dentition was performed. None of the subjects had crowns or removable prostheses. All teeth were determined to be healthy and representative of young adults in their early 20s. Each twin underwent a complete oral examination including alginate impressions [54].

The impressions were immediately cast in plaster, and subsequently epoxy-resin replicas of the anterior teeth were made and used to create test bites in a variety of materials, including plaster of Paris and silicone impression materials. The test bites were then treated by the wax radiographic technique for overlay production, and the resultant radiographs were analyzed by computer.

A large number of measurements were carried out by the investigators who carefully noted asymmetries in each of the anterior teeth, angulations of test bites, and the depth of the test bites [54]. Although the article stated that efforts were taken to standardise the production of these test bites, there was no discussion of how this was obtained. One crucial aspect would have been the amount of pressure applied to the epoxy replicas when creating the test bite. Many of the individual features claimed by the authors were dependent on the depth of penetration of the test bite into the substrate, and therefore a standardisation of this pressure would have been necessary. The substrate, plaster of Paris, has very dissimilar properties to that of human skin [54].

It should be noted that many of the differences between the bitemarks described by the authors could be explained by the depth of substrate penetration (and hence increased width of tooth outline) by the replicas. The authors noted that the teeth did not meet at the same horizontal plane at the incisal edges in each twin. This is described as an individualising difference between the twins rather than as an artefact of experimental variation. Figure 10 shows the difference in test bite outline produced from the same dentition applied to wax at a variety of different pressures [54].

Even if it was to be accepted that the variation caused by inconsistent pressure application is negligible, the selection of substrate is questionable. Are investigators interested in the representation of uniqueness in plaster of Paris or human skin? Should a study that determined morphological human dental uniqueness in wax or plaster be extrapolated to fulfil a legally sound statement that a bitemark on skin is unique? With the current interest in the proper application of the scientific method, this would be unlikely to meet the legal burden. Sognnaes and colleagues concluded that, in terms of dental arch form and individual tooth position, even identical twins are not dentally identical [54]. As previously mentioned, the effect of different wear-and-tear rates, exposure to environmental factors, dental treatments, and disease experience among such individuals will obviously cause differences over time.

The twin study, despite the described problems, is one of two papers frequently cited as resounding evidence for the uniqueness of the human dentition. The other is Rawson's 1984 article Statistical Evidence for the Individuality of the Human Dentition [55].

Rawson, a coauthor on the twin study, in coauthorship with another dentist, two dental students, and a statistician, wrote arguably the most cited and well-known bitemark paper describ-

Figure 10 The effect of pressure on the overlay production process. This figure demonstrates the overlays produced from the same dental cast that has been impressed in dental wax using increasing amounts of pressure.

ing an empirical experiment. In an attempt to prove finally the uniqueness of the anterior segment of human teeth, Rawson examined 397 bites and applied a statistical probability theory to the results. The significance of this paper warrants the comprehensive assessment of its validity that follows.

Twelve hundred wax bites were obtained from forensic odontologists in various geographic locations in the United States. Each bite was made on a custom wax wafer 1-mm thick supported by a 1-mm hard cardboard backer. The subjects were instructed to bite to the maximum depth of 1 mm. This design removed the variation of incisal penetration found in the twin study. A calibrated 1-cm scale was also impressed upon the wax.

From the 1200 samples received, 384 bites were selected, although this number was later increased to 397. There is no indication that this was a randomised sample. To adhere to strict scientific methods, the bites should have been selected in a random fashion to prevent any selector or observer bias being introduced. Rawson stated that the screening process involved an assessment of the clarity and accuracy of the marks as well as the completeness of an accompanying questionnaire. Another aspect of the study that is unclear is at what point the sampling was performed. Was it before or after the radiographic treatment of the bites?

The bitemark indentations were filled with zinc powder and then radiographed using a technique designed to minimize any enlargement. Following the exposure of one side of the wax, the zinc was removed and the procedure repeated for the other side. A study described earlier determined that the radiographic process for overlay production was relatively accurate, but it found that hand-traced overlays were less accurate and generally unsuitable for use [37]. Rawson's study used a combination of the two techniques, thus increasing the chance of errors considerably. In this study, the radiographic overlays were enlarged three times and then hand traced on to gridded computer paper. The article stated that the resolution of bitemark examinations should be within ± 1 mm of the center point of a tooth and ± 5° of rotation. Results of the Bowers and Sweet study suggested that this resolution might be difficult to obtain using the hand-tracing method [56].

Following the selection of the bites, the population sample was described. A comparison of these figures to U.S. census data found that the population sampled in the study was a reasonable measure of the U.S. population, although African-Americans were underrepresented and Asians slightly overrepresented.

Following the tracing of the biting edges, several elements of tooth position were assessed. A center point for each tooth was determined and the x and y coordinates noted. The angulation of each of the teeth was measured, and all the data were entered into a computer for analysis. It was determined that the minimum number of positions that a tooth can occupy is 150 and the greatest 239.9. These figures were determined by multiplying the number of positions of x by y and by the angles observed. The occurrence of fractions of positions (i.e., 239.9) is a reflection of this multiplication. Rawson elected to use 150 as the number of possible positions for each tooth, as this represented a conservative sample. Using this premise, the article then stated that the probability of finding two sets of dentition with all six teeth in the same position was 1.4×10^{13}. With an assumed world population of 4 billion (4×10^9), Rawson stated that a match at five teeth on a bitemark would be sufficient evidence to positively identify an individual as the biter to the exclusion of all others [55].

One concern with this use of the product rule to multiply individual probabilities to establish an overall likelihood is that of independence of the variables [1]. The article assumed that the position of each of the teeth was entirely independent of the position of any others. However, neither this nor any other study has established the independence of these features. Indeed, the studies described previously have shown this to be incorrect—e.g., the dependence of mesiopalatal rotation described by MacFarlane [52]. It is likely that every tooth position influences another—intraquadrant, intra-arch, and between opposing arches. This lack of independence renders Rawson's certainties of individualization invalid. Rawson's results also showed a possible sampling error, as evidenced by the data sets regarding possible tooth position for each unit. It should be intuitively anticipated that the left and right quadrants should represent a mirror image of each other in terms of possible tooth center positions. This was not the case. The upper right lateral incisor was reported to have 239.9 possible locations while the upper left lateral incisor had 161.5 locations [55].

It can be argued that this paper, without the statistical treatment, confirms the anecdotal evidence of almost any practising dentist that the human dentition is unique. It can be stated that, with an extremely high resolution of measurement, such as in this article, the minutia of the dentition can be described and proven unique. Indeed, if one was to measure 100 meter-length rules, one would find that each would be individual with regards to its length, if measured with sufficient resolution. It is, therefore, not the uniqueness of the teeth that is questioned, it is the rendition of these asserted unique features on human skin that is the unknown quantity. Rawson alluded to this point within his article [57]: "whether there is a representation of that uniqueness in the mark found on the skin or other inanimate objects" [55].

Rawson has proven what his article claims, although perhaps not to the mathematical or statistical certainty expressed. The article determined that the dentition is unique; however, when this paper is cited, authors often extend this conclusion to incorporate the uniqueness of bitemarks. The survey of odontologists described previously asked a number of questions of the respondents in relation to the question of dental uniqueness. Ninety-one percent of the forensic dentists questioned believed that the human dentition was unique, with only 1% stating that it wasn't; 8% were unsure. Seventy-eight percent believed that this uniqueness was replicated on human skin during the biting process, while 11% believed that it wasn't, and 11% were unsure [49]. Ninety-six percent of ABFO diplomates in this survey stated that the human dentition was unique and accurately registered on human skin during the biting process. When questioned about the product rule and its application in the determination of dental uniqueness, 60% of the respondents did not know what the product rule was, 22% thought that its use was justified, 9% believed that it shouldn't be used, and 9% were unsure [49].

While not a scientifically designed study, it is worth mentioning the case report of Keyes from 1925 [58]. The case report concerned a bitemark in a case of homicide (of a police officer) in which marks from the lower teeth of the suspect could be clearly seen. No maxillary teeth marks were present on the injury, and the explanation for this was that the officer was wearing a rubber coat which may have prevented these teeth from contacting the skin. Keyes describes his attempts to quantify the uniqueness of the bitemark by examining over 2000 mouths, none of which, he claimed, "fitted" the bitemark as well as the suspects. Keyes describes the fact that as the excised skin had changed following removal it was impossible to "match" the defendant's teeth to the mark, but that the alignment was correct [58]. In none of the 2000 mouths was a similar alignment seen. While this evidence was, quite correctly, not accepted in court, it represents the first anecdotal evidence of dental uniqueness. It could be argued that we are still relying similarly anecdotal evidence nearly 80 years later [58].

The human dentition is certainly unique; this has been established, although, as previously stated, not in a mathematically sound fashion [5]. The larger question facing the odontological community is whether or not the replication of these unique features on such a poor registration material as skin, is possible. But perhaps the odontological community has spoken, the final question in the recent survey asked, "Should an appropriately trained individual positively identify a suspect from a bitemark on skin"—70% of the respondents stated yes [49]. However, it is the judicial system that must assess validity, reliability, and a sound scientific base for expert forensic testimony. A great deal of further research is required if odontology hopes to continue to be a generally accepted science [59].

7. CONCLUSION

It is healthy that within any discipline some contentious issues exist; indeed, without an inquisitorial approach and a rejection of current theories or practice, no science would advance. In this regard forensic dentistry is no different, and within the speciality it is bitemark analysis that attracts the most discussion. The efforts of the ABFO should be commended in their attempts to standardize protocol and promote best practice. However, if we truly want an evidence-based, scientific discipline, then the research must be available, and when it is, it should be assessed, evaluated, and, if it is determined to be of quality, the recommendations should be implemented.

REFERENCES

1. Fleiss JL. The Design and Analysis of Clinical Experiments. New York: John Wiley & Sons., 1986.
2. Ligthelm AJ, van Niekerk PJ. Comparative review of bitemark cases from Pretoria, South Africa. J Forens Odontostomatol 1994; 12(2):23–9.
3. Hale A. The admissibility of bitemark evidence. South Calif Law Rev 1978; 51(3):309–34.
4. Sweet D, Pretty IA. A look at forensic dentistry. Part 2. Teeth as weapons of violence—identification of bitemark perpetrators. Br Dent J 2001; 190(8):415–8.
5. Pretty IA, Sweet D. The scientific basis for human bitemark analyses—a critical review. Sci Justice 2001; 41(2):85–92.
6. Brunette D. Critical Thinking. London: Quintessence Books, 1998.
7. Rothwell BR. Bite marks in forensic dentistry: a review of legal, scientific issues. J Am Dent Assoc 1995; 126(2):223–32.
8. Keiser-Nielsen S. Copenhagen Dental School Department of Forensic Dentistry—25 years of activity. Tandlaegebladet [??](In Danish.) 1989; 93(18):712–4.

9.   Atkinson SA. A qualitative and quantitative survey of forensic odontologists in England and Wales, 1994. Med Sci Law 1998; 38(1):34–41.

10. McNamee AH, Sweet D. Adherence of forensic odontologists to the ABFO guidelines for victim evidence collection. J Forens Sci 2003; 48(2):382–5.

11. Layton JJ. Identification from a bite mark in cheese. J Forens Sci Soc 1966; 6(2):76–80.

12. Solheim T, Leidal TI. Scanning electron microscopy in the investigation of bite marks in foodstuffs. Forens Sci 1975; 6(3):205–15.

13. Sweet D, Hildebrand D. Saliva from cheese bite yields DNA profile of burglar: a case report. Int J Legal Med 1999; 112(3):201–3.

14. Rudland M. The dimensional stability of bite marks in apples after long-term storage in a fixative. Med Sci Law 1982; 22(1):47–50.

15. Simon A, Jordan H, Pforte K. Successful identification of a bite mark in a sandwich. Int J Forens Dent 1974; 2(3):17–21.

16. Corbett ME, Spence D. A forensic investigation of teeth marks in soap. Br Dent J 1984; 157(8):270–1.

17. Barbenel JC, Evans JH. Bite marks in skin—mechanical factors. J Forens Sci Soc 1974; 14(3):235–8.

18. Zhang Z, Monteiro-Riviere NA. Comparison of integrins in human skin, pig skin, and perfused skin: an in vitro skin toxicology model. J Appl Toxicol 1997; 17(4):247–53.

19. Sheasby DR, MacDonald DG. A forensic classification of distortion in human bite marks. Forens Sci Int 2001; 122(1):75–8.

20. DeVore DTBite marks for identification? A preliminary report. Med Sci Law 1971; 11(3):144–5.

21. Vale GL, Noguchi TT. Anatomical distribution of human bite marks in a series of 67 cases. J Forens Sci 1983; 28(1):61–9.

22. Pretty IA, Sweet D. Anatomical location of bitemarks and associated findings in 101 cases from the United States. J Forens Sci 2000; 45(4):812–4.

23. Bernstein ML. Two bite mark cases with inadequate scale references. J Forens Sci 1985; 30(3):958–64.

24. Harvey W. Dental Identification and Forensic Odontology. London: Kimpton Publishers, 1976.

25. Hyzer WG, Krauss TC. The bitemark standard reference scale—ABFO No. 2.. J Forens Sci 1988; 33(2):498–506.

26. Guidelines for bite mark analysis. American Board of Forensic Odontology, Inc.. J Am Dent Assoc, 1986:383–6.

27. Bernstein ML. The application of photography in forensic dentistry. Dent Clin North Am 1983; 27(1):151–70.

28. Bang G. Analysis of tooth marks in a homicide case. Observations by means of visual description, stereo-photography, scanning electron microscopy and stereometric graphic plotting. Acta Odontol Scand 1976; 34(1):1–11.

29. Jonason CO, Frykholm KO, Frykholm A. Three dimensional measurement of tooth impression of criminological investigation. Int J Forens Dent 1974; 2(6):70–8.

30. Jakobsen J, Holmen L, Fredebo L, Sejrsen B. Scanning electron microscopy, a useful tool in forensic dental work. J Forens Odontostomatol 1995; 13(2):36–40.

31. Nambiar P, Bridges TE, Brown KA. Quantitative forensic evaluation of bite marks with the aid of a shape analysis computer program, Part 2. "SCIP" and bite marks in skin and foodstuffs. J Forens Odontostomatol 1995; 13(2):26–32.

32. Nambiar P, Bridges TE, Brown KA. Quantitative forensic evaluation of bite marks with the aid of a shape analysis computer program, Part 1. The development of "SCIP" and the similarity index. J Forens Odontostomatol 1995; 13(2):18–25.

33. Barsley RE, West MH, Fair JA. Forensic photography. Ultraviolet imaging of wounds on skin. Am J Forens Med Pathol 1990; 11(4):300–8.

34. Lightelm AJ, Coetzee WJ, van Niekerk PJ. The identification of bite marks using the reflex microscope. J Forens Odontostomatol 1987; 5(1):1–8.

35. Rao VJ, Souviron RR. Dusting and lifting the bite print: a new technique. J Forens Sci 1984; 29(1):326–30.

36. Wood RE, Miller PA, Blenkinsop BR. Image editing and computer assisted bitemark analysis: a case report. J Forens Odontostomatol 1994; 12(2):30–6.

37. Sweet D, Bowers CM. Accuracy of bite mark overlays: a comparison of five common methods to produce exemplars from a suspect's dentition. J Forens Sci 1998; 43(2):362–7.

38. Sweet D, Parhar M, Wood RE. Computer-based production of bite mark comparison overlays. J Forens Sci 1998; 43(5):1050–5.

39. Dailey JC. A practical technique for the fabrication of transparent bite mark overlays. J Forens Sci 1991; 36(2):565–70.

40. West MH, Barsley RE, Frair J, Seal MD. The use of human skin in the fabrication of a bite mark template: two case reports. J Forens Sci 1990; 35(6):1477–85.

41. Naru AS, Dykes E. The use of a digital imaging technique to aid bite mark analysis. Sci Justice 1996; 36(1):47–50.

42. Pretty IA, Sweet D. Digital bitemark overlays—An analysis of effectiveness. J Forensic Sci 2001; 46(6):1385–91.

43. Pretty IA, Hall RC. Forensic dentistry and human bite marks: issues for doctors. Hosp Med 2002; 63(8):476–82.

44. Naru AS, Dykes E. Digital image cross-correlation technique for bite mark investigations. Sci Justice 1997; 37(4):251–8.

45. Sweet D, Lorente M, Lorente JA, Valenzuela A, Villanueva E. An improved method to recover saliva from human skin: the double swab technique. J Forens Sci 1997; 42(2):320–2.

46. Sweet D, Lorente JA, Valenzuela A, Lorente M, Villanueva E. PCR-based DNA typing of saliva stains recovered from human skin. J Forens Sci 1997; 42(3):447–51.

47. Pretty IA, Sweet D. Adherence of forensic odontologists to the ABFO bite mark guidelines for suspect evidence collection. J Forens Sci 2001; 46(5):1152–8.

48. Drinnan AJ, Melton MJ. Court presentation of bite mark evidence. Int Dent J 1985; 35(4):316–21.

49. Pretty IA. A web-based survey of odontologists opinions concerning bitemark analyses. J Forensic Sci., 2003; 48(5):1117–20.

50. Pretty IA, Sweet D. A Comprehensive Examination of Bitemark Evidence in the American Legal System. Reno. NV: American Academy of Forensic Science, 2000.

51. Pretty IA, Sweet D. A look at forensic dentistry, Part 1. The role of teeth in the determination of human identity. Br Dent J 2001; 190(7):359–66.

52. MacFarlane TW, MacDonald DG, Sutherland DA. Statistical problems in dental identification. J Forens Sci Soc 1974; 14(3):247–52.

53. State v. Garrison, 120 Ariz. 255, 585 P.2d 563, 1978.

54. Sognnaes RF, Rawson RD, Gratt BM, Nguyen NB. Computer comparison of bitemark patterns in identical twins. J Am Dent Assoc 1982; 105(3):449–51.

55. Rawson RD, Ommen RK, Kinard G, Johnson J, Yfantis A. Statistical evidence for the individuality of the human dentition. J Forens Sci 1984; 29(1):245–53.

56. Goldstein M, Sweet DJ, Wood RE. A specimen positioning device for dental radiographic identification—image geometry considerations. J Forens Sci 1998; 43(1):185–9.

57. Alt KW, Walz M. Dental print media and their value in forensic odontology. J Forens Odontostomatol 1999; 17(1):5–9.

58. Keyes FA. Teeth marks on the skin as evidence in establishing identity. Dental Cosmos 1925; 67: 1165–1167.

59. Aksu MN, Gobetti JP. The past and present legal weight of bite marks as evidence. Am J Forens Med Pathol 1996; 17(2):136–40.

XII
Research

29
Research Projects and Recent Developments

Robert B. J. Dorion
Laboratoire de sciences judiciaires et de médecine légale,
Ministry of Public Security for the Province of Quebec,
Montreal, Quebec, Canada

1. HISTORY FROM 1975

A glance of the American Academy of Forensic Sciences' 27th annual meeting in Chicago in February 1975 lists 12 papers in odontology with two odontology plenary sessions. The three noteworthy papers on bitemark evidence included a lecture by Dr. Miles Standish on "the methods of developing bitemark evidence," Dr. Richard Souviron on "the dental role in child abuse," and Dr. Curtis Mertz on "a survey of impression in materials for forensic odontology." The plenary sessions included the topic of "dental evidence in crimes against children," moderated by Dr. Lowell Levine, and "the oral manifestation and legal aspects of child abuse," moderated by Drs. Stanley Schwartz and Edward Woolridge.

The report on bitemark evidence [1] results was presented to the American Academy of Forensic Sciences (AAFS) odontology section in 1977 but never published. It might be of interest from a historical perspective to examine the report in order to appraise the current situation. The committee's mandate was to assess and develop criteria for bitemark investigation. A three-part questionnaire was sent to all members of the odontology section of the AAFS as well as to selected individuals throughout the world with known bitemark experience. There were 31 respondents. Among the non-American respondents were R.B.J. Dorion, G. Johanson, S. Kogon, J. Purves, K. Suzuki, G. C. Swann, W. Harvey, S. Keiser-Nielsen, and P. R. Van Ostenberg. Warren Harvey's classic textbook, Dental Identification & Forensic Odontology, had just been published in 1976 [2]. There were five chapters dealing with bitemark evidence: bites and bite marks; experimental human bite-marks; characteristics of individual teeth and identification from bite marks—Preliminary statistical data; Saliva in forensic odontology; and the preparation of models of teeth and bitemarks in food and on bodies.

A hand written letter from Warren Harvey's wife can best express the importance of the AAFS survey:

June 21st 1976

Dear Dr. Dorion,

My husband Dr. Warren Harvey was a member of the American Academy of Forensic Sciences and received your questionnaire at the beginning of April. You may not have heard that he died on May 7th. He was busy until his death answering the questionnaire in longhand and in great detail, as you will see. I have done my best to decipher his notes, and have typed them out (I am not, as you will see, a trained typist) and am sending them to you in case they are of interest! I know it is long past the date they were asked for.

This was the last academic task my husband completed before he died, and it gave him great satisfaction to try and answer to the best of his ability.

Sincerely yours,

Sheila Harvey

Dr. Harvey's nine-page typewritten letter ends with, "As I am writing in bed recovering from a coronary, will you please accept my apologies for the format. I have had to adopt doctors' orders to answer the longest exam paper I've ever had. I wish I was 20 years younger and could start to work with you—if you would have me!"

The questionnaire, divided into three parts, related solely to the contributors' personal experience in bitemark evidence. The first part analyzed personal experience by bitemark type—animal, human, and "false" or pseudo-bites—and by category of bitemarks on live or deceased individuals (Fig. 1). It then analyzed the status of the victim and suspect whether alive or deceased (Fig. 1). The distribution by bitemark type and country is seen in Fig. 2.

The reported U.S. statistics are overstated as more than one expert investigated the same case. In the Malone case (1976), for example, there were four odontologists—two for the prosecution, and two for the defense.

The criteria for discerning between bitemarks of human and animal origin were divided into categories of subjective and objective analysis. The related court experience in these cases was among the 44 questions to part 1. Figure 3 categorizes the number of cases ending in court with or without opposition. Figure 4 categorizes the number of court cases involving human bitemarks by country.

Part 2 of the questionnaire included 21 questions relating to bitemarks on inanimate objects. The responses included bitemarks on: cheese, apple, sandwich, candy, chewing gum, wood, leather jacket, and baked clay. Thirteen cases were reported with only one having gone to court. The information received was insufficient to form a reliable conclusion for evaluating procedural and technical methods that were and should be used in the latter case.

Lastly, Part 3 of the questionnaire asked contributors to suggest the three most important recommendations they could make to the committee. As a result of the recommendations psychiatric/psychological profiling by dentists based on the bitemark was abandoned. It was thought that psychiatric/psychological profiling was not within the realm of the forensic dentist's knowledge and expertise and also because the factors affecting bitemark dynamics (Fig. 3) were so numerous as to render questionable any profiling based on on the bitemark alone. For example, what would be the psychiatric/psychological profiling attributed to drag marks produced by the dentition? In one case the drag marks can be produced as a result of slippage and closure of the dental arches against tissue; in another, as a result of the pulling action of either the victim and/or the bitemark perpetrator. If the forensic dentist cannot definitely attribute the specific action used to produce the bitemark, how can the forensic dentist attribute a psychological/

	Bitemarks on live individuals – number of cases	Bitemarks on deceased – number of cases
Bitemarks of animal origin	128	63
Bitemarks of human origin	46	267
"False" bitemarks	7	22
Total number of bitemark cases	181	352

Figure 1 Bitemark distribution by type.

	BITEMARKS ON LIVE INDIVUDUALS NUMBER OF CASES							BITEMARKS ON DECEASED INDIVIDUALS NUMBER OF CASES						
BITEMARKS OF ANIMAL ORIGIN	1		1	2	114	10					2	60	1	
BITEMARKS OF HUMAN ORIGIN	1	1	5	7	30		2	2	2	7	15	232	7	2
FALSE BITEMARKS			2		4		1				1	21		
TOTAL NUMBER OF CASE	2	1	8	9	148	10	3	2	2	7	18	313	8	2
COUNTRY (EXPERTS)	ENGLAND (1)	DENMARK (1)	JAPAN (1)	CANADA (4)	US (22)	WALES (1)	SWEDEN (1)	ENGLAND (1)	DENMARK (1)	JAPAN (1)	CANADA (4)	US (22)	WALES (1)	SWEDEN (1)

Figure 2 Bitemark distribution by country.

	TOTAL EXPERIENCE	OTHER THAN US EXPERIEMCE	US EXPERIENCE
NUMBER OF CASES ENDING IN COURT (DUPLICATION)	77	34	43
FORENSIC DENTIST OPPOSE VIEWS IN COURT	12	2	10
FORENSIC DENTIST CORROBORATE VIEWS COURT	29	16	13
TOTAL NUMBER OF CASES	57	37	20

Figure 3 Bitemark distribution by court case.

BITEMARKS ON HUMAN TISSUE	4	0	15	8	20	7	3
COUNTRY	ENGLAND	DENMARK	JAPAN	CANADA	US	WALES	SWEDEN

Figure 4 Bitemark distribution by court case and country by 1976.

psychiatric profile to the action? The first and last article, to this author's knowledge, on the psychiatric bitemark profiling by a psychiatrist appeared in the American Academy of Forensic Sciences Journal in 1979 [3].

Use of the word "sucking" in bitemark interpretation also became restricted in use. While it is clear that sucking can be an activity associated with bitemarks, it is not possible to categorically differentiate the presence of a sucking injury from other forms of trauma. One clue might be the presence of salivary DNA that can be associated to a specific bruise, yet devoid of any teethmarks. On the other hand, that same bruise could result from other trauma and someone spiting on the victim!

The American Academy of Forensic Sciences (AAFS) and the American Society of Forensic Odontology (ASFO) are involved in the continuing education of its members. The American Board of Forensic Odontology (ABFO) is, in addition, involved with certification of individuals practicing forensic dentistry. The board realized that to assess a person's competency, it would also have the responsibility of setting standards and guidelines for the practice of forensic dentistry. This not only included setting guidelines for the identification of the deceased but also for the recognition and analysis of bitemarks. To this end the board established the Research, the Bitemark, and the Examination committees. The results of the AAFS odontology section bitemark survey in 1974 and that of the ABFO in 1983 were used as the basis for organizing bitemark workshops with the first held in 1984 which ultimately set standards and guidelines for ABFO members. The board also recognized that the most experienced persons in bitemark evidence were board members and that the board had a responsibility to educate nonmembers who were seeking continuing education credits to ultimately apply for board eligibility. As a result, it organized bitemark Workshop 5 (2002) and Workshop 6 (2003) for nonmembers.

2. BITEMARK CASES IN QUEBEC

This author itemized by category the forensic dental cases in which he acted as a consultant for the Laboratoire de Sciences Judiciaires et de Médecine Légale between 1973 and 1995 [4]. These did not include private cases or consultations from within and without the province. Formal dental identification accounted for 84.48% of cases; nonforensic dental identification (historic or cemetery specimens) 4.94%, crime scene recovered dental specimens 5.25%, and bitemarks accounted for 5.33% of cases. The 328 bitemarks were categorized as follows: 207 human; 73 animal; 15 self-inflicted; 8 on inanimate objects; 11 of unknown or unidentifiable origin; and 14 were nonbitemarks. There would appear to be a higher number of cases and a higher number of bitemarks per case in Quebec than in other jurisdictions as reported by two collegues [5,6]. Does this mean that there are more biters in this population or that the pathologists are better diagnosticians? When giving a lecture a number of years ago in a midsize American city, the lone medical examiner with over 15 years experience claimed, ''We have never had a bitemark in this jurisdiction.'' How many did he fail to recognize? Failure to diagnose is probably the No. 1 problem, closely followed by failure to consult. Both are professionally unacceptable. As of this writing, July 2004, this author was consulted in 2929 forensic cases since 1973 at the Laboratoire de Sciences Judiciaires et de Médecine Légale. The strength of the system is in its team approach in solving a problem.

3. ABFO BITEMARK WORKSHOPS

The ABFO workshops (Fig. 5) addressed different aspects of bitemark evidence (G. Bell, personal communication, 2003):

1. Bitemark Workshop #1. Purpose was to establish general guidelines regarding all aspects of bitemark evidence.

2. Bitemark Workshop #2. Establish guidelines and standards in regard to bitemark terminology and methodology, in addition to a review of the scientific principle.

3. Bitemark Workshop #3. A review of past and current literature in regard to bitemark evidence and analysis. An attempt to establish guidelines in regard to injury analysis in relation to amount and quality of evidence collected. Establish bitemark report writing guidelines.

4. Bitemark Workshop #4. Review and update bitemark evidence collection in regard to the dentition responsible for the bite injury. Practical use of previously established guidelines and standards in regard to bitemark case analysis and methods of comparison and the use of the bitemark forensic report writing guidelines.

5. Bitemark Workshop #5 2002. For persons other than ABFO diplomates.

6. Bitemark Workshop #6 2003. For persons other than ABFO diplomates.

The purpose of ABFO Bitemark Workshop #4 was to determine if the amount and the quality of the bitemark evidence would have any impact on the participant's ability to associate the available evidence with the suspects' dentition. Some persons have misinterpreted the purpose

	YEAR	PLACE	CHAIR	PURPOSE
1	1984	Anaheim	Krauss, Vale	General Bitemark Guidelines Scoring System negated in 1988
2	1994	San Antonio	Bell	Methodology, Terminology (*1995) Scientific principle
3	1997	New York	Bell, Dorion	Review of literature, Injury analysis Report writing
4	1999	Orlando	Bell	Educational exercise on quality and evidentiary value of BM - not proficiency test
5	2002	Atlanta	Bell	Teach non Diplomates Guidelines and Methodology
6	2003	Chicago	Dial	Teach non Diplomates Guidelines and Methodology

Figure 5 ABFO bitemark workshops.

of and the statistical analysis derived from the workshop. The ABFO's board of directors authorized a position paper regarding the workshop [7] in 2003.

The 32 participating diplomates in Workshop #4 were given varying amounts of information on four bitemark cases along with seven sets of dental models. Each case included differing amounts and types of evidence available for analysis.

The workshop was designed as an educational exercise and not as a proficiency examination. It was meant to establish a consistency of agreement among examiners when confronted with cases of varying levels of evidentiary value. A proficiency examination is designed to assess competency within a discipline. Proficiency tests are administered to verify if the examinee has maintained sufficient minimum skills to perform the tasks at hand.

The examiners were asked to analyze each case and to answer the following:

1. What is the degree of certainty that this injury is a bitemark? (Range of values: indeterminable, incompatible, unlikely, possible, probable, reasonable certainty, or definite.)

2. What is the forensic value of the case? (Range of values: case has high forensic value and could support a reasonable certainty/very probable identification as well as an exclusionary finding; case has medium forensic value and could support a possible or consistent with type of identification as well as an exclusionary finding; case has low forensic value and would not support a linking type of finding but could be used for an exclusionary finding; or case has no forensic value and should not be used in an investigation to either link or exclude.)

3. What is the link between the bitemark and the noted dentition? (Range of values: nondiagnostic, inconclusive, incompatible, improbable, possible, probably, or reasonable medical certainty.)

There were several limitations associated with the cases and procedures utilized in this workshop, including:

1. Three of the four bitemark cases were not witnessed or confessed to. They relied on the submitter's opinion to establish the baseline conclusions for each case. It is possible that the submitter may have been incorrect in his original analysis of the case.

2. A number of the participants were allowed to take part, even though they did not submit required reports. This resulted in inconsistencies in the analysis of the workshop results.

3. Based on conversations with the participants and the results obtained, it was apparent that a number of the participants did not fully understand the values they were entering. This lack of understanding resulted in incompatible answers to the three questions listed above.

4. It was also obvious that many of the participants did not treat these cases as seriously as they would have with actual cases in terms of thoroughness and time spent in analysis.

Following the tabulation of participants' answers from the workshop, there was a desire by some of the diplomates to have a statistical analysis conducted on the participants' responses. The thinking was that this could bolster the credibility of bitemark analysis. Following completion of the statistical analysis, the executive committee and the board of directors voted to publish the report. Kristopher Arheart and Iain Pretty, who had accomplished the statistical analysis for the board, were asked to write that report.

Realizing the limitations in the construction of the workshop and wishing to avoid the appearance of concealing its results, the executive committee and directors of the ABFO voted to submit the findings of the workshop to a refereed scientific journal for publication. The motivation was also to demonstrate the proactive position the ABFO has taken in the field of bitemark analysis, pointing out that, in spite of the best of intentions, problems can occur in the construction of a workshop of this type, which would preclude obtaining valid statistics.

The ABFO initially submitted the write up of the workshop results to the Journal of Forensic Sciences for publication. The article was ultimately rejected because the JFS editorial reviewers were of the opinion that the workshop was not constructed appropriately for a statistical analysis. It was the reviewers' opinion that a statistical analysis of this type of workshop would be erroneous because the participants were actually evaluating the subjective determination of an original examiner in three out of the four cases being examined. Such an objection would imply that any statistical analysis of this workshop would not be valid. Remaining convinced that the information obtained from this workshop should be published, in spite of questionable validity of the statistical analysis, the board pursued submission of the article to another refereed journal.

Kristopher Arheart and Iain Pretty subsequently published the results of this workshop in Forensic Science International. Arheart and Pretty concluded that the results of this workshop survey indicate that "analysis of bitemark evidence is a relatively accurate procedure among experienced forensic odontologists when the results are examined in combination." However, the authors also noted that this study involved only four cases and that "these cases are not representative of the range of cases encountered in the real world." They further state, "Therefore, the findings of this study generalize only to cases having moderate to high forensic value. In future studies, a larger number of cases covering a wide range of forensic values should be used to increase the generalization or cross-section and to facilitate the use of individual receiver operating characteristic (ROC) analyses."

Because of the limitations of the case material in the Bitemark Workshop #4, one cannot draw accurate statistical conclusions that would be applicable to actual casework. The analysis of ABFO Bitemark Workshop #4 indicates a need for further study of the agreement among examiners confronted with varying degrees of evidentiary value in bitemark analysis. It is the responsibility of each individual examiner to determine if sufficient evidence exists to go forward with a meaningful bitemark analysis.

4. BITEMARK 2000

While attending Liverpool University Dental Hospital a fourth dental student at the time, Dr. Dave J. Roberts, participated in a project at the Laboratoire de Sciences Judiciaires et de Médecine Légale in Montreal in the summer of 2000.

4.1. Objectives

The project had as objectives:

1. The comparison of bitemarks to preorthodontic and postorthodontic dental casts.

2. To investigate whether the recently pioneered method of digital examination and comparison of bitemarks to dental casts can be performed by a person with no forensic experience.

3. To investigate whether comparison was possible without access to the actual casts or to the bitemarks.

4. To investigate the objectivity of the method.

5. To investigate possible additions to the existing standards for the bitemark analysis.

6. To study the effects that orthodontic therapy has in distinguishing one bitemark from another.

4.2. Introduction

Factors that contribute to the uniqueness of the human dentition [8] include variations in dental alignment, rotation, wear, size of teeth, anomalies, diestemas, fillings, chipping, fractures, notching, etc. Spatial orientation, namely the position and angulation of each tooth within each dental arch, is another important criteria. The permutations and combinations of these variables render a highly unique 3D quality to a given dentition. Few would argue against the uniqueness of the human dentition, but what happens when the dentition is modified by orthodontic treatment to obtain a ''perfect'' dentition? This type of analysis is important to show the uniqueness of a dentition despite orthodontic intervention. Orthodontics is a field in dentistry that alters individual physical features by leveling, reorienting, and realigning the dentition. How do the dental changes influence the observer's ability to correctly identify the offending dentition from a bitemark? Can software programs assist in evaluating the bitemarks made by the ''ideal'' dentition? Can software programs contribute to observer objectivity? Can subjectivity be eliminated?

A bitemark contains information about its creator, but that information may not be completely transferred to the substrate or decipherable. Transferring three-dimensional dental characteristics in a two-dimensional form (photographs or digitized images) leads to loss of information. Additionally, the third dimension of depth is lost as a result of the skin's and underlying muscle's elasticity.

Bitemark analysis is both a qualitative and a quantitative evaluation. The qualitative component refers to the accuracy and readability of the transferred information from dentition to substrate. The more accurate and readable, the better the quality of the bitemark. The quantitative component refers to how many dental characteristics are transferred to the substrate. Are there two or 12 teeth in the bitemark?

While research has been done on quantifying the dentition, little experimentation exists on its influence on the bitemark pattern for obvious ethical, practical and economic considerations but also for the tremendous number of variables influencing a bitemark pattern (Fig. 3 in Chapter 17). Experimenting on animals has also come under scrutiny in recent years by certain members of the public and the media.

4.3. Materials and Methods

An Agfa Snapscan 1212P was used to scan maxillary and mandibular sets of casts in occlusal view at 300 dpi with an ABFO No. 2 scale as control (Fig. 11, left photo). The criteria for choosing the casts for the study were (1) the set of 50 preorthodontic models had to show a variety of malocclusions and disharmonies, and (2) the set of 50 postorthodontic models had to show a reasonable orthodontic outcome. Each of the sets of casts was assigned and labeled with a unique identifier number. Casts were placed in maximum contact of the anterior teeth against the scanner window. The casts were then scanned in frontal and in edge-to-edge position (Fig. 11, left photo). The position of the upper and lower cast was stabilized by a front surface mirror between them and held by elastics. The casts were in direct contact and perpendicular to the scanner window. In cases where the anterior teeth were not in contact with the mirror, the position was forced by placing Play-Doh between the posterior section of the cast and front surface mirror. The purpose of this scan was to register the incisal relationship of the anterior teeth with the horizontal plane, notably for the teeth more likely to register in the bitemark.

The material chosen to receive the bitemarks was Styrofoam. Sections of flat Styrofoam were cut in 600 mm × 600 mm × 3 mm squares and a stereotypical bitemark was created by pressing each arch into the Styrofoam by freehand and dragging it along the Styrofoam. Features usually found in a bitemark, such as drag and slippage, were thus created. A freehand method was warranted because it would have been difficult to create a stereotypical bitemark on a flat surface with models mounted on an articulator. A flat plane was used to facilitate digitalising the bitemarks and to minimize distortion problems. Each of the Styrofoam squares was assigned and labeled with a unique identifier number and scanned with the ABFO No. 2 reference scale.

Dr. Dave Roberts, a dental student at the time, examined the computer based digitized bitemarks and casts. The dental casts and the bitten Styrofoam were not made available, thus eliminating the possibility of fabricating test bites and observing three-dimensional dental features from the casts and the bitemarks. It should be noted that under normal circumstances these materials would be available for analysis by the expert.

4.4. Software

The software can only assist in the selection process in the ideal dentition and only on a very limited basis. Ideal dentitions have few differentiating points. The search for details becomes of paramount importance. Did the use of computer-generated overlays eliminate subjectivity? No, it did not, as the production of overlays in itself requires human input. The operator must adjust for ''sensitivity'' and the number of times a particular software tool is used. This is inherently subjective as the operator produces the ''ideal'' overlay. There are no set rules to acquire consistently accurate ideal dental overlays, and it would be difficult to define any since the precise biting surface(s) can vary from case to case. For example, in certain cases the bitemark incorporates only the incisal edges or parts thereof. In other cases it may incorporate the lingual surfaces only. This is where the additional information derived from transillumination may come in handy. Secondly, the operator cannot duplicate identical positions of cast placement on the scanner. But while the overlay production does not completely eliminate subjectivity, there is a shift toward objectivity and reproducibility. The computer can define outlines with greater precision than the human eye, and the history of overlay construction can be logged to meet SWGIT guidelines (Chapter 8), including adjustments for brightness and contrast to enhance the dental characteristics.

4.5. Discussion

Photoshop tools that create the incisal outline overlay rely on differences in shading and variances in color. The equipment, the software, and the scanning technique utilized also affects the process of creating a 2D image from a 3D object. These factors necessitated that some adjustment of the methodically produced overlay was needed to ensure that details were not missed. But this simple action of adjustment added a degree of subjectivity to the comparison. The digital techniques of comparison of the dentition to bitemark in the year 2000 did not include frontal views of the dentition. A great deal of information about the teeth is gained from a frontal view such as the levels of the teeth, prominent canines, chips in the incisal edges, etc., that is not available from occlusal views.

Roberts, a novice to forensic odontology and bitemark comparison, claimed that the technique of digital comparison of biter-bitemarks was exceedingly easy to comprehend and to perform [9]. The method did not assume extensive knowledge of either odontology or even computer literacy, but computer skills and some knowledge of Adobe Photoshop 5 was helpful is expediting the comparison process. The step-by-step guide given was more than adequate to allow a layman to compare bitemarks to dental casts.

4.6. Scoring and Results

For many of the dentitions, Roberts began the comparison without the frontal view but found it more difficult to eliminate bitemarks from the initial list without the use of the frontal view. When the frontal view was used, the time taken for the identification was significantly reduced. The positive identification of the preorthodontic models with the respective bitemarks took approximately 21 hours, while the postorthodontic comparison took approximately 63 hours. This is triple the amount of time spent in comparison.

Preorthodontic comparison success rate was 100% (50 commitments to positive matches; 50 correct matches). This is an incredible success rate especially for a novice who knows little of bitemark evidence and who was restricted to the use of digitized images only.

The post orthodontic comparison success rate was 78% (41 commitments to positive matches out of 50, with one mismatch). Each correct positive match was attributed 2%, and in the case of a mismatch, 2% was deducted. The reasoning behind the 2% deduction for mismatches was to discourage guesswork on the part of the examinee. Did committing to 41 out of the 50 cases suggest that the bitemarks resembled each other too closely or that the dentitions are no longer unique? Roberts claims that given only the digitized images of the dentitions and the bitemarks that he could not commit to a positive identification for the remaining comparisons.

4.7. Comments on the Selection of Preorthodontic Models

Roberts was asked to comment on the degree of difficulty of the project upon completion. The process of comparing preorthodontic models to the bitemarks was a relatively easy task that took approximately 3 days. Postorthodontic cases took about 9 days of comparison. Primarily the preorthodontic casts were easier to distinguish among themselves, rendering the initial method of comparison as one of exclusion. The initial focus was on (1) tooth position and rotations within the same arch (i.e. the angle and relation between the two central incisors, followed by the relation of the laterals and their angular position in the arch and the adjacent teeth, and so on), and (2) the presence of a central diastema — often an obvious point on both casts and bites (whether one exists or not). These points were normally enough to reach a reasonable conclusion, then additional details confirmed the identity.

The line of thinking adopted by the observer was to choose a set of models, mentally note the major discriminatory factors in the arch alignment, and then compare those factors to the bitemarks by eliminating the obvious impossibilities. The process excluded many bites, leaving a handful of possibilities. The elimination process would eventually lead to a single possibility. The frontal views of the casts were not really necessary, but occasionaly the extra points of consistency helped in a final decision. In only a handful of cases was it necessary to apply details of intercanine width and/or individual tooth characteristics to reach a conclusion.

4.8. Comments on the Selection of Postorthodontic Models

The postorthodontic models and the bitemark comparisons were a completely different story, according to Roberts. Initially, mental notes on tooth angulation were useful in a few cases, but on the whole the eye was unable to distinguish differences in tooth position as the arches were too neatly aligned. The frontal views of the casts were incredibly important in identifying the biter since the variations of the incisal horizontal relationship proved to be of paramount importance. In fact, it was found that noting the horizontal level of the teeth in both arches, and the expectation of prominence in the bitemark was a prime exclusionary factor in the selection process. For example, if the canines of the lower arch were very prominent, one might expect not to find them in the bitemark was unlikely.

Whether both arches coincided with the bite in the comparison was very valuable. Intercanine width was the next point for which exclusion could be made. On the whole, intercanine width was highly variable, but many casts fell within similar parameters. When it came down to selecting one bite over another, more details were needed. This included tooth width and minute dental details such as tooth chipping and notching of the incisal edges. The presence of

PRE-ORTHODONTIC	POST-ORTHODONTIC
• Angulations (relation to arch/other teeth) • Positions (relation to arch/other teeth) • Level of teeth • Intercanine width • Individual tooth characteristics	• Level of teeth • Individual tooth characteristics • Intercanine widths • Positions (relation to arch/other teeth) • Angulations (relation to arch/other teeth)

Figure 6 Preorthodontic criteria.   **Figure 7** Postorthodontic criteria.

drag marks in the bitemark was a good point of reference. All these points together — the horizontal relationships of the incisal edges, notching, intercanine width, tooth widths, chips and occasional tooth angulations (still present in some post-orthodontic cases)—helped in the selection of biter to bitemark. The points of reference in descending order of usefulness are outlined in Figures 6 and 7.

Figures 8 through 14 represent scanned dental casts in occlusal and frontal views. The casts in some cases have been "layered" to demonstrate the incisal edges of the anterior teeth (hollow volume overlay; HVO) while in others the horizontal incisal relationships. Various combinations of the latter are used to demonstrate their relationship to the various bitemarks.

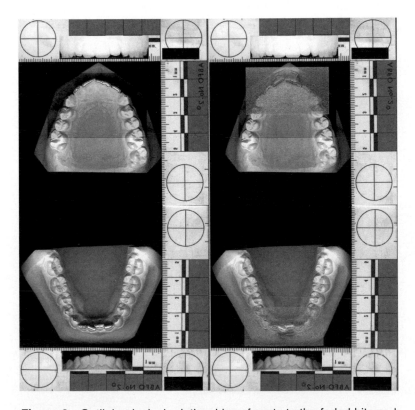

Figure 8 Outlining incisal relationships of casts to the faded bitemark.

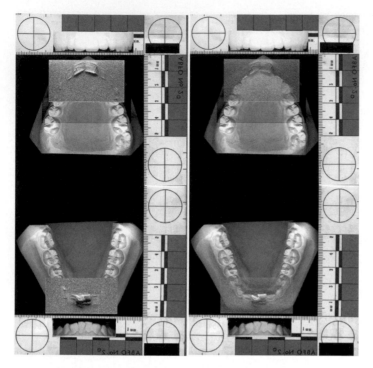

Figure 9 Bitemark (left) and fading bitemark (right).

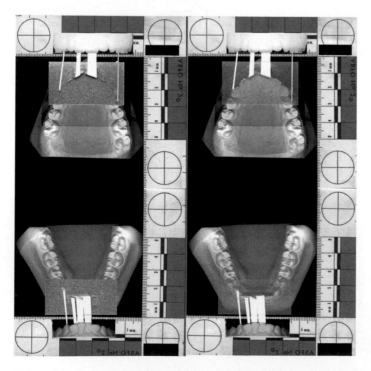

Figure 10 Outlining horizontal incisal relationships to bitemarks and casts.

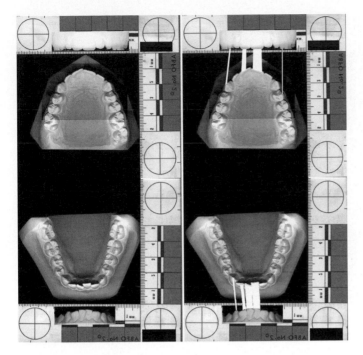

Figure 11 Highlighting tooth positions with the horizontal incisal relationships (maximum contact with tissue).

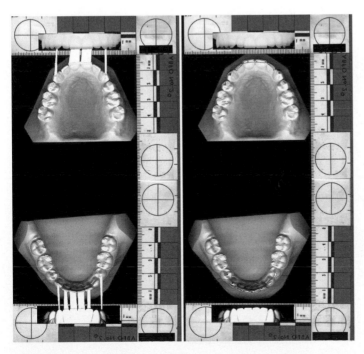

Figure 12 Postorthodontic casts showing horizontal high points (left) and corresponding incisal edges (right).

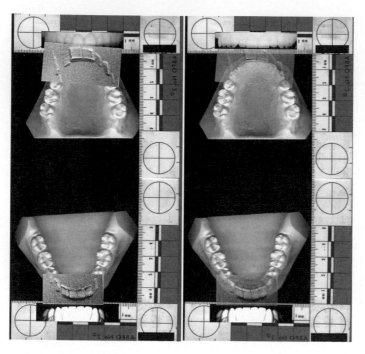

Figure 13 Postorthodontic casts showing bitemark and faded bitemarks (right) to corresponding incisal edges.

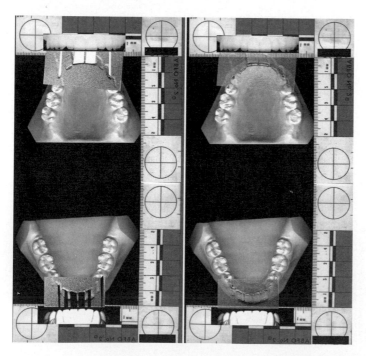

Figure 14 Postorthodontic casts highlighting incisal edges and incisal relationship with the bitemarks.

5. BITEMARK COMPARISON

Methods used in the bitemark comparison have changed over the years. There is no question that the methods currently employed are more accurate and less subjective than they were in the 1970s. At that time, hand-drawn overlays were made of the suspect dentition and compared directly to a 1:1 life-size photograph of the bitemark. Figure 15 demonstrates the ''scraping'' action of the incisal edges dragging over the back. The alignment of the individual teeth is easily demonstrable.

Dorion [10] discussed the method of using a photocopy machine to produce dental cast overlays. Alternatively, a scanner was used for the same purpose. The software programs used in 1997 were Photoshop 3.0, ImagePals 2.0, and SigmaScan/Image 1.2.

In the 1980s video comparison techniques became popular. In the following example a suspect's dental casts are compared to the excised fixed and transilluminated bitemark on a breast (Fig. 16). Three-dimensional vinyl templates and Styrofoam were introduced as bite registration medium in bitemark analysis in 1990. Clear vinyl hygroscopic templates 0.02 mm in thickness, commonly known in dentistry as temporary splint material, is heated and molded to a dental cast under vacuum.

In the intervening years, computer-generated overlays have been favored over the hand-drawn variety. In the following example computer overlays are used to demonstrate the differences between two suspect dentitions in an infanticide case (Fig. 17). This is by no means an ideal bitemark since it is dated, healing, and lacks individual dental characteristics. On the other

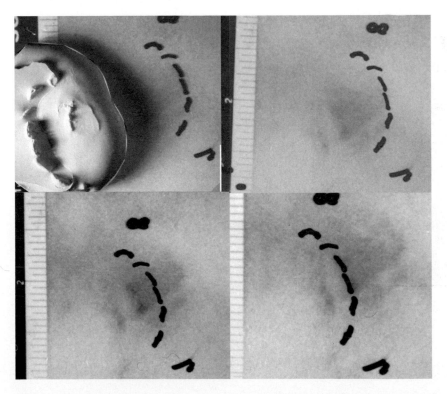

Figure 15 Hand-drawn overlay of suspect dentition over bitemark photograph.

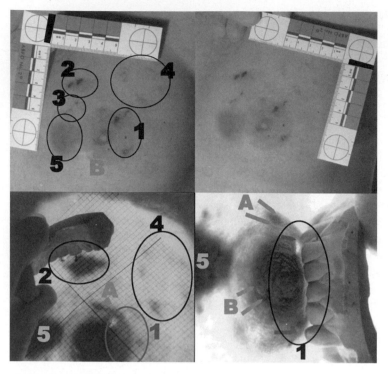

Figure 16   Bitemarks on breast (top), and dental comparison of transilluminated specimen. Also see color photograph insert section.

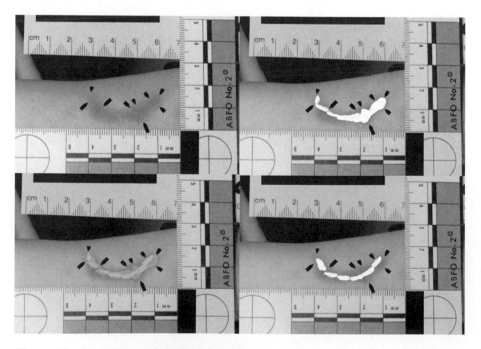

Figure 17   Superimposed dental comparisons.

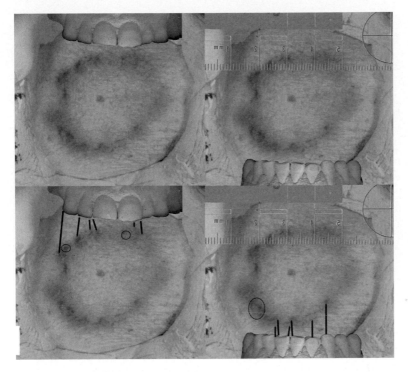

Figure 18 Frontal view of dentition with corresponding area of bitemark.

hand, the bruise has certain parameters that when taken as a whole can be analyzed in relationship to a suspect dentition. The current example is a case of exclusive opportunity, which limits the suspect population to two adults.

Retrospective studies and comparisons are interesting in light of the new technologies. The new technologies were applied to a bitemark case of a female homicide victim from the mid-1980s. The effects of the new technologies are not only more visually appealing but are more intelligible to the layman. In Figures 18–21, the fixed bitemark specimen demonstrates dental characteristics of tooth alignment, size, and detail not apparent prior to excision (Fig. 21). Why certain details become more apparent following fixation is unclear.

The buccal cusp of the perpetrator's upper left first bicuspid (dental cast flipped to match the corresponding contusion on the bitemark photograph) is fractured and missing. The interrelationship between the underlying subcutaneous hemorrhage and the surface contusions/lacerations representing class and individual dental characteristics are decidedly more visual and intelligible.

Having the occlusal as well as the frontal view of the dentition makes it more three-dimensional like. This editor has chosen the maxim ''a picture is worth 1000 words'' as the focus of this textbook for obvious reasons.

6. SUMMARY

Human bitemark analysis is by far the most challenging and difficult aspect of forensic dentistry. Bitemarks as a research theme has exploded as witnessed by the 32 papers delivered at the American Academy of Forensic Sciences' annual meeting between 1999 to 2003 can attest [6,9,11–40].

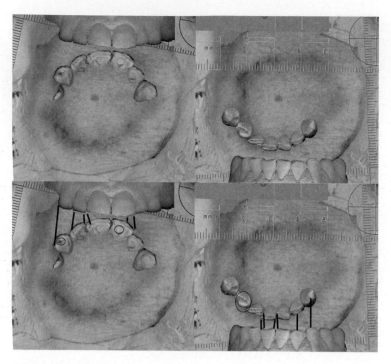

Figure 19   Occlusal and incisal view of the dentition and corresponding bitemark.

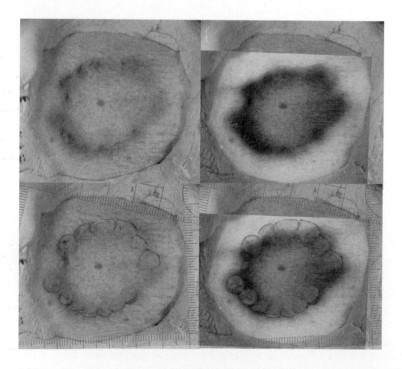

Figure 20   Bitemark comparison technique and transillumination. Also see color photograph insert section.

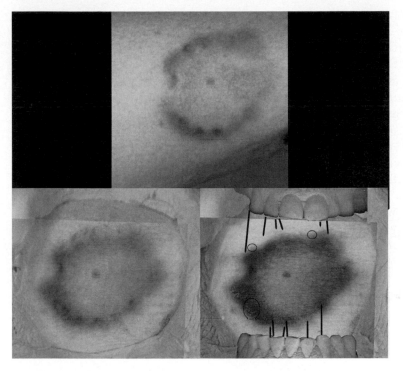

Figure 21 Bitemark comparison technique and transillumination. Also see color photograph insert section.

One preliminary study [37], yet to be published as of this writing, on the aging of bitemark wounds inflicted before, at, and after death on pigskin, is particularly interesting. Bitemark comparison techniques, metric analysis, specimen transillumination, and histological slides were analyzed. Paired bitemarks on each side of the pig were excised and fixed for 35 days in formalin. Avon correctly states that no form of artificial simulation can precisely replicate the mechanics or response of tissue to a bite (Fig. 3 in Chapter 17).

Why are certain bitemark cases controversial? Controversial bitemark cases are usually associated with one or more of the following issues:

1. The examiner's lack of knowledge, training, and/or experience
2. Failure to follow established protocol
3. Examination of substandard material (quantity and/or quality)
4. Failure to obtain all of the available information before examination/conclusions
5. Using untested, unproven, or unpublished methods or procedures or those that cannot be demonstrated and/or duplicated.

In many controversial bitemark cases, the expert was asked to rely on limited information either about the case itself or the material provided. The expert may only have had access to limited and poorly defined photographs to base the conclusions. As a result, the expertise has been brought to question. Even the most accomplished forensic dental expert should be in the position to qualify the conclusions based on the material received. Poor-quality photographs cannot be compared to the wealth of information available when standard protocol is maintained.

Where can one obtain formal education in forensic odontology? The first university in North America to grant a postdoctorate master's degree in Dental Diagnostic Science with an option in forensic dentistry was the University of Texas in San Antonio. The University of British Columbia's Bureau of Legal Dentistry (BOLD) in Vancouver was the next to offer an MS degree in forensic odontology. McGill University in Montreal will be the first to offer an on line certificate-granting course in forensic odontology in September 2004 (www.mcgill.ca/dentistry/forensic). It also plans to offer a postdoctorate master's degree program in forensic odontology in the near future. The online course will have theoretical and practical components. Course registrants will, in addition, need to spend time on practical training and examination at the Laboratoire de Sciences Judiciaires et de Médecine Légale in Montreal.

Continuing-education credits in forensic odontology can be obtained from a number of universities, institutions, forensic facilities, and organizations. The Armed Forces Institute of Pathology in Washington has been giving a 1-week beginners' training course in forensic odontology since the early 1970s.

Advancement in any discipline results from the observer's knowledge, training, education, experience, and experimentation. Experimentation must follow certain fundamental principles that may be repeated by others. One can utilize one's basic knowledge as a building block to assist in undeveloped or underdeveloped disciplines. Several examples have been cited in this textbook including the development of photography, computer science, and imagery for forensic dental use.

7. KNIVES

Possession of a firearm without a permit in Canada is illegal. In the province of Quebec 25.6% of homicides in 1998 were committed with a handgun and 15% with other firearms (total 40.6%). Knives accounted for 26.3% of homicide deaths. If one considers that most firearms involved in the commission of homicide are either unregistered or stolen, the statistics on the use of knives as a murder weapon becomes impressive since everyone has access to them (Fig. 22). As an instrument of death, therefore, the forensic implications are important.

On May 5, 1995, Tara Manning was raped and stabbed over 30 times in her bedroom while her father and brother lay sleeping in their Montreal suburban house. This case was the basis for changing Canadian criminal law that permitted authorities to obtain DNA samples from suspects. Samples could be obtained for hair, blood, or saliva. Dental impressions could also be taken. The latter was recommended to the Law Reform Commission of Canada as early as 1980 by this author. The law of the land is slow to catch up to science.

The forensic dentist may be the best-qualified person to perform forensic comparisons of knife impressions on cartilage. Cartilage is a biological substance as is bitten skin; both are encountered at autopsies. Cartilage must be preserved in the same media as bitemarks. Cartilage is a much better impression material than skin. Knife test cuts must be performed on similar material to cartilage (usually dental impression material). Impressions of the knives and test cuts must be used for comparative purposes. No person is more highly qualified than a dentist to take accurate impressions of the biological substrate, cartilage in this case, and of the knives. The comparison between suspect knife and cartilage can be performed digitally, as are bitemarks to a suspect's dentition currently.

There are few scientific articles [41], little research, and no classification of knives for forensic purposes. This author proposed a standard for the photography and for the classification of knives [22].

DEATH STATISTICS IN CANADA		
CANADIAN MEN		
No. of Deaths	**Cause of Death**	**Frequency**
487	Homicides all causes	1 death every 18 hrs.
178	Homicide, by firearm	1 death every 2 days
142	Homicide, by cutting/piercing instrument	1 death every 3 days
CANADIAN WOMEN		
No. of Deaths	**Cause of Death**	**Frequency**
245	Homicide, all causes	1 death every 32 hrs.
69	Homicide, by firearm	1 death every 5 days
68	Homicide, by cutting/piercing instrument	1 death every 5 days

Causes of Death 1992 (Ministry of Industry, Science and Technology, Statistics Canada, Health Statistics Division, Sept. 1994); and, Method of Committing Homicide Offences, Canadian the Provinces/Territories, 1992 (Ministry of Industry, Science and Technology, Statistics Canada, Canadian Center for Justice Statistics, 1992)

Figure 22 Firearm and cutting instrument homicide statistics in Canada (1992).

An ABFO No. 2 scale is placed on the upper left quadrant of the photograph. The suspect knife is photographed by placing the handle to the right and the cutting edge facing upward, then downward (Figs. 23, 24). This is the key to the classification.

In Figure 23 the right knife edge (handle to the right and the cutting edge facing upward) is highly beveled (top photo) and curved. The left knife edge (handle to the right and the cutting edge facing downward) is highly beveled (bottom photo) and curved. This knife is classified as right and left highly beveled curved blade.

In Figure 24 the right knife edge is highly beveled (top photo) and serrated, the left knife edge is highly beveled (bottom photo) and serrated. This knife is classified as right and left highly beveled, serrated.

Figure 25 demonstrates a test cut from a serrated knife into a roll of fixed dental impression material. Note the mirror images of the striations resembling hills and valleys. Where there are hills in the upper impression, there are corresponding valleys in the lower impression. The upper and the lower impression materials represent a section of the right side and of the left side of the blade.

Knife impressions and test cuts can be made using vinyl polysiloxane impression material. Test cuts are made perpendicular to the set impression material. For contrast, the cartilage is ''stroked'' with India ink.

Figures 26–28 represent digital comparisons between a homicide victim's cartilage, test cuts made in impression material, and the suspect knife. This material was given to defense attorneys prior to trial. A plea bargain was obtained.

With every new discipline, innovation, or technique there are answers for which questions have yet to be asked. Research, time, experience, and thoughtful consideration will resolve the issue at hand.

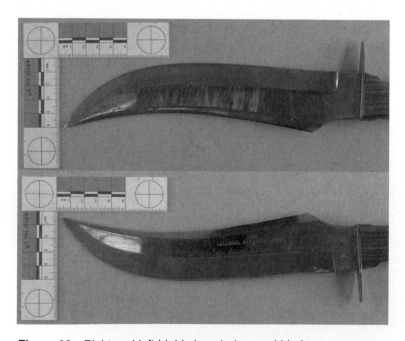

Figure 23 Right and left highly beveled curved blade.

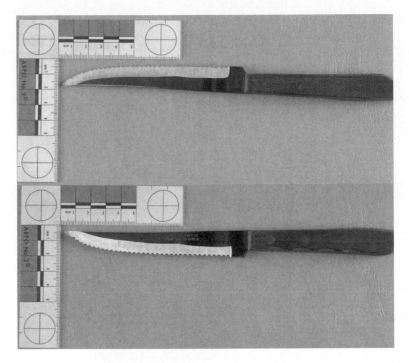

Figure 24   Right and left highly beveled serrated straight blade.

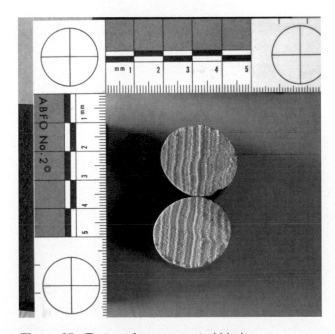

Figure 25   Test cut from a serrated blade.

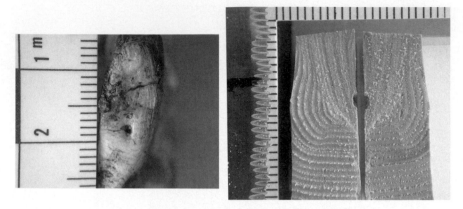

Figure 26 Cartilage, knife, and knife impression (left to right).

Figure 27 Knife, knife impression, cartilage (left to right) Note insert in knife impression corresponding to cartilage stiations.

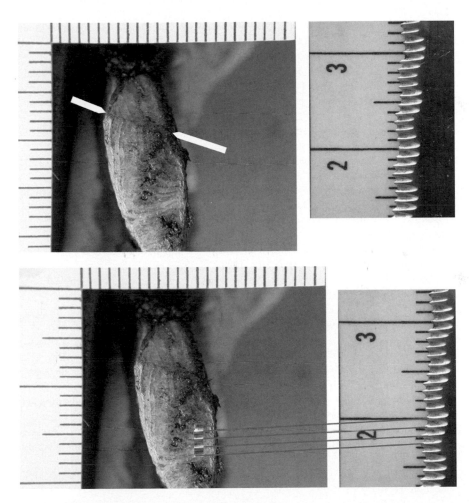

Figure 28 Cartilage and knife correspondence.

REFERENCES

1. Dorion RBJ. Chairman, Committee for Recommended Methods, American Academy of Forensic Sciences, Odontology Section, February 1977.
2. Harvey W. Dental Identification and Forensic Odontology. London: Kimpton Publishers, 1976.
3. Morrison HL. Psychiatric observations and interpretations of bitemark evidence in multiple murders. J Forens Sci 1979; 24(2):492–502.
4. Dorion RBJ. Forensic dentistry in Quebec from 1973 to 1995. JCSFS 1996; 29(4):259–68.
5. Vale GL, Noguchi TT. Anatomical distribution of human bite marks in a series of 67 cases. J Forens Sci 1983; 28(1):61–69.
6. Pretty IA, Sweet D. The anatomical location of bite marks and associated findingsin 101 cases from the United States. J Forens Sci 2000; 45(4):812–814.
7. ABFO position paper on Bitemark Workshop #4. ASFO News 22(2):5.
8. R. D. Rawson, R. K. Ommen, G. Kinard, J. Johnson, A. Yfantis. Statistical Evidence for the Individuality of the human dentition. J Forens Sci 1984; 29(1):245–253.
9. Dorion RBJ. Bitemark project 2000—objectivity, AAFS meeting, Odontology Section, Seattle, February 23, 2001.
10. Dorion RBJ. Bitemark computer imaging, enhancement, measurement, analysis and overlays. AAFS, Odontology Section, New York, February 21, 1997.
11. Gardner CD, Mincer HH, Smith OC, Symes SA. Application of epiluminescence microscopy (ELM) to the evaluation of bite marks, AAFS meeting, Odontology Section, February 1999.
12. Riley CK, Norling BK, Alder ME. Dimensional stability and accuracy of a non-traditional modeling material: a pilot study, AAFS meeting, Odontology Section, February 1999.
13. Johnson LT, Dhuru V, DelCampo G. The accuracy of elastomeric forensic models, AAFS meeting, Odontology Section, February 1999.
14. Gould GA. Bite mark analysis: a device to assist in the orientation of upper and lower arches, AAFS meeting, Odontology Section, Orlando, February 18, 1999.
15. Gardner CD, Mincer HH, Smith OC, Symes SA. Application of epiminescence microscopy (ELM) to the evaluation of bite marks, AAFS meeting, Odontology Section. February 18, 1999.
16. Johnson LT, Dhuru V, delCampo G. The accuracy of elastomeric forensic models, AAFS meeting, Odontology Section, Orlando, February 18, 1999.
17. Crowley KM, Evans RJ, Gillies R, Bamberg M, Kollias N. Identification of saliva on skin using fluorescence spectroscopy, AAFS meeting, Odontology Section, Orlando, February 18, 1999.
18. Kim JJ, Sweet D. Evaluation of the use of ABF0 bitemark guidelines in various geographic locations. AAFS, Odontology Section, February 13 1999.
19. Perrier M, Horisberger B, Mangin P. A bite mark case presentation: examination and computer imaging analysis. AAFS, Odontology Section, February 13 1999.
20. Brzozowski CC, Nawrocki LA, Friedman BK. A comparison of dimensional stability of excised patterned injuries using various fixatives: a preliminary study. AAFS, Odontology Section, February 13, 1999.
21. Georget CE, Baston WT. Recording and computerizing superimposition of human bite marks. AAFS, Odontology Section, February 13 1999.
22. Dorion RBJ. Knives, tissue resection, preservation and transillumination, AAFS meeting, Odontology Section, Orlando, February 18, 1999.
23. Bowers CM, Pretty IA. Critique of the knowledge base for bitemark analysis during the 60's, 70's, and early '80s, AAFS meeting, Odontology Section, Reno, February 24, 2000.
24. Brzozowski CC, Nawrocki LA, Friedman BK. A comparative study of materials and methods used for collecting, stabilizing, and preserving excised tissue, AAFS meeting, Odontology Section, Reno, February 26, 2000.
25. Wiley BR, Rawson RD. Classifying bitemark severity—a proposed modification of forensic odontological nomenclature, AAFS meeting, Odontology Section, Seattle, February 23, 2001.
26. Pretty IA, Sweet D. The effectiveness of bitemark overlays, AAFS meeting, Odontology Section, Seattle, February 23, 2001.

27. Valenzuella A, Martin–de las Heras S, Fuentes D, Torres JC. Production of bitemark comparison overlays from 3-D scanned images, AAFS meeting, Odontology Section, Seattle, February 23, 2001.

28. Senn DR, Alder ME, Brumit PC, White M. Scanning electron microscopy and digital imaging software in bite mark analysis: technique in case report, AAFS meeting, Odontology Section, Seattle, February 23, 2001.

29. Sweet D. Blind testing as a scientific protocol — use of a dental lineup for bitemark suspects, AAFS meeting, Odontology Section, Seattle, February 23, 2001.

30. Firestone SR, Friedman BK. Objective bitemark analysis using an electronic occlusal diagnostic system, AAFS meeting, Odontology Section, Atlanta, February 15, 2002.

31. Weems RA, Embry JH. Dynamic courtroom presentation of bitemark evidence via digital overhead camera and LCD projector. AAFS, Atlanta, February 15, 2002.

32. Parks ET. Bitemark analysis utilizing the computer pitfalls and brick walls. AAFS, Atlanta, February 15, 2002.

33. Lasser AJ, Warnick AJ, Berman GM. A unique way to analyze bite marks using 3-D laser scanners and comparative software. AAFS, Atlanta, February 15, 2002.

34. Johansen RJ, Bowers M. Digital analysis of evidence photographs (bitemark): automated rectification of photographic distortion, resizing to life size, and rotation of images. AAFS, Atlanta, February 15, 2002.

35. Taylor RV, Blackwell SA, Yoshino MU, Ogleby CL, Tanijiri T, Clement JG. 3-dimensional noncontact morphometric comparisons of human dentitions with simulated human bite marks. AAFS, Odontology Section, Atlanta, February 15, 2002.

36. McCormack O, Hall RC, Pretty IA. Wound contraction and older bite mark injuries: aspects of interest to odontologists. AAFS, Odontology Section, Chicago, February 21, 2003.

37. Avon SL, Wood RE, Blenkinsop B. An in-vivo porcine model of contusive bite mark injuries in human bite mark analysis. AAFS, Odontology Section, Chicago, February 21, 2003.

38. Tewes W. Topographic mapping to improve objectivity in bite mark analysis for Abode Photoshop hollow volume construction. AAFS, Odontology Section, Chicago, February 21, 2003.

39. Firestone SR, Friedman BK. Objective bite mark analysis using an electronic occlusal diagnostic system. Part II. AAFS, Odontology Section, Chicago, February 21, 2003.

40. Brumit PC, McGivney J. A mathematical approach to bitemark analysis using Bite2000 software, AAFS, Odontology Section, Chicago, February 21, 2003.

41. Houck M. Skeletal trauma and the individualization of knife marks in bone. In Reichs KJ, Ed. Forensic Osteology. 2nd ed.. Spring Field, IL: Charles C. Thomas, 1998.

30

Genotypic Comparison of Oral Bacteria Isolated from Bitemarks and Teeth

Geoffrey R. Tompkins
Department of Oral Sciences, University of Otago School of Dentistry, Dunedin, New Zealand

1. INTRODUCTION

Major advances in nucleic acid technology over the past 20 years have led to the development of spectacularly discriminative applications to forensic analyses. An individual's unique genetic profile can now be determined from very small samples of blood, semen, hair, or epithelial cells, and such profiles, in conjunction with other biochemical and immunological tests, have the potential statistical capability to distinguish all humans [1]. Despite these advances, the recovery of the biter's DNA from a bitemark inflicted on human skin (living or not) remains a difficulty because nucleic acid–degrading enzymes (nucleases) present in saliva rapidly degrade DNA [2]. The temperature of living skin undoubtedly promotes the activity of the nucleases; the half-life for DNA maintained at 37°C in saliva has been estimated at less than 1 min [3]. As recently as 1994, it was generally held that a "DNA fingerprint" could not be generated from a saliva sample [4]. David Sweet and his collaborators have, to an extent, overcome this difficulty by the development of a double-swabbing method to recover intact oral epithelial cells from bitemarks [2]. The biter's DNA is protected from the salivary nucleases by sequestration within the epithelial cells. However, even under controlled experimental conditions, using human cadavers and drops of saliva, this DNA recovery method is not always successful [2], and anecdotal reports suggest that the success rate is lower in field situations.

Owing to the difficulty of recovering human DNA, we have investigated the isolation and analysis of other potentially discriminative markers that may be deposited in bitemarks. Specifically, we have assessed the feasibility of recovering and genotypically matching oral bacteria from the teeth of a suspected biter to those isolated from a bitemark. From the outset, though, it is emphasized that this approach is not intended as an alternative to recovering the biter's own DNA, but rather as a backup method that may provide valuable supportive evidence in situations where human DNA is not recovered. Every attempt should be made to recover human DNA derived from the biter, as this provides the most compelling evidence to associate an individual with a crime and, more importantly, can unequivocally exonerate a suspect [5].

2. ORAL MICROBIOLOGY

The human mouth contains a diversity of microbial habitats, and recent estimates indicate that as many as 500 distinct species of bacteria may inhabit the oral cavity [6]. Of these, the genus

593

Streptococcus represents the most numerically prolific group [7]. Members of this genus are not only the most common bacteria on the surfaces of the teeth but include the colonizing ''pioneers'' that attach to the tooth surface within minutes of removal by mechanical prophylactic procedures [7,8]. Thus, in the absence of aggressive antimicrobial treatment, the human teeth are inevitably coated with millions of bacteria, many of which belong to the genus *Streptococcus*. Most species of *Streptococcus* are largely benign (nonpathogenic) and live on various surfaces within the mouth, including the teeth and the oral soft tissues [9]. Streptococci are rarely present on healthy human skin. The more pathogenic species such as *S. pyogenes* (the causative agent of streptococcal pharyngitis which prequels rheumatic fever, scarlet fever, and other potentially fatal conditions) and *S. pneumoniae* (the most common etiologic agent of community-acquired pneumonia) have been intensively studied taxonomically, but the more common oral species, with the possible exception of the group known as the mutans streptococci (implicated in the initiation of dental caries), are relatively poorly defined. The majority of benign supragingival plaque streptococci are often collectively referred to as the ''mitis group'' and include the species *S. sanguinis* (*S. sanguis*), *S. parasanguinis*, *S. mitis*, *S. oralis*, *S. gordonii*, and *S. crista* [10].

Traditional taxonomic methods, such as the ability to ferment specific carbohydrates, offer poor discrimination between the oral streptococci, suggesting that the species distinctions may be ill founded [11]. However, attempts to resolve these issues by molecular methods have revealed tremendous genotypic diversity within the group. Thus, although they are physiologically and biochemically similar, the arrangement of their genetic material is quite heterogeneous. Taxonomic comparisons by restriction fragment-length polymorphism (RFLP) analysis of whole genomic DNA and by arbitrarily primed polymerase chain reaction (PCR) techniques, have served only to emphasize the genotypic diversity [12–14]. For example, of a collection of 72 isolates compared by arbitrarily primed PCR, none shared identical amplicon profiles [14]. An underlying reason for this diversity may stem from the widespread ability of these bacteria to exchange and rearrange genetic material by the process known as genetic transformation. Competence for transformation in the oral streptococci is chromosomally encoded [15] and occurs under experimental conditions designed to mimic the oral environment [3].

The ubiquity and number of streptococci colonizing the human teeth would seem to imply that such bacteria are deposited on every surface bitten by human teeth. In view of the extreme genotypic diversity displayed by these organisms, the question arises whether bacteria recovered from bitemarks inflicted on human skin can be genotypically matched, with any degree of specificity, to bacteria isolated from the teeth responsible for the bite.

3. PIONEERING WORK

Elliot and colleagues originally proposed the concept of recovering oral bacteria from bitemarks for forensic purposes. In their studies, freshly collected human saliva was applied as droplets to living human skin, and the sites were sampled at intervals to determine the number of viable bacteria [16]. The study concentrated on isolating *S. salivarius*, which, although not strictly a tooth-colonising organism, is probably the most abundant bacterium in the mouth [17] and likely to be deposited in most bitemarks. The experiment involved the highly selective and differential bacteriological culture medium Mitis-Salivarius agar [18] to isolate and culture viable streptococci from the skin surface. The study found that *S. salivarius* can be recovered for at least 3 hours following deposition of the saliva but that bacterial viability decreases rapidly over this period. The experiment was not extended beyond 7 hours. A subsequent publication reported the application of a mass spectrometric method to distinguished strains of *S. salivarius* [19]. Thus, although not a genotypic approach, the essential principle of recovering and distinguishing (at the subspecies level) oral bacteria derived from the biter was investigated. Unfortunately, the research program seems to have concluded before determination of the statistical resolution of *S. salivarius* strain distinction by this method, and, to my knowledge, there have been no reports of field application.

4. RECOVERY OF ORAL STREPTOCOCCI FROM BITEMARKS

Over a decade later, our group initiated studies on a similar approach but elected to focus on the streptococci associated with the tooth surface, rather than *S. salivarius*. There were two reasons for this choice. Firstly, essentially every healthy human being harbours large numbers of these organisms on their teeth and therefore it may be anticipated that significant numbers of such bacteria are likely to be deposited in a bitemark. Secondly, several studies [12–14] report the extreme genotypic diversity of the (non-*salivarius*) oral streptococci (there is little such information on *S. salivarius*).

In our studies, it was felt that it was essential to deposit the bacteria in the most authentic way possible and thus the experiments involved participants biting themselves as firmly as they could on the upper arm. The application for approval for these experiments apparently provided some diversion for the human ethics committee but it was important to deposit the bacteria in an authentic manner. It is surprising how hard an individual can bite him/herself, and many of the self-inflicted bites produced a marked contusion with subsequent bruising. Our study also used Mitis-Salivarius agar to recover viable streptococci. Our sampling was concentrated on the imprints of the mandibular incisors and canines as these teeth generate the principal force in biting and therefore the shearing interaction between skin and tooth is likely to be the greatest, which should result in deposition of larger numbers of bacteria. The experiment was protracted such that bitemarks were sampled for up to 24 hours following the bite. The finding reiterated those of the earlier study [16] by demonstrating that the numbers of recoverable bacteria decreased exponentially following deposition on the skin surface [20]. Nevertheless, thousands of bacteria were recoverable after a 24-hour interval provided the bitemark remained relatively undisturbed, whereas only one or two colonies (at most) were ever recovered from unbitten (control) upper-arm sites [20]. Female assault victims, on average, seek medical attention within 11 hours of an attack [21], and thus there should be an opportunity to recover viable oral bacteria derived from the biter in many instances where biting occurs. Extrapolation of the data suggests that viable bacteria would not be recoverable from living skin beyond 30 hours, but we have not yet studied survival of streptococci on nonliving skin.

Under authentic circumstances, however, there are a number of factors that conceivably reduce either the viability or recoverability of deposited bacteria. Firstly, there may be a physical struggle that would generate heat and perhaps sweat at the skin surface. Thus the effect of 10 min of moderate exercise (running on a treadmill) was assessed immediately before biting and demonstrated that indeed this led to decreased bacterial recoverability [22]. Furthermore, prior application of moisturizing lotion (containing preservatives), manual rubbing immediately after biting, and (not surprisingly) washing with soap, all reduced bacterial recoverability [22]. However, with the exception of washing with soap, informative numbers of bacteria could be recovered from all experimental subjects. Bacteria could also be recovered from a variety of tested fabric types through which bites were inflicted [22].

5. GENOTYPIC IDENTIFICATION OF ORAL STREPTOCOCCI

Having established that authentically deposited oral bacteria survive in bitemarks long enough for practical purposes, the next phase of the study aimed (1) to determine whether recovered bacteria could be genotypically matched to those isolated from the teeth responsible for the bite, and (2) to get an indication of the exclusivity of streptococcal strains isolated from different individuals. Genotypic comparison of bacterial strains was initially accomplished by RFLP analysis of whole genomic DNA (genotypic "fingerprinting") [22]. Although this is more labor-intensive than PCR-based approaches, it offers potentially greater resolution. The study demonstrated, by comparing 10 bacterial isolates from the teeth with 10 from the self-inflicted bitemarks of eight subjects, that at least one strain (usually more) could be matched between the two sites [22]. Furthermore, specific bacterial genotypes were unique to each individual within the study [22]. In other words, there was no evidence of bacterial strain sharing between participants (53 genotypes isolated in total). We had anticipated that one or two strain(s) would dominate the teeth of an individual, but the results suggested that there are likely to be several frequently isolatable strains [22]. Furthermore, the study indicated that the skin exerts a selective pressure on the deposited bacteria. Thus, the bacterial strains surviving for protracted periods on the skin were not necessarily the most dominant strains on the tooth surface. In subsequent investigations we felt we needed to look at greater numbers of isolates. As a result, an arbitrarily primed PCR method was adopted which allowed more rapid identification of larger numbers of bacteria.

The PCR assessment was structured as a simulated crime situation in which an investigator compiled a genomic database of bacteria isolated from the teeth of eight volunteers. He was then given two Mitis-Salivarius agar plates containing bacterial colonies cultured from swabbed samples from self-inflicted bitemarks (plated within 10 min of swabbing), purportedly from two of the eight individuals, and attempted to identify the biters. In the course of this study, 50 streptococcal isolates from the teeth of each participant and from each of the two bitemarks were genotypically typed. Examples of PCR amplicon profiles comparing bacteria isolated from teeth and bite marks are shown in Figure 1. Analyses of the dental isolates indicated that in most individuals one or two genotypes compose around 60% of isolates but that there may be as many as 23 strains harbored by an individual [23]. The study also supported the previous observation that strains predominating on the tooth surface were not always the prevalent strains recovered from the bitemarks. A total of 105 genotypes were isolated from the eight individuals, and again none of the bacterial genotypes were shared between individuals [23]. The investigator was confidently and correctly able to identify one of the biters by comparing the bacterial genotypes from the bitemark to those in the database. However, he was unable to determine the origin of the second bitemark sample, which in fact was not one of the original eight volunteers from his database (i.e., was included as a negative control). Over 1 year later, the teeth of the same eight individuals were again sampled, and PCR analyses indicated that identifiable bacterial genotypes had been retained by each of the participants (Rahimi, submitted). This strain stability implies that there is a reasonable likelihood that bacteria recovered from an authentic bitemark associated with criminal activity may be matched to the biter some months (and possibly years) following an attack.

6. FUTURE RESEARCH AND APPLICATION

As this work is still in the developmental stage, we have not applied the method to an authentic assault case. Forensic application will require a statistical determination of the frequency with which two unrelated individuals harbor genotypically identical bacterial strains. This is currently not known, and such a determination may at first appear to be a monumental task (which is why it was preferred initially to establish the practical feasibility of the approach), but the finding that most people harbor at least six distinguishable streptococcal strains may make the undertaking feasible because the chance of two individuals sharing more than one strain decreases logarithmically according to the number of identified matching strains. Thus, if the probability of

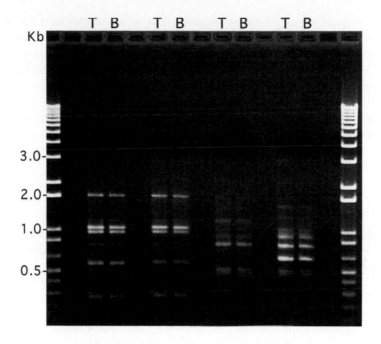

Figure 1 Comparison of AP-PCR products derived from four *Streptococcus* colonies isolated from a self-inflicted bitemark (B) with four from the lower incisors of the biter (T). Calibration markers are in the extreme lanes. (Courtesy of M. Rahimi.)

two unrelated individuals harboring an indistinguishable strain is 1/100 (probably a conservative figure), then the chance of two individuals sharing four indistinguishable strains is $\sim 10^{-8}$, which is compelling especially in association with other evidence. Note that this calculation makes certain assumptions, in particular, that individual genotypes are acquired independently of each other. To determine the statistical resolution, it may therefore be necessary to isolate and compare only ~ 1000 streptococcal isolates. Thus far, the focus is purely on bitemarks, but suck and kiss marks could also be a valuable source of oral bacteria in the absence of bitemarks, and therefore areas for future research.

As discussed, the time limitation of 24 hours should provide the opportunity for successful recovery of oral bacteria from a bitemark in many instances of assault involving adults. However, young children are also the frequent victims of assault involving biting but child physical and sexual abuse are usually chronic problems [24]. The victims are therefore less likely to receive immediate medical attention, and there will be less opportunity to sample recent bitemarks. The exception would be when physical abuse has been excessive and emergency assistance is sought within hours of the assault. Under these circumstances there may be opportunity to sample a very recent bitemark in order to recover oral streptococci.

A question sometimes raised following presentations of this work pertains to the use either of antiseptic mouthwashes or of systemic antibiotics to suppress the streptococci to a level at which they either cannot be recovered from the teeth of a suspect (following an incident) or are not deposited in the bitemark (if a mouthwash is applied before the incident). These are valid issues that have yet to be addressed, but it would seem unlikely that perpetrators would think to protect themselves in such a way unless advised to do so for the purposes of swab sampling.

Of interest, though, two individuals initially enrolled as participants in the studies were found to harbor only one streptococcal genotype each on their teeth. On further questioning, it transpired that both individuals regularly used a chlorhexidine-containing mouthwash and were thus considered unacceptable for the study. If the use of a mouthwash generally provides such a striking and unusual result (i.e., a single streptococcal genotype), then it may be obvious when such intervention has occurred.

Other potential limitations (some of which apply broadly to forensic use of DNA technologies) include issues such as the likelihood of bacterial strain sharing within a family. Others include the difficulty of generalising findings derived from one ethnic or cultural group to another, and the comprehension of the methodology by jurors.

7. CONCLUSIONS

These studies have established that streptococci deposited in bitemarks inflicted on living human skin by human teeth survive long enough to allow isolation within the time period that the majority of sexual assault victims might seek medical attention. Bacteria recovered from bitemarks can be genotypically compared with those isolated from the teeth of suspects, with a high degree of confidence that matches will be made to isolates from the teeth of the biter. The long-term stability of bacterial strains harbored by an individual indicates that the biter, even if apprehended months later, is likely to retain the same bacterial genotypes on his/her teeth. It is noteworthy that one of the first successful prosecutions involving ''DNA evidence'' involved genotypic identification of a viral strain [25]. Thus, there is precedent for the involvement of micro-organisms as forensic aids.

ACKNOWLEDGMENTS

The support of the New Zealand Dental Research Foundation, the New Zealand Lottery Board, and the Maurice and Phyllis Paykel Trust is gratefully acknowledged.

REFERENCES

1. Krawczak M, Schmidtke J. DNA Fingerprinting. Oxford: Bios Scientific Publishers, 1998:1–16.
2. Sweet D, Lorente JA, Valenzuela A, Lorente M, Villanueva E. PCR-based DNA typing of saliva stains recovered from human skin. J Forensic Sci 1997; 42:447–451.
3. Mercer DK, Scott KP, Bruce-Johnson WA, Glover LA, Flint HJ. Fate of free DNA and transformation of the oral bacterium *Streptococcus gordonii* DL1 by plasmid DNA in human saliva. Appl Environ Microbiol 1999; 65:6–10.
4. Blumenthal I. Child Abuse: A Handbook for Health Care Practitioners. London: Edward Arnold, 1994:93–105.
5. Balding DJ, Donnelly P. How convincing is DNA evidence? Nature 1994; 368:285–286.
6. Paster BJ, Boches SK, Galvin JL, Ericson RE, Lau CN, Levanos VA, Sahasrabudhe A, Dewhirst FE. Bacterial diversity in human subgingival plaque. J Bacteriol 2001; 183:3770–83.
7. Socransky SS, Manganiello AD, Propas D, Oram V, van Houte J. Bacteriological studies of developing supragingival dental plaque. J Periodont Res 1977; 12:90–106.
8. van Houte J, Gibbons RJ, Banghart SB. Adherence as a determinant of the presence of *Streptococcus salivarius* and *Streptococcus sanguis* on the human tooth surface. Arch Oral Biol 1970; 15:1025–1034.
9. Krasse B. The proportional distribution of *Streptococcus salivarius* and other streptococci in various parts of the mouth. Odont Rev 1954; 5:203–211.
10. Rudney JD, Larson CJ. Identification of oral mitis group streptococci by arbitrarily primed polymerase chain reaction. Oral Microbiol Immunol 1999; 14:33–42.

11. Truong TL, Menard C, Mouton C, Trahan L. Identification of mutans and other oral streptococci by random amplified polymorphic DNA analysis. J Med Microbiol 2000; 49:63–71.
12. Rudney JD, Neuvar EK, Soberay AH. Restriction endonuclease-fragment polymorphisms of oral viridans streptococci, compared by conventional and field-inversion gel electrophoresis. J Dent Res 1992; 71:1182–1188.
13. Alam S, Brailsford SR, Whiley RA, Beighton D. PCR-based methods for genotyping viridans group streptococci. J Clin Microbiol 1999; 37:2772–2776.
14. Wisplinghoff H, Reinert RR, Cornely O, Seifert H. Molecular relationships and antimicrobial susceptibilities of viridans group streptococci isolated from blood of neutropenic cancer patients. J Clin Microbiol 1999; 37:1876–1880.
15. Jenkinson HF. Genetics of *Streptococcus sanguis*. In Fischetti VA, Ed. Gram-Positive Pathogens. Washington: American Society for Microbiology, 2000:287–294.
16. Brown KA, Elliot TR, Rogers AH, Thonard JC. The survival of oral streptococci on human skin and its implication in bite-mark investigation. Forens Sci Int 1984; 26:193–197.
17. Gibbons RJ, Kapsimalis B, Socransky SS. The source of salivary bacteria. Arch Oral Biol 1964; 9: 101–103.
18. Chapman GH. The isolation of oral streptococci from mixed cultures. J Bacteriol 1944; 48:113–114.
19. Elliot TR, Rogers AH, Haverkamp JR, Groothuis D. Analytical pyrolysis of *Streptococcus salivarius* as an aid to identification in bite-mark investigation. Forens Sci Int 1984; 26:131–137.
20. Robinson FG, Owens S, Birchmeier KR, Tompkins GR. Recovery of oral streptococci from bitemarks inflicted on skin of living humans. Proc Am Acad Forens Sci 1997; 3:103.
21. Peipert JF, Domagalski LR. Epidemiology of adolescent sexual assault. Obstet Gynecol 1994; 84: 867–871.
22. Borgula LM, Robinson FG, Rahimi M, Chew K, Birchmeier KR, Owens SG, Kieser JA, Tompkins GR. Isolation and genotypic comparison of oral bacteria from experimental bite marks. J Forensic Odonto-Stomatology 2003; 21:23–30.
23. Rahimi M, Heng NCK, Kiesser JA, Tompkins GR. Forensic PCR analysis of bacteria recovered from bite marks. International Association for Dental Research 80th General Session, San Diego. J Dent Res 81 Special Issue A:149, 2002.
24. Hobbs CJ, Hanks HGI, Wynne JM. Child Abuse and Neglect: A Clinician's Handbook. London: Churchill Livingstone, 1999:165–189.
25. Albert J, Wahlberg J, Uhlen M. Forensic evidence by DNA sequencing. Nature 1993; 361:595–6.

Appendix I

ABFO BITE MARK ANALYSIS GUIDELINES (1990)* (OUTLINE)

I. Description of Bitemark

Λ. Demographics
B. Location of bitemark
C. Shape
D. Color
E. Size
F. Type of injury
G. Other information

II. Collection of Evidence from Victim

A. Photography
B. Salivary swabbing
C. Impressions
D. Tissue samples

III. Collection of Evidence from Suspect

A. History
B. Photography
C. Extraoral examination
D. Intraoral examination
E. Impressions
F. Sample bites
G. Study casts

IV. Evaluation of Evidence

ABFO BITE-MARK METHODOLOGY GUIDELINES (1995)* (OUTLINE): METHODS TO PRESERVE BITEMARK EVIDENCE

1. Bite Site Evidence

A. Saliva swabs of bite site
B. Photographic documentation of bite site

---

* The ABFO Bite Mark Analysis Guidelines (1990), ABFO Bite-Mark Methodology Guidelines (1995), and Methods of Comparing Bitemark Evidence (1995) are copyrighted material and are reprinted in outline form with kind permission from the American Board of Forensic Odontology, Inc.

        1. General considerations
        2. Lighting considerations
        3. Scale considerations
        4. Additional photographic considerations
    C. Impressions of bite site
        1. Victim's dental impressions
        2. Impressions of the bite site
    D. Tissue specimens
        1. General considerations
        2. Tissue fixative—10% formalin is a common fixative used

2. Evidence Collection of Suspected Dentition

    A. Dental records
    B. Photographic documentation of the dentition
        1. Extraoral photographs
        2. Intraoral photographs
    C. Clinical examination
        1. Extraoral considerations
        2. Intraoral considerations
    D. Dental impressions
    E. Saliva samples

METHODS OF COMPARING BITEMARK EVIDENCE (1995)

    A. Generation of overlays
    B. Test bite media
    C. Comparison techniques
    D. Technical aids employed for analysis

Appendix II—Bitemark Checklist

1. VICTIM

1.A. Demographics

Name of victim _____

Address _____

_____

Race _____ Sex _____ DOB ___/___/___ Age _____ Height _____ Weight _____

Victim alive _____ deceased _____

Date reported missing ___/___/___ Date of recovery ___/___/___

Police case No. _____ Coroner/Me case No. _____

Referring agency _____ TEL _____ FAX _____

Contact person _____ TEL _____ FAX _____

Name of physician/pathologist _____

Address _____

_____

_____ TEL _____ FAX _____

Date:Time:Place of Autopsy ___/___/___ : _____ : _____

Cause of death _____ Manner of death _____

Name of first dental examiner _____

Dental examiner first contacted by _____

Date of contact ___/___/___

Date:Time:Place of exam ___/___/___ : _____ : _____

Officer in charge _____

Address _____

_____

_____ TEL _____ FAX _____

Coroner/ME _____

Address _____

_____

_____ TEL _____ FAX _____

Person authorizing billing _____

Address _____

_____

_____ TEL _____ FAX _____

Prosecutor/DA _____

Address _____

_____

_____ TEL _____ FAX _____

Case No. _____ Court No. _____

Brief description of facts:

_____
_____
_____

1.B. Saliva Swab of Bite Site

Name of collector _____
Are bite sites protected: No _____ Yes/How _____
Site collection _____
Control site _____
Date collected ___/___/___
Analysis by _____ Results _____
Victim blood type _____
Other bodily fluids collected _____ Results _____
From where _____

1.C. Photographic Documentation of Bite Site

Any prior photography (other than dental examinner)

Name of person	Date	Time	Place
_____	___/___/___	_____	_____
_____	___/___/___	_____	_____

Examiner photographs: Self _____ Other _____

	Type	Date	Time	Date	Time
Video	_____	___/___/___	_____	___/___/___	_____
Film: Color	_____	___/___/___	_____	___/___/___	_____
B&W	_____	___/___/___	_____	___/___/___	_____
Slides	_____	___/___/___	_____	___/___/___	_____
UV	_____	___/___/___	_____	___/___/___	_____
IR	_____	___/___/___	_____	___/___/___	_____
Other	_____	___/___/___	_____	___/___/___	_____
Digital	_____	___/___/___	_____	___/___/___	_____

Filters _____
Lighting _____
Scale ABFO No.2 _____ Other _____

1.D. Location and Description of Bitemark

Any prior examination (other than by dental examiner)

Name of person	Date	Time	Place
_____	___/___/___	_____	_____
_____	___/___/___	_____	_____
_____	___/___/___	_____	_____
_____	___/___/___	_____	_____

	A	B	C
Anatomic location	_____	_____	_____
Clothing at bite site	_____	_____	_____
Surface contour	_____	_____	_____
Tissue: fixed/mobile	_____	_____	_____
Underlying tissue	_____	_____	_____

Shape of bitemark   _____   _____   _____
Size: Vertical linear   _____   _____   _____
   Horizontal linear   _____   _____   _____
Color   _____   _____   _____
Petechial hemorrhage   _____   _____   _____
Contusion (ecchymosis)   _____   _____   _____
Abrasion   _____   _____   _____
Laceration   _____   _____   _____
Incision   _____   _____   _____
Avulsion   _____   _____   _____
Indented/without bruising   _____   _____   _____
with Bruising   _____   _____   _____
Perforation   _____   _____   _____
Multiple marks   _____   _____   _____
Artifacts   _____   _____   _____
Embalmed   _____   _____   _____
Lividity   _____   _____   _____
Decomposition   _____   _____   _____
Other   _____   _____   _____
Orientation   _____   _____   _____
Type of mark:
   Animal   _____   _____   _____
   Human   _____   _____   _____
   Unknown   _____   _____   _____
Dental characteristics:
   Child   _____   _____   _____
   Mixed   _____   _____   _____
   Adult   _____   _____   _____
Infliction:
   Self   _____   _____   _____
   Second party   _____   _____   _____
Timing and how determined:
   Antemortem   _____   _____   _____
   Perimortem   _____   _____   _____
   Postmortem   _____   _____   _____
BM/Body recov (dys-hrs)   _____   _____   _____
Body recov/exam (dys-hrs)   _____   _____   _____
Exam/excision (dys-hrs)   _____   _____   _____

1.E. Impressions

I. Victim dental impressions:
   Who took impressions   _____
   Date/time/place   _____
   Impression material   _____
   Mfg. lot No./exp. date   _____
   Dental stone – Master   _____
   Duplicate   _____
   Mfg. lot No./Exp. date   _____
Wax bite _____ Aluwax _____Styrofoam _____ Celluloid _____ Other _____

II. Bitemark impressions:

Who took impressions   _____

Date/time/place   _____

Impression material   _____

Mfg. Lot No./exp. date   _____

Dental Stone – Master   _____

Duplicate   _____

Mfg. Lot No./exp. date   _____

Other _____

1.F. Tissue Specimens

	A	B	C
Bitemark excised by	_____	_____	_____
Date:time	__/__/: _____	__/__/: _____	__/__/: _____
Method:			
No excision	_____	_____	_____
Simple excision	_____	_____	_____
Sutured ring	_____	_____	_____
Dorion type 3	_____	_____	_____
Combination	_____	_____	_____
Other	_____	_____	_____
Fixative (name & %)	_____	_____	_____
Transillumination	_____	_____	_____
SEM	_____	_____	_____
Histology	_____	_____	_____
Bacteriology	_____	_____	_____
Saliva	_____	_____	_____
DNA	_____	_____	_____

Name of other specialist consulted _____

Address _____

_____

_____ TEL _____ FAX _____

2. SUSPECT

2.A. Demographics

Name of suspect _____

Address _____

_____

Race _____ Sex _____ DOB ___/___/___ Age _____ Height _____ Weight _____

Suspect alive _____ deceased _____

Case No. _____

Referring agency _____ TEL _____ FAX _____

Contact person _____ TEL _____ FAX _____

Person authorizing billing _____

Address _____

_____

_____ TEL _____ FAX _____

Defense attorney _____

Address _____

_____

_____ TEL _____ FAX _____

Case No. _____ Court No. _____

Authorization for exam:

   Court order _____   NO. _____

   Search warrant _____   NO._____

   Informed consent: by suspect _____ BY Guardian _____

   Other _____

   Witness to consent   Date   Time   Place

1. _____   __/__/__   _____   _____

2. _____   __/__/__   _____   _____

Name of dental examiner _____

Dental examiner called by _____

Date:Time:Place of exam   __/__/__ : _____ : _____

2.B.   Suspect's Dental History

Last dental appointment _____

Name of last treating dentist _____

Address of last dentist _____

_____

Type of records available from last dentist _____

Nomenclature used in record: FDI _____ Universal _____ Other _____

Dental record: Retained _____ Seized _____ Court order _____

	Last date on record	Date seized
Written record	__/__/__	__/__/__
Odontogram	__/__/__	__/__/__
Radiograph	__/__/__	__/__/__
Models/dental casts	__/__/__	__/__/__
Dental impressions	__/__/__	__/__/__
Dental photographs	__/__/__	__/__/__
Other	__/__/__	__/__/__

Brief medical history

_____

_____

2.C.   Photographic Documentation of the Dentition

Any prior photograph (other than by dental examiner)

    Name of person   Date   Time   Place

_____   __/__/__   _____   _____

_____   __/__/__   _____   _____

Examiner photographs: Self _____   Other (name) _____

	Type	Date	Time	Date	Time
Video	_____	__/__/__	_____	__/__/__	_____
FILM:					
Color	_____	__/__/__	_____	__/__/__	_____

B&W	_____	__/__/__	_____	__/__/__	_____
Slides	_____	__/__/__	_____	__/__/__	_____
UV	_____	__/__/__	_____	__/__/__	_____
IR	_____	__/__/__	_____	__/__/__	_____
Other	_____	__/__/__	_____	__/__/__	_____
Digital	_____	__/__/__	_____	__/__/__	

Filters _____

Lighting _____

Scaled ruler ABFO No.2 _____ Other _____

Extraoral view	Front	Right	Left
Centric occlusion	_____	_____	_____
Rest position	_____	_____	_____
Protusive	_____	_____	_____
Edge to edge	_____	_____	_____
Intraoral view			
Occlusal maxillary	_____	_____	_____
Occlusal mandibular	_____	_____	_____
Other	_____	_____	_____

X-rays _____

2.D. Clinical exam

Name of dental examiner _____

Date:time:place of exam _____

	Normal	Abnormal	Remarks
Extraoral			
TMJ	_____	_____	_____
Facial symmetry	_____	_____	_____
Muscle tone and balance	_____	_____	_____
Deviation on opening	_____	_____	_____
Max vertical opening	_____	_____	_____
Surgery or trauma	_____	_____	_____
Facial hair	Yes_____	No_____	
Other	_____	_____	
Intraoral			
BITE CLASSIFICATION	_____		
OCCLUSAL DISHARMONIES	_____		
TONGUE SIZE, FUNCTION	_____	_____	_____
PERIODONTAL CONDITION	_____	_____	_____
MISSING TEETH	_____	_____	_____
BROKEN TEETH	_____	_____	_____
TOOTTH MOBILITY	_____	_____	_____
MISALIGNMENT	_____	_____	_____
RESTORED TEETH	_____	_____	_____
DENTAL CHARTING	_____	_____	_____

2.E. Impressions

I. SUSPECT'S DENTAL IMPRESSIONS:
Who took impressions   _____

Date:time:place _____

Impression material _____

Mfg Lot No./exp. date _____

Dental stone—Master _____

Duplicate _____

Mfg Lot No./exp. date _____

Wax bite _____ Aluwax _____ Stryrofoam _____ Celluloid _____

II. Bitemark impression *on suspect*:

Who took impressions _____

Date:time:place _____

Impression material _____

Mfg Lot No./exp. date _____

Dental stone—Master _____

Duplicate _____

Mfg Lot No./exp. date _____

2.F. Suspect's Saliva Swab

Name of collector _____

Site collection _____

Control site _____

Date collected ___/___/___

Analysis by _____ Results _____

Suspect blood type _____

Other bodily fluids collected _____ Results _____

From where _____

Appendix III—Bitemark Digital Imaging Processing

Case specialist _____ Unit/team _____

Digital image file No. (original) _____

Capture device and specifications:

    Photographer _____ Date _____ Time _____

    Specialist _____ Date _____ Time _____

Digital camera	Flatbed scanner	Film scanner
Type _____	Type _____	Resolution _____
Lens _____	Resolution _____	Mode _____
F-stop _____	Reflect/trans _____	
Shutter Speed _____	Mode _____	

Lighting _____

    See attached computer printout if available

Imaging history:

    Photographer _____ Date _____ Time _____

    Specialist _____ Date _____ Time _____

Software package(s) utilized:

1) _____   4) _____

2) _____   5) _____

3) _____   6) _____

See attached computer printout if available.

File name (enhanced version): _____

Output device: _____ (circle) GS/RGB/CMYK

Storage: DVD/CD Serial # _____

Archive: DVD/CD Serial # _____

Lab # _____ Page # _____ of _____

Appendix IV—Sample Consent Form

DECLARATION OF VOLUNTARY ACCEPTANCE FOR AN ODONTOLOGICAL EXAMINATION

By the present, I, _____ ,The
Undersigned, authorize Dr. _____
to perform the following:

A) Take dental impressions;
B) A dental examination including the taking of radiographs;
C) Take a video and pictures of my dentition;
D) Visually examine any and all corporal wounds;
E) Take impressions of any and all corporal wounds;
F) Take a video and pictures of any and all corporal wounds;
G) Take saliva samples;
H) Take samples of substances on the surface of my body.

I hereby voluntarily accept, without duress, coercion, threats, promises of reward or immunity, to undergo these examinations.

I do hereby release and forever hold harmless Dr. _____
from any liability flowing from these examinations.

I further agree that the results of these examinations may be made available to competent authorities for judicial, scientific and publication purposes.

Signature   _____
Address   _____
     _____

Witness:
1) _____
2) _____

Date: _____
Time: _____
Place: _____

Appendix V—Dental Nomenclature

DENTAL CONVERSION TABLE FOR TOOTH DESIGNATION DECIDUOUS DENTITION

	Upper right					Upper left				
Palmer	E+	D+	C+	B+	A+	+A	+B	+C	+D	+E
F.D.I.	55	54	53	52	51	61	62	63	64	65
Hareup	05+	04+	03+	02+	01+	+01	+02	+03	+04	+05
Other	V	IV	III	II	I	I	II	III	IV	V
Other	5D	4D	3D	2D	1D	1D	2D	3D	4D	5D
Other	d5	d4	d3	d2	d1	d1	d2	d3	d4	d5
Other	5m	4m	3m	2m	1m	1m	2m	3m	4m	5m
Other	A	B	C	D	E	E	D	C	B	A
Other	dm2	dm1	dc	di2	di1	di1	di2	dc	dm1	dm2
F.D.I. (modified)	55	54	53	52	51	61	62	63	64	65
Other	E	D	C	B	A	A	B	C	D	E

	Lower right					Lower left				
Palmer	E–	D–	C–	B–	A–	–A	–B	–C	–D	–E
F.D.I.	85	84	83	82	81	71	72	73	74	75
Hareup	05–	04–	03–	02–	01–	–01	–02	–03	–04	–05
Other	V	IV	III	II	I	I	II	III	IV	V
Other	5D	4D	3D	2D	1D	1D	2D	3D	4D	5D
Other	d5	d4	d3	d2	d1	d1	d2	d3	d4	d5
Other	5m	4m	3m	2m	1m	1m	2m	3m	4m	5m
Other	A	B	C	D	E	E	D	C	B	A
Other	dm2	dm1	dc	di2	di1	di1	di2	dc	dm1	dm2
F.D.I. (modified)	75	74	73	72	71	81	82	83	84	85
Other	E	D	C	B	A	A	B	C	D	E

Table first published in the Journal of the Canadian Society of Forensic Science and reprinted with kind permission. RBJ Dorion. Dental nomenclature. CSFSJ 8(3):107–110, 1975.

DENTAL CONVERSION TABLE FOR TOOTH DESIGNATION PERMANENT DENTITION

	Upper right								Upper left							
	3rd Molar	2nd Molar	1st Molar	2nd Bicuspid	1st Bicuspid	Cuspid	Lateral	Central	Central	Lateral	Cuspid	1st Bicuspid	2nd Molar	1st Bicuspid	2nd Molar	3rd Molar
Miscellaneous	UR8	UR7	UR6	UR5	UR4	UR3	UR2	UR1	UL1	UL2	UL3	UL4	UL5	UL6	UL7	UL8
Hareup	8+	7+	6+	5+	4+	3+	2+	1+	+1	+2	+3	+4	+5	+6	+7	+8
Palmer	8⌋	7⌋	6⌋	5⌋	4⌋	3⌋	2⌋	1⌋	⌊1	⌊2	⌊3	⌊4	⌊5	⌊6	⌊7	⌊8
Universal	1	2	3	4	5	6	7	8	9	10	11	12	13	14	15	16
F.D.I.	18	17	16	15	14	13	12	11	21	22	23	24	25	26	27	28
U.S. Army	8	7	6	5	4	3	2	1	1	2	3	4	5	6	7	8
U.S. Navy	1	2	3	4	5	6	7	8	9	10	11	12	13	14	15	16
Bosworth	8	7	6	5	4	3	2	1	1	2	3	4	5	6	7	8
Lowlands	M3	M2	M1	P2	P1	C	12	11	11	12	C	P1	P2	M1	M2	M3
Some European countries	D8	D7	D6	D5	D4	D3	D2	D1	G1	G2	G3	G4	G5	G6	G7	G8
Holland	sdM3	sdM2	sdM1	sdP2	sdP1	sdC	sd12	sd11	sg11	sg12	sgC	sgP1	sgP2	sgM1	sgM2	sgM3
F.D.I (modified)	18	17	16	15	14	13	12	11	21	22	23	24	25	26	27	28
Other	16	15	14	13	12	11	10	9	8	7	6	5	4	3	2	1

	Lower right								Lower left							
Other	32	31	30	29	28	27	26	25	24	23	22	21	20	19	18	17
F.D.I. (modified)	38	37	36	35	34	33	32	31	41	42	43	44	45	46	47	48
Holland	diM3	diM2	diM3	diP2	diP1	diC	dil2	dil1	gil1	gil2	giC	giP1	giP2	giM1	giM2	giM3
Some European countries	d8	d7	d6	d5	d4	d3	d2	d1	g1	g2	g3	g4	g5	g6	g7	g8
Lowlands	M3	M2	M1	P2	P1	C	12	11	11	12	C	P1	P2	M1	M2	M3
Bosworth	H	G	F	E	D	C	B	A	A	B	C	D	E	F	G	H
U.S. Navy	17	18	19	20	21	22	23	24	25	26	27	28	29	30	31	32
U.S. Army	16	15	14	13	12	11	10	9	9	10	11	12	13	14	15	16
F.D.I.	48	47	46	45	44	43	42	41	31	32	33	34	35	36	37	38
Universal	32	31	30	29	28	27	26	25	24	23	22	21	20	19	18	17
Palmer	8⌋	7⌋	6⌋	5⌋	4⌋	3⌋	2⌋	1⌋	⌊1	⌊2	⌊3	⌊4	⌊5	⌊6	⌊7	⌊8
Hareup	8–	7–	6–	5–	4–	3–	2–	1–	–1	–2	–3	–4	–5	–6	–7	–8
Miscellaneous	LR8	LR7	LR6	LR5	LR4	LR3	LR2	LR1	LL1	LL2	LL3	LL4	LL5	LL6	LL7	LL8

Table first published in the Journal of the Canadian Society of Forensic Science and reprinted with kind permission. RBJ Dorion Dental Nomenclature. CSFSJ 8(3):107–110, 1975.

Index